PAGE 36

ON THE ROAD

...ATION GUIDE
...d listings
and insider tips

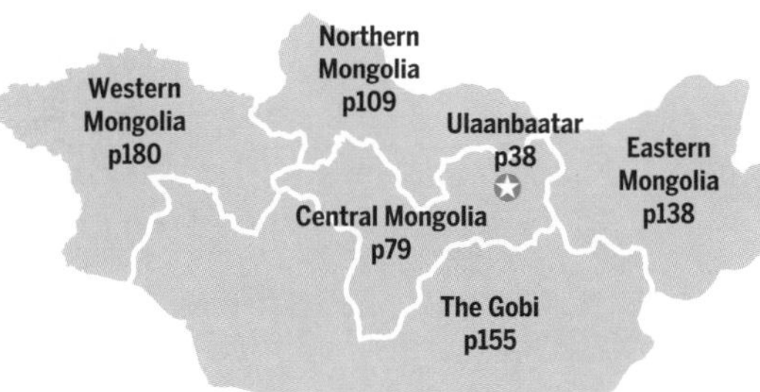

PAGE 245

SURVIVAL GUIDE

YOUR AT-A-GLANCE REFERENCE
How to get around, get a room, stay safe, say hello

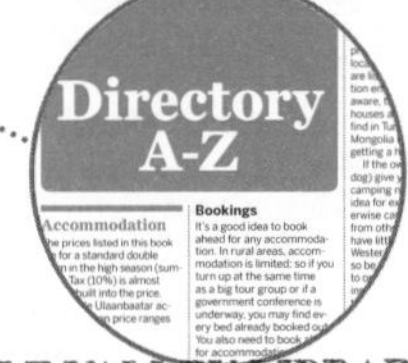

THIS EDITION WRITTEN AND RESEARCHED BY

Michael K...
Dean Sta...

Mongolia

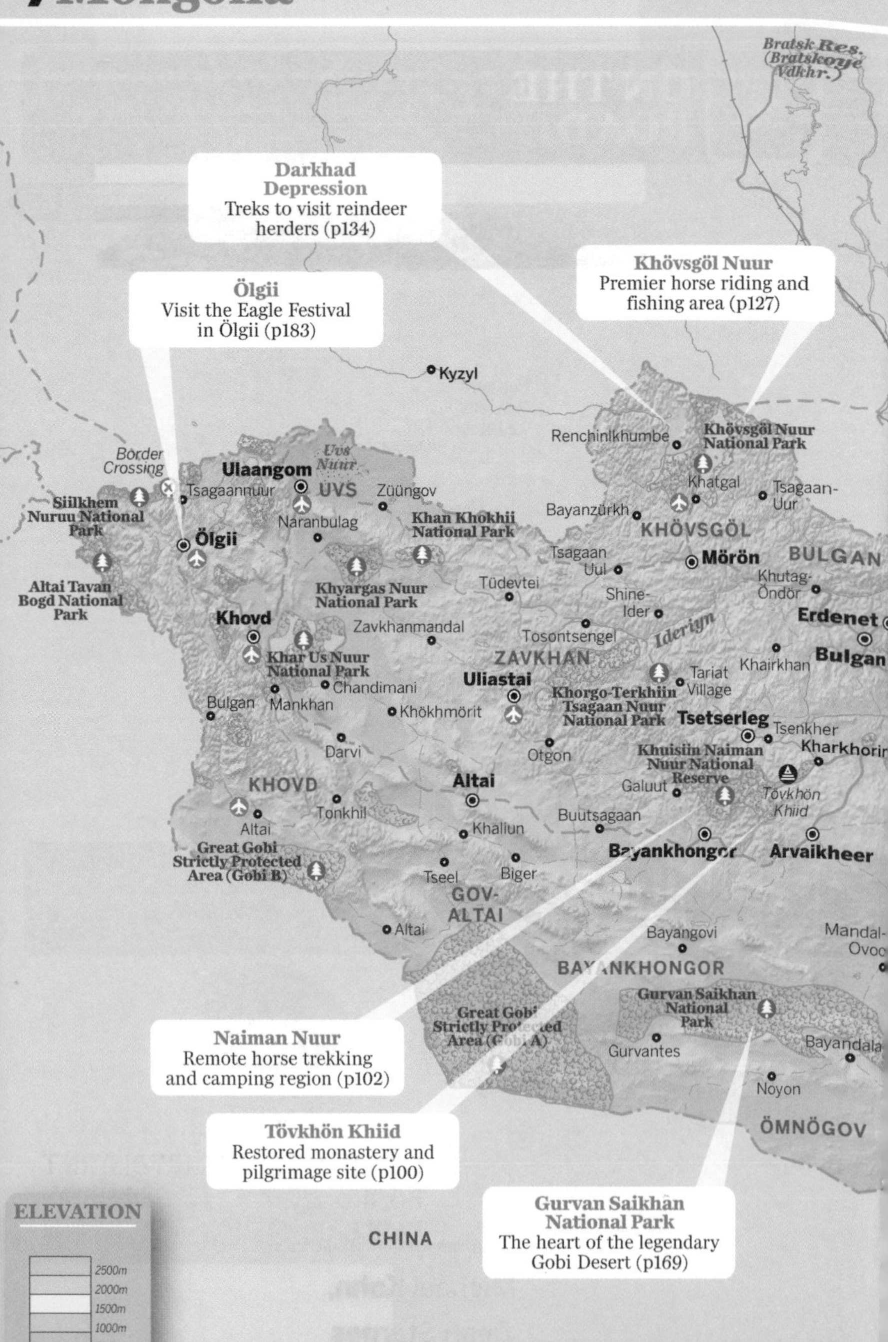

Darkhad Depression
Treks to visit reindeer herders (p134)
Khövsgöl Nuur
Premier horse riding and fishing area (p127)
Ölgii
Visit the Eagle Festival in Ölgii (p183)
Naiman Nuur
Remote horse trekking and camping region (p102)
Tövkhön Khiid
Restored monastery and pilgrimage site (p100)
Gurvan Saikhan National Park
The heart of the legendary Gobi Desert (p169)
Kyzyl
Renchinlkhumbe
Khövsgöl Nuur National Park
Khatgal
Tsagaan-Uur
Bayanzürkh
KHÖVSGÖL
Mörön
BULGAN
Tsagaan Uul
Shine-Ider
Khutag-Öndör
Erdenet
Bulgan
Border Crossing
Ulaangom
Uvs Nuur
UVS
Züüngov
Tsagaannuur
Siilkhem Nuruu National Park
Naranbulag
Khan Khokhii National Park
Ölgii
Altai Tavan Bogd National Park
Khyargas Nuur National Park
Tüdevtei
Khovd
Zavkhanmandal
Tosontsengel
Ideriyn
Khar Us Nuur National Park
ZAVKHAN
Khairkhan
Tariat Village
Chandimani
Uliastai
Khorgo-Terkhiin Tsagaan Nuur National Park
Bulgan
Mankhan
Khökhmörit
Tsetserleg
Tsenkher
Kharkhorin
Darvi
Otgon
Khuisiin Naiman Nuur National Reserve
KHOVD
Altai
Galuut
Tövkhön Khiid
Tonkhil
Altai
Buutsagaan
Khaliun
Great Gobi Strictly Protected Area (Gobi B)
Arvaikheer
Tseel
Biger
GOV-ALTAI
Altai
Bayangovi
Mandal-Ovoo
Gurvan Saikhan National Park
Gurvantes
Bayandalai
Noyon
ÖMNÖGOV
CHINA
ELEVATION
2500m
2000m
1500m
1000m
500m
0

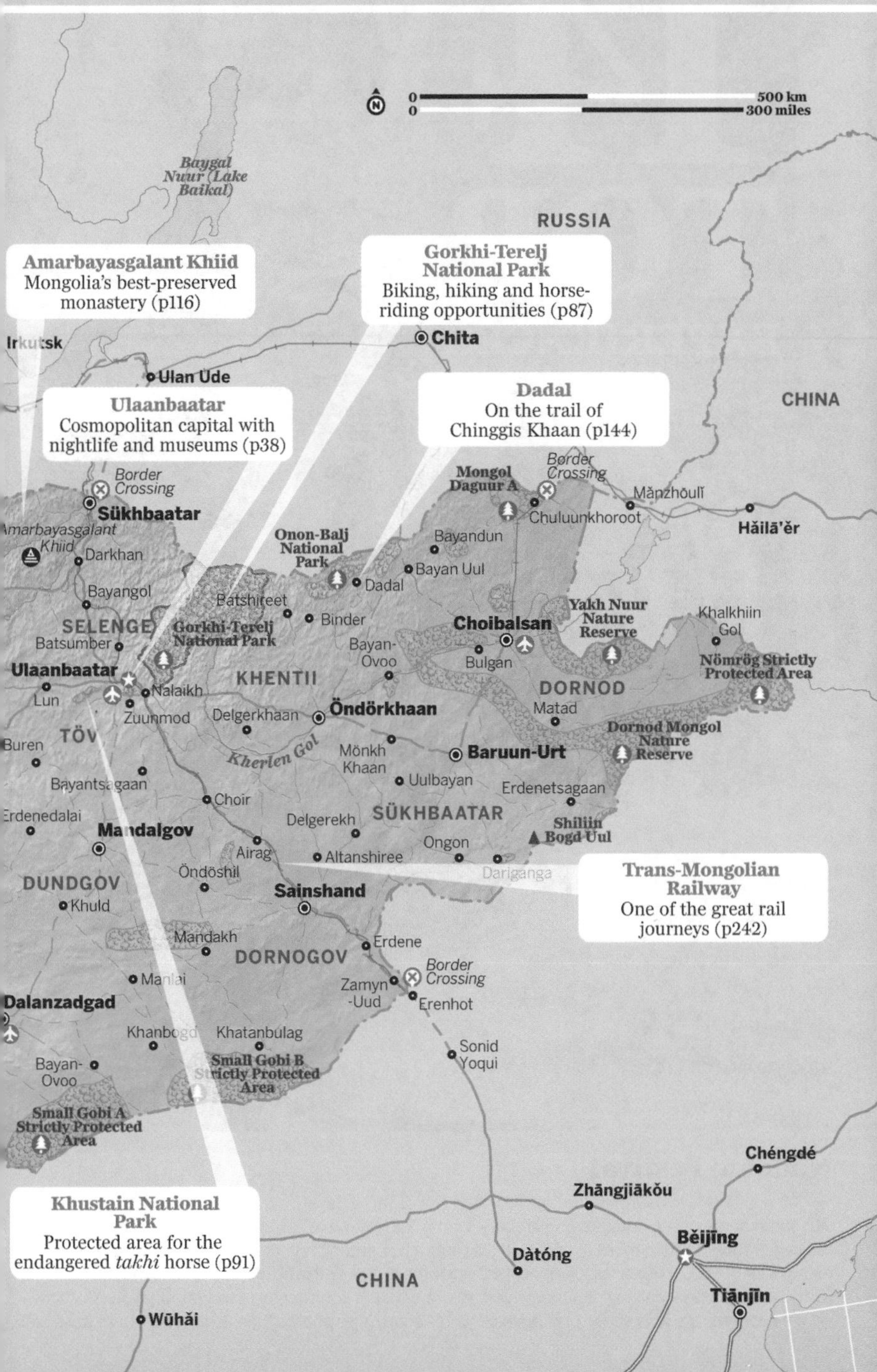

0 — 500 km
0 — 300 miles
Baygal Nuur (Lake Baikal)
RUSSIA
Amarbayasgalant Khiid
Mongolia's best-preserved monastery (p116)
Gorkhi-Terelj National Park
Biking, hiking and horse-riding opportunities (p87)
Irkutsk
Chita
Ulan Ude
Ulaanbaatar
Cosmopolitan capital with nightlife and museums (p38)
Dadal
On the trail of Chinggis Khaan (p144)
CHINA
Border Crossing
Sükhbaatar
Amarbayasgalant Khiid
Darkhan
Bayangol
SELENGE
Batsumber
Ulaanbaatar
Lun
Nalaikh
Zuunmod
TÖV
Buren
Bayantsagaan
Erdenedalai
Mandalgov
DUNDGOV
Khuld
Dalanzadgad
Mongol Daguur A
Border Crossing
Chuluunkhoroot
Mănzhōulǐ
Hǎilā'ěr
Onon-Balj National Park
Bayandun
Bayan Uul
Dadal
Batshireet
Binder
Gorkhi-Terelj National Park
KHENTII
Bayan-Ovoo
Choibalsan
Bulgan
Yakh Nuur Nature Reserve
Khalkhiin Gol
Nömrög Strictly Protected Area
DORNOD
Matad
Delgerkhaan
Öndörkhaan
Kherlen Gol
Mönkh Khaan
Baruun-Urt
Dornod Mongol Nature Reserve
Uulbayan
Erdenetsagaan
Choir
Delgerekh
SÜKHBAATAR
Shiliin Bogd Uul
Airag
Altanshiree
Ongon
Dariganga
Öndöshil
Sainshand
Trans-Mongolian Railway
One of the great rail journeys (p242)
Mandakh
DORNOGOV
Erdene
Manlai
Border Crossing
Zamyn-Uud
Erenhot
Khanbogd
Khatanbulag
Sonid Yoqui
Bayan-Ovoo
Small Gobi B Strictly Protected Area
Small Gobi A Strictly Protected Area
Chéngdé
Khustain National Park
Protected area for the endangered takhi horse (p91)
Zhāngjiākǒu
Běijīng
Dàtóng
CHINA
Tiānjīn
Wūhǎi

14 TOP EXPERIENCES

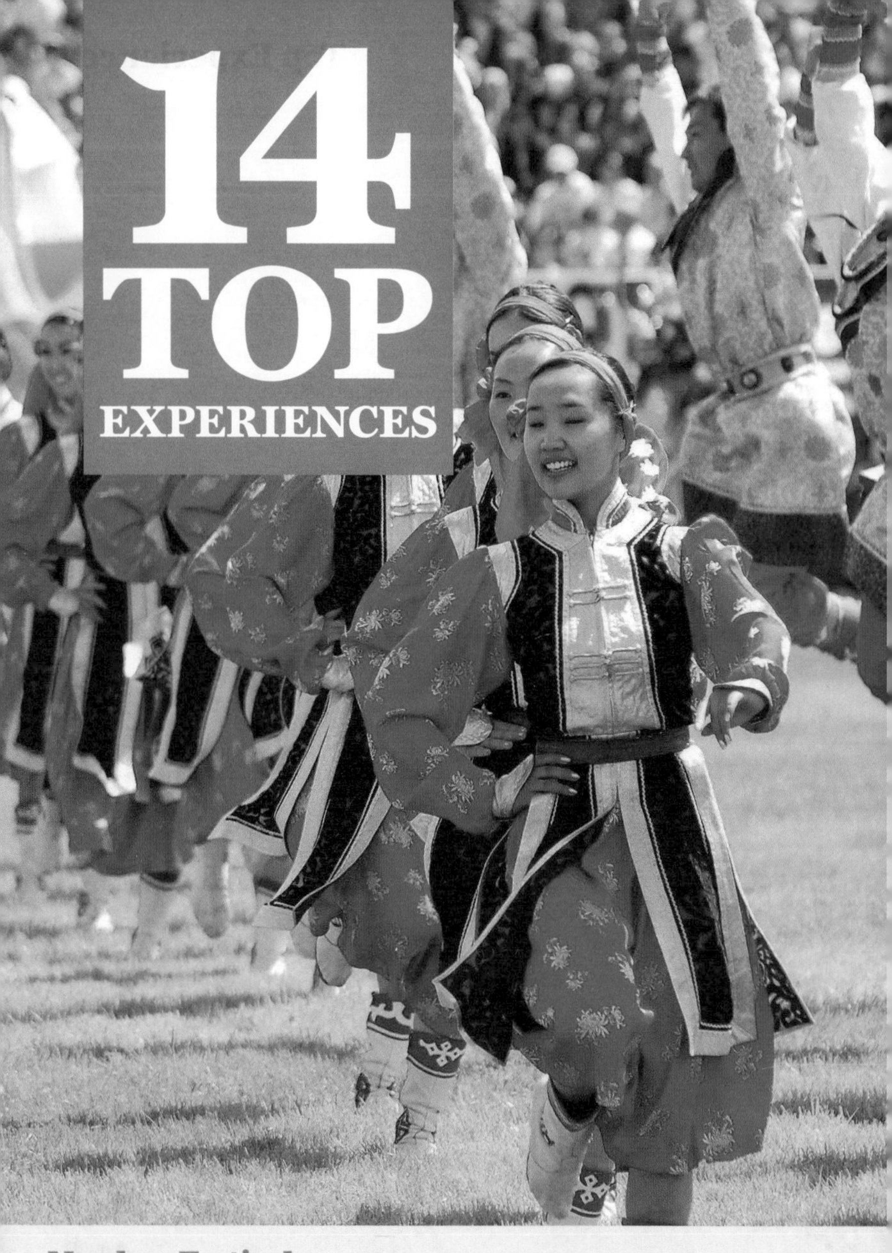

Naadam Festival

1 Mongolians love their naadam (p222). With two or three days of serious wrestling action, awesome horse racing and dazzling archery, who wouldn't? While 'naadam' literally means games, the celebration is much more than that. It's all about fun, getting together with friends and relatives, eating a lot of *khuushuur* (mutton pancakes) and emptying a vodka bottle or two. The most traditional festivals happen in small towns, where every member of the community is somehow involved. These village naadams are also super-photogenic – you'll snap more photos than you ever thought possible.

Staying in a Ger

2 Of all the experiences you are likely to have in Mongolia, the most memorable will be your visits to gers (p225). From the outside, gers look like simple tents, but step inside and you'll be surprised by the amount of furnishings and modern appliances a nomadic family can have. There are beds, tables, chairs, dressers, a stove and often a TV and radio. Visitors are always welcome inside a ger and you don't even need to knock (Mongolians never do). Instead, when approaching a ger, call out 'Nokhoi khor', which means 'Hold the dog'.

MICHAEL KOHN / LONELY PLANET IMAGES ©

Horse Riding

3 Mongolians have been traversing their country on horseback for thousands of years. You should do the same. Short day rides are possible right around Ulaanbaatar (p53) – but the best areas are Gorkhi-Terelj National Park (p82) and Bogdkhan Uul Strictly Protected Area (p83). Multiday horse treks can be made at Khövsgöl Nuur (p129), Khan Khentii Strictly Protected Area (p88) and Naiman Nuur (p102). It can take some getting used to the half-wild Mongolian horses. Fortunately, local guides know their animals well – pay attention and follow their lead.

Gobi Desert

4 The idea of going to the Gobi (p155) for a vacation would probably have Marco Polo turning in his grave. The Venetian traveller, and others like him, dreaded crossing this harsh landscape. Thankfully, travel facilities have improved in the past 800 years, and it's now possible to make a reasonably comfortable visit. There are shaggy camels to ride and dinosaur fossils to dig up, but the real highlight is the scenic Khongoryn Els (p169) – towering sand dunes that whistle when raked by high winds.

Wildlife Watching

5 Mongolia provides an ideal landscape for watching wildlife (p237). In the east you'll spot hundreds (sometimes thousands) of gazelle streaking across the plains at supersonic speeds. In mountainous areas, especially in the Gobi, you stand a good chance of seeing argali sheep and ibex, and in the taiga north of the Darkhad Depression (p134) you can see majestic reindeer. The easiest place to watch wildlife is at Khustain National Park (p91), home to *takhi* (wild horses). And no matter where you travel, there are enormous birds circling overhead. Roosting cormorants, Khetsuu Khad (p201), Khyargas Nuur National Park

Mongolian Hospitality

6 It may sound clichéd, but the truth is that you won't find a more hospitable people than the Mongols. Stop for directions at a ger and soon bowls of sweets appear, then cups of tea, then possibly lunch and even a bed if you're in need of a nap. Camp by a group of nomads and chances are you'll get a visit by children bearing fresh milk and cheese. It's all part of a time-honoured tradition, allowing for the mutual survival of Mongolians themselves as they travel across their vast nation.

Hiking

7 With its rugged mountains, serene river valleys and fields of wildflowers, the Mongolian back-country is begging to be explored on foot. Hiking (p28) is a new activity in Mongolia, but with some improvisation, it's certainly possible. Although there are no warming huts and few marked trails, you'll find shelter in gers and encounter locals who are more than willing to show you the way. There are no sherpas, but a pack horse (or yak) will do nicely. Good maps, a sturdy tent and a sense of adventure will help see you through.

GRAHAM TAYLOR / LONELY PLANET IMAGES ©

Khövsgöl Nuur

8 The natural highlight of Mongolia is Khövsgöl Nuur (p127), a 136km-long lake set on the southern-most fringe of Siberia. For Mongolians the lake is a deeply spiritual place, home to powerful *nagas* (water spirits) and a source of inspiration for shamans that live there. For foreigners Khövsgöl is a place for adventure, with horse riding, fishing, kayaking, trekking and mountain biking a few of the possibilities. Hard-core adventurers can even embark on a 15-day trek around its glorious shoreline.

Trans-Mongolian Railway

9 A trip on the Trans-Mongolian (p242) is not merely a cheap way to travel – it is also a journey unto itself. A couple of days on the train will mean meeting new friends, plenty of time to catch up on your reading and some dreamy views of the quiet, empty Mongolian plateau. When riding the rails, make sure to travel as the locals do – bring loads of salami, bread and pickles, and a deck of cards or chessboard. Also bring a good phrasebook so that you can communicate with your cabin mates.

MICHAEL KOHN / LONELY PLANET IMAGES ©

Ulaanbaatar

10 Mongolia is said to be the least-densely populated country on the planet. You would have a hard time believing that if you only visited its capital. The crush of people, cars and development in Ulaanbaatar can be overwhelming and exciting all at once. Beyond the heady nightlife, chic cafes and Hummers, the city has a peaceful side, too. Turn a prayer wheel at Gandan Khiid (p49), saunter across Sükhbaatar Sq (p41) and climb up Zaisan Memorial (p48) to take a break from this bewildering place. Military band member in front of Parliament House (p41)

On the Trail of Chinggis Khaan

11 Amateur historians shouldn't miss the chance to track down Chinggis Khaan. Pack a copy of *Mongoliin Nuuts Tovchoo (The Secret History of the Mongols)*, climb into your jeep and head east. Start at the place Chinggis found his famous golden whip, Tsonjin Boldog (p87), which is now a hill topped with a huge statue of the great conqueror. Continue on to Khökh Nuur (p143), the site of his coronation before 100,000 soldiers. The trail gets wilder the further you go, until you finally reach his birthplace at Dadal (p144). Chinggis Khaan statue, designed by D Erdembileg, atTsonjin Boldog

MICHAEL KOHN / LONELY PLANET IMAGES ©

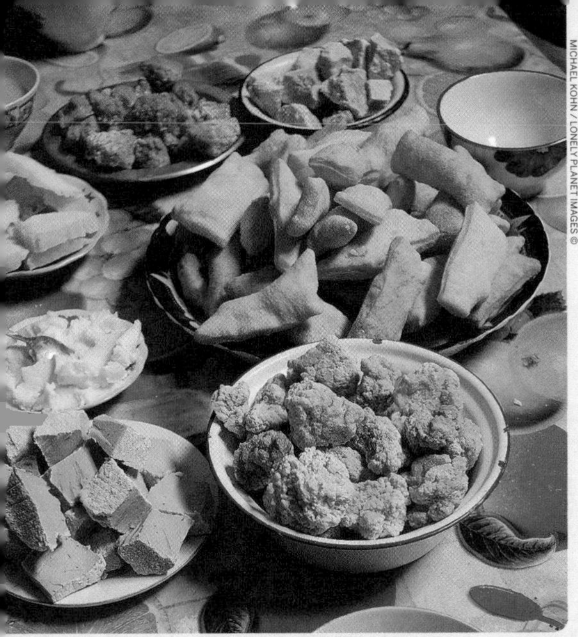

Mongolian Food & Drink

12 When it comes to cuisine (see p231), Mongolians make the most of limited ingredients. Meat (especially mutton), flour and milk products, such as dried curd and cheese, feature prominently in traditional meals. The best meals tend to be at a ger in the countryside, where a family feast includes meat, animal organs, intestines and even the head. There are other dishes too, such as *buuz* (steamed mutton dumplings) and *khuushuur*, which you can find in every city. Drinking fermented mare's milk *(airag)* is a uniquely Central Asian experience, one your stomach won't soon forget.

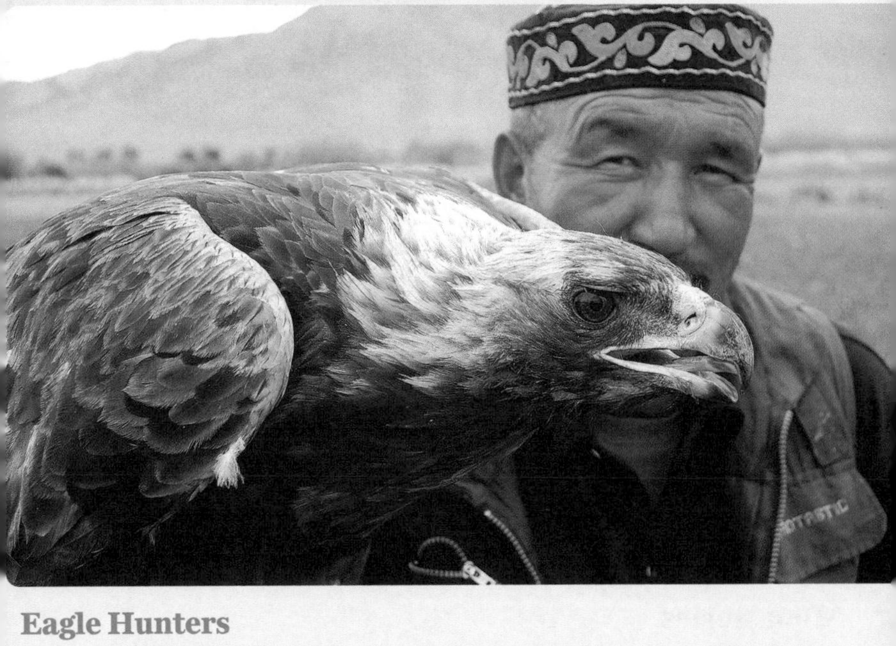

Eagle Hunters

13 For centuries, using eagles to catch prey has been a traditional sport among Central Asian nomads. Even Marco Polo mentioned the great raptors kept by Kublai Khaan. The sport is alive and well today, but you'll only find it in a small corner of Mongolia. Travel to Bayan-Ölgii and link up with the Kazakh hunters that capture and train these magnificent birds. The best time to visit is in early October, when you can attend the colourful Eagle Festival (p183) in Ölgii city.

Monasteries

14 The time-worn Buddhist monasteries *(khiid)* that dot the landscape are the most immediate window on Mongolia's spiritual roots. Lamas young and old sit quietly in the pews, carrying on the legacy of a religion brought here from Tibet centuries ago. The laypeople that visit the monasteries pay homage with the spin of a prayer wheel and whispered mantras. As well as a place of pilgrimage, the monasteries are also rare slices of tangible history, filled with precious Buddhist icons, Sutras and the delicate paintings that grace their ancient walls. Erdene Zuu Khiid (p95)

welcome to Mongolia

Wild, untamed Mongolia is fabled for being remote from civilisation. But the reality is different. The capital, Ulaanbaatar, is awash with Hummers and wi-fi hotspots. Nomadic herders chat to each other on mobile phones and kids practice their break dance moves in the shadow of Chinggis Khaan's statue.

Open for Business

For most of the 20th century, Mongolia was sealed off from the world; a place so distant and so exotic that the very name of the country became a byword for remoteness and isolation. Mongolia has spent the past 20 years fighting that stereotype, and for tourists, that means that Mongolia is now open for business. Visas are relatively easy to acquire compared to other Central Asian republics; a handful of nationals won't even require one. Mongolia appreciates that tourism is a key growth sector of its economy and is an important revenue earner for local communities. It's important to remember that despite the warm welcome you will receive, it's not a pleasure cruise. Mongolia is still a poor country with rudimentary infrastructure and mostly basic facilities outside the capital.

Why Mongolia?

Mongolians know they live in a unique country. Ask anyone why it is so special and they will probably start gushing about the beautiful countryside, the vast steppes, rugged mountains, clear lakes, abundant wildlife and, of course, their animals. It's this true wilderness experience that many people find so appealing. But just as appealing is Mongolia's nomadic culture, still going strong in the 21st century. The chance to sleep in a nomads' ger, help herd the sheep, ride horses and milk a cow or two is the 'back to rural roots' experience that many Westerners crave. Experiencing the Mongolian way of life is really only possible because of the tremendous hospitality that exists in Mongolia. In a world of walls, locks and fences, it can be tremendously refreshing to meet a people who are willing to open their doors to complete strangers.

Not Just Grass & Horses

There are few countries in the world with such a stark difference between the rural and urban populations. While nomadic Mongols live the simple life, their cousins in Ulaanbaatar are lurching headlong into the future. The capital is changing at a dizzying pace and many Mongolians have bought wholeheartedly into the global economy, capitalism and consumerism. If you've travelled elsewhere in Asia, this unbridled consumerism might not be anything new – what sets Mongolia apart from its neighbours is its embrace of Western-style democracy. Despite leaving communism behind just 20 years ago, the country is often held up as a model emerging democratic state, which is nothing short of a miracle for a country surrounded by democracy-challenged countries like Russia, China and Kazakhstan. Mongolia is eager to be part of the global community; by visiting the country and sharing your experiences with locals, you are contributing in some way to the remarkable developments happening in this extraordinary land.

need to know

Currency

» tögrög (T)

Language

» Mongolian and Kazakh

When to Go

High Season
(Jun-Aug)

» Expect hot, dry weather in June and July.

» Late July and August are warm but expect rain.

» Book flights and accommodation in advance, especially around Naadam.

Shoulder
(May & Sept)

» Some ger camps may be closed.

» Weather can be changeable so plan for a cold snap.

» Fewer tourists at this time.

Low Season
(Oct-Apr)

» Some ger camps and guesthouses close; some hotels offer discounts.

» Frigid in December and January. Winds and dust storms in March and April.

» Activities such as dog sledding, ice skating and skiing.

Your Daily Budget

Budget less than
US$50

» Dorm beds: US$5–12 a night

» Free camping: the countryside

» Meals at simple restaurants: US$3–5

» A 650km bus ride: around US$20

Midrange
US$50–120

» Double room at a standard midrange hotel: US$70 a night

» Ger camps with room and board: average US$35

» Meals at midrange restaurants in Ulaanbaatar: US$8–10

Top end over
US$120

» Top-end hotels and ger camps are only found in a few areas; expect to pay at least US$150

Money

» ATMs are widely available in Ulaanbaatar and regional capitals. Most businesses only accept cash, although you can use credit cards at some businesses in Ulaanbaatar.

Visas

» Most nationalities can purchase a 30-day visa at a Mongolian consulate or embassy. Certain nationalities can visit visa free.

Mobile Phones

» Mongolia has four carriers (two GSM and two CDMA). With an unlocked phone, buy a local SIM card and top up with units.

Driving

» Public transport is slow and destinations are limited. Most visitors hire a guide and driver for countryside tours.

Websites

» **Mongolia Expat** (www.mongoliaexpat.com) slew of articles on living in Mongolia.

» **Mongol Expat** (www.mongolexpat) Good resource for expats living in Mongolia, with up-to-date listings, classifieds and events, plus a bus route map.

» **Mongolia National Tourism Centre** (www.mongoliatourism.gov.mn) Info on events, sights and trip planning.

» **Lonely Planet** (www.lonelyplanet.com/mongolia) Destination info, hotel bookings, traveller forum and more.

Exchange Rates

Australia	A$1	T1250
Canada	C$1	T1267
China	Y1	T190
Euro zone	E1	T1694
Japan	Y100	T1503
New Zealand	NZ$1	T944
Russia	R1	42.8
USA	US$1	T1253
UK	US£1	T2023

For current exchange rates, see www.xe.com.

Important Numbers

Country code	☎976
Directory assistance/ information	☎109
Ambulance	☎103
Fire	☎101
Police	☎102

Arriving in Mongolia

» Bus connections from Ulaanbaatar's airport to the city are inconvenient and private taxis are risky (some may overcharge). It's best to organise a pick-up from the airport through your guesthouse or hotel. A taxi should cost US$12–20.

» The Ulaanbaatar train station is close to the city centre – from here you can catch a public bus or walk. Like the airport, though, it's best to organise a pick-up. A taxi should cost US$2–5 to most downtown areas.

Don't Leave Home Without

» Small gifts. Mongolians love exchanging gifts, so bring small items from home: pocket knives, torches (flashlights), T-shirts and books/pens for children.

» Tents, sleeping bags and other equipment are available for sale in Mongolia but you'll save money by bringing your own gear.

» ChapStick, sunblock, sunglasses, bandanas and anything else that will protect you from Mongolia's relentless sun, dust and wind.

» New US dollars; it's difficult to change bills that predate 2000. Moneychangers won't accept ripped or crumpled bills.

» A torch for seeing your way around a campsite or dark stairwell.

if you like...

Hanging with the Locals

Mongolians are very outgoing people and it's easy to get to know them at a bar, cafe or in their ger on the steppes. A great time to meet locals is during festivals and holidays when everyone is in good spirits (especially after drinking spirits).

Xanadu Interesting artist-types often congregate at this Ulaanbaatar gallery/bar (p47)

Grand Khaan Irish Pub Young Mongols can be found drinking on the wooden porch of this bar on UB's Seoul St (p63)

Zaisan Memorial Trudge up the steps with a bunch of Mongolian friends to drink some beers at sunset (p48)

Naadam horse races Big groups of Mongolians camp out at the horse race field near Ulaanbaatar (p222)

In the countryside It's inevitable that you'll pop into a ger for directions or to meet up with your driver's cousins; these unplanned interactions often lead to new friendships.

Volunteering with Asral Volunteering is a great way to build relationships with local people (p46)

Spotting Wildlife

Mongolia is home to some of the most varied wildlife you can find in Asia. Unfortunately much of it has been wiped out by poachers in recent years. Still, there is much to see, especially in national parks and strictly protected areas. Bring binoculars, a high-powered camera lens, and patience.

Ikh Nartiin Chuluu Nature Reserve One of the best places in the country to spot wildlife in their natural habitat, including argali sheep and ibex (p165)

Dornod Mongol Strictly Protected Area Tens of thousands of gazelle inhabit this park in an incredibly remote corner of the country (p146)

Nömrög Strictly Protected Area This geographically distinct region is home to some stunning flora and fauna; possible sightings include otter, bear and moose (p150)

Mongol Daguur Strictly Protected Area Excellent place for ornithologists hoping to spot white-napped crane (p146)

Khustain National Park Easily accessible from Ulaanbaatar, this is the place to visit for sightings of the *takhi* horse (p91)

Hiking

After travelling around in a cramped Russian jeep for a few days you'll relish the opportunity for a long hike. As it's not a popular activity among Mongolians, there's no hiking infrastructure, but it's easy enough to follow a horse trail through the mountains.

Renchinlkhumbe Trail One of the best multiday hikes in the country goes from the gorgeous shores of Lake Khövsgöl over the mountains to the quaint village of Renchinlkhumbe (p130)

Bogdkhan Uul For a long day hike or an overnight walk, start at Mandshir Khiid and walk over the mountain to Ulaanbaatar (p84)

Gorkhi-Terelj National Park The main valley in the park is crowded but hike over a mountain or two and you'll find yourself in almost total isolation (p82)

Otgon Tenger Uul Strictly Protected Area The locals don't want you climbing this mountain (it's sacred) but it's perfectly OK to hike around its base (p203)

Altai Tavan Bogd National Park The park has a lot of varied terrain to tackle. You can hike along the side of the glacier at Tavan Bogd, or go down to the lake area for a trek around Khoton Nuur (p188).

If you like... mountaineering
Tavan Bogd (Five Saints) is the most challenging peak for dedicated climbers (p189).

If you like... clubbing
Ulaanbaatar has booming nightclubs and a thriving hip-hop scene with local DJs, rappers and folk-rock fusion bands (p66).

Hidden Gems

Most people set off for the Flaming Cliffs, Lake Khövsgöl and Karakorum but it's certainly worth checking out some of the country's lesser known sites. By visiting these places you'll escape the crowds and get Mongolia without the hype.

Dadal There is much to see here, including the beautiful Onon-Balj National Park as well as historic places associated with Chinggis Khaan (p144)

Dariganga Explore a landscape of volcanic craters and historic sites hidden in the southeast of the country (p153)

Khamaryn Khiid Foreign tourists have yet to discover it but Mongolian visitors frequently make a pilgrimage to this 'energy centre' (p163)

Chandmani Learn throat singing from an old master at this remote village in western Mongolia (p194)

Tsengel Trek out to the westernmost village in the country, a rough-and-ready town, home to a number of eagle hunters (p188)

Chandman-Öndör A magical land of green fields, wide rivers and log cabins, this is a rarely visited corner of Khövsgöl aimag (p133)

Arts & Crafts

Mongolia's arts scene is surprisingly vibrant. Local artists are skilled at blending modern styles with traditional Mongolian themes and you'll have many opportunities to purchase their works. Start your search at the following places.

Red Ger Art Gallery Probably the best place in Ulaanbaatar to find paintings by top Mongolian artists (p47)

Bayan-Ölgii Aimag Museum Gift Shop A great place to browse for Kazakh antiques and *tush* (wall hangings) (p186)

Bow-making Workshop Meet a traditional bow maker at his workshop in Dulaankhaan, learn the secrets of this ancient craft and maybe go home with a new bow (p113)

Mongolian Quilting Shop Purchase a homemade quilt produced at a craft cooperative in Ulaanbaatar (p70)

Mary & Martha Mongolia Locate this hidden shop on UB's Peace Ave and you'll discover a trove of unique handmade items; good for Kazakh products (p70)

The Obscure

A lot of strange stuff happens in Mongolia. One day you're driving a tank, the next day you're eating sheep's head stew. Keep your itinerary loose and expect the unexpected.

Mongol Tsergiin Khuree Shooting Range If you like the idea of driving a Russian tank or shooting an RPG, pay a visit to this military shooting range, an hour from Ulaanbaatar (p83)

Creepy Bars Ulaanbaatar has a lot of these, including a Nazi-themed bar that is sure to make you cringe; ask some Mongolian friends to take you to their local bar and see what you discover.

Ninjas Out in the wilds of Mongolia there are some 100,000 illegal goldminers, nicknamed Teenage Mutant Ninja Turtles (Ninjas for short). With the price of gold soaring, you could join them and pay off your trip.

Choir This Soviet-era city was once home to thousands of Red Army troops; crumbling statues and mosaic propaganda slogans (p165) can still be found here.

Kharkhorin Penis Statue This rock-hard statue was recently erected on a hill near Kharkhorin (p99)

Urlag Down some vodka shots and toast the Dear Leader at this North Korean restaurant (p62)

month by month

Top Events

1 **Naadam**, July

2 **Golden Eagle Festival**, October

3 **Khatgal Ice Festival**, February

4 **Tsagaan Sar**, February

5 **Bulgan Camel Festival**, February

January

Cold. Damn Cold. Frozen toes and eyelashes cold. But that doesn't mean you can't visit the country. Hotels, restaurants and most other services still operate. This is a good time for short winter walks in Terelj.

February

Cold temperatures across the country (typically minus 15ºC during the day and minus 25ºC at night), although skies are usually clear. Deep snows can block roads but driving over lakes and rivers is possible.

Tsagaan Sar

The Lunar New Year. This is a good time to meet Mongolians and, if you're lucky, get invited to a family celebration. Note: this may occur in late January or early March.

Khatgal Ice Festival

A newish celebration (p130) that includes ice skating, horse-sledding races, ice fishing and thickly dressed locals. It'll be bitterly cold but skies are usually clear.

Bulgan Camel Festival

This event happens during Tsagaan Sar. You'll see camel polo, camel racing and other camel games.

Ice Ankle-bone Shooting Competition

Staged on the frozen Tuul River in Ulaanbaatar. The competition (p55) is similar to curling, except with ankle-bones replacing the blocks of Scottish granite.

Winter Sports

Long-distance ice skating and dog sledding are possible at Lake Khövsgöl (certain tour companies organise this); or try downhill skiing at Sky Resort.

March

This month suffers from strong winds, subzero temperatures, snow and dust storms. You may get all four seasons in one day and the inclement weather often cancels flights. Melting snows will reveal a brown, harsh landscape. The long winter and lack of fodder will make livestock thin – a bad time for horse riding.

Navrus

The Kazakh spring festival begins in Bayan-Ölgii on 22 March. Visit a family feast and watch traditional games and contests.

April

The weather in April is similar to March, with frequent dust storms and cold snaps. The second half of the month can see slightly better, more consistent weather. However, if the winter has been severe, livestock will die off rapidly at this time, causing hardship for herders. Melting snow can cause flooding and vehicles are prone to falling through ice.

May

The weather will be warming up this month and the tourist season will start tepidly as some ger camps open. Snowfalls may still occur, especially

in the north. Central areas will see a rainstorm or two.

Ikh Duichin

Buddha's Birthday is held on 18 May. The day is marked by *tsam* dancing at Gandan Khiid in Ulaanbaatar and by special services in most other monasteries.

June

Temperatures will reach the mid to high 20s, allowing for more comfortable travel conditions. The weather tends to be dry this month but an occasional rainstorm will bring relief to the parched grasslands.

Roaring Hooves Festival

Often held at a remote location in the Gobi Desert, this international music festival can be staged anywhere in the country. See www.roarinhooves.com for details.

Fishing Season Starts

Fishing season kicks off on 15 July in Mongolia.

Blue Valley Awards Festival

A mid-June festival of horse games and song competitions, held in Renchinlkhumbe (Khövsgöl aimag).

July

This is peak travel season. Weather is good although a heat wave usually hits around this time; temperatures in the Gobi can reach 40°C.

Naadam

Mongolia's premier summer sports festival (p222) erupts in July. The date is fixed in Ulaanbaatar (11–12 July) but will change from year to year in other cities and towns. Good village naadams can be found at Dadal or Khatgal.

Altai Horse Games Festival

This festival (p184) is held the third weekend in July in Tavan Bogd National Park. It features traditional Kazakh horse games like *kokbar* (tug of war with a goat).

Sunrise to Sunset Ultramarathon

This 100km race (there is also a 42km segment for wimps) is held along the shores of Lake Khövsgöl. Check www.ultramongolia.org.

August

In terms of weather, this tends to be the best month in Mongolia. Temperatures are pleasant and there is enough rainfall to keep the dust down and turn the grasslands an electric green. On the downside, heavy rains can turn jeep tracks into mud pits, causing vehicles to get bogged.

Gongoriin Bombani Hural

Religious festival held at Amarbayasgalant Monastery. Bring your tent and camp in the fields with the other festival-goers.

Mongolia Bike Challenge

New event that brings together serious mountain bikers for a cycling rally.

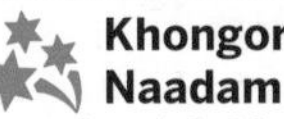

Khongoryn Els Naadam

A naadam is held nearby these iconic sand dunes (usually 15 August).

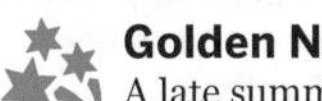

Golden Naadam

A late summer naadam (usually 21 August) that takes place at Terelj.

Playtime

Two-day alternative music fest (p55), held in Gachuurt. A great opportunity to meet young Mongol music fans and check out the newest local bands.

September

As summer ends you can expect changeable weather. Temperatures will be fair but you should bring a fleece layer and light jacket. A cold snap may occur and you might even see a brief snowstorm.

Gobi Marathon

Go for a 42km run in one of the world's most inhospitable deserts. See www.gobimarathon.org for information. Try not to die.

Altai Eagle Festival

One of several eagle festivals held in Bayan-Ölgii. This one is held in Sagsai in late September.

Fishing

September is a great time for fishing. The weather will be good and rivers will be calm after the August rains.

October

October is cool and sees snow flurries up north but is still fine for travel, especially in the Gobi. By now most ger camps are closed except for a few around Terelj.

Eagle Festival

The Eagle Festival (p183) in Bayan-Ölgii is growing in popularity. If you're in Mongolia in October, it's certainly worth a trip way out west.

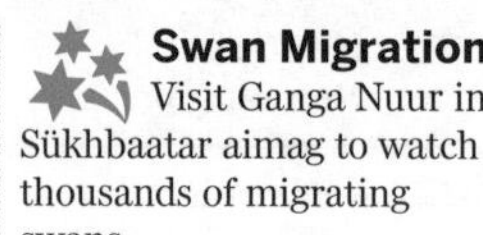

Swan Migration

Visit Ganga Nuur in Sükhbaatar aimag to watch thousands of migrating swans.

November

The mercury dips below zero and will continue to plummet. Despite the cold there are still a few visitors around – some take trips down to the Gobi where it's a touch warmer.

Eagle Hunting

November is a good time to visit Bayan-Ölgii and watch the eagle hunters in action.

December

Brace yourself, the Mongolian winter is upon you. Sky Resort near Ulaanbaatar will open (good for beginning skiers).

New Year's Eve

Mongolians celebrate New Year's enthusiastically, usually with lots of beer, vodka and fireworks.

itineraries

Whether you've got six days or 60, these itineraries provide a starting point for the trip of a lifetime. Want more inspiration? Head online to lonelyplanet.com/thorntree to chat with other travellers.

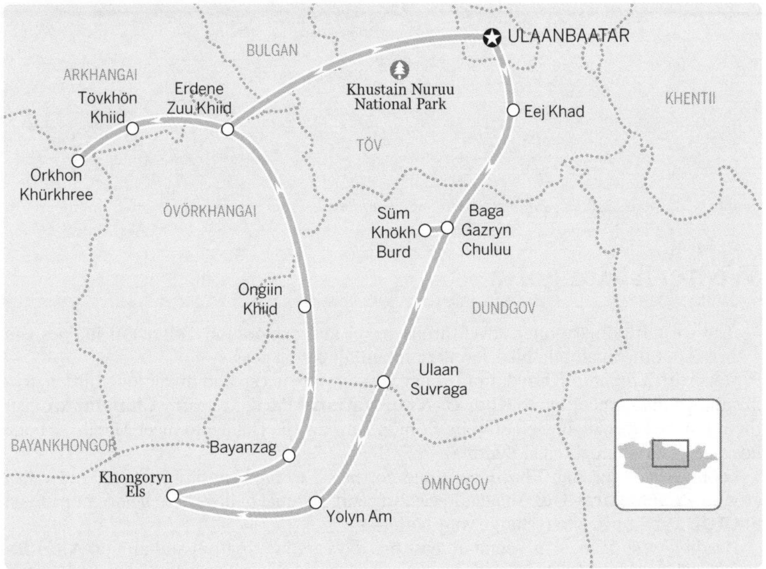

Two Weeks
The Big Loop

Spend a day in **Ulaanbaatar** visiting Gandan Monastery and the main museums. On day two, head south to the eerie rock formations of **Baga Gazryn Chuluu** and the ruined castle at **Süm Khökh Burd**, stopping at **Eej Khad**, Mother Rock, en route. From Süm Khökh Burd, stop by **Ulaan Suvraga** on your way south.

At least three days are needed to explore Ömnögov: check out the spectacular ice canyon at **Yolyn Am**, the massive sand dunes at **Khongoryn Els** and the dinosaur quarry at **Bayanzag**.

From Bayanzag, go north to the ruins of **Ongiin Khiid desert monastery**, a perfect place to organise a camel trek.

Leaving the Gobi, your first stop is **Erdene Zuu Khiid**, the country's oldest monastery. Head west up the Orkhon Valley, to **Tövkhön Khiid** and then onto the **Orkhon Khürkhree**. The waterfall is the perfect place to unwind after a long trip to the Gobi, so spend a couple of nights here (and wash away the Gobi dust in the falls).

If there's time on your way back to Ulaanbaatar, spend a night at **Khustain Nuruu National Park**.

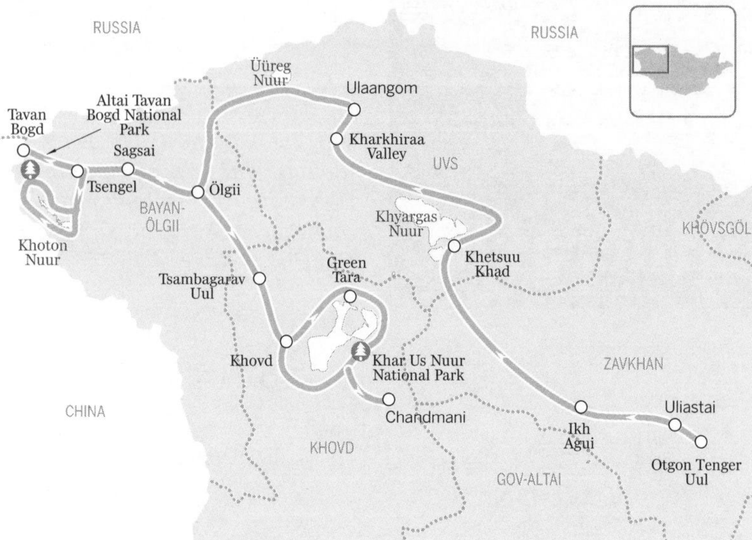

One Month

Western Mongolia

The western aimags offer adventurous travel and exploration. Adrenalin junkies can break out the mountain bike, kayak or mountaineering gear.

Start with a flight to **Khovd**, from where you can hire a jeep and driver for a bird-watching and wildlife expedition to **Khar Us Nuur National Park**. At nearby **Chandmani**, visit the renowned throat singers. Stop by Dörgön sum for the chance to meet Megjin, a bona fide Green Tara (enlightened Buddha).

Looping back through Khovd, continue northwest to the beautiful pastures and valley around **Tsambagarav Uul**. You could easily spend a couple of days here before moving on to **Ölgii**, a great place to recharge your batteries.

Heading west from Ölgii, spend at least five days getting to, from and around **Altai Tavan Bogd National Park**. With more time, consider doing a horse trek around **Khoton Nuur**. With proper equipment, permits and some logistic support, it's even possible to scale Mongolia's highest peak, the 4374m **Tavan Bogd**, though a visit to the base camp and glacier is more feasible.

On the way to or from Tavan Bogd, stop in **Tsengel** or **Sagsai**, authentic Kazakh villages that offer a taste of life in the Wild West. From Sagsai it's even possible to go rafting back to Ölgii.

The best time to make this journey is in late September or early October, which gives you the chance to watch the spectacular Eagle Festival in Ölgii or Sagsai.

From Ölgii, the main road winds northeast, passing **Üüreg Nuur** en route to **Ulaangom**. Allow a week for trekking around **Kharkhiraa Valley**. An experienced driver can get you from Ulaangom to **Uliastai**, visiting **Khyargas Nuur** and **Ikh Agui** en route. If you arrive at Khyargas Nuur before mid-September, you'll have a chance to see hundreds of squawking cormorants that roost here in summer.

From pretty Uliastai you can get a flight to Ulaanbaatar, but not before mounting a horse or hiking to **Otgon Tenger Uul**.

If you've done this itinerary in reverse order, it may be possible to catch a flight from Khovd to Urumqi in Xinjiang. Contact AeroMongolia or EZ Nis in Ulaanbaatar for more information.

Two Weeks

Eastern Mongolia

Eastern Mongolia offers a delightful romp through grasslands, forest and some unique historical sights. Best of all, it's almost completely devoid of tourists.

Heading east from UB, you'll pass the new **Chinggis Khaan statue** on the way to **Khökh Nuur**, a pretty alpine lake that saw the coronation of the great *khaan*. Continue northeast, visiting **Baldan Bereeven Khiid**, **Öglögchiin Kherem**, **Batshireet** and **Binder** as you travel through Khentii's scenic countryside. There are ger camps all along this route where you can stop for horse-riding trips in the mountains.

Dadal is another good place for horse trekking or just kicking back with some locals, and is an excellent destination for Naadam. Make sure to visit Zundoi-Davag, a retired hunter who has assembled a small museum at his home.

Following the Ulz Gol further east, you'll pass pretty Buriat villages, such as **Bayan-Uul** and **Bayandun**, and nature reserves including **Ugtam Uul**. If you're interested in meeting a shaman you may be fortunate enough to meet one by asking around in this area. Continue south towards **Choibalsan**.

An alternative route to Choibalsan goes via the nature reserve **Toson Khulstai** and ancient ruins at **Kherlen Bar Khot**.

From Choibalsan take the train to **Chuluunkhoroot** to visit **Mongol Daguur B**, a protected area for wader birds, or travel across the empty steppes to **Khalkhiin Gol**, a remote landscape of lakes, rivers, wildlife and historical sights. Highlights include giant Buddha statues carved into a hillside and monuments dedicated to soldiers who died here during WWII.

You'll need another couple of days to visit the lush **Nömrög Strictly Protected Area** and **Sangiin Dalai Nuur**. From Nömrög, tackle the rough terrain in **Dornod Mongol Strictly Protected Area** to spot some truly massive herds of gazelle.

The **Dariganga region**, with its sand dunes, cinder cones and scattered stone statues, requires two or three days. Horse trekking is also possible here. If you happen to be in the area in early October, this is the time to catch the large migration of swans at Ganga Nuur.

Return to Ulaanbaatar via **Baruun-Urt** and **Öndörkhaan**, or travel to **Sainshand** for a taste of the Gobi and a visit to **Khamaryn Khiid**.

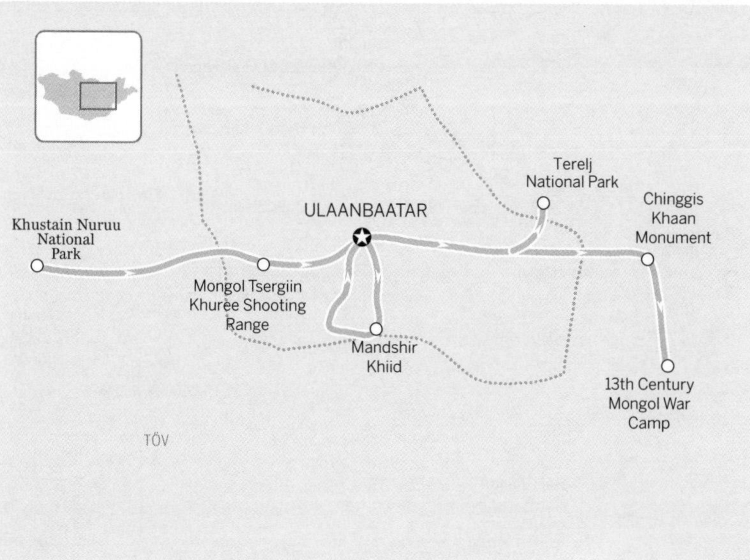

One Week
Around Ulaanbaatar

If you've got some spare time to kick around Ulaanbaatar, there is enough to see and do around the city to keep you busy for a few days.

After a day of sightseeing around UB, head to **Khustain Nuruu National Park** for the night to watch the wild *takhi* horses. On the way to or from the park, stop at the **Mongol Tsergiin Khuree Shooting Range**, where you can sharpen up your tank-driving skills.

Back in Ulaanbaatar, catch a ride to **Mandshir Khiid** in Töv aimag, from where you can hike back over the mountain to Ulaanbaatar. This can be done either as a full day trip or as an overnight hike.

Next, head east to **Terelj National Park**. There are a number of activity options here, including mountain biking, horse riding, rock climbing, hiking and river rafting. If you have your own vehicle, push on a little further east to see the enormous **Chinggis Khaan Monument** at Tsonjin Boldog. The company that built the statue also runs the nearby **13th-Century Mongol War Camp**, where you can watch mini naadams and see artisans create traditional products.

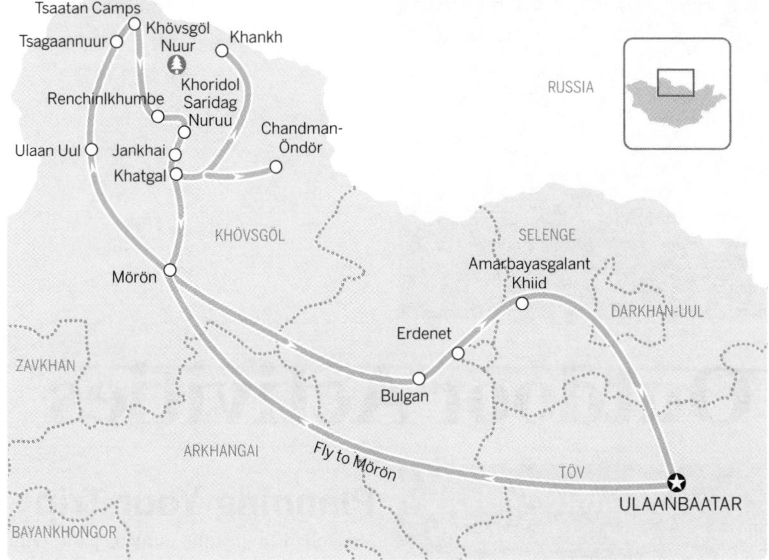

One Month
Northern Mongolia

Start week one of this trip by flying to **Mörön** from Ulaanbaatar. Hire a vehicle in Mörön and drive to **Tsagaannuur**, breaking up the journey with a night at Ulaan Uul. In Tsagaannuur, drop into the TCVC and hire a guide and horses to get you out to the taiga and **Tsaatan camps**. Plan for a week of travel in the area.

To start week two, get a lift to **Renchinlkhumbe** and then trek your way over the **Khoridol Saridag Nuruu** to the shores of **Lake Khövsgöl**. Then walk down the lakeshore until you reach **Jankhai**. Spend a few days relaxing at Nature's Door Guesthouse and then continue on to **Khatgal**.

From Khatgal, the adventurous will make their way all the way up to **Khankh** on the northern shore of the lake. Alternatively, there are some gorgeous areas east of the lake in the **Chandman-Öndör** area. You'll need another week to explore this region.

The trip back to Ulaanbaatar goes through a remote part of Bulgan aimag to the pleasant aimag capital of **Bulgan**. Further east, after passing through **Erdenet**, make a short detour to visit the magnificent **Amarbayasgalant Khiid**.

Outdoor Activities

Most Popular Activity

Mongolians practically invented horse riding, making this one of the most iconic activities you can do here. Short horse rides are possible just about everywhere you go. Multiday horse treks are best done in the mountainous areas of Arkhangai, Khövsgöl and Khentii.

Best Off-Season Activity

Visit Mongolia in winter and you can try your hand at dog sledding. French tour guide Joel Rauzy harnesses up teams of strong huskies to pull your sled through the Mongolian wilderness.

Best Area for Adventure

Khövsgöl aimag has great potential for adventure tourism. The varied terrain is ideal for horse riding or mountain biking. This is also one of the premier areas for fishing. In winter you can even go ice skating across Lake Khövsgöl.

Best Way to Mix Adventure & Local Culture

If you are looking for a fun, adventurous trip that also introduces you to the local culture then consider a Ger to Ger trip (see p29). These combine hiking and horse riding as you move from one ger to the next – a great way to meet locals in the Mongolian backcountry.

Planning Your Trip

Mongolia is a gigantic outdoor park. With scattered settlements, few roads and immense areas of steppe, mountain and forest, the entire country beckons the outdoor enthusiast. But the lack of infrastructure is a double-edged sword: while there are many areas that have potential for ecotourism, only a few (for example, Khövsgöl Nuur, Terkhiin Tsagaan Nuur and Terelj National Park) can really handle independent travellers. Signing up with a tour group, on the other hand, gives you instant logistical help. Tour agencies can act like mobile support centres, using vans, trucks and helicopters to shuttle clients and their gear around. Independent travellers hoping to explore remote areas of the country will need to be completely self-sufficient. This chapter provides tips on how to deal with these logistical hurdles.

For details of overseas companies that organise activities, see p263; for companies based in Mongolia, see p52.

When to Go

Summer offers the best weather for horse riding, hiking and mountain biking but winter sports are also possible – think ice fishing, dog sledding and long-distance ice skating. Independent travellers arriving in summer will have a good chance to link up with others to share costs.

SAFE CYCLING TIPS

» Dogs can be ferocious and will chase you away from gers. If you stop and hold your ground they will back off; it helps to pick up a rock. The faster you cycle away, the more they want to chase you.

» Cyclists usually follow river valleys. However, in Mongolia it's often better to go over the mountains. Roads along rivers are usually sandy or consist of loose stones that make riding difficult.

» Most cyclists consider the best trip to be a cross-country adventure but in Mongolia (where there are vast areas of nothingness) consider focusing on one small area and doing a loop. There are great routes to explore in Khövsgöl and Bayan-Ölgii aimags.

» Bring all the spare parts you may need, including brake pads, cables and inner tubes. Spare parts are hard to find in Mongolia, but you could try the Seven Summits (p68) in Ulaanbaatar.

Best Times

» **July & August** Weather is fair across the country and summer rains will bring life back to the pasturelands. This is an especially good time for horse trekking.

» **September** This is perhaps the best month for fishing. It's also a great time for trekking in northern Mongolia where you can watch the leaves change colour.

» **February** If you are considering a winter sport like cross-country skiing, February is a good time to do it. There will be a decent amount of snow cover by now and temperatures will be warming slightly by the day.

Avoid

» **March & April** Spring weather is plagued by strong winds and dust storms. This is not a good time for horse trekking as animals will be weak after the long winter. The landscape – bare, brown earth – is at its least photogenic.

» **December & January** These are the coldest months of the year and you'll get the least amount of daylight. Temperatures can plummet to -35°C at this time.

Cycle Touring

Mongolia is an adventure cyclist's dream. There are few fences, lots of open spaces and very little traffic. Roads are mainly dirt but the jeep trails are usually hard-packed earth, allowing you to cover 40km to 50km per day.

Overlanding by bike does require careful planning and thought; you'll need to be totally self-sufficient in terms of tools and spare parts. Other factors include washed-out bridges, trails that disappear into rivers or marshland and, in late summer, heavy rain and mud. On the plus side, locals will be pleasantly intrigued by your bike. You'll have lots of chances to swap it for a horse and go for a short canter, but don't forget to show your Mongolian counterpart the brakes!

Guided tours are led by **Bike Mongolia** (www.bikemongolia.com).

Routes

The following trips require several days. They can be made solo provided you are equipped with a tent, sleeping bag, food, tools and spare parts. Another option is to use vehicle support: hire a jeep and driver to take you out to the best biking areas and keep all your gear in the vehicle while you ride unhindered. Gobi areas, due to their lack of water and facilities, are places to avoid.

» **Chinggis Khaan Trail** This trail in northern Khentii offers plenty of cultural heritage and nice riding terrain. Get a ride from Ulaanbaatar (UB) to Tsenkhermandal in Khentii aimag, then cycle north to Khökh Nuur, buried deep in the Khentii Mountains. Continue northwest to Khangil Nuur and the very bumpy road to Balden Bereeven Khiid. Another 17km brings you to the deer stones and then Öglögchiin Kherem. Continue to Batshireet, Binder and, finally, Dadal. This trip takes four to six days.

» **Khövsgöl aimag** A nice route leads south from Mörön to Tariat in Arkhangai, via the towns of Shine-Ider, Galt and Jargalant. The more popular route is from Mörön up to Khatgal and then along either side of Khövsgöl Nuur. The slightly more adventurous could cycle in the spectacular Chandman-Öndör area.

» **Ölgii to Ulaanbaatar** This mammoth 1450km expedition will take three or four weeks. In summer, the prevailing winds in Mongolia travel from west to east, which means that you'll enjoy tail winds if you start in Ölgii and end in Ulaanbaatar. Ending in UB also gives you something to look forward to – a cold beer at the Grand Khaan! The northern route, via either Mörön or Tosontsengel, is more interesting than the southern Gobi route.

Fishing

With Mongolia's large number of lakes *(nuurs)* and rivers *(gols),* and a sparse population that generally prefers red meat, the fish are just waiting to be caught. The best places to dangle your lines:

» **Khövsgöl Nuur** (p129) For grayling and lenok.

» **Terkhiin Tsagaan Nuur** (p107) Has a lot of pike.

The season is mid-June to late September. You can get a fishing permit from the national park office. Permits are valid for two days or 10 fish, whichever comes first. For the truly intrepid, visit either lake in winter for some hard-core ice fishing.

Serious anglers will want to try out Mongolia's rivers – the fly-fishing is some of the best anywhere. The major target is taimen, an enormous salmonoid that spends its leisure time hunting down unfortunate rodents that fall in the rivers. These monsters can reach 1.5m in length and weigh 50kg. Unfortunately they are also prized by poachers and are thus carefully guarded by locals along the river. To avoid any problems, you must fish for taimen with a reputable outfitter. Catch and release is mandatory, using only single barbless hooks (never use treble hooks). Outfitters run fishing trips on the Ider, Chuluut, Selenge, Orkhon, Onon and Delgermörön Gols.

While it's relatively easy to get a fishing permit in a national park, buying one for other areas is much more difficult. Anglers must have a special permit authorised by the **Ministry of Nature & Environment and Tourism** (☎051-266 286; www.mne.mn; Negdsen Undestnii Gudamj 5/2, Government Bldg II, Ulaanbaatar), which costs US$120 a week. But to get the permit you need a contract with the *sum* (district) where you plan to fish and approval by the aimag (province). Obviously this is not possible for casual tourists – the whole system has been set up so that it can be effectively managed by tour operators. Before signing up, make sure your outfitter has the necessary agreements and permits; some take the risk of fishing illegally, which can get you in big trouble if you're caught.

Four responsible fly-fishing tour operators:

Mongolia River Outfitters (www.mongoliarivers.com)

Fish Mongolia (www.fishmongolia.co.uk)

Sweetwater Travel (www.sweetwatertravel.com/mongolia.htm)

Hovsgol Travel (www.hovsgoltravel.com)

The cost for two people on an 11-day package trip will be between US$3000 and US$6000 all-inclusive, more if you take a Cessna flight direct to the camps from UB.

Several shops in Ulaanbaatar sell fishing equipment, the best is Ayanchin Outfitters (p68).

For more information check www.taimen.mn.

Hiking

With a good map and compass, hikers can explore the best of Mongolia's back country. The biggest obstacle faced by hikers is finding transport to the mountains once they get far from Ulaanbaatar. However, in the regions around Bogdkhan Uul (p84) and Terelj (p88), which are not far from Ulaanbaatar, there are enough mountains to keep hikers busy for a few days.

Pay any fees and procure any permits required by local authorities. Be aware of local laws, regulations and etiquette about wildlife and the environment. Decent topographic maps are available in Ulaanbaatar.

Mosquitoes and midges are a curse. The situation is at its worst during spring and early summer, with the marshy lakes and canyons in the western deserts the most troublesome areas.

» In western Mongolia, prime hiking areas include the Altai Tavan Bogd National Park (p188), around Khoton Nuur or between the lakes and Tavan Bogd. In Uvs aimag try the Kharkhiraa and Türgen uuls (p199), which have hiking trails of three to seven days.

» In northern Mongolia there is great hiking in the Khövsgöl Nuur area (p129).

» Down in the Gobi, it's possible to hike in Gurvan Saikhan National Park (p169), especially around Yolyn Am.

GER TO GER

As the most innovative tourism concept in Mongolia, the **Ger to Ger program** (Map p42; ☎313 336; www.gertoger.org; Arizona Plaza, Suite 11, Baruun Selbe 5/3, Ulaanbaatar) should be near the top of every traveller's wish list. By combining hiking, sports, Mongolian language and visits with local families, the experience promises total cultural immersion.

The concept is simple. Travellers can choose one of several routes in Dundgov, Arkhangai, Bulgan or Terelj, or a combination of routes if they have more time. Prior to departure they are educated in local social graces, culture and appropriate Mongolian phrases. Transport is organised to the starting point and then the trekkers begin walking from ger to ger, which can be anywhere from 5km to 30km apart. Once the trekkers have reached the appointed ger, the local family prepares a meal and helps them set up camp (tents and gear are carried by pack animals).

Because distances vary between gers, there may be different modes of transport between them – you may take a yak cart for one stretch or go by horse on another. The program is not forced on the host families; they are still nomadic and may move their ger if they have to (gers along the route keep in regular contact and will know the location of other families). Participant families are also paid fairly (many have tripled their incomes) and a portion of the proceeds goes to community development.

Although you'll pay for the majority of the trip in Ulaanbaatar, you may want to bring extra cash, because some routes include a visit to a local cooperative where you can buy products made by herders (handmade cashmere sweaters and the like can be great bargains).

Horse & Camel Trekking

Horse treks in Mongolia range from easy day trips with guides to multiweek solo adventures deep in the mountains. Inexperienced riders should begin with the former, organising their first ride through a ger camp or tour operator. The prettiest, most accessible places to try are the camps at Terelj and Khövsgöl Nuur, where you can normally hire a horse and guide for less than US$20 a day.

Even the most experienced riders will benefit from a lesson on how to deal with a Mongolian horse. The local breed is short, stocky and half-wild; Mongolian horsemen can provide instruction on saddling, hobbling and caring for your horse. You'll also get tips on the best places in which to ride and where to purchase saddles and other equipment. Try Stepperiders (p85) in Töv aimag.

Of the dozens of possible horse treks, several are popular and not difficult to arrange.

» Tsetserleg to Bayankhongor is a rugged wilderness trip that crosses a series of alpine passes.

» In the east, try the Binder area (p144) of Khentii aimag, which can include a ride to Dadal near the Siberian border.

» The most popular horse-trekking area is Khövsgöl Nuur (p127), largely because there is such a good network of guides and available horses. Some travellers have horse-trekked from Terkhiin Tsagaan Nuur to Khövsgöl Nuur. By land (following the twisting river valleys) it's around 295km and takes at least two weeks by horse.

» Closer to Ulaanbaatar, the areas of Terelj and Bogdkhan are both excellent if you don't have a lot of time.

» In western Mongolia there is great horse trekking around Otgon Tenger Uul (p203); it can take six days to circle the mountain.

» In Altai Tavan Bogd National Park (p188), try a horse trek around Khoton Nuur. There is also horse trekking around Tsast Uul and Tsambagarav Uul. Tour operators in Ölgii can help set something up, or just turn up in any nearby village and ask around for horses.

At touristy places such as the ger camps at Terelj and in the south Gobi you can ride a camel, though these are more like photo sessions than serious sport. Some of the ger camps at Ongiin Khiid (p160) can arrange a multiday camel trek.

HORSE HINTS

» Mongolians swap horses readily, so there's no need to be stuck with a horse you don't like, or which doesn't like you, except perhaps in April and May, when all animals are weak after the long winter and before fresh spring plants have made their way through the melting snows. The best time for riding is in the summer (June to September).

» Mount a horse (or camel) only from the left. They have been trained to accept human approach from that side, and may rear if approached the wrong way.

» The Mongolians use the phrase '*chu!*' to make their horses go. Somewhat telling about the obstinate nature of Mongolian horses is that there is no word for 'stop'.

» If you are considering a multiday horse trip, remember that horses attract all kinds of flies.

» A saddle, bridle, halter and hobble can all be bought at the outdoor market in Ulaanbaatar. An English hybrid saddle can be bought for T55,000 to T65,000, pack-saddles for half that. Riders with long legs might consider bringing narrow stirrup leathers from home.

» Buying a horse is best done with the help of a Mongolian friend. A decent quality horse will run to at least T300,000. Herders will be reluctant to sell their best (ie quiet and calm) horses and may try to sell you a nag. Buyer beware. Test ride any horse you are considering and try loading up potential pack horses to make sure they don't crumple under the weight. To hire a horse you'll likely pay T7000 to T15,000 per day. Horse guides charge around T20,000 per day.

» The most important thing to consider when planning a trip is where to get water. Following a river is a good idea, or you can ask around for a well, though these can be dry. As a rule of thumb, where there are animals and people, there is water.

Kayaking, Canoeing & Rafting

Mongolia's numerous lakes and rivers are often ideal for kayaking and rafting. There is little white water but, during the summer rains, rivers can flow at up to 9km/h.

» One of the most popular river trips is down the Tuul Gol, from the bridge at the entrance to Terelj and back to Ulaanbaatar.

» There are more adventurous options that begin in Khövsgöl aimag. Boat or kayak trips on the Eg Gol can start at Khatgal. A trip on the Delgermörön Gol starts at Bayanzürkh. In this area, contact **Fish Mongolia** (www.fishmongolia).

» In Bayan-Ölgii it's possible to raft down the Khovd Gol from Khurgan Nuur, past Ölgii city and onto Myangad in Khovd aimag.

» Rafting is organised along the Tuul and Khovd Rivers by agencies based in Ulaanbaatar (p52), including Juulchin, Khövsgöl Lodge Company and Nomadic Journeys.

Some cowboy outfitters offer canoe trips but may not be reliable or qualified to run them. If you are serious about this sport, contact the **Mongolian Institute of Outdoor Learning** (MIOL; ☎9915 8130; www.miol.org), which trains river guides.

There is nothing stopping you from heading out on your own. The Seven Summits (p68) rents inflatable kayaks for about US$25 a day.

The best time for kayaking or rafting is July to September, after some decent rain.

Bird-Watching

Mongolia is rich in birdlife; for a comprehensive overview see http://birdsmongolia.blogspot.com. These are the best places to get out your binoculars and telephoto lens:

» **Ganga Nuur** (p153) Migratory swan.

» **Khar Us Nuur and Khar Nuur** (p194) Goose, wood grouse and relict gull, and migratory pelican.

» **Khyargas Nuur and Airag Nuur** (p201) Migratory cormorant and pelican.

» **Mongol Daguur Special Protected Area** (p146) White-naped crane and other waterfowl.

» **Sangiin Dalai Nuur** (p159) Mongolian lark, eagle, goose and swan.

» **Uvs Nuur** (p199) Spoonbill, crane and gull.

Golf

Although not the first sport that comes to mind when planning an adventure in Mongolia, golfing is possible. There are two courses in Terelj National Park (p89).

Dedicated golfers travelling across the green steppes of Mongolia may begin to wonder if it is possible to simply golf across the country. In fact, someone has beaten you to it. Extreme golfer Andre Tolme accomplished the feat in 2003–04 (he shot the round in 12,170 strokes). You can read more about his adventure at www.golfmongolia.com.

Ice Skating

In winter you won't have to worry about falling through the ice, as many lakes and rivers freeze right down to the bottom. Many Mongolians are keen ice-skaters – at least those who live near water, or in big cities with rinks.

» The Children's Park (National Amusement Park) in Ulaanbaatar has ice-skating and skate hire.

» Long-distance skating is possible on Lake Khövsgöl. A one-week trip with support costs around US$1300; contact Nomadic Journeys (p54).

Mountaineering

Mongolia also offers spectacular opportunities for mountain climbing. In the western aimags there are dozens of glaciers, and 30 to 40 permanently snow-capped mountains. You must have the necessary experience, be fully equipped and hire local guides. The best time to climb is July and August. Karakorum Expeditions (p53) is a leader in this area.

Rock Climbing

There are excellent opportunities for rock climbing in Mongolia, although the sport is still in its infancy with few established routes. For now the best place to climb is in Terelj, where routes have been established on a 35m-high rock near the Buveit ger camp (p89). Plans have been laid to keep climbing gear at the ger camp, where you can turn up and climb at a cost of US$40 to US$50 per day. With your own gear, it's US$35. Climbing routes have also been established at Ikh Gazryn Chuluu (p161) in Dundgov; climbers will need to bring their own equipment. Wind of Mongolia (p54) runs rock-climbing tours.

Skiing

The only downhill ski resort in Mongolia is Sky Resort (p51), which will only be of interest to beginners. There is much potential

MONGOLIA'S HIGHEST PEAKS

» **Tavan Bogd** (4374m; p189) In Bayan-Ölgii, on the border of Mongolia, China and Russia. This mountain cluster is full of permanent and crevassed glaciers.

» **Mönkh Khairkhan Uul** (4362m; p196) On the border of Bayan-Ölgii and Khovd aimags. You will need crampons, an ice axe and ropes.

» **Tsambagarav Uul** (4202m; p187) In Khovd; it is relatively easy to climb with crampons and an ice axe.

» **Tsast Uul** (4193m; p187) On the border of Bayan-Ölgii and Khovd aimags. It's accessible and the camping here is great.

» **Sutai Uul** (4090m; p178) On the border of Gov-Altai and Khovd aimags.

» **Kharkhiraa Uul** (4037m; p199) In Uvs; a great hiking area.

» **Türgen Uul** (3965m; p199) One of the most easily climbed with spectacular views; in Uvs.

» **Otgon Tenger Uul** (3905m; p203) Mongolia's holiest mountain, located in Zavkhan aimag. Its sanctity means that climbing is strictly prohibited.

for cross-country skiing, although there are no developed trails and hiring equipment is difficult. If you have your own equipment, the best places to try are Nairamadal, about 20km west of Ulaanbaatar city centre, Khandgait or Terelj. The best months for skiing are January and February – but be warned: the average temperature during these months hovers around a very chilly -25°C.

Offbeat Activities

» **Dog sledding** Trips, organised by Wind of Mongolia (p54), are offered in Terelj (December to February) for US$60 to US$80 per day, and in Khövsgöl Nuur (March to April); cross-lake trips take eight days (all-inclusive US$2600).

» **Polo** Legend has it that Chinggis Khaan's troops used to play polo using their enemies' heads as the ball, but this practice seems to have died out. Modern polo (sans severed heads) is occasionally played by local clubs. See www.genghiskhanpolo.com for details.

regions at a glance

Most first-time travellers to Mongolia spend a day or two in the capital Ulaanbaatar before setting off for the countryside. The most popular destination is the iconic Gobi; a trip here usually loops in part of Central Mongolia as it's fairly easy to combine the two regions. Northern Mongolia, specifically Lake Khövsgöl, is the second most popular destination. All three of these areas have built up a solid tourist infrastructure, with lots of ger camps along established routes.

Western Mongolia sees fewer visitors, largely because of its great distance from Ulaanbaatar and the cost of getting a flight there. However, the West does offer some spectacular scenery and is a great place for the adventurous. The East is Mongolia's least-known and least-visited region (only 3% of tourists head this way), a blessing for explorers wanting an off-the-beaten path experience.

Ulaanbaatar

Shopping ✓✓
Museums ✓
Entertainment ✓✓

Shopping
Ulaanbaatar is the best place for shopping. Pick up cashmere jumpers, artwork, crafts, antiques, traditional clothing, CDs and souvenirs. Meet artists by visiting their studios and buying their art directly.

Museums
Mongolia's best museums and a must for a deeper understanding of the country. Some are neglected; others recently renovated and modernised. The National Museum is a must-see.

Entertainment
Options include Mongolian culture shows, operas, dramas, concerts and fashion shows, especially during summer tourist season. Bars and nightclubs cater to both foreigners and locals.

p38

Central Mongolia

Historic Sites ✓
Nature ✓✓
Horse Riding ✓✓✓

Historic Sites
Arkhangai aimag has deer stones and ancient Turkic monuments carved with runic script. There are also ancient monasteries that survived Stalin's purge; the best is Erdene Zuu with walls built from the ruins of Karakorum.

Nature
There's marvellous scenery in the Khan Khentii Strictly Protected Area. Or head west to the Khangai Mountains to explore the Orkhon waterfall, the Great White Lake and the remote Naiman Nuur.

Horse Riding
The Orkhon valley is great for horse trekking, especially from the Orkhon waterfall to Naiman Nuur. Terkhiin Tsagaan Nuur is also good, or closer to UB, try the forests north of Terelj.

p79

Northern Mongolia

Fishing ✓✓✓
Culture ✓✓✓
Hiking ✓✓✓

Fishing
Fishing holes in northern Mongolia are world class. The big prize here is taimen, the world's largest salmonoid. Help protect these endangered creatures and go with an experienced tour operator.

Culture
Khövsgöl is a culturally distinct part of Mongolia. The aimag features the unique Tsaatan, a tribe of reindeer herders, and if you're lucky, you can visit a shaman ceremony while in the north.

Hiking
There is wonderful backcountry to be explored in Khövsgöl aimag. Hikes can last from one day to over a week. One of the most popular is along the west shore of Khövsgöl Nuur and through the mountains to Renchinlkhumbe.

p109

Eastern Mongolia

Wildlife ✓✓✓
Historic Sites ✓✓
Horse Riding ✓✓✓

Wildlife
Spotting gazelles on the eastern steppe rivals any wildlife experience you can have in Asia. Nömrög, in the country's far east, is another place to see wildlife, including moose, otter and bears.

Historic Sites
In Khentii take a trip along the Chinggis Khaan trail, visiting sites associated with his life. The adventurous can also head to Khalkhiin Gol to see the enormous Janraisag Buddha and some WWII battlefields.

Horse Riding
The horse trekking through the mountains of Khentii, especially around Dadal, is among Mongolia's best. Follow the rivers, camp amid gorgeous scenery and learn horse-handling skills from Buriats who make their home here.

p138

The Gobi

Camel Riding ✓✓✓
Scenic Drives ✓✓
Palaeontology ✓✓✓

Camel Riding
Trekking across sand dunes on a camel is the iconic Gobi experience. Pack camping gear and plenty of water – trekking happens around Khongoryn Els and Ongiin Khiid.

Scenic Drives
Head out of Dalanzadgad to Gurvan Saikhan NP. Visit the Vulture's Canyon and Singing Sand Dunes, enjoying the simple pleasure of travelling across a vast landscape unhindered by human development.

Palaeontology
The palaeontological record in the Gobi is astounding – a little digging and you might uncover a cache of fossilized bones and dinosaur eggs. Try Bayanzag, where Roy Chapman Andrews uncovered hundreds of dinosaur skeletons in the 1920s.

p155

Western Mongolia

Historic Sites ✓✓
Hiking ✓✓✓
Eagle Hunting ✓✓✓

Historic Sites
The Altai Mountains are rich in Bronze Age sites, many unmarked and undocumented. Tavan Bogd National Park has petroglyphs, massive burial mounds and ancient stone statues of warriors. The rock art gallery at Tsagaan Sala is one of the most impressive in Central Asia.

Hiking
Western Mongolia is ripe for experienced hikers in search of a challenge. Try the area around the lakes in Tavan Bogd National Park or in the Kharkhiraa Uul region of Uvs aimag.

Eagle Hunting
Visit Bayan-Ölgii between November and March and you may see Kazakh eagle hunters capture prey. A stunning experience, it requires time, patience, a good guide and luck.

p180

Look out for these icons:

Our author's recommendation

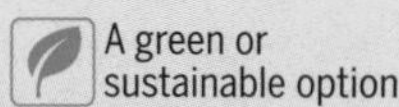
A green or sustainable option

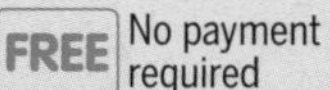

No payment required

See the Index for a full list of destinations covered in this book.

On the Road

Ulaanbaatar
Улаанбаатар

☎011, 021, 051 / POP 1,112,300 / AREA 1368 SQ KM

Includes »

Best Places to Eat

» Millie's Café (p63)
» Namaste (p64)
» Bull (p61)
» Veranda (p63)

Best Places to Stay

» Lotus Guesthouse (p56)
» Zaya's Hostel (p55)
» Hotel Örgöö (p56)
» Corporate Hotel (p57)

Why Go?

If Mongolia's yin is its pristine countryside, then Ulaanbaatar (UB) conforms nicely to its yang. An enormous city of pulsating commerce, heavy traffic, sinful nightlife and bohemian counter-culture, the Mongolian capital elicits as much shock as it does excitement. The contrasts within the city can be exasperating too; Armani-suited businessmen rub shoulders with mohawked punks and *del*-clad nomads fresh off the steppes. One minute you're dodging the path of a Hummer H2 and the next you're mystified by groaning Buddhist monks at Gandan Khiid. It's a wild place that bursts into life after slumbering through a long winter. UB is not the easiest city to navigate, as many buildings get lost in a forest of concrete towers, but with a little patience, travellers can take care of all their logistical needs, watch traditional theatre, sample international cuisine and party till three in the morning. This ever-changing city may be the biggest surprise of your Mongolian adventure.

When to Go

Ulaanbaatar

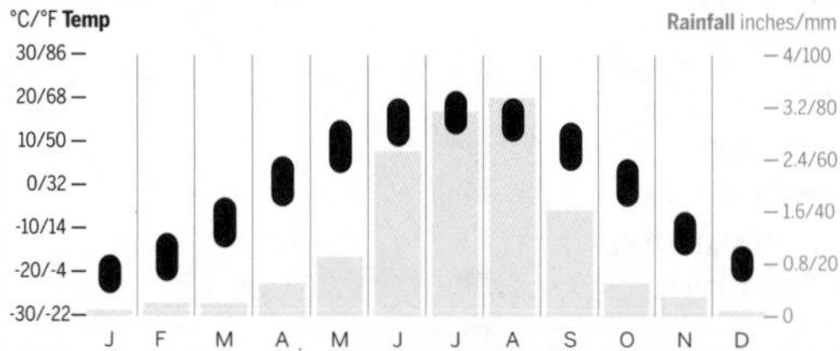

Mid-July The city to a halt to make way for Naadam and its wrestling, archery and horse racing.

August Lounge at street cafes and swill beer during the last throes of summer.

31 December A New Year's Eve in the world's coldest capital is one you won't soon forget.

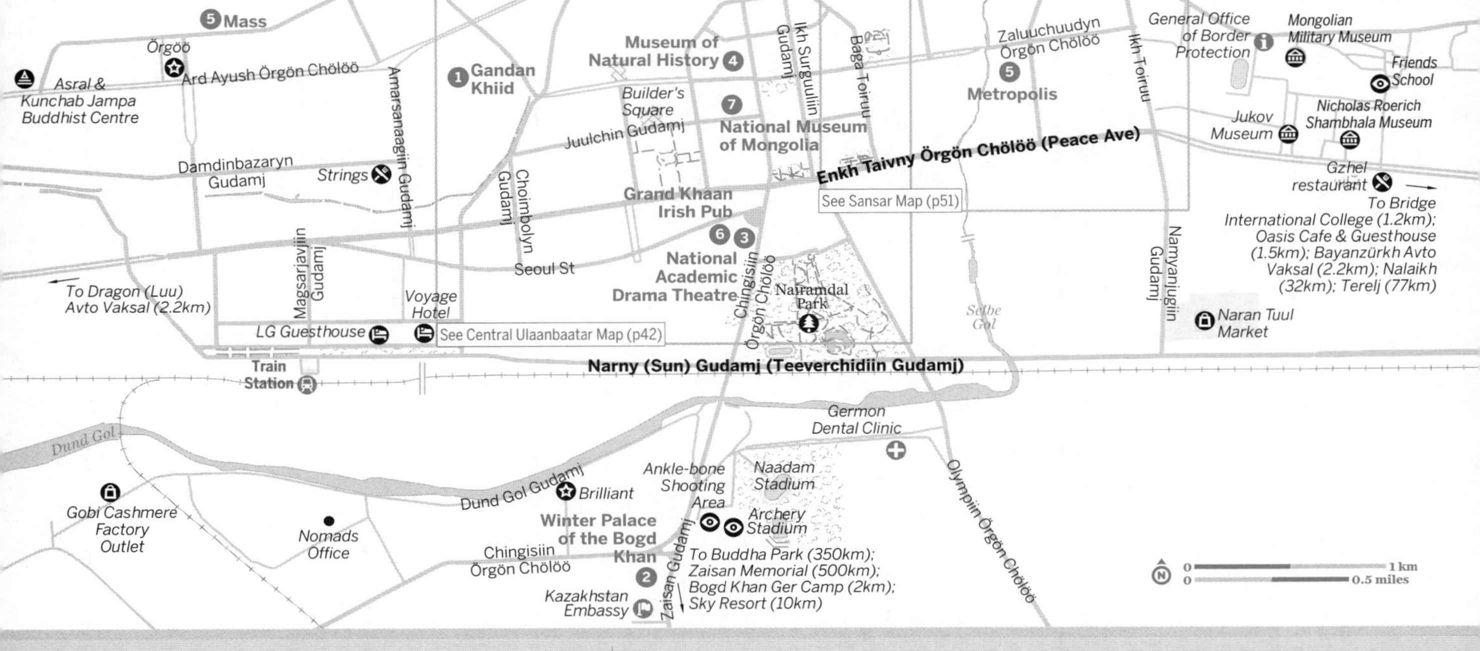

Ulaanbaatar Highlights

1 Walk the prayer circuit around **Gandan Khiid** (p49), the country's largest monastery

2 Wonder at the eccentric collection of animals, curios and artefacts at the **Winter Palace of the Bogd Khan** (p50)

3 Take in a performance of traditional dance and music at the **National Academic Drama Theatre** (p66)

4 Come face to skull with the extraordinary dinosaur collection in the **Museum of Natural History** (p46)

5 Party til the wee hours at one of UB's hottest nightclubs, such as **Metropolis** or **Mass** (p66)

6 Kick back with a litre of Chinggis on the terrace of the **Grand Khaan Irish Pub** (p63), a popular summer social spot

7 Weave through Mongolia's ancient past at the **National Museum of Mongolia** (p46)

History

The first recorded capital city of the Mongolian empire was created in 1639. It was called Örgöö and was originally located at the monastery of Da Khuree, some 420km from Ulaanbaatar in Arkhangai aimag (province). The monastery was the residence of five-year-old Zanabazar who, at the time, had been proclaimed the head of Buddhism in Mongolia. Because it consisted of felt tents, the 'city' was easily transported when the grass went dry. Some 25 movements were recorded along the Orkhon, Selenge and Tuul Gols (rivers). Throughout such movement the city was given some fairly unexciting official and unofficial names, including Khuree (Camp) in 1706.

In 1778 Khuree was erected at its present location and called the City of Felt. Later the city became known as Ikh Khuree (Great Camp) and was under the rule of the Bogd Gegeen (Living Buddha). The Manchus, however, used Uliastai as the administrative capital of Outer Mongolia.

In 1911 when Mongolia first proclaimed its independence from China, the city became the capital of Outer Mongolia and was renamed Niislel Khuree (Capital Camp). In 1918 it was invaded by the Chinese and three years later by the Russians.

Finally, in 1924 the city was renamed Ulaanbaatar (Red Hero), in honour of the communist triumph, and declared the official capital of an 'independent' Mongolia (independent from China, not from the Soviet Union). The *khangard* (garuda), symbolising courage and honesty, was declared the city's official symbol. In 1933 Ulaanbaatar gained autonomy and separated from the surrounding Töv aimag.

From the 1930s the Soviets built the city in typical Russian style: lots of ugly apartment blocks, large brightly coloured theatres and cavernous government buildings. Tragically, the Soviets also destroyed many old Russian buildings as well as Mongolian monasteries and temples. Today the city booms with new private construction projects, although a comprehensive infrastructure plan has been slow to implement. It has also enjoyed cultural resurgence with lots of museums, galleries, theatre performances and clubs bringing out the best in 21st-century Mongolian culture.

Orientation

Most of the city spreads from east to west along the main road, Enkh Taivny Örgön Chölöö, also known as Peace Ave. At the centre is Sükhbaatar Sq, often simply known as 'the Square' *(talbai)*, which is just north of Peace Ave. Sprawling suburbia is limited by the four mountains that surround the city: Bayanzürkh, Chingeltei, Songino Khairkhan and Bogdkhan.

The city is divided into six major districts, but there's a multitude of subdistricts and microdistricts. Mongolians rarely use street names and numbers, so tracking down an address can be difficult. Another problem is many buildings are not on any road at all, instead set behind another building (sometimes behind a number of buildings).

A typical address might be something like: Microdistrict 14, Building 3, Flat 27. However, you are unlikely to know which microdistrict it refers to, building numbers can be hard to spot and most street signs are in Mongolian Cyrillic. As a result, most locals will give you an unofficial description, such as 'Door 67, building 33, last door of a white-and-red building, behind the Drama Theatre'. To find your way around Ulaanbaatar, a good map, phrasebook and sense of direction are vital. Because of the confusing state of affairs, business cards usually have small maps on the back.

If you think your destination might be hard to find, call ahead. The staff will send someone out to meet you at a nearby landmark. Most places you are likely to call (tour operators, hotels, etc.) will probably have an English speaker.

Maps

Several maps of Ulaanbaatar are available; a good one is the 1:10,000 *Ulaanbaatar City Map*. Basic but free maps are usually available at the Tourist Information Office on Sükhbaatar Sq.

The most extensive selection of maps is at Seven Summits (p68). The **Cartography Co Map Shop** (Map p42; ☎9115 6023; Ikh Toiruu; ⌚9am-6pm Mon-Fri, 10am-4pm Sat year-round, 10am-4pm Sun May-Sep) on Ikh Toiruu, near the Elba Electronics shop, is another place to check, although the stock is starting to age.

Sights

Most sights are located within a 15-minute walk of Sükhbaatar Sq. The Winter Palace of the Bogd Khan and the Zaisan Memorial are a short bus ride south of the city. Gandan Khiid is about 2km to the northwest.

ULAANBAATAR IN...

Two Days

Ulaanbaatar's main sights can be seen in a couple of days. On your first morning in town pay a visit to the **National Museum of Mongolia** then take a turn around **Sükhbaatar Square**. Grab lunch at **Millie's** and then visit the nearby **Choijin Lama Temple Museum**. Watch a Mongolian cultural show in the evening. The following day get up early for hot apple pastries at **Michele's French Bakery** and then head up to **Gandan Khiid** in time to catch the monks chanting. Next visit the **Museum of Natural History** then, later in the day, head south to the **Winter Palace of the Bogd Khan**. Finally, climb the steps to **Zaisan Memorial** to watch the sun set over the city.

Four Days

On day three visit the **Zanabazar Museum of Fine Arts** and then head over to **Naran Tuul Market**. In the evening down a pint or two on the deck of the **Grand Khaan Irish Pub** and then hit **Metropolis** nightclub after midnight. On day four take a day trip out of town to swim in the river at Gachuurt, mountain bike to the observatory or hike over the Bogdkhan Uul. Have dinner at **Hazara** then listen to live music at **River Sounds**.

SÜKHBAATAR SQUARE

Sükhbaatar Square
Сүхбаатарын Талбай PUBLIC SQUARE

In July 1921 in the centre of Ulaanbaatar, the 'hero of the revolution', Damdin Sükhbaatar, declared Mongolia's final independence from the Chinese. The square now bears his name and features a **statue of Sükhbaatar** (Map p42) astride his horse. The original concrete statue has been replaced by a bronze one.

Sükhbaatar would have been very disappointed to learn that the square was also where the first protests were held in 1990, which eventually led to the fall of communism in Mongolia. Today, the square is occasionally used for rallies, ceremonies and even rock concerts, but is generally a serene place where only the photographers are doing anything. Near the centre of the square, look for the large plaque that lists the former names of the city – Örgöö, Nomiin Khuree, Ikh Khuree and Niislel Khuree.

The enormous marble construction at the north end was completed in 2006 in time for the 800th anniversary of Chinggis Khaan's coronation. At its centre is a seated bronze **Chinggis Khaan statue**, lording it over his nation. He is flanked by Ögedei (on the west) and Kublai (east). Two famed Mongol soldiers (Boruchu and Mukhlai) guard the entrance to the monument.

Behind the Chinggis monument stands **Parliament House**, which is commonly known as Government House. An inner courtyard of the building actually holds a large ceremonial ger used for hosting visiting dignitaries.

To the northeast of the square is the tall, modern **Cultural Palace**, a useful landmark containing the Mongolian National Modern Art Gallery and several other cultural institutions. At the southeast corner of the square, the salmon-pinkish building is the **State Opera & Ballet Theatre**.

The clay-red building to the southwest is the **Mongolian Stock Exchange**, which was opened in 1992 in the former Children's Cinema. For a blast from the past, walk east of the square to the **Lenin statue** (located in front of the Ulaanbaatar Hotel). Across from the Central Post Office is a **statue of S Zorig**, who at the age of 27 helped to lead the protests that brought down communism in 1990.

National Amusement Park
Үндэсний Соёл Амралтын Хүрээлэн
AMUSEMENT PARK

(Childrens Park; Map p42) Known to almost everyone as the 'Children's Park', this small amusement park features rides, games and paddleboats. The target audience is the 13-and-under set, so it's perfect if you are travelling with small kids. The park entrance is on the southeast corner. Admission is free (and there's also free parking). For the rides you buy individual tickets, around T2500 to T4000 a pop. It's open year round; in winter there's ice skating for T2000 per 90 minutes.

Central Ulaanbaatar

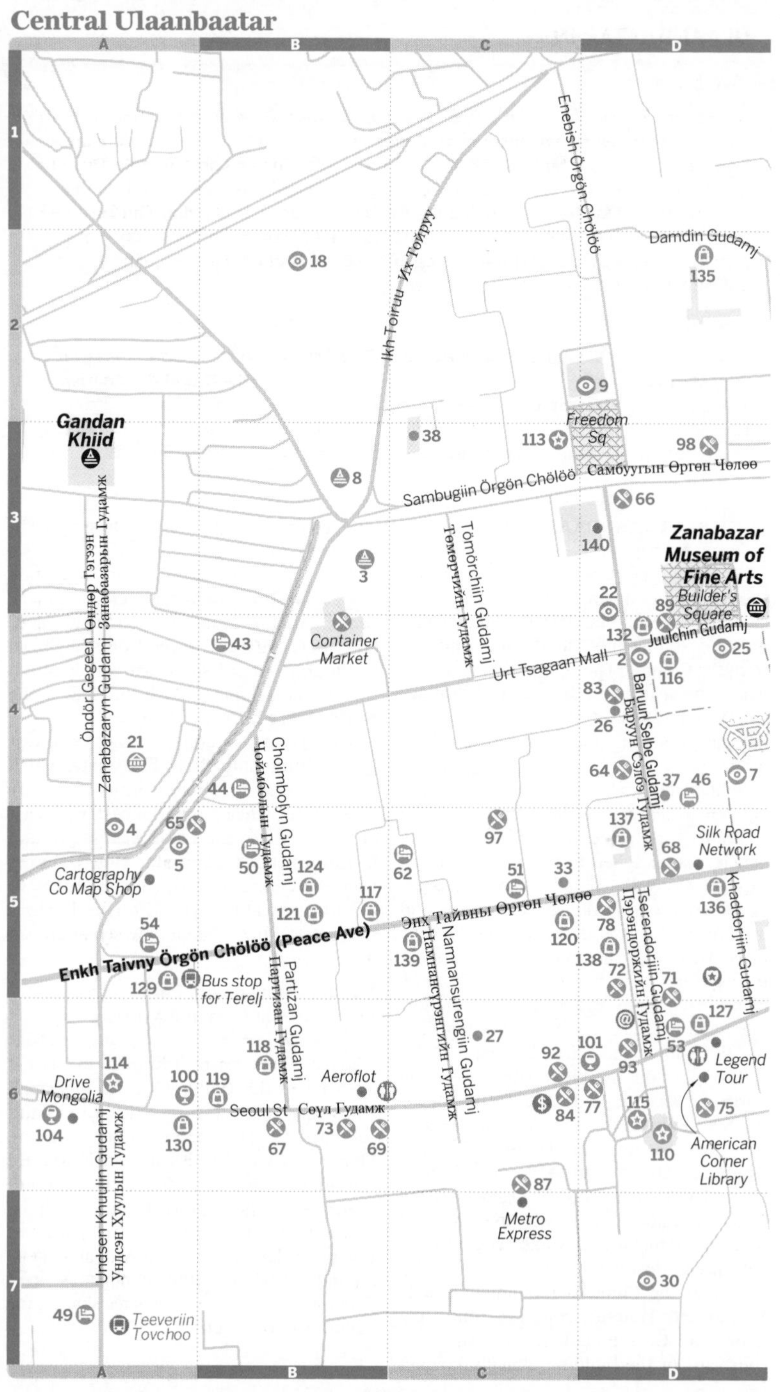

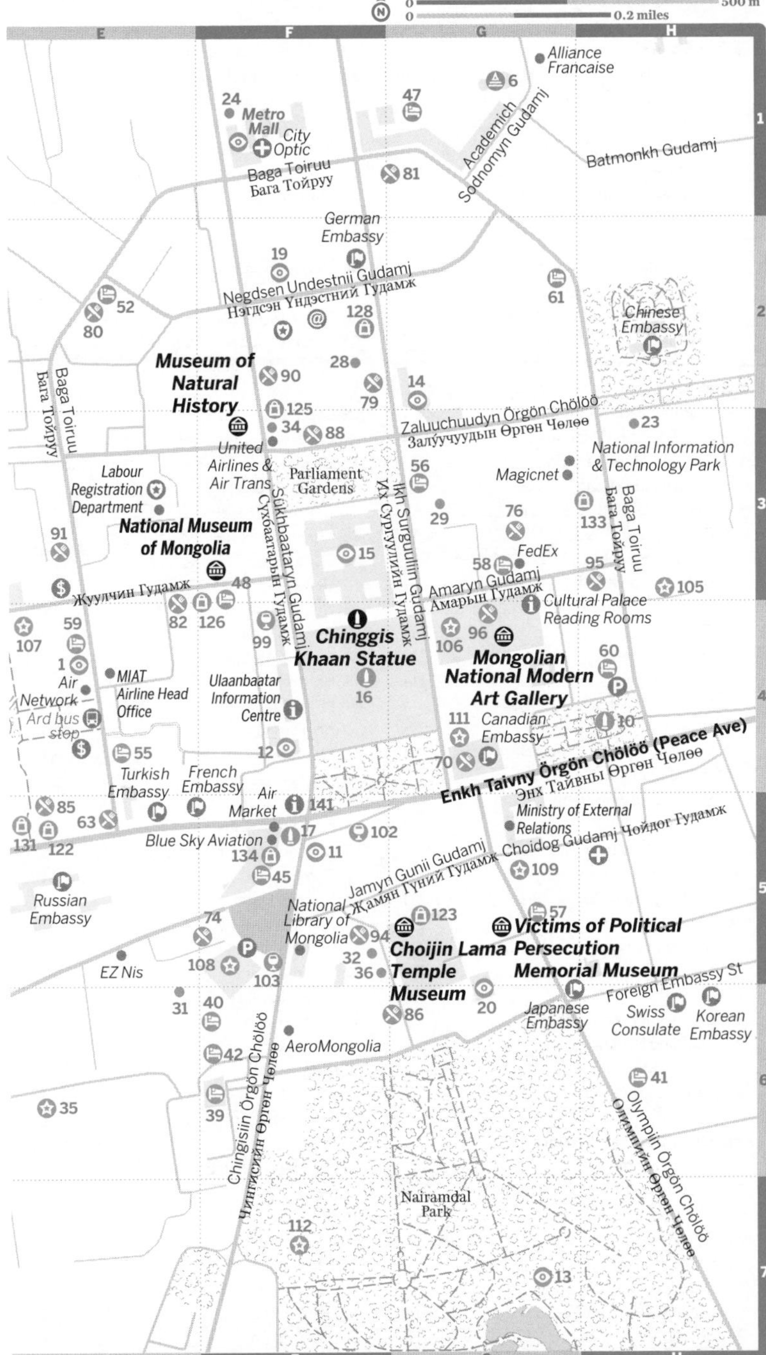

500 m
0.2 miles
Alliance Francaise
Metro Mall
City Optic
Baga Toiruu
Бага Тойруу
Academich Sodnomyn Gudamj
Batmonkh Gudamj
German Embassy
Negdsen Undestnii Gudamj
Нэгдсэн Үндэстний Гудамж
Chinese Embassy
Museum of Natural History
Zaluuchuudyn Örgön Chölöö
Залуучуудын Өргөн Чөлөө
United Airlines & Air Trans
Parliament Gardens
National Information & Technology Park
Magicnet
Labour Registration Department
National Museum of Mongolia
Sükhbaataryn Gudamj
Сүхбаатарын Гудамж
Ikh Surguuliin Gudamj
Их Сургуулийн Гудамж
FedEx
Жуулчин Гудамж
Amaryn Gudamj
Амарын Гудамж
Cultural Palace Reading Rooms
Chinggis Khaan Statue
Mongolian National Modern Art Gallery
MIAT Airline Head Office
Air Network
Ard bus stop
Ulaanbaatar Information Centre
Canadian Embassy
Enkh Taivny Örgön Chölöö (Peace Ave)
Энх Тайвны Өргөн Чөлөө
Turkish Embassy
French Embassy
Air Market
Ministry of External Relations
Blue Sky Aviation
Choidog Gudamj Чойдог Гудамж
Jamyn Gunii Gudamj
Жамян Гүний Гудамж
Russian Embassy
National Library of Mongolia
Choijin Lama Temple Museum
Victims of Political Persecution Memorial Museum
EZ Nis
Foreign Embassy St
Japanese Embassy
Swiss Consulate
Korean Embassy
AeroMongolia
Chingisiin Örgön Chölöö
Чингисийн Өргөн Чөлөө
Olympiin Örgön Chölöö
Олимпийн Өргөн Чөлөө
Nairamdal Park

Central Ulaanbaatar

Top Sights

Chinggis Khaan Statue F4
Choijin Lama Temple Museum G5
Gandan Khiid A3
Mongolian National Modern Art Gallery G4
Museum of Natural History F3
National Museum of Mongolia F3
Victims of Political Persecution Memorial Museum G5
Zanabazar Museum of Fine Arts D3

Sights

1 Ananda Meditation Centre E4
2 Arts Council of Mongolia D4
3 Bakula Rinpoche Süm B3
4 Centre of Shaman Eternal Heavenly Sophistication A5
5 Citinet A5
Cultural Palace .... (see 106)
6 Dashchoilon Khiid G1
7 Ger to Ger Head Office D4
8 Gesar Süm B3
9 Lenin Centre D2
10 Lenin Statue H4
11 Mongolian Artists' Exhbition Hall F5
12 Mongolian Stock Exchange F4
13 National Amusement Park G7
14 National University of Mongolia G2
Palace of Culture .... (see 106)
15 Parliament House F3
State Opera & Ballet Theatre .... (see 111)
16 Statue of Sükhbaatar F4
17 Statue of Zorig F5
18 Tasgany Ovoo B2
Ulusnet .... (see 140)
19 UN Development Program F2
20 Wedding Palace G6
21 Wildlife Museum A4
22 Xanadu Art Gallery D3

Activities, Courses & Tours

Active Mongolia .... (see 134)
23 American Center for Mongolian Studies H3
24 Black Ibex F1
25 Federation for the Preservation of Mahayana Tradition D4
26 Horseback Mongolia D4
27 Hovsgol Travel Company C6
28 Institute of International Studies F2
29 Juulchin G3
30 Karakorum Expeditions D7
31 Khövsgöl Lodge Company E6
M Bowling .... (see 140)
32 Mongolia Expeditions F5
33 Nomadic Expeditions C5
34 Nomadic Journeys F3
35 Speed Inline Skate E6
36 Stone Horse F5
37 Tseren Tours D4
38 Wind of Mongolia C3

Sleeping

39 Bayangol Hotel F6
Bolod's Guesthouse .... (see 45)
40 Chinggis Guesthouse F6
41 Continental Hotel H6
42 Corporate Hotel F6
43 Gana's Guest House B4
44 Genex Hotel B4
45 GobiTours & Guesthouse F5
46 Golden Gobi D4
47 Guide Hotel G1
48 Hotel Örgöö F3
49 Idre's Guest House A7
50 Kharaa Hotel B5
51 Khongor Guest House C5
52 Lotus Guesthouse E2
53 Mongolian Properties D6
54 Narantuul Hotel A5
55 Nassan's Guest House E4
56 Puma Imperial G3
57 Springs Hotel G5
58 Tuushin G3
59 UB Guesthouse E4
60 Ulaanbaatar Hotel H4
61 Zaluuchuud Hotel G2
62 Zaya's Hostel C5

Eating

63 40K E5
64 American Burgers & Fries D4
65 Arab Kebab Café A5
BD's Mongolian Barbeque .... (see 100)
66 Berlin D3
67 Bull B6
68 Café Amsterdam D5
69 California B6
70 Central Tower Restaurants G4
71 Delhi Darbar D5
72 Emerald Bay D5

73 Good Price....B6
74 Grand Khaan Irish Pub....F5
75 Ikh Mongol....D6
76 iLoft....G3
77 Kenny Rogers Roasters....D6
78 Khaan Buuz....D5
79 Le Bistro Français....F2
80 Little Buddha....E2
81 Los Bandidos....G1
82 Luna Blanca....E4
83 Mama Mia....D4
84 Marco Polo....C6
85 Michele's French Bakery....E5
86 Millie's Café....G6
87 Minii Delguur, Passage & Merkuri Markets....C6
Monet....(see 70)
88 Mongol Khuushuur....F3
89 Narya Café....D4
90 Nomad Legends Mongol Club....F2
91 Sacher's Café....E3
92 Saffron....C6
93 Sakura Bakery....D6
94 Silk Road....F5
State Department Store....(see 137)
Stupa Café....(see 25)
95 Tender....H3
96 Urlag....G4
Veranda....(see 94)
Werner's Deli....(see 87)
97 Yori Michi....C5
98 Zochin Buuz....D3

Drinking

99 Budweiser Bar....F4
100 Detroit....A6
101 Dublin....D6
Grand Khaan Irish Pub....(see 74)
102 Greenland....F5
103 MB Beer Plus....F5
104 Premiership Sports Pub....A6
Sky Lounge....(see 70)
View Lounge Club....(see 42)

Entertainment

Arts Council of Mongolia....(see 2)
105 Central Sports Palace....H3
106 Cultural Palace....G4
107 Face Club....E4
Medusa....(see 9)
108 National Academic Drama Theatre....F5
109 River Sounds....G5
110 State Circus....D6
111 State Opera & Ballet Theatre....G4
112 State Youth & Children's Theatre....F7
113 Tengis....C3
114 Torgo Fashion Salon....A6
115 Tsuki House....D6

Shopping

116 Amarbayasgalant Antique....D4
117 Antique & Art Gallery....B5
118 Argasun....B6
119 Ayanchin Outfitters....B6
120 Books In English....C5
121 Canon Showroom....B5
122 Cashmere House....E5
123 Choijin Lama Temple Museum Shop....G5
124 Computerland....B5
125 Egshiglen Magnai National Musical Instrument Shop....F2
126 Fuji Film....F3
127 Hi-Fi CD Shop....D6
128 Librairie Papillon....F2
Mary & Martha Mongolia....(see 68)
129 Mon Nip Camera Shop....A5
130 Mongolian Quilting Shop....A6
131 Möngön Zaviya....E5
132 Nomads Culture Antique Shop....D4
133 Nomin Ikh Delgur....H3
134 Seven Summits....F5
135 Shonkhor Saddles....D2
136 Souvenir House....D5
137 State Department Store....D5
138 Tsagaan Alt Wool Shop....D5
139 Ulaanbaatar Department Store....C5
Valiant Art Gallery....(see 86)
Xanadu....(see 86)

Information

Guide Tourist Information Centre....(see 63)
140 Mobicom (Tedy Centre)....D3
Post Office Central....(see 141)
141 Tourist Information Centre....F5

ASRAL & KUNCHAB JAMPA LING BUDDHIST CENTRE

Located in the northwest corner of the city, **Asral** (Map p39; ☎304 838, 9810 7378, 9595 2272; www.asralmongolia.org) is an NGO and a Buddhist social centre that supports impoverished families. Its main aim is to stop disadvantaged youths from becoming street children. It also provides skills and jobs for unemployed women; an on-site felt-making cooperative turns out some lovely products.

The Buddhist arm of the organisation has classes on Buddhism and meditation, although for now these are only offered in Mongolian. In summer, a high Tibetan lama, Panchen Otrul Rinpoche, visits the centre and provides religious teachings.

Asral encourages travellers to visit the centre. You can meet the felt-makers and buy their products or even volunteer your time. The centre is always looking for English teachers or gardeners to work on a small farm in Gachuurt (in summer). The centre is in the 3/4 district opposite the Gobi Sauna, slightly off the main road. It's best to call before you visit: ask for Davaa, the English-speaking director. Take bus 21, 29 or 13 to the last stop and continue walking for 300m. Asral is a two-storey cream-coloured building on your right.

WEST OF SÜKHBAATAR SQUARE

National Museum of Mongolia
Монголын Үндэсний Музей MUSEUM

(Map p42; www.nationalmuseum.mn; cnr Juulchin Gudamj & Sükhbaataryn Gudamj; adult/student T2500/1200, camera T10,000; ⊙9.30am-6pm daily 15 May-31 Aug, 9.30am-5.30pm Tue-Sat 1 Sep-14 May) Mongolia's National Museum has been revamped and is not to be missed.

The 1st floor has some interesting exhibits on Stone Age sites in Mongolia, as well as petroglyphs, deer stones (stone sculptures of reindeer and other animals) and burial sites from the Hun and Uighur eras. Look for the remarkable **gold treasure** (including a golden tiara), found in 2001 by archaeologists digging near the Kul-Tegin Monument in Övörkhangai.

The 2nd floor houses an outstanding collection of costumes, hats and jewellery, representing most of Mongolia's ethnic groups. Take a gander at some of the elaborate silverwork of the Dariganga minority or the outrageous headgear worn by Khalkh Mongols. Some of the outfits contain 20kg to 25kg of silver ornamentation!

The 3rd floor is a must-see for fans of the Mongol horde. The collection includes real examples of 12th-century Mongol armour, and correspondence between Pope Innocent IV and Guyuk Khaan. Written in Latin and Persian and dated 13 November 1246, it bears the seal of the *khaan*. There is also a display of traditional Mongolian culture with, among other things, a furnished ger, traditional farming and domestic implements, saddles and musical instruments. In the 20th-century-history section, look out for D Sükhbaatar's famous hollow horsewhip, inside which he hid a secret letter written in 1920 by the Bogd Khan enlisting the aid of the Russian Red Army.

The final hall contains an excellent display of Mongolia's recent history and the 1990 Democratic Revolution.

Museum of Natural History
Байгалийн Түүхийн Музей MUSEUM

(Map p42; cnr Sükhbaataryn Gudamj & Sambugiin Örgön Chölöö; adult/student T2500/1000, camera T5000, video T10,000; ⊙10am-4.30pm, closed Mon & Tue mid-Sep–mid-May) With its rambling halls, ancient exhibits and smell of formaldehyde and dust, the Museum of Natural History feels stuck in another age. There are displays on Mongolia's geology, flora and fauna, including the requisite section with stuffed and embalmed animals, birds and even fish. Although badly in need of renovation, the museum can help the traveller get acquainted with Mongolia's remarkable biodiversity and varied landscapes.

One of the few new exhibits, on the ground floor, chronicles various Mongolian expeditions: to the top of Mt Everest, to Antarctica and to space.

Certainly, the most impressive section is the Palaeontology Hall and its array of complete **dinosaur skeletons** (to photograph them costs an extra T5000), including a 3m-tall, 5-tonne, flesh-eating tarbosaurus. For a bird's-eye view, clamber up the stairs outside the hall to a gallery on the 3rd floor.

The gallery that is next door to the hall is full of interesting knick-knacks, such as petrified wood, dinosaur eggs and some huge leg bones, which look like something out of *The Flintstones*. Look out for the world-famous 'fighting dinosaurs', a Velociraptor and Protoceratops that were buried alive (probably when a sand dune collapsed on top of them) in the midst of mortal combat, some 80 million years ago (note that this exhibit is frequently on loan). For more on Mongolia's remarkable dinosaurs see p174.

Zanabazar Museum of Fine Arts

Занабазарын Уран Зургийн Музей MUSEUM

(Map p42; Juulchin Gudamj; adult/student T2500/1000; ⏲10am-6pm May-Sep, 10am-5pm Oct-Apr) This fine-arts museum has a superb collection of paintings, carvings and sculptures, including many by the revered sculptor and artist Zanabazar. It also contains other rare, and sometimes old, religious exhibits such as scroll *thangka* (paintings) and Buddhist statues, representing the best display of its kind in Mongolia. A bonus is that most of the exhibit captions in the museum are in English.

The second room contains some fine examples of the sculptor's work, including five Dhyani, or Contemplation, Buddhas (cast in 1683) and Tara in her 21 manifestations.

Also worth checking out are the wonderful *tsam* masks (worn by monks during religious ceremonies) and the intricate paintings, *One Day in Mongolia* and the *Airag Feast,* by the renowned artist B Sharav. These paintings depict almost every aspect of nomadic life.

Worthy of a visit in itself, the **Red Ger Art Gallery** on the 1st floor showcases modern artwork by Mongolia's top contemporary painters. English-speaking guides are available. From the gallery, continue towards to the back of the building to find two more halls, one featuring prints and the second containing folk art.

The building itself carries some historical value. It was built in 1906 and for many years served as Ulaanbaatar's biggest department store. Shortly after the 1921 Communist Revolution, Soviet Red Army troops were stationed here.

FREE Xanadu ART GALLERY

(Map p42; ☎310 239; www.xanaduartgallery.org; Baga Toiruu west; ⏲noon-10pm Mon-Sat, 2-6pm Sun) This gallery has a funky vibe with its modern art displays, coffee bar and couches. Interesting artsy folk often hang out here and a free movie is often screened on Sundays at 3pm.

SOUTH OF SÜKHBAATAR SQUARE

Choijin Lama Temple Museum

Чойжин Ламын Хийд-Музей MUSEUM

(Map p42; admission student/adult T1000/2500, camera T12,000, video T25,000; ⏲9am-7.30pm mid-May–Sep, 10am-4pm Oct–mid-May) This temple museum is a hidden gem of architecture and history, smack in the middle of downtown Ulaanbaatar. It was the home of Luvsan Haidav Choijin Lama ('Choijin' is an honorary title given to some monks), the state oracle and brother of the Bogd Khan. Construction of the monastery commenced in 1904 and was completed four years later. It was closed in 1938 and probably would have been demolished had it not been saved in 1942 to serve as a museum demonstrating the 'feudal' ways of the past. Although religious freedom in Mongolia recommenced in 1990, this monastery is no longer an active place of worship.

There are five temples within the grounds. As you enter, the first temple you see is the **Maharaja Süm**. The **main temple** features statues of Sakyamuni (the historical Buddha), Choijin Lama and Baltung Choimba (the teacher of the Bogd Khan), whose mummified remains are inside the statue. There are also some fine *thangka* and some of the best *tsam* masks in the country. The *gongkhang* (protector chapel) behind the main hall contains the oracle's throne and a magnificent statue of *yab-yum* (mystic sexual union).

The other temples are **Zuu Süm**, dedicated to Sakyamuni; **Yadam Süm**, which contains wooden and bronze statues of various gods, some created by the famous Mongolian sculptor Zanabazar; and **Amgalan Süm**, containing a self-portrait of Zanabazar himself and a small stupa apparently brought to Ulaanbaatar by Zanabazar from Tibet.

Free cultural performances are held here in summer at 5pm; this is a great chance to see *tsam*-mask dancing and listen to *khöömii* (throat singing). The complex is located off Jamyn Gunii Gudamj, with the entrance on the south side.

Victims of Political Persecution Memorial Museum MUSEUM

(Map p42; www.memorialmuseum.info; cnr Gendeniin Gudamj & Olympiin Örgön Chölöö; admission T3000, camera T5000, video T10,000; ⏲9am-5pm) This little-known museum houses a series of haunting displays that chronicle the communist purges of the 1930s – an aggressive campaign

DON'T MISS

ZAISAN MEMORIAL & BUDDHA PARK

The tall, thin landmark on top of the hill south of the city is the Zaisan Memorial (Зайсан Толгой; off Map p39). Built by the Russians to commemorate 'unknown soldiers and heroes' from various wars, it offers the best views of Ulaanbaatar and the surrounding hills. The enormous tank at the bottom of the hill – part of the Mongolia People's Tank Brigade – saw action against the Nazis during WWII. West of the memorial is the Buddha Park, featuring a 16m-tall standing Sakyamuni image. Below the statue is a small room containing *thangkas*, Sutras and images of the Buddha and his disciples. To get there, catch bus 7 to the memorial. This bus departs from the Bayangol Hotel or Baga Toiruu near Ard.

to eliminate 'counter-revolutionaries'. During the campaign, intellectuals were arrested and put on trial, sent to Siberian labour camps or shot. Mongolia lost its top writers, scientists and thinkers. One hall reveals this tragedy most vividly with a display of human skulls pierced by bullet holes.

The museum was inspired by the deeds of former prime minister P Genden, who was executed in Moscow by the Komitet Gosudarstvennoy Bezopasnosti (KGB; Committee for State Security) in 1937 for refusing Stalin's orders to carry out the purge. Stalin found a more willing puppet in Marshall Choibalsan, whose purge ended in the deaths of more than 28,000 Mongolians, mostly lamas. The house containing the museum once belonged to Genden and it was his daughter, Tserendulam, who converted it into a museum in 1996. Only some displays are in English. To gain a full understanding of the museum, it's best to bring your own English-speaking guide.

The large, white, square building located just southwest of the museum is called the Wedding Palace (Map p42; Khurimiin Ordon). Built in 1976 by the Russians, it has since been used for tens of thousands of wedding ceremonies, including the marital vows of a few foreigners.

FREE Mongolian Artists' Exhibition Hall

Монголын Зураачдын Үзэсгэлэн Танхим — ART GALLERY

(Map p42; cnr Peace Ave & Chingisiin Örgön Chölöö; ⌚9am-6pm) If you want to see more Mongolian art, and maybe buy some, head into the Mongolian Artists' Exhibition Hall, on the 2nd floor of the white marble building diagonally opposite the CPO. This is a rotating collection of modern and often dramatic paintings, carvings, tapestries and sculptures. The displays often change and there's a good souvenir shop.

NORTH OF SÜKHBAATAR SQUARE

Dashchoilon Khiid — MONASTERY

(Map p42; Academich Sodnomyn Gudamj; admission free) originally built in 1890 and destroyed in the late 1930s, this monastery was partially rebuilt and is now located in three huge concrete gers that once formed part of the State Circus. There are plans afoot to expand the monastery to include a six-storey building which will house a **17m-high statue of Maidar**. So far, the only part of the statue to exist is the 108-bead rosary, donated by monks from Japan (each bead weighs 45.5kg, making it the largest rosary in the world). You can get to Dashchoilon from a lane running off Baga Toiruu – look out for the orange-and-brown roof.

Mongolian National Artists Union

Уран Бүтээлчдийн Урлан — ART GALLERY

(Map p51; ☎325 849; www.uma.mn; cnr Erkhuugiin Gudamj & Ikh Toiruu; ⌚9am-1pm & 2-6pm) A unique cultural experience in Ulaanbaatar is a visit to the studios of the Mongolian National Artists Union. The artists are welcoming and you can offer to buy their work on the spot. It's all in a hard-to-find blue building set off the road, behind a gas station; look for the bronze statue of a seated monk above the door. Inside it's a bit of a maze and all the doors are closed so it's best to bring a guide or Mongolian friend. The **Arts Council of Mongolia** (Map p42; ☎reservations 319 015; www.artscouncil.mn; cnr Juulchin Gudamj & Baruun Selbe Gudamj) conducts tours here for US$25 per group of five.

EAST OF SÜKHBAATAR SQUARE

Mongolian National Modern Art Gallery

Монголын Уран Зургийн Үзэсгэлэн — ART GALLERY

(Map p42; www.art-gallery.mn; admission T3000; ⌚10am-6pm May-Sep, 9am-5pm Oct-Apr) Sometimes called the Fine Art Gallery, it contains a large and impressive display of modern and uniquely Mongolian paintings and sculptures, with nomadic life, people and landscapes all depicted in styles ranging from impressionistic to nationalistic. The Soviet romantic paintings depicted in *thangka* style are especially interesting, but the most famous work is Tsevegjav Ochir's 1958 *The Fight of the Stallions*.

The entrance is in the courtyard of the Palace of Culture. The main gallery is on the 3rd floor and there are temporary exhibits on the 2nd floor. In the courtyard of the Cultural Palace (near the entrance to the Gallery) you'll notice that part of the structure was damaged by fire. This occurred when political protestors stormed through the area on 1 July 2008, burning and looting as they went.

GANDAN MONASTERY AREA

Gandan Khiid Гандан Хийд MONASTERY

(Gandantegchinlen Khiid; Map p42; Öndör Gegeen Zanabazaryn Gudamj; admission T3500, camera T5000, video T10,000; ⌚8.30am-7pm) Around the start of the 19th century, more than 100 *süm* (temples) and *khiid* (monasteries) served a population of about 50,000 in Ulaanbaatar. Only a handful of these buildings survived the religious purges of 1937. It wasn't until the early 1990s that the people of Mongolia started to openly practise Buddhism again. This monastery is one of Mongolia's most important, and also one of its biggest tourist attractions. The full name, Gandantegchinlen, translates roughly as 'the great place of complete joy'.

Building was started in 1838 by the fourth Bogd Gegeen, but as with most monasteries in Mongolia, the purges of 1937 fell heavily on Gandan. When the US Vice President Henry Wallace asked to see a monastery during his visit to Mongolia in 1944, Prime Minister Choibalsan guiltily scrambled to open this one to cover up the fact that he had recently laid waste to Mongolia's religious heritage. Gandan remained a 'show monastery' for other foreign visitors until 1990 when full religious ceremonies recommenced. Today more than 600 monks belong to the monastery.

As you enter the main entrance from the south, a path leads towards the right to a courtyard containing two temples. The northeast building is Ochidara Temple (sometimes called Gandan Süm), where the most significant ceremonies are held. As you follow the *kora* (pilgrim) path clockwise around this building, you see a large statue behind glass of Tsongkhapa, the founder of the Gelugpa sect. The two-storey Didan-Lavran temple in the courtyard was home to the 13th Dalai Lama during his stay here in 1904.

At the end of the main path as you enter is the magnificent white Migjid Janraisig Süm, the monastery's main attraction. Lining the walls of the temple are hundreds of images of Ayush, the Buddha of longevity, which stare through the gloom to the magnificent Migjid Janraisig statue.

The original statue was commissioned by the eighth Bogd Khan in 1911, in hopes that it might restore his eyesight – syphilis had blinded him; however, it was carted away by Russia in 1937 (it was allegedly melted down to make bullets). The new statue was dedicated in 1996 and built with donations from Japan and Nepal. It is 26m high and made of copper with a gilt gold covering. The hollow statue contains 27 tonnes of medicinal herbs, 334 Sutras, two million bundles of mantras, plus an entire ger with furniture!

To the east of the temple are four colleges of Buddhist philosophy, including the yellow building dedicated to Kalachakra, a wrathful Buddhist deity.

To the west of the temple is the Öndör Gegeen Zanabazar Buddhist University, which was established in 1970. It is usually closed to foreigners.

You can take photos around the monastery and in Migjid Janraisig Süm, but not inside the other temples. Try to be there for the captivating ceremonies – they generally start at around 9am, though you may be lucky and see one at another time. Most chapels are closed in the afternoon.

FREE **Centre of Shaman Eternal Heavenly Sophistication** Мөнх Тэнгэрийн Шид Бөө Шүтээний Төв SHAMAN CENTRE

(Map p42; ☎9929 8909; Öndör Gegeen Zanabazaryn Gudamj; admission free; ⌚10am-6pm Sun-Fri May-Sep) Ulaanbaatar's official Shaman Centre is a ramshackle collection of squalid gers teetering on the slope that leads to Gandan Monastery. While not particularly mystifying at first sight, this is the real deal, with a bona fide shaman at its helm, holding daily court. The resident shaman, Zorigtbaatar, is known for his fiery orations that whip up the faithful into a frenzy. The main ger contains a smattering of icons, from a stuffed owl to bottles of vodka. If there is a ceremony going on, and you want your fortune told, you'll need to make a small donation. If you want to see a ceremony, call ahead to confirm times.

Wildlife Museum MUSEUM
(Map p42; Öndör Gegeen Zanabazaryn Gudamj; admission T3000; ⏲10am-6pm) The Wildlife Museum (formerly known as the Hunting Museum) is on the 2nd floor of the Baigal Ordon (Nature Palace) on the street leading to Gandan Khiid. The museum shows off centuries-old trapping and hunting techniques that are used by both nomads and urban cowboys. It's usually locked, so ask for the key from the watchman downstairs.

Gesar Süm TEMPLE
(Map p42; cnr Sambugiin Örgön Chölöö & Ikh Toiruu west; admission free; ⏲9am-8pm) Belonging to Gandan Khiid, Gesar Süm is named after the mythical Tibetan king. The lovely temple is a fine example of Chinese-influenced architecture. It is a popular place for locals to request, and pay for, *puja* (a blessing ceremony). Allegedly, the temple was placed here to stop the movement of the hill behind it, which was slowly creeping towards the centre of the city. It's easy to visit the temple as it lies between Gandan and the city centre.

Tasgany Ovoo (Map p42), about 300m north of Gesar Süm, is worth a look if you haven't yet seen an *ovoo,* a sacred pyramid-shaped collection of stones.

Bakula Rinpoche Süm MONASTERY
(Map p42; admission free; ⏲9am-6pm) The Bakula Rinpoche Süm, also known as the Pethub Stangey Choskhor Ling Khiid, was founded in 1999 by the late Indian ambassador, himself a reincarnated lama from Ladakh. The Rinpoche's ashes were interred inside a golden stupa inside the temple in 2004. The monastery, used mainly as a centre for Buddhist teaching, also has a **Centre for Buddhist Medicine** (☎9199 7894; ⏲9am-5pm Mon-Fri, 9am-noon Sat). The monastery is not a must-see unless you are interested in learning about traditional medicine. The complex is located where Ikh Toiruu meets Sambugiin Örgön Chölöö, behind a high white wall.

KHAN UUL DISTRICT & ZAISAN

Winter Palace of the Bogd Khan
Богд Хааны Өвлийн Ордон MUSEUM
(Map p39; Chingisiin Örgön Chölöö; admission T2500, camera T10,000, video T15,000; ⏲9am-5.30pm 15 May-15 Sep, 9.30am-4.30pm Fri-Tue 16 Sep-14 May) Built between 1893 and 1903, this palace is where Mongolia's eighth Living Buddha, and last king, Jebtzun Damba Hutagt VIII (often called the Bogd Khan), lived for 20 years. For reasons that are unclear, the palace was spared destruction by the Russians and turned into a museum. The summer palace, on the banks of Tuul Gol, was completely destroyed.

There are six temples in the grounds. The white building to the right as you enter is the Winter Palace itself. It contains a collection of gifts received from foreign dignitaries, such as a pair of golden boots from a Russian tsar, a robe made from 80 unfortunate foxes and a ger lined with the skins of 150 snow leopards. Mongolia's Declaration of Independence (from China) is among the exhibits.

The Bogd Khan's penchant for unusual wildlife explains the extraordinary array of **stuffed animals** in the palace. Some of it had been part of his personal zoo – look out for the photo of the Bogd's elephant, purchased from Russia for 22,000 roubles.

The Winter Palace is a few kilometres south of Sükhbaatar Sq. It is a bit too far to walk, so take a taxi or catch bus 7 or 19.

EASTERN ULAANBAATAR

Nicholas Roerich Shambhala Museum MUSEUM
(Map p39; ☎9988 1210; www.roerichmongolia.org; Peace Ave; adults/students T2500/200; ⏲11am-6pm) The great Russian artist and philosopher Nicolas Roerich (1874–1947) passed through Mongolia in 1926–1927 on one of his Asian odysseys. The log cabin where he stayed that winter has been converted into a museum and art institute. The artwork that hangs in the building consists largely of Roerich replicas, painted by Mongolian artists. In summer, the museum hosts events and lectures by Buddhist scholars. Call ahead to see what's on. The museum is in the Russian district, 300m east of the Jukov Monument on eastern Peace Ave (it's off the main road, so look for the sign).

SANSAR

International Intellectual Museum MUSEUM
(Map p51; www.iqmuseum.mn; Peace Ave 10; admission T3000; ⏲10am-6pm Mon-Sat) Also known as the Mongolian Toy Museum, this museum is in a pink building behind the round 'East Centre'. It has a collection of puzzles and games made by local artists. One puzzle requires 56,831 movements to complete, says curator Zandraa Tumen-Ulzii.

Ulaanbaatar City Museum MUSEUM
(Map p51; Peace Ave; admission T1500; ⏲9am-6pm Mon-Fri) The Ulaanbaatar City Museum offers a brief but insightful view of Ulaanbaatar's history through old maps and photos. The

most interesting item is a huge painting of the capital as it looked in 1912, in which you can clearly make out major landmarks such as Gandan Khiid and the Winter Palace of the Bogd Khan.

Activities

Orchlon Pool SWIMMING
(Map p51; ☎9905 2427; Chingisiin Örgön Chölöö; 2hr session T15,000) This indoor heated pool is the best place to swim.

Ulaanbaatar Indoor Pool SWIMMING
(Map p51; ☎318 180; Zaluuchuudyn Örgön Chölöö; per hr T6000; ⏰8am-8pm Mon-Sat 10am-7pm Sun) Right across the road from Orchlon pool, it's less modern, but cheaper.

Sky Resort SKIING
(off Map p39; ☎9100 7847; www.skyresort.mn; ⏰11am-9pm Mon-Fri, 9am-10pm Sat & Sun) A new ski resort that includes two chairlifts and full ski services (equipment rental, lessons, cafeteria) and even night skiing! A full-day lift ticket costs T21,000 on a weekend or T16,500 on a weekday. Half-day tickets are also available. A golf course is also being planned. To get here, go to Zaisan and take the road east for about 10km. Skiing is possible between mid-November and March.

Speed Inline Skate INLINE SKATING
(Map p42; ☎315 414; per hr T2000, skate hire T1000; ⏰10am-10pm) Indoor roller-skating rink. Pads cover the support beams but you still need to be careful.

Ice Rink ICE SKATING
(⏰9am-4pm Sat & Sun) In winter, ice skating is possible at the American School, south of Zaisan (but you need your own skates). You can also skate at the Children's Park.

M Bowling Centre BOWLING
(Map p42; ☎319 866; Baruun Selbe Gudamj; 1 frame before 7pm T5000, after 7pm T7000; ⏰11am-midnight Tue-Sun) Located in the Tedy Centre (Mobicom).

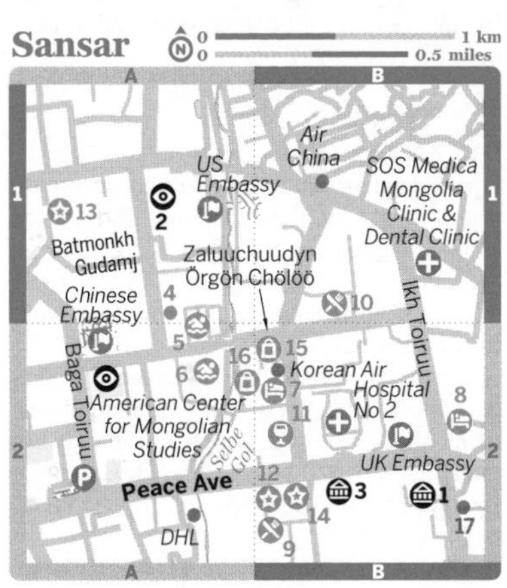

Sansar

Sights
1 International Intellectual Museum ... B2
2 Mongolian National Artists Union ... A1
3 Ulaanbaatar City Museum ... B2

Activities, Courses & Tours
4 Active Adventure Tours Mongolia ... A1
5 Orchlon Pool ... A2
6 Ulaanbaatar Indoor Pool ... A2

Sleeping
7 Chinggis Khaan Hotel ... B2
8 Kempinski Hotel Khan Palace ... B2

Eating
9 Hazara ... B2
10 Namaste ... B1
Sakura ... (see 8)

Drinking
11 Sexy Jazz Lounge ... B2

Entertainment
12 City Nomads ... B2
13 Hollywood ... A1
Metropolis ... (see 16)
14 Wrestling Palace ... B2

Shopping
15 Altai Cashmere ... B2
16 Sky Shopping Centre ... A2

Information
17 Hovsgol Travel Company ... B2

Courses

The following language schools in Ulaanbaatar offer short- and long-term courses with flexible schedules. You might be able to organise a 'language exchange' with a Mongolian student through one of the universities. The English language department of any school would be the obvious place to begin your search.

Recommended schools in Ulaanbaatar include the following:

Bridge International College MONGOLIAN LANGUAGE
(off Map p39; ☎461 744, 9919 4729; www.bridge.edu.mn; PO Box 955, Ulaanbaatar-13) Receiving consistently positive reviews, this language centre offers an intensive two-week survival course, as well as longer courses and individual tuition. Private and group lessons are available. Located at the back of the Catholic Church, near Sunjin Grand hotel.

Friends School MONGOLIAN LANGUAGE
(Map p39; ☎454 513, 9978 9321; www.friendscompany.mn; Apt 64/2 Bayanzürkh District, 5th Microdistrict) Short-term survival Mongolian classes are available. The location is northeast of the Jukov monument; check the website for map and directions.

Institute of International Studies MONGOLIAN LANGUAGE
(Map p42; ☎9911 4250, 328 681; dashpurev@magicnet.mn) Located opposite the university. Offers flexible group and private Mongolian-language lessons. It usually charges T5000 per hour.

Federation for the Preservation of Mahayana Tradition BUDDHISM
(FPMT; Map p42; ☎321 580; www.fpmtmongolia.mn; Builder's Sq, Juulchin Gudamj) The centre is involved in the regeneration of Buddhist culture in Mongolia and offers free lectures and courses on various aspects of Buddhist tradition and meditation. Lectures are given in English (at the time of writing, Wednesday at 6pm); look for the pink-tiled building with a stupa in front.

Ananda Meditation Centre YOGA, MEDITATION
(Map p42; ☎9913 2100; Baga Toiruu, Bldg 23, Apt 4) Offers yoga courses nightly at 6.30pm (Hatha yoga with chanting and meditation) in the building next to the Bohemian (Czech) Restaurant. It's best to call ahead to reserve a space. Note that it's in a private apartment, accessed through the back of the building.

National University of Mongolia MONGOLIAN LANGUAGE, CULTURE
(NUM; Map p42; ☎320 159; www.num.edu.mn; Ikh Surguuliin Gudamj 1, PO Box 46a/523, 210646) Northeast of Sükhbaatar Sq, the school offers specialised classes on Mongolian culture and language, and has a foreign-student department. The office is in the main building, room 213. If your primary goal is to learn Mongolian, the private language schools do a better job.

American Center for Mongolian Studies MONGOLIAN LANGUAGE, CULTURE
(Map p42; ☎7735 0486; www.mongoliacenter.org; Mongolian University of Science & Technology, Room 407, Baga Toiruu;) Has a good website listing courses and can recommend study possibilities.

Tours

ULAANBAATAR

It is not particularly easy to join an organised tour of Ulaanbaatar if you have arrived as an independent traveller. You can try to contact one of the companies offering tours under Around Ulaanbaatar and see what they have available.

Central Ulaanbaatar is reasonably compact, so it's easy enough see it on your own using this guide and a map. Although not really necessary, if you do hire a taxi to drive you around, a guide-cum-interpreter could be handy.

The **Arts Council of Mongolia** (Map p42; ☎319 015; www.artscouncil.mn; cnr Juulchin Gudamj & Baruun Selbe Gudamj) sponsors the 'Mongolian Buddhism Tour', which explores Ulaanbaatar's Buddhist legacy beyond the main tourist attractions. The tour lasts from 10am to 4pm and includes lunch. Prices vary depending on the size of your group, but count on paying about US$70 per person.

AROUND ULAANBAATAR

Of the hundred or more travel agencies offering tours that have sprung up around Ulaanbaatar in the past few years, the following are recommended as being generally reliable. Per day costs start at around US$100 a day (for two people), including food, accommodation, tickets to sights, a guide (who will double as a cook), driver and jeep. These costs can go up or down depending on several factors (eg whether staying in tents or a ger camp).

Most of the guesthouses around town also run tours, grouping together solo travellers

MOUNTAIN BIKING NEAR ULAANBAATAR

The best short bike ride from Ulaanbaatar goes from Zaisan to the Observatory. From the city centre, travel south to the Zaisan Memorial. From Zaisan, continue in an easterly direction. The road follows the southern bank of the Tuul River for 11km until you reach the ski hill (Sky Resort). The Observatory is a little bit further along; follow the switchbacks uphill until you reach it. From the Observatory you can descend briefly through the forest to the left (as you are looking downhill), pick up the trail at Sky Resort, and return to Ulaanbaatar on the same road. It's a two- to three-hour return trip.

and couples that wash upon their doorsteps. These trips offer bargain-basement prices and run fairly standard jeep tours of the countryside. Competition is stiff between guesthouses and some will be none too pleased if you take a tour with a rival outfit. For the most basic driving tour, prices start at around US$45 per day per person, provided you have four or more people. Some budget tours don't include food or accommodation; however, they usually include stoves for cooking your own food and tents for camping out.

Guides employed by the guesthouses are often students on a summer break, who may have limited knowledge of Mongolian history or off-the-beaten-path destinations. Tour operators, on the other hand, hire specialists in history and culture or they may be particularly skilled trekking, mountain-biking or horse-riding guides. If you are planning a fishing expedition, note that some low-end companies take tourists fishing without a permit – if you are concerned, check with the operator before signing up for the trip or steer clear of the cheaper options.

In summer you may be approached by students or other young Mongols who organise their own tours, charging around US$90 per day for up to six people. Freelance guides charge less than established tour operators because their overhead is so low, but there is more risk involved when dealing with them. To minimise your risk, don't hand over all your money up front, ask to pay a little before the trip and the rest at the end of the tour (if all goes well). Some of the more entrepreneurial guides have started their own minicompanies; they are somewhat nomadic, shifting their base of operations around each summer. Do your homework before signing up for a trip with them (ask for references or search online to see what past travellers have posted). **Daka Nyamdorj** (☎9984 4844; www.happymongolia.net) is an experienced English-speaking freelancer who can help with logistics and local tours.

Active Adventure Tours Mongolia CYCLING, HORSE RIDING
(Map p51; ☎345 662; www.tourmongolia.com; Erkhuugiin Gudamj) Good for bike and horse trips, this eco-conscious Mongolian-run outfit also runs traditional homestays and employs sustainable tourism practices by hiring local guides rather than shipping them out from UB.

Active Mongolia ADVENTURE
(Map p42; ☎329 456; www.activemongolia.com) This reliable Scottish-German operation specialises in rugged hiking, rafting and horseback trips, plus mountain biking. Most of the trips are to the aimags Khövsgöl, Arkhangai and Khentii. It's based at Seven Summits, opposite the CPO. Contact Sylvia Hay.

Hovsgol Travel Company BOATING, HORSE RIDING
(Map p42; ☎460 368; www.hovsgoltravel.com; PO Box 2003; Namyanjugiin Gudamj) Specialises in boat and horse trips around Khövsgöl. Runs the popular Camp Toilogt.

Horseback Mongolia HORSE RIDING
(Map p42; ☎9968 9075; www.horseback-mongolia.com; Baruun Selbe Gudamj) French-managed company that offers horse trips around the country. Quality saddles, horse tack and equipment are available. Very competitive rates.

Juulchin JEEP TOURS, HORSE RIDING
(Map p42; ☎328 428; www.juulchin.com; Tavan Bogd Plaza, Amar Gudamj 2) Offers 15-day group tours departing at six different dates each summer. Its office is next to the Puma Imperial Hotel.

Karakorum Expeditions CYCING, HIKING
(Map p42; ☎320 182, 315 655; www.gomongolia.com; PO Box 542) The leader in bike and hiking tours in western Mongolia, it also offers trips to China. The company has a good philosophy: a big plus is that it organises

snow-leopard research trips and wildlife tours. Contact Graham Taylor.

Khövsgöl Lodge Company HORSE RIDING, HIKING (Map p42; ☎9911 5929; www.boojum.com; Sükhbaatar District, Bldg 33, Room 16) This experienced outfit is part of the US-based Boojum Expeditions. It is in an apartment block behind the Drama Theatre, but you are better off calling first to get someone to meet you. Contact Bobo or Anya.

Mongolia Expeditions ADVENTURE (Map p42; ☎329 279, 9909 6911; www.mongolia-expeditions.com; Jamyn Gunii Gudamj 5-2) Specialises in adventure travel, including cycle touring, mountaineering, caving and rafting trips, as well as less vigorous options such as flower-watching tours. Sponsors the Mongolia Bike Challenge.

Nomadic Expeditions JEEP TOURS, HORSE RIDING (Map p42; ☎313 396; www.threecamellodge.com; Peace Ave 76) This is the Mongolian office of the US-based travel company. Runs countrywide tours but is especially good for the Gobi, where it runs the excellent Three Camel Lodge.

Nomadic Journeys TREKKING (Map p42; ☎328 737; www.nomadicjourneys.com; Sükhbaataryn Gudamj 1) A joint Swedish-Mongolian venture, this business concentrates on low-impact tourism, runs fixed-departure yak, camel and horse treks and can also arrange rafting trips on the Tuul Gol. Its trip in Terelj is unique – you walk while yaks haul your own portable ger on a cart. Contact Jan Wigsten or Manduhai.

Nomads HORSE RIDING, TREKKING (Map p39; ☎/fax 328 146; www.nomadstours.com; Khan Uul District, PO Box 1008) Offers a wide range of fixed-departure tours, including popular horse treks in Khentii and through Terelj, visiting Günjiin Süm. The office is located in Khan Uul District, 600m south of the train station.

Rinky Dink Travel Mongolia LOCAL CULTURE (☎9517 8001; www.rinkydinktravel.com; PO Box 1927) This is a small tour company that keeps its trips simple, safe and fun. It has homestays in ger districts and takes you out of Ulaanbaatar to meet nomad families. It is involved in social development programs in poor neighbourhoods and invites tourists to volunteer for its projects. We've received strong reader feedback on this outfit. There is no actual office – you just contact the company and it will pick you up.

Tseren Tours FAMILY TOURS, BIKING (Map p42; ☎9911 1832, 327 083; www.tserentours.com; Baruun Selbe Gudamj 14/1) Dutch- and Mongolian-run outfit that does countrywide tours, biking trips and stays with nomad families. Specialises in family-friendly tours. Good for budget travellers.

Wind of Mongolia ADVENTURE (Map p42; ☎316 222, 9909 0593, 9904 6585; www.windofmongolia.mn; Chingeltei District, Bldg 5, Door 1, Apt 4) This French-run tour operator offers creative and offbeat trips, including rock climbing, dog sledding (in winter) and tours that focus on Buddhism. Contact Joel Rauzy. As the office is buried amid apartment blocks and difficult to find, it's best to phone ahead so that staff can meet you.

Black Ibex JEEP TOURS, LOGISTICAL SUPPORT (Map p42; ☎7012 0011; www.discovermongolia.mn; Sükhbaatar Gudamj, Metro Business Centre, Room 1101) Countrywide tours at reasonable rates. Good for logistics such as vehicle hire and train tickets.

Stone Horse HORSE RIDING (Map p42; ☎9592 1167; www.stonehorsemongolia.com; Jamyn Gunii Gudamj 5-1, Viva Bldg, Room 104) Offers horse treks in the Khan Khentii Mountains (trips start from just one hour out of Ulaanbaatar). Professional outfit with quality horses and eco-conscious policies. Also offers reasonably priced homestay opportunities with herders near Ulaanbaatar.

Festivals & Events

The biggest event in Ulaanbaatar is undoubtedly the **Naadam** (Festival), held on 11 and 12 July. Some visitors may not find the festival itself terribly exciting, but the associated activities during the Naadam week and the general festive mood make it a great time to visit. For more information, see p222.

Around Naadam and other public holidays, special cultural events and shows are organised. It is worth reading the local English-language newspapers and asking a Mongolian friend, guide or hotel staff member to find out what may be on.

At the end of July, on a date set by the lunar calendar, you can see **tsam-mask dancing** at Dashchoilon Khiid.

The last week in October sees the **city's birthday** – it was founded in 1639. Events and concerts are usually put on at this time at the Cultural Palace or State Opera & Ballet Theatre. See www.artscouncil.mn for details.

In early February the city hosts an **Ice Ankle-bone Shooting Competition**, which is something like bowling on ice (but with a ball made of cowhide). It's held on the Tuul River.

The annual two-day music festival **Playtime** features the country's top rock bands and hip hop artists. It's held at a venue outside the city, usually in August. Check the Hi-Fi Music Store (or any CD shop) for location and tickets.

Sleeping

There is a wide range of places to stay in the capital city, with some of the best deals at the bottom and top ends. During the week surrounding Naadam, accommodation may be in short supply and prices are often higher.

If you are planning to stay in Ulaanbaatar for an extended period or you are travelling in a small group, it's worth looking around for an apartment to rent. A reasonable, furnished, two-bedroom apartment with a kitchen in an old Russian building in the city centre costs around US$400 to $700 per month (steep discounts are available in winter). Check the classified sections of the local English-language newspapers. **Mongolian Properties** (Map p42; ☎324 545; www.mongolia-properties.com; Seoul St 48/13) has apartments for rent on a long-term basis. Its target audience is wealthy expats, so prices are on the high end of the price spectrum. Another recommended agent is **Mongolian Real Estate** (☎310 445; www.mongolianrealestate.com). You could also ask at the guesthouses, which sometimes rent out apartments for around US$20 to US$30 per night for short-term stays.

UB BUNK RATES

Hotel rates in Ulaanbaatar are, on the whole, significantly higher than in the countryside, especially in the mid to high price range. In UB we define prices as follows:

$ Less than US$40 (under T57,000)

$$ US$40 to US$90 (T57,000 to T115,000)

$$$ More than US$90 (more than T115,000)

ZAISAN AREA

Bogd Khan Ger Camp TOURIST GER CAMP **$**
(off Map p39; ☎9191 9129; ger T35,000-45,000, without bathroom T15,000-20,000) Sports around 100 gers, some basic with shared bathroom and others decked out with furniture and modern attached bathroom. It's 3km south of the Tuul Gol (behind Zaisan). Although there is no regular transport, this may be a good option around Naadam when most hotels are booked out.

STATE DEPARTMENT STORE AREA

TOP CHOICE **Zaya's Hostel** GUESTHOUSE **$**
(Map p42; ☎331 575; www.zayahostel.com; Peace Ave; dm/s/d/tr US$12/25/30/36; @ wi-fi) While most guesthouses in town are located in old Russian flats, this one is in a modern building with hardwood floors, sparkling bathrooms, a comfortable lounge, fresh paint and new furnishings. Owner Zaya speaks English, enjoys a good conversation and is happy to help travellers looking for volunteer opportunities. She is not too keen on groups of noisy backpackers, however, so if you are looking for a party guesthouse, skip this one. The hostel is on the 3rd floor of an orange building, about 100m north of Peace Ave (find the Seoul Hotel, then continue further down the same alley). When reserving a room make sure to ask for Building 2, which is much nicer and more modern than the rooms in Building 1 (on the south side of Peace Ave).

Khongor Guest House GUESTHOUSE **$**
(Map p42; ☎316 415, 9925 2599; www.khongor-expedition.com; Peace Ave 15, Apt 6; dm/s/d US$5/10/14; @ wi-fi) This popular guesthouse is run by a friendly couple, Toroo and Degi, who work hard to help guests with logistical matters, tours, visa issues and airport or train-station runs. Their countryside tours get positive reports from travellers and business is casual – tours are usually paid for when you get back. The guesthouse is a simple affair with small private rooms and slightly larger dorms. Each bed comes with a privacy curtain, light and safety box. There's a spacious lounge with three computers and a kitchen. The entrance of the guesthouse is around the back of the third building west of the State Department Store. Credit cards are accepted.

Golden Gobi GUESTHOUSE **$**
(Map p42; ☎322 632, 9665 4496; www.goldengobi.com; dm US$6, d with/without bathroom US$23/19; @ wi-fi) This family-run place has a fun, youthful vibe, with colourful walls, two

GOING UNDERGROUND

While the streets of Ulaanbaatar heave with traffic and congestion, a group of people have found quiet and warm refuge beneath the pavement. Since the early 1990s, homeless people (both adults and children) have made homes in the sewer systems of Ulaanbaatar. The sewers are particularly useful in winter when the hot water pipes keep them warm.

Life is unimaginably rough for Ulaanbaatar's homeless. Many suffer malnutrition, syphilis, scabies and body lice. Homeless men find themselves in and out of jail (where conditions are sometimes worse than the streets), and women often end up in prostitution.

Homeless numbers, however, are dropping, thanks to improved social services and shelters. UB now has around 20 shelters for street children, many run by foreign NGOs, with beds for around 500 kids. Several aid agencies work with the children, including **Save the Children** (www.savethechildren.org), the National Centre for Children and the **Lotus Children's Centre** (www.lotuschild.org) and the **Christina Noble Foundation** (www.cncf.org).

The Lotus Children's Centre is also happy to meet visitors – tours are set up by the Lotus Guesthouse, or by emailing lotusguest@gmail.com. Money is not usually requested, but the centres will accept donations.

lounges and lots of soft sofas. Dorms and private rooms are clean and comfortable, but a little stuffy in summer. It's very popular with young backpackers; you'll probably hear its name mentioned in a Beijing or Moscow hostel long before you arrive. Reaction to this place among travellers is either red hot or icy cold; most people overwhelmingly praise the staff for friendly attitudes and helpful service, while a handful report hostile encounters. It's inside a courtyard about 100m east of the State Department Store.

Kharaa Hotel HOTEL **$$**
(Map p42; ☎313 717; Choimbolyn Gudamj 6; s/d US$65/75; P @) One of the few hotels in this range to have been renovated with a tasteful, restrained style. Each of the 29 rooms contains a fridge, TV and desk. Views are best from the street side of the building.

Narantuul Hotel HOTEL **$$$**
(Map p42; ☎330 565; www.narantuulhotel.com; Peace Ave; s/d/tr US$88/98/108; @ wi-fi) This friendly hotel has modern, well-appointed rooms with decent space. On the downside it can get hot in here in mid-summer. It has two restaurants, a business centre, a sauna and a beauty salon.

Genex Hotel HOTEL **$$**
(Map p42; ☎319 326; www.generalimpex.mn; Choimbolyn Gudamj 10; s/d US$35/60; @) At Genex Hotel bland but clean rooms overlook a quiet street near Gandan Monastery and Peace Ave. A tacky, pseudo-European atmosphere prevails. The luxe rooms are a little odd-looking, with two queen-size beds pushed into a triangular-shaped alcove.

WEST OF SÜKHBAATAR SQUARE

TOP CHOICE **Lotus Guesthouse** GUESTHOUSE **$**
(Map p42; ☎325 967, 9909 4943; www.lotuschild.org; Baga Toiruu West; dm US$8-10, r US$15-25; @ wi-fi) This homey place feels more like a boutique hotel than a guesthouse. Rooms are individually styled, some with traditional Mongolian furniture. It has a bright, cosy atmosphere and is extremely clean. The location is nice, on a quiet bend of the Little Ring Rd, away from the hustle and bustle of Peace Ave but still close to the centre. It's run by the Lotus Children's Centre, an NGO that helps orphaned children, and it employs young Mongolians who used to live in the orphanage. An annex, in an apartment away from the centre, takes overflow if the main block is full.

Hotel Örgöö BOUTIQUE HOTEL **$$$**
(Map p42; ☎313 772; www.urgoohotel.com; M100 Bldg, Juulchin Gudamj; d/ste incl breakfast US$150/200; wi-fi) This recently renovated boutique hotel has just 10 rooms, each one decked out in brown and beige furnishings, with flat panel TVs and modern bathrooms. The entire place is spotless and the location is prime, overlooking a little park near the National Museum. It's an easy walk from here to Sükhbaatar Sq and other downtown sights.

UB Guesthouse GUESTHOUSE $
(Map p42; ☎311 037, 9119 9859; www.ubguest.com; Tserendorjiin Gudamj; dm/s/d US$6/16/20; @ wi-fi) This long-time guesthouse has several rooms stretching around a Soviet-era apartment block. It's clean (guests are required to remove their shoes upon entering) but the common room is a bit small and the place does get very busy in summer. The Korean-Mongolian management has plenty of experience in helping backpackers with logistics and trip planning. The location is ideal – between Sükhbaatar Sq and the State Department Store. Enter from the back of the building, behind Golomt Bank.

Nassan's Guesthouse GUESTHOUSE $
(Map p42; ☎321 078; www.nassantour.com; Baga Toiruu West; dm/s/d/tr US$7/20/24/28; @ wi-fi) Friendly Nassan has been in the guesthouse business for almost 20 years and runs a clean and friendly downtown hostel. Rooms are bright and have newly renovated bathrooms and kitchen facilities. It's fairly spacious and somewhat off the radar, making it a great place to stay when other downtown guesthouses are bursting at the seams. Access is through a gated courtyard at the back of the building, which provides extra security. It's just north of the Flower Centre.

EAST OF SÜKHBAATAR SQUARE

Ulaanbaatar Hotel HOTEL $$$
(Map p42; ☎320 620; www.ubhotel.mn; Baga Toiruu; s T150,000, d T180,000, luxe T255,000; @ wi-fi) The Ulaanbaatar Hotel is the grand old dame of Mongolia. Opened in 1961, this was where Soviet dignitaries stayed during their visits to the 'Red Hero'. It still carries an air of the Khrushchev era with its high ceilings, chandeliers, a marble staircase and a lavish ballroom. Rooms are well-appointed but some are a bit small. The hotel also contains two restaurants and a travel agency, business centre and sauna.

Zaluuchuud Hotel HOTEL $$
(Map p42; ☎324 594; www.zh.mn; Baga Toiruu 43; s/d/ste incl breakfast US$35/65/90; @) One of Ulaanbaatar's oldest hotels, the Zaluuchuud (Young People) is a midrange hotel at the lower end of the midrange price category. It has a quiet location in the University area but don't expect much in the way of service. Not all the rooms are the same size, so you might try asking for an en suite standard, which includes a bedroom and a sitting room with TV. Room 300 is a good choice.

Tuushin HOTEL $$
(Map p42; ☎323 162; www.tuushinhotel.mn; Amaryn Gudamj 2; economy s/d incl breakfast US$35/65, standard s/d incl breakfast US$65/80; @) This was one of the Ulaanbaatar's better hotels in the 1990s but is somewhat forgotten these days. Although dated, its rates are low and the location is great, just a few steps away from Sükhbaatar Sq. The only difference between the economy and standard rooms is that the latter have street views.

Puma Imperial HOTEL $$$
(Map p42; ☎313 043; www.pumaimperialhotel.mn; Ikh Surguuliin Gudamj; s/d/f incl breakfast US$78/115/120; P @ wi-fi) Popular with visiting journalists and diplomats wanting to be close to the Square. None of the rooms have a particularly good view.

Springs Hotel HOTEL $$$
(Map p42; ☎320 738; www.springshotel.mn; Olympic Street 2a; s/d incl breakfast US$88/110; @ wi-fi) This hotel feels squeezed between other buildings but there are good views from the upper floors. It's a popular place for business travellers and has an in-house Korean restaurant.

NORTH OF SÜKHBAATAR SQUARE

Guide Hotel HOTEL $
(Map p42; ☎353 582, 353 887; bisoft_2010@yahoo.com; Baga Toiruu north; d/half-luxe incl breakfast US$35/60; wi-fi) Between Dashchoilon Khiid and Baga Toiruu, this hidden hotel offers clean and comfortable rooms. Its best feature is its large and modern bathrooms, plus the free Swedish breakfast. It's one of the few recommended places in this price range that is an actual hotel, rather than a guesthouse.

SOUTH OF SÜKHBAATAR SQUARE

TOP CHOICE **Corporate Hotel** HOTEL $$$
(Map p42; ☎334 411; www.corporatehotel.mn; Chingisiin Örgön Chölöö 9-2; s/d US$170/220, luxe s/d US$210/280; non-smoking @ wi-fi) With its slender tower and minimalist design, the Corporate looks like a slice of Tokyo lost in the tangle of Ulaanbaatar's ungainly Soviet architecture. Thanks to the unique design of the building, most rooms are on corners, with windows facing in two directions. It has a restaurant, sauna, jacuzzi, fitness room and a spectacular roof-top bar on the 11th floor.

Bayangol Hotel HOTEL $$$
(Map p42; ☎328 869; www.bayangolhotel.mn; Chingisiin Örgön Chölöö 5; s/d T145,000/180,000; P non-smoking @) One of Ulaanbaatar's biggest and

GER DISTRICT DIGS

As Ulaanbaatar's centre booms with high-rise construction sites and multimillion-dollar property developments, its ger (yurt) districts remain trapped in time. By staying in one you'll get a real sense of traditional Mongolian family life, at the same time gaining an appreciation of the difficulties that ger residents must endure. Several tour companies offer walks through ger districts, but to achieve the full living experience contact **Rinky Dink Travel Mongolia** (p58), which can set you up with a homestay in a ger district and place you as a volunteer in its social development projects. A typical stay might include digging a pit toilet, repairing a fence, doing art projects with street kids or teaching English. You'll live like the locals (pit toilets, no running water, difficult transport) but you'll also encounter some of the friendliest people anywhere and gain a rare perspective on the city. Visits can last from three days to several weeks.

most reliable hotels, the Bayangol consists of two 12-storey towers that dominate the skyline south of the Square. Rooms have been renovated and even come with a personal computer with internet access. It's popular with groups.

GobiTours & Guesthouse GUESTHOUSE **$**
(Map p42; ☎322 339, 9820 1991; www.gobitours.com; Peace Ave 61, Door 20, Room 25; dm US$6, r US$18-20; @ 📶) A welcoming and friendly guesthouse with two spacious dorms. The owners are from Dalanzadgad and have good contacts there if you are planning a Gobi tour. Very central, it's in the L-shaped white apartment block opposite the post office. Near the State Department Store there's a second apartment branch, which has private rooms.

Bolod's Guesthouse GUESTHOUSE **$**
(Map p42; ☎9820 6816; www.bolodtours.com; Peace Ave 61, Door 20, Room 22; dm US$7; @ 📶) Intimate guesthouse with bright comfortable dorms. Bolod has a strong interest in Mongolian history and culture and offers off-beat travel tours to unique sights, including an artillery range near Ulaanbaatar. It's located in the same building at the GobiTours & Guesthouse. It's closed in winter (15 October to 15 May) but Bolod has an apartment in the suburbs and can make arrangements for you to stay there.

Chinggis Guesthouse GUESTHOUSE **$**
(Map p42; ☎325 941, 9517 5043; chinggis_house@yahoo.com; Bldg 33, Door 67; dm/s/d US$8/15/20; @) A clean and friendly four-room apartment establishment, Chinggis Guesthouse offers some private rooms and a central location. It is situated back behind the National Academic Drama Theatre and Bayangol Hotel.

Continental Hotel HOTEL **$$**
(Map p42; ☎323 829; www.ubcontinentalhotel.com; Olympiin Örgön Chölöö; s/d US$84/112; P @ 📶) This rather incongruous hotel bears a striking resemblance to the White House. Facilities include a small fitness centre, with a charge of US$9 per hour.

OLD BUS STATION (TEEVERIIN TOVCHOO) AREA

LG Guesthouse GUESTHOUSE **$**
(Map p39; ☎328 243, 9989 4672; www.lghostel.com; Narny Gudamj; dm US$6-8, s/d US$16/20; @ 📶) With 12 rooms, this is one of the largest guesthouses in the city. It has dorms and private rooms with attached bathroom, a common area, a kitchen where you can cook your own meals and a restaurant on the ground floor. Bathrooms are clean and have hot-water boilers – important in summer when other places only have cold water. It's a little out of the centre, on the road towards the train station.

Voyage Hotel HOTEL **$$**
(Map p39; ☎327 213; Narny Gudamj; www.voyagehotel.mn; s/d/half-luxe/luxe US$30/50/65/90; @) Representing good value, the 30-room Voyage has attentive staff and pleasant rooms. Facilities include two restaurants (European and Korean), free internet and sauna. The low price is a reflection of its less-than-perfect location, on the busy road to the train station.

Idre's Guest House GUESTHOUSE **$**
(Map p42; ☎7011 0846; www.idretour.com; Undsen Khuulin Gudamj; dm US$5, r with/without bathroom US$18/15; @ 📶) Amiable host Idre has constructed a single-floor guesthouse with several dorms and reasonably sized private rooms. It has a central lounge, a small kitchen and a book exchange. It's located near the old long-distance bus station, not the flash-

est neighbourhood in town but still a fairly easy walk into the centre of the city. Idre also runs ger accommodation in Töv aimag, near Mandshir Khiid.

GANDAN MONASTERY AREA

Gana's Guest House HOSTEL $

(Map p42; ☎9911 6960; www.ganasger.mn; Gandan Khiid ger district, House No 22; dm/d US$5/15; @) If you fancy staying in a ger district, drop by this longtime backpacker hangout. Owner Gana has accommodation in private rooms inside a main block, or you could stay in a ger on the roof. To find it, head up Öndör Gegeen Zanabazaryn Gudamj and turn right down an alley, 150m before Gandan Khiid. It's a little difficult to find, so you may want to call ahead for a pick up. You can also get there from the footbridge on Ikh Toiruu. The guesthouse is closed in winter.

EASTERN ULAANBAATAR

Oasis Café & Guesthouse GUESTHOUSE $$

(off Map p39; ☎463 693, 9928 4702; www.intergam-oasis.com; Nalaikh Gudamj; dm T18,000, d without bathroom T58,000, both incl breakfast; P@ᯤ) Austrian-German-run place with beautiful accommodation in dorms, gers and private rooms with attached bathroom. It has a large yard and a brightly painted cafe, which serves excellent Austrian meals and pastries. Because it has secure parking, it's popular among overlanders with their own motorbike or car. Motorcycles may be available for hire. Located 5km east of Sükhbaatar Sq (in the Amgalan district; GPS: N47° 54.706', E106° 58.857'). The nearest landmark is the large round Catholic Church; the guesthouse is 300m past the church.

SANSAR

Chinggis Khaan Hotel HOTEL $$$

(Map p51; ☎313 380; www.chinggis-hotel.com; Tokyogiin Gudamj 10; s US$84, d US$107-119; P@) The Chinggis Khaan is Mongolia's biggest, brashest hotel. It has all the facilities you could dream of, including an indoor pool, a travel agent and an attached shopping mall. Rooms are well appointed and of international four-star standard; choose one that faces west for a view of the Bogd Khan mountain and downtown Ulaanbaatar.

Kempinski Hotel Khan Palace HOTEL $$$

(Map p51; ☎463 463; www.kempinski.com/en/ulaanbaatar; East Cross Rd; s/d US$98/120; P❄@) Ulaanbaatar's newest luxury hotel is a Kempinski-managed Japanese-invested venture on the east end of Peace Ave. Rooms are plush, with a tasteful design and little niceties such as humidifier, robes and slippers. The hotel also has free internet, a fitness centre and sauna, but no swimming pool. Expats say the breakfast is the best in town.

Eating

A crop of midrange to upscale restaurants have opened up along Seoul St. Cheaper places can be found all along Peace Ave, near the State Department Store. A string of restaurants have also sprung up along Baga Toiruu West. In summer you can get shashlik (meat kebab), usually served with onions and cucumber, from any number of street Uzbek vendors. A few are usually located outside the State Department Store.

Self-Catering

For self-caterers, there are many shops around the city that sell foods imported from China, Korea, the US and Europe. Fresh fruits and veggies are also available; some items are home-grown in Mongolia, although most of what you'll find is imported from China. Some tasty local products include yoghurt, cheese, apples, berries, tomatoes and cream. Bread is available everywhere but the best are found at small bakeries like Sachers, West of Sükhbaatar Sq and Michele's French Bakery in the State Department Store area. Most markets are open from about 10am to 8pm daily.

State Department Store SUPERMARKET $

(Map p42; Peace Ave 44) This supermarket is on the ground floor of the State Department Store.

Minii Delguur & Merkuri Markets MARKETS $

(Map p42; ⌚10am-7pm Mon-Sat, 10am-6pm Sun) Merkuri (Мэркури) is sort of a flea market for food where you can bargain with individual vendors for all manner of imported goods, meat, cheese, fruit and vegetables. It's around the back of Minii Delguur, a more standard form of supermarket off Tserendorjiin Gudamj.

Werner's Deli DELI $$

(Map p42; Passage Market; ⌚10am-7pm Sun-Fri, 11am-5pm Sat) Genuine German deli serving all cold cuts and sandwiches, Werner's is located at the back of the Passage Market (the same complex as Minii Delguur and Merkuri Market).

Mama Mia DELI $$
(Map p42; Baruun Selbe Gudamj) French-owned deli that sells meats, cheeses and ready-food like lasagne and quiche.

Good Price IMPORTED GROCERIES $$
(Map p42; Seoul St) Shop that sells imported food products from the US, including sauces, canned vegetables and dried fruit.

STATE DEPARTMENT STORE AREA

Delhi Darbar INDIAN $$
(Map p42; Tserendorjiin Gudamj; dishes T8000-10,000, ⏲noon-11pm; 🍴) Owner Ishmael has two North Indian restaurants. This popular option is near the State Department Store (the other is in the Puma Imperial Hotel). Grab a spot inside a little tent with floor cushions and enjoy some delicious naan, tandoori chicken and curries. It's on the 2nd floor above a coffee shop.

Yori Michi JAPANESE UDON $
(Map p42; opposite Manduhai Hotel; meals T5000; ⏲noon-midnight) Authentic Japanese udon restaurant and bar run by the affable Kobe-native Kimuru. Udon is the staple (try a bowl with tempura) while grilled chicken and beer are served after dark. To find it, walk towards the Mandukhai Hotel: it's in the long white building (No 12) before the hotel, the fifth blue door on the left. The sign on the door is tiny and faded, so the place is easy to miss.

40K ITALIAN, AMERICAN $$
(Map p42; Peace Ave & Baga Toiruu; meals T6000-9000; ⏲noon-11pm; 📶🍴) On a stretch of road jam-packed with mediocre restaurants and cafes, this one stands head and shoulders above the rest. It's run by the owner of Silk Road and has a similar menu but this place feels more urban chic, set on a busy corner of Peace Ave and literally attached to a bank. The name refers to the neighbourhood, so called after the 40,000 apartments built here in the 1950s.

American Burgers & Fries BURGERS & SANDWICHES $$
(Map p42; Baruun Selbe St; meals T5000-9000; ⏲11.30am-midnight; 📶🍴) The name says it all. Affable owner Robert serves up some delicious, authentic burgers and hot dogs. Sub'Baatar, a popular sandwich restaurant, has moved in here, so you also have the option of ordering sub sandwiches. It's popular with Peace Corps volunteers and overseas students, so there is always a fun, youthful crowd hanging out here. Free delivery (☎8869 7827) is available in the city centre.

Michele's French Bakery FRENCH BAKERY $
(Map p42; ⏲8am-7pm; 📶🍴) A popular haunt among Ulaanbaatar expats and travellers alike, this bakery and coffee shop serves an array of reasonably priced treats, including apple turnovers (T900) and chocolate croissants (T900). Come in the morning when these items are fresh out of the oven. You can also enjoy paninis (T3900) and crepes (T4900) while listening to a great music playlist. An excellent place to load up on snacks before heading off on an expedition. It's located on a narrow lane behind the Cashmere House.

Café Amsterdam CAFE $
(Map p42; Peace Ave; items T2500-5000; ⏲7am-10pm; 📶🍴) Mongolia's first literary cafe. The Dutch and Mongolian owners offer lattes, sandwiches, fresh vegetable soup and English breakfast, as well as shelves of books that you can borrow, trade or buy. It has an ideal location on Peace Ave, and in summer you'll find its terrace packed with travellers. Guest speakers and/or films can be seen on Wednesday evenings at 8pm – check the noticeboard for upcoming events.

Narya Café CAFE $
(Map p42; Builder's Sq, Juulchin Gudamj; light meals T2500-5500; ⏲8.30am-8pm Mon-Fri, 9am-7pm Sat & Sun; 📶🍴) The Latin music playing in the background, ochre-painted walls and contemporary artwork make for a pleasant welcome when entering this laid-back cafe. The menu offers reasonably priced sandwiches, soups and home-baked muffins. There is also a shop downstairs where you can get imported goods and bakery items.

Stupa Café VEGETARIAN CAFE $
(Map p42; Builder's Sq, Juulchin Gudamj; snacks T2500-4000; ⏲10am-8pm Mon-Fri, 10am-7pm Sat & Sun; 🌿🍴) This charming cafe serves light vegetarian meals and sweet snacks. It also has a shelf full of English-language books and magazines, which you can read while enjoying a sandwich, coffee or tea. It's part of the FPMT Buddhist centre and profits go towards supporting the restoration of Buddhism in Mongolia.

Sakura Bakery JAPANESE $
(Map p42; Tserendorjiin Gudamj; mains T4000-5400; ⏲10am-7pm) This authentic Japanese cafe has a dedicated following who come for the simple curry lunches, excellent cakes

ULAANBAATAR CHEAP EATS

There are dozens of Mongolian fast-food restaurants *(guanz)* and they can be found on every block in the city. Some are chain restaurants and you'll start to recognise prominent eateries, including Zochin Buuz (Зочин Бууз), Khaan Buuz (Хаан Бууз) and Mongol Khuushuur (Монгол Хуушуур). They serve up *buuz* (steamed mutton dumplings), plus soups and *bifshteks ondogtei* (beefsteak with egg); many of these operate 24 hours. Meals cost T2500 to T5000. Look for them at these locations:

Khaan Buuz (Map p42) Opposite the State Department Store.

Zochin Buuz (Map p42; Sambuugiin Örgön Chölöö) It's 80m east of the fire station.

Mongol Khuushuur (Map p42) Behind Government House.

and friendly atmosphere. Manga fans will appreciate the collection of comic books.

Emerald Bay MEDITERRANEAN $$
(Map p42; Tserendorjiin Gudamj; mains T7000-15,000; 11am-11pm;) Excellent Mediterranean menu includes pork *gyros* (T9500) and grilled salmon (T15,000). Vegetarians should be able to find a salad or soup to their liking. It also has a nice patio overlooking Tserendorjiin Gudamj where you can sit and watch Ulaanbaatar go about its business.

Berlin FAST FOOD $
(Map p42; Sambugiin Örgön Chölöö; meals from T2500;) Cafeteria-style place with good-value burgers, spaghetti and goulash.

GANDAN MONASTERY AREA

Arab Kebab Cafe MIDDLE EASTERN $$
(Map p42; Duruv Zam; kebabs from T3500; 11am-midnight;) Run by a friendly Syrian chap named Ishmael, this small restaurant serves up simple Middle Eastern cuisine, including donor kebabs, *plov* (pilaf), *lavash* (flat bread) and Arabic coffee. It's also possibly the only place in UB where you can puff on a *shisha* (water pipe). The entire place is covered in plastic green foliage, as Ishmael likes to say, 'Even in winter, its summer in my cafe'.

SEOUL STREET

TOP CHOICE **Marco Polo** PIZZA, PASTA $$
(Map p42; Seoul St 27; meals T10,000-20,000; 10am-midnight;) The brick-oven pizza here is considered by many to be the best in town. It also has delicious lasagne, baked chicken and a variety of salads. The wooden tables on the patio make for great streetside seating in summer. Try not to let the kiddies wander off unaccompanied – Ulaanbaatar's most notorious strip club is right upstairs!

Bull HOT POT $$$
(Map p42; Seoul St; meal per person T15,000; 11.30am-10pm;) A local favourite, this hot-pot place gets a steady stream of patrons at its two Seoul St locations. Order an array of raw vegetables and meats, which are brought to your table on platters, then cook the ingredients in your personal cauldron of boiling broth. It's a great alternative to the meat-heavy menus you'll experience at most other restaurants in town.

Saffron FUSION $$
(Map p42; Seoul St; meal T8000-20,000; 11am-midnight;) This bistro feels like a good place for a power lunch: perhaps it's the inspiring modern art that hangs from the walls, or the fact that it's attached to the headquarters of Mongolia's biggest bank. Choose from a range of light but tasty dishes that sometimes combine European and Asian flavours. Chicken, fish and beef dishes are prominent and there are some vegetarian items (try the saffron risotto). Enter through Khan Bank.

California ECLECTIC $$
(Map p42; Seoul St; dishes T12,000; 8am-midnight;) One of Ulaanbaatar's most popular restaurants, this place has an array of eclectic menu items, including a Thai steak salad with Caesar dressing, authentic chicken tacos and *shorlog* (shish kebab with cream sauce). There's a huge variety of other items to choose from and the portions are generous. It's also one of the few places in town that is open for breakfast. The interior is often smoky but there's a nice outdoor (smoke-free) patio.

Kenny Rogers Roasters SOUL FOOD $$
(Map p42; Seoul St; meals T9000-14,000; 10.30am-11pm;) Kenny Rogers–themed restaurant serving generous portions of

roasted chicken, corn bread, mac and cheese and other American soul foods. Indoor seating in booths is comfortable and there's an outdoor patio. Good for families.

BD's Mongolian Barbeque STIR-FRY $$
(Map p42; Seoul St; meal per person from T6900; 11am-11pm;) If you've ever had Mongolian food in a Western country, this place might look familiar. Load your bowl full of veggies, meats, noodles, a raw egg and sauces, then hand it over to a grill master who cooks up your meal before your eyes. It is by no means traditional Mongolian food but it's a popular place for families and hungry travellers (there is an all-you-can-eat option for T13,900). Great for salads and vegetable stir-fries.

Ikh Mongol STEAKS $$
(Map p42; Seoul St; meal with beer T8000-12,000; noon-midnight;) This place specialises in gut-busting platters of meat and big jugs of beer. Needless to say, it's not a great place for calorie-watchers. It has daily live music (10pm) and a large beer patio built on two levels. Despite its size, it can still be hard to get a table in summer. It's located on the east side of the Circus.

WEST OF SÜKHBAATAR SQUARE

TOP CHOICE **Luna Blanca** VEGETARIAN $$
(Map p42; M-100 Bldg, Juulchiin Gudamj; meals T5000-10,000; 10am-9pm;) This is one of the best places in UB to get a vegetarian meal. The vegan kitchen whips up pastas, tofu dishes, veggie kebabs, soups and salads. The food is not spectacular but it is a nice change of pace and the atmosphere is clean, smoke-free and friendly. The spaghetti is recommended.

Sachers Café GERMAN BAKERY $
(Map p42; Baga Toiruu west; snacks T500-2000, light meals T5000; 9am-9pm;) Birgette, the grandmotherly Bavarian native that runs this place, bakes up a wide array of pretzels, cakes, pastries and breads. There are some delicious light meals too, including homemade soups, ready-made sandwiches and hot dishes (try the *kaesekrainer,* a sausage with cheese filling). It has a nice outdoor patio, where you can enjoy reading local or international English newspapers (in English, German and Japanese). The interior seating is cosy in winter and the bathrooms are about as good as you'll find anywhere.

Little Buddha GRILL, MONGOLIAN $$
(Map p42; Baga Toiruu West; meals T5000-11,000; 9am-9pm;) This colourful restaurant has Western-style meals, grilled meats and even breakfast. The chilled-out vibe makes it a nice place to just sit with a cup of tea and watch some BBC on the tube. The friendly owner, Tseiko, speaks English and German. In winter, Tseiko disappears and the menu turns to standard Mongolian fare.

EAST OF SÜKHBAATAR SQUARE

Monet EUROPEAN $$$
(Map p42; Sükhbaatar Sq 2; meals T35,000-60,000, business lunch 9000-16,000; noon-10pm;) Located on the 17th floor of the Central Tower, this swish restaurant offers unbeatable city views stretching out in three directions. A window divides the patrons from the kitchen, so you can peer at chefs as they create their masterpieces, mostly European cuisine like grilled salmon, seafood risotto, rack of lamb and fresh salads. The two-course business lunch, priced under US$10 (available Monday to Friday noon to 3pm), is good value for money. Smart casual dress is required.

Urlag NORTH KOREAN $$
(Map p42; Amaryn Gudamj; meals T7000; noon-9pm;) If you've never been to a North Korean restaurant before, here's your chance. Dishes to try include the marinated beef, eggplant stir-fry and the tempura vegetables. Order a bottle of genuine North Korean vodka (T10,000) and toast Kim Jung Un with your North Korean waitress. It's hidden away in the Culture Palace, opposite the Tuushin Hotel.

Central Tower Restaurants MONGOLIAN, INTERNATIONAL $$
(Map p42; Peace Ave; meals T5000-15,000;) The new Central Tower contains several restaurants that cater to various budgets and tastes. Head up to the 3rd floor for the Waka Waka Food Court (Mongolian cafeteria), Biwon Korean Restaurant, Bugis Coffee Shop and the Square (Western-style pub grub).

iLoft CAFE $
(Map p42; Amaryn Gudamj; snacks from T3500; 10am-6pm) This friendly, posh nook has soft seating, stunning black-and-white decor and a hip vibe. Drinks, sandwiches and desserts are available. It's quiet by day but in the evening the adjacent hall is home

to loud parties and events. It's located behind the Tuushin Hotel.

Tender MONGOLIAN, RUSSIAN **$**
(Map p42; Amaryn Gudamj; meals T2500-6000; ⏲10am-midnight) Serves hearty portions of goulash, schnitzel and fried pork, plus some Korean dishes. Has a low-key, non-touristy vibe, bright orange walls and Brezhnev-era tablecloths.

NORTH OF SÜKHBAATAR SQUARE

Le Bistro Français FRENCH **$$$**
(Map p42; Ikh Surguuliin Gudamj 2; meals T15,000-35,000; ⏲9am-10pm Mon-Fri, 10am-10pm Sat & Sun; 📶📋) The soft lighting, cream-coloured walls and French art give this bistro a peaceful, romantic ambience. Try the quiche Lorraine for a starter, followed by a lamb goulash or beef fillet, washed down with a French red wine. Classic French delicacies like frogs legs and escargot are sometimes available. Ice cream and crepe desserts are excellent. It's popular with expats and Mongolian corporate big shots looking for some Rive Gauche atmosphere. Ice cream and crepe desserts are excellent.

Los Bandidos MEXICAN, INDIAN **$$**
(Map p42; Baga Toiruu north; dishes T7500-15,000; ⏲11.30am-midnight; 📶📋) One of the more eclectic places in town, Los Bandidos serves both Mexican and Indian cuisine. The Mexican dishes are surprisingly good, although each dish is essentially the same thing, just presented in a different format. They serves nachos, fajitas, enchiladas and burritos, as well as meals hot from the tandoori oven.

Nomad Legends Mongols Club MONGOLIAN **$$**
(Map p42; Sükhbaataryn Gudamj 1; meals T6000-8000; ⏲noon-midnight; 📋) This tiny restaurant is a good place to try some Mongolian food in a somewhat upscale atmosphere. Try a Mongolian milk tea or plate of *khuushuur* (fried meat pancake).

SOUTH OF SÜKHBAATAR SQUARE

TOP CHOICE **Millie's Café** AMERICAN, LATIN **$$**
(Map p42; ☎330 338; Marco Polo Bldg; mains T7000-9500; ⏲8am-8pm Mon-Sat; 📶📋) This place is an Ulaanbaatar institution. Drop by Millie's at noon any day of the week and you'll find the place packed with hungry expats and locals sipping excellent smoothies and gobbling steak sandwiches, cheeseburgers and homemade lemon pie. Come early for legendary chocolate cake (usually finished by 1pm). Owner Millie is a gracious host while the Cuban chef Daniel adds a bit of Latin zing to the place.

Veranda WESTERN **$$**
(Map p42; Jamyn Gunii Gudamj 5/1; mains T7500-12,000; ⏲noon-midnight; 📋) One of the most popular places in town, this Italian restaurant excels at meat dishes, such as a nice lamb roll with blackcurrant sauce on a bed of greens. The house speciality is the Veranda, a tender, flavourful grilled beef tenderloin that goes well with one of the Italian wines on offer. Kick back on a couch or sit on the balcony, enjoying fine views of the Choijin Lama Temple Museum.

Silk Road INTERNATIONAL **$$**
(Map p42; Jamyn Gunii Gudamj 5/1; meal with drink T10,000; ⏲12.30-midnight; 📋) A long-time Ulaanbaatar eatery, Silk Road is so named for its bas-relief scenes of the ancient route from China to Europe. The menu also carries a trans-Eurasian theme, with sprinklings of Indian, Central Asian and Mediterranean treats, including shish kebabs, chicken tikka and pork *gyros* (pitta with meat and vegetables). It's in the same building as Veranda.

Grand Khaan Irish Pub PUB **$$**
(Map p42; Seoul St; meal with beer T7000; ⏲11am-midnight; 📶📋) Big crowds, lots of smoke, free-flowing beer and loud music set the scene for Ulaanbaatar's most popular night spot. Waitresses dash past with big jugs of beer and it can be a challenge to get their attention. The pub-grub menu includes an array of salads. An attached cafe (open 8am to 10pm) serves coffee, croissants and English breakfasts.

EASTERN ULAANBAATAR

Gzhel UKRAINIAN **$$**
(Map p39; East Peace Ave – 55, Bayanzürkh District; dishes T7000-9000; ⏲11am-11pm Mon-Fri, noon-10pm Sat & Sun) This Ukrainian restaurant has a schmaltzy Eastern European atmosphere, right down to the frilly blue and white outfits worn by the waitresses. The kitchen specialises in fish dishes, so try the raw fish appetisers to start, followed by the lemon salmon. The *pelmeni* (small, meat-filled ravioli) is also good. Live Ukrainian music is sometimes played here, usually Tuesdays and Thursdays from 7pm. It's on the east side of the city, next to the gold-domed Russian church.

BARS WITH A VIEW

If you are looking for a bar with a great view, you've got two good options in UB. The **View Lounge Club** (Map p42; ⏲5pm-midnight), on the top floor of the Corporate Hotel, and the **Sky Lounge** (Map p42; ⏲noon-midnight), on the 17th floor of the Central Tower, are both worth checking out. They serve pricey drinks (beers T5000, cocktails T7000 to T12,000) and have a dimly lit, Manhattanesque style, with big windows overlooking the city below. If you're in party mode, try the Sky Lounge on Thursday or Friday (admission T5000 to T10,000) when the tables are cleared and DJs spin the latest Mongolian electronica.

SANSAR

TOP CHOICE **Namaste** INDIAN $$$
(Map p51; Zaluuchuudin Örgön Chölöö; dishes T6500-8000; ⏲11.30am-11pm; 📄) If awards were given out for the most comfortable seating in UB, this place would win hands down. Relax on one of the soft red velvet couches and enjoy some superb kebabs, cheese naans, tandoori roti and juicy chicken meatballs. Try the delicious *saag gosht* (beef in spinach sauce). There are vegetarian options and classic street food like *gol-gappa* (pastry with chickpeas). The entrance is through the Flower Hotel.

Hazara INDIAN $$
(Map p51; Peace Ave 16; dishes T6000-8000; ⏲noon-2.30pm & 6-10pm; 📄) Tucked behind the Wrestling Palace, this North Indian restaurant has consistently been one of the best restaurants in Ulaanbaatar since it opened in the late 1990s. Each table is covered by a colourful *samiyan* (Rajasthani tent), so it's easy to escape to India for an hour or two while you dine on excellent *murgh makhni*, a naan basket and saffron rice.

Sakura JAPANESE $$
(Map p51; Khan Palace Hotel, East Cross Rd; meals T6000-8000; 📄) Known as one of the better places in town for an authentic Japanese meal, Sakura is located inside the Khan Palace Hotel.

THREE/FOUR DISTRICT

Strings SANDWICHES, STIR-FRY $$
(Map p39; ☎367 845; Damdinbazaryn Gudamj; dishes T7000-14,500; ⏲noon-midnight; 📄) A Hard Rock Cafe knock-off with big portions of food, live music and fun atmosphere. 24K, a Filipino rock band, plays here most nights (call to confirm the schedule). For a filling meal try the fajitas, the Hawaiian pork stir-fry or a teriyaki chicken sandwich. If you are only here for drink, a T5000 to T8000 cover may apply. The restaurant is attached to the White House Hotel. Head up Amarsanaagiin Gudamj for 400m and turn left.

Drinking

There are many good, clean and safe bars and pubs in Ulaanbaatar, most of them are located downtown, around the Drama Theatre or on Seoul Street. There are an equal number of dark and dingy nightspots, usually out in the suburbs, the 3/4 District and Ikh Toiruu (north of the Kempinski Hotel). Theme bars are the latest trend – there are Irish bars, sports bars, American bars and, bizarrely, one with paraphernalia from the Third Reich. Better yet, skip the Nazi bar and try something more Mongolian, like a cup of *airag* (*koumiss;* fermented mare milk), available at sidewalk gers in summer. Besides the places following, enjoy a drink at one of the open-air beer and shashlik stands that open in summer near the State Department Store.

Dublin IRISH PUB
(Map p42; Seoul St; meals from T7000; ⏲noon-midnight) With a cosy atmosphere, cream-coloured walls and dark wood finish, Dublin transplants a bit of Ireland to the steppes. It's a popular expat hangout, but also frequented by young Mongols. There is plenty of alcohol on tap, as well as Irish coffee and tasty pub grub.

MB Beer Plus BREW PUB
(Map p42; Chingisiin Örgön Chölöö 4; ⏲10am-midnight) This is the plastic-looking building next to the Drama Theatre. Giant brass brewing vats serve as a centrepiece downstairs while upstairs you can rent out a swanky private room (for about T15,000 per hour).

Budweiser Bar BAR
(Map p42; Sükhbaataryn Gudamj; ⏲6pm-2am) This bar proudly serves the original Budweiser beer brewed in the Czech Republic.

It has an iconic location on Sükhbaatar Sq and retains a somewhat old-school, smoky but friendly ambience.

Sexy Jazz Lounge LOUNGE
(Map p51; Tokyogiin Gudamj; ⏲11am-midnight; 📶) This place attempts to recreate a 1960s jazz lounge atmosphere. It's a little cramped but can be a fun place for a drink. If you're peckish, the menu includes hamburgers and other American fare, plus authentic milkshakes.

Premiership Sports Pub PUB
(Map p42; Seoul St; ⏲1pm-midnight) Lovers of football (and beer) will want to pay a homage to this large and friendly pub, decorated with memorabilia from the English Premier League.

Detroit BAR
(Map p42; Seoul St; ⏲5pm-2am) This Motor City–inspired bar has a foosball table, a darts board and plenty of sports paraphernalia. Besides alcohol, you can order burgers, fries and sandwiches. Live music is staged on Wednesdays and Fridays. It's under BD's Mongolian Barbeque.

Greenland BEER GARDEN
(Map p42; Peace Ave; ⏲noon-midnight Jun-Aug) Oktoberfest-style tent, opposite Sükhbaatar Sq. It's open in summer only.

☆ Entertainment

Both the *UB Post* and the *Mongol Messenger* English-language newspapers contain weekly events listings. The **Arts Council of Mongolia** (Map p42; www.artscouncil.mn) produces a monthly cultural-events calendar, which covers most theatres, galleries and museums. You can pick up a brochure in hotel lobbies and many restaurants. Theatres and galleries sometimes post English ads outside or you could just buy a ticket and hope for the best.

Other online resources include the **Ulaanbaatar Events** (www.facebook.com/ulaanbaatar.events) page on Facebook, which is good for listings on parties, raves and concerts. The **Mongol Expat** (www.mongolexpat.com) website is handy for expat events, including sports events and meet ups at a local pub.

Theatre

TRADITIONAL MUSIC & DANCE

A performance of traditional music and dance will be one of the highlights of your visit to Mongolia and should not be missed. You'll see outstanding examples of the unique Mongolian throat-singing, known as *khöömii;* full-scale orchestral renditions of new and old Mongolian music; contortionists guaranteed to make your eyes water; traditional and modern dancing; and recitals featuring the unique horse-head violin, the *morin khuur.*

The Tumen Ekh Song & Dance Ensemble at the **State Youth & Children's Theatre** (Map p42; ☎9665 0711; www.tumen-ekh.mn; Nairamdal Park; admission T12,000; ⏲6pm May-Oct) is the most popular cultural show in town, featuring traditional singers, dancers and contortionists. It's a great chance to hear *khöömii* and see some fabulous costumes. You can buy CDs (T20,000) of the performance after the show. There is a cafe and gallery in the traditional-style hall.

The Moonstone Song & Dance Ensemble at **Tsuki House** (Map p42; ☎318 802; admission US$7; ⏲4pm, 6pm & 8pm May-Oct) puts on a Mongolian cabaret. You get the lot: contortionists, throat singers, musicians, *tsam* mask dancers and an electrifying shaman dance done in contemporary fashion. One drink is included in the price of the ticket and food is available. Tsuki House is the modern glass building next to the Circus (on the north side).

The **Mongolian National Song & Dance Ensemble** (☎323 954; www.mon-ensemble.mn) puts on performances for tourists throughout the summer in the **National Academic Drama Theatre** (Map p42; ☎324 621; cnr Seoul St & Chingisiin Örgön Chölöö; admission T7000; ⏲6pm). Shows are less frequently staged at the **Cultural Palace** (Map p42; ☎321 444) on the northeast corner of Sükhbaatar Sq.

You can also see traditional song and dance at the Choijin Lama Temple Museum (see p47) in summer at 5pm.

OPERA & BALLET

Built by the Russians in 1932, the **State Opera & Ballet Theatre** (Map p42; ☎7011 0389; admission T5000-8000; ⏲closed Aug) is the salmon-pinkish building on the southeast corner of Sükhbaatar Sq. On Saturday and Sunday evenings throughout the year, and sometimes also on weekend afternoons in the summer, the theatre holds stirring opera (in Mongolian) and ballet shows.

Mongolian original operas include *Three Fateful Hills* by famous playwright D Natsagdorj, and the more recent *Chinggis Khaan,* by B Sharav. Other productions include an exhilarating (but long) rendition of *Carmen,* plus plenty of Puccini and Tchaikovsky.

A board outside the theatre lists the shows for the current month in English. Advance purchase is worthwhile for popular shows because tickets are numbered, so it's possible to score a good seat if you book early. The box office is open 10am to 1pm and 2pm to 5pm Wednesday to Sunday.

DRAMA

National Academic Drama Theatre (Map p42; ☎324 621; cnr Seoul St & Chingisiin Örgön Chölöö; admission T10,000; ⊙ticket sales 10am-7pm) During most of the year, this large, fire-engine-red theatre shows one of a dozen or so Mongolian-language productions by various playwrights from Mongolia, Russia and beyond. Schedules are sporadic. Check listings in the *UB Post*. You can buy tickets in advance at the booking office, which is on the right-hand side of the theatre.

On the left-hand side of the theatre, as you approach it from the road, is a door that leads to a **puppet theatre** (☎321 669; admission T1500-2500; ⊙noon, 2pm, 4pm Sat & Sun), which is great if you are travelling with children.

Nightclubs

Ulaanbaatar has a lively nightlife that has matured in recent years – you can experience everything from small jazz bars and cocktail lounges to gargantuan dance halls and the odd strip club. Places go out of fashion pretty quickly, so you'll need to ask the locals about what is popular.

Metropolis NIGHTCLUB
(Map p51; Sky Shopping Centre; admission T5000; ⊙10pm-4am) The most stylish place in Ulaanbaatar, Metropolis (mispronounced 'Metro Police' by most locals) has a large dance floor and a VIP voyeur terrace. The DJ plays an eclectic mix of disco, salsa, pop, rock and techno. Drinks go for T4000 to T6000. It's set inside a large vault next to the entrance to the Sky Shopping Mall. It's closed the first day of the month.

Face Club NIGHTCLUB
(Map p42; Juulchin Gudamj; admission T3000; ⊙7pm-3am) The Face Club is a lively little place with a Tahitian theme. It has live bands and DJs. It's the most centrally located nightclub in town.

Hollywood NIGHTCLUB
(Map p51; Academich Sodnomyn Gudamj; admission T3000; ⊙8pm-late) This throbbing nightclub, with DJ and elevated dance floor, is on a little lane between Dashchoilon Khiid and Ikh Toiruu. It's popular with students who attend the nearby university.

Mass NIGHTCLUB
(Map p39; 3/4 District; admission T5000; ⊙10pm-late) This is Ulaanbaatar's biggest nightclub. Trance, techno and hip hop blares from the noisiest sound system on the steppes. It's a little tricky to find; from the main road in the 3/4 District turn right just after the Nomin supermarket and then take another right at the T-junction; Mass is about 50m down on the left, set back a little bit from the road.

Brilliant NIGHTCLUB
(Map p39; Dund Gol Gudamj, Khan Uul District; admission T5000; ⊙11.30pm-late) Young, hip urbanites have discovered this nightclub buried in an industrial part of UB. It's about 1km from Peace Bridge, along the canal; the entrance is through the alley, off the street. The shopping plaza here is known as Arvan-Yos Uilchilgeenii Töv (19th Shopping Mall).

Medussa NIGHTCLUB
(Map p42; 3/4 District; admission T5000; ⊙10pm-late) This long-time favourite is located in basement below the Lenin Centre, next to Tengis movie theatre. DJs here like to experiment, you'll hear R&B-hip hop mixes, baroque pop, trip hop, electronica and every sound in between.

Live Music

River Sounds (Map p42; ☎320 497; Olympiin Örgön Chölöö; admission T5000; ⊙8pm-3am) This is one of the best places to hear music as it's a dedicated live-music venue with jazz bands and the occasional indie rock band.

Another popular place is Strings (p64), which has a house band playing classic rock covers. A few brew houses and bars also have live music, including Detroit (p65), Grand Khaan (p63) and Ikh Mongol (p62). Check the UB Post for schedules.

The contemporary Mongolian folk band Altan Orgil puts on a performance at **City Nomads** (Map p51; ☎454 484; Peace Ave), a Mongolian-style restaurant near the Wrestling Palace. The band performs nightly in July and August, and Tuesday and Friday the rest of the year, always at 7.30pm. But Altain Orgil has hardly cornered the market on this type of music – about 10 other bands also play at local clubs, bars and restaurants.

DON'T MISS

MODERN MONGOLIAN MUSIC MASHUPS

There is a thriving contemporary music scene in Ulaanbaatar. While you are in town, make sure to pick up some CDs of the newest artists. Even better, try to catch a live performance. You can hear live music at many downtown bars like Ikh Mongol or Grand Khaan Irish Pub. Popular music genres include pop, rap and hip hop, as well as a totally Mongolian brand of folklore-rock fusion music that includes drums and guitars along with traditional instruments.

For folklore-rock, **Altan Urag** (www.altanurag.mn) is regarded as one of the best. Their mashups of Western percussion and Mongolian string instruments will have you entranced. Their website has a full range of videos (we like 'Raakh II' and 'Abroad'). We are also huge fans of the **Boerte Ensemble**, which fuses all sorts of instruments into a mellow sound good for long road trips. There are several good videos on wn.com/XOBORXYH. Another band enjoying some success is **Khusugtun** (www.khusugtun.com); they were recently recorded by BBC's Human Planet series.

If you are into hip hop, look out for upcoming artists **Opozit**, **Quiza**, **Tatar** and **Tsetse**. The emulation of American inner city gangsta rap speaks volumes about Mongolia's eagerness to embrace Western culture; however, if you can get someone to translate the lyrics you'll hear distinct Mongolian flavour as popular topics include lost loves, mothers, wild nature and blue skies.

Rock groups include the **Lemons**, **Pips** and **Nisvanis**. For mellow R&B, the best are **BX**, **Maraljingoo** and **Bold**. **Nominjin** (www.nominjin.com) is an up-and-coming R&B voice on the international scene; she sings in both English and Mongolian. You can hear most of these artists on YouTube.

This recent breakout in Mongolian music has not gone unnoticed. Australian film-maker Benj Binks has documented the phenomena in film **Mongolian Bling** (www.mongolianbling.com).

Cinemas

Örgöö CINEMA
(Map p39; ☎7011 7711; www.urgoo.mn; Ard Ayush Örgön Chölöö; regular show T4000, VIP seat T8000) This comfortable theatre has air-conditioned halls and a modern projection system. It's located in the heart of the 3/4 District, on the main road just past the Nomin Supermarket.

Tengis CINEMA
(Map p42; ☎326 575; www.tengis.mn; Liberty Sq; regular show T2500, matinee T1500) Similar to Örgöö but the sound system here is so loud it may cause your ears to bleed.

Gay & Lesbian Venues

There are no dedicated gay bars as such but some members of the gay community will meet at one place or another for a few weeks and then move on. Attitudes towards gays are loosening up a little but it's better to err on the side of discretion when asking about meeting places.

Circus

State Circus (Map p42; ☎320 795) In the recognisable round building with the blue roof south of the State Department Store. Despite the name, the circus no longer preforms here. Concerts are sometimes held here in summer.

Sport

The annual Naadam features wrestling, horse racing and archery; see p222 for more details. In the lead-up to Naadam, you should be able to catch some informal, but still competitive, wrestling at the Naadam Stadium. For wrestling at other times of the year, check out the schedule at the **Wrestling Palace** (Map p51; ☎456 443; Peace Ave; admission T1000-5000), which is the ger-shaped building south of the Chinggis Khaan Hotel. Wrestling, basketball and boxing are also held at the **Central Sports Palace** (Map p42; Baga Toiruu) during the year. In late 2010, a brand new sports complex was opened near the airport. Big concerts and international sports competitions are held here.

Fashion Show

Mongolian models strut their stuff on the catwalk at the **Torgo Fashion Salon** (Map p42; ☎324 957; www.torgo.mn; Big Ring Rd; admission T8000) nightly at 6pm from 1 June to 25

September. The designs, by local designers, usually blend traditional Mongolian outfits into contemporary fashions. You can buy products here or just kick back, watch the show and listen to the accompanying music.

Shopping

Just about everything you can think of is available in UB, from ancient Buddhist antiques to the latest generation iPhone. Some higher-end places accept credit cards but cash is still king at most shops.

The antique trade is booming in Mongolia, but you need to be careful about what you buy, as some of it is illegal to export. Make sure the seller can produce a certificate of authenticity. Some dealers will suggest shipping the antiques in the mail to avoid customs at the airport – if you get caught, be sure to send us a postcard from prison.

Souvenir shops are found absolutely everywhere in Ulaanbaatar – just toss a stone in the air and chances are you'll hit one. You can pick up cheap and authentic gifts such as landscape paintings, wool slippers, Mongolian jackets and felt dolls. There is also a lot of kitsch, such as Chinggis Khaan T-shirts and key chains. On the streets you will undoubtedly encounter amateur artists selling watercolours for under US$1. Contemporary Mongolian artwork can be purchased at a small number of galleries around town. For more information see the section on art galleries.

The biggest souvenir outlet is on the 5th floor of the State Department Store. You'll also spot shops inside gers mounted on carts, notably outside the Bayangol Hotel and National Museum of Mongolia.

Traditional musical instruments make perfect gifts for friends who are musically inclined. The *morin khuur* (horse-head fiddle) is particularly nice as a piece of decorative art (and Mongolians consider it good luck to have one in the home).

Cashmere also makes good gifts. The major cashmere and wool factories are Goyo, Gobi Cashmere and Altai. The State Department Store has cashmere on the 2nd and 5th floors. Tserendorjiin Gudamj, between the State Circus and the State Department Store, has around a dozen fashion shops.

Be aware that Western-quality camping gear is not cheap in Mongolia, so you may want to bring stuff from home. Cheap Chinese-made products are available if you're desperate, though most of it breaks down before you even leave the city. Besides the shops listed, there is a decent camping section on the 3rd floor of the State Department Store. For secondhand stuff, check the noticeboards at the guesthouses and at Café Amsterdam.

For a country with such a rich tradition in horse riding there is a surprising lack of shops selling saddles and tack. The best selection is still at the Naran Tuul Market. You may also be able to pick up a secondhand saddle from another traveller (check guesthouse noticeboards).

English-language bookshops are small and limited. Besides the ones listed here, you could try poking around the newspaper kiosk in the CPO or the bookshop on the 6th floor of the State Department Store.

Photo-developing studios are everywhere, including the State Department Store. Our favourites are listed below.

Seven Summits OUTDOOR GEAR
(Map p42; ☎329 456; www.activemongolia.com/7summits; btwn Peace Ave & Seoul St) Stocks German-made Vaude gear, GPS units, maps, stoves and gas, travel books and accessories. It also hires out gear, including tents, sleeping bags, gas stoves, mountain bikes and inflatable kayaks. It's opposite the CPO.

Ayanchin Outfitters OUTDOOR GEAR
(Map p42; www.ayanchin.mn; Seoul St 21) This place sells Western camping, fishing and hunting equipment, plus GPS units, mainly imported from the US.

Amarbayasgalant Antique ANTIQUES
(Map p42; Juulchin Gudamj 37/31) A quality shop for the serious buyer, it sells enormous Sutras, traditional headdress, Buddhist statues and other rare items. Some of the items are creations of Zanabazar and not for sale. Great for browsing.

Valiant Art Gallery ART GALLERY
(Map p42; www.mongolianartgallery.com; Marco Polo Bldg) Highly regarded gallery run by a Polish art lover. If you are after high-quality art, make this your first stop. Also runs an auction house in the Altai Centre, next to the State Department Store.

Books in English BOOKSTORE
(Map p42; Peace Ave) Sells used books including guidebooks. It's tough to spot, located in the basement of an apartment block. Keep your eyes peeled for the yellow and blue sign.

Librairie Papillon BOOKSTORE
(Map p42; Ikh Surguuliin Gudamj) Ulaanbaatar's finest bookshop. Has plenty of classic books

in English but the collection of French books is by far the most interesting.

Nomin Ikh Delgur BOOKSTORE
(Map p42; Baga Toiruu east) This place is well stocked with Mongolian-language books and has a few English titles on the 2nd floor.

Xanadu BOOKSTORE
(Map p42; Marco Polo Bldg; ⏲10am-6pm Mon-Sat) Sells mostly Lonely Planet titles.

Shonkhor Saddles OUTDOOR GEAR
(Map p42; ☎311 218, 9191 1190; shonkhorjockey@yahoo.com; Damdin St) Produces and sells horse paraphernalia. The workshop is buried under an apartment behind School No 5 but it's very hard to find and is often closed. It's best to call first (have a Mongolian call for you). Or you can meet the owners; they manage the Internet Centre opposite the German Embassy. Ask for Tomor or Naraa.

Egshiglen Magnai National Musical Instrument Shop MUSICAL INSTRUMENTS
(Map p42; Sükhbaataryn Gudamj) At this shop on the east side of the Museum of Natural History, *morin khuur* range from T150,000 to T700,000. There are also *yattag* (zithers) and two-stringed Chinese fiddles.

Hi-Fi CD Shop MUSIC STORE
(Map p42; Seoul St) Mongolian music CDs make great gifts for friends back home and this place has one of the best collections. Also check the State Department Store.

Cashmere House CASHMERE
(Map p42; Peace Ave; ⏲11am-7pm Mon-Sat) Excellent cashmere garments can be purchased here. It's opposite the Russian embassy.

Gobi Cashmere Factory Outlet CASHMERE
(Map p39; Peace Ave; ⏲11am-7pm) Has slightly lower prices than Cashmere House, although much of it is last year's stock. It's in the industrial suburbs and hard to find on your own. If you take a taxi, have your hotel write down the address for the driver.

Red Ger Art Gallery FINE ART
(Map p42; Juulchin Gudamj) The best contemporary artwork in the country is on sale inside the Zanabazar Museum of Fine Arts; it's open during museum hours.

Choijin Lama Temple Museum Shop SOUVENIRS
(Map p42) The gift shop inside the Choijin Lama Temple is a great place to pick up hand-stitched slippers, designer Mongolian garments, brass cups and jewellery. You can also get pouches of sheep ankle-bones with instructions on fortune telling and traditional games.

Naran Tuul market MARKET
(Наран Туул Зах; Map p39; admission T50; ⏲9am-7pm Wed-Mon) East of the centre, this is also known as the Black Market (Khar Zakh), but it's not the sort of place where you go to change money illegally and smuggle goods – though this certainly happens.

A covered area has a decent selection of clothes and accessories, such as bags, leather boots and fake North Face jackets. This is also one of the cheapest places to get traditional Mongolian clothes such as a *del* (T30,000 for a summer *del*, T60,000 for a winter *del*) and jacket (T20,000 to T40,000). Towards the back of the market you'll find saddles, riding tack and all the ingredients needed to build your own ger. The back area is also where you'll find antique and coin dealers, but they don't issue any official documentation (unlike the antique shops in town), making it illegal to export their stock. New items, such as the snuff bottles (made in China anyway), can be purchased without worry.

The market is notorious for pickpockets and bag slashers, so don't bring anything you can't afford to lose. Don't carry anything on your back, and strap your money belt to your body.

A taxi to the market should cost about T2000 from the centre of town. To walk from the Square will take about 40 minutes. Try to avoid Saturday and Sunday afternoons, when the crowds can be horrendous.

Computerland ELECTRONICS
(Map p42; Peace Ave; ⏲10am-7pm Mon-Sat) Techie travellers will find joy in this three-storey building crammed with dozens of private dealers selling everything from flash drives to the latest laptops. It is located behind the Canon Showroom, which also has a computer shop.

State Department Store SHOPPING CENTRE
(Их Дэлгүүр; Map p42; Peace Ave 44) Known as *ikh delguur* ('big shop'), this is virtually a tourist attraction in itself, with the best products from around the city squeezed into one building.

The 1st floor has a supermarket at the back and a foreign-exchange counter. The 2nd and 3rd floors have outlets for clothing, cashmere and leather goods. The 4th floor has a children's section. The 5th floor has electronics in the back and a large room containing souvenirs, traditional clothing, maps and books about Mongolia. The 6th floor has a food court and bookstore.

Sky Shopping Centre SHOPPING CENTRE
(Map p51) If you are based on the east side of town, this may be more convenient than the State Department Store and offers similar goods and services (at slightly higher prices). It's behind the Chinggis Khaan Hotel.

Other shops offering a good selection:

Antique & Art Gallery ANTIQUES
(Map p42; Peace Ave) Sells a range of jewellery, art and brassware.

Nomads Culture Antique Shop ANTIQUES
(Map p42; Juulchin Gudamj 35) Smaller than the Antique & Art Gallery, but with similar products; opposite Amarbayasgalant.

Argasun MUSICAL INSTRUMENTS
(Map p42; Partizan Gudamj 48) A *morin khuur* workshop near Aeroflot.

Altai Cashmere CASHMERE
(Map p51; Zaluuchuudyn Örgön Chölöö) Large cashmere outlet near the Chinggis Khaan Hotel on the east side of town.

Mary & Martha Mongolia SOUVENIRS
(Map p42; www.mmmongolia.com; Peace Ave) Fair-trade shop selling handicrafts, felt products and modern Kazakh wall hangings.

Mongolian Quilting Shop SOUVENIRS
(Map p42; mongolianquilt@gmail.com; Peace Ave; 9am-7pm Mon-Fri) Sells handmade quilts produced by low-income families. The money earned here goes to the New Life NGO, which directly supports the women who produce the quilts.

Möngön Zaviya FELT PRODUCTS
(Map p42; Peace Ave; 10.30am-8.30pm Mon-Fri, 11am-7.30pm Sat & Sun) Great for picking up silver cups, belt buckles and jewellery.

Souvenir House SOUVENIRS
(Map p42; cnr Peace Ave & Khaddorjiin Gudamj) One of the largest souvenir shops in town.

Tsagaan Alt Wool Shop FELT PRODUCTS
(Map p42; www.mongolianwoolcraft.com; Tserendorjiin Gudamj) This nonprofit store, which sends money directly back to the craftspeople, has all manner of wool products, including toys, clothes and artwork.

Canon Showroom PHOTOGRAPHY
(Map p42; Peace Ave) Sells new Canon cameras, video cameras and accessories.

Mon Nip Camera Shop PHOTOGRAPHY
(Map p42; Peace Ave 30) Sells a range of cameras, tripods and other photographic equipment.

Fuji Film PHOTOGRAPHY
(Map p42; M-100 Bldg, Juulchin Gudamj) Northwest of Sükhbaatar Sq.

Information

Emergency

It might take a few minutes to get hold of an English speaker for these numbers.

Emergency aid/ambulance (103)

Fire (101)

Police emergency (102)

Robbery Unit (318 783)

Internet Access

In Ulaanbaatar an internet cafe (Интэрнэт Кафэ) is never more than a block or two away; just look for the signs, which are usually in English. Hourly rates are reasonable at about T500 to T800, but double that price at hotel business centres. Connections are generally good. You can scan photos in many places for around T200.

Internet cafe (Map p42; Peace Ave; per hr T600; 24hr) Located inside the CPO.

Internet Center (Map p42; per hr T500; Negdsen Undestnii Gudamj) Next to the Orange coffee shop. Also good for scanning and colour printing. We highlight this place because the people that run it also have Shonkhor Saddles (p69).

Internet Centre (Map p42; Tserendorjiin Gudamj 65; per hr T800; 9am-midnight) One of the largest internet cafes, with at least 35 computers.

Laundry

Almost all of the hotels in Ulaanbaatar offer a laundry service for between T500 and T1500 per kilogram, but they may not advertise it – so just ask. If you can be bothered, it's not difficult to do some laundry yourself – the markets and shops sell small packets of detergent and bleach.

Metro Express (470 789, 9919 4234) Has 10 branches scattered across the city, including one next to the Minii Delguur supermarket (Map p42). A load of laundry costs T8500 and turn-around time is about four hours.

Left Luggage

Most hotels and guesthouses can store luggage while you are off getting lost in the Gobi. There is usually no fee if you've stayed a few nights.

WI-FI ACCESS

Ulaanbaatar is awash with wi-fi hotspots. Most likely your hotel or guesthouse will offer it. It's even available in Sükhbaatar Sq. A very fast and stable connection is available on the 3rd floor of the Central Tower (at the Bugis Coffee Shop). The 6th floor of the State Department Store (at the food court) also has wi-fi. Most of the cafes listed in this guide also have free wi-fi, the best include Café Amsterdam, Michele's French Bakery, Sacher's Bakery, 40K, Narya Café and Millie's Café. At the airport, you'll hit a hotspot at the domestic check-in area (with a spotty connection in other parts of the airport).

Libraries

Alliance Française (Map p42; Academich Sodnomyn Gudamj; ⏲10am-1pm & 2.30-8pm; Mon-Fri; @) French-language literature. Of all the libraries, this one has the most comfortable chairs.

American Center for Mongolian Studies (Америкийн Монгол Судлалын Төв; Map p42; ☎7735 0486; www.mongoliacenter.org; Mongolian University of Science & Technology, Room 407, Baga Toiruu; ⏲10am-6pm Mon-Fri; @) Has a small library of books on Mongolia. Hosts twice-monthly lectures by Western and Mongolian academics, authors and other people of interest (check the website for events).

American Corner Library (Map p42; Seoul St; ⏲10am-6pm Mon-Fri; @) American books and DVDs. It's inside the Natsagadorj Library.

Cultural Palace Reading Rooms (Map p42; Cultural Palace, Amaryn Gudamj) The Cultural Palace has eight small reading rooms, each one set up by a different NGO or country. These include German, Swiss, Korean, Japanese, Russian and Taiwanese rooms. The German room on the 2nd floor has comfy sofas, big tables and fast wi-fi. The Swiss room on the 1st floor has a large selection of English language books. You can get there through the same entrance as the National Art Gallery - turn left for the libraries and right for the gallery.

National Library of Mongolia (Map p42; Chingisiin Örgön Chölöö; ⏲9am-5pm Mon-Fri Jun-Sep, 9am-8pm Mon-Fri & 9am-5pm Sat & Sun Oct-May) Has a vast collection of English-language books and documents about Mongolia. The stacks are only accessible to the library staff, so you'll need to browse the card catalogue, get the call number and request the book from the librarian. If you don't have a library card (T4000), you'll need to leave some ID for a deposit.

Media

Ulaanbaatar's two English-language newspapers, *Mongol Messenger* (weekly) and *UB Post* (twice weekly), are well worth picking up for local news and entertainment information. *That's Ulaanbaatar,* a free magazine packed with updated tourist information, is available at hotels and tourist offices. You can listen to the BBC World Service on 103.1PM.

Medical Services

The best place for most of your health care needs is the SOS clinic but life or death emergencies are sent to Seoul or Beijing. Pharmacies (*aptek;* Аптек) are common in Ulaanbaatar, stocking Mongolian, Russian, Chinese and Korean medicine. Check expiry dates carefully. The **US embassy website** (mongolia.usembassy.gov/medical_information.html) has an extensive list of medical services .

City Optic (Map p42; ☎7011 4567) An optometrist, located on the 1st floor of the Metro Mall.

Germon Dental Clinic (Map p39; ☎9914 7526) A reputable German dentist. Located near Naran Town.

Hospital No 2 (Map p51; ☎450 129, 310 945; cnr Peace Ave & Tokyogiin Gudamj) Considered to be the best Mongolian hospital in UB. It's 200m west of the British embassy. Consultations cost around US$20.

Songdo Hospital (Map p42; ☎7012 9000; Choidog Gudamj; ⏲8.30am-5pm Mon-Fri & 8am-noon Sat) Modern Korean-run hospital with examinations starting at T6000.

SOS Dental Clinic (Map p51; ☎464 330) The best place for dental work. In the same building as SOS Medica Mongolia Clinic.

SOS Medica Mongolia Clinic (Map p51; ☎464 325; 4a Bldg, Big Ring Rd; ⏲9am-6pm Mon-Fri) This clinic has a staff of Western doctors on call 24 hours (after hours call ☎9911 0335). Its services don't come cheap (examinations start from around US$195), but it's the best place to go in an emergency.

Money

Banks, ATMs and moneychangers are widespread. Banks with the best services include Golomt, Khan Bank and Trade & Development Bank. ATMs (you'll find them in department stores, mini markets and hotel lobbies) dispense tögrögs; you can get dollars or euros from a bank teller, with your debit card and passport (expect a fee of around 1% to 3% from your home bank).

The money changer on the ground floor of the State Department Store is handy.

Both Golomt and Trade & Development Bank (T&D Bank) will allow you to receive money wired from abroad. It will cost the sender about US$40 to wire any amount of money; there is no charge for receiving cash. For general information on money, see p252.

Trade & Development Bank (T&D Bank; Map p42; ⏲9am-4pm Mon-Fri) Will change travellers cheques into tögrög for a 1% fee or into US dollars for a 2% fee. Will also replace lost Amex travellers cheques.

Valiut Ariljaa (Map p42; Baga Toiruu west; ⏲8.30am-9pm) There are several exchange offices on this square, known by locals as Ard Kino. The exchange offices here have some of the best rates in town.

Permits

If you are travelling to border areas such as Altai Tavan Bogd National Park in Bayan-Ölgii, the **General Office of Border Protection** (Map p39; ☎286 788, 454 142; Border Defence Bldg; ⏲10am-12.30pm & 2-5pm Mon-Fri), in the east of the city, is the place to go for permits. Permits are free but you must send a Mongolian on your behalf to apply. The office requires a passport photocopy and a map showing your route. The office is in a grey building just west of the Mongolian Military Museum.

Police

The **police** (☎311 002, 102; www.ubpolice.mn) are located on Sambugiin Örgön Chölöö and on Negdsen Undestnii Gudamj.

Post

Central Post Office (CPO, Töv Shuudangiin Salbar; Map p42; cnr Peace Ave & Sükhbaataryn Gudamj; ⏲7.30am-9pm Mon-Fri, 9am-8pm Sat & Sun) Located near the southwest corner of Sükhbaatar Sq. The Postal Counter Hall is the place to post mail, packages and check poste restante (counter No 9; you'll need to show your passport). EMS express (priority) mail can also be sent from here. There is also a good range of postcards, small booklets about Mongolia in English and local newspapers for sale. A travel agency (masquerading as a tourist office) can answer some of your questions. On Sunday, although it's open, most services are nonexistent. DHL and FedEx are more reliable than anything the CPO can offer.

DHL (Map p51; ☎310 919; www.dhl.mn; Peace Ave 15a; ⏲9am-6pm Mon-Fri, 9am-noon Sat) Near the Edelweiss Hotel.

FedEx (Map p42; ☎320 591; fedex@tuushin.mn; Amaryn Gudamj 2; ⏲9am-6pm Mon-Fri) Inside the Tuushin Hotel. A 500g letter to Australia is US$36; to the UK and USA it is US$45.

Telephone & Fax

For local calls, you can use the phone at your hotel, often for free. Other hotels, including those with business centres, and some of the street stalls with telephones charge T200 for a call to a landline (six digits) or a mobile number (eight digits). You can also make local calls from the CPO or at any number of street-side peddlers whose entire business is selling phone calls on ubiquitous portable white phones. Many internet cafes are equipped with headsets and webcams for easy Skype calls.

International phone calls from the CPO are also possible between 9am and 8pm. A call to the US costs T500 and to the UK costs T700.

Most midrange to top-end hotels have a fax that can be used by guests for about T1500 to T2000 per page. The CPO offers a less user-friendly service, with cheaper rates. Hotels charge around T500 to receive a fax on your behalf.

Toilets

Public toilets are rare in Ulaanbaatar. There are two on Seoul St opposite Master Foods. At the time of writing, one was being built in front of the Ulaanbaatar Hotel.

Tourist Information

Guide Tourist Information Centre (☎7010 1011; cnr Baga Toiruu West & Peace Ave; ⏲9am-9pm May-Sep, 10am-7pm Oct-Apr) Located in the Erel Bank Building. Probably the most helpful of the tour offices.

Tourist Information Centre (Map p42; ☎7007 8916; Peace Ave) Located in the back hall of the CPO, this info desk has English-speaking staff who can give general info on city tours and nationwide travel. The desk also sells maps and books about Mongolia.

Ulaanbaatar Information Centre (Map p42; ☎7011 8083; www.ubtourism.mn; Sükhbaataryn Gudamj; ⏲9am-6pm) Located on the west side of Sükhbaatar Sq. This office (run by the city) has free city maps and a rack of brochures but the staff here seem pretty indifferent to visitors.

Travel Agencies

Staff at backpacker guesthouses can help with visa registration and train tickets. All the guesthouses mentioned in this book offer reliable help. For a small fee, some guesthouses even help visitors staying at other hotels.

The Russian embassy usually refers travellers to **Legend Tour** (Map p42; ☎315 158, 9984 2999; www.legendtour.ru; Seoul St, Mongol Nom Bldg, 2nd fl) for visa help. It's on the 2nd floor of a building opposite Master Food Supermarket.

Make sure you are clear on the full itinerary and any additional costs.

The following agencies are good for organising air tickets. For details of local agencies offering tours either within or outside of Ulaanbaatar, see p52.

Air Market (Map p42; ☎305 050; www.airmarket.mn; cnr Peace Ave & Chingisiin Örgön Chölöö; ⏱9am-8pm)

Air Network (Map p42; ☎322 222; airnetwork@magicnet.mn; Baga Toiruu west; ⏱9am-7pm Mon-Fri, 10am-3pm Sat & Sun)

Air Trans (Map p42; ☎313 131; airtrans@magicnet.mn; cnr Sükhbaataryn Gudamj & Sambugiin Örgön Chölöö; ⏱9am-7pm Mon-Fri, 10am-3pm Sat) Very reliable air-ticketing agency.

Silk Road Network (Map p42; ☎320 405; silkroad@mongolnet.mn; Peace Ave, east side of State Department Store; ⏱10am-8pm)

Dangers & Annoyances

Ulaanbaatar is a fairly carefree and easygoing city but there are a few concerns to keep in mind.

Theft

Pickpockets and bag slashers are a growing and common problem, although theft is seldom violent against foreigners, just opportunistic.

Pickpockets usually hang around on Peace Ave, between the post office and the State Department Store. Be extra vigilant here or use alternative streets (Seoul St is better).

Pickpockets also target public buses, the Naran Tuul Market and the footpaths near banks, hotels and upscale restaurants. Hang onto your bag when sitting in cafes. Be very careful around the stadium during Naadam.

Perpetrators are mostly teenagers. They work brazenly in broad daylight and on busy streets. One may distract you while his buddy picks your pocket.

» Leave passports, credit cards, large amounts of cash and valuables locked up in your hotel (preferably in a safe). Just carry the cash you need for food, admission fees and incidentals.

» Never keep valuables in your pants pocket, or anywhere else a thief could reach (a shirt pocket is safer).

» If carrying a backpack, hold it in front of you and padlock the zippers together.

» Money belts are handy but not fail-safe (thieves might slice the belt with a razor).

» If you are a robbed, you may need to file a report with the police to satisfy your insurance company.

REGISTRATION

The Office of Immigration, which registers passports, is located about 1.8km from the airport. If you need to register your passport or need to apply for a visa extension, you should go straight to this office when you land (if during working hours). This will save you having to make a second trip out to the airport for registration. To get there from the airport, walk out to the main road, turn right and walk 900m, then turn right again and walk 350m. The large round building (a sports arena) is a nearby landmark.

Violent Crime

Reports of violence against foreigners have increased in recent years. While Europeans are targets, Mongolian youth gangs typically espouse anti-Chinese and anti-Korean sentiments and have attacked businesses owned by Asian expats. Most incidents occur in the alleys, courtyards and ger districts beyond the well-lit boulevards. Avoid these areas after dark. Be vigilant when leaving nightclubs and bars in Ulaanbaatar; try to leave with a group, not alone.

Some foreigners have reported being assaulted and robbed in a taxi. Use an official taxi – as opposed to a private vehicle – late at night.

Alcoholism

Alcoholism is a big problem in Ulaanbaatar, especially among out-of-work middle-aged and older Mongolian men. It's worse around Naadam time, but drunks are usually more annoying than dangerous. In bars and nightclubs, you're only asking for trouble if you flash money around or get into arguments about Chinggis Khaan or other sensitive issues.

Queues

The concept of lining up has spread in recent years and queues at supermarkets, banks and shops are generally civilised. But sometimes they feel more like the front row of a punk rock concert, complete with flying elbows, grunts and small mosh pits. Being polite won't really help, nor will getting angry.

Traffic

Probably the most dangerous thing you can do in Ulaanbaatar is cross the street – even when the traffic lights are in your favour. Pedestrian rights are zilch and drivers have a habit of speeding up when pedestrians are on the road – not really trying to kill you, it's their way of warning you to look out. A particularly dangerous crossing is right in front of the State Department Store.

Other Annoyances

Some stairwells aren't lit, so it's a small torch (flashlight) is handy. Blackouts and hot-water shortages are common throughout the year.

Police often mean well but language barriers and cultural differences can make dealing with them a challenge.

The number of street children and beggars in Ulaanbaatar has noticeably decreased but there are still a few around. The best way to help out is to make a donation to a local orphanage. If you want to offer something to a street kid, handing out food and drinks is better than money (as any money collected is often taken from them by older boys or gangs).

Getting There & Away

Air

Chinggis Khaan International Airport is 18km southwest of the city. The airport has ATMs and banking services, a post office and internet access for T50 per minute. A tourist booth opens when planes arrive.

Mongolia has three domestic carriers: MIAT, AeroMongolia and EZ Nis. On domestic routes with MIAT and AeroMongolia you can carry 15kg but EZ Nis allows 20kg. You'll pay around T1500 per kilogram over the limit. For details of international flights to Ulaanbaatar, see p261. Flight days always change, so check updated schedules. The airlines accept credit cards for international and domestic flights. If paying cash, foreigners are supposed to use US dollars only.

AeroMongolia (Map p42; ☎330 373; www.aeromongolia.mn; Monnis Bldg, ground fl)

Blue Sky Aviation (Map p42; ☎312 085; www.blueskyaviation.mn; Peace Ave) Has one nine-seat Cessna 208 aeroplane available for charter flights. The office is in the same building as Seven Summits, opposite the post office.

EZ Nis (Map p42; ☎333 311; www.eznis.com; 8 Zovkhis Bldg) The newest airline in the country has an office on Seoul St.

MIAT (Map p42; ☎333 999; www.miat.com; ⏲9am-6pm Mon-Sat, 9am-3pm Sun) Head office is on Baga Toiruu west, near the Trade & Development Bank. It only offers international flights.

Foreign airline offices include the following:

Aeroflot (Map p42; ☎320 720; www.aeroflot.ru; Seoul St 15; ⏲9am-6pm Mon-Fri, 10am-3pm Sat) US dollars and credit cards are accepted.

Air China (Map p51; ☎452 548; www.fly-airchina.com; Ikh Toiruu Bldg 47; ⏲9am-1pm & 2-5pm Mon-Fri, 10am-4pm Sat, 9am-noon Sun) Located on Big Ring Rd in the northeast of town.

Korean Air (Map p51; ☎317 100; www.koreanair.com; 2nd fl, Chinggis Khaan Hotel; ⏲9am-6pm Mon-Fri) Payment in US dollars and tögrög.

United Airlines (Map p42; ☎323 232; www.united.com; Air Trans office, Sükhbaataryn Gudamj 1; ⏲9am-6pm Mon-Fri, 10am-4pm Sat) Handy for booking flights out of Seoul and Beijing.

Bus

Two stations handle most bus traffic. The eastern depot, **Bayanzürkh Avto Vaksal** (off Map p39; ☎7015 3386), is 6km east of Sükhbaatar Sq. The western bus station, called the **Dragon (Luu) Avto Vaksal** (Dragon bus stand; off Map p39; ☎7017 4902), is on Peace Ave, 7km west of Sükhbaatar Sq.

In addition to the buses listed here, minivans run daily to the same destinations (at a similar price), departing when full.

The old bus station, **Teeveriin Tovchoo** (Map p42; Undsen Khuulin Gudamj), is about a 10- to 15-minute walk from the centre. Little happens here now, although you can still get occasional vehicles to Zuunmod and Eej Khad, both in Töv aimag.

Buses are always full so buy your ticket as early as possible. Tickets can be purchased two days prior to travel.

Hitching

Hitching is a necessary form of transport in the countryside, but is less certain and more difficult to organise out of Ulaanbaatar. Most Mongolians get out of the capital city by bus, minibus, train or shared jeep/taxi, and then hitch a ride on a truck for further trips around the countryside, where there is far less public transport. Unless you can arrange a ride at a guesthouse, you should do the same.

Minivan & Jeep

Minivans and buses heading for destinations in the north and west (but not east) leave from the **Dragon (Luu) Avto Vaksal** (Dragon bus stand; off Map p39), the same place as the main bus departures. Minivans for destinations in eastern Mongolia depart from the Naran Tuul market. For the Gobi, the Mandalgov-bound minivans use the Dragon bus stand while vans for Ömnögov usually use Naran Tuul.

Overall, the Dragon bus stand is better for the casual traveller (riders at Naran Tuul are often traders with lots of bulky luggage to deal with). Note that there are no vehicles at Naran Tuul on Tuesdays, when the market is closed. On Tuesdays the minivans leave from the Bayanzukh bus station.

ULAANBAATAR BUS TIMETABLES

Departing from Dragon Bus Station

DESTINATION	PRICE	DURATION (HR)	FREQUENCY	DEPARTURES
Altai (Алтай)	T37,000	25	Tue, Wed, Fri, Sun	10am
Arvaikheer (Арвайхээр)	T14,000	8	2 daily	8am, 2pm
Bayankhongor (Баянхонгор)	T21,000	15	daily	8am
*Bayan-Ölgii (Баян-Өлгий)	T68,500	50	Mon, Wed, Fri	3pm
Bulgan (Булган)	T13,500	8	Mon, Wed, Fri	8am
Darkhan (Дархан)	T6000	3½	hourly	9am-8pm
Erdenet (Эрдэнэт)	T11,000	7	4 daily	10am, noon, 2pm, 4pm
Kharkhorin (Хархорин)	T12,000	8	daily	8am
*Khovd (Ховд)	T55,000	48	6 weekly Wed-Mon	3pm
Mandalgov (Мандалговь)	T12,000	6	2 daily	8am, 2pm
Mörön (Мөрөн)	T26,500	18-22	daily	8am
Tsetserleg (Цэцэрлэг)	T22,000	12	daily	8am
Zunnmod (Зуунмод)	T1300	1	hourly	8am-8pm
*Ulaangom (Улаангом)	T55,000	46	Wed, Fri, Sun	3pm
*Uliastai (Улиастай)	T33,000	20	Mon, Wed, Fri	9am

*May be a minivan

Departing from Bayanzürkh Bus Station

DESTINATION	PRICE	DURATION (HR)	FREQUENCY	DEPARTURES
Baruun-Urt (Баруун-Урт)	T21,500	11	daily	8am
Choibalsan (Чойбалсан)	T25,500	13	daily	8am
Öndörkhaan (Өндөрхаан)	T10,000	5	daily	8am
Dalanzadgad (Далланзадгад)	T22,500	12	2 daily	8am, 4pm
Baganuur (Багануур)	T4000	2	2 daily	11am, 5pm

Minivans are privately run, so drivers will try to stuff as many people and as much luggage as they possibly can into their vehicle. There is no set schedule; never expect to leave straight away, even if the van is full. Some might not be leaving for another day. If you can find out when it will leave, you could ask the driver to save your seat, and return later.

For destinations reachable by paved road you might find a Korean compact car.

Van destinations are posted on the dashboard (in Cyrillic). Prices are usually about 10% to 15% higher than the bus trip (eg to Öndörkhan, bus T10,000, minivan around T12,000). Most travellers prefer buses, as they tend to leave on time and are considered safer and more reliable.

Taxi

Taxis (shared or private) can only travel along paved roads, so they are only useful for trips around Töv aimag, to the towns along the main road to Russia (Darkhan, Erdenet and Sükhbaatar), and to Kharkhorin and Öndörkhan.

The cost of hiring a taxi to these places near Ulaanbaatar should start at around T400 per kilometre. The taxi drivers may want more for waiting if you are, for example, visiting Mandshir Khiid, or because they may be returning with an empty vehicle if dropping you off somewhere remote. This is not unreasonable, but it *is* negotiable.

To avoid any argument about the final charge make sure that you and the driver have firstly agreed on the cost per kilometre, and have

DOMESTIC TRAIN TIMETABLE

DESTINATION	TRAIN NO	FREQUENCY	DEPARTURE	DURATION (HR)	FARE*
Choir	284	Fri, Sun	5.40pm	6	T4800/9700/14,900
Darkhan	271	daily	10.30am	8	T5000/10,000/15,300
Darkhan	211 (fast)	daily	3.50pm	5	T5000/10,000/15,300
Erdenet	273	daily	8.20pm	11	T6800/12,300/20,300
Sainshand	285	daily	10.15am	10	T7400/13,200/21,500
Sükhbaatar	263	daily	9.10pm	7¾	T6300/11,800/18,900
Sükhbaatar	271	daily	10.30am	7¾	T6300/11,800/18,900
Zamyn-Üüd	276	daily	4.30pm	15½	T9600/16,800/27,300
Zamyn-Üüd	34 (fast)	Mon, Wed, Fri	8pm	12	T22,100/T39,200

*seat/hard sleeper/soft sleeper

discussed any extra charges. Then write down the number shown on the odometer/speedometer before you start.

Train

The train station (Map p39) has a left-luggage office, some small kiosks and a restaurant.

From Ulaanbaatar, daily trains travel to northern Mongolia and on to Russia, via Darkhan and Sükhbaatar, and southeast to China, via Choir, Sainshand and Zamyn-Üüd. There are also lines between Ulaanbaatar and the coal-mining towns of Erdenet and Baganuur.

To buy a ticket you must show identification; a passport or driving licence will do (student ID won't work).

DOMESTIC

The **domestic railway ticket office** (☎21-24137; ⊙8am-12.30pm & 2.30-9pm) is located in the modern-looking building on the east side of the train station (Map p39). Boards inside the office show departure times (in Cyrillic) and ticket prices. There's also a full timetable at the information desk on the station platform.

Tickets can be booked up to a month in advance for an extra T800 to T1200 (depending on the ticket), which is not a bad idea if you have definite plans and want a soft seat during peak times (mainly July to August). If you speak Mongolian, there is an **enquiries number** (☎21-24194).

INTERNATIONAL

The yellow **International Railway Ticketing Office** is about 200m northwest of the train station (Map p39). Inside the office, specific rooms sell tickets to Irkutsk and Moscow in Russia, and to Beijing, Ereen and Hohhot in China. The easiest place to book a ticket is in the **foreigners booking office** (☎21-24133, enquiries 21-243 848; Room 212; ⊙8am-8pm Mon-Fri). It's upstairs and staff here speak some English. On weekends you can use the downstairs booking desk.

Getting Around

To/From the Airport

If it's your first visit to Mongolia, the best way to get into the city is to organise a pick-up from your hotel/guesthouse (just email them with your flight details). This may be free (usually if you book three nights' accommodation) or cost around US$12 to $15. Taxi drivers will find you in the airport terminal but will almost certainly try to overcharge first-time visitors. After agreeing a price, some might demand more (up to US$50) when you reach your destination; drivers also might hold your luggage hostage until you pay their price; to avoid this, keep your luggage with you in the car, rather than in the boot.

There is no dedicated airport bus that runs straight to/from the terminal and the city. However, if you don't mind walking a little, you can use either bus 11 or 22 (T300). These connect the city centre and the district of Nisekh, close to the airport. At the airport, go out of the terminal and across the parking lot to the main road (a 500m walk). At the main road turn right and walk about 400m, until you reach the bus turn out (there is no sign but you'll see others waiting). Only do this during daylight (for safety reasons). A bus comes by every 15 minutes or so until 9pm. Once in the city you can get off at the bus stop near the main library (opposite the Drama Theatre).

Getting to the airport is a little easier. Bus 11 stops at Ard (near the MIAT office) on Baga Toiruu, and also near the Bayangol Hotel. Bus 22 stops near Tengis Movie Theatre but it won't drop you at the terminal. You still have to haul your luggage 500m from the bus stop on the highway.

To/From the Train Station

It's a 25-minute walk from the train station to the State Department Store. International trains arrive early in the morning while the city is still quiet, so with a backpack it's easy to walk into town. Guesthouses and hotels may pick you up if contacted ahead of time (some hostel owners will be at the station anyway, trawling for guests).

The nearest bus stop is across the street from the station. Bus 20 will get you to the State Department Store and Sükhbaatar Sq. Some taxi drivers at the station, like those at the airport, may agree on one price and then charge more once you reach the hotel. If this happens, stay calm and be patient and polite. Don't give into their demands. Eventually they will get bored with trying to rip you off and will just accept a reasonable price.

Some try to enlist the aid of their guesthouse/hotel manager. This only works sometimes. As with earlier advice, keep your luggage in their car so they can't hold it hostage in the boot. If you must use a taxi, head out of the station and up the road to escape the sharks, then flag down a taxi and pay the standard rate of T400 per kilometre.

Bicycle

Mongolian drivers are downright dangerous so riding a bike around town can be hazardous to your health. There are no bike lanes and you should never expect to have right of way. Seven Summits (p68) rents mountain bikes for US$26 per day (or US$19 per day for five or more days). Mongolia Expeditions (p54) rents bikes for a similar price. If you want to buy a mountain bike, try Seven Summits, the State Department Store or the Naran Tuul Market (the latter sells new and used bikes).

Bus & Minivans

Local public transport is reliable and departures are frequent, but buses can get crowded. Conductors collect fares (at the time of writing, T300 for a bus or T200 for a trolleybus for any trip around Ulaanbaatar, including to the airport) and usually have change. Pickpockets and bag slashers occasionally ply their trade on crowded routes. Seal up all pockets, hold your bag on your chest and be careful when boarding.

Minivans no longer run through the heart of Peace Ave but you'll encounter them on some outlying roads. The touts announce the destination at each stop. If you can't understand them tell someone your destination and with luck you'll end up in the right van. Generally, most of them end up either at the Naran Tuul Market or the train station.

The route number is next to the (Cyrillic) destination sign on the front of the trolleybus or bus. The route is often marked on the side of the bus. For short trips it's just as cheap to take a taxi, especially for two or more passengers.

ULAANBAATAR'S MAIN BUS ROUTES

Bus 1 Runs the full length of Peace Ave between the Bayanzürkh and Dragon bus stations.

Bus 7 From Ard to Bayangol Hotel, Winter Palace and Zaisan.

Bus 11 From Ard to Bayangol Hotel, then to the airport.

Bus 17 From Berlin Burger to Ard, then west on Peace Ave to Dragon bus station.

Bus 10 From Sansar, past the University, to Tengis Movie Theatre and then 3/4 district.

Bus 20 From Bagshiin Deed (near Ulaanbaatar Hotel) to Peace Ave, then down Seoul St to the train station.

Bus 22 From Berlin Burger to Ard and on to the airport.

Bus 23 From Peace Ave to the Naran Tuul Market.

Bus 27 Runs the full length of Peace Ave between Bayanzürkh and Dragon bus stations.

Bus 32 Runs between Bayanzürkh and Dragon bus stations (via Naran Tuul Market).

Bus 44 From National University past Chinggis Khaan Hotel to the Naran Tuul Market.

Trolleybus 2 Same route as Bus 27.

Trolleybus 4 From train station to Bayanzürkh bus station.

Trolleybus 5 Along Peace Ave to the 3/4 Microdistrict.

Car

Drive Mongolia (Map p42; ☎312 277, 9911 8257; www.drivemongolia.com) offers driving tours of Mongolia, allowing you to drive the car with a backup support vehicle.

Foot

Exploring Ulaanbaatar on foot has its challenges. Footpaths are often in bad shape (or non-existent) and wild traffic makes crossing streets difficult. However, most of the time the traffic congestion is so bad that walking will actually prove faster than going by taxi or bus if you are only going a kilometre or two.

Taxi

In Ulaanbaatar, there are official and unofficial taxis; in fact, just about every vehicle is a potential taxi. All charge a standard T400 per kilometre (check the current rate, as it increases regularly). Don't agree to a set daily price because it will always be more than the standard rate per kilometre. Nowadays, all taxis and even some private cars have meters.

Taxi drivers will try to take advantage of you if you are new to the city. The more confident you appear, the better chance you have of getting a fair deal. Before you get in the cab, have some idea of the route and the price. Always have the driver reset the odometer to zero and agree a per kilometre rate before setting off.

To find a taxi, just stand by the side of a main street and hold your arm out with your fingers down. After dark, avoid using a private car, stick to an official taxi.

Noyon Zuuch Taxi Company (☎1950) Is reliable and has English speakers.

Safe Taxi Company (☎9979 8185) British-run venture, established to provide safe and reliable transport around the city and airport transfers. No cash transactions with the driver: pay a flat-fee fare at hotels and restaurants around the city; your destination is printed on a chit that you show to the driver. Expats and Mongolians can buy a pre-paid account and summon a taxi by text message.

Central Mongolia

POP 298,500 / AREA 199,000 SQ KM

Includes »

Best Places to Eat

» Ayanchin (p89)
» Terelj Hotel (p90)
» Hotel Mongolia (p91)
» Fairfield (p104)

Best Places to Stay

» Duut Resort (p105)
» Dreamland Ger Camp (p99)
» Ecotourism Ger Camp (p89)
» In a tent near Naiman Nuur (p102)

Why Go?

Roll out of Ulaanbaatar in a Russian jeep and you'll only need to put a hill or two between yourself and the city before the vast steppes of central Mongolia begin to unfold before your eyes. Verdant swaths of empty landscapes are sprinkled with tiny gers stretching to the horizon while magical light plays across the valleys. This is the Mongolian heartland, loaded with both historical sites and natural beauty, with plenty of scope to horse trek in the forested mountains, camp by some pretty lakes or soak in hot springs. Because the region is relatively close to Ulaanbaatar (and many sights in this chapter are right beside the city), infrastructure is a little better than other areas, with many sites reachable by paved road. The most scenic sub-region is the Khangai Mountains but you'll find equally stunning scenery in the Khan Khentii region, northeast of Ulaanbaatar.

When to Go

Tsetserleg

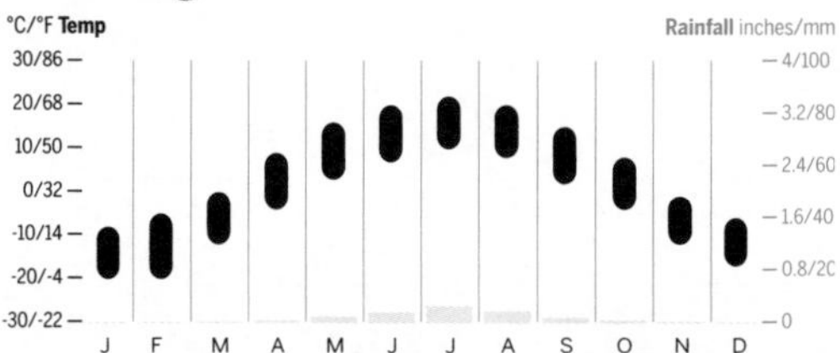

Mid-July Naadam festivals in many *sums* and aimag capitals.

August Good for horse treks, hiking and biking.

February Experience Tsagaan Sar (Mongolian New Year) with a family of herders.

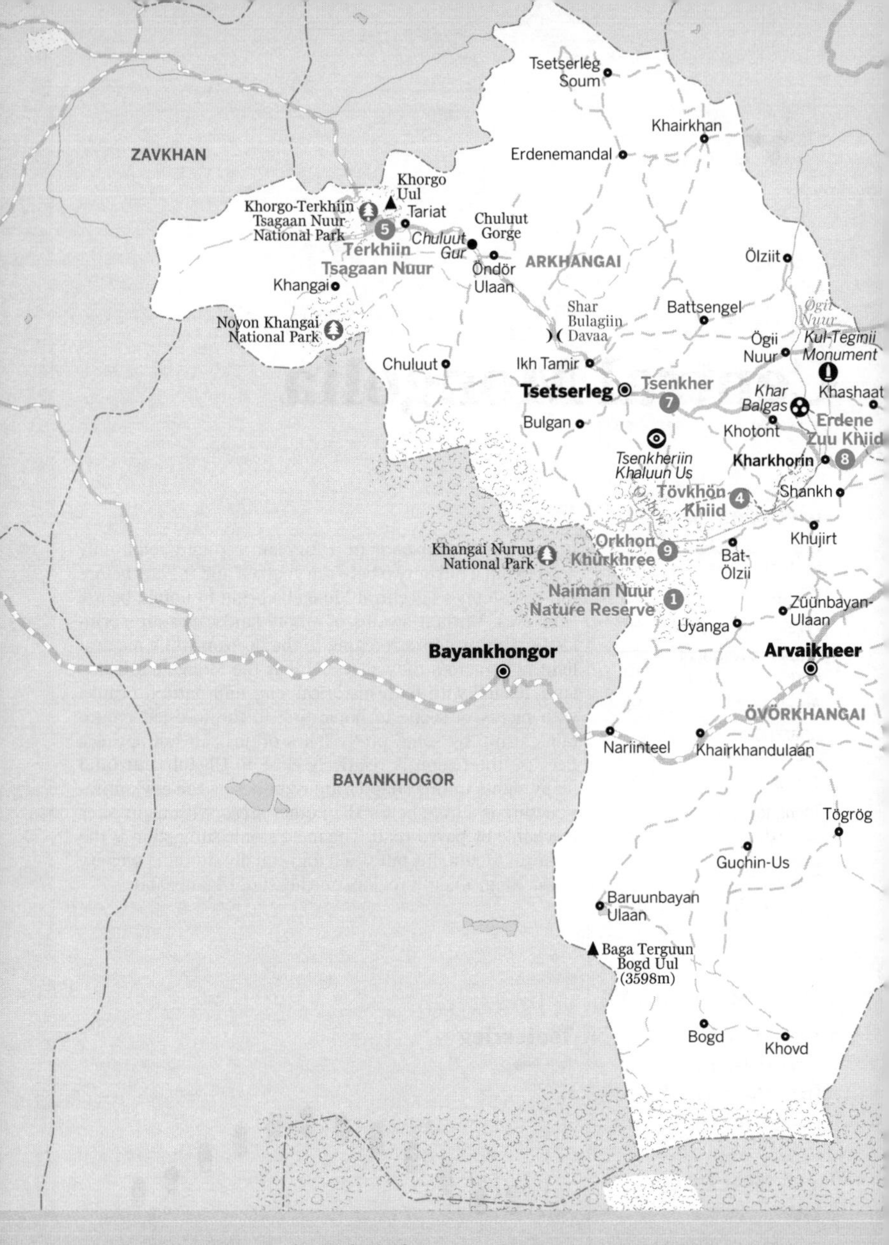

Central Mongolia Highlights

1. Saddle up for a horse trek to the beautiful, remote **Naiman Nuur Nature Reserve** (p102)
2. Bike or hike over the hills and through the valleys of **Gorkhi-Terelj National Park** (p82)
3. Focus your camera on the magnificent *takhi* (wild horse) at **Khustain National Park** (p91)
4. Hike into the forests to **Tövkhön Khiid** (p100), the site of Zanabazar's workshop
5. Camp by **Terkhiin Tsagaan Nuur** (p107), a

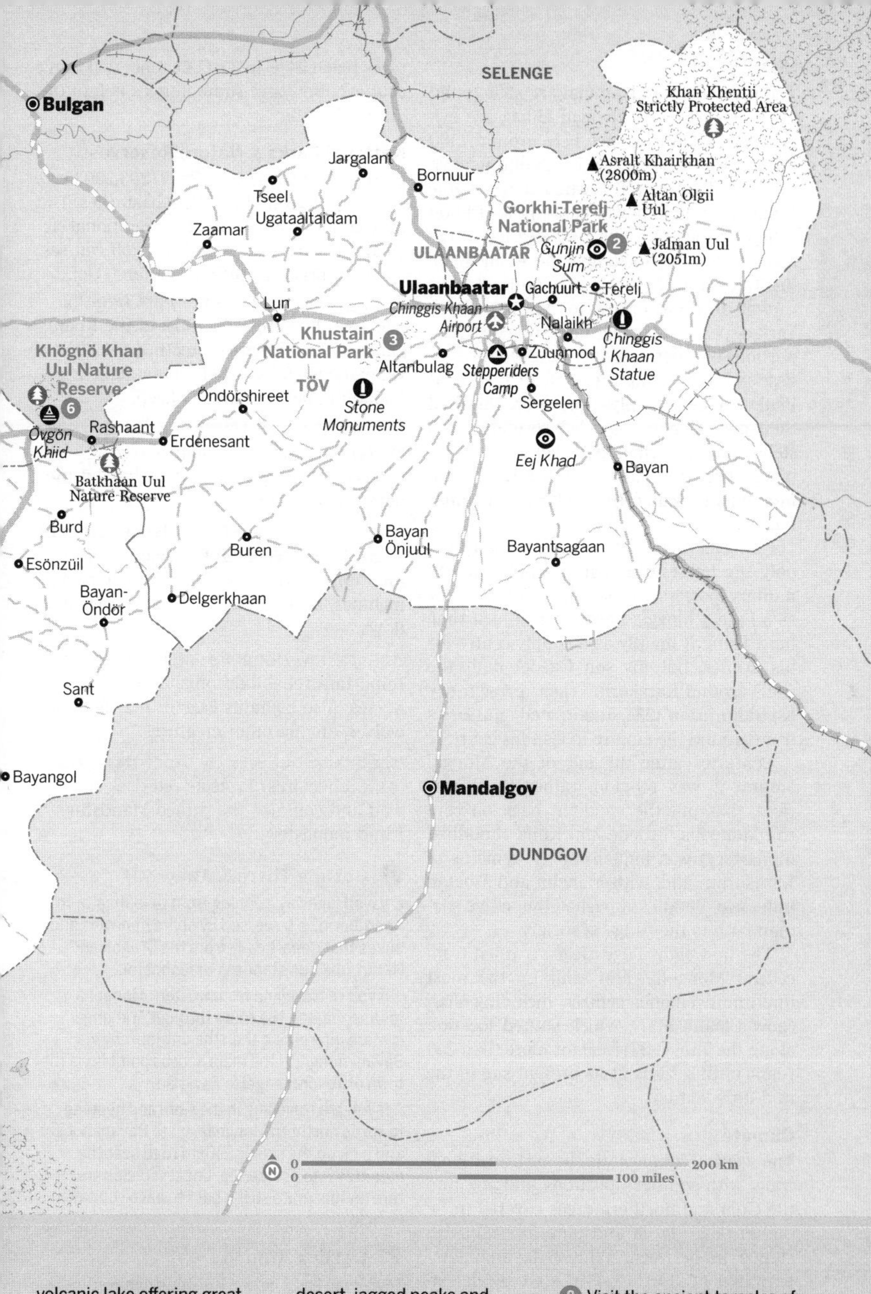

volcanic lake offering great fishing and lovely sunsets

6 Explore the **Khögnö Khan Uul Nature Reserve** (p101), a curious landscape of scrubby desert, jagged peaks and Buddhist temples

7 Relax in the hot springs of **Tsenkher** (p105), on the scenic fringe of the Khangai Mountains

8 Visit the ancient temples of **Erdene Zuu** (p95), Mongolia's first Buddhist monastery

9 Gaze upon **Orkhon Khürkhree** (p101), Mongolia's tallest waterfall

History

The many deer and 'animal art' stele found in the valleys of Arkhangai aimag are evidence of tribal existence here around 1300 BC, but the region really came into its own in the 3rd century BC, when the nomadic Xiongnu set up a power base in the Orkhon valley. Various 'empires' rose and fell in the Xiongnu's wake, including the Ruan-Ruan, the Tujue and the Uighurs, who built their capital at Khar Balgas in AD 715. These Turkic-speaking peoples held sway over vast portions of inner Asia and harassed the Chinese (whose attempts to defend the Great Wall were never really successful). They had their own alphabet and left several carved steles that describe their heroes and exploits. The most famous is the Kul-Teginii Monument, located relatively close to Khar Balgas.

Chinggis Khaan and his merry men were only the latest in a string of political and military powers to use the Orkhon valley as a base. Chinggis never spent much time here, using it mainly as a supply centre for his armies, but his son Ögedei built the walls around Karakorum (near present-day Kharkhorin) in 1235, and invited emissaries from around the empire to visit his court.

Centuries after the fall of the Mongol empire it was religion, rather than warriors, that put the spotlight back on central Mongolia. Erdene Zuu Khiid (Buddhist monastery) was built from the remains of Karakorum and, with Manchu and Tibetan influence, Buddhism pushed the native shaman faith to the fringe of society.

The first eight Bogd Gegeens ruled from central Mongolia, and built up the most important religious centres, including Urga (now Ulaanbaatar), which shifted location along the Tuul Gol (river) for more than 250 years, until settling at its present site in the mid-18th century.

Climate

The central aimags lie in a transitional zone, with southern portions nudging into the Gobi and northern areas covered in Siberian taiga (larch and pine forests), with steppe in between. Winter daytime temperatures of -30°C to -15°C are typical, lasting from late November to early February. March and April suffer from strong, dry winds and changeable weather. July and August are good times to travel as the wet weather finally turns the steppe into a photogenic shade of green. Summer temperatures reach 24°C to 30°C. October will bring cool evenings and snow flurries before the onset of winter.

National Parks & Nature Reserves

Gorkhi-Terelj National Park (293,200 hectares) A playground for Ulaanbaatarites. The park contains numerous ger (traditional circular felt yurt) camps and two golf courses. It's more pristine north of the Terelj Gol.

Khangai Nuruu National Park (888,455 hectares) Encompasses most of the Khangai mountain range, protecting crucial watersheds and a variety of animals including ibex and argali sheep.

Khögnö Khan Uul Nature Reserve (46,900 hectares) This nature reserve protects wolves and foxes that inhabit the desert-steppe area.

Khorgo-Terkhiin Tsagaan Nuur National Park (77,267 hectares) Protected area for migratory birds as well as fish. The park includes lakes, cinder cones and volcanic flows.

Khustain National Park (50,620 hectares) Important rehabilitation site for *takhi* horses. Also contains gazelle, marmot and wolves, among other creatures.

Bogdkhan Uul Strictly Protected Area (41,700 hectares) Protects red deer, fox, wolf and contains the ruined Mandshir Khiid monastery.

Getting There & Away

A paved highway, running from Ulaanbaatar to Kharkhorin, is traversed by share minivans and buses that depart daily from the Dragon and Naran Tuul bus stands in Ulaanbaatar.

If you're travelling from western Mongolia to Ulaanbaatar, the route through Arkhangai is more interesting than the dull journey via Bayankhongor – the main access point is via the town of Tosontsengel in Zavkhan.

If you are travelling in the Gobi and heading towards northern Mongolia, go to Bayankhongor and pick up the scenic 210km road over the mountains to Tsetserleg. Local vehicles are rare on this route so it's best to have your own vehicle.

Getting Around

Töv aimag has a network of good unpaved and paved roads, so you can easily use public transport to make day or overnight trips from the capital.

For the other aimags, share jeeps will travel from the nearest provincial centre to other destinations, but off the main paved road traffic

READY, AIM, FIRE!

If you've ever dreamed of playing Rambo, the **Mongol Tsergiin Khuree Shooting Range** (Mongolian Army Camp; ☎450 922) outside Ulaanbaatar (UB) is your chance to launch rockets and drive tanks. The camp is located about 50km west of Ulaanbaatar and several tour companies in UB can organise the trip. Try contacting Bolod's Guesthouse or Mongolia Expeditions. Shooting an AK-47 will cost US$16 for a 30-round clip and launching an RPG is around US$60. To drive a tank you need to pay US$25 to start and additional US$35 per kilometre. The camp, open May to November, is state owned and belongs to a branch of the Mongolian military. You should bring some form of ID, like a passport, to register for a shooting permit.

throughout these regions is light. In Övörkhangai, public transport will get you to Erdene Zuu Khiid, Khujirt and Arvaikheer, but if you want to visit Tövkhön Khiid or Orkhon Khürkhree you'll need your own transport. Horse is the best way to reach Naiman Nuur. In Arkhangai, the main road is one of the few routes in Mongolia where hitchhikers can easily get to a few places of interest, including Taikhar Chuluu and Terkhiin Tsagaan Nuur.

A jeep is fine for getting around, but travelling by horse is the best way to get up the river valleys and into the mountains.

TÖV ТӨВ

POP 88,500 / AREA 81,000 SQ KM

The 'Central' province surrounds Ulaanbaatar (UB) and its forested mountains offer a welcome escape from the city. There are no knock-out sights but you can go horse trekking and camping, spot *takhi* horses at Khustain Nuruu or check out the brand-new silver statue of Chinggis Khaan outside Nalaikh.

Although Töv lies close to industrial Ulaanbaatar, its economy remains almost exclusively agricultural. Recent *zuds* (extreme winters) have drawn even more herders here from other aimags and analysts report that Töv is 600% over capacity for livestock. This has resulted in a worrying amount of desertification, especially in the southern part of the province.

Fortunately, most of the Khan Khentii Strictly Protected Area (in the northeast part of the province) remains in pristine condition. And because it's relatively close to Ulaanbaatar, you don't need to mount a major expedition to see this gorgeous corner of the country.

Zuunmod Зуунмод

☎01272 / POP 14,300 / ELEV 1529M

In great contrast to the big city on the other side of the mountain, Zuunmod is a peanut-sized place, even smaller than most Mongolian provincial capitals. There is little reason to linger in the capital of Töv but you'll probably pass through on the way to Mandshir Khiid or Bogdkhan Uul Strictly Protected Area.

The main sight in town is the **Aimag Museum** (admission T1000; ⌚9am-1pm & 2-6pm), opposite the southeast corner of the park – look for the sign in English. There are exhibits on local history and a section of stuffed animals including an enormous moose. It also has some interesting black-and-white photos of Mandshir Khiid, including the once-regular *tsam* (lama dances, performed by monks wearing masks during religious ceremonies).

Minivans run through the pretty countryside (on a paved road) between Zuunmod and Ulaanbaatar (T1500, one hour, hourly) between 7am and 8pm, from Ulaanbaatar's old bus stand (Teeveriin Tovchoo). The bus stop in Zuunmod is just a short walk west of the main street.

A chartered taxi from Ulaanbaatar will cost between US$15 and US$20 one way. Taxis can be hired in Zuunmod from the taxi stand on the east side of the park. The fare to Mandshir Khiid is around T10,000 to T15,000 plus waiting time.

Bogdkhan Uul Strictly Protected Area Богдхан Уул

The Bogdkhan Uul (2122m) is said to be the world's oldest nature reserve. Established in 1778, the park was guarded by 2000 club-wielding lamas. Animal poachers were hauled away in chains, beaten within an inch of their lives, and locked inside coffin-like jail cells.

These days it's perfectly safe and legal to walk on the mountain and you can enjoy some terrific **hiking** and **horse-riding** trails. Wildlife is more difficult to spot than it used to be, but you still stand a good chance of seeing red deer.

For information on hiking to the main peak from Zaisan Memorial or Mandshir, or combining the two in an overnight hike from Mandshir to Ulaanbaatar, see p84. For details on hiring a horse, see p85.

Entrance to the park costs T3000.

Sights

Mandshir Khiid MUSEUM/NATIONAL PARK
(МАНДШИР ХИЙД; GPS: N47° 45.520', E106° 59.675'; admission T5000; 9am-sunset) For the 350 monks who once called this place home, the gorgeous setting around this monastery (elevation 1645m) must have been a daily inspiration. Like most monasteries in Mongolia, Mandshir Khiid was destroyed in 1937 by Stalin's thugs, but was partially restored in the 1990s. Just 6km northeast of Zuunmod and 46km by road from Ulaanbaatar, the monastery is a perfect half-day trip from the capital, or can be used as a starting point for hikes into the Strictly Protected Area.

The main temple has been restored and converted into a museum, but the other buildings remain in ruins. The monastery and museum are not as impressive as those in Ulaanbaatar – it is the beautiful forest setting that makes a visit worthwhile.

As you enter from the main road from Zuunmod you'll be required to pay an admission fee of T5000 per person, which covers the T2000 museum entrance fee and the T3000 national park fee. You'll have to buy both tickets even if you don't plan on entering the museum.

From the gate it's a couple of kilometres to the main area, where there is a shop, a lacklustre **nature museum** (admission T2000), a restaurant and several gers offering accommodation. Look for the huge two-tonne **bronze cauldron**, which dates from 1726 and was designed to boil up 10 sheep at a time.

The remains of the monastery (and monastery museum) are about 800m uphill from the nature museum. The **monastery museum** has *tsam* masks, exhibits on the layout of Mandshir and some photos that show what it looked like before Stalin's followers turned it into rubble. Look out for the controversial **Ganlin Horn**, made from human thigh bones.

If you have time, it's worth climbing up the rocks behind the main temple, where there are some 18th-century Buddhist **rock paintings**. The views from the top are even more beautiful, and you'll find yourself in the midst of a lovely pine forest.

Activities

Hiking

Bogdkhan Uul has a broad and flat summit, so many routes cross it. Most hikers get dropped off on one side and hike to the other on a day or overnight hike. The summit, known as **Tsetseegün Uul** (2256m), is a popular destination but including this part of the mountain requires a bit more time. From Mandshir Khiid straight to Zaisan, plan on walking about six to seven hours. From Mandshir Khiid to the Observatory, figure on six hours.

Don't underestimate the weather up here. Even in summer strong thunderstorms can tear across the mountain without much warning. In June 2010, an American hiker died of hypothermia after getting stranded on the mountain during a major thunderstorm. Even if you are just doing it as a day hike, bring warm, waterproof clothing, a compass, food and water. Yellow paint on the trees marks the trail, but it can be hard to spot.

Some scrambling over fields of granite boulders is necessary, and the chance of slipping and injuring yourself should not be taken lightly. It would be wise to inform a friend or guesthouse owner in Ulaanbaatar of your itinerary and the time of your expected return.

MANDSHIR KHIID TO ULAANBAATAR ROUTE

This approach to Tsetseegün from the south side is the easiest route by far. As you face the monastery, cut over to your right (east) until you get to the stream. Just follow the stream until it nearly disappears and then head north. About three hours' walking should bring you out over a ridge into a broad boggy meadow, which you'll have to cross. If you've walked straight to the north, the twin rocky outcrops of the summit should be right in front of you. When you start to see Ulaanbaatar in the distance, you're on the highest ridge and close to the two large *ovoo* (a shamanistic pyramid-shaped collection of stones as an

WORTH A TRIP

BORNUUR

A small *sum* (district) located 5km off the Ulaanbaatar–Darkhan road, Bornuur (Борнуур) contains an interesting **museum** (admission T1000; ⏲10am-5pm) of local artefacts and Buddhist relics. Some exhibits are a bit gruesome, including a stack of human skulls pulled out of a mass grave. They are the skulls of local lamas who were executed by communist forces in 1937. G Purevbat, a lama and master of Buddhist sculpture and painting, created the museum using artefacts from his personal collection.

offering to the gods) on the **summit** (GPS: N47° 48.506', E107° 00.165'). From the *ovoo* you can return to Mandshir or descend to Ulaanbaatar.

A second route from the monastery begins from the left (west) side of the temples, passing a stupa on the way up to the ridge. This route, marked with yellow tags, is faster but you'll miss the *ovoo* on Tsetseegün.

Coming down from Tsetseegün the quickest way is to head due north, towards the Observatory, and descend to the valley where you'll cross the train tracks. You can catch a taxi from here to town for around T5000. A longer route takes you to the **Zaisan Memorial**, on the southern fringe of the city. Be careful not to drop down too soon or you'll end up at **Ikh Tenger**, one valley short of Zaisan. Ikh Tenger is where the president lives with machine-gun-wielding guards, who will be none too pleased if you drop by unannounced. If you see a barbed -wire fence you are in Ikh Tenger; to get out, just continue west along the fence and over the next ridge.

ZAISAN ROUTE

It is more of an uphill battle to Tsetseegün if you start from the Zaisan Memorial. From the memorial, head up the road past the ger camp and enter the forest. Look for the yellow trail markers, which veer left when you've reached the top. From here, the slope levels off and becomes an easy walk through a pleasant forest for the next two hours. If you stick to the yellow tags you'll follow the quickest route to Mandshir but will miss reaching Tsetseegün. All up, this is a 15km walk.

OBSERVATORY ROUTE

This is the easiest route on the Ulaanbaatar side (mainly because you hit the fewest boulders) but is also the least interesting. The walk to Tsetseegün and over to Mandshir takes about six hours.

The problem is that getting to the Observatory ('Khureltogoot' in Mongolian) is difficult. You could catch a bus to Nalaikh and get out at the toll gate, then walk the last 6km up the hill. Otherwise, you'll have to take a taxi.

Horse Riding

In summer, some of the ger camps around Mandshir Khiid rent out horses. Horses are also available from **Stepperiders Camp** (☎9908 3061, 9665 9596; www.stepperiders.com; GPS: N 47° 43.649', E106° 47.418'), just off the main Ulaanbaatar–Zuunmod road. Stepperiders is run by Minde, a recommended local horse guide who can give lessons, instructions and support to independent travellers planning their own expedition. This is a perfect place to test ride a Mongolian horse before a longer trip. Rides start at around US$45 per day and include pick-up, drop-off, guides, horses, food and even entry fees to the national park. As this camp is something of a hang-out for dedicated riders, you may be able to find partners for a trip.

Sleeping

The area around the monastery is one of the best camping spots near Ulaanbaatar. You should get permission from the caretaker at the monastery if you are camping nearby, or just hike off into the woods.

Mandshir Ger Camp TOURIST GER CAMP **$$**
(☎01272-22535, 9192 4464; 4-bed ger T35,000) In a lovely spot amid trees about 200m northeast of the monastery's car park, this convenient place has hot showers but Mongolian-style toilets. There's a restaurant in the grounds, but it may only be open if a tour group is staying there, so take some food. Horse hire here is US$5 per hour.

Ovooni Enger Ger Camp TOURIST GER CAMP **$$**
(☎01272-22011; 2-/4-person ger T30,000/60,000) Another good option, 800m off the road to Mandshir (look for the sign just after entering the park gate).

MOTHER ROCK

During communism, visiting the sacred Eej Khad (Mother Rock) was a political crime, as it showed respect for religion, which was basically banned at the time. Some people, however, still went in secret.

Sometime in the late 1970s the communists decided to do away with the 'feudal' site once and for all. Workers tried dynamite to blow it up, and a tractor to haul it away, both to no avail. The next day workers awoke to find their tractor burnt and destroyed. Soon after the incident, the official who ordered Eej Khad's destruction died and his family members became ill. It is said that all the other members of the team suffered a string of bad luck. Most Mongolians can recite a similar tale of provocation and retribution at the holy rock.

Getting There & Away

The most accessible entrances to the park are reached via Zaisan Memorial, the Observatory and Mandshir.

The monastery is easy enough to visit in a day trip from Ulaanbaatar or Zuunmod (from where it's a 7km drive). If you are walking from the north of Zuunmod it's 6km; you can either walk along the main northern road after visiting Dashchoinkhorlon Khiid, or save some time by walking directly north from Zuunmod, eventually joining up with the main road.

Trekking to Mandshir by horse is a good idea, but Zuunmod is not set up for tourists and it will require some effort to track a horse down. You could ask around the ger suburbs of town, at Stepperiders (p85), or make enquiries at one of the guesthouses, such as Idre's Guest House, in Ulaanbaatar. At Mandshir itself, wranglers from the nearby ger camps rent horses for US$5 per hour.

Eej Khad (Mother Rock) Ээж Хад

Vanloads of pilgrims can be found venturing a rough 48km south of Zuunmod to the sacred **Mother Rock** (Map p80; Eej Khad; GPS: N47° 18.699', E106° 58.583'). Mongolians often come here to seek solace and advice, and make offerings of vodka, milk and *khatags* (silk scarves). Pilgrims ask for three wishes to be granted, circle the rock three times and make three separate visits.

There are several sacred rocks nearby that are thought to generate good luck, including one called **Dog Rock**, which Mongolians rub their body against to cure ailments.

Minivans depart from Teeveriin Tovchoo (T9000 round trip) at 9am (between April and October). It's also possible to stop here on your way to the Gobi, but be prepared for some off-roading as the jeep trails south of here will quickly peter out.

Nalaikh Налайх

This small city, 35km southeast of the capital, is part of the Ulaanbaatar autonomous municipality because it once supplied the capital city with its coal. The state mine shut down years ago but small-scale private excavations (legal and illegal) continue in the mines.

A community of Kazakhs settled here in the 1950s to work at the mines and they still represent a quarter of the population. To find Nalaikh's **mosque**, face the bright-blue town hall, turn 180 degrees and walk about 25 minutes over a small hill. It's very basic and has a greenish tin roof. About 200m past the mosque is the family home of Ibrahim (also known as Erakhun), a Kazakh who operates a small **ger museum** in his yard. The museum only works in summer but Ibrahim is happy to have you visit his home at other times of the year. Visiting the home is a great chance to experience small-town life without going too far from UB.

At least four buses (T700) per hour depart from Teeveriin Tovchoo to Nalaikh, the first at 7.30am and the last at 7pm. You can catch this bus on Peace Ave.

Around Nalaikh

Around 19km southeast of Nalaikh is an 8th-century Turkic **stele of Tonyukok** (GPS: N47° 41.661', E107° 28.586'). The stele is covered in runic script and there are *balbals* (stone figures believed to be Turkic grave markers) and grave slabs nearby. To get to the stele you'll need to have your own transport. From Nalaikh, take the main highway towards Baganuur and travel for 16km until you see a sign that says 'Tonyukok'. Turn right onto this track and travel another 11km to reach the stele. Just past the site, a huge hangar contains a few relics found around the site; you could ask the local watchman to let you inside, though there is little to see.

Mongolia's newest landmark is a 40m-high silver **Chinggis Khaan statue** (Map p87; ☎11-328 960; www.genco-tour.mn; GPS: N47° 48.494', E107° 31.860'; admission foreigners T10,000, Mongolians T5000; ⏲9am-sunset), located just off the main road between Nalaikh and Erdene, at a place called Tsonjin Boldog. The dramatic statue, built with private funds, has a lift (elevator) rising up its tail, from where there are steps to the horse's head. It was built here, so the legend goes, because this was the spot where Chinggis Khaan found a golden whip. The complex includes a **museum** (of pre-Mongol Hunnu artefacts), cafe and souvenir shop. A six-minute **film** describes how the monument was built. For an extra T1000 you can don Chinggis Khaan armour for a photo shoot in front of an enormous Mongolian boot.

The same company that built the statue also has an elaborate replica of a **13th-century Mongol war camp** (per person US$60), complete with towers and catapults. It also has **workshops** displaying the production of traditional clothing, jewellery, bows, arrows and battle gear. Rodeos and mini-naadams (games) are sometimes available. The price includes lunch. The camp is located 18km south of Erdene *sum*. Contact **Genco Tour** (www.genco-tour.mn) for details.

Terelj Area Тэрэлж

Terelj *sum* (district), about 55km northeast of Ulaanbaatar, is a playground for urban-weary Ulaanbaatarites. At 1600m, the area is cool and the alpine scenery magnificent, and there are great opportunities for hiking, rock climbing, swimming (in icy cold water), rafting, horse riding and, for hard-core extreme-sports fanatics, skiing in the depths of winter.

Terelj was first developed for tourism in 1964 and 30 years later it became part of **Gorkhi-Terelj National Park**. It's a bit crowded with ger camps these days but you can easily get away from the hustle and bustle. Be prepared for mosquitoes, especially in late summer.

There is a T3000 entry fee to the park for each person, which you'll have to pay at the park entrance, 6km from the main road.

Terelj village (GPS: N47° 59.193', E107° 27.834') is about 27km from the park entrance, at the end of a paved road. It's in a nice location near the river but there's not much here apart from a few shops and a ger camp.

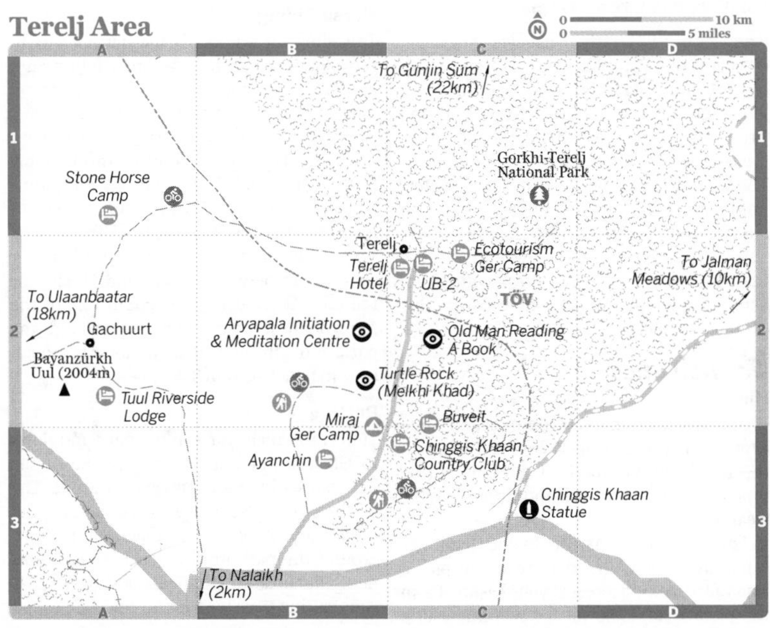

Sights

Günjiin Süm TEMPLE

(Гунжийн Сум; GPS: N48° 11.010', E107° 33.377') Surrounded by magnificent forests and not far from a lovely river, the Baruun Bayan Gol, this Buddhist temple (elevation 1713m) was built in 1740 by Efu Dondovdorj to commemorate the death of his Manchurian wife, Amarlangui. Once part of a huge monastery containing about 70 sq metres of blue walls, five other temples and a tower, Günjiin Süm is one of very few Manchurian-influenced temples in Mongolia to survive over the centuries. Only a couple of buildings and walls remain.

Unlike most other monasteries in Mongolia, Günjiin Süm was not destroyed during the Stalinist purges, but simply fell into ruin from neglect, vandalism and theft.

The temple is not a must – there are many better and more accessible temples and monasteries in Ulaanbaatar and Töv – but more of an excuse for a great **overnight trek**, on horse or foot, or as part of a longer trip in the national park.

Günjiin is about 25km by foot (or horse) from the UB-2 hotel (heading in a northwest direction). The jeep trail is longer (about 40km in total), as you need to skirt around the mountains, but easier if you don't want to walk the hills. You can do the trip on your own with a good map and compass (or GPS) but it's best to take a local guide.

Khan Khentii Strictly Protected Area

(Khentii Nuruu; Map p80; admission fee T300) To the northeast, Gorkhi-Terelj National Park joins the Khan Khentii Strictly Protected Area, comprising more than 1.2 million hectares of the Töv, Selenge and Khentii aimags. The Khan Khentii park is almost completely uninhabited by humans, but it is home to endangered species of moose, brown bear and weasel to name but a few, and to more than 250 species of birds. If you come from Terelj, the fee at the gate there covers this protected area as well.

Activities

Hiking

If you have good maps, a compass and some experience (or a proper guide), hiking in the Terelj area is superb in summer, but be prepared for mosquitoes and unpredictable weather.

For more sedate **walks** in the Terelj ger camp area, follow the main road and pick a side valley to stroll along at your leisure. From the main road, look out for two interesting rock formations: **Turtle Rock** (Melkhi Khad; GPS: N47° 54.509', E107° 25.428'), in a side valley to the south of Terelj, which really looks like one at a certain angle; and the less dramatic **Old Man Reading a Book**, which can be spotted on the left side of the road when travelling south from Terelj village. Head north 3km from Turtle Rock to reach the **Aryapala Initiation & Meditation Centre** (GPS: N47° 56.121', E107° 25.643'; admission T2000) set on a spectacular rocky hillside. The temple at the top of the hill is a new creation. If you are lucky, you might arrive during a prayer session, when you can sit and hear monks chanting.

Some suggested easier hikes are to Günjiin Süm or along the Terelj or Tuul Gols towards Khan Khentii. This is a great area for wildflowers, particularly rhododendron and edelweiss.

Places of interest on more difficult, longer treks in Khan Khentii:

Altan-Ölgii Uul (2656m) The source of the Akhain Gol.

Khagiin Khar Nuur A 20m-deep glacial lake, about 80km up Tuul Gol from the ger camps at Terelj.

Yestii Hot Water Springs These springs reach up to 35°C, and are fed by the Yuroo and Yestii Gols. Yestii is about 18km north of Khagiin Khar Nuur.

Horse Riding

Travelling on a horse is the perfect way to see a lot of the park, including Günjiin Süm and the side valleys of Tuul Gol. To travel long distances, you will need to have experience, or a guide, and bring most of your own gear. Horses can be hired through any of the ger camps, but you'll pay high tourist prices (around US$35 to US$40 a day). A mob of horse boys hang around Turtle Rock offering horse riding at US$5 per hour, or somewhere between US$12 and US$20 for the day. Alternatively, approach one of the Mongolian families who live around the park and hire one of their horses, though they may not be much cheaper.

Rafting

Tuul Gol, which starts in the park and flows to Ulaanbaatar and beyond, is one of the best places in the country for rafting. The best section of the river starts a few kilometres north of Terelj village, and wraps around the park until it reaches Gachuurt, near Ulaanbaatar. Nomadic Journeys (p54) runs rafting trips here for around US$45 per

MOUNTAIN BIKING AROUND TERELJ

Terelj to Gachuurt (Central)

This rugged route takes in two passes along the way. Get a ride all the way to the town of Terelj and then start riding on the road that heads west; it's about 2km to the next small settlement of gers. The trail continues west and starts heading into the wilderness, up a valley with a forest to your left. The ridge tops out at 1859m and descends to another valley. The trail climbs again, slightly to the right, to another 1859m ridge, from where you begin a long descent towards Gachuurt. At the end of the valley (it's about 15km) you'll reach Tuul Gol, which you follow back to Gachuurt town. All up it's a 30km ride and should take around five hours.

Turtle Rock Loop

This convenient route begins and ends at Turtle Rock in the Gorkhi valley. From Turtle Rock ride west down the slope until the road goes right into a ger camp (the camp was built over the trail). Go around the camp and then it's a 30-minute climb to the top of the hill. From the top you get some great views of the rock formations in the next valley. The trail continues south past several ger camps and eventually leads back to the main road and back to Turtle Rock. This loop is 15km.

day (minimum four people). You can also get a raft from the Seven Summits (p68).

Golf

The **Chinggis Khaan Country Club** (☎9911 0707; www.chinggisgolf.com) is just off the road in Gorkhi valley. Green fee is T85,000 (including caddy) and club hire is T24,000. A second course is at the UB-2 hotel.

Tours

Most foreign and local tour companies include a night or two in a tourist ger at Terelj in their tours. Several local agencies based in Ulaanbaatar, such as Nomadic Journeys and Nomads, run some of the more interesting trips around Terelj.

Sleeping & Eating

Unless you hike out into the hills it's best to get permission for camping, either from the nearest ger or, for a fee, a ger camp. Pitch your tent away from the main road, don't use wood fires and take all of your rubbish out.

During the peak season of July and August (and also at the more popular camps), it's not a bad idea to book ahead. Outside the normal tourist season (July to September), it's also a good idea to ring ahead to make sure the camp is open and serves food. A few places stay open in winter.

Apart from the ger camps listed here, many individual families rent out a spare ger and/or hire horses, normally at cheaper rates than the ger camps. You'll have to ask around as none advertises.

ROAD TO TERELJ VILLAGE

Miraj TOURIST GER CAMP **$**
(☎325 188, 9911 9426; per person with/without meals T52,000/27,000) Located 14km along the main road from the park entrance, Miraj is clean, comfortable and reasonably priced. Horses cost US$5 per hour or US$12 per day, and hot showers are available. There are a couple of other camps up this valley.

Buveit TOURIST GER CAMP **$$**
(☎322 870, 9911 4913; per person with/without meals US$45/20) About 13km along the main road from the park entrance, Buveit is in a beautiful secluded valley 3km east of the main road. It also has five-bed cabins for US$60. Marked rock-climbing routes are nearby and the camp might be able to supply climbing gear.

Ayanchin TOURIST GER CAMP **$$$**
(☎319 211, 9909 4539; ger bed T80,000, r T160,000) This American-built camp has a Western-style lodge and modern shower and toilet block. At meal times (meals US$5 to US$11), enjoy a steak, pasta, sandwich or burger on the sunny deck. It's about 10km from the main entrance, marked with a big billboard.

TERELJ VILLAGE AREA

Ecotourism Ger Camp TOURIST GER CAMP **$$**
(☎9973 4710; bergroo@hotmail.com; GPS: N47° 58.722', E107° 28.907'; ger with/without 3 meals

US$35/US$14) For an offbeat experience, you could wade across Terelj Gol and hike to a pleasant ger camp run by a Dutchman named Bert. Bert makes Dutch cheese at the camp, and if you want to get your hands dirty, get up at the crack of dawn and help him milk the cows. He also organises horse trips up to Günjiin Süm. To find the place on your own, go to the UB-2 hotel and walk around the right side of the building, cross the iron bridge over the river, follow the path to a second river, cross it and then walk east. Follow the electric poles until you get to pole 40; from here you will see the gers on the right. It's 2.5km from the UB-2. If that sounds complicated, call Bert and he will meet you at the UB-2.

Terelj Hotel HOTEL **$$$**
(☎9900 7206; www.tereljhotel.com; s/d from US$160/200; @📶🏊) Mongolia's first luxury hotel and spa is an incongruous neoclassical building set on the edge of tiny Tererlj village. Opened in 2008, the hotel is a self-contained complex with a gourmet French restaurant, professional spa, indoor swimming pool, library and children's play centre. Rooms are immaculate, spacious and tastefully decorated. If you've got cash to burn, the presidential suite costs about the same as Mongolia's per capita GDP. It's a nice place to come if you want to splurge on a fancy meal (dishes T12,000 to T30,000), even if you're staying elsewhere.

UB-2 HOTEL **$$**
(☎9977 4125; ger bed T29,500, r from T80,000) This is a branch of the Ulaanbaatar Hotel. It's a midrange place with clean but somewhat dim rooms and renovated bathrooms. It's not bad on its own but looks a little sad compared to the incredibly swanky Terelj Hotel next door. On the downside, the food at the restaurant is disappointing. Facilities here include a golf driving range and par-three golf course (green fees T40,000, club hire T15,000).

NORTHERN TERELJ

Jalman Meadows TOURIST GER CAMP **$$$**
(4-day package per person US$195) Nomadic Journeys runs this remote and low-impact ger camp in the upper Tuul valley, which makes a nice base if you are headed to Khagiin Khar Nuur, which is an eight-hour horse ride away. The camp has a library of books on Mongolia and a number of great activities, including mountain biking, yak carting, river boating and even portable saunas! You'll need to book well in advance for these trips. The price includes transfers to and from Ulaanbaatar.

ℹ Getting There & Away

Bicycle

A mountain bike would be an excellent way of getting around some of the Terelj area if you could stand the 70km of uphill riding to get there and cope with the traffic in Ulaanbaatar along the way. The Seven Summits in Ulaanbaatar rents bikes.

Bus

The road from Ulaanbaatar to Terelj, which goes through part of the national park, is in pretty good nick. A bus (T2300) departs at 11am and 4pm in summer, or 3pm in winter (1 October to 15 May), from Peace Ave, opposite the Narantuul Hotel. Get there with 15 minutes to spare as they sometimes depart early. Going the other way, it leaves Terelj at 8am and 7pm; catch it near the UB-2 hotel, on the road. When heading into the park they may charge T5000 but this includes park admission. You may have to pay an extra T2500 for a bike or heavy luggage. For additional information, contact the bus conductor, **Ms Nara** (☎9665 4818). It's a good idea to call ahead to confirm departure times.

Hitching

Hitching *out* of Ulaanbaatar can be difficult because vehicles going to Terelj could leave from anywhere. The cheapest way to hitch to Terelj is to take a minivan for Baganuur or Nalaikh and get off at the turn-off to Terelj, where you are far more likely to get a lift.

Hitching *back* to Ulaanbaatar from along the main road through Terelj is not difficult, as almost every vehicle is returning to the capital.

Taxi

A taxi from Ulaanbaatar is easy to organise; jeeps aren't necessary because the road is paved all the way. You should only pay the standard rate per kilometre, which works out at about US$35 one way, but the driver may understandably want more because his taxi may be empty for part of the return journey. You can also arrange with your taxi to pick you up later.

When there's enough demand, shared taxis to Terelj sometimes leave from Naran Tuul market jeep station in Ulaanbaatar (Map p39). This is more likely on summer Sundays when locals make a day trip to the area.

Gachuurt Гачуурт

Around 20km east of Ulaanbaatar, the town of Gachuurt offers the chance to quickly trade city traffic and bustle for riverside walks, horse riding, camping, fishing and rafting. The town is a rapidly growing suburb of the capital, popular with wealthy

DON'T MISS

TRAIL RIDE DAY TRIPS NEAR UB

A number of tour operators can organise horse riding day trips near Ulaanbaatar. They are usually in Terelj National Park, which can get crowded on weekends. A handful of companies offer specialised day trips on horseback in the backcountry, away from the ger camps. These are some of the best:

» Stepperiders (p85) in Bogdkhan Uul

» Xanadu (p91) near Gachuurt and Terelj

» Stone Horse (p91) near Gachuurt to Terelj route

Mongolians who build gated villas on the hills surrounding the town. Despite the increased development, it remains an idyllic setting and a popular half-day trip from Ulaanbaatar.

Activities

Xanadu ADVENTURE
(☎9987 2912, 9975 6964; www.mongolienomade.mn in French) Frenchman Côme Doerflinger runs adventure trips through his outfit based in Gachuurt. He mainly runs horse trips (around T25,000 per day), and has French, Russian and English saddles. Côme also has kayaks and canoes that you can use to float down Tuul Gol, and mountain bikes which are great for excursions up Gachuurt's side valleys towards Terelj. Côme also offers accommodation at his camp.

Stone Horse Expeditions HORSE RIDING
(☎9592 1167; www.stonehorsemongolia.com) Another Western-run company, Stone Horse is located 16km north of Gachuurt and offers a variety of trips, including one-day horse rides (T130,000) that include a pre-ride snack, riding introduction and a gourmet lunch. Longer trips (up to 14 days) include lodging at the staging area and camping equipment when on the trail. They use comfortable saddles and have quality horses. All trips are organised ahead of time so don't just turn up at the camp, phone first.

Jetboating BOAT
(☎8809 2094; 30min ride T60,000) A new activity in the Gachuurt area is New Zealand–style jetboating.

Sleeping & Eating

Gachuurt offers reasonable camping opportunities. About 2km before the town centre, near Tuul Gol, there are spots to pitch your tent. Just try to avoid the clusters of ger camps.

Tuul Riverside Lodge TOURIST GER CAMP $$
(☎9909 9365; www.tuulriverside.com; ger incl breakfast from US$25) This upmarket option has en suite gers that include bath and shower. It's good for a short break from Ulaanbaatar (total driving time is one hour) or family holiday. It's about 10km past Gachuurt, at the foot of Bayanzurkh mountain, on the backroads to Terelj.

Hotel Mongolia HOTEL $$
(☎315 513; www.hotel-mongolia.com; ger s/d US$80/120, s/d US$80/120, ste US$180-250) Ögödei Khaan would feel right at home at Hotel Mongolia, the unmissable walled palace resembling ancient Karakorum, a few kilometres short of Gachuurt, on the right side of the road. Luxurious rooms have private bath and shower, and the price includes breakfast. The hotel includes a business centre, souvenir shops and a field behind the walls where mini-naadams are held according to tour-group bookings. Even if you don't stay here, it's worth visiting for the kitsch ambience and excellent Asian-style restaurant (meals T6000 to T12,000), which serves a few delicacies such as horse's stomach. On hot summer days you can lounge on the 'beach' by the river.

Getting There & Away

Buses pick up passengers every hour or so from the east end of Peace Ave in Ulaanbaatar, near the Jukov statue, a couple of kilometres east of the city centre, bound for Gachuurt (T600, 25 minutes). You can also easily get a taxi from UB (T8000).

Khustain National Park
Хустайн Нуруу

Also known as Khustain Nuruu (Birch Mountain Range), this park was established in 1993 and is about 100km southwest of Ulaanbaatar. The 50,620-hectare reserve protects Mongolia's wild horse, the *takhi*, and the reserve's steppe and forest-steppe environment. In addition to the *takhi,* there are populations of *maral* (Asiatic red deer), steppe gazelle, deer, boar, manul (small wild cat), wolf and lynx. A visit to the park has become a popular overnight excursion from Ulaanbaatar in recent years.

Entry to the park is a one-off fee of US$5 (free for locals). It's worth spending at least one night in the park, as you are most likely to see *takhi* and other wildlife at dusk or dawn.

The park is run by the Hustai National Park Trust, which is supported by the Dutch government and the Mongolian Association for the Conservation of Nature and the Environment (Macne).

The information centre at the entrance to Khustain National Park has a ger with displays on the park and the *takhi,* a small souvenir shop and videos that include a documentary on Mongolian horses, featuring Julia Roberts. Ten kilometres south into the park's core area is the former park headquarters. Another 13km or so west is Moilt camp.

Sights & Activities

In an effort to make the park self-financing, horse riding, hiking and jeep excursions are offered. There's a good **hike** that takes you from the visitors centre to Moilt camp (22km) in about five hours.

A fun **horseback trek** heads to Turkic **stone monuments** (Map p80; GPS: N47° 33.201', E105° 50.991') southwest of the park and then on to Tuul Gol. Horse rental is US$12 per day. Contact the park for details.

With your own jeep you can drive to Moilt camp. Park regulations require you to take a park guide (free within the park) and stick only to existing tracks. **Wildlife watching** is best at dusk and at dawn. The *takhi* could be in any number of places, and park guides can direct your driver to the best spots.

The park runs a three-week **volunteer program** where you can help with research. See www.ecovolunteer.org for details.

A community-based **tourism project** at Khustain allows visitors to stay with nomad families, ride horses, learn felt-making and experience daily life in the countryside. The per-day cost is US$30 for a solo traveller, or US$25 per person for two or more people. Prices include meals and horse riding is an additional US$3 per hour.

Sleeping

Independent camping is not allowed inside the park so you have to camp outside the park boundary. The best place to go is the south side of the park by Tuul Gol.

To book accommodation in the park, contact **Hustai National Park Trust** (☎021-245 087; www.hustai.mn; Hustai Bldg, 2nd khoroo, Bayangol District) in Ulaanbaatar. It is about 2km west of the State Department Store, off Peace Ave.

Ger camp TOURIST GER CAMP **$$**
(per person with/without meals US$48/20, tent US$5; @) There is a small ger camp at the entrance to the park (the payment for accommodation includes the park entrance). Travellers report that the food here is pretty mediocre, so it's probably best to just pay for the bed and cook your own meals.

Moilt camp CABINS **$**
(per person US$15) Basic wooden cabins clustered in a pretty valley.

Getting There & Away

To get to the park, travel 100km west from Ulaanbaatar, along the road to Kharkhorin, where there is a signpost pointing you 13km south to the park entrance. A minivan (one way US$15) travels from the park to Ulaanbaatar and back twice a week, departing the park at 3pm Friday and 2pm Sunday, returning from Ulaanbaatar at 6pm Friday, 5pm Sunday. The van only has 10 seats so you definitely need to make an advanced booking. In UB it leaves from the **Hustai Park office** (☎021-245 087), which is very difficult to find so call ahead for directions.

ÖVÖRKHANGAI
ӨВӨРХАНГАЙ

POP 117,500 / AREA 63,000 SQ KM

Övörkhangai contains one of Mongolia's top attractions, the Erdene Zuu monastery in Kharkhorin. This is Mongolia's oldest monastery and it has become a regular stop on most tour circuits. But while travellers flock to this site and then rush off to the points west, many miss some of the best parts of Övörkhangai, including the Naiman Nuur lake area and the spectacular Tövkhön Khiid. The southern part of the aimag, past Arvaikheer, is uninteresting desert steppe.

If travelling by rented jeep, it is easy to combine a visit to these sights with some other places that are clustered near the borders of Arkhangai, Bulgan and Töv aimags, including Khögnö Khan Uul Nature Reserve and the sand dunes of Mongol Els. The

TAKHI – THE REINTRODUCTION OF A SPECIES

The year was 1969 and a herder in western Mongolia spotted a rare *takhi* (wild horse) in the distance. It was an extraordinary find as so few *takhi* were left in the wild. Alas, it was also the final sighting; with no new reports thereafter, scientists had to declare the species extinct in the wild – the result of poaching, overgrazing by livestock and human encroachment on their breeding grounds.

All was not lost for the *takhi*, however, as a dozen individual horses were known to exist in zoos outside Mongolia – their ancestors had been captured by game hunters in the early 20th century. A small group of conservationists dedicated themselves to breeding the animals with the hope that one day they could be reintroduced to Mongolia.

The conservationists did not fare so well with Mongolia's suspicious communist government, but when democracy arrived in the early 1990s they were welcomed with open arms. By that time the worldwide population was around 1500, scattered around zoos in Australia, Germany, Switzerland and the Netherlands.

Between 1992 and 2004, *takhi* were reintroduced into Mongolia at Khustain National Park, Takhiin Tal in Gov-Altai, and Khomiin Tal in Zavkhan. Today there are more than 250 *takhi* in Khustain, 80 in Takhiin Tal and 12 in Khomiin Tal. Given the political and logistical challenges to the project, their reintroduction is nothing short of miraculous, making it one of the best conservation stories of our times.

The *takhi*, also known as Przewalski's horse (named after the Polish explorer who first 'discovered' the horse in 1878), are now descended from the bloodline of three stallions, so computerised records have been introduced to avoid inbreeding. They are the last remaining wild horse worldwide, the forerunner of the domestic horse, as depicted in cave paintings in France. They are not simply horses that have become feral, or wild, as found in the USA or Australia, but a genetically different species, boasting two extra chromosomes in their DNA make-up.

Within the parks, the laws of nature are allowed to run their course; an average of five foals are killed by wolves every year in Khustain. The park gets locals onside by hiring herders as rangers, offering cheap loans to others and offering employment at a cheese-making factory on the outskirts of the park.

For more information, check out www.treemail.nl/takh.

paved road, which reaches Kharkhorin and the aimag capital of Arvaikheer, is also a definite attraction.

Arvaikheer Арвайхээр

☎01322 / POP 23,400 / ELEV 1913M

A nondescript but friendly aimag capital, Arvaikheer is of little interest except as a place to eat and rest, refuel the jeep or arrange onward public transport. If you find yourself between rides, the museum is worth a look.

There is no need to go to Arvaikheer if you only want to visit Kharkhorin and northern Övörkhangai, as a paved road runs to Kharkhorin from Ulaanbaatar.

Sights

Gandan Muntsaglan Khiid MONASTERY
(ГАНДАН МУНТСАГЛАН ХИЙД; GPS N 46º 16.338', E 102º 46.151') This comparatively large monastery, about 900m north of the town square, contains a fine collection of *thangka* (scroll paintings), including one depicting the original monastery, which was destroyed in 1937. The current monastery was opened in 1991, and now has about 60 monks in residence. It is located 900m northwest of the town square, through the ger districts.

Aimag Museum MUSEUM
(☎22075; admission T1500, camera T3500; ⏲9am-1pm & 2-6pm Mon-Fri, 10am-5pm Sat & Sun) Since Övörkhangai lies partly in the forested Khangai region and the Gobi Desert, the Aimag Museum boasts a better-than-average selection of stuffed mountain and desert animals. There are also some fossils and arrows, local artwork and leftovers from Karakorum.

Zanabazar Memorial Museum MUSEUM
(admission T1500, camera T3500; ⏲9am-12.30pm & 2-6pm Mon-Fri) Next door to the Aimag Museum, the Zanabazar Memorial Museum has

Arvaikheer

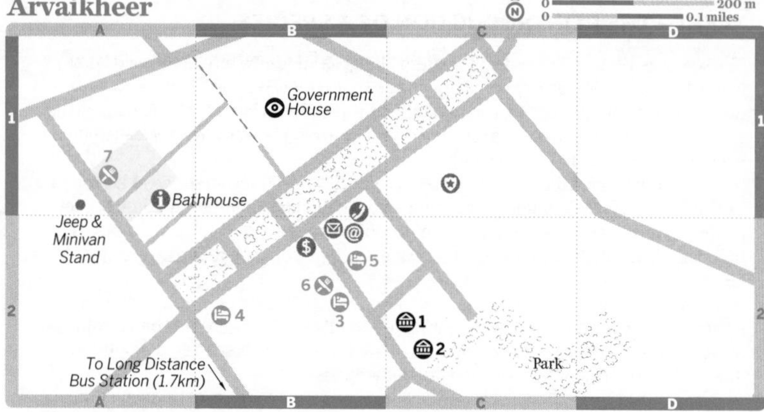

Arvaikheer

Sights

Sleeping

Eating

a collection of religious artwork connected to the master sculptor (p118). Ask at the Aimag Museum for the key.

Sleeping

Time Hotel HOTEL $$
(9855 2891; r US$15, half-luxe US$17-20, luxe US$30-35) This is the best hotel Arvaikheer has to offer, a compact place with clean, modern rooms and reliable hot water. The restaurant on the ground floor is also one of the best in town. The sign outside simply says: 'Hotel'.

Mandarvaa Hotel HOTEL $
(9932 9695; s/d T8000/16,000, half-luxe s/d T15,000/30,000) The Mandarvaa Hotel is fairly reliable but only the half-luxe and luxe rooms include bathroom and shower. Hot water comes on for a couple of hours in the morning and evening – check the times with reception.

Zalaa Hotel HOTEL $
(9904 2832; per person from T12,000) A clumsy building with wobbly halls and a mishmash of furniture. Rooms are basic but clean and shared bathrooms are located at the end of the hall. The restaurant downstairs has basic meals.

Eating & Drinking

There are *guanz* (canteens) around town, several of them in the **container market**.

Time Hotel Restaurant MONGOLIAN $
(meals T2800-5000) This is the best place in town to get a meal, with a choice of pastas, Mongolian meals and even a few vegetarian dishes.

Altan Holbo Bar MONGOLIAN $
(dishes T2000; 9am-8pm Mon-Sat) A wood-panelled pub that offers mugs of beer and hearty Mongolian meals.

Information

The police station is southeast of the town square.

Bathhouse (shower/sauna T1500/5000; 9am-10pm Tue-Sun)

Internet cafe (per hr T500; 9am-10pm Mon-Fri, 10am-5pm Sat & Sun) In the Telecom office.

Khan Bank (9am-8pm Mon-Fri, 10am-3pm Sat & Sun)

Telecom office (24hr) The post office is also here, on the southeast side of the main square.

Getting There & Away

You can travel quickly along the 430km paved road between Ulaanbaatar and Arvaikheer. The paved road finishes just west of Arvaikheer; from there it is about another 200km along the usual rough road to the next aimag capital of Bayankhongor. With a jeep, an experienced driver and lots of time you could venture south to Dalanzadgad, 377km away in Ömnögov aimag, either via Saikhan-Ovoo or (more adventurously) via Guchin Us, Khovd and Khongoryn Els.

Air

At the time of writing there were no flights to Arvaikheer, although there is an airport in Bayankhongor, about 200km away.

Bus

Two daily buses travel from Arvaikheer to Ulaanbaatar (T14,000, eight hours), departing at 8am and 2pm. The bus station is southwest of the centre, near the highway.

Hitching

The Ulaanbaatar–Arvaikheer route is pretty busy so hitching a ride should be fairly easy. Going further west along the main road to Bayankhongor won't be as easy, but it is possible (although it's a pretty uninteresting highway – the better route is through Arkhangai).

Jeeps & Minivans

Minivans and jeeps run along the paved road between Arvaikheer and Ulaanbaatar daily (T15,000, seven hours). Look for them on the west side of the market. Shared vehicles travel to Khujirt (T7000, two hours) and Kharkhorin (T8000, three hours); as usual, when the driver says departure time is 'now' that means 'sometime today (or tomorrow)'.

Shankh Khiid
Шанх Хийд

Shankh Khiid, once known as the West Monastery, and Erdene Zuu are the only monasteries in the region to have survived the 1937 purge. Shankh was founded by the great Zanabazar in 1648 and is said to have once housed Chinggis Khaan's black military banner. At one time the monastery was home to more than 1500 monks. As elsewhere, the monastery was closed in 1937, temples were burnt and many monks were shipped off to Siberia. Some of those that survived helped to reopen the place in the early 1990s.

The **monastery** (GPS: N47° 03.079', E102° 57.236'; admission T1000, camera T1000) is about 26km south of Kharkhorin. You'll see it on the right side of the road as you approach the village of Shankh.

Kharkhorin (Karakorum)
Хархорин (Каракорум)

☎01325 / POP 8000 / ELEV 1913M

In the mid-13th century, Karakorum was a happening place. Chinggis Khaan established a supply base here and his son Ögedei ordered the construction of a proper capital, a decree that attracted traders, dignitaries and skilled workers from across Asia and even Europe.

The good times lasted around 40 years until Kublai moved the capital to Khanbalik (later called Beijing), a decision that still incites resentment among some Mongolians. Following the move to Beijing and the subsequent collapse of the Mongol empire, Karakorum was abandoned and then destroyed by vengeful Manchurian soldiers in 1388.

Whatever was left of Karakorum was used to help build Erdene Zuu Khiid in the 16th century, which itself was badly damaged during the Stalinist purges.

The charmless Soviet-built town of Kharkhorin was built a couple of kilometres away from Erdene Zuu. There is little of interest in the town and it's a big disappointment if you've come expecting the glories of the Middle Ages, but a surge in tourism has improved local infrastructure. There are several ger camps in the area, each with a restaurant, plus some basic cafes in the centre of town.

Sights

Erdene Zuu Khiid MONASTERY

(ЭРДЭНЭ ЗУУ ХИЙД; ☎ticket desk 82285, 9926 8286; grounds/temples free/US$3, camera/video US$5/10; ⏲9am-6pm May-Sept, 10am-5pm Oct-Apr) Founded in 1586 by Altai Khaan, Erdene Zuu (Hundred Treasures) was the first Buddhist monastery in Mongolia. It had between 60 and 100 temples, about 300 gers inside the walls and, at its peak, up to 1000 monks in residence.

The monastery went through periods of neglect and prosperity until finally the Stalinist purges of 1937 put it completely out of business. All but three of the temples in Erdene Zuu were destroyed and an unknown number of monks were either killed or sent to Siberian gulags.

However, a surprising number of statues, *tsam* masks and *thangkas* were saved – possibly with the help of a few sympathetic military officers. The items were buried in

Kharkhorin

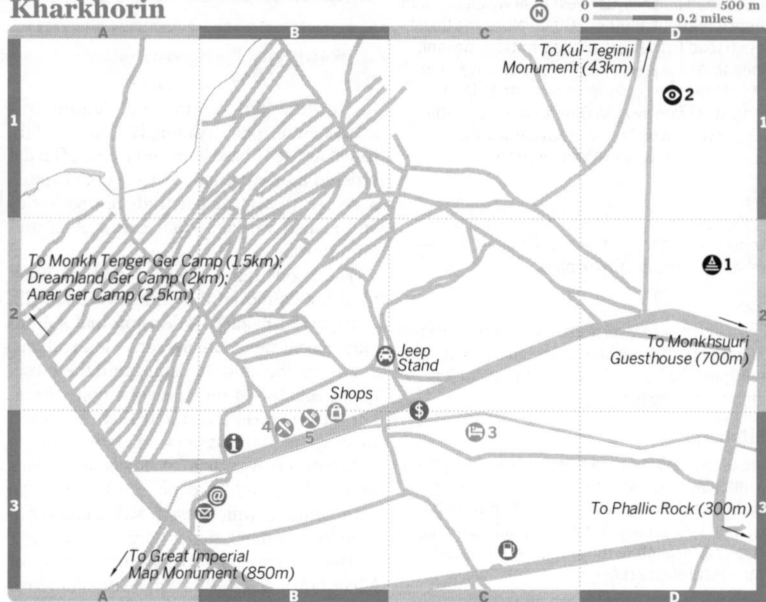

Kharkhorin

Sights

1 Erdene Zuu Khiid D2
2 Stone Turtles D1

Activities, Courses & Tours

Morin Jim .... (see 4)

Sleeping

3 Bayan Burd C3
Morin Jim .... (see 4)

Eating

4 Morin Jim B3
5 Tsagaan Lavai B3

nearby mountains, or stored in local homes (at great risk to the residents).

The monastery remained closed until 1965, when it was permitted to reopen as a museum, but not as a place of worship. It was only with the collapse of communism in 1990 that religious freedom was restored and the monastery became active again. Today Erdene Zuu Khiid is considered by many to be the most important monastery in the country, though no doubt it's a shadow of what it once was.

Entrance to the monastery grounds is free. If you want to see inside the temples, however, you'll have to go to the ticket desk and souvenir shop on your left as you enter the grounds from the south and buy a ticket for US$3, which includes a guided tour of the site.

The monastery is an easy 2km walk from the centre of Kharkhorin.

Temples

The monastery is enclosed in an immense walled compound. Spaced evenly along each wall, about every 15m, are 108 **stupas** (108 is a sacred number to Buddhists). The three temples in the compound, which were not destroyed in the 1930s, are dedicated to the three stages of Buddha's life: childhood, adolescence and adulthood.

Dalai Lama Süm was built in 1675 to commemorate the visit by Abtai Khaan's son, Altan, to the Dalai Lama in Tibet. The room is bare save for a statue of Zanabazar and some fine 17th-century *thangkas* depicting the Dalai Lamas and various protector deities.

Inside the courtyard, **Baruun Zuu**, the temple to the west, built by Abtai Khaan and his son, is dedicated to the adult Buddha. Inside, on either side of Sakyamuni (the historical Buddha), are statues of Sanjaa ('Dipamkara' in Sanskrit), the Past Buddha, to the

NOMADS TO NINJAS

Miners indulging in Mongolia's great new gold rush are turning verdant plains and pure rivers inside out in search of buried fortunes. But for once, it's not just the megacorporations from Ulaanbaatar who are to blame, it's the Ninjas.

When severe winters at the beginning of the millennium wiped out entire herds and family fortunes, many impoverished nomads turned to illegal goldmining in central and northern Mongolia.

The green, shell-like buckets strapped to their backs, coupled with their covert, night-time operations, earned them the moniker 'Teenage Mutant Ninja Turtles', or Ninjas for short.

The Ninjas, who often pan what larger mining operations dredge from the flooded plains, attract businesspeople who sell them food and supplies. The result has been the development of 'Ninja ger boomtowns', each with ger-butchers, ger-shops, ger-karaoke bars, ger-video game parlours and ger-goldsmiths. Police have tried, often vainly, to break up the settlements, but the Ninjas return in larger numbers.

The Ninjas, who number more than 100,000, pose a serious threat to the environment and themselves. Unlike the licensed mining companies, they don't clean up after themselves; their work sites are often littered with discarded batteries and open pits. Mercury and cyanide, used to separate gold from the rock, add more problems. Health workers report that miners who use these methods have levels of mercury in their urine that are five to six times the safe limit.

Despite the health concerns, the number of people performing artisanal mining increases each year, thanks largely to skyrocketing gold prices (which in 2010 reached US$1400 per troy ounce). A Ninja miner can earn US$20 to US$40 per day, well above the national average.

But this is dangerous business – a couple of dozen Ninjas are buried alive in mine shafts each year and shootouts have occurred between Ninjas and legitimate goldmining companies. Recognising the problems, the government is in the process of drafting a law to legalise Ninja mining, in the hope of controlling their activities and regulating the Ninja economy.

left; and Maidar ('Maitreya' in Sanskrit), the Future Buddha, to the right. Other items on display include some golden 'wheels of eternity', *naimin takhel* (the eight auspicious symbols), figurines from the 17th and 18th centuries, and *balin* (wheat dough cakes, decorated with coloured medallions of goat or mutton fat), made in 1965 and still well preserved. Look out for the inner circumambulation path leading off to the left, just by the entrance.

The main and central temple is called the **Zuu of Buddha**. The entrance is flanked by the gods Gonggor on the left and Bandal Lham (Palden Lhamo in Sanskrit) on the right. Inside, to the right of the statues of the child Buddha, is Otoch Manal (the Medicine Buddha), while to the left is Holy Abida (the god of justice). The temple also contains statues of Niam and Dabaa, the sun and moon gods respectively, a few of the *tsam* masks that survived the purges, some carved, aggressive-looking guards from the 16th and 17th centuries, and some displays of the work of the revered sculptor and Buddhist, Zanabazar.

In the temple to the east, **Zuun Zuu**, there's a statue depicting the adolescent Buddha. The statue on the right is Tsongkhapa, who founded the Yellow Hat sect of Buddhism in Tibet. The figure on the left is Janraisig (Chenresig in Tibetan, Avalokitesvara in Sanskrit), the Bodhisattva of Compassion.

As you walk north you will pass the **Golden Prayer Stupa**, built in 1799. The locked temple next to this is said to be the first temple built at Erdene Zuu.

The large white temple at the far end is the Tibetan-style **Lavrin Süm**, where ceremonies are held every morning, usually starting at around 11am; the times vary so ask at the office. Visitors are welcome, but photographs during ceremonies are not.

Other Sights

Apart from the main temples, there are several other interesting things to see. The **gravestones** of Abtai Khaan (1554–88) and

THE ANCIENT CAPITAL

Mongolia's ancient capital may be gone, but Karakorum is certainly not forgotten. By piecing together the accounts of the city written by visiting missionaries, ambassadors and travellers, we have some idea of what the imperial capital once looked like.

Frankly, it wasn't much. The missionary William of Rubruck (1215–95) dismissed the city as being no bigger than the suburb of Saint Denis in Paris. Giovanni de Piano Carpine (1180–1252), an envoy sent to the Mongols in 1245 by Pope Innocent IV, described the city vaguely as 'at the distance of a year's walk' from Rome.

The city never had much time to expand; it was only active for 40 years before Kublai moved the capital to Khanbalik (Beijing). Few Mongols even lived there, most preferring to stay in their gers several kilometres away on the steppe. It was mainly inhabited by artisans, scholars, religious leaders and others captured by the Mongols during their foreign raids.

Its main feature was a brick wall with four gates that encircled the city. Each gate had its own market, selling grain in the east, goats in the west, oxen and wagons in the south and horses in the north.

The Mongol khaans were famed for their religious tolerance and split their time equally between all the religions, hence the 12 different religions that coexisted within the town. Mosques, Buddhist monasteries and Nestorian Christian churches competed for the Mongols' souls. Even powerful figures such as Ögedei's wife and Kublai's mother were Nestorian Christians.

The centrepiece of the city was the Tumen Amgalan (Palace of Worldly Peace) in the southwest corner of the city. This 2500-sq-metre complex, built in 1235, was the palace of Ögedei Khaan. The two-storey palace had a vast reception hall for receiving ambassadors, and its 64 pillars resembled the nave of a church. The walls were painted, the green-tiled floor had underfloor heating, and the Chinese-style roof was covered in green and red tiles.

A team of German archaeologists recently uncovered the foundations of the palace, close to one of the stone turtles (see below). You can also see a model of the palace in the National Museum of Mongolian History in Ulaanbaatar.

The most memorable aspect of the city was a fountain designed in 1253 by the French jeweller and sculptor Guillaume Bouchier (or Bouchee) of Paris, who had been captured by the Mongols in Hungary and brought back to embellish Karakorum. The fountain was in the shape of a huge silver tree, which simultaneously dispensed mare's milk from silver lion heads, and wine, rice wine, *bal* (mead) and *airag* (fermented mare's milk) from four golden spouts shaped like snakes' heads. On top of the tree was an angel. On order, a servant blew a pipe like a bugle that extended from the angel's mouth, giving the order for other servants to pump drinks out of the tree.

Rubruck disparagingly described various pleasure domes and epic feasts (during one of which the Mongol guests guzzled 105 cartloads of alcohol). There were also quarters of artisans and traders, populated by a great mix of people brought back to Karakorum from all over Asia. So cosmopolitan was the city that foreign coins were legal tender.

his grandson Tüshet Khaan Gombodorj (the father of Zanabazar) stand in front of the Dalai Lama Süm and are inscribed in Mongol, Tibetan and Arabic scripts. In the northeast of the monastery are the base stones of a gigantic ger (now called the **Square of Happiness and Prosperity**), set up in 1639 to commemorate Zanabazar's birthday. The ger was reported to be 15m high and 45m in diameter, with 35 concertina-style walls, and could seat 300 during the annual assemblies of the local khaans.

Stone Turtles HISTORIC SITE

Outside the monastery walls are two stone turtles (also called Turtle Rocks). Four of these sculptures once marked the boundaries of ancient Karakorum, acting as protectors of the city (turtles are considered symbols of eternity). The turtles originally had an inscribed stone stele mounted vertically on their back.

One is easy to find: just walk out of the northern gate of the monastery and follow the path northwest for about 300m. Often, an impromptu **souvenir market** is set up next to one stone turtle. You'll need a guide or directions to find the other one, which is on the hill south of the monastery, about 600m past the phallic rock.

Ancient Karakorum RUINS

Just beyond the stone turtle, stretching for about 1km south and east, is the site of ancient Karakorum. The foundations of Karakorum's buildings are all underground and little has been excavated, so you need lots of imagination when contemplating the grandness of it all. The plain was littered with bricks, ruined walls and pillars until the mid-16th century, when everything was picked up and used to build the walls and temples of nearby Erdene Zuu. Next to the stone turtle you can see an area of raised earth surrounded by a wire fence. This was the alleged site of Ögedei Khaan's palace.

Phallic Rock MONUMENT

(GPS: N47° 11.152', E102° 51.235') Near Kharkhorin, a 60cm-long stone penis attracts steady streams of curiosity-seekers. The 'phallic rock', which points erotically to something interestingly called a 'vaginal slope', is hidden up a small valley, about 2km southeast of Erdene Zuu Khiid (look for the sign from the main road).

Legend has it that the rock was placed here in an attempt to stop frisky monks, filled with lust by the shapely slope, from fraternising with the local women. On the hill next to the historic stone penis is a newer penis, chiselled smooth and standing erect.

Great Imperial Map Monument MONUMENT

This large new monument, built in 2004, is on a hill overlooking Kharkhorin to the southwest. The three sides honour various empires established on the Orkhon Gol, including the Hunnu period (300–200 BC), the Turkic period (AD 600–800) and the Mongol period (13th century). There are superb panoramic views from here.

Tours

Most of the ger camps below can help to arrange horse trips around Kharkhorin. The best tour operator is **Morin Jim** (☎9605 2980, 9924 2980; www.horsetrails.mn), a French-run operation based in Kharkhorin (at the Morin Jim cafe). Horse trips cost T30,000 per day (not including food).

Sleeping

The rash of ger camps have taken over the best camping spots, but if you head out towards the main cluster of camps west of town near the Orkhon Gol you should be able to find somewhere to pitch a tent.

Kharkhorin is inundated with ger camps and the fierce competition keeps prices in check. Most camps are in a lovely valley 2km west of town.

Mönkh Tenger TOURIST GER CAMP $$

(☎9978 1996; www.munkh-tenger.com; per person US$17; @) This is the first ger camp you see in the middle of the valley. It's relatively new so still in good condition compared to others in the valley. It has about 20 gers, a restaurant, hot showers and laundry facilities. Free internet access is a plus.

Dreamland TOURIST GER CAMP, HOTEL $$$

(☎9191 1931, 9908 8605; www.asa-travel.com; 3-bed economy ger d US$60-84, lodge d US$92-172; ❄@) What would Chinggis Khaan think of a ger that had an attached bathroom with flush toilets and a private shower, a king-sized bed, air-conditioning and cable TV? Those are some of the options you'll get at this luxurious ger camp, owned and operated by a Mongolian sumo champion. A beautiful Japanese-style sauna and bathhouse completes the picture. The restaurant is also recommended.

Mönkhsuuri TOURIST GER CAMP $

(☎9937 4488; msuri_gh@yahoo.com; GPS: N47° 11.781', E102° 51.345'; per person T5000) This simple camp 1km southeast of Erdene Zuu is popular with backpackers and has a fun, communal vibe. Breakfast costs T2000 and both lunch and dinner are T3000 each. A hot shower is T2500. Mönkhsuuri is a friendly and helpful host; she works as a guide at Erdene Zuu Khiid and is most easily contacted there. Her daughter speaks English.

Anar TOURIST GER CAMP $$

(☎9919 0766; per person US$17) This place is bigger and more commercialised than the others in the valley; it comes complete with Chinggis Khaan statues and a ger gift shop. Meals are also available (breakfast US$2, lunch US$7, dinner US$3). It's in a great location in the southwest corner of the valley, and offers plenty of walking and horse-riding opportunities.

Bayan Burd HOTEL $
(☎82315, 9909 7372; dm/half-luxe/luxe T7000/11,000/17,000) This small hotel could do with some renovation but it's not a bad place to stay if you want to be close to the town centre. All rooms are clean and comfortable, and the luxe room with attached toilet is good value. No rooms have hot water but you can use the hot shower downstairs (shower/sauna T1500/6000).

Morin Jim GUEST GER $
(☎9924 2980; ger T8000) The owner of the Morin Jim cafe has placed several gers behind his restaurant. It's basic but has hot showers (T1000) and the management speaks English.

Eating

All the ger camps serve meals, the best being the Dreamland camp.

Dreamland WESTERN $$$
(☎9191 1931, 9908 8605; www.asa-travel.com; dishes T8000-15,000; ⏰9am-8pm; @) This branch of Ulaanbaatar's California restaurant serves Western meals and offers some of the best food in Kharkhorin.

Morin Jim Café WESTERN/MONGOLIAN $$
(☎9924 2980; meals T4000-6000; ⏰8am-11pm; 📋) A French-run place in town, with a mixed Western and Mongolian menu that includes *buuz* (steamed mutton dumplings), goulash and fried chicken.

Tsagaan Lavai VEGETARIAN $
(dishes T2000; ⏰9am-8pm Mon-Sat; ✎) A vegetarian cafe near Morin Jim.

Information

Internet cafe (per hr T500; ⏰9am-10pm Mon-Fri, 10am-5pm Sat & Sun) Located in the Telecom office.

Kharkhorin Tourist Information Centre (☎9901 8917; zuch_20@yahoo.com; ⏰8am-10pm; @) This private information centre offers travel info, has internet access (T500 per hour) and can help organise horse treks.

Telecom office (⏰24hr) The post office is also here, on the western edge of the main road through town.

XAC Bank (⏰9am-5.30pm Mon-Fri) Changes money and gives cash advances on MasterCard.

Getting There & Away

Erdene Zuu and the nearby sights are a 2km walk from town; otherwise ask around for a lift (about T600).

Air

There are no regularly scheduled flights here, although EZ Nis sometimes does a charter package deal that includes flights, hotels and food.

Bus

A daily bus goes from Kharkhorin market to Ulaanbaatar at 11am (T12,000, eight hours).

Hitching

Hitching along the main road between Ulaanbaatar and Kharkhorin is fairly easy, but remember that a lot of vehicles will be carrying tourists, so they may not want to pick up a hitchhiker. Getting a lift between Arvaikheer and Kharkhorin is less likely, but if you're patient something will come along.

Minivans & Jeeps

Minivans run daily to Ulaanbaatar (T15,000, seven hours) from the container market, leaving sometime after 8am, whenever they are full. As the road is sealed, this is one of the more bearable long-distance trips in the countryside. There are far fewer vehicles going to Khujirt (T3000) and Arvaikheer (T6000) – maybe once a day if at all. Going the other way, the minivans leave when full from Dragon Centre.

A post office van runs Monday and Thursday to Khujirt (T4000) and Arvaikheer (T6500) at 11.30am. Ask at the post office for details.

The road from Kharkhorin to Khujirt (54km) is being upgraded. The aimag capital, Arvaikheer, is 138km to the southeast. The 160km road between Kharkhorin and Tsetserleg is likewise being upgraded.

West of Kharkhorin

TÖVKHÖN KHIID ТӨВХӨН ХИЙД
Hidden deep in the Khangai mountains, this incredibly scenic **monastery** (GPS: N47° 00.772', E102° 15.362') has become a major pilgrimage centre for Mongolians. Zanabazar founded the site in 1653 and lived, worked and meditated here for 30 years. The monastery was destroyed in 1937 but rebuilt with public funds in the early 1990s.

Situated at the top of Shireet Ulaan Uul, Zanabazar apparently liked the unusual formation of the peak; the rocky outcrop looks like an enormous throne. It was here that Zanabazar created many of his best artistic endeavours, some of which can be found now in the Zanabazar Museum of Fine Arts (p47) in Ulaanbaatar.

Several **pilgrimage sites** have grown up around the temple and hermits' caves, including one that is said to be Zanabazar's boot imprint. Locals will also instruct you to squeeze through the narrow **rebirth cave**, representative of a woman's uterus, although this is not recommended if you have a fear of heights, are susceptible to claustrophobia or have the frame of a sumo wrestler.

The temple is in **Khangai Nuruu National Park** (admission T3000) and best reached with your own vehicle. A good 4WD can drive the steep road up to the monastery in 20 minutes, but old Russian jeeps and vans can't make the trip so you'll have to walk (one hour) up the hill through the forest. From the car park it's 2.5km. The route is obvious and in summer locals offer horse rides (T1000) to the top. Swarms of flies will probably plague your ascent; wrap a T-shirt, bandana or towel around your head to keep them away. A small shop at the top sells bottled water and snacks.

It's not possible to camp at the monastery, but there are a couple of family-run ger camps by the entrance to the national park.

The monastery is around 60km from Kharkhorin. Just follow the Orkhon Gol southwest for around 50km and turn north, up a side valley. This brings you to the ger camps and the trailhead up the eastern side of the mountain. Note that if you are coming from Orkhon Khürkhree (see below), you will arrive at the western slope of the mountain and will end up taking a different trail to the top. From this side you'll also find boys offering horse rides to the monastery.

ORKHON KHÜRKHREE
ОРХОН ХҮРХРЭЭ

After a strong rain this magnificent seasonal **waterfall** (GPS: N46° 47.234', E101° 57.694'), also called Ulaan Tsutgalan (Улаан Цутгалан), is one of the best sights in central Mongolia. About 250m downstream from the waterfall you can climb down to the bottom of the **gorge**; it's 22m deep and dotted with pine trees.

Ask your tour operator about the status of the falls. The water doesn't run all year and will only start to flow after the first good summer rain. Late July and August are the best times to see it. If it's not running you could consider rearranging your travel schedule to visit later in the summer. If you arrive when the waterfall is not in flow, take solace in the fact that the region is still gorgeous, and a fine area for **camping** and **horse riding**.

There are a few different ways to approach the waterfall; all of them involve rough travel on very rocky roads. Coming directly from Ulaanbaatar, most traffic will go on the road via Khujirt. The road from Kharkhorin is longer but by taking this route you can stop at Tövkhön Khiid on the way. From Arvaikheer, it's possible to take a remote backcountry road via Züünbayan-Ulaan and Bat-Ölzii; but you'll need an experienced driver and a very sturdy 4WD to attempt it.

In summer, a handful of nomad families open up a guest ger, charging T10,000 per ger. **Möngön Khürkhree** (per person without food T6000) is the only permanent ger camp near the waterfall (it's the one surrounded by the fence). The camp is basic but it does have a restaurant, flush toilets and hot showers (which take ages to heat up). You can hire horses here for T4000 per hour.

Bayan Uul Camp (☎9904 9993; GPS: N46° 48.709', E102° 02.650'; ger T15,000-20,000) has hot showers (T2000), meals and basic gers. It's by the Orkhon River (on the road from Kharkhorin), 7km before the waterfall.

If you have a rod and reel, you could try catching your dinner. Good spots for catching lenok trout can be found downstream from the waterfall.

Nomads that live in the area can organise overnight horse trips, usually up to Naiman Nuur (p102). **Bold** (☎9521 5377) is one herder that makes the trip. His ger is usually on the road to the waterfall or just past it; call ahead or just ask around. He charges T7000 per day per horse and T7000 per guide. A pack yak will cost T8000 per day.

East of Kharkhorin

There are several interesting places between Kharkhorin and Khustain National Park en route to/from Ulaanbaatar.

KHÖGNÖ KHAN UUL NATURE RESERVE ХӨГНӨ ХАН УУЛ

Located just off the main Ulaanbaatar–Kharkhorin highway, this 46,900-hectare nature reserve sees a steady stream of visitors. Its arid terrain of rocky semidesert is good for short hikes and there are a few old temples to explore, both ruined and active. You might spot ibex, wolves and many varieties of hawk.

Sights

Erdiin Khambiin Khiid RUINS
(GPS: N47° 25.561', E103° 41.686'; admission T2000) At the southern foot of the mountain are these ruins, with a couple of new temples and the remains of one older temple. About five monks reside here in the summer months.

WORTH A TRIP

NAIMAN NUUR НАЙМАН НУУР

The area of Naiman Nuur (Eight Lakes), which was created by volcanic eruptions centuries ago, is now part of the 11,500-hectare **Khuisiin Naiman Nuur Nature Reserve**. Despite the name, there are actually nine, not eight, lakes. The **lakes** (GPS: N46° 31.232', E101° 50.705') are about 35km southwest of Orkhon Khürkhree (waterfall), but the roads are often virtually impassable. Locals around the waterfall can hire horses for the two-day trip to the lakes. This area is environmentally fragile; vehicles that attempt to make the trip end up tearing new tracks through the grasslands, so local communities are working on ways to prevent cars from coming here. If your driver says he can make it by car, insist on going by horse. Companies such as Nomads and Nomadic Expeditions (p54) run tours here, including horse-riding trips.

The head lama is a charming woman who professes soothsaying abilities.

The mountain is in Bulgan aimag but most easily accessed from the Ulaanbaatar–Arvaikheer road.

Övgön Khiid RUINS
(Өвгөн Хийд; GPS N47° 26.267', E103° 42.527') These ruins are a lovely 45-minute (2km) walk along a well-defined path up the valley to the right. The monastery was built in 1660 and destroyed (and the monks massacred) by the armies of Zungar Galdan Bochigtu, a rival of Zanabazar's, in 1640.

Sleeping

Camping is excellent in the valley, though the only water comes from a hard-to-find well at its lower end. The following ger camps have horses for rent for about US$3 per hour.

Övgön Erdene Tour Camp TOURIST GER CAMP $
(Monastery Ger Camp; ☎9977 0410; with/without meals T35,000/25,000) This well-built ger camp and wood lodge is a short walk from the temple. It's run by the monks at the Övgön Khiid.

Khögnö Khan TOURIST GER CAMP $
(☎9910 2885; GPS N47° 24.430', E103° 40.364'; with/without meals T58,000/24,000) Located 4km southwest of Övgön Khiid in an attractive setting. Horse riding is available here for US$7 per hour

Getting There & Away

To get to Khögnö Khan Uul from Kharkhorin by jeep, turn north off the main road, 80km east of Kharkhorin. The road passes several ger camps until, after 8km, you reach Khögnö Khan ger camp, where you turn right for the remaining 4km or so to the monastery ruins. There is a shortcut if you are coming from Ulaanbaatar (the turn-off is marked by a sign that says 'Ar Mongol', 1.2km after the Bichigt Khad ger camp).

There is no public transport to the monastery but you can take a Kharkhorin-, Khujirt- or Arvaikheer-bound minivan from Ulaanbaatar, get off at the turn-off on the main road and then hitch (or more likely walk) the remaining 12km.

MONGOL ELS МОНГОЛ ЭЛС

As you approach the border of Övörkhangai from Ulaanbaatar, one surprising sight that livens up a fairly boring stretch of road is the sand dunes of Mongol Els. If you don't have the time to visit the Gobi (where there are not a lot of sand dunes anyway), these are certainly worth wandering around. At the turn-off to the sand dunes there is a group of camel herders who hang around and sell camel rides. Expect to pay about T5000 for a guided 20-minute camel ride.

ARKHANGAI АРХАНГАЙ

POP 92,500 / AREA 55,000 SQ KM

Arkhangai is something of an oasis in the centre of Mongolia's harsh climatic zones; to the south lies the hot Gobi Desert and to the north lies the frigid Siberian taiga. Arkhangai is right in the middle, a mixed landscape of rugged mountains, peaceful forests, rushing streams and rolling steppe. All this wild nature and mixed topography makes for some interesting independent travel options: horse riding, mountain biking, fishing and trekking are all possible in Arkhangai.

The Khangai Mountains in the southern part of the aimag rise to a height of 3300m. The mountains are by no means impenetrable and it's possible to travel through the passes on horse and jeep trails to Bayankhongor aimag. In winter, nomads use the passes on traditional *otors* (treks) to find grazing land for their animals.

Most travellers make stops at the Tsenkher hot springs and Tsetserleg before heading off to Terkhiin Tsagaan Nuur (Great White Lake) for a few days of R&R. From the White Lake there are trails north to Khövsgöl aimag. With a few extra days up your sleeve you could dangle a fishing line at Ögii Nuur and check out the historic Turkic-era stone monuments of Kul-Tegin.

Tsetserleg Цэцэрлэг

01332 / POP 17,900 / ELEV 1691M

Nestled comfortably between rugged mountains, with tree-lined streets and a quaint temple overlooking the town, Tsetserleg gets our vote for Mongolia's most beautiful aimag capital.

Tsetserleg is a perfect place to break up your journey if you are combining a visit to Kharkhorin or Khujirt with a trip to Terkhiin Tsagaan Nuur or Khövsgöl Nuur. There are some decent restaurants and hotels, busy temples and a striking aimag museum. Nature lovers will appreciate the hiking opportunities and good camping spots. Tourist activities revolve around the Fairfield cafe and guesthouse, an attraction in its own right.

Sights

Museum of Arkhangai Aimag MUSEUM

(admission T3500, camera T7000; 9am-6pm) This is one of the best aimag museums in the country. It's housed in the temple complex of **Zayain Gegeenii Süm**, which was first built in 1586 but expanded in 1679, when it housed five temples and up to 1000 monks. Miraculously, the monastery escaped the Stalinist purges because it was made into a museum.

The main hall concentrates on traditional Mongolian lifestyle, with exhibits of costumes, traditional tools, a ger, musical instruments, weaponry and saddles. The displays have some useful English captions. The second hall concentrates on religious icons. The other two rooms of the former main prayer hall are empty, while the last hall focuses on local artwork. Look out for the unique traditional playing cards.

Galdan Zuu Temple TEMPLE

Up the hill from the aimag museum, this temple has been renovated with donations given by the locals. It stands behind an impressive 7m statue of the Buddha. Behind the temple is a large, nearly vertical, rocky hill called Bulgan Uul, where there are some **Buddhist inscriptions**.

Buyandelgerüülekh Khiid MONASTERY

(Буяндэлгэрүүлэх Хийд) Tsetserleg's small monastery (next to the museum) has a handful of monks who hold services at 11am in summer and 10am in winter. The **main statue** here is Shakyamuni; you'll also see a picture of the last Zayan Gegeen (to the left of the throne), who was the traditional head of the monastery in Tsetserleg.

Gangin Gol VALLEY

In the north of town a trail leads to the pretty Gangin Gol, which offers great **hiking** potential. At the mouth of the valley is a ger camp and a pitiful **nature museum** of stuffed animals, which isn't worth the T1000 the caretaker will demand. From the camp you can hike up the mountain to the left (east), and walk along the ridge until you reach the peak of Bulgan Uul (1953m), the mountain that overlooks Tsetserleg.

MOBILE GER CAMP

Gers are an environmentally sustainable form of housing because when they begin to have an impact on the land, the owners can move them to fresh pastures. Sadly, most ger camps in Mongolia these days are as stationary as any hotel.

Mobile Ger Camp (11-345 662; per night incl 3 meals US$35;) in Gurvanbulag bucks this trend. The camp is run by a cooperative of local herders. They are not professional hotel operators but real nomadic Mongolians who accept guests in a guest ger. The community is located in the buffer zone of Khögnö Khan Nature Reserve. Activities in the area include horse riding and travelling by ox cart to nearby natural sights. Mostly, this is a great opportunity to watch nomads going about their daily routines and sample some local foods.

The camp is located about 7km south of Gurvanbulag *sum* centre, along the Tarnii Ovort Gol (river). It's not exactly in the same place every year but you should be able to find it if travelling north from the main highway towards Gurvanbulag. If in doubt, just ask the locals.

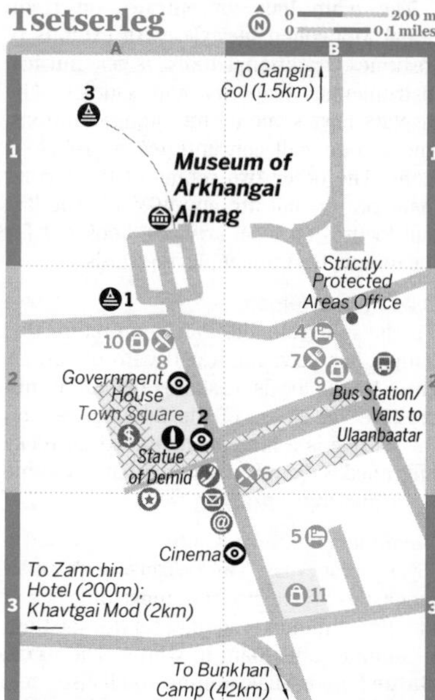

Tsetserleg

Dancing Fountain FOUNTAIN
Tsetserleg's newest landmark keeps the local kids cool on hot summer days. It puts on a colourful light show after dark.

Sleeping

Gangin Gol has some great camping spots, though someone may come and collect a dubious 'fee' for camping in a 'nature reserve' (it's not). A few hundred metres past the ger camp is a grassy enclosure that's perfect for camping. There are also some nice spots a few kilometres south of town on the banks of the river.

TOP CHOICE **Fairfield Guesthouse** GUESTHOUSE $$
(21036, 9909 8612; www.fairfield.mn; per person incl breakfast T17,500) Attached to the restaurant of the same name, this nine-room guesthouse is a popular choice and one of the only hotels in the countryside where you need a reservation in summer. Nonattached rooms are clean and cosy and there is an excellent breakfast. Hot showers are clean and reliable. The hotel is a travellers' hub with a book exchange and a popular cafe. It can also arrange horse trekking trips (guides T11,000, horses T12,000). A delicious, Western-style breakfast is included in the price.

Sundur Hotel HOTEL $
(22359; s/d/luxe T15,000/40,000/60,000; @) The cheapest rooms here have only a toilet and no shower, but all others have nice bathrooms with hot water (at fixed times of the day only – check the times with reception). Rooms are no-frills but clean and bright. There's a decent restaurant downstairs that serves Mongolian food.

Khavtgai Mod TOURIST GER CAMP $
(9975 3150; per person US$10) On a hillside a couple of kilometres out of town to the west, this camp has a good location in the forest and valley views. It's fine for a quick night's sleep but the facilities aren't great and there is no shower.

Zamchin Hotel HOTEL $
(22274; r per person T10,000, half-luxe T26,000; @) A reliable place, Zamchin has a restaurant, sauna and hot shower. Rooms are spacious but it's away from the centre, on the western road out of town.

Eating

TOP CHOICE **Fairfield** CAFE $
(21096; meals T3500-6500; 9am-6pm Mon-Sat;) This British-run cafe is one of the highlights of Tsetserleg and should feature prominently on your itinerary. A full English breakfast (T12,100) consists of bacon, sausage, eggs, toast and pancakes – enough for two people. Lunch and dinner options include lasagne, chilli con carne,

beef in beer sauce and some vegetarian dishes. Pastries are served all day long and are great snacks to take with you on the road. The cafe is also a good place to ask about travel conditions and look for a ride if you are hitching around the country. Note that it's closed on Sundays – plan accordingly.

Tsakhiur MONGOLIAN **$**
(meals T2000; ⏲10am-10pm) A little fancier than other places, this upmarket restaurant (it has tablecloths) is near the department store at the north end of town. It serves local favourites such as goulash and *puntutste khuurag* (clear or glass noodles).

Cactus Bar CAFE **$**
(meals T2500-3000; ⏲10am-10pm) Has a few good Mongolian dishes on the menu and even some rare items like fried fish. It is opposite the Telecom office.

Shopping

Everyday goods are best bought at the **department store** at the northern end of town. The Fairfield has a fair-trade gift shop.

The daily **market** *(khunsnii zakh)*, on the corner of the main road and the road to Ulaanbaatar, has enough products for a pre-trekking shopping trip.

Art Shop SOUVENIRS
(⏲10am-7pm) Sells Mongolian *dels* (traditional coats) and jackets, plus locally produced art and artefacts. It's next to the Fairfield Guesthouse.

Information

Internet cafe (per hr T500; ⏲8am-10pm) In the Telecom office.

Khan Bank (⏲9am-1pm & 2-4pm Mon-Fri) Changes cash and has an ATM.

Strictly Protected Areas office (khangainuruu@yahoo.com; ⏲9am-6pm) Has information on Arkhangai's national parks and can give advice on tourist sites, fishing licences and park fees.

Telecom office (⏲8am-10pm) The post office is also here; it's on the main road in town, on the south side of the main square.

Getting There & Away

There are no flights to Tsetserleg, so the only way here is by bus or shared vehicle.

Bus

A daily bus departs Tsetserleg at 8am for Ulaanbaatar (T18,000, 12 hours). Purchase the ticket at least one day ahead. The Fairfield cafe can get your ticket for a T500 commission. The driver may impose a 15kg limit and charge you T3000 for an extra bag.

Hitching

All types of vehicles go to/from Tsetserleg and, generally, along the main road through Arkhangai. Wait on the main road into and out of town (heading east or west), and something will eventually stop.

Minivan & Jeep

Microbuses and minivans run between Tsetserleg and Ulaanbaatar (T20,000, 10 hours). In Tsetserleg, minivans will wait by the bus stand. Drivers in Tsetserleg have developed a dual-pricing system so that tourists are charged twice as much as locals. Bargaining hard doesn't help much and you may have to pay the 'tourist prices'.

Minivans and Jeeps to other places will wait at a lot near the market. You can probably find a vehicle going to Tariat (T15,000) and possibly Erdenet (T20,000 to T25,000).

There are two routes between Tsetserleg and Ulaanbaatar – directly east via Ögii Nuur (453km) or along the longer but better road via Kharkhorin (493km). From Tsetserleg to Kharkhorin it's 115km (two hours). Tosontsengel is a mere 350km to the northwest.

Tsenkher Hot Springs
Цэнхрийн Халуун Рашаан

Set between forested hills, these **hot springs** (GPS: N47° 19.241', E101° 39.411') are becoming an increasingly popular detour from the main road. Four ger camps have been built around the springs; each pumps water into splash pools that cost around US$5 to enter. If you are already in Tsetserleg, it's possible to head south on a jeep trail 27km to get here. If you are coming from Ulaanbaatar, the turn-off is at Tsenkher *sum*. From the *sum* centre it's 24km to the hot springs.

Sleeping

TOP CHOICE **Duut Resort** TOURIST GER CAMP, LODGE **$$$**
(☎9898 1499; duutresort@yahoo.com; ger with/without 3 meals US$60/30, lodge s/d US$100/160) Not only is this the top place to stay at the hot springs, it's also one of the best ger camps in the country. The lodge, made entirely from local timber, is beautifully constructed and furnished. It includes a cosy restaurant that serves reasonably priced Western and Mongolian meals for around T7000 to T9000 per person. The two hot springs pools are located out back and a communal shower block is located in the lodge. Non-guest use of the pool is US$8.

RETREAT TO THE KHANGAI

Horse lovers, poets, writers, photographers, yogis, Buddhist practitioners or plain old refugees of commercialism are all welcome at the Bunkhan Camp, a lovely ger camp set deep in the Khangai mountains. The camp, 42km south of Tsetserleg, is operated by an American couple, anthropologist Carroll Dunham and photographer Thomas Kelly, and their Mongolian partners Gerlee and Toroo.

Workshops lasting two weeks include wilderness poetry, meditation, yoga and photography, with space for 10 to 12 people at a time. It's a great place to unwind, meet like-minded people and commune with nature. Horses are available and visitors can go on pack trips to nearby Blue Lake. The camp is kid-friendly, with plenty of options for fishing, archery and horse riding. Costs average out to US$150 per day for adults and US$80 per day for kids. For more information see www.wildearthjourneys.com.

Tsenkher Jiguur TOURIST GER CAMP, LODGE **$$** (☎9816 1744; www.visit2mongolia.mn; ger incl 3 meals US$46;) Although not in the same league as Duut Resort, this place has better than average accommodation and attractive pools lined with rocks (rather than concrete). There are separate pools for men and women. Nonguest use of the pool is US$6.

Ögii Nuur Өгий Нуур

On the road between Ulaanbaatar and Tsetserleg, near the border with Bulgan aimag, this **lake** (GPS: N47° 47.344', E102° 45.828') is a wonderful place for birdlife. Cranes and ducks, among other species, migrate to the area around late April. A **visitors centre** (GPS: N47° 45.023', E102° 46.314') located on the southern shore of the lake helps travellers get acquainted with the wildlife. The lake is also popular for **fishing**.

Ögii Nuur can only be reached from the direct road linking Tsetserleg with Ulaanbaatar. The lake makes a nice overnight stop with plenty of camping spots. There are also four ger camps by the lake, the best being **Khatan Ögii** (GPS: N47° 45.114', E102° 47.489'; ger from T30,000), which has accommodation in gers and *orts* (tepees).

Khar Balgas Хар Балгас

The ruined citadel of Khar Balgas (Kara Balgasun in Turkic) is in Khotont *sum* on the banks of the Orkhon Gol. The city was founded in AD 751 as the capital of the Uighur Khaganate, which ruled Mongolia from 744 to 840.

There's not much to see except the outer walls (with gates in the north and south), a **Buddhist stupa** and the ruler's **kagan** (castle), in the southwest corner. From the walls you can see the rows of stupas on either side and the remains of irrigated fields in the surrounding countryside. The city had an elaborate plumbing system, which brought water into the city from the nearby river.

The **ruins** (GPS: N47° 25.782', E102° 39.490') lie about 33km northwest of Kharkhorin. Take the road to Tsetserleg for 20km, then follow rough dirt tracks another 13km to the site.

Tsetserleg to Terkhiin Tsagaan Nuur

Cutting straight through Arkhangai Aimag, this 180km stretch of road is one of the most scenic in Mongolia. It's rough in patches but road crews continue the slow process of upgrading.

The first place worth stopping is **Taikhar Chuluu** (Тайхар Чулуу) rock formation, just 22km east of Tsetserleg. The rock is the subject of many local legends, the most common one being that a great *baatar* (hero) crushed a huge serpent here by hurling the rock on top of it. Locals claim there are some ancient Tibetan inscriptions on the rock, though you'll be lucky to spot them through 30 years of Mongolian graffiti. There is even an *ovoo* at the top. You could camp anywhere along the Khoid Tamir Gol. **Taikhar Ger Camp** (☎9911 4060; per person US$14), next to the rock, has hot-water showers and flush toilets. Taikhar Chuluu is about 2km north of Ikh Tamir along the river – you can see it from the main road.

The next landmark is **Chuluut Gur** (GPS: N48° 05.666', E100° 19.025'), the bridge over the Chuluut River (*gur* means bridge). Near the bridge are a few tyre repair shops and several *guanze* selling basic meals. About 2km past the bridge (on the south side of the road) is the **Chuluut Ger Camp** (☎9911 8066; ger T25,000), the best place to stay in the area.

About 30km east of Tariat is the dramatic **Chuluut gorge**, which makes a pleasant picnic stop. Once you reach Tariat it's another 6km to the lake.

Khorgo-Terkhiin Tsagaan Nuur National Park
Хорго-Тэрхийн Цагаан Нуур

Amid volcanic craters, pine-clad lava fields and the occasional herd of grazing yaks, the Great White Lake, as it's known in English, is the natural highlight of Arkhangai aimag. According to legend, the lake was formed when an elderly couple forgot to cap a well after fetching water. The valley was flooded until a local hero shot a nearby mountain top with his arrow; the shorn top covered the well and became an island in the lake (Noriin Dund Tolgoi).

The freshwater **Terkhiin Tsagaan Nuur** is not as forested or as large as Khövsgöl Nuur, but it is closer to Ulaanbaatar, relatively undeveloped and just about perfect for **camping** (though there are a few flies in summer). The lake, birdlife and mountains are now protected within the 77,267-hectare Khorgo-Terkhiin Tsagaan Nuur National Park. The national park fee of T3000 applies.

The lake, which was formed by lava flows from a volcanic eruption many millennia ago, is excellent for **swimming**, though a bit cold in the morning – try the late afternoon, after the sun has warmed it. Hidden along the shore are stretches of sandy beach, perfect for lounging with a book or fishing line.

The **fishing** is great, though you should get a permit for around T3000 per day. There are several park rangers who sell permits, or try asking at the park entrance by the bridge in **Tariat**.

One must-do excursion takes you to the top of **Khorgo Uul** volcano. A road leads 4km from Tariat village to the base of the volcano, from where it's a 10-minute walk up to the **cone** (GPS: N48° 11.187', E99° 51.259'). The volcano is in the park so you'll need to pay the park fee of T3000 if you haven't already.

There is also the option of exploring the lake by **boat**. Khorgo I ger camp has a rowboat and Maikhan Toilgoi has a jet ski.

Sleeping

Except for a few annoying flies, Terkhiin Tsagaan Nuur is an excellent place for camping. There is good fishing, endless fresh water, and flat ground for pitching a tent. The western end of the lake, where it joins the Khoid Terkhiin Gol, is muddy. The best place to camp is the northern part, away from the ger camps. The area is cold year-round, and often windy, so a good sleeping bag is vital.

DON'T MISS

KUL-TEGINII MONUMENT КУЛ-ТЭГИНИЙ ХӨШӨӨ

When Chinggis Khaan decided to move his capital to Karakorum, he was well aware that the region had already been the capital of successive nomad empires. About 20km northeast of Khar Balgas lies the remainder of yet another of these, the Turkic *khaganate* (pre-Mongol empire). All that's left of the *khaganate* is the 3m-high inscribed monument of Kul-Tegin (AD 684–731), the *khagan* (ruler) of the ancient empire.

The **monument** (GPS: N47° 33.837', E102° 49.931') was raised in 732 and is inscribed in Runic and Chinese script. You can see a copy of the stele in the entrance of the National Museum of Mongolian History in Ulaanbaatar.

Just over 1km away is another **monument to Bilge Khagan** (683–734), older brother of Kul-Tegin. Ten years after the death of Bilge, the Turkic *khaganate* was overrun by the Uighurs.

A Turkish-funded archaeological expedition has built a **museum** at the site. In fact, the outdoor monuments are replicas and the originals have been moved inside the museum. If the museum is locked, the watchman at the ger next door should be able to let you inside.

The museum and monuments are 45km north of Kharkhorin. The Turkish government has built a paved road from Kharkhorin to the site, so getting here is easy. At the time of writing, the paved road was being extended in the direction of Ögii Nuur, another 28km north.

About 3km before the museum (if coming from Kharkhorin) is **Tsaidam Ger Camp** (☎9923 6888; per person US$10), which has comfortable gers and hot showers.

LOCAL KNOWLEDGE

JAMSRANJAV BAYARSAIKHAN: ARCHAEOLOGIST

Jamsranjav Bayarsaikhan is a seasoned archaeologist based at the National Museum of Mongolia in Ulaanbaatar. He spoke with us about his recent excavations in Arkhangai.

'One of the most interesting places to visit in Central Mongolia is the Khannui Valley. Very few people get there because it's off the main tourist route, but for me this is one of the most beautiful valleys in the country.

'Khannui is also a historically significant region with a huge ritual complex, the remains of a 14th-century settlement and around 30 deer stones. This is one of the largest concentrations of deer stones in Central Asia. Around the deer stones there are about 1700 horse mounds. These mounds contain horse skulls, which were buried according to local custom. Even today, nomadic people honour horse skulls – you can see them placed on *ovoos*' (shamanistic collections of stones, wood or other offerings to the gods).

Bayarsaikhan offers some additional advice for visitors: 'If travellers come here I recommend they bring a Polaroid camera. It would please herders very much to receive an instant picture of their family. I also recommend that foreigners join an archaeological dig in Mongolia – it's a great way to see Mongolia and gain an appreciation for its history.'

To contact the National Museum about joining an archaeological dig, visit www.nationalmuseum.mn.

Several camps are built up along the shore of the lake (mostly the northern and eastern shores), but they are all fairly spread out so it's not too crowded. On the northern shore of the lake you'll also see some 'ger hotels' that charge T8000 per person (or T15,000 for a ger). A shop nearby sells soft drinks, confectionery and fishing equipment.

Khorgo I TOURIST GER CAMP $$
(☎011-322 870, 9916 2847; GPS: N48° 12.246', E99° 50.834'; with/without meals US$45/20) In a lovely location in the Zurkh Gol Khundii (Heart River valley) by the northeast section of the lake, Khorgo I has hot showers and there is excellent hiking nearby. To get there, take the road north of Tariat into the park and take the branch to the right when you get near the volcano.

Maikhan Tolgoi TOURIST GER CAMP $
(☎9911 9730, 9908 9730; GPS: N48° 10.821', E99° 45.725'; without meals US$20) Set on a headland on the northern shore of the lake, this is perhaps the most attractive camp on the lake. It has flush toilets, hot showers (US$7) and a cosy restaurant. A jet ski is available to rent for T40,000 per hour.

Tsagaan Nuur TOURIST GER CAMP $
(☎9981 7465; GPS: N48° 10.621', E99° 48.691'; per person without meals US$10) This is the first camp on the north shore of the lake. Horses are T7000 per hour, each meal is $3. The owners also rent fishing rods for T15,000 per hour.

Hotel HOTEL $
(☎9981 9094; per person T5000) Tariat village, about 6km east of the lake, has a basic but clean unnamed hotel, next to the Mobicom shop. Facilities include a pit toilet around the back.

Eating

All the camps around the lake provide reasonably priced meals. Self-caterers can stock up on supplies in either Tariat or the shops by the lake. In Tariat, you could try **Ma Bagsh** (☎9962 7615; meals T1500; ⏲9am-midnight), which was closed at the time of research but will hopefully be open by the time you read this. It's near the bridge.

Information

Internet cafe (per hr T500; ⏲10am-7pm Mon-Sat) In Tariat village.

Khan Bank (⏲9am-1pm & 2-5pm Mon-Fri) In Tariat village, this bank will change US dollars.

Getting There & Away

From Tariat, occasional minivans run to/from Ulaanbaatar and Tsetserleg. For Tsetserleg expect to pay T20,000 and to Ulaanbaatar about T40,000. For elsewhere you are better off hitching.

From the lake to Tosontsengel (179km), the main road climbs over Solongotyn Davaa, a phenomenally beautiful area. You can see patches of permanent ice from the road. The road has been upgraded to an all-weather gravel road but is still rough in patches. For the route to Mörön, see p136.

Northern Mongolia

POP 463,000 / AREA 192,800 SQ KM

Includes »

Best Places to Eat

- » Garage 24 (p132)
- » Texas Pub (p115)
- » Molor Erdene (p120)
- » Stupa Ger Camp (p118)

Best Places to Stay

- » Comfort Hotel (p115)
- » Nature's Door (p132)
- » Toilogt (p132)
- » Anak Ranch (p113)

Why Go?

Log cabins, pine forests and monstrous fish do not conform to the classic image of Mongolia's empty steppes. But strung along its northern border is a region so lush and rugged that one might confuse it with bits of Switzerland. Selenge, Bulgan and Khövsgöl aimags actually have more in common with Siberia than Mongolia. Winters are long and cold, with snow staying on the ground until May. Summers bring wildflowers and the melting snow fills up lakes and rivers, many of which flow north to Lake Baikal in Siberia. This habitat provides an ideal home for wildlife as well as rich grasslands for nomadic herders. Close to the Russian border you can even meet reindeer herders, or just relax by the glorious shores of Lake Khövsgöl. Northern Mongolia is also the place to go if you are interested in shamanism, which is being revived and encouraged.

When to Go

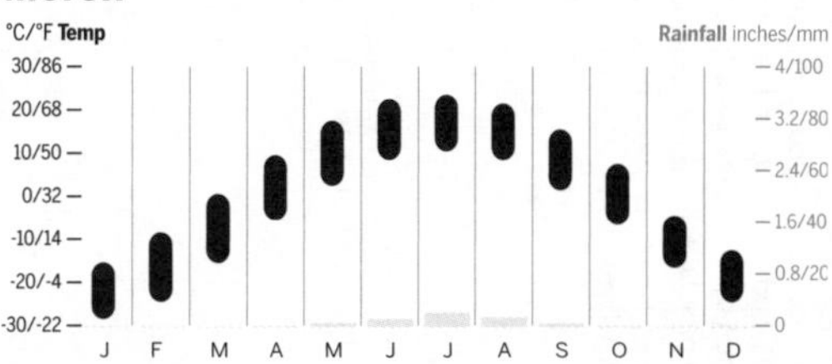

Mid-July Catch Naadam in Khatgal, Renchinlhumbe or another small village.

Late August–September Visit the taiga: fewer bugs and dry ground make for better trekking.

Late February Skiing, skating and ice fishing at the Khatgal Ice Festival.

Northern Mongolia Highlights

1 Drop a fishing line into **Khövsgöl Nuur** (p127), and while away an afternoon by Mongolia's loveliest alpine lake

2 Explore the remote **Darkhad Depression**, where you can mount an expedition to visit Tsaatan reindeer herders (p134)

3 Wander around the grounds of **Amarbayasgalant Khiid** (p116), the architectural highlight of the country

4 Visit the bow-and-arrow-making workshop in **Dulaankhaan** (p113), one of the last in Mongolia

5 Journey to **Chandman-Öndör** (p133), a little-visited region of fish-filled streams, hot springs and sacred caves

6 Study the curious deer-stone carvings at **Uushigiin Uver** (p127), one of the best examples of ancient rock art in Mongolia

7 Watch the scenery roll past your window on a **rail journey** from Ulaanbaatar to Erdenet

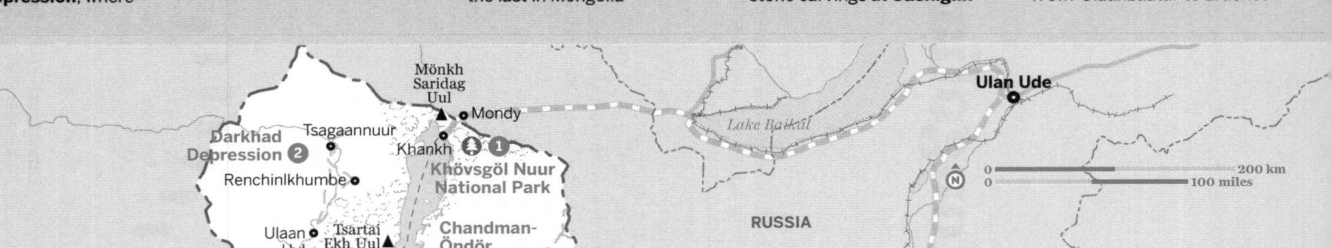

History

For thousands of years northern Mongolia was the borderland between the Turkic-speaking tribes of Siberia and the great steppe confederations of the Huns, Uighurs and Mongols. Some of the Siberian tribes still survive in Mongolia, notably the Tsaatan people of northern Khövsgöl. Evidence of the steppe nomads is also found in Khövsgöl in the form of numerous burial mounds and deer stones.

Settled history really began in the 18th century under Manchu rule when thousands of monks poured into the area from Tibet and China to assist in the construction of monasteries. As the nomads were converted to Buddhism, local shamans were harassed into giving up traditional practices. The largest centre of religion, Amarbayasgalant Khiid, had more than 2000 lamas.

During communism, religious persecution boiled over into a 1932 rebellion that left thousands of monks and Mongolian soldiers dead. Meanwhile, an attempt by the monks to form an insurrectionist government ended in failure. Later, the Russians improved their standing with the locals by developing a variety of industries. Darkhan and Selenge became important centres of agriculture, Bulgan became home to the Erdenet copper mine, and Khövsgöl developed a thriving industry of timber mills, fisheries and wool processing.

Climate

In the region around Khövsgöl aimag, the terrain is mainly taiga (subarctic coniferous forest) of Siberian larch and pine trees, where there's plenty of rain (often 600mm a year). Snowfall can exceed 2m in some regions during winter. After winter the lakes and rivers remain frozen until May; travel can be hazardous at this time, as trucks and jeeps can fall through the thin ice. Travelling in winter means faster drive times around the aimag, as vehicles won't get bogged in the mud. July is warm and relatively dry, but this is also the time of the tourist crunch, leaving ger (traditional circular felt yurt) camps teeming. September, when the leaves change colour, is visually spectacular.

ℹ Getting There & Away

A good paved road runs from Ulaanbaatar all the way to the Russian border and also west from Darkhan to Bulgan City and beyond. Darkhan, Sükhbaatar and Erdenet can all be reached by rail. If your destination is Khövsgöl Nuur, the quickest way into the area is either a flight from Ulaanbaatar to Mörön or by road via Bulgan. Main jeep tracks also run from Ulaangom and Tosontsengel in the west to Mörön, but tracks heading north from Tsetserleg in central Mongolia are more difficult to find. To travel between Selenge aimag and the east, you'll have to come back through Ulaanbaatar first, or go by horse.

ℹ Getting Around

Improvements made to the roads that travel to the Russian border, Erdenet and Bulgan make it easier to get into the region. The fun starts as you travel further west, with the usual dirt roads and rocky terrain. Trains will take you as far as Erdenet, while horses are a popular form of transport in the mountains. Although there is very little organised adventure travel, some tour companies offer mountain-biking trips in the region. A few crazies have even paddled kayaks down the Selenge Gol (Selenge River) to Sükhbaatar City!

SELENGE СЭЛЭНГЭ

POP 193,500 (INCL DARKHAN-UUL) / AREA 42,800 SQ KM

Mongolia's breadbasket, Selenge is a fertile landscape of rolling wheat fields, apple orchards and meandering rivers. Wide-scale agriculture has settled many nomads and nowadays wood cabins and trucks far outnumber gers and camel caravans. For travellers, the main reasons to visit are the majestic but remote monastery, Amarbayasgalant Khiid, and some beautiful scenery.

Darkhan is the major population centre, although the city is actually part of its own tiny aimag, Darkhan-Uul. The aimag capital, Sükhbaatar, is comparatively small, but as a border town it remains a viable part of the local economy.

In the southeast, the open-pit coal mine at Sharyngol produces approximately two million tonnes of coal each year to provide electricity for the Erdenet mine in Bulgan aimag. Selenge's biggest revenue earner is the Canadian-owned Boroo gold mine, which produces nearly 4300kg of gold per year.

The mighty Selenge Gol starts in the mountains of western Mongolia and flows into Lake Baikal in Siberia, draining nearly 300,000 sq km of land in both countries. The other great river, the Orkhon Gol, meets the Selenge Gol near Sükhbaatar.

Sükhbaatar Сүхбаатар

01362 / POP 19,700 / ELEV 626M

With its hilly backdrop, riverside location and unhurried pace of life, Sükhbaatar makes a pleasant stopover for travellers heading into or out of Russia.

If you have time, drop by the **Khutagt Ekh Datsan** temple near the town square. Unusual for a Mongolian monastery, its head lama is a woman. The other main attraction in the area is **Eej Mod** (Mother Tree), a sacred tree located 10km south of Sükhbaatar. There are actually several sacred trees in the grove; some have died while others are dying. Locals frequently come here to pray to the spirits that inhabit the trees; a rite that predates Buddhism. According to shamanic beliefs, the spirits have the power to grant wishes (on the condition that the devotee visits three times). A sign points you in the right direction as you head south on the main road; from the sign it's another 1.7km to the tree.

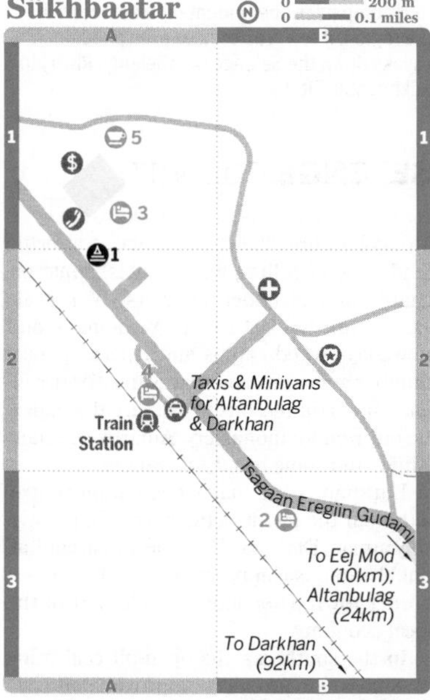

Sükhbaatar

Sights

1 Khutagt Ekh Datsan....A2

Sleeping

2 Delphin Hotel....B3
3 Kharaa Hotel....A1
4 Station Hotel....A2

Eating

5 Khairkhan Cafe....A1

Sleeping & Eating

Delphin Hotel HOTEL $$
(9929 7911, 9949 6868; Tsagaan Eregiin Gudamj; d/tr T20,000/30,000, half-luxe/luxe T50,000/120,000) This new place has bright rooms with some modern furniture. The luxe room is an over-the-top kitsch extravaganza, with gaudy furnishings, wolf pelts and Greek statuettes. The manager might be across the street in the Delphin restaurant.

Kharaa Hotel HOTEL $
(23876; s/d/luxe T8000/15,000/30,000) Close to the town square and good for budget travellers. Look for the 'Hotel Bar' sign.

Station Hotel HOTEL $
(40371; per hr T1500, s/d T10,000/12,000) Basic rooms in a building attached to the train station; travellers can take a room and pay per hour.

Khairkhan Cafe MONGOLIAN $
(22141; meals T2000-4000; 9am-10pm) Friendly restaurant near the town square. Good dumplings available.

Information

Private moneychangers appear at the station whenever a train arrives. If you are leaving Mongolia, try to get rid of all your tögrög – they are worthless anywhere in Russia (including on the Trans-Mongolian Railway in Russia). The police station is to the south of town.

The daily **market**, behind the Selenge Hotel, is lively and friendly and, as a border town, well stocked.

Internet cafe (per hr T500; 8am-10pm) Adjacent to the Telecom office.

Khan Bank (9am-7pm Mon-Fri, 10am-3pm Sat) Changes money and has an ATM. There is also an ATM at the train station.

Telecom office (Tsagaan Eregiin Gudamj; 8am-10pm) The post office is also located here.

Getting There & Away

Minivan & Taxi

The road to Ulaanbaatar (311km) through Darkhan (92km) is well paved, so jeeps are not necessary. Share vehicles to Ulaanbaatar (T20,000, six hours), Darkhan (T7000, two hours) and

Altanbulag (T2000, 20 minutes) depart from outside the train station.

Train

International trains going to/from Moscow, Irkutsk or Beijing stop at Sükhbaatar for two or more hours (usually late at night or very early in the morning) while customs and immigration are completed. See p268 and p267 for more information about international trains.

Direct, local trains travel between Ulaanbaatar and Sükhbaatar (hard seat/hard sleeper/soft sleeper T6300/11,800/18,900, about 10 hours), with a stop at Darkhan. Train 272 departs for Ulaanbaatar at 6.25am; train 264 departs Sükhbaatar at 9.05pm.

The **train station** (☎40124) sells local tickets and also tickets for Ulan Ude (T31,700), Irkutsk (T64,150) and Moscow (T229,500), but you'll need a Russian visa. The ticket office opens up an hour or two before the train leaves.

OPEN FOR BUSINESS?

Opening times mentioned in this chapter (for museums, monasteries etc) are never exact. Places open and close at the whim of the manager (or key holder) so be flexible when visiting these sites of interest.

Altanbulag Алтанбулаг

Just 24km northeast of Sükhbaatar is Altanbulag, a small, peaceful border town opposite the Russian city of Khyakhta. Both Khyakhta and Altanbulag are of some historical importance to Mongolians. In 1915 representatives from Russia, China and Mongolia met in Khyakhta to sign a treaty granting Mongolia limited autonomy. At a meeting in Khyakhta in March 1921, the Mongolian People's Party was formed by Mongolian revolutionaries in exile, and the revolutionary hero Sükhbaatar was named minister of war.

In Altanbulag, Selenge's **aimag museum** (admission T2000; ⏲10am-5pm Mon-Fri) contains lots of dusty communist propaganda and exhibits dating back to Mongolia's independence movement of 1921. Relics include some of Sükhbaatar's personal effects – his boots, gun and even his desk. The curator assured us that Sükhbaatar's office was housed in the small red building outside the museum.

Minivans run between Sükhbaatar and Altanbulag at various times during the day. If there is nothing going you could charter a taxi (T8000).

The border is located right at the edge of Altanbulag. You cannot cross the border by foot, so you'll need to hitch a ride with a local or take any public transport available. The border is open between 8am and 5pm, and you can expect delays of several hours.

Dulaankhaan Дулаанхаан

Forty-seven kilometres south of Sükhbaatar, this tiny village is worth a stop if you have your own vehicle. Dulaankhaan is home to a **bow and arrow workshop** (☎9913 1491, 9901 1924), one of only three in Mongolia. Bows and arrows are made from ibex and reindeer horn, bamboo and even fish guts. Only around 100 sets are crafted every year and each bow takes about four months to complete. A set sells for about T350,000 (bow plus four arrows). If there are no finished bows available you can order one and they will ship it overseas.

To find the workshop, cross the railroad tracks to enter the village then look for the long building next to the bank. There is no

WORTH A TRIP

DOWN ON THE RANCH

Anak Ranch (☎9983 8205, 9909 9762; www.anakranch.com) is a working ranch where guests can get their hands dirty doing farm work. You can milk cows, herd the sheep, make cheese and lasso a half-wild horse or two. There is also plenty of time to relax, enjoy a barbecue, hike and fish. Price includes everything: food, accommodation, horse riding etc... The ranch is close to the town of Orkhon, which is 11km off the main Darkhan–Sükhbaatar road. You can take a bus to Darkhan then a taxi to Orkhon (T20,000). A much slower way of reaching Orkhon is by train; from Ulaanbaatar, trains depart at 9.10pm (train 263) or 10.30am (train 271). If you contact the ranch ahead of time, someone will meet you at the station with horses.

sign but you can ask for Boldbaatar – everyone knows him.

The village is 6km west of the Sükhbaatar–Darkhan Hwy. Expect to pay about T15,000 for a taxi from Sükhbaatar. There is nowhere to stay in the village so carry on to Sükhbaatar or Darkhan, or camp nearby.

Darkhan Дархан

01372 / POP 73,500

This minor city on the Trans-Mongolian Railway has the look and feel of Ulaanbaatar c 1996. The city has a clutch of cafes and restaurants, burgeoning local commerce shops and a few modern hotels, but lacks the sprawl, traffic and congestion that afflicts the capital.

Darkhan was created by the Soviets in the 1960s as an industrial base for the north. During communism it worked as a model urban cooperative of factory workers, tractor drivers, coal miners and government officials. The economy took a nosedive in the early 1990s but is slowly picking up again, thanks to grain production and coal mining. The city is not actually part of Selenge aimag, but an autonomous municipality, Darkhan-Uul.

Darkhan is divided into an 'old town' near the train station and a 'new town' to the south. The new town contains most of the shops, restaurants, hotels and other amenities of use to the traveller.

Sights

Kharaagiin Khiid MONASTERY

(ХАРААГИЙН ХИЙД; 8am-6pm) Probably the most interesting sight in Darkhan is this monastery. Housed in a pretty log cabin in the old town, it has a host of protector deities and a tree encased in blue *khatag* (silk scarves).

Museum of Darkhan-Uul MUSEUM

(admission T2500; 9am-1pm & 2-6pm Mon-Fri) This museum contains a well-laid-out collection of archaeological findings, traditional

Darkhan

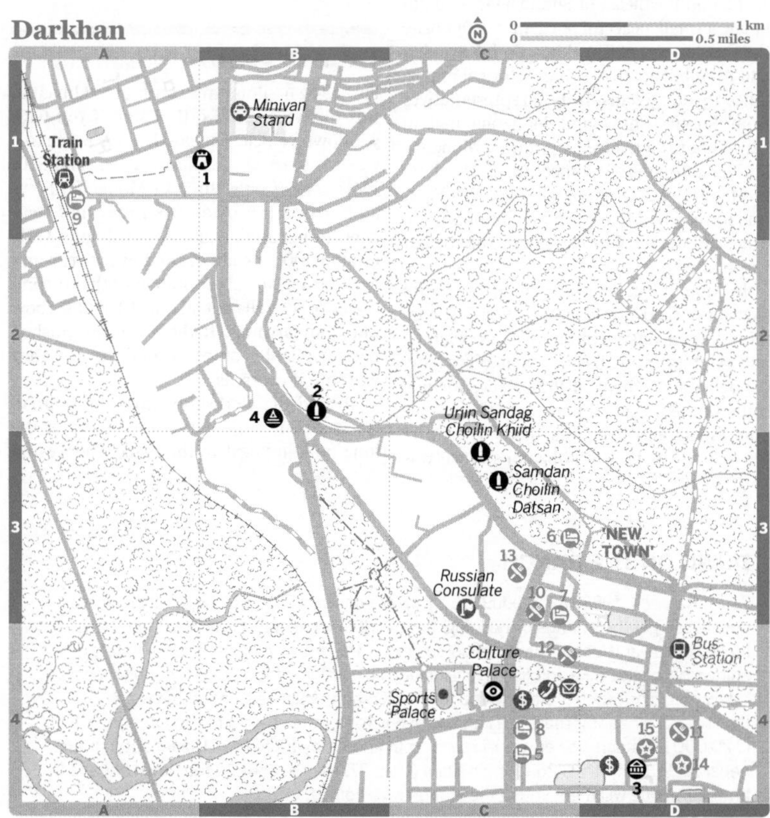

clothing, religious artefacts and a few obligatory stuffed animals. Its most valued piece is the original painting of Lenin meeting Sükhbaatar, a classic work of myth-making, painted by B Tsultem in 1953. The museum is upstairs in a building on the northern side of the shopping square, across from the minibus and taxi stand.

Morin Khuur Statue & Seated Buddha MONUMENTS
These two new monuments are across the road from each other, near the roundabout between the new and old towns. They are connected by a pedestrian bridge. Both are congregating points for locals who hang out here at sunset.

Sleeping

Despite the size of Darkhan, it isn't hard to get away from the town and find a nearby secluded camping spot. Southwest of the train station are some empty fields – but get away from the drunks who hang around the station. The fields to the north of the Darkhan Hotel are also good.

TOP CHOICE **Comfort Hotel** HOTEL $$
(☎29090; r/half-luxe/luxe incl breakfast T35,000/48,000/75,000; @) Darkhan's best hotel has spotless, well-maintained rooms with pastel shades and a cosy atmosphere. Internet is available in the rooms (if you have a laptop). It's popular so book ahead.

Kharaa Hotel HOTEL $
(☎26019; tw/half-luxe/luxe incl breakfast T20,000/27,000/35,000; @) This place has some renovated rooms with hardwood floors and new furnishings but the service is a little lacklustre. They claim to have cable internet but you need to supply your own cable. It's set back behind the Urtuchin and Comfort hotels. An egg and bread breakfast is included.

Darkhan Hotel HOTEL $
(☎20001; s/d/half-luxe T13,500/20,000/25,000, luxe incl breakfast T40,000-60,000) This Soviet-era monster has scruffy old standard rooms with attached bathroom and hot water. If you have a group, go for the renovated half-luxe rooms, a great bargain. The hotel has a restaurant, a sauna (T6000) and a fitness room.

Hotel Friends HOTEL $
(☎24142; s/d/luxe T10,000/16,000/20,000) This cheapie takes up the ground floor of an apartment block. Rooms are a little poky but its clean and friendly. It's located off the main road, hidden amid other apartment blocks.

Train station hotel HOTEL $
(☎42263; d/luxe T7000/10,000) The train station has a hotel on the top floor. To find the entrance, walk out of the station, onto the platform, turn right and look for a door at the end of the building.

Eating

Texas Pub AMERICAN $$
(meals T4000-7000; ⏰11am-midnight; 📄) A long-time Darkhan favourite, the Texas Pub has recently been renovated and sports a fresh, modern look (but still retaining its Texas theme). Burgers, fries, steaks and sandwiches are available.

Bulgogi Family KOREAN $$
(meals T4000-8000; ⏰10am-midnight) A popular Korean food place with spicy soups and tasty *bibimbab* (rice, meat, vegetables and an egg, choice of hot or cold). Pass on the extremely fatty grilled pork dish.

Sondor Cafe CAFE $
(meals T1500-4000; ⏰10am-midnight; 📄) This cute cafe and bakery serves up pizzas and pastas.

Nomin Supermarket SUPERMARKET $
Southeast of the central park in the new town, this is the best place to shop if you are self-catering.

Darkhan

Sights
1 Kharaagiin Khiid B1
2 Morin Khuur Statue B2
3 Museum of Darkhan-Uul D4
4 Seated Buddha B2

Sleeping
5 Comfort Hotel C4
6 Darkhan Hotel C3
7 Hotel Friends C3
8 Kharaa Hotel C4
9 Train Station Hotel A1

Eating
10 Bulgogi Family C3
11 Nomin Supermarket D4
12 Sondor Cafe C4
13 Texas Pub C3

Entertainment
DD Night Club .... (see 14)
14 Erdenes Plaza D4
15 Queens Night Club D4

✪ Entertainment

You'll find a cluster of discos just south of the Nomin Supermarket. The best is **DD Night Club** (⏲6pm-midnight), a surprisingly chic discotheque that would not look out of place in LA, Berlin or Hong Kong. Also popular is **Queens Night Club** (⏲6pm-midnight), just across the road. Both charge T1000 to enter. DD Night Club is located inside the **Erdenes Plaza**, which has a movie theatre, karaoke club, internet cafe and game room.

ℹ Information

Golomt Bank (⏲9am-6pm Mon-Fri, 10am-3pm Sat) It is 200m west of the taxi stand. There are also ATMs at the Erdenes Entertainment Centre, the train station and the bus station.

Internet cafe (per hr T500; ⏲24hr) At the same location as the Telecom office.

Telecom office (⏲24hr) ATM and post office are also located here. It's on the northern edge of a vast park in the middle of the new town.

ℹ Getting There & Away

Bus

Buses depart hourly between 9am and 8pm for Ulaanbaatar (T6000, 3½ hours). Two buses a day leave for Erdenet (T6000, three hours) at 11am and 5pm. For Khövsgöl (T28,000, 13 hours) buses depart on Monday, Wednesday, Friday and Sunday.

Minivan, Taxi & Jeep

Plenty of shared taxis (T12,000) and minivans (T6000) do the three-hour run to Ulaanbaatar, departing from the bus station in the new town. The station also has share taxis to Erdenet (T12,000, 2½ hours).

For Sükhbaatar (T6000, two hours), vans leave from outside the market in the new town. Roads to Ulaanbaatar (219km), Sükhbaatar (92km) and Erdenet (180km) are all paved. For Amarbayasgalant Khiid hire your own jeep or taxi at the bus stand near Kharaa Hotel. A round trip should cost about T100,000 but you'll need to bargain.

Train

Darkhan is the only train junction in Mongolia: all northern trains to/from Ulaanbaatar, and all trains to/from Erdenet, stop here.

Travelling to Ulaanbaatar (hard seat/hard sleeper/soft sleeper T5000/10,000/15,300), a daytime train (272) leaves Darkhan at 8.48am, arriving in Ulaanbaatar at 4.20pm. An overnighter (264) departs Darkhan at 11.40pm, arriving at 6.10am. Other trains leave in the middle of the night.

The daily five-hour trip between Darkhan and Erdenet (hard seat/hard sleeper/soft sleeper T4100/7700/12,000) leaves Darkhan at an ungodly 3am.

The daily Ulaanbaatar–Sükhbaatar train (271) leaves Darkhan for Sükhbaatar at 5.55pm (hard seat/hard sleeper/soft sleeper T2300/4200/6200, two hours). See p268 and p266 for details about international trains that stop at Darkhan.

ℹ Getting Around

Darkhan is spread out, so you will probably have to take a taxi or hop in a minivan (T250) that connects the new and old towns.

Amarbayasgalant Khiid
Амарбаясгалант Хийд

The star attraction of Selenge aimag, this monastery is considered to be one of the top three Buddhist institutions in Mongolia (along with Erdene Zuu in Kharkhorin and Gandan in Ulaanbaatar) and the country's most intact architectural complex. It is well worth visiting on the way to/from Khövsgöl Nuur, or other areas in northern or western Mongolia. As it's about five hours away from Ulaanbaatar on a decent road, you could also do it as an overnight trip from the capital.

Amarbayasgalant Khiid (www.amarbayasgalant.org; GPS N49° 28.648', E105° 05.122'; admission T3000) was built between 1727 and 1737 by the Manchu emperor Yongzheng, and dedicated to the great Mongolian Buddhist and sculptor Zanabazar (see p118), whose mummified body was moved here in 1779. It is in the Manchu style, down to the inscriptions, symmetrical layout and imperial colour scheme.

The monastery was largely spared during the 1937 purge, possibly because of sympathetic and procrastinating local military commanders. These days about 60 monks live in the monastery, compared with more than 2000 in 1936. The oldest monk is 102 years old.

The **temples** in the monastery are normally closed, so you'll have to ask the monks to find the keys and open them up if you want to see any statues or *thangkas* (scroll paintings). About six temples are open to tourists. The monk with the keys can usually be found in the monks' quarters, the yellow concrete buildings on the right side (south) of the monastery.

The main hall has a **life-size statue of Rinpoche Gurdava**, a lama from Inner Mongolia who lived in Tibet and Nepal before returning to Mongolia in 1992 and raising much of the money for the temple's res-

Amarbayasgalant Khiid

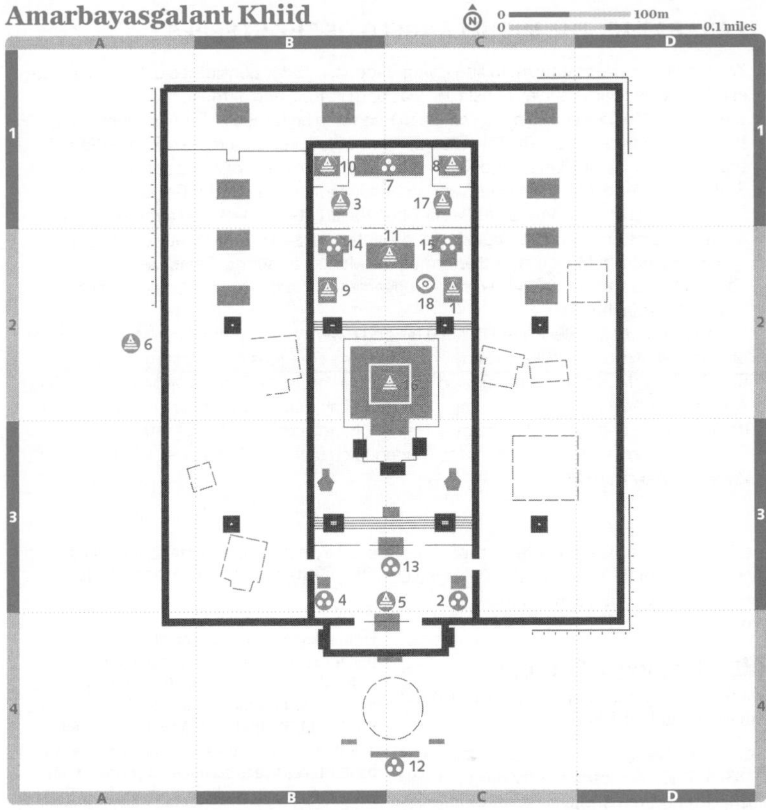

Amarbayasgalant Khiid

Sights

1 Ayush Temple ... C2
2 Bell Tower ... C3
3 Dorje Shugden Temple ... B1
4 Drum Tower ... B3
5 Entrance Temple ... C3
6 Jaryn Khashuur Stupa ... A2
7 Living Rooms of Bogd Gegeen ... C1
8 Maider (Maitreya) Temple ... C1
9 Manal Temple ... B2
10 Narkhajid Temple ... B1
11 Sakyamuni Buddha Temple ... C2
12 Screen Wall ... C4
13 Temple of Protector Gods ... C3
14 Tomb of 4th Bogd Gegeen ... B2
15 Tomb of Zanabazar ... C2
16 Tsogchin Dugan (Main Temple) ... C2
17 Yam Temple ... C1
18 Yellow Ger ... C2

toration. It's normally possible to climb up to the roof for fine views of the valley.

Ceremonies are usually held at 10am, so arrive early or stay overnight to see them.

A couple of new monuments – a large **Buddhist statue** and a **stupa** – are situated on the hills behind the monastery. You could continue hiking up the mountains for even better views of the valley.

Festivals

The most interesting time to visit Amarbayasgalant Khiid is 14 to 15 August, when the **Gongoriin Bombani Hural** (prayer ceremony) is held. As part of the rituals, the

ZANABAZAR: THE MICHELANGELO OF THE STEPPES

Zanabazar, an artist, statesman and Living Buddha, is today considered one of the greatest Renaissance artists in all of Asia. He was born in 1635 and at the tender age of three was deemed to be a possible *gegeen* (saint), so when he turned 14 he was sent to Tibet to study Buddhism under the Dalai Lama. He was also proclaimed the reincarnation of the Jonangpa line of Tibetan Buddhism and became the first Bogd Gegeen (reincarnated Buddhist leader of Mongolia). He is also known in Mongolia as Öndür Gegeen.

When he returned from his studies in Tibet, the artist-lama kick-started a Mongolian artistic renaissance. Besides sculpting and painting he also invented the *soyombo*, the national symbol of Mongolia, and reformed the Mongolian script. Zanabazar was also a political figure and his struggle with the Zungar leader Galdan led to Mongolia's submission to the Manchus in 1691.

Zanabazar died in Beijing in 1723 and his body was later entombed in a stupa in Amarbayasgalant Khiid. You will see many of Zanabazar's creations in monasteries and museums in Mongolia, and there is a fine collection of his art in the Zanabazar Museum of Fine Arts in Ulaanbaatar. You can recognise images of Zanabazar by his bald, round head, the *dorje* (thunderbolt symbol) he holds in his right hand and the bell in his left hand.

For more on Zanabazar, look for the *Guidebook to Locales Connected with the Life of Zanabazar*, by Don Croner.

locals hike up to the eight white stupas. Festival-goers usually camp in the fields near the monastery – like a Buddhist version of Woodstock.

Sleeping & Eating

There are excellent camping spots all around Amarbayasgalant Khiid.

Stupa Ger Camp TOURIST GER CAMP **$**
(☎8806 7397; per person with/without meals US$32/15) Located 300m west of the monastery, this camp has flush toilets, hot showers and a restaurant. It is operated by the monks of Amarbayasgalant so any money you spend here goes towards the continued preservation of the temples. The food is surprisingly good – the menu was designed by the owner of the Silk Road restaurant in Ulaanbaatar.

IF Tour Ger Camp TOURIST GER CAMP **$$**
(☎9918 9981; iftour@magicnet.mn; ger/r/cabin T25,000/35,000/40,000) This camp is just west of the Amarbayasgalant Ger Camp. You can choose between a ger, individual cabin or a room inside the lodge. It's clean and comfortable and stays open year-round. Horse hire can also be organised for T5000 per hour.

Getting There & Away

Hitching

The monastery is not on the way to anywhere but a couple of cars a day come here in summer so you may be able to bum a lift. The cheapest and best way from Ulaanbaatar is to catch a train to Darkhan, take a shared jeep to Khötöl, hitch (which is easy) from there to the turn-off, then hitch another ride (much more difficult) to the monastery.

Jeep

From Ulaanbaatar, travel north to the T-intersection for Erdenet (just short of Darkhan). Take the Erdenet road for 90km and then turn right onto a dirt track; look for the **sign** (GPS: N49° 12.809', E104° 59.128') that says 'Amarbayasgalant 35km'. Altogether, the journey to/from Ulaanbaatar takes five to six hours. If you don't have your own car you could charter one from Darkhan for about T100,000 (but you'll need to negotiate).

BULGAN БУЛГАН

POP 145,400 (INCL ORKHON) / AREA 49,000 SQ KM

Bulgan's lack of major tourist sights has kept it off the beaten track. Most visitors to northern Mongolia charge through the aimag en route to more popular sights such as Khövsgöl Nuur and Amarbayasgalant Khiid, but travellers with a bit of time on their hands can find some interesting, rarely visited sights in Bulgan, as well as some beautiful scenery that makes for nice cycle touring.

A small mountain range, the Bürengiin Nuruu, bisects the aimag and, though it only reaches a maximum altitude of 2058m, it provides plenty of lush habitat for wild animals and livestock. In the south of the aimag are two unique historical sights, Tsogt Taijiin Tsagaan Balgas and Khar Bukh Balgas, which are both geographically more in line with sights found in central Mongolia.

This section includes the small aimag of Orkhon, which contains the city of Erdenet. This aimag was formed in 1994 after being previously run as a federal municipality under the capital, Ulaanbaatar.

Erdenet Эрдэнэт

☎01352 / POP 73,450

In the autonomous municipality of Orkhon, and not technically part of Bulgan aimag, Erdenet is a little slice of Russia in Mongolia. The reason for Erdenet's existence is the copper mine, which employs about 8000 people and is the lifeblood of the city.

Up to one-third of the population of Erdenet was Russian during communist times, though now only about 1000 Russians still work as technical advisers at the mine. You'll hear plenty of Russian on the streets and will find restaurant menus featuring *peroshki* (meat-filled fried pastries) rather than *buuz* (steamed mutton dumplings).

Erdenet is a sprawling city, though everything you will need is along the main street, Sükhbaatar Gudamj. The train station is located more than 9km east of the centre.

Sights

Copper Mine MINE

(www.erdnetmc.mn, in Mongolian) The open-cut mine, easily seen to the north of the city, was one of the biggest infrastructure projects developed in Mongolia during the communist era. Copper and molybdenum concentrate from Erdenet still account for about 30% of Mongolia's exports.

The mine is worth a visit if you've never seen one like this before. You'll need to show your passport to the guard at the gate. No one seems to mind if you look around on your own, but it would be wise to check in at the administration building, up the hill from the guard station, on the left. A taxi to the mine and back from the town centre costs about T5000, including waiting time.

Friendship Monument MONUMENT

This communist monument, about 200m northeast of the Selenge Hotel, is worth a quick look. On the way from the town centre you pass a fine **Marx mural** and a **picture of Lenin** bolted to the wall. Head north of the Friendship Monument into the hills above town for good views of the city. After walking for around 30 minutes you'll find yourself in a lovely pine forest. In late summer the hills are thick with grass and wildflowers.

FREE **Mining Museum** MUSEUM

(☎73405, 9936 1898; ⏲9am-noon & 2-5pm Wed-Sun) This Soviet-built museum belongs to the copper-mining company, Erdenet Concern. It's pretty small and not terribly thrilling but it is free and worth a look if you're killing time. It's on the 2nd floor of the Culture Palace on the town square. If it's locked you'll need to visit the administrative offices and find the person with the key (or call ahead).

Museum of Orkhon Aimag MUSEUM

(admission T1000; ⏲9am-5pm Mon-Fri) Opened in 1983 and hidden in a concrete complex on the right side of the Marx mural, this small museum includes a few oddities including a model of the copper mine (you can see it in 'day' or 'night') and a model of a modern ger with a TV inside. Look out for the two-headed calf, which hopefully is no indication of what the mine is doing to the local water supply.

Activities

If you have some time to kill, check out the **Sports Palace** (☎73436; Sükhbaatar Gudamj; ⏲8am-8pm). You can hit the **sauna** (T3000 per hour), watch some **wrestling** or go **ice skating** in winter at the stadium at the back. There's an indoor **pool** (T3000), open weekdays only, but the staff may make life difficult by insisting on a medical examination (T2000) before they let you swim.

Sleeping

Erdenet has a reasonable selection of hotels but no guesthouse or ger camp.

Although the city is comparatively large, it is still possible to camp nearby. The best places to try are north of the Friendship Monument, or south of the stadium, over the other side of Tsagaan Chuluut Gol and among the pretty foothills. But unless you plan on staying longer in Erdenet, it's best to carry onto to either Bulgan or Amarbayasgalant Khiid, where the camping is better.

TOP CHOICE **Molor Erdene** HOTEL $$$

(☎20309; d/half-luxe/luxe incl breakfast T50,000/60,000/80,000; P@) Molor Erdene is the best hotel Erdenet has to offer. Rooms are large and comfortable, with an internet cable for laptop users (although the connection is slow). There's a decent breakfast of eggs, toast and sausage.

Selenge Hotel HOTEL $$

(☎27359; s T18,000, tw/half-luxe/luxe T24,000/30,000/32,000) This classic Soviet-style hotel has large rooms with private bathrooms. It

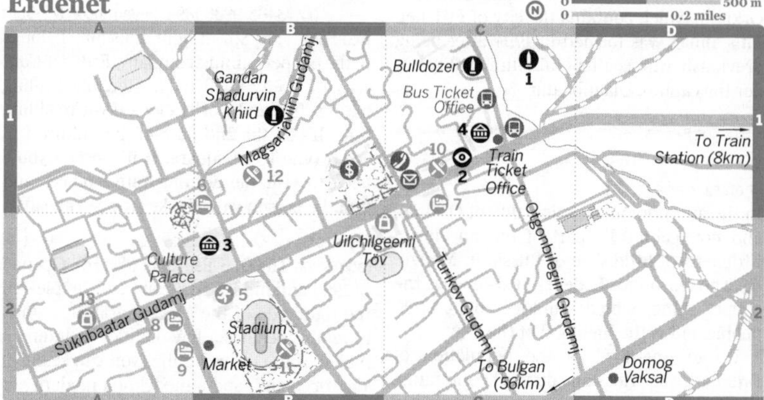

Erdenet

Sights

1	Friendship Monument	C1
2	Marx Mural	C1
3	Mining Museum	B2
4	Museum of Orhon Aimag	C1

Activities, Courses & Tours

5	Sports Palace	B2

Sleeping

6	Molor Erdene	B1
7	Selenge Hotel	C1
8	Sonor Khairkhan	A2
9	Uyanga Hotel	A2

Eating

10	Art Café	C1
11	Daily Market	B2
	Molor Erdene	(see 6)
12	Onix	B1

Entertainment

	Allegro nightclub	(see 12)

Shopping

13	Nomin Supermarket	A2

was renovated a few years ago but is already starting to fall apart in places. Still it's not a bad deal for budget travellers and the location is good. There's a sauna and a karaoke lounge, which attracts an interesting crowd of locals.

Sonor Khairkhan HOTEL $$
(☎28120; d/half-luxe/luxe incl breakfast T28,000/38,000/48,000) This place is nothing spectacular but fills a need if you are looking for a midrange hotel in the centre. Rooms are clean, there is a good hot-water supply and TV. It's near the daily market.

Uyanga Hotel HOTEL $
(☎8812 6939; r T15,000) Basic hotel, but fine for a night if you're on a tight budget. It's opposite the market.

Eating

Molor Erdene HOT POT $$
(per person around T8000; Molor Erdene Hotel; ⏲10am-midnight) Hot-pot aficionados will delight in this excellent restaurant. Order raw veggies, platters of meat and dumplings then drop all the ingredients in boiling pots to stew in front of your eyes. It's in the hotel of the same name.

Art Café CAFE $
(meals T2000-5000; ⏲10am-10pm) This orange-coated cafe and bar on the main road is good for a Mongolian meat-and-potato lunch, accompanied by a Russian soup or salad.

Onix PUB $$
(meals T3000-7000; Magsarjaviin Gudamj; ⏲9am-midnight) This new pub has flashy decor and a mix of Mongolian and Western dishes. Combine this with the Allegro Disco next door and you've got a pretty hip evening in Erdenet. The entrance is from the south side of the building.

Entertainment

Allegro Disco NIGHTCLUB
(⏲6pm-midnight) Erdenet's youth mingle here and dance to the latest Mongolian pop and rap hits. The entrance is on the south side of the building.

Shopping

Carpet Factory CARPETS
(☎20111; ⏰9am-7pm Mon-Fri, 10am-7pm Sat & Sun) If a couple of tonnes of copper is a bit inconvenient to carry around, a carpet would make a fine souvenir. The city's carpet factory produces more than a million sq metres every year using machinery from the former East Germany. The factory is open year-round but production is low in summer (June to August) when supplies of wool are scarce. If you ask the guard it may be possible to take a tour of the entire operation. Even if you can't tour the factory you'll certainly be allowed in the shop. Prices are similar to those at the Ikh Delguur in Ulaanbaatar, but the selection here is much better. Floor carpets measuring 2m by 3m start from T120,000. The factory is just off the main road to the train station, about 2km from the Friendship Monument.

Nomin Supermarket SUPERMARKET
(⏰9am-8pm) A good place to buy food or pick up supplies.

Information

Golomt Bank (⏰8am-7.30pm Mon-Fri, 9am-5.30pm Sat & Sun) Changes US dollars and euros and gives cash against Visa and MasterCard.

Internet cafe (Sükhbaatar Gudamj; per hr T500; ⏰8am-10pm) Internet access at the Telecom office.

Telecom office (cnr Sükhbaatar Gudamj & Natsagorjiin Gudamj; ⏰24hr) ATM and post office are also located here.

Getting There & Away

Travellers often bypass Erdenet and go straight from Ulaanbaatar to Mörön. Alternatively, take the sleeper train from Ulaanbaatar to Erdenet and catch a shared vehicle to Mörön. However, this can be slower because you'll have to wait a day or two for a ride to Mörön. Erdenet-to-Moron vehicles are typically jam-packed with as many people as they can hold. It's easier to get a lift from Erdenet than from Bulgan.

Bus, Minivan & Jeep

Four daily buses depart from Erdenet's bus stand to Ulaanbaatar's Dragon bus stand (T11,000, seven hours, 371km) at 10am, noon, 2pm and 4pm. Going the other way they depart Dragon at the same times. The bus stand in Erdenet is a little parking lot near the Friendship Monument, from which private vans (T11,000) and sedans (T20,000) also depart, when full.

Shared vehicles to Mörön (T25,000, 10 hours, three to four times per week), Bulgan (T4000, one hour, two or three times per day) and Tsetserleg (T20,000, seven hours, three times per week) leave from the **Domog Vaksal** (station) in the southeast part of town.

The roads from Erdenet to Darkhan (180km) and to Bulgan City (55km) are both paved.

Train

Train 273 departs Ulaanbaatar for Erdenet (via Darkhan) at 8.50pm, arriving at 8.05am (hard seat/hard sleeper/soft sleeper T6800/12,300/20,300). The sleeper is definitely worth the extra tögrög: the hard-seat carriages are packed to the roof. The train returns to Ulaanbaatar from Erdenet at 7.40pm, arriving in UB at 7.05am.

To Darkhan, train 273 (hard seat/soft seat/soft sleeper T5000/10,000/15,300, five hours) arrives at 11.55pm. For Sükhbaatar in Selenge aimag, change trains in Darkhan.

You can buy tickets at the train station, but it's better to queue on the day of, or before, departure at the **train ticket office** (☎22505; ⏰9am-noon & 2-6pm) in the northeast end of town.

Buses (T300) meet arriving trains or you can take a taxi (about T8000). Buses to the train station leave from the car park opposite the train ticket office.

Bulgan City Булган

☎01342 / POP 11,000 / ELEV 1208M

Bulgan is one of Mongolia's prettiest aimag capitals. There is a grassy pine-clad park in the middle of town and a lazy main street where you are just as likely to see a horseman as you are a passing vehicle. With Erdenet so close by, the town has never had a chance to develop much – there are only a couple of small hotels and restaurants, and very few jeeps. Despite the minimal facilities, it's not a bad place to spend a night if you are travelling between Mörön and Ulaanbaatar.

Sights

Aimag Museum MUSEUM
(☎22589; admission T2000; ⏰9am-6pm) This museum on the main street has some information on obscure sights in the aimag; a display on J Gurragchaa, Mongolia's first man in space; and some interesting old photos. The ethnography section has a few interesting exhibits, including period surgical instruments, *airag* churners and saddles.

Dashchoinkhorlon Khiid MONASTERY
(ДАШЧОЙНХОРЛОН ХИЙД; GPS N48° 47.821', E103° 30.687') Like most monasteries in Mongolia, this one (built in 1992) replaced the original

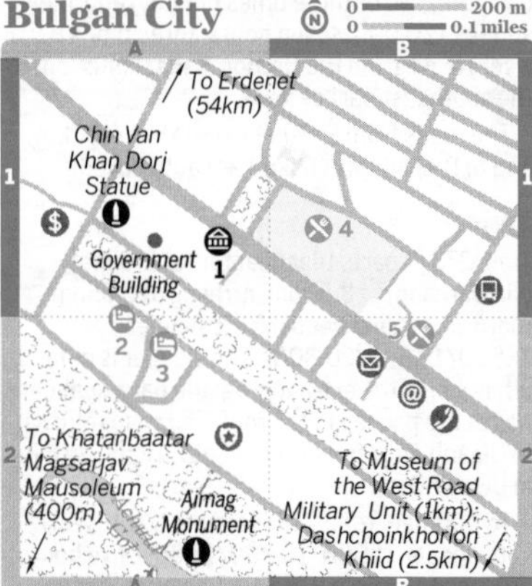

Bulgan City

Sights
1 Aimag Museum ... A1

Sleeping
2 Bulgan Hotel ... A2
3 Khantai Hotel ... A2

Eating
4 Guanz ... B1
5 Loving Hut ... B2

monastery, Bangiin Khuree, which was destroyed in 1937. About 1000 monks lived and worshipped at Bangiin Khuree before they were arrested and, presumably, executed. The remains of several stupas from the old monastery complex can be seen nearby.

The modern monastery contains statues of Tsongkhapa and Sakyamuni, and features a painting of the old monastery layout. About 30 monks now reside here. It's about 2.5km southwest of Bulgan City, hidden behind some hills. The rundown pavilion next to the temple, called Divajin, was built in 1876.

Khatanbaatar Magsarjav Mausoleum MAUSOLEUM
(ХАТАНБААТАР МАГСАРЖАВЫН БУНХАН) Located 1km southwest of the Bulgan Hotel, across the stream and at the top of a hill, this curious silver building looks like a concrete ger but is actually a mausoleum in the shape of a hat. It allegedly contains the remains of Khatanbaatar Magsarjav, a key figure in the 1911 Revolution, who helped to liberate the city of Khovd from Chinese rule. There are some murals of battle scenes inside, but to see them you'll need to get the keys from the caretaker. Ask at the Aimag Museum.

Museum of the West Road Military Unit MUSEUM
(БАРУУН ЗАМЫН ТУСГАЙ АНГИЙН ШТАФ; ☎9814 9546; admission T1000; ⏲9am-6pm) The West Road Military Unit was a key force in freeing Mongolia from White Russian rule in 1921. Its history is described in this small museum, 2.5km south of Bulgan. The building itself dates from 1668 and was used as a shop until being transformed into a military post in 1921. Choibalsan and Khatanbaatar Magsarjav both stayed here during Mongolia's military campaigns of the early 20th century. The museum contains, among other things, Choibalsan's saddle and sword. The person with the key to the museum lives in the ger next door.

Sleeping

The best place to pitch your tent is over the southern side of the river, the Achuut Gol; go past the market and find a discreet spot. If you have your own transport, consider camping a few kilometres north of town, along the road to Mörön.

TOP CHOICE **Khantai Hotel** GUESTHOUSE $
(☎22964; per person T10,000) This small B&B offers six spotless double rooms, one with a gorgeous balcony overlooking the park. The bathroom and shower are both downstairs and there is 24-hour hot water. The friendly owner sometimes offers breakfast (eggs, bread and rice milk) for an extra cost. In late summer she might add blueberries and cream to the menu.

Bulgan Hotel HOTEL $
(☎22811; tw/luxe T8000/26,000) This charmingly rundown Soviet hotel is in a peaceful location overlooking the park. With its moose on the wall, (defunct) Russian slot machines in the lobby and a billiard table upstairs, it has more character than most places in the countryside. The standard rooms are depressing but luxe rooms include cable TV and hot-water shower. The friendly granny who manages the place can usually be found in the bar next to the lobby.

Eating

Don't expect much from Bulgan's restaurant scene. There are a few hole-in-the-wall **guanze** (canteens) on the main street serving standard plates of goulash.

Loving Hut VEGETARIAN $
(meals T2000-3000; ⏲10am-8pm; ✎) For something different, try this basic vegetarian cafe located inside the All Mart department store.

Information

Bathhouse (showers T1100, sauna T2200; ⏲10am-7pm Thu-Mon) Look for the small grey brick building with a green roof.

Internet cafe (per hr T500; ⏲9am-9pm) In the same building as Telecom.

Telecom office (⏲9am-9pm) In the middle of the main drag, about 150m southeast of the jeep stand. The post office is also located here.

Xac Bank (Chin Van Khandorj Gudamj; ⏲9am-5pm Mon-Fri) Exchanges US dollars and will give a cash advance on debit cards.

Getting There & Away

At the time of research there were no flights to Bulgan and there is little prospect these will resume in the near future.

Bus, Minivan & Jeep

A bus departs Bulgan for Ulaanbaatar (T13,500, seven hours) on Tuesday, Thursday and Saturday at 8am. When there is demand, minivans and jeeps go between Bulgan and Ulaanbaatar (T20,000, six hours), but most people take a minivan to Erdenet (T4000, one hour, 55km) and then take the overnight train or a bus. One daily bus goes to Erdenet (T3000) at 4pm.

Vehicles to Mörön (or anywhere else) are very rare as these tend to leave from Erdenet. Usually on Thursday a postal truck goes to Khutag-Öndör (T10,000, three hours), but check.

There are two routes between Ulaanbaatar and Bulgan City: the rougher but more direct southern route (318km) via Dashinchilen, or the paved northern route (434km) via Darkhan and Erdenet. If you want to visit Amarbayasgalant Khiid, the northern route is the way to go.

Bulgan City is 248km from Darkhan and 353km from Mörön. The Bulgan–Mörön road was under construction at the time of research.

Hitching

Bulgan is on the main road from Erdenet to Mörön. However, most cars leaving Erdenet are already packed to the gills so they may not have room for one more. You could wait by the roadside for a vehicle to pass but it's worth checking the jeep stand to see if any drivers are looking for passengers.

Around Bulgan

There are a couple of obscure historical monuments around Bulgan. About 20km south of the city, just north of Orkhon village, are seven standing deer stones, so called because the stones are carved with reindeer and other animals. The stones, known as **Seeriyn Adigyn Bugan Khoshoo** (GPS: N48° 38.537', E103° 32.735'), mark what are thought to be Neolithic grave sites.

About 60km west of Bulgan City is the extinct volcano of **Uran Uul** (GPS: N48° 59.855', E102° 44.003') and nearby Togoo Uul, part of the 1600-hectare **Uran-Togoo Tulga Uul Nature Reserve**. It's a decent place to camp if you are headed to/from Khövsgöl aimag.

KHÖVSGÖL ХӨВСГӨЛ

POP 124,100 / AREA 101,000 SQ KM

Tourist brochures tout it as the Switzerland of Mongolia, and this is no idle boast. Khövsgöl is a land of thick forests, rushing rivers, sparkling lakes and rugged mountains. It

WORTH A TRIP

DASHINCHILEN ДАШИНЧИЛЭН

There are a couple of minor ruins in Dashinchilen *sum* (district), in the south of the aimag, which are of interest if you are travelling between Ulaanbaatar and Tsetserleg, via Ögii Nuur.

On the western side of the Tuul Gol, about 35km northeast of Dashinchilen, are the impressive ruins of **Tsogt Taijiin Tsagaan Balgas** (GPS: N48° 01.422', E104° 21.091'), a 17th-century fort that was the home of the mother of Prince Tsogt, a 17th-century poet who fought against Chinese rule. There is a **stone stele** nearby. The ruins are hard to find without a GPS so ask in Dashinchilen and keep asking at gers en route.

About 12km west of the *sum* capital, the ruined **Khar Bukh Balgas** (Khar Bakhin Fortress; GPS: N47° 53.198', E103° 53.513') is worth exploring and easy to reach as it's just a few kilometres north of the main road. The fortress, inhabited by the Kitan from 917 to 1120, is sometimes known as Kitan Balgas. A small **museum** nearby is unlocked by a caretaker when visitors arrive.

does rain a lot during summer, but this only adds to the scenery: rainbows hang over meadows dotted with white gers, grazing horses and yaks.

While the Khalkh dominate the south, there are also pockets of minority ethnic groups, including Uriankhai, Khotgoid and Darkhad people. The Tsaatan, who live in the taiga in the far north of the aimag, herd reindeer and live in tepees resembling those of Native Americans.

The main geographic feature of the province, and its major tourist draw, is enormous Khövsgöl Nuur. Most travellers fail to explore areas beyond the lake and this is a shame; the rest of the aimag has much to offer. The Darkhad valley, Chandman-Öndör and Jargalant all make fine destinations, with many opportunities for fishing, hiking and cycle touring.

Mörön Мөрөн

☎01382 / POP 36,100 / ELEV 1283M

Mörön (mu-roon) is a bustling mid-sized city and a transport hub in northern Mongolia. It slumbers quietly through the long winter but comes alive in summer when tourists pass through on their way to Khövsgöl Nuur. The market is a constant hive of activity, there's a better than average crop of hotels and restaurants, and it's one of the few places outside Ulaanbaatar to have a functioning tourist office. Some travellers never see the city, as tour operators whisk their clients from the airport directly to Khövsgöl Nuur, but it's not a bad place to be if you're waiting for a flight or bus out of town.

Sights

Aimag Museum MUSEUM

(☎9913 0344; Peace St; admission T2000; ⏰9am-6pm Mon-Fri) Given the variety of wildlife in the aimag, stuffed animals are, not surprisingly, the main feature of the museum. There's a large tusk from a woolly mammoth, but you won't see one of those in the flesh – they haven't inhabited this region for more than 40,000 years. An ethnographic room displays a shaman outfit, hunting weapons and traditional jewellery. Photographic exhibits of the Tsaatan people are also intriguing.

Danzandarjaa Khiid MONASTERY

(ДАНЗАНДАРЖАА ХИЙД) The history of this monastery is unclear, but the original (Möröngiin Khuree) was built around 1890 and was home to 2000 monks. It was rebuilt and reopened in June 1990 and now has 40 monks of all ages. It's a charming place, designed in the shape of a concrete ger, and contains a great collection of *thangka*.

Khövsgöl Park PARK

This contains a giant map of Khövsgöl aimag with each *sum* (district) represented. The map is meant to show off all the highlights of the aimag. It's somewhat slapdash in design, but it's still a fun place to wander around during summer. A large **Buddha statue**, donated by South Koreans, is located nearby.

Tours

The guesthouses listed below can help to arrange transport out of Mörön. Local English-speaking guide **Saraa** (☎9938 5577; saraa_m3@yahoo.com) can also help with logistics and travel in the area.

Sleeping

If you have a tent there are good camping spots by the river, the Delgermörön Gol. Twenty-seven kilometres east of Mörön, on the road to Bulgan City, a tiny, unmapped and unnamed lake offers good camping. If you are heading west, there are great spots on the river past Burentogtokh.

50° 100° Hotel HOTEL $$

(☎22206; d/half-luxe/luxe US$30/45/50; P) This popular hotel has a range of rooms, a good hot-water supply and friendly staff who will come outside to help with your luggage. The renovated rooms come with a modern bathroom and cable TV. Some beds are rock hard, so check this out before settling on a room. It's named after a particular geographical phenomenon in Khövsgöl, where the 50° north latitude meets 100° east longitude.

Bata Guesthouse GUESTHOUSE $

(☎9138 7080; bata_guesthouse@yahoo.com; GPS N49° 39.053', E100° 10.018'; per person incl breakfast T7000; @) This *hashaa* guesthouse (basically a fenced-in yard) is a 20-minute walk from the centre, 400m past the market. Turn right at the water pump house and walk for another 150m; it's on the left. Look out for the 'Bata Guesthouse' sign. Locals know the address as '5-8-4'. The owner, Bata, speaks English and can help arrange transport around the aimag. He also arranges homestays with nomad families and can rent you a motorbike to visit Uushigiin Uver. Laundry service and showers (T1500) are available.

Gan Oyu Guesthouse GUESTHOUSE $

(☎22349, 9938 9438; ganoyu_n@yahoo.com; Peace St; dm incl breakfast T10,000; @) This

Mörön

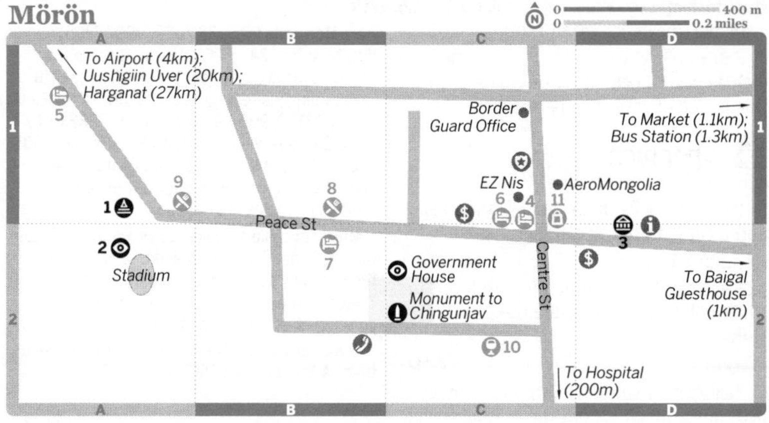

Mörön

Sights

1 Danzandarjaa Khiid A1
2 Khövsgöl Park A2
3 Museum D2

Sleeping

4 50° 100° Hotel C1
5 Altan Ulias A1
6 Gan Oyu Guesthouse C1
7 Tsetseg Hotel B2

Eating

50° 100° Hotel .... (see 4)
8 Jaragalan Café B1
9 Tes Supermarket A1

Drinking

10 Neg Ye C2

Shopping

11 Antique Souvenir House C1
Handicraft Shop .... (see 4)

good-value guesthouse has spotless dorm rooms and a hot-water shower. It is on the 2nd floor of an apartment block next to the 50° 100° Hotel. For a cheaper option, ask about its off-site ger camp, with four-bed gers for T20,000. Laundry service available.

Baigal Guesthouse GUESTHOUSE $
(☎9938 8408; baigal999mn@yahoo.com; GPS N49° 38.176', E100° 10.798'; per person incl breakfast T8000) A similar option to the Bata, about 800m past the wrestling stadium. Breakfast is toast, bread, jam and eggs (Baigal raises chickens so you can be sure the eggs are fresh). Hot showers T1000.

Tsetseg Hotel HOTEL $$
(☎5038 3007; s/d/tr T20,000/30,000/40,000) Simple, clean rooms but only doubles have attached bathrooms. Look for the white brick building northwest of the square.

Altan Ulias TOURIST GER CAMP $$
(☎22206; GPS N49° 38.483', E100° 08.618'; per person US$25) This ger camp, owned by the 50° 100° Hotel, has clean and simple rooms in the lodge or comfortable gers. The toilets and showers are also clean.

Eating & Drinking

Khairkhan Zoog VEGETARIAN $
(meals T1500-3000; 9am-9pm;) Vegetarian restaurant serving Mongolian veggie treats. Across the street from the market.

TOP CHOICE **50° 100° Hotel** RESTAURANT $$
(mains T3000-6000; 9am-midnight;) Located in the hotel of the same name, the 50° 100° serves up pizzas, lasagne, steak and some mysterious dishes like 'president enjoyed chicken'. Complete your meal with an outstanding cinnamon roll or apple pie. Vegetarians should find a soup or salad.

Neg Ye PUB $
(10am-7pm) Easily spotted, this local watering hole features two giant beer barrels outside its entrance. The local drink of choice is Kvas, a brew made from fermented rye bread. The alcohol content is so low (1%) that you'd need to drink a few gallons of the

stuff to feel any of its effects. Food is also available (meals T2000 to T5000).

Tes Supermarket SUPERMARKET
(⏲10am-8pm) Located on the main road, this is one of several supermarkets.

Shopping

Antique Souvenir House SOUVENIRS
(⏲9am-9pm) Sells maps, books, antiques and locally produced handicrafts.

Handicraft Shop HANDICRAFTS
(⏲9am-6pm) Sells handicrafts produced in Khövsgöl Aimag. It's inside the 50° 100° Hotel.

Market MARKET
(⏲9am-7pm) If you have forgotten any expedition gear, check out the market; you'll find torches (flashlights), tents, stoves, fishing equipment, bags and bike parts. Quality and variety won't be great but it will do in a pinch. Close to the market is a strip of **vehicle repair shops** that can help out if you need to fix a flat or pick up spare car parts.

Information

Border Guard office (☎24136, 24662; ⏲9am-noon & 2-6pm Mon-Fri) Can usually issue permits for border towns such as Tsagaannuur, although it's best to get them in Ulaanbaatar if you can.

Golomt Bank (⏲9am-5pm Mon-Fri) Changes cash. If it's closed you can use the Golomt Bank ATM inside the Shin Ogooj supermarket.

Internet cafe (per hr T500; ⏲9am-11pm Mon-Fri, 10am-5pm Sat & Sun) Attached to the Telecom office.

Orgil Bathhouse (per person T1500; ⏲8am-midnight) On the east side of the market, this is the newest bathhouse in town.

Telecom office (⏲24hr) Opposite the town square. The post office is also located here.

Tourist Information Centre (☎9938 6070, 9938 2050; hovsgul _info@yahoo.com; Peace Ave; ⏲10am-6pm Mon-Fri) Supplies maps and books for the region and can give some basic tips on transport and accommodation. It's in the lobby of the Aimag Museum.

Getting There & Away

Be wary of people meeting you at the airport or bus station in Mörön. Some may claim to be affiliated with one guesthouse or another, when in fact they are freelancers looking to sweep you off to their own ger camp or hostel.

Air

AeroMongolia (☎9138 7080, 9997 7705) flies here for T243,600 one way. It seems to change offices every year but was last seen in the building just east of the 50° 100° Hotel. **EZ Nis** (☎21199, 9904 9930) charges T282,000/T535,280 one way/return; its office is in the 50° 100° Hotel. Between these two airlines there should be at least one flight a day in summer. Winter schedules are cut back.

Mörön occasionally serves as a refuelling stop for flights headed further west, so you could theoretically combine a trip to the west with Khövsgöl Nuur. Check EZ Nis for details. Buy your ticket as early as possible.

Mörön airport is about 5km from the centre of town. A taxi will cost T5000.

Bus

Daily direct buses depart Mörön for Ulaanbaatar (T26,500, 18 to 22 hours), Erdenet (T25,000, 12 hours) and Darkhan (T28,000, 15 hours). They leave from the bus station (*teeveriin tovchoo*) east of the market (past the second of two MT petrol stations). They usually leave around 1pm but you need to get your ticket well in advance, especially in late summer when the buses fill up with students headed for Ulaanbaatar. Direct buses to the capital travel on the rough road via Ikh Uul, Khairkhan and Ölziit. This could change in the coming years, however, as the northern route via Bulgan is being paved and, when complete, will be the faster route.

Hitching

The Ulaanbaatar–Erdenet–Mörön road is fairly busy, so hitching a ride shouldn't be a problem. But be warned: the trip by truck between Ulaanbaatar and Mörön is a tough 27 or more nonstop hours (expect to pay at least T20,000 for a lift). Some travellers do it one way for the 'experience', and then gratefully fly back. It's best to fly here from Ulaanbaatar, as it's easier to get a seat. It's also easier to hitch *to* UB rather than *from* it, as all traffic tends to funnel back to the capital.

Minivan & Jeep

Minivans run between Mörön and Ulaanbaatar daily (T45,000, 17 hours, 671km), departing from the main bus station.

The local jeep stand to *sum* around Khövsgöl is a small lot about 250m north of the market, hidden behind a building. Vehicles leave most afternoons to Khatgal (T10,000, three hours). Vehicles to Tsagaannuur (T30,000) leave two or three times a week.

When there is demand, Bata Guesthouse organises shared jeep trips to Ulaanbaatar via Terkhiin Tsagaan Nuur.

From Mörön it is 273km to Tosontsengel in Zavkhan aimag and 353km to Bulgan City.

DEER STONES

Found across Mongolia, deer stones are ancient burial markers that date from the Bronze Age. The ancient steppe tribes believed that, after death, a soul departed this world and ascended to the sky on the backs of deer. The deer carved onto the stones are representational of this act. Many deer stones are also carved with a belt, from which hang various tools including axes and spears. These accessories would be required for successfully navigating the afterlife. Of the 700 deer stones known to exist worldwide, 500 are located in Mongolia. The best collection of deer stones is at Uushigiin Uver.

Uushigiin Uver Ушигийн Өвөр

A Bronze Age site, **Uushigiin Uver** (GPS N49° 39.316', E99° 55.708'; admission T3000) contains 14 upright carved deer stones, plus sacrificial altars *(keregsuur)*. This remarkable collection is located 20km west of Mörön, and about 1km north of the Delgermörön Gol. The area is enclosed by a fence and small placards describe the stones. The most unique, stone 14, is topped with the head of a woman; there are only a handful of such deer stones in Mongolia. The carved stones are 2500 to 4000 years old, and the nearby mountain range contains about 1400 burial tombs. A caretaker living near the area can show you around and provide commentary. Despite the uniqueness of the site, an ugly ger camp built nearby detracts from its allure. Be wary of anyone out here selling unofficial tickets to the site – the caretaker is the only source of legitimate tickets.

Perched on a ridge over the Delgermörön valley, the attractive **Harganat** (☎9903 7022; www.besudtour.com; GPS N49° 38.521', E99° 50.030'; with/without meals US$30/15) ger camp has hot showers and tasty meals. It's run by a helpful English-speaking local named Bat who can assist with tours of the area. Even if you're not staying, it's a nice place for lunch after visiting the deer stones at Uushigiin Uver. In summer, swans swim in the river below, but the real time to visit is mid-September, when more than 100 swans make their home here. It is 7km past Uushigiin Uver.

Khövsgöl Nuur National Park Хөвсгөл Нуур

Known as the Blue Pearl of Mongolia, Khövsgöl Nuur is an extraordinary lake that stretches 136km deep into the Siberian taiga. The lake and the mountains that surround it form the basis for this popular national park, a major destination for both Mongolian and international tourists.

In surface area, this is the second-largest lake (2760 sq km) in Mongolia, surpassed in size only by Uvs Nuur, a shallow, salty lake in the western part of the country. But Khövsgöl Nuur (sometimes transliterated as Hövsgöl or Hovsgol) is Mongolia's deepest lake (up to 262m deep) as well as the world's 14th-largest source of fresh water – it contains between 1% and 2% of the world's fresh water (that's 380,700 billion litres!). Geologically speaking, Khövsgöl is the younger sibling (by 23 million years) of Siberia's Lake Baikal, 195km to the northeast, and was formed by the same tectonic forces.

The lake is full of fish, such as lenok and sturgeon, and the area is home to argali sheep, ibex, bear, sable, moose and a few near-sighted wolverines. It also has more than 200 species of bird, including the Baikal teal, bar-headed goose (*kheeriin galuu* in Mongolian), black stork and Altai snowcock.

The region hosts three separate, unique peoples: Darkhad, Buriat and Tsaatan (aka Dukha). Shamanism, rather than Buddhism, is the religion of choice in these parts.

The lake water is still clean but a rise in livestock using the area for winter pasture has led to some pollution of the shore and feeder rivers, so you are better off purifying your water.

Climate

Spring (April–May) is a pleasant time to visit as it rains less than August and the flowers and birdlife are at their best. However, it will still be very cold, with snow on the ground and ice on the lake (some ice usually remains until early June).

The summer (June–August) is a little more crowded (not so crowded that it would spoil your trip), but it can still be cold, and it often rains. The meadows around the lake are sprinkled with beautiful wildflowers during this time. Autumn (September–October) is

Khövsgöl Nuur National Park

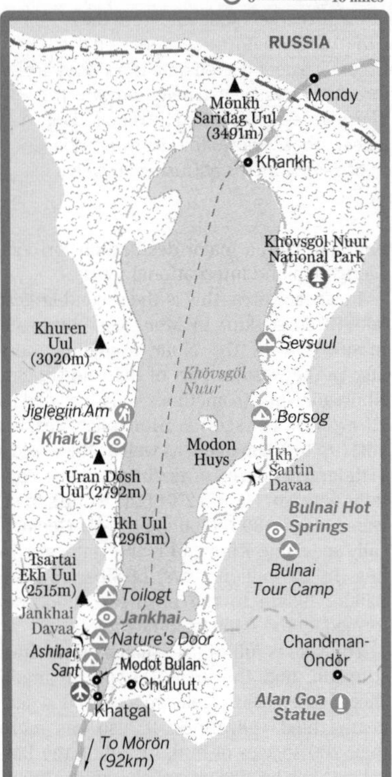

another pleasant time to visit, when the leaves are changing colour.

Winter (November–March) is bitterly cold, though blue skies are the norm. Khövsgöl Nuur freezes to a depth of 120cm, allowing passenger trucks to cross the length of the lake in winter. Oil trucks once made this journey in vast numbers but this practice was stopped in 1990 when it was determined that they were polluting the water. About 40 trucks have fallen through the ice over the years.

Sights

KHATGAL ХАТГАЛ

As the southern gateway to Khövsgöl Nuur, Khatgal is the largest town on the lake. With some of the best budget accommodation in Mongolia, it is a good launching pad for the lake and most people spend at least a day here preparing for, or relaxing after, a trip. The town is actually on the arm of the lake that funnels into the Egiin Gol, so you don't get much of an idea of the lake's size from here.

Khatgal used to be a busy depot for trucks headed to and from Russia, but the town's economy is now based mainly on tourism.

There are easy **walks** up the lakeshore or, for an easier view of the lake, just climb the hill immediately north of Nature's Door camp (p132). You can also check out the **Mogoi Mod** (Snake Tree; GPS N50° 27.080', E100° 07.274'), 4km from town, past the airport, towards Jankhai Davaa (Jankhai Pass). This tree, which curves into a unique spiral, is honoured with *hadak* (ritual scarves).

WESTERN SHORE

From Khatgal, a reasonable road first heads southwest before swinging northeast across several dry riverbeds and over the pass, Jankhai Davaa, 17km from Khatgal, where you receive your first magical glimpse of the lake. The road continues past the gorgeous headlands of **Jankhai**, once a Russian scientist station, and **Toilogt** (GPS: N50° 39.266', E100° 14.961'), pronounced 'toy-logt' but routinely mispronounced 'toilet' by most travellers, where there is a rash of ger camps. The road then gradually deteriorates.

About 30km north of Toilogt is **Khar Us** (GPS: N50° 56.132', E100° 14.835'), a series of springs surrounded by meadows of beautiful wildflowers. In June locals flock here to eat the bailius fish for its medicinal properties (these fish are smoked and served with wild green onions, or sometimes boiled). This makes a great destination to reach on horseback – four days from Khatgal.

A jeep can travel about 10km past Toilogt, after which the trail becomes overgrown and is best managed on horseback for the trip up to **Jiglegiin Am** (GPS: N51° 00.406', E100° 16.003'), almost exactly halfway up the western shore. From Jiglegiin Am you could take the western trail to Renchinlkhumbe, on the way to Tsagaannuur. For that trip, see p130.

If you need a ride up the western shore, contact **Ganbaa** (☎9838 9755), a local driver who makes a daily run up to Jankhai for T5000 per person.

EASTERN SHORE

The eastern shore is less mountainous than the west, but offers spectacular views across Khövsgöl Nuur. It gets far fewer visitors than the western shore, making it a great destination for travellers seeking an off-the-beaten-path experience. The main drawback to this side of the lake is the appalling road that heads up to Khankh. Expect mud, rocks, roots and the odd collapsed bridge.

From Khatgal, head for the bridge over the Egiin Gol. The trail meanders over some hills and continues past an interesting *ovoo* (shamanistic collection of stones, wood or other offerings to the gods) at the pass **Ikh Santin Davaa** (GPS: N50° 52.622', E100° 41.185') to a gorgeous spot called **Borsog** (GPS: N50° 59.677', E100° 42.983'), six hours by jeep and 103km from Khatgal.

If your spine hasn't suffered permanent damage, you could carry on further to a couple of gers known as **Sevsuul**. The road actually improves a little here, then hugs the lake and is usually passable all the way to Khankh.

From Khatgal, allow at least 12 hours by jeep to travel about 200km to **Khankh** (Turt), a former depot for oil tankers headed to and from Siberia. Khankh is more Buriat and Russian than Mongolian because most visitors are Russian holidaymakers from Irkutsk.

Remember that if you reach Khankh, you will have to come *all* the way back along the same bone-crunching eastern road: there is no way any vehicle can get from Khankh down the western shore. At the moment going all the way around the lake is only possible by boat or horse. The nearby border crossing with Russia is closed to third country nationals.

Activities

Fishing

If you love fishing, then you'll get excited about Khövsgöl Nuur. If you don't have fishing gear already, you can buy some at the shops in Khatgal (Buren Khaan shop has the best selection).

Around a dozen species of fish inhabit the lake, including grayling, omol, Siberian roach, perch and lenok. A fishing permit costs T10,000 and is valid for three days or 10 fish, whichever comes first. You can get them from Khatgal's Government House. Fishing is not allowed between 15 April and 15 June. The fine for fishing illegally is US$40 (or jail, depending on the mood of the ranger).

Hiking

This is one of the best ways to see the lake and the mountains surrounding it. You will need to be self-sufficient, although there are a few gers in the area from which to buy some meat or dairy products. The trails around the lake are easy to follow.

Of the mountains in the southwestern region, the most accessible is Tsartai Ekh Uul (2515m), immediately west of Jankhai, where the hiking is excellent. Also try the numerous other mountains in the mountain range of Khoridol Saridag Nuruu, such as Khuren Uul (3020m), not far north of the trail to Renchinlkhumbe; Ikh Uul (2961m), a little northwest of Toilogt; and the extinct volcano of Uran Dösh Uul (2792m).

Longer treks are possible around the Ikh Sayani Nuruu range, which has many peaks over 3000m. It is right on the border of Russia, so be careful not to accidentally cross it or you may be shot at by border guards.

Horse Riding

The only place to organise a horse trek around the lake is in Khatgal. The guesthouses here can arrange everything within 24 hours. Prices are negotiable but reasonable at about T8000 to T10,000 per horse per day, and about T15,000 to T20,000 per day for a guide. Ger camps along the lake can organise horse hire for day trips.

A guide is recommended for horse-riding trips in the region and, in fact, park regulations stipulate that foreigners should have one local guide for every four tourists. Guides will expect you to provide food while on the trail.

A complete circuit of the lake on horseback will take from 10 to 15 days. A return trip by horse from Khatgal to Tsagaannuur, and a visit to the Tsaatan, will take 15 to 20 days. An interesting two-week trip could take you east of the lake to Chandman-Öndör and Dayan Derkhiin Agui, a sacred cave. A trip to the Bulnai hot springs would take eight to nine days. You'll definitely need a guide.

Shorter trips include one to Toilogt, through the mountainous Khoridol Saridag Nuruu Strictly Protected Area, or up to Khar Us and back in five or six days.

Kayaking & Boating

The lake is full of glorious coves, perfect for kayaking, and you could even check out **Modon Huys**, an island almost exactly in the middle of the lake. Nomadic Expeditions (p54) in Ulaanbaatar runs kayaking trips in the region. Garage 24 and MS Guesthouse (p131) rent kayaks for about T35,000 per day.

Garage 24 has a Zodiac boat and can run travellers up to its camp and beyond to the island and the northern reaches of the lake. MS Guesthouse also has a motor boat. Ask about the two-day boat trip to Jiglegiin Am (T450,000 for up to five people, including meals).

TREKKING FROM KHÖVSGÖL TO DARKHAD

One of the most adventurous treks in Mongolia, done by either horse or foot, begins in Khatgal, goes up the western shore of the lake and over the Jiglegiin Davaa (Jiglegiin Pass) to Renchinlkhumbe.

From Khatgal to Jiglegiin Am, about halfway up the western shore of Khövsgöl Nuur, will take five days (four hours' riding each day). You start to feel the isolation after Ongolog Gol (the end of the jeep road), from where it's a 10-hour journey to Khar Us. There are endless camping spots along this route.

From Khar Us it's just three hours to Jiglegiin Am, where you can find accommodation in a cabin (T2000) and get a cooked meal (T1000) – it's best to have exact change. The jeep trail that heads up to Jiglegiin Davaa (2500m) is very muddy even after a long dry spell – this is where a pair of Russian NBC overboots will come in handy. Expect to get to the pass in around three hours.

From the pass it's a gentle walk down to the Arsayn Gol, which you'll need to cross at least twice. There are also some side streams to cross. These crossings are usually OK but if it's been raining hard you can be stuck for hours or even days. In dry spells the river can disappear completely so you need to fill up with water whenever possible.

After a seven-hour walk from the pass you should be at Ooliin Gol (25km west of Jiglegiin Am), where there are some camping spots. It's then another seven hours to Renchinlkhumbe. When you reach the broad expanse of the Darkhad, make a beeline south for the town.

The final three hours of the trek are often marred by horrific swarms of flies and mosquitoes – a sanity-saving measure is to wrap your head with a towel or T-shirt. The bugs seem to disappear when you've reached the village.

From Renchinlkhumbe it's another two-day trek to Tsagaannuur, from where you can organise a trip to the Tsaatan camps. Alternatively, return to Khatgal via the old Russian logging route that runs through the mountains. If you don't intend to go to Tsagaannuur, you could skip Renchinlkhumbe and take a shortcut back to Khatgal. This involves following the Arsayn Gol around 35km upstream, eventually picking up the logging route.

This route involves moderate trekking in good weather. However, the area is prone to heavy rain and flash flooding that can stop you in your tracks. Hikers and horse riders are frequently made to wait on river banks (sometimes for several days) until water levels drop low enough for them to cross. Bring wet-weather gear, warm clothes and preferably a guide to get you across. If you don't have a guide, at least bring a good map, such as the *Lake Khövsgöl National Park Satellite Map* (Conservation Ink). Contact MS Guesthouse in Khatgal for further details on this trek.

Several large boats remain moored at the Khatgal docks, including the *Sükhbaatar*, a passenger ferry. In summer (July to mid-August) the *Sükhbaatar* has daily two-hour boat trips up the lake shore, usually departing at 11am and 3pm and costing T9000. The captain usually won't leave unless he has around 50 paying passengers.

Occasionally, a group will charter a boat for the trip up to Khankh. Ask around the Khatgal guesthouses for possible departures.

Festivals & Events

The **Khatgal Ice Festival**, held on 28 February, includes ice fishing, cross-country skiing, ice skating and horse-sledding competitions. Khatgal's **naadam** (traditional sports festival) is held on 11 July. A second naadam on 11 August is sponsored by MS Guesthouse; profits from the event go towards ecoprojects in the area.

In mid-summer the **Sunrise to Sunset Ultra-marathon** is held further up the lakeshore. Mongolian and international runners compete in 42km or 100km divisions; for more info and dates, check the website: www.ultramongolia.org.

Sleeping

KHATGAL

If you have a tent you can camp along the shores of the Egiin Gol, either in town or in the beautiful valleys further south.

At the beginning of the season the main ger camps in town set a standard price in order to avoid a price war. The price might shift during the season but it will probably be the same no matter which camp you go to. At time of research the price was T10,000 per person for a ger and T3000 for camping.

The exception is the smaller guest gers (small family-run operations with just one or two gers) that may try to undercut the coalition of larger camps. These are cheaper but offer basic facilities and limited services.

MS Guesthouse TOURIST GER CAMP **$**
(☎9979 6030; lake_hovsgol@yahoo.com; @) This camp, in the extreme south of town, is the first collection of gers you see when you arrive in town. Perhaps the most congenial of ger camps around Khatgal; the staff makes visitors feel at home, with communal meals and activities. Owner Ganbaa is very knowledgeable about hiking and horse-trekking routes in the area. The camp has hot showers, clean pit toilets and a lodge where you can order meals (T1200). This place is open all year, and may be your only option in winter.

Garage 24 LODGE **$**
(☎9908 0416, 9314 2878; www.4thworldadventure.com) This environmentally conscious backpacker hang-out is built from a reclaimed Soviet-era truck garage. The cosy lodge, warmed by a fireplace, feels like an old English country home. It has bunk beds and a dining area where you can get the best food in northern Mongolia. Mountain bikes, kayaks, horses and camping gear are available for hire (although some equipment may be at the Jankhai camp). The staff is friendly but little English is spoken. Garage 24 is in the north of town, at the base of the hill, not far from the storage drums of the petrol station.

Bonda Lake TOURIST GER CAMP **$**
(☎9860 7649; mongoliantrips@yahoo.com) This long-time Khatgal camp is located on the main road heading north, just past the shops. It has four-bed gers and one ger with a double bed. The hot showers work well and the English-speaking owner has kayaks for rent. Ask for Bayara.

Khövsgöl Inn LODGE **$**
(☎9911 5929, 9906 5929; klm@boojum.com) Beds at this simple lodge are available in dorms and private rooms. It's usually pretty quiet unless a group books it out. It's affiliated with the Saridag Inn at Renchinlkhumbe and the Jigleg Camp on the lake so you can get info here if you are headed that way. It's about 200m behind the MS Guesthouse. Contact Uka.

Sunway GUESTHOUSE **$**
(☎9975 3824, 9838 9990; horsetrek_khuvsgul@yahoo.com) Small guesthouse, with a wood ger and a felt ger, on the northwestern side of town below the hills. The owner, Esee, is an experienced trekking guide.

MODOT BULAN

This area extends due north of Khatgal, up the Egiin Gol mouth for about 6km. Most people miss it because the road up the coast bypasses this section. If you're exploring the lake by foot, you can walk here and continue up the shore, which is blissfully ger-camp-free for another 7km. The road is short but rough.

Ashihai TOURIST GER CAMP **$$$**
(☎011-315 459, 9968 5185; www.ashihai.mn; per person with/without meals US$59/30) This camp nearly qualifies as a work of art. Beautifully decorated gers are embroidered with traditional patterns and the interior contains exquisitely carved furniture. Gers are elevated onto wood platforms and offer lake views. The camp has a fine location on a spit of land overlooking the lake and the bay.

Sant Ger Camp GER CAMP **$**
(☎9304 3797; 4-bed ger T35,000) After crossing the small hill beyond Khatgal, this is the first camp you'll encounter. Built in 2010, it has gers, small wooden cabins, hot showers and a sauna.

Khövsgöl Dalai TOURIST GER CAMP **$**
(☎011-7011 0045, www.huvsguldalai.mn; 4-bed ger T35,000) Solid, no-frills ger camp, with a dining hall and sauna.

WESTERN & EASTERN SHORES

You'll find designated campsites, marked by yellow signs with a triangle, near the Nature's Door camp, just past Jankhai camp, and two in the bay between Jankhai and Toilogt. Away from these areas you can pretty much pitch your tent anywhere you want, though try to stay 100m from other gers.

The best camping spots on the western shoreline are anywhere between Jankhai and Ongolog Nuur, 10km north of Toilogt. If you have your own jeep and want to experience one of the worst roads in Mongolia, the best spot to camp on the eastern shoreline is at Borsog.

There are several ger camps in stunning locations on the western shore (but only one or two on the east). Nearly all have electricity, running water, flush toilets and showers. Most will offer a lower price if you bring and cook your own food. The majority open in mid-June and close around the end of August or early September.

Several families from Khatgal have opened 'ger hotels' (*ger buudal*) along the lake shore, charging visitors around T5000. These usually include one or two guest gers but no bathroom facilities. The ger hotels have become controversial in the community as the operations are not eco-friendly. Park rangers meet stiff resistance when trying to move them out of the park.

If you are looking for an eco-conscious ger camp, the best ones are Nature's Door and Toilogt.

The main group of camps start where the road meets the lake, after descending from Jankhai Davaa.

TOP CHOICE **Nature's Door** TOURIST GER CAMP **$$**
(☎9908 0416, 9314 2878; per person with/without meals US$40/20) This popular backpacker hang-out has plush cabins, a lodge and excellent Western food options. Most people stay in the gers but the flashy cabins are also an option. Camping (US$3) allows you access to the hot-water showers. As an eco-conscious camp, Nature's Door gets high marks for composting and recycling. The staff speaks English and the food is some of the best you'll get on the lake. Nature's Door is associated with Garage 24 in Khatgal; it's about 5km northeast of Jankhai Davaa.

Toilogt TOURIST GER CAMP **$$$**
(☎011-460 368; www.hovsgoltravel.com; per person with/without meals US$45/25) Run by the Hovsgol Travel Company, this eco-conscious camp is 5km north of Jankhai, and off the main road to the right. Facilities here are of high standard and the camp offers bikes, boats and horses for hire. Concerts are occasionally organised for guests. The camp has a boat that can transfer you here from Khatgal but you'll need to give advance notice to the Ulaanbaatar office.

Khuvsgol Sor TOURIST GER CAMP **$$**
(☎9919 0330, 9811 4601; khuvsgul_travel@yahoo.com; per person with/without meals US$30/15) This is the first camp after the pass (Jankhai Davaa). Unlike many others on this part of the lake, this one is hidden in the trees and off the main road, providing some sense of isolation. Quality cabins and bathrooms available.

Jigleg Camp LODGE **$**
(dm T5000) Serves as a handy pit stop for trekkers on their way to Renchinlkhumbe (it's right at the Jigleg trail head). The camp is 90km north of Khatgal. Book through Khövsgöl Inn in Khatgal.

KHANKH

Northern Gate Ger Guesthouse GUESTHOUSE **$**
(☎9979 6030; per person T15,000) Operated by the people from MS Guesthouse in Khatgal. It's just outside the town (within walking distance) but can be hard to find. Call for direction, or ask a local.

Last Frontier TOURIST GER CAMP **$$**
(☎8808 9141; www.sayan-radian.ru; GPS N51° 30.566', E100° 39.296'; per person with 3 meals US$40) A second option in Khankh if Northern Gate is full.

Eating

There are a few basic shops in Khatgal selling things such as beer, soft drinks, chocolate bars and a limited selection of vegetables. If possible, stock up in Mörön or Ulaanbaatar. The following places are all in Khatgal.

Garage 24 WESTERN **$$**
(☎9908 0416, 9314 2878; meals T5000-10,000;) Garage 24 has a Western-oriented menu that will come as a welcome break after a few days of hard trekking in the wilderness. The English breakfast includes bacon, toast, beans and sausage. Lunch and dinner menu items include shepherd's pie and pizza. Give some advance warning as preparations take around an hour.

MS Guesthouse MONGOLIAN **$$**
(☎9979 6030; meals T3500-7000;) MS is another nice place to eat and will occasionally prepare *khorkhog* (mutton dish cooked using hot stones) and authentic Mongolian barbecue for guests and visitors.

Flower MONGOLIAN **$**
(meals T900; ⏲9am-10pm) Amid the row of downtown shops and *guanz*. This one serves soups and large portions of *tsuivan* (flat noodles) among other dishes.

Information

On the main road, 12km before Khatgal, you'll be required to pay an **entrance fee** (per person foreigners/Mongolians T3000/300) at a gate to the national park. If there's no one there you can buy permits at the information centre or from the ranger, who patrols the lakeside on horseback. With your permit you should receive a useful visitors' pamphlet explaining the permits and how to limit your impact on the lake. Hang onto the ticket as you may be asked to show it more than once.

Information Centre (Мэдээллийн Төв; ⌚9am-8pm) Located near the MS Guesthouse in Khatgal. It has some interesting, museum-style displays on the lake but the staff speak only Mongolian and has very little practical information on touring the area. If it's locked look for the caretaker in a ger around the back.

Internet cafe (per hr T1500; ⌚8am-10pm) Located in Khatgal, on the main road, just south of the shops. It's pretty basic, just a computer hooked up to a mobile phone.

Khan Bank (⌚9am-1pm & 2-5pm Mon-Fri) Changes cash. The closest guaranteed ATM is in Mörön.

Telecom office (☎01382-26513/36; ⌚8am-11pm) The post office is also located here.

 Getting There & Away

Air

At the time of research there were no flights to either Khatgal or Khankh.

Hitching

For lifts from Mörön, hang around the market or the petrol station – and keep asking. In Khatgal, most trucks will stop in front of the post office.

From Khatgal, hitching a ride to Jankhai or Toilogt shouldn't be difficult in the summer, but you'll probably end up paying a fair bit. Ask the guests at the camps for a lift. You should be self-sufficient with camping gear and food.

Hitching around the eastern shore is much more difficult; you could wait for days for a lift.

Jeep

Minivans and jeeps regularly make the trip between Mörön and Khatgal (three hours) for T7000 per person or T70,000 for the jeep. Enquire at the stand at the northern end of the market in Mörön.

Transport also meets the Ulaanbaatar flight at Mörön airport to take passengers directly to Khatgal. Some jeep owners try to charge foreigners up to US$50 for the run; local drivers with the 'ХӨА' licence plate are likely to be fairer. Contact Bata Guesthouse in Mörön for transport to Khatgal.

A chartered jeep should not cost more than the normal T450 per kilometre. There are plenty of jeeps in Mörön but few in Khatgal, where it is best to ask at the guesthouses. Khatgal is 101km from Mörön over a raised gravel road.

Chandman-Öndör

Чандмань-Өндөр

Nestled between pine-clad mountains and consisting almost entirely of log cabins, the village of Chandman-Öndör comes straight from the pages of a Brothers Grimm fairy tale. The surrounding area is one of wide meadows, alpine forests and wildflowers, making it a good trip for hardy travellers.

The town **museum** (admission T500) shows off local history. More interesting is the **Alan Goa Museum** (admission T500), housed inside the ger-shaped log cabin. Alan Goa was an ancestor of Chinggis Khaan and revered locally.

Every three years (August 2012, 2015) a large **naadam** is held here to honour Alan Goa. It attracts Mongols from Inner Mongolia, Kalmyks, Tuvans and Buriats as well as a host of Khalkh Mongols.

The only place to stay in town is **Alan Goa Töv** (per person T6000), a fenced-off grassy area in the centre of town where some gers are set up in summer. Ask for Oyunchimeg.

Oyunchimeg can play the *shanz,* a sort of python-skin banjo, and will give lessons for a small fee.

Around 11km from town on the road to Mörön is a painted **statue of Alan Goa** (GPS: N50° 24.994', E100° 58.548'). About 5km west of the statue on the main road to Tsagaan-Uur is a **deer stone**.

Shared jeeps going to Chandman-Öndör (T11,000) occasionally leave from the northern side of the market in Mörön. From Khatgal you need your own jeep. The 85km ride is very rough and takes five to six hours. It's muddy in places and the chances of getting bogged are pretty high (the worst bit is in a valley around 48km out of Khatgal). Don't attempt it after heavy rain.

In the rainy season, the best way here is by horse; the trek from Khatgal takes four to five days. The route is spectacular, the lone drawback being swarms of flies in the boggy areas on the second day of the trek.

Around Chandman-Öndör

Chandman-Öndör is the jumping-off point for several sites, including the **Bulnai hot springs** (Булнайн Рашаан; per person T5000), about 60km northwest of town. This Soviet-era resort has wood cabins over the springs, some of which reach 48°C. The **Bulnai Tour Camp** (per person T30,000) near the springs has log cabins with four beds, plus a restaurant.

Heading east of Chandman-Öndör, the road follows the Arig Gol. After 41km you'll pass a row of 13 **shamanic tepees** (GPS: N50° 30.727', E101° 17.478') made from sticks. These represent the 12 years according to the Asian calendar, plus one central *ovoo*. After another 13km you'll spot a **sacred tree** honoured with blue silk scarves. The town of Tsagaan-Uur, reached after another 5km, has shops and *guanze*. The bridge east of town washed away in 2006 and the river crossing is now a bit dicey. About 15km east of Tsagaan-Uur you'll spot another large wood ovoo.

Around 38km past Tsagaan-Uur (and 97km past Chandman-Öndör) is the Dayan Derkh Monastery (GPS: N50° 26.804', E101° 53.328'), set on a beautiful bend of the Uur Gol. The log cabin temple, rebuilt in 2006 over the remains of an older monastery, is home to seven lamas. Another 15km east of the temple is the Dayan Derkhiin Agui (Даян Дэрхийн Агуй), a cave considered holy by local Buddhists and shamanists. According to legend, the monastery was founded after the famed shaman Dayan Derkh turned to stone rather than be captured by Chinggis Khaan, whose wife the shaman had stolen. In winter you could reach the cave by vehicle, in summer the only way is by horse (a six-hour return journey). Herders in the area may be able to rent you a horse for T5000. In theory you need a border permit for Tsagaan-Uur and Dayan Derkhiin Agui, although there is rarely anyone around to check.

The road from Dayan Derkh Monastery to Erdenebulgan requires two difficult river crossings. A tractor might be available to haul you across (ask at the monastery), but you'll need to pay around T55,000 for this service (the crossings are 20km apart so the tractor needs to follow you).

About 26km downstream from the monastery is the confluence of the Eg and Uur Gols. Head west at the Eg and after about 35km you'll reach the town of Erdenebulgan, which offers basic food and lodging.

Alternatively, continue down the Eg-Uur Gol, a rough and remote journey into northern Bulgan aimag.

In the northeast of the aimag, the area around the Khökh, Arig and Kheven Gols is particularly good for **camping** and **hiking** enthusiasts.

Darkhad Depression
Дархадын Хөндий

About 50km west of Khövsgöl Nuur, behind a wall of mountains, sits a harsh but mystical landscape of prairie, forest and 300-odd lakes scattered over a wide plain called the Darkhad Depression. The depression is roughly the same size as Khövsgöl Nuur and was also originally formed as a glacial lake.

The difficulty in reaching the region ensures the unique Tsaatan people, who are among the inhabitants of the valleys (see p135), are able to continue their traditional lifestyle – but tourism is rapidly making an impact. The area is also one of Mongolia's strongest centres of shamanism.

This is one of the best-watered regions in Mongolia and the lakes are full of white carp and trout. Salmon and huge taimen can also be found here.

One definite drawback to visiting the region is the insects that invade the area in summer. Be warned: these little critters have insatiable appetites for foreign skin and will ruin your trip if you are not fully prepared with mosquito nets and repellent.

RENCHINLKHUMBE РЭНЧИНЛХҮМБЭ

Renchinlkhumbe is 42km west of the Jiglegiin Am trailhead on Khövsgöl Nuur, an adventurous two-day journey on foot or horseback. Most travellers heading further into the taiga will rest here for at least one night.

A nice time to visit the town is in mid-June when it hosts the **Blue Valley Awards Festival**, a great time to see traditional horse games and singing competitions.

Renchinlkhumbe hosts an excellent local **naadam** (11 July) complete with 'barrel racing' (horse racing around barrels) and mounted archery events, along with the usual wrestling, horse racing and standing archery.

The local ger camp, Saridag Inn (☎9526 0401; GPS N51° 06.852', E099° 40.135'; camping/r/ger per person T5000/8000/10,000) is run by Khövsgöl Lodge Company. Its hot-water showers and sit-down toilets are legendary. Contact Mishig.

TSAGAANNUUR ЦАГААННУУР

About 40km beyond Renchinlkhumbe is Tsagaannuur, the last stop before the Tsaatan encampments in the taiga.

Tsagaannuur occasionally puts on a **Reindeer Festival** in summer, which includes reindeer polo, reindeer racing, arts and crafts, and a big bonfire. However, bringing the reindeer down to this elevation (1535m) is definitely not good for their health, and the festival has become somewhat controversial within the community.

The TCVC (Tsaatan Community & Visitors Centre) offers guesthouse accommodation (dm incl breakfast T10,000) at its new facility in Tsagaannuur. Tsaatan work at the guesthouse and the money you spend will go directly back to the community.

THE REINDEER HERDERS

Not far from Khövsgöl Nuur live the Tsaatan (literally 'Reindeer People'). Their entire existence is based around their herds of reindeer, which provide milk, skins for clothes, antlers for carving and medicine, transport and, occasionally, meat.

The Tsaatan are part of the Tuvan ethnic group, which inhabits the Tuvan Republic of Russia. There are only about 500 Tsaatan in total (250 live in taiga), spread over 100,000 sq km of northern Mongolian taiga landscape. They are truly nomadic, often moving their small encampments *(ail)* every two or three weeks, looking for special types of grass and lichen loved by the reindeer (of which there are over 1200). The Tsaatan do not use gers, but prefer *orts*, similar to Native American tepees, traditionally made from birch bark but now from store-bought canvas. The Tsaatan are strong practitioners of shamanism.

Visiting the Tsaatan is difficult and exhausting. The climate is exceedingly harsh, the area is prone to insects, the terrain is rough and mountainous, and it's easy to get lost without a good local guide. Plan to be self-sufficient with a quality sleeping bag, food and waterproof tents.

Irresponsible tourism, research and evangelical activities have put the Tsaatan culture and their reindeer at risk. Tourist dollars have already lured Tsaatan members down to Khövsgöl Nuur, an inhospitable elevation for their sensitive reindeer. If you go, use the Tsaatan Community & Visitors Centre (TCVC), a legitimate source of income for their community.

If you are intent on making the trip, read up about permits (p135).

There are other guesthouses in town run by locals; these include **Ganbaa's Guesthouse** (☎9954 3317) and **Erdene Guesthouse** (☎9950 8657). Prices change each season but you should expect to pay around T7000 per person for bed and breakfast. Local guesthouses will try to sell you a horse trip to visit the Tsaatan, most likely undercutting the prices at the TCVC.

Food and cooking fuel is scarce in the taiga, usually with just enough for the Tsaatan families. The Tsaatan tell horror stories of travellers coming to the taiga empty-handed and noshing on their meagre supplies for a few days. Proper preparation includes bringing all the food and fuel you need from Tsagaannuur or (even better) Mörön.

A **bathhouse** (per person T1500) is located 100m west of the school.

Information

To visit Tsagaannuur (and probably Renchinlkhumbe) you will need a **border permit**. As there are few English speakers in Tsagaannuur, it's recommended that you bring an English-speaking guide who can help smooth out any permit issues. Some travellers have obtained permits from border guards in Mörön, but this option could change so it's best to get permits in Ulaanbaatar. It's strongly advised that you also register in Mörön.

Border permits are free and are processed in one to three working days. Delays are common, so apply as early as possible. You'll need a map of where you intend to travel, passport copies and ideally a letter of support from a Mongolian organisation of some sort. In a pinch, guesthouses can arrange the permit in Khatgal through their Mörön contacts. This involves handing over your passport for a few days (which many travellers are unwilling to do).

Check the TCVC website (www. visittaiga.org) for possible updates.

Tsaatan Community & Visitors Center (TCVC; ☎9552 3972, 9552 3973; www.visittaiga.org) in Tsagaannuur provides background info on the Tsaatan and important tips on travel in the area. It can organise guides, horses and other logistics for trips to the taiga. It's a good idea to contact the TCVC a few days before your visit to give them a head start on organising guides and horses. The TCVC cannot help in organising your border permit.

Getting There & Away

AIR Tsagaannuur has an airstrip but it hasn't been used in about 20 years.

HITCHING Since all traffic to Tsagaannuur starts from Mörön there isn't much point getting on the road and trying to hitch. You'll be much better off hanging around in Mörön and asking around for a ride from there. Vehicles that do leave Mörön will be packed to the gills so you'll need to wait in town anyway to secure a seat.

HORSE There is really only one way to get to the taiga: by horse. Horses can be hired in Tsagaannuur and this is best done through the TCVC. Some travellers make the journey all the way from Khatgal – a return trip from Khatgal to Tsagaannuur, with a visit to the Tsaatan, will take from 15 to 20 days. You could go from Khatgal to Tsagaannuur on an easy trail in about five days (bypassing Jiglegiin Am), but you would miss Khövsgöl Nuur. If you do come from Khatgal, it's best to leave your horses and guide in Tsagaannuur and switch to fresh horses and a Tsaatan guide, provided by the TCVC, because the terrain becomes very boggy after Tsagaannuur and is extremely hard on horses that have already made the trip up from the lake. Horse hire in Tsagaannuur starts from T15,000 per day.

JEEP By chartered jeep you can get to Tsagaannuur from Mörön (but rarely from Khatgal) in a bone-crunching 10 to 12 hours, depending on the state of the road. You'll have to pay for all the petrol and pay the driver about US$60 a day. Contact the guesthouses in Mörön and ask if they can set you up with a vehicle, or arrange one through a UB tour operator. Two or three times a week a van will come up here from Mörön – a seat will cost T30,000 to T50,000. Ask at the jeep stand in Mörön.

AROUND TSAGAANNUUR

The Tsaatan live in two groups, known as the east *(zuun)* and west *(baruun)* taiga (this is a little confusing as the west taiga is actually southwest of the east taiga). From Tsagaannuur, it can take four to 12 hours to reach either the west or east taiga by horse (the camps move but are usually closer in the early summer or late autumn). There are several **tepee hotels** (per person T8000) in both taigas; these are operated by the Tsaatan themselves. The east taiga is 20km north of the Shishged Gol, which is crossed by **ferry**. You can even put a car on the ferry for a charge of T7000.

Once you are in the taiga, you'll need your own tent, camping supplies and 100% DEET to keep the bugs at bay. The TCVC offers meal kits that you can bring to the taiga to be cooked by the Tsaatan families. Once you've left Tsagaannuur, figure on spending around US$45 to US$50 a day for horses, guides, accommodation and meals.

Plenty of tour operators run trips in the region. A specialist in the area is Dino de Toffol, whose Italian company **Lupo World Trekking** (www.world-trekking.com) brings small groups into the area and contributes some of the profits back into the community.

Mörön to Terkhiin Tsagaan Nuur

A popular route out of Khövsgöl is south to Terkhiin Tsagaan Nuur in Arkhangai aimag. This is also an excellent road for cyclists. About 97km southwest of the aimag capital is **Zuun Nuur** (GPS: N49° 03.727', E99° 31.096'), a large lake and the scenic highlight of the region. There is good camping here or

TCVC

If you are planning a trip to the taiga, one great way to get there is with the Tsaatan themselves. The Tsaatan Community & Visitors Centre (TCVC), based in Tsagaannuur, can help organise your trip, has guides, rents horses and offers information about the location of the Tsaatan camps. The centre is fully owned and operated by the Tsaatan and works to both help travellers as well as give the Tsaatan a chance to control tourism to their community.

The concept of the TCVC began in the mid-2000s after years of unregulated tourism to the Tsaatan camps. While tour operators in Ulaanbaatar (as well as guesthouses in Khatgal and Tsagaannuur) were financially benefiting from running trips to the taiga, the Tsaatan themselves were often left empty-handed, despite being the main attraction to the area. The TCVC is the Tsaatan's response to the problem. By using the TCVC to organise your trip to the taiga, it's guaranteed that the money you spend goes directly to the Tsaatan. The system is new and not yet perfected so ask for a receipt when you pay for your trip to make sure your money goes into their bank account.

A portion of the money you spend (around 60% to 80%) will go directly to the guide, cook or homestay owner. The remaining cash goes into a community fund for small loans, scholarships and environmental protection. In its first year the fund accumulated T18 million (around US$15,000).

If you are heading this way with a tour operator from Ulaanbaatar (or elsewhere), it's still possible to use the TCVC; just request that your tour operator use the TCVC during the Tsagaannuur leg of your journey. Boojum Expeditions (p264) and Panoramic Journeys (p264) both have a well-established relationship with the TCVC. Among the guesthouses in Ulaanbaatar, Idre's (p58) has also worked closely with the TCVC.

WINDHORSE – PORTABLE GER CAMP

The unique Windhorse Ger Camp (mongoliawindhorse@gmail.com; per person incl 3 meals from US$90) is an upscale bush camp located in the Darkhad valley. The fact that it's portable (like a traditional Mongolian *ail*) means that there's no concrete or permanent structures that can scar the landscape, making this camp about as eco-friendly as you can find.

Although basic in concept, the camp offers first-rate services; it includes a dining ger, a shower ger and a bathroom tent with chemical toilets. Solar panels provide a limited energy source. Gourmet cuisine and quality wine can be ordered. Horses with Western saddles are available to ride and the camp can organise pack trips into the taiga to visit the Tsaatan or across the Saridag mountains to Lake Khövsgöl.

We cannot place the camp under one regional heading because the location is not fixed. In 2010 Windhorse was based about 35km north of Ulaan Uul Soum, but the location can change from year to year depending on the whims of its owner. To confirm its location you'll need to email ahead for directions. Reservations are required.

you can stay at the Zuun Nuur Ger Camp (☏9907 5445; GPS N49° 02.870', E99° 29.359'; per person US$10), on the southern side of the lake (meals T4000 to T7000). The lake is 13km north of Shine-Ider village.

Around 30km south of Shine-Ider, right on the main road, is an area of standing stones and graves (GPS: N48° 45.808', E99° 23.084'). A further 8km brings you to a scenic pass and the historic Gelenkhuugiin Suvraga (GPS: N48° 41.182', E99° 22.650'), an old stupa built in 1890 by local hero Khainzan Gelenkhuu (1870–1937), who leapt off a 200m cliff with a set of sheepskin wings and flew as if he were some kind of Icarus-incarnate. From the pass it's an easy 19km to Jargalant.

Jargalant is a pretty town near the confluence of the Ider and Khonjil Gols. The *sum* is perhaps most famous for being homeland of a herder named Öndöör Gongor (Tall Gongor, 1879–1931), who was 2.57m tall (you can see pictures of him in the local museum).

The museum (☏5038 8118; admission T500; ⏲8am-7pm) in Jargalant contains old photos, stuffed animals and religious objects. Two of the rooms are not lit, so bring a torch (flashlight). It's run by a local elder named Shagdarsuren who will proudly show off some of his wood craft and demonstrate the use of hand-powered drills and other tools. The other attraction in town is Jargalantiin Dugan (also called Dashbijeliin Süm), an old monastery that dates back to 1890. It's rundown and boarded up but you could still have a look around.

The best place to stay in Jargalant is the Jargal Jiguur (☏011-450 093; admin@ajnewtour.mn; GPS N48° 33.615', E99° 22.061'; per person US$15), a ger camp 3km south of town (meals US$6 to $8; shower US$2). The highlight of the camp is a mineral spring pool (you can see the natural pool across the river; just follow the pipes).

A cheaper option is Wild Nature Guest Ger (☏9550 5617; GPS N48° 33.989', E99° 21.984'; per ger T15,000, shower US$2), between Jargal Jiguur and the town. The guest ger is run by a friendly local lady named Batchimeg; she will bring you delicious fresh cream and berries in the morning.

From Jargalant it's another 80km to Terkhiin Tsagaan Nuur. About 6km south of town are several **burial mounds**, including one with a tree growing from it. Some 26km south of Jargalant there is a small ger hotel (GPS: N48° 33.989', E99° 21.984') and, on the hill behind it, a **Buddhist temple** constructed in 2001 to replace an older temple on the same spot. About 46km from Jargalant is Orokhiin Davaa (GPS: N48° 17.484', E99° 23.130'), the final pass on the way to Terkhiin Tsagaan Nuur. There is a delicious cold water **spring** by the road on the north side of the pass.

Eastern Mongolia

POP 200,100 / AREA 287,500 SQ KM

Includes »

Best Places to Eat

» Oasis (p142)
» Bolor Centre (p149)
» Winners Pub (p149)

Best Places to Stay

» Titem (p148)
» East Palace (p148)
» Dorjsuren's Homestay (p145)

Why Go?

Eastern Mongolia is where heaven and earth fuse into one part – a blank slate of blue sky colliding with an equally empty sea of yellow grass. The occasional wooden shack or ger reminds you that humans do inhabit this enormous landscape, but for the most part it's an unspoilt amphitheatre of bounding gazelle, scurrying marmots and jeep tracks that squiggle endlessly into the distance. Biologists tout the region as one of the world's last great unharmed grassland ecosystems – imagine the scenery from *Dances with Wolves*. The discovery of oil threatens to bring change, however, so get here before the prairie disappears. Besides the grasslands, the major feature of the region is the Khan Khentii Mountains. This was the homeland of Temujin, the embattled boy who grew up to become Chinggis Khaan. Travelling by horseback or jeep, there are many opportunities to visit places associated with the world's greatest conqueror.

When to Go

Choibalsan

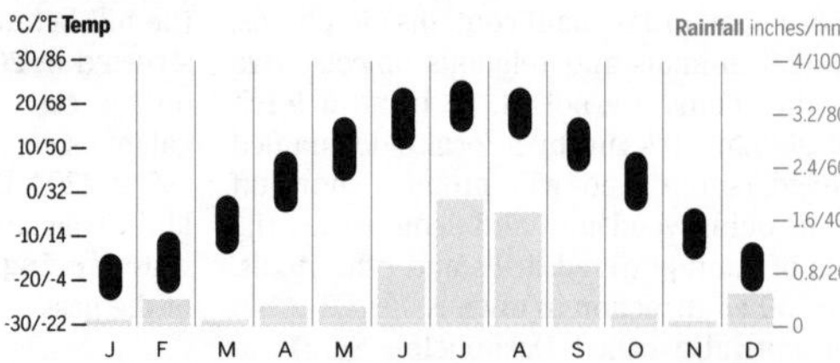

Mid-July Naadam festival held in many towns and villages.

September Autumn brings a riot of oranges and yellows to the Khentii Mountains.

Late September to mid-October Thousands of migratory swans descend on Ganga Nuur.

Eastern Mongolia Highlights

1 Spend a few days around **Dadal** (p144), a pretty village of log cabins and Chinggis Khaan legends

2 Hire sturdy horses and set off on an expedition to **Burkhan Khalduun** (p144), the hill sacred to Chinggis Khaan

3 Restore your soul with a sunrise ascent of sacred **Shiliin Bogd Uul** (p154)

4 Tour the area around **Dariganga** (p153), rich in cultural relics and eerie volcanic landscapes

5 Travel across the empty steppes to the war memorials at **Khalkhiin Gol** (Khalkhiin River; p150)

6 Seek moose, otter and bear at the biologically unique **Nömrög Strictly Protected Area** (p146)

7 Photograph majestic gazelle bounding across the steppes in **Dornod Mongol Strictly Protected Area** (p146)

History

The Tamtsagbulag Neolithic site in Dornod, active more than 4000 years ago, is proof that agriculture predated nomadic pastoralism on the eastern steppes. But it was the Kitan, a Manchurian tribal confederation, who made the first big impression on the region, building forts and farming communities in the 10th century, including Kherlen Bar Khot in Dornod.

Another Manchu tribe, the Jurchen, deposed the Kitan in the early 12th century, renamed itself the Jin, and returned eastern Mongolia to its warring ways. It wasn't until Chinggis Khaan united the fractured clans in 1206 that peace took over.

It was from Avarga (modern Delgerkhaan) that Chinggis launched expeditions south towards China. When the capital was moved to Karakorum in 1220, the region withdrew into obscurity. It wasn't until 1939 that eastern Mongolia was again in the headlines, this time as a battlefield between Japanese and Soviet forces. Heavy losses forced the Japanese military machine south, a crucial turning point in WWII.

The discovery of zinc and oil in the region in the 1990s brought the promise of development. Uranium is also found in the northeast. These natural resources have altered the local landscape, with oil wells and other mining infrastructure now dotting parts of Dornod. More development is planned as the government hopes to connect Sainshand and Choibalsan by rail, largely to facilitate the transfer of coal from the Gobi to Russia.

Climate

Eastern Mongolia's climate and landscape have more in common with northeastern China than with Central Asia. Temperature extremes are less severe and winds less violent than in the west. While the Khan Khentii Mountains get a lot of rain in the summer, annual precipitation on the steppes is around 250mm. Winter daytime temperatures fall to -20°C but skies are usually blue.

Getting There & Away

A paved road between Ulaanbaatar (UB) and Öndörkhaan is complete, allowing for a relatively hassle-free entry into the region. Decent dirt roads connect other areas, although the far north can get boggy after heavy rains.

Buses for Öndörkhaan, Baruun-Urt and Choibalsan depart from Ulaanbaatar's Bayanzurkh bus station. Private vehicles wait at the Naran Tuul jeep station. Another route into the region is through northern Khentii – daily minivans from Naran Tuul travel to Dadal via Ömnödelger and Binder (these are not well advertised so you may need a local to help you contact the drivers).

Getting Around

Public transport can get you to some places of interest, including Dadal and Dariganga. But if you want to maximise your time and see what the region really has to offer you'll need your own vehicle, preferably hired in Ulaanbaatar. A GPS will come in handy when trying to find some remote sites mentioned in this chapter. The best way to explore northern Khentii, including the Khan Khentii Strictly Protected Area, is on horseback – both Batshireet and Dadal are great places to launch an expedition. The train that connects Choibalsan and Chuluunkhoroot is something of an adventure, but useless for serious exploration.

KHENTII ХЭНТИЙ

POP 71,500 / AREA 82,000 SQ KM

Khentii is Chinggis Khaan territory. The great man grew up here, established his empire on its grasslands and, from Delgerkhaan, launched his military machine to the heart of Asia. As a nomad empire, the Mongols left few physical reminders of their existence, but with a jeep, a copy of *The Secret History of the Mongols* and a GPS unit you could launch your own expedition to scour the land for clues to their past. So far researchers have identified more than 50 historical sites relating to Chinggis Khaan's life.

The aimag is named for the Khentii Nuruu (Khentii Mountain Range), which covers the northwestern corner of the aimag and is part of the giant 1.2-million-hectare Khan Khentii Strictly Protected Area. The forests provide a home for wildlife and you stand a good chance of seeing deer and elk. The lush scenery, however, can make jeep travel arduous business – vehicles get bogged and in some areas the best way forward is on the back of a horse.

National Parks

Khan Khentii Strictly Protected Area (1.2 million hectares) Mostly in Töv aimag, the strictly protected area includes the northwest corner of Khentii, protecting taiga, steppe and the sacred mountain Burkhan Khalduun.

Onon-Balj National Park (415,752 hectares) Protects taiga and steppe along the Mongolia-Russia border. It's divided into two parts; part A is west of Dadal and part B covers the area to the northeast.

Öndörkhaan Өндөрхаан

☎01562 / POP 15,200 / ELEV 1027M

With tree-lined streets, scattered Chinggis Khaan monuments and a small collection of well-preserved 18th-century buildings, Öndörkhaan (High King) is an intriguing aimag capital. The surrounding area is barren steppe, but the Kherlen Gol flows through the southern part of Öndörkhaan, providing a fishing hole for locals and riverside campsites for tourists. Most of the residents live in wooden buildings, so gers are relatively few.

Öndörkhaan is a useful pit stop on the way to the sights in Dornod or Sükhbaatar, but you don't need to come here if you're exploring northern Khentii. The most interesting route to Dadal is not from the aimag capital but along the back roads from Tsenkhermandal.

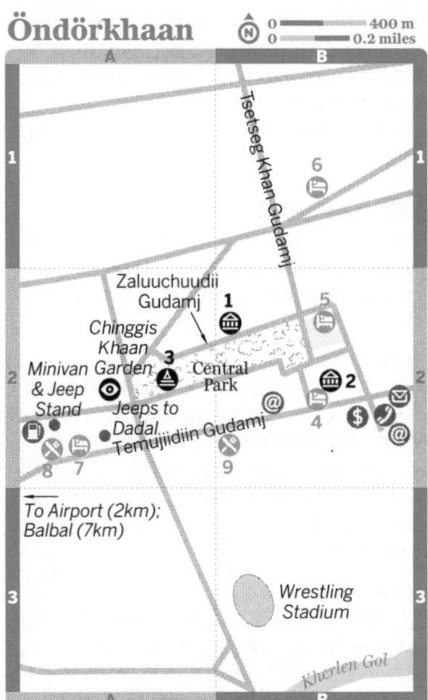

Öndörkhaan

Sights

1	Aimag Museum	B2
2	Ethnography Museum	B2
3	Shadavdarjaliin Khiid	A2

Sleeping

4	Erdes Hotel	B2
5	Jargalan Hotel	B2
6	Khuvchin Jonon	B1
7	Negdelchin Hotel	A2

Eating

8	Nature Pub	A2
	Negdelchin Hotel	(see 7)
9	Oasis	B2

Sights

Ethnography Museum MUSEUM

(admission T1500, camera T5000; 9am-1pm & 2-6pm Tue-Sat) The Ethnography Museum, next to the City Hall, is housed inside the 18th-century home of the Tsetseg Khaan, a Mongolian prince who governed most of eastern Mongolia during the Manchu reign. One building holds a portrait of the last Tsetseg Khaan, painted in 1923. Other buildings contain ethnic costumes, Mongolian toys and religious artefacts. The last building, in the corner of the compound, houses 13th-century weaponry including arrowheads and daggers. Also, look out for the ceremonial ger with delicately carved wood furnishing and ornaments. The curator will unlock each building for you.

Aimag Museum MUSEUM

(admission T1000; 9am-1pm & 2-6pm Tue-Sat) The small Aimag Museum, north of the park, contains a mastodon tusk, a Protoceratops skull, some Chinggis Khaan–era armour and the usual array of stuffed animals, including a saluting bear.

Shadavdarjaliin Khiid MONASTERY

Shadavdarjaliin Khiid, in the western part of town near the Sports Palace, is a lively place with 15 monks. The original monastery in this area was built in 1660 and housed the first Buddhist philosophy school in Mongolia. At its peak the monastery was home to more than 1000 monks. In the spring of 1938 the Stalinist purge reached Khentii and the monks were all arrested. The buildings remained standing until the 1950s, when they were torn down.

Balbal HISTORIC MONUMENT

(GPS: N47° 16.722', E110° 36.098') A well-preserved Turkic-era *balbal* (stone figure be a Turkic grave marker) is 7km west of Öndörkhaan, past the airport. The squat-figured statue, covered in blue silk *hadak* (ritual scarves), has a disproportionately large head with pronounced eyebrows and deep-set eyes. His long hair is curled behind his ears, an unusual feature for this type of statue. Locals refer to the statue as 'Gelen', a religious title.

Sleeping

If you want to camp, head south past the wrestling stadium, and walk along the Kherlen Gol to the west until you've found a quiet spot.

Negdelchin Hotel HOTEL $$
(☎22333; d T20,000-30,000, luxe T45,000) The recently renovated Negdelchin sports some of the best rooms in town. The cheaper doubles are small and do not have an attached bathroom. Try a luxe room for a little more space. There is a decent Chinese restaurant downstairs.

Khuvchin Jonon HOTEL $
(☎23845, 9956 2222; r per person T6000, half-luxe/luxe T18,000/22,000) About 350m north of Government House, this 17-room hotel is newish but already starting to deteriorate. Still, it's a decent budget offering although only the luxe rooms have private showers.

Erdes Hotel HOTEL $$
(☎23007; dm US$10, half-luxe per person US$18-20, luxe US$30) This overpriced Soviet dinosaur has scruffy rooms with shared bath but a nice location in the centre of town. Consider splashing out for the better half-luxe room with private bath. It's on the main road, 150m west of the Telecom office.

Eating & Drinking

Oasis CAFE $
(Temujiidiin Gudamj; meals T2500-5000; ⏰10.30am-8.30pm; 📋) Adding a little diversity to the restaurant scene in Öndörkhaan, this small cafe serves tacos, pizzas, pastas, shakes and burgers, plus some Korean dishes. It's on the 2nd floor of a building, between the Modern Bar and an internet cafe.

Negdelchin CHINESE $$
(Temujiidiin Gudamj; meals T4000-7000; ⏰8.30am-10.30pm) In the hotel of the same name, this place serves tasty Chinese dishes in a clean atmosphere.

Information

Internet cafe (per hr T500; ⏰10am-10pm) This private internet cafe keeps long hours on weekends.

Telecom internet cafe (per hr T500; ⏰9am-10pm Mon-Fri, 10am-6pm Sat & Sun) In the Telecom office.

Telecom office (⏰24hr) On the eastern end of the main road; the post office is also located here.

Xac Bank (⏰9am-5pm Mon-Fri) Changes dollars and offers cash advances on Visa. There is also an ATM in the Erdes Hotel.

Getting There & Away

Air

There are no flights to Öndörkhaan.

Bus, Minivan & Jeep

A daily bus heads to Ulaanbaatar (T10,000) at 8am. There is a daily bus to Choibalsan and another to Baruun-Urt but both originate in Ulaanbaatar so they will most likely be full by the time they arrive (and there is no way to book ahead). Both buses pass through between 1pm and 2pm – there may be seats available or the driver might let you sit in the aisle on a plastic stool. Wait for the buses at the Hangard petrol station near the minivan stand.

Daily taxis and minivans go between Ulaanbaatar and Öndörkhaan (taxis T15,000, vans T10,000, five hours, 331km). Very few (if any) private vehicles take passengers further east – your best bet is to wait for the bus.

Postal trucks run to Dadal (T12,400) on Monday and Thursday, to Binder (T8300) on Tuesday and Thursday, and to Batshireet (T9300) on Monday and Thursday; they usually leave in the early morning. Finding a jeep to hire can be difficult; it's best to bring your own jeep and driver from Ulaanbaatar.

Hitching

Öndörkhaan is the gateway for eastern Mongolia, so all vehicles heading to Dornod aimag and Sükhbaatar aimag will come through here. Getting a lift to Ulaanbaatar, Choibalsan and Baruun-Urt is comparatively easy. Most drivers will expect some form of payment.

Delgerkhaan Дэлгэрхаан

Locals, and some historians, claim that Avarga, not Karakorum, was the first capital of the Mongol empire. The ancient tent-city was located on a 20km-wide plain, Khödöö Aral (Countryside Island), so named because it is encircled by the Kherlen and Tsenkheriin Gols. The area is in modern-day Delgerkhaan *sum* (district).

Because the city was composed of gers rather than buildings, there are no historical ruins left to look at. Instead, the main sight is a relatively new **Chinggis Statue** (GPS: N47° 06.157', E109° 09.356'), 13km south of Delgerkhaan village. It was built in 1990 under the sponsorship of Unesco, to commemorate the 750th anniversary of the writing of *The Secret History of the Mongols*. The symbols on the side of the statue are the brands used by about 300 different clans in the area for marking their livestock.

One kilometre east of the statue is the **Avarga Toson Mineral Spring**, from which Ögedei Khaan drank and was cured of a serious stomach ailment. The spring is covered by an *ovoo* (a shamanistic collection of stones), but you can fill your water bottles at a pump house near the site.

To reach the area, travel on the paved road to Jargaltkhaan, then travel 42km southwest on a decent dirt road to Delgerkhaan.

Khökh Nuur Хөх Нуур

According to *The Secret History of the Mongols,* it was at **Khökh Nuur** (Blue Lake; GPS: N48° 01.150', E108° 56.450') that Temujin first proclaimed himself a *khaan* (emperor) of the Mongol tribe. It's a great place for a coronation site; a beautiful lake at the foot of what is called **Heart-Shaped Mountain**.

The lake is about 35km northwest of Tsenkhermandal (which is just north of the Ulaanbaatar–Öndörkhaan road). As you approach the lake a caretaker from the nearby ger camp demands a fee of T1000, claiming it's a protected area (it's not). The only other drawback is the flies that invade the place in midsummer.

You'll need your own transport and a driver who knows where it is. Someone from nearby Tsenkhermandal might take you there by jeep or motorcycle. The area is sometimes labelled Khar Zurkhen (Black Heart) on maps, which refers to a mountain behind the lake.

The **Khökh Nuur Ger Camp** (☎9911 2825; www.khukhnuurtours.com; per person incl 3 meals US$30) has popped up right by the lake; it's the only place to stay in the area although you can camp pretty much anywhere (campers can use the hot shower for T3500).

A further 49km away is the larger lake of **Khangil Nuur** (GPS: N48° 08.619', E109° 22.132'). It's a fine place to camp or break for lunch.

Baldan Bereeven Khiid
Балдан Бэрээвэн Хийд

This **monastery** (GPS: N48° 11.910', E109° 25.840'; admission T2000) in Ömnödelger *sum* was first built in 1700. At its peak it was one of the three largest monasteries in Mongolia and home to 5000 lamas. Communist thugs destroyed it in the 1930s. Now only ruins remain, but impressive ruins they are. Near the monastery is the **Eej (Mother) Cave**, which acts a purifying place for anyone who passes through it. A *manach* (watchman) will ask for T2000 to visit the site.

The road to the monastery heads north from Khangil Nuur and goes straight over the hills; it is about 9km. A flatter but more circuitous route goes northeast from Khangil Nuur. The area is perfect for camping but the closest place to stay is the **Bayangol Ger Camp** (☎011-451 016, 9918 3067; GPS: N46° 09.621', E105° 45.590'; with/without food US$30/15), 15km to the west.

About 17km past the monastery, on the way to Binder, are two **deer stones** (GPS: N48° 11.916', E109° 35.712'), which served as burial markers during the Bronze and Iron ages.

Öglögchiin Kherem
Өглөгчийн Хэрэм

Literally 'Almsgivers Wall', but also known as 'Chinggis Khaan's Castle' or 'Red Rock', this 3.2km-long **stone wall** (GPS: N48° 24.443', E110° 11.812'), believed to date from the 8th century, stretches around a rocky slope in Batshireet *sum*. It was once thought to be a defensive work or a game preserve, but recent archaeological digs by a Mongolian-American research team have identified at least 60 ancient graves within the walls, indicating that it may have been a royal cemetery. As you walk inside the grounds you may see small red signs, marking the location of graves excavated in 2002. The site is 8km west of the road to Batshireet.

Öglögch Wall Ecolodge (☎11-354 662, 9860 4175; www.tourmongolia.com; per person with/without 3 meals US$40/20) is about 2km before the wall. This well-run place can organise a variety of trips in the area, including mountain-bike rides, rafting and horse riding. The camp makes a concerted effort to limit its environmental impact; it also promotes local income-generating projects.

Close to the turn-off to Öglögchiin Kherem is **Rashaan Khad** (GPS: N48° 22.766', E110° 17.950'), a huge rock with 20 different types of (barely discernable) script carved upon it. About 2km past the turn-off towards Binder are more **deer stones** (GPS: N48° 25.098', E110° 17.825').

Binder & Batshireet
Биндэр & Батширээт

At the confluence of the Khurkh and Onon Gols, the village of **Binder** is a good place to rest on your way to or from Dadal. There are a couple of cafes, a **ger camp** (with 3 meals US$20) 7km from the village and a small **Chinggis Khaan monument** 2km east of the village. If you are travelling onto Dadal you'll need to cross the Onon Gol, just north of town. When the river is high a local named **Mishka** (☎9890 7076, G-Mobile network only) will offer to tow your jeep across for T10,000 with a tractor. Everyone in town knows him.

Batshireet, 45km northwest, is worth the detour for some excellent **camping**, **fishing** and **horse-riding** opportunities. From this small Buriat community of 3000 people you can follow the Eg Gol to the Onon and trek back to Binder. More challenging trails lead west towards the Khan Khentii Strictly Protected Area and Burkhan Khalduun. Note that if you head up the Eg River you'll enter a protected area (US$3 admission).

The town has a couple of basic hotels, including **Altan Endert** (per person T10,000) located near the Telecom office. It can arrange horses for T5000 per day. There is fine camping in Batshireet; the best spots are 7km north of town on the Onon Gol.

Because it's near Russia, you'll need a permit for Batshireet from the Border Protection Office in Ulaanbaatar. Expect a visit from the police, who will want to see your permit, original passport and trekking route.

Burkhan Khalduun
Бурхан Халдуун

Remote **Burkhan Khaldun** (God's Hill; GPS: N48° 45.728', E109° 00.629'), elevation 2350m, is one of the sites mooted as the burial place of Chinggis Khaan. Whether or not Chinggis was buried here, *The Secret History of the Mongols* does describe how the *khaan* hid here as a young man and later returned to give praise to the mountain and give thanks for his successes.

Because of its auspicious connections, Mongolians climb the mountain, which is topped with many **ovoos** (GPS: N48° 45.430', E109° 00.300'), to gain strength and good luck. The hill itself is in a very remote location. To get there you'll need to head to Möngönmorit in Töv, and then travel north along the Kherlen Gol.

Around 22km due north of Burkhan Khalduun (as the falcon flies) is **Khalun Us Rashant** (Hot Water Springs; GPS: N48° 57.206', E109° 00.217'). The site has more than a dozen **hot springs**, a collection of log bathhouses and a small **Buddhist temple** (built in honour of Zanabazar, who frequented the site). You can also reach the area by horse from Batshireet (it's possible to drive there in winter when the ground freezes).

Dadal Дадал

As written in *The Secret History of the Mongols,* it is now generally accepted that the great Chinggis was born at the junction of the Onon and Balj Gols (though his date of birth is still subject to great conjecture). The assumed spot is in Dadal *sum,* near the town of the same name.

Dadal is a gorgeous area of lakes, rivers, forests and log huts (very few people live in gers), reminiscent of Siberia, which is only 25km to the north. Even if you are not a Chinggisphile, there is no shortage of scenery to admire and hike around in. The village itself is a quaint place of stained log cabins and trotting horses. Don't miss sampling the local bread, some of the best you can find outside Ulaanbaatar.

The 415,752-hectare **Onon-Balj National Park**, extending north from the village towards Russia, offers enticing **camping spots**, **fishing holes** and chances for spotting **wildlife**. Buy your national park ticket (T3000) in the Dadal Government House.

Sights

Deluun Boldog MONUMENT

About 3.5km north of Dadal village is a collection of hills known as Deluun Boldog. On top of one of the hills is a **stone marker** (GPS: N49° 03.158', E111° 38.590'), built in 1990 to commemorate the 750th anniversary of the writing of *The Secret History of the Mongols*. The inscription says that Chinggis Khaan was born here in 1162. Some historians may not be entirely convinced about the exact date or location of his birth, but it's a great place to come into the world: the scenery and hiking around the valleys and forests are superb.

Chinggis Khaan Statue MONUMENT

The Chinggis Khaan Statue, located in the Gurvan Nuur camp, was built in 1962 to commemorate the 800th anniversary of Chinggis' birth. The monument was built at the height of the communist era and after it was complete the folks who built it were the subject of a purge by the president. Somehow the monument itself was allowed to stand.

Khajuu Bulag SPRING

(GPS: N49° 02.767', E111° 36.865') These mineral water springs, where the great man once drank, are bout 2.2km west of Deluun Boldog. Take your bottles and fill them to the brim because this is the freshest (flowing) spring water you will ever taste. You could also hike up into the hills behind town, where there is a large **ovoo**.

Hunting Museum MUSEUM

For an offbeat adventure, you could drop by the home of **Zundoi-Davag**, a 94-year-old hunter who has built a private museum filled with the animals he has trapped over the years. Zundoi-Davag will be happy to show you his trophies and regale you with hunting stories. He will also show off his impressive collection of antique guns and may let you practise shooting his bow and arrow. His **summer camp** (ger) is about 5km northwest of Dadal, literally over the hill and through the woods. His **winter ger** (GPS: N49° 04.345', E111° 29.776') is in the same direction, but 11km northwest of Dadal. A local should be able to take you there on horseback or motorbike (a motorbike costs about T3000/T6000 to the summer/winter ger). A jeep might cost double that. On the way to the winter camp you'll see a little **stick hut**, built to commemorate the home of Bodon Chuur, an ancestor of Chinggis Khaan.

Dadal Museum MUSEUM

(admission T2500) The tiny village museum has a hodgepodge of mementos and photographs, mostly dating to the communist era. Just outside is a wooden ger with a few artefacts dating to Mongolia's imperial era. The locals seem quite proud of the wooden ger but we preferred the main museum. You'll need to find the caretaker to get in, around the Government House, next door.

Stupa Memorial MONUMENT

On the western part of the village, this new memorial was built to honour the 607 people from Dadal who died in the political repression of the 1930s. The memorial contains three stupas and a list of the victims. The Buriats were treated much more harshly than Khalkh Mongols during the purge era, largely due to rumours that some Buriats were in league with the Japanese.

Activities

There are several **hiking** and **horse-riding** routes out of Dadal. Locals recommend the 30km hike to the junction of the Onon and Balj Gols, or the 45km trek further along the Onon Gol to the gorge at the confluence of the Onon and Agats Gols. You'll need to inform the border patrol of your itinerary and it would be wise to take a local guide; ask at the ger camps or track down Dorjsuren, who runs the eponymous homestay.

There is good **fishing** in the area. You might be able to get a permit at the Government Office (T10,000, good for five days) but it's better to get a permit with the help of a licensed tour operator.

Festivals

Dadal is a great place to be for Naadam, which occurs on 11 to 12 July. You can get up close and personal with the archers and jockeys, and perhaps make up the numbers in the wrestling tourney!

Sleeping

This is perfect camping country, so if you have your own tent and food supplies there is no need to stay in a hotel or ger camp. Just find a secluded spot away from the village.

TOP CHOICE **Dorjsuren's Homestay** HOMESTAY $

(☎9997 7534, 9822 4720; dorjsurengalsan2009@yahoo.com; GPS: N49° 01.280', E111° 38.562'; per person about T6000) Dorjsuren, a retired maths teacher, has a small log cabin for guests next to his home. The classic (but basic) Buriat-style lodge includes a toilet and hot-water shower block. There's a cast-iron stove for cooking and Dorjsuren can hunt down bread, eggs, milk, cream and vegetables. Breakfast costs T2000. It is a 10-minute walk southeast of the centre, across the river, but there is no sign, so ask for directions from the Telecom office. Dorjsuren can arrange a variety of activities in the area; costs for trips and transport in the area are reasonable.

Chinggisiin Gurvan Nuur TOURIST GER CAMP $ (☎9877 5001; Three Lakes; GPS: N49° 02.005', E111° 39.267'; per person T10,000) This rundown but peaceful Soviet-era resort has a nice location on the shore of a lake about 2km from Dadal village. Meals are T1500, a hot shower T4000. There are no gers. A good hiking trail starts from the back of the camp.

Eating

Dadal has a few *guanze* (canteens/restaurants) that serve up hot soup and goulash, the best of which is probably **Buren Khaan Tsainy Gazar** (meals T1000-2000).

Information

Dadal is in a sensitive border area so it's wise to register with the police (T2000). If you are heading any further out of town, it's also a good idea to register with the border guards, on the western side of Dadal. Don't expect anyone to speak English. The closest thing Dadal has to a tourist information centre is the **WWF office** (GPS: N49° 01.770', E111° 38.412') located between the village and Chinggisiin Gurvan Nuur ger camp. Staff here sell tickets to the Onon-Balj National Park and offer jeep hire (at inflated prices). **Internet** (per hr T1500) is available at a small shop in the village.

If you want a better understanding of the region or a crash course on Chinggis Khaan lore, contact **Mr Tserendorj**, Dadal's retired historian. Dorjsuren (of Dorjsuren's Homestay) can put you in touch.

Getting There & Away

One minivan or jeep a day usually goes to Ulaanbaatar (T30,000, 515km), taking anywhere from 12 to 18 hours, depending on the weather or the number of pit stops your driver makes.

A postal truck travels from Öndörkhaan (T12,400) every Monday and Thursday morning at around 8.30am, returning to Öndörkhaan on the same day. Most traffic from Öndörkhaan takes the road via Norovlin.

There are few vehicles for hire in Dadal, but if you ask around the shops something should be available. Expect to pay T60,000 per day plus petrol.

For travel from Dadal to Öndörkhaan or Dornod (but not Binder), you'll need to cross the Onon Gol at a lone **bridge crossing** (GPS: N48° 50.403', E111° 38.746'). Dadal is 254km north-by-northeast of Öndörkhaan and 301km northwest of Choibalsan. It's only 75km as the crow flies to Bayan-Uul (in Dornod) but the actual distance via the bridge is about 140km.

DORNOD ДОРНОД

POP 73,600 / AREA 123,500 SQ KM

One of Mongolia's most stunning landscapes, Dornod is pure steppe, with pancake-flat grasslands in all directions. There are few roads, towns or fences, making this an important ecological zone and habitat for white-tailed gazelle, which can outrun even the best jeep driver.

Dornod, which means 'east', has a number of worthy attractions, geared for both historians and ecotourists. These include Buir Nuur and Khalkhiin Gol, both the scenes of fierce fighting against the Japanese; Khökh Nuur, the lowest point in the country; and some lovely nature reserves. If you've already visited other more popular areas of Mongolia, Dornod offers scope for some challenging, offbeat exploration.

The northern *sums* of Bayan-Uul, Bayandun and Dashbalbar are home to the Buriats, who still practise shamanism. If you ask around you may be able to meet a shaman or, if you are lucky, watch a shamanist ceremony.

National Parks & Nature Reserves

Dornod aimag is the focus of several environmental projects that protect one of the world's last undisturbed grasslands. The protected areas of the aimag include the following:

Dornod Mongol Strictly Protected Area (570,374 hectares) Holds one of the last great plain ecosystems on earth, protecting seas of feather-grass steppe and 70% of Mongolia's white-tailed gazelle, which roam in herds of up to 20,000.

Mongol Daguur Strictly Protected Area (103,016 hectares) This is divided into northern 'A' and southern 'B' sections. Mongol Daguur A is hill steppe and wetland bordering Russia's Tari Nuur and Daurski Reserve, protecting endemic species such as the Daurian hedgehog; Mongol Daguur B, along the Ulz Gol, protects the *tsen togoruu* (white-naped crane) and other endangered birds. The area is part of a 1-million-hectare international reserve, linking the Siberian taiga with the inner-Asian steppe.

Nömrög Strictly Protected Area (311,205 hectares) An unpopulated area, which contains rare species of moose, crane, otter and bear. Ecologically distinct from the rest of Mongolia, the area takes in the transition zone from the eastern Mongolian steppe to the mountains and forest of Manchuria.

GAZELLE

A highlight of eastern Mongolia, as you bounce along in your jeep, is the sight of thousands of Mongolian gazelle darting across the steppes. When pre-eminent biologist George Schaller first visited in 1989, he proclaimed the immense herds to be one of the world's greatest wildlife spectacles.

Sadly, indiscriminate poaching for subsistence and bush-meat sale has reduced their numbers by as much as 50% in the past 10 years. It's believed that up to 200,000 of these creatures are illegally shot every year, about 20% of their entire population. An estimated 60% of herding households shoot about eight gazelle per year. There is a growing foreign souvenir market for gazelle-leg horse-whips (US$15) – please do not purchase these.

Habitat loss to overgrazing, road construction and the erection of barriers further puts their numbers at risk. Mining is another threat: oil exploration in southeast Dornod has brought large-scale infrastructure and thousands of workers into a once-uninhabited region.

US-based international conservation NGOs such as the **Wildlife Conservation Society** (www.wcs.org) and **The Nature Conservancy** (www.tnc.org) now work to protect gazelle habitat on the eastern steppe. BBC Planet Earth featured the gazelles and the eastern steppe on their grassland series (go to youtube.com and search 'Mongolian gazelle').

Toson Khulstai (469,928 hectares) The nature reserve protects large herds of white-tailed gazelle; easy detour if travelling between Khentii and Dornod.

Ugtam Uul Nature Reserve (46,100 hectares) Forested area that contains wildlife and the ruins of an old temple.

Choibalsan Чойбалсан

☎01582 / POP 39,800 / ELEV 747M

Lying on the banks of the Kherlen Gol, 324km downstream from Öndörkhaan, is Choibalsan, Mongolia's easternmost capital and the regional centre for trade and industry. The city has a better-than-average selection of hotels, plenty of shops and one of Mongolia's busiest markets. It's in two parts: a half-abandoned district to the west and a more functional eastern section, where most of the action takes place.

Centuries ago, the city was a trading centre and part of a caravan route across northeast Asia. It grew into a town in the 19th century and was called Bayan Tumen. In 1941 it was named after the Stalinist stooge Khorloogiin Choibalsan, an honour bequeathed while the dictator was still in power. It's now a major economic centre for eastern Mongolia.

Although the city is spread out along a narrow 5km corridor north of the Kherlen Gol, most of the facilities needed by visitors are near the Kherlen hotel. The market is 1.5km east of the main square. The train station is about 5.5km past the market.

Sights

Aimag Museum & Gallery MUSEUM
(admission T5000; 10am-5pm Mon-Fri, 10am-3pm Sat & Sun) In the former Government House in the old part of town, this is one of the best of its kind outside of Ulaanbaatar. It contains some interesting paintings, fascinating old photos and some Choibalsan memorabilia including his desk and shortwave radio (a real antique gem). The aimag map marks the location of some ruined monasteries. Outside is a recreated WWII bunker, like the ones used at Khalkhiin Gol. If the museum is locked, just ring the buzzer next to the door.

Natural History Museum MUSEUM
(10am-5pm Mon-Fri, 10am-3pm Sat & Sun) This museum on the western side of the square has a collection of stuffed wildlife from around the aimag, plus exhibits on geology and flora. It's free if you've already paid for the Aimag Museum.

Mongolian Heroes' Memorial MONUMENT
This large arch with a soldier on horseback charging towards the enemy is one of the more dramatic pieces of Stalinist architecture in Mongolia. It's in the western town square. A small Soviet tank next to the monument saw action during the 1939 Khalkhiin Gol war.

Danrig Danjaalin Khiid MONASTERY
(Данриг Данжаалин Хийд) According to the chief monk, this monastery was built around 1840 and was once very active. It

Choibalsan

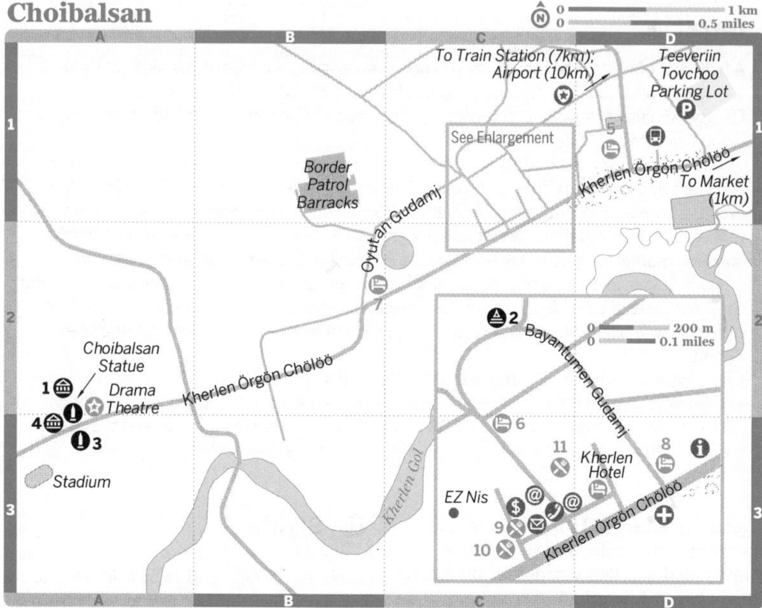

Choibalsan

Sights

1 Aimag Museum & Gallery A2
2 Danrig Danjaalin Khiid C2
3 Mongolian Heroes' Memorial A3
4 Natural History Museum A3

Sleeping

5 Bolor Centre D1
6 Chadanguud C3
7 East Palace B2
8 Titem D3

Eating

Bolor Centre .... (see 5)
9 Khishig Supermarket C3
10 Top Café C3
11 Winners Pub C3

contained three northern temples and four southern temples, but less than half the 800 monks could be accommodated at one time, so most had to pray outside. It was closed in 1937. The monastery reopened in 1990 and has two small temples where about 15 monks worship. It's located about 400m behind the Kherlen Hotel.

Sleeping

The best place to camp is anywhere south of the main street; walk for a few hundred metres and you will be sharing some great spots along the Kherlen Gol with a few curious cows.

Titem HOTEL **$$$**

(☎21026; Kherlen Örgön Chölöö; s/d incl breakfast from T40,000/80,000; P) When Mongolia's president visits Choibalsan, he stays here. The newly renovated Titem (also known as the Tovan Hotel) is the best in Choibalsan and one of the best outside Ulaanbaatar. Well-lit rooms come with a flat-panel TV, fan and comfortable beds.

East Palace HOTEL **$$$**

(☎9906 6777; Kherlen Örgön Chölöö; s/tw incl breakfast from T50,000/90,000) Choibalsan's newest hotel has comfortable, modern rooms with bright colours and lots of sunlight, as well as a sauna and fitness room. It's about 600m west of the centre.

Bolor Centre HOTEL **$$**

(☎21010; Kherlen Örgön Chölöö; d/luxe T20,000/37,000) The recently built Bolor Centre has clean rooms with high ceilings and what appears to be a reliable water supply. As long as the management can keep it maintained, this should remain a good midrange option.

Chadanguud HOTEL $$
(☎22355; d/half-luxe/luxe T24,000/38,000/40,000; P@) The Chadanguud (which is the name of a Buriat clan) has a sauna and laundry service, plus hot showers and reliable cable internet in the rooms (if you have your own laptop) and wi-fi in the lobby. On the downside, the rooms are scruffy and the bathrooms don't function properly – the toilets barely flush and tap water is occasionally the colour of coffee.

Eating

Both the Titem and the East Palace hotels have decent restaurants.

Bolor Centre CHINESE $$
(⏰9am-10.30pm) The Chinese restaurant at the Bolor Centre is a great alternative to the numerous mutton-based restaurants around town. There are good stir-fries, hot soups and a recommended eggplant dish. Bring a group of friends to share the big portions. This is the same location as the Bolor Hotel, on the main road, between the town and the market.

Winners Pub PUB $
(⏰noon-11pm Mon-Sat) The first theme pub in Choibalsan sports English Premier League paraphernalia on the walls and a variety of Western and Mongolian dishes.

Top Café MONGOLIAN $
(⏰7am-11pm Mon-Fri, 9.30am-9pm Sat & Sun) This place serves tasty Mongolian food, stir-fries and spaghetti in a colourful dining room. Top is located in a row of metal shacks, just west of the Khishig Supermarket.

Khishig Supermarket SUPERMARKET $
(⏰9am-10pm Mon-Sat, noon-7pm Sun) Next to the post office.

Shopping

Choibalsan's proximity to China means that its **market** (⏰9am-7pm) is better stocked compared with other aimag capitals. It has lots of fresh fruit and vegetables, as well as an interesting shop selling ger furniture, saddles, Mongolian hats and boots. The back of the market plays host to gambling stalls where locals play cards, dominoes and *shagai* (a dice game using ankle bones).

Information

Eastern Mongolia Strictly Protected Areas Office (☎23373, 9986 3888; ⏰9am-5pm Mon-Fri) Next to the Titem Hotel. Information on visiting protected areas in both Dornod and Sükhbaatar aimags. Arranges permits and sells tickets to protected areas and nature reserves.

Golomt Bank (Kherlen Örgön Chölöö) Gives cash advances against Visa and MasterCard. Next to Khishig Supermarket.

Internet Centre (per hr T500; ⏰8am-10pm) Next to the Telecom office.

Library Internet Cafe (per hr T500; ⏰10am-6pm Mon-Fri) One building east of the Telecom office.

Post office (Kherlen Örgön Chölöö) Next door to the Telecom office.

Telecom office (Kherlen Örgön Chölöö; ⏰24hr) Located in the commercial centre, in an old concrete slab that surrounds a small courtyard on three sides.

Getting There & Away

Air

EZ Nis (☎21177, 9904 9934) flies to/from Ulaanbaatar four days a week (one way/return T272,900/546,800), and a flight to Hailar (in China) two days a week (p261). The office is near the Trade & Development Bank. The airport is about 10km east of the centre; around T10,000 by taxi.

Bus, Minivan & Jeep

A bus departs for Ulaanbaatar (T25,500, 13 hours, 655km) at 7am, every day except Tuesday, from **Teeveriin Tovchoo** (☎9866 1845) at the eastern end of town. Going the other way it leaves Ulaanbaatar's Bayanzürkh bus station at the same time. From the same station it's also possible to get a seat in a minivan for T29,700 to Ulaanbaatar or T15,000 to Öndörkhaan, which doesn't have a specific departure time but generally leaves when full.

Private minivans and jeeps run between Ulaanbaatar and Choibalsan daily (T30,000), departing from Ulaanbaatar's Naran Tuul jeep station. Minivans from Choibalsan market depart when full. Private vans and jeeps (also from the market) go to Öndörkhaan (T15,000, 324km), Baruun-Urt (T14,000, 191km) and, less frequently, nearby *sums* such as Bayandun (T15,000).

Recommended local drivers include **Dondog** (☎9957 3463, 9957 7186) and **Munkhbat** (☎9958 7769). Both charge around T60,000 per day plus petrol.

A postal minivan to Khalkhiin Gol (T14,500, 10 hours) leaves on Wednesday, departing at 8am.

Hitching

Choibalsan is a large city by Mongolian standards, so hitching a ride on a truck or any other vehicle in or out of the city should not be difficult. Hang around the market and keep asking.

Train

A direct rail line from Choibalsan to Russia was built in 1939 to facilitate the joint Soviet-Mongolian war effort against Japan. It still functions, albeit only twice weekly. As a foreigner, you can go as far as Chuluunkhoroot on the Mongolian side of the border (no permit is apparently required).

The train leaves Choibalsan at 4pm every Monday and Thursday and takes seven to eight hours. The return trip leaves Chuluunkhoroot at 8.30pm on Tuesday and Friday. Tickets cost T4500 for hard seat (the only class). For further details call the **station** (☎21502).

The train moves very slowly (averaging about 25km per hour) but its saving grace is the friendly locals who liven up the trip. Take food and plenty of water as the carriage can get stiflingly hot during the day.

The train station is about 7km northeast of the centre. You can get there by bus, but go early because buses are full close to train departure times.

Kherlen Bar Khot
Хэрлэн Бар Хот

These small-scale **ruins** (GPS: N48° 03.287', E113° 21.865') and 10m-high brick tower from a 12th-century city were once part of the ancient state of Kitan.

Kherlen Bar Khot is about 90km west of Choibalsan, on the main road between Choibalsan and Öndörkhaan. It is worth a look if you have your own vehicle.

Buir Nuur Буйр Нуур

This vast lake on Mongolia's eastern thumb is well known for the large stocks of fish. Amur Carp is the main species of fish in the lake, although it also contains taimen, grayling and lenok, among others. Most of the fish end up on the plates of Chinese restaurants; the northern shore is actually in China, a fact exploited by Chinese fishermen. The 40km lake has a maximum depth of 50m and is especially popular with mosquitoes, so bring lots of repellent or you'll need a blood transfusion!

The lake is also great for bird-watching. Head for the northeast area around the Khalkhiin Gol delta.

The only way to Buir Nuur is by chartered jeep from Choibalsan, 285km away over a flat dirt road.

Khalkhiin Gol
Халхын Гол

The banks of the Khalkhiin Gol, in the far eastern part of Dornod, are of particular interest to war historians because of the battles against the Japanese in 1939. The region is about a nine-hour drive east of Choibalsan.

Numerous **war memorials** are found in the area, most of them on the road to Khalkh Gol (town). The memorials are real socialist masterpieces, built to honour the Russian and Mongolian soldiers who died here. The **Yakolevchudiin Tank Khoshuu** (Monument for Yakolev Tank Brigade; GPS: N47° 48.810', E113° 32.850') is 23km northwest of the town. The largest memorial is the 10m-high **Yalaltiin Khoshuu**, just outside Khalkh Gol (marked on some maps as Sümber).

A **museum** (admission T1000) in Khalkh Gol offers some explanations (in Mongolian) about the history of the battles. The friendly caretaker will show you around the museum and probably issue you a commemorative pin to mark your visit. There may be no electricity, so bring a torch (flashlight) to see the exhibits. A small **hotel** (per person T8000) in Khalkh Gol, about 200m from the museum, has a pit toilet and electricity powered by a generator.

At **Ikh Burkhant** (GPS: N48° 03.287', E113° 21.865'), a huge image of **Janraisag** ('Avalokitesvara' in Sanskrit) is carved into the hillside. The carving was commissioned in 1864 by local regent Bat Ochiriin Togtokhtooriin, or Tovan (*van* means 'lord') and was renovated in the mid-1990s. It is right on the roadside, about 32km northwest of Khalkh Gol.

In the other direction, it's another 70km or so to the spectacular but remote **Nömrög Strictly Protected Area** (admission T3000). It only receives a handful of visitors each year, but those who go are rewarded with virgin fields and pine forests untouched by livestock or humans. The **border post** (GPS: N46° 59.019', E119° 21.522') at Nömrög is as far as you can go by vehicle. The border guards can rent you horses at inflated prices (around T18,000 to T20,000 per day) for further explorations of the strictly protected area (SPA). A border guard must accompany you in the SPA; they may be reluctant but as long as you have a border permit for the area they are required to do so.

Khalkh Gol is about 325km from Choibalsan. If you ask around the market in

WORTH A TRIP

NORTHERN DORNOD

A loop around northern Dornod makes for a good three- or four-day jeep trip. From Choibalsan you can head northeast to **Khökh Nuur**, a medium-sized freshwater lake at an altitude of 560m (the lowest point in Mongolia). The lake has a subtle beauty and is an important migration point for waders and shore birds.

From Khökh Nuur you could head northwest to **Mongol Daguur B Strictly Protected Area**, an area along the Ulz Gol and another important habitat for wader birds. The nearest town in the area is Chuluunkhoroot (Stone Corral), near the border crossing with Russia. The only place to stay around here is in a spare room at the **Mongol Daguur Information Office** (9587 9714; per night T5000). If you've ended up here without transportation (eg by train or shared minivan), the ranger at the information office might be able to show you around the protected area on the back of his motorbike.

Heading west from Chuluunkhoroot, you'll pass through the quiet village of Dashbalbar and then **Ugtam Uul Nature Reserve** (46,160 hectares). The reserve includes Ugtam mountain (1236m), Tsagaan Ovoot Uul (1236m) and the ruins of some monasteries. The park is situated along the Ulz Gol in the northwest of the aimag, about 35km from the village of Bayandun.

Jeep tracks lead further west to Bayandun and Bayan-Uul, both fine areas for camping and horse riding. There are relatively few gers here since most Buriats prefer log homes. There is a good road from Bayan-Uul back to Choibalsan (187km, 3½ hours) or you could take the rough road further west to Dadal via Norovlin (140km, four hours).

One last sight to look out for in the area is the **Wall of Chinggis Khaan** (Чингисийн Хэрэм). Despite the name, it was probably built during the Liao dynasty to prevent rampaging Mongol hordes from heading east. Locals know it as the Chingissiin Zam, or Chinggis' Rd, which gives some indication of just how worn down the wall has become. The best place to start looking is about two-thirds of the way along the northern road from Choibalsan to the Russian border, near the village of Gurvanzagal.

Choibalsan, a shared van (T15,000) may eventually turn up bound for Khalkh Gol, but from here you'd still need to hire a vehicle to visit the sights (and there may not be any vehicles for hire). It's best to hire your own vehicle and split the cost between travellers.

Information

Khalkhiin Gol is near the Chinese border and a military base and there is one military check en route from Choibalsan. You'll need a **border permit** issued from Ulaanbaatar to get through it. Watch out for fake permits given out at Khalkh Gol (for Nömrög). If you have a border permit from the border office in Ulaanbaatar (which should be free), you could probably get past the border guards at Khalkh Gol, without risking having to buy a phoney permit.

In addition to the border permit you need a **ticket** for the SPA. At the time of research these were being sold at the SPA office in Choibalsan but there were plans to open a new SPA Nömrög office in Khalkh Gol town (at the museum). Just to be safe, check on this when you get to Choibalsan (at the Protected Areas Office) or contact the Nömrög ranger **Mr Batbold** (8855 7082).

SÜKHBAATAR
СУХБААТАР

POP 55,000 / AREA 82,000 SQ KM

Pancake-flat Sükhbaatar is wedged between the Gobi Desert and the pure steppes of Dornod. It contains elements of both – shifting sand dunes and barren rock feature prominently in the southwest, while the knee-high grass in the east provides important habitat for huge herds of gazelle.

The southern *sum* of Dariganga contains some 20 extinct volcanoes. This is the most interesting part of the aimag, a legendary region of horse thieves, holy mountains and ancient stone statues. A highlight is watching a glorious sunrise from sacred Shiliin Bogd Uul.

Sükhbaatar is well off the tourist track but can be incorporated into a greater tour of eastern Mongolia. Because it receives so few visitors it feels as if you have the aimag to yourself.

National Parks

Ganga Nuur Nature Reserve (28,000 hectares) Protects dunes and the Ganga

Nuur, an important habitat for migrating swans.

Lkhachinvandad Uul Nature Reserve (58,500 hectares) On the border with China, this steppe area has plenty of gazelle and elk. It's reached via Erdenetsagaan.

Baruun-Urt Баруун-Урт

☎01512 / POP 11,500 / ELEV 981M

Sükhbaatar's capital is located smack in the middle of eastern Mongolia's vast plains. It's a fairly desolate location, with no river or lake nearby, and the town is one of the smallest provincial capitals in the country. However, the local economy is picking up, thanks largely to a nearby Chinese-invested zinc mine. During our last visit we found new streets and footpaths paved, street lamps installed, the main square renovated and a shiny new bus stand and market.

In winter it's possible to walk out into the empty, barren, frozen steppe and feel as if you've landed on the moon. The ground underneath your feet, however, contains high levels of sulphur, which has seeped into the local water supply – you are better off buying bottled water or filtering the tap water.

Sights

Museum MUSEUM
(admission T2000; ⏲9am-6pm Mon-Fri) Baruun-Urt's surprisingly good museum has a fine collection of costumes representing the three ethnic groups that inhabit the region: the Khalkh (the majority), the Dariganga (30,000 live in the south of Sükhbaatar aimag) and the Uzemchin (about 2000 live in Dornod aimag and Sükhbaatar aimag). Look out for the brass-studded Uzemchin wrestling jacket.

There are also beautiful examples of products from Dariganga's renowned silversmiths and blacksmiths, some stuffed gazelle, and two rooms dedicated to the famed poet, author and politician Ochirbatyn Dashbalbar (1957–99), including his electric razor and record collection.

From the square, walk 400m south and turn right. The museum is located just past the drama theatre.

Erdenemandal Khiid MONASTERY
(Эрдэнэмандал Хийд) According to the monks, this monastery was originally built in 1830, about 20km from the present site. At the height of its splendour, there were seven temples and 1000 monks in residence, but the Stalinist purges of 1938 had the same result as elsewhere. The new monastery, surrounded by a wall topped with 108 stupas, is about 400m west of the square.

Sleeping

Baruun-Urt is short on hotels; they tend to fill up if a mining crew rolls through town. You may want to call ahead to reserve a room.

This is the only aimag capital where camping is not a good idea. The town is in the middle of dusty plains and there is no river nearby. The only passable option is by a creek in the northeast of town.

Tansag Hotel HOTEL $$
(☎22444; half-luxe s/d T25,000/30,000, luxe s/d T35,000/45,000, all incl breakfast) Easily the best in town, the Tansag has six rooms in a new building on the east side of the main square. It has fairly reliable hot water and a filling omelette breakfast. Cable internet is available in the rooms if you have a laptop.

Solo Hotel HOTEL $
(☎21499, 9890 9555; d/tr T25,000/24,000) This hotel was somewhat shoddily built – all wobbly floorboards and lopsided hallways – but the double rooms on the 3rd floor aren't too bad. Rooms come with bathrooms but the shower is downstairs. Triples on the 2nd floor have shared bathrooms.

Sharga Hotel HOTEL $
(☎8851 9445; r/luxe T16,000/25,000) Next to the town square, this old hotel of communist yore has passable standard rooms and better deluxe rooms with sitting room, TV and private bathroom. Hot water comes and goes as it pleases.

Eating

There will be no surprises with the mutton-heavy menu at the **Tansag Hotel**, but it's still the best in town. You can get a decent plate of pasta, salad or *buuz* (steamed mutton dumplings) at **Shilmel Zoog** (☎9am-8pm; 🚭), a clean and friendly cafe behind the Deej Market.

Entertainment

The locals enjoy going out, especially on weekends, and there are a few fun dance and karaoke places in town. The youngsters patronise **Smile Pub** (☎9am-midnight), on the west side of the square, which has a small disco upstairs from a restaurant. A slightly older crowd can be found dancing under the blazing strobe lights at **Ikh Uul Pub** (☎noon-midnight), close to the jeep stand. Also near the jeep stand are a couple of karaoke joints, including **Yesui Kafe** (10am-midnight) and **Khongor Restaurant** (10am-midnight).

Information

Government House (Square) Ask for the latest info about permits to border areas here.

Internet cafe (per hr T500; 9am-10pm Mon-Fri, 10am-6pm Sat & Sun) Inside the Telecom office.

Khan Bank (9am-1pm & 2-5pm Mon-Fri) Changes US dollars and has a 24-hour ATM. Located in the same entrance as the Sharga Hotel.

Telecom office (24hr) The post office is also located here. It's on the south side of the main square.

Getting There & Away

Air

At the time of writing there were no flights to Baruun-Urt.

Bus

One daily bus (T21,500, 11 hours) departs to/from Ulaanbaatar at 8am. In Baruun-Urt, at the time of writing, the bus stand was 1km east of the square but a new bus stand was under construction in the town centre. The same bus can drop you in Öndörkhaan (229km) for T9900. In Ulaanbaatar the bus leaves from the Bayanzurkh bus station. Tickets are usually sold out one or two days before departure.

Jeep & Minivan

Shared jeeps and minivans leave Ulaanbaatar daily (T24,000, 560km) from the Naran Tuul jeep station. From Baruun-Urt, vehicles wait at a small jeep stand behind the department store (but may move to the new jeep stand about 200m northeast). Expect to pay around T20,000 for Öndörkhaan (229km) because drivers will be looking for a full fare all the way to UB. If you just want to go to Öndörkhaan, it's much cheaper to take the bus. The Öndörkhaan to Baruun-Urt road is slowly being paved; at the time of research the tarmac extended for 50km out of Öndörkhaan. Traffic is very light in the direction of Choibalsan (191km) and you may have to wait a day or two for a lift. If you hire a car to get you there you'll be expected to pay the return fare.

Hitching

This is difficult because few vehicles come here. Still, with some patience you'll get a lift to Choibalsan, Öndörkhaan and even Zamyn-Üüd. In Baruun-Urt, ask around at the jeep stand or the petrol station.

Dariganga Дарьганга

The vast grasslands of Dariganga are speckled with volcanic craters, small lakes and sand dunes, the sum of which makes the area one of the most scenic in eastern Mongolia. Before communism this area was a haven of aristocracy and its grasslands were the royal grazing grounds of horses belonging to the emperor in Beijing. Silversmiths and blacksmiths made their homes here, providing local women with stunning jewellery that now features prominently in the national museum in Ulaanbaatar. Dariganga's best days are now behind it, but it's still worth the effort of getting down here. With a jeep and a good driver you can set off from town to explore the lakes, volcanoes, caves, sand dunes and ancient stones nearby. The sacred mountain of Shiliin Bogd Uul is also not too far away.

Sights

The skyline of Dariganga is dominated by **Altan Ovoo** (Golden Ovoo), a wide former crater topped by a **stupa**, which only men are allowed to visit. The stupa was built in 1990 on top of the ruins of the original Bat Tsagaan stupa, which was built in 1820 and destroyed in 1937.

In the area around Dariganga there are dozens of broken *balbals* – mostly dating back to the 13th- or 14th-century Mongol period, although some are earlier. According to tradition, you should place an offering of food in the cup held in the statue's left hand. There are also three *balbals*, known as the **king, the queen and the prince** (GPS: N45° 18.540', E113° 51.224'), on the northern edge of town, near some hay sheds. In the village itself, you can visit the welcoming **Ovoon Khiid** (Овоон Хийд), which was built in 1990 and is served by a handful of monks.

There are six lakes in the vicinity of Dariganga; all are part of the Ganga Nuur Nature Reserve. The three main lakes, Kholboo Nuur, Tsagaan Nuur and Ganga Nuur, are good for swimming, though a bit muddy.

The magnificent **Ganga Nuur** (Ганга Нуур; GPS: N45° 15.994', E113° 59.874') is about 13km southeast of Dariganga. From the end of September until mid-October it is home to thousands of migrating swans. Along the shore, in a fenced compound, is delicious and safe spring water. Entry to the lake is T1000 per person and T500 per car (but you can park by the gate and walk).

The sand dunes in the region are known as **Moltsog Els** (Молцог Элс) and stretch for 20km, coming to within walking distance of Dariganga village.

 Sleeping & Eating

There is little to differentiate Dariganga's three ger camps, which lie about 1.5km south of the village. **Dagshin Amaralt**, **Zigistei Nuur** and **Ovor Khurem** ger camps all have cabins (no gers, actually) and basic facilities for about T10,000 per person. If prodded, the caretakers can provide meals. None of the camps has a shower or phone, but you can get both of these in the village.

There is nothing stopping you camping anywhere you want as long as you stay away from the ger camps. If you have a vehicle, camp on the shores of Ganga Nuur.

Dariganga has a few basic shops on the main road, alongside two or three *tsainii gazar* (tea houses/cafes).

 Information

Although they are not usually checked, **permits** (available from the border office in Ulaanbaatar) are required for Dariganga and Shiliin Bogd. The fine for travelling without one is T40,000 per head.

If you are coming from Dornod you shouldn't have any trouble getting to Shiliin Bogd and on to Dariganga; this allows you to travel directly from Khalkhiin Gol area and Dornod Mongol SPA, bypassing Choibalsan and Baruun-Urt. This is the most scenic drive in eastern Mongolia and will be faster than heading back through Choibalsan. Just make sure you have this route listed on your border permit.

Getting There & Away

Occasional shared jeeps (T12,000, four hours) connect Dariganga with Baruun-Urt. A postal truck runs every Thursday from Baruun-Urt at 8am but you should reserve a ticket the day before. Call the **Baruun-Urt post office** (☎01512-21675) to confirm.

One or two jeeps and even motorbikes are available for charter in Dariganga. Travellers report being able to hire horses through one of the ger camps.

Shiliin Bogd Uul
Шилийн Богд Уул

At 1778m, **Shiliin Bogd Uul** (GPS: N45° 28.350', E114° 35.349'), about 70km east of Dariganga, is the highest peak in Sükhbaatar aimag. The extinct volcano is sacred to many Mongolians: the spirit of any man (and man only!) who climbs it, especially at sunrise, will be revived. The region is stunning, isolated and close to the Chinese border – so be careful.

A jeep can drive about halfway up the mountain, and then it's a short, but blustery, walk to the top. There are plenty of *ovoos* and awesome views of craters all around. About 3km to the south, the fire break that squiggles into the distance is the border with China. If you are camping, Shiliin Bogd offers one of the greatest sunrises in a country full of great sunrises.

On the road between Dariganga and Shiliin Bogd, 8km past Ganga Nuur, look out for the statue of **Toroi-Bandi** (GPS: N45° 17.308', E114° 04.466'), the Robin Hood of Mongolia, who stole horses from the local Manchurian rulers, then eluded them by hiding near Shiliin Bogd Uul. The statue, dedicated in 1999, pointedly faces China.

The only two roads to Shiliin Bogd start from Erdenetsagaan (70km) and Dariganga (70km). It's better to go to Dariganga first, where you are more likely to find a jeep for hire or a lift.

Around Shiliin Bogd Uul

Assuming that you have a jeep to get to Shiliin Bogd Uul in the first place, you can make a good loop from Dariganga, to take in Ganga Nuur on the way to Shiliin Bogd Uul, and Taliin Agui and Khurgiin Khundii on the way back to Dariganga.

Taliin Agui (Талын Агуй; GPS: N45° 35.405', E114° 30.051'), 15km northwest of the mountain, is one of the largest caves in Mongolia. If the ice covering the entrance has melted (it's normally covered until mid-summer), you can squeeze through the narrow entrance. The large, icy cavern has three chambers to explore (the back wall looks like a dead end but you can squeeze under the overhang). You'll need a torch to see anything, and be careful on the slippery floor.

A **ger camp** (ger T25,000) is located near the cave. Meals are available (T2500) or you can cook your own food in the lodge. The ger camp also acts as landmark for the cave (which would otherwise be difficult to spot).

The Gobi

POPULATION: 313,400 / AREA: 612,000 SQ KM

Includes »

Best Places to Stay

» Yolyn Am (p170)

» Secret of Ongi Tourist Camp (p161)

» Three Camel Lodge (p168)

» Camping at Khongoryn Els (p170)

Best Places to See Wildlife

» Ikh Nartiin Chuluu (p165)

» Yolyn Am (p170)

» Takhiin Tal (p179)

Why Go?

To be sure the Gobi is a bleak place; vast, harsh and silent, and there are many who will question your sanity if you choose to travel there. But it is the profound emptiness and terrible isolation that draws adventurers to its fold. In a world of smartphones, Facebook and 24/7 cable news, there are few places on the planet where it is still possible to fall completely off the radar like you do in the Gobi.

However, it is also a place of secrets. Ice-filled canyons, abandoned monasteries, salt flats, sand dunes, rust-coloured badlands, dinosaur fossils and legend conspire to fill the empty spaces. So get ready to scratch the sand from your scalp and shake the dust from your clothes, for somewhere in the desert there's a camel with your name on it, and an adventure is waiting to unfold.

When to Go

Dalanzadgad

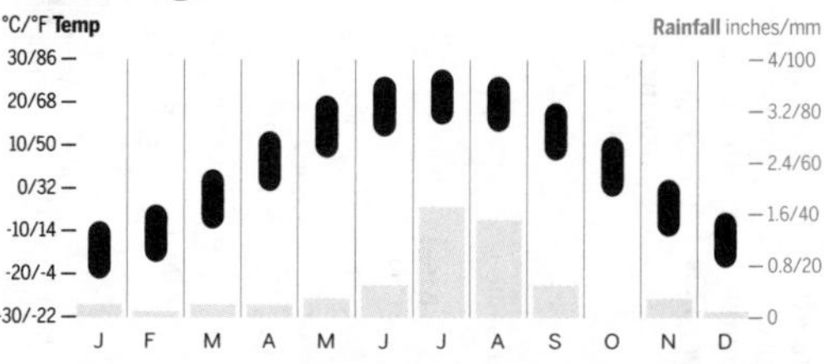

March–May Windstorms increase and airborne sand can strip paint off cars.

June–September Most ger camps will now be in full swing for the tourist season.

December–February Bulgan celebrates Lunar New Year with flair despite bitter cold.

Gobi Highlights

1. Take one step forwards and slide three steps backwards as you attempt to summit the dunes at **Khongoryn Els** (p170)
2. Trek through the ice-filled canyon of **Yolyn Am** (p170), on the lookout for ibex
3. Go fossil hunting at **Bayanzag** (p170), the 'flaming cliffs' that house rich deposits of dinosaur bones and fossilised eggs
4. Shimmy up a granite face while rock climbing in the eerie **Ikh Gazryn Chuluu** (p161)
5. Get within spitting distance of an unruly camel during a **camel trek**
6. Make a pilgrimage to Shambhala at **Khamaryn Khiid** (p163)
7. Learn a nomadic song from a **chance encounter with a herdsman**
8. Soak away your ailments in the **Shargaljuut hot springs** (p175)

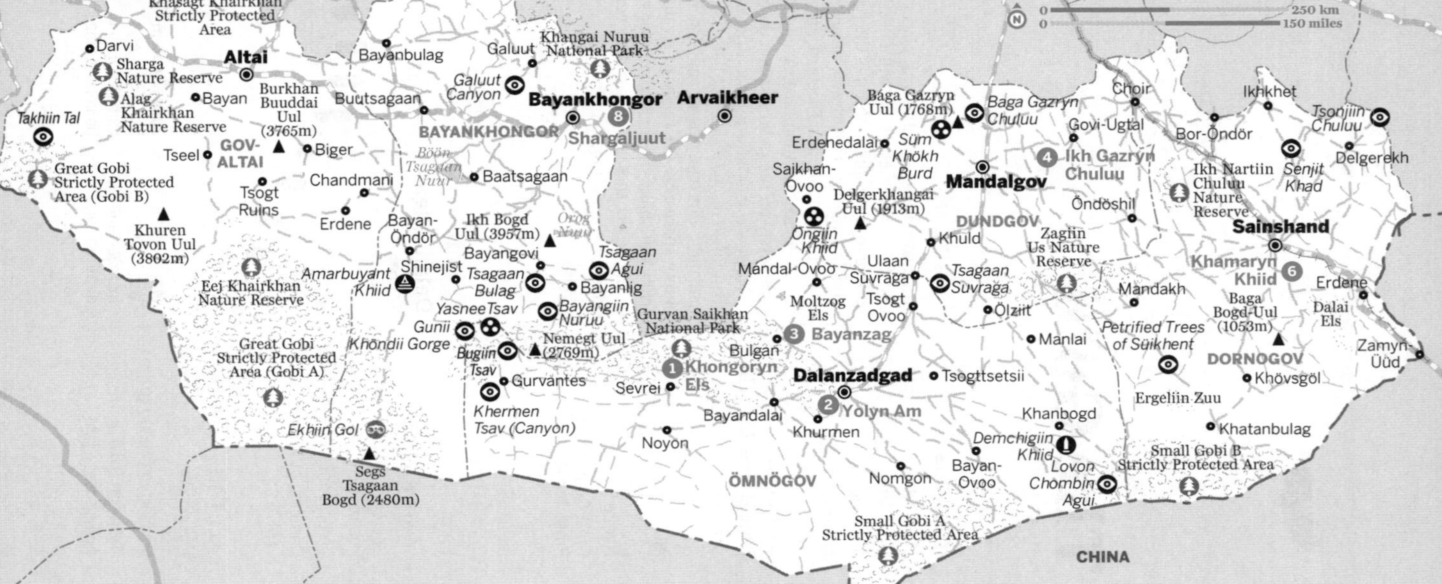

Getting There & Away

There is plenty of public (overcrowded buses) and private (overcrowded minivans and jeeps) transport heading from Ulaanbaatar (UB) to all the Gobi aimag (province) capitals. Remember the travel times given are indicative only and don't take into account breakdowns and time spent in *guanzs* (canteens) drinking *airag* (fermented mare milk) and watching sumo. Flying is also an option to Dalanzadgad, Altai and Bayankhongor. If you are travelling on local trains in China, it's possible to enter Mongolia at Dornogov aimag.

Getting Around

Gobi infrastructure is almost non-existent, but the lack of roads does not prevent vehicles from getting around. On the contrary, the rock-hard jeep trails are the best in the country and sometimes jeeps reach speeds of 100km/h, causing much excitement if an unexpected rise sends them airborne.

Breakdowns in the Gobi can be deadly and you shouldn't think of setting off without a reliable jeep and driver, a good sense of direction and plenty of water.

Annoyingly, public transport between aimag capitals is practically nil, and harder still out to national parks and other attractions. As it's easier to get off a bus heading back to Ulaanbaatar than trying to hop on an already full one on its way out, a good plan is to travel to your furthest destination first and work your way back to the capital.

If you are hitching, you will have the best chance of success if you ask around at markets, bus stations or any places selling petrol.

DUNDGOV ДУНДГОВЬ

POP 47,700 / AREA 78,000 SQ KM

Dundgov (middle Gobi) is something of a misnomer. The aimag would be best described 'North Gobi', as this area is the northernmost extent of the Gobi Desert. Lying just a few hours' drive south of Ulaanbaatar, it's also one of the most convenient Gobi regions to explore.

Dundgov's allure lies in its mysterious rock formations, which mainly appear at two locations: Baga Gazryn Chuluu and Ikh Gazryn Chuluu. At both you'll find large granite pinnacles and winding canyons that make for great hiking and climbing. The water that manages to collect in these areas can support some wildlife, including argali sheep and ibex.

COMMUNITY-BASED TOURISM

If you're interested in staying with local families and experiencing nomadic life in the Gobi, the community-based Ger to Ger project may be of interest. All trips must be booked out of Ulaanbaatar. See p29 for details.

If you are heading south, it's worth visiting the ruined monastery Ongiin Khiid and the still-intact monastery at Erdenedalai en route.

National Parks

Ikh Gazryn Chuluu Nature Reserve (60,000 hectares) Extraordinary rock formations, argali sheep and ibex.

Zagiin Us Nature Reserve (273,606 hectares) Protected mountain Gobi area, saxaul trees, salt marshes and black-tailed gazelle.

Mandalgov Мандалговь

01592 / POP 10,300 / ELEV 1427M

Mandalgov came into existence in 1942 and originally consisted of only 40 gers. Today it's a sleepy town that offers the usual amenities for an aimag capital: a hotel, a monastery, a museum and a few shops. A walk to the top of Mandalin Khar Ovoo, just north of the town centre, affords sweeping views of the bleak terrain. There is more to see in western Dundgov, but Mandalgov is a useful stop-off on the way to Dalanzadgad.

Sights

Aimag Museum MUSEUM

(Buyan Emekhiin Gudamj; admission T1300; 9am-6pm Mon-Fri) This Aimag Museum is divided into two main sections: a natural history section and a more interesting ethnography and historical section. There's also a collection of priceless *thangkas* (scroll paintings), old flintlock rifles, bronze arrowheads, silver snuffboxes, pipes and chess sets carved out of ivory.

Dashgimpeliin Khiid MONASTERY

(Дашгимпэлийн Хийд) In 1936 there were 53 temples in Dundgov; a year later the Mongolian KGB reduced nearly all to ashes and rubble. In 1991 Dashgimpeliin Khiid was opened for the people of Mandalgov. Thirty monks now serve the monastery and services are held most mornings from 10am. It's 300m northeast of the Mandal Hotel.

Mandalgov

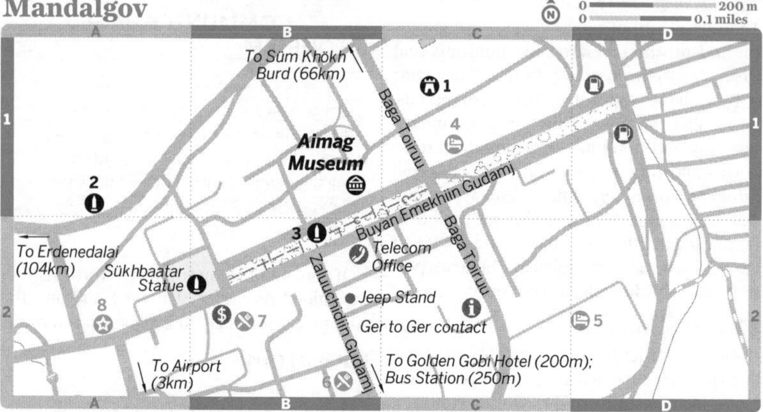

Monument Park PARK

Communism has been preserved in this small park, which includes statues of Sükhbaatar, Yuri Gagarin (first man in space), Lenin, a pair of happy workers, various livestock, a Soviet–Mongolian friendship monument and an outstanding collection of weeds.

Sleeping

Like other Gobi aimag capitals, Mandalgov has no great camping spots; the city has no river and it is flat and dusty. Perhaps walk north of town and find somewhere past Mandalin Khar Ovoo or the monastery.

Gobi Hotel HOTEL $

(☎9115 2771; Buyan Emekhiin Gudamj; dm/s/d T9000/20,000/30,000, half-luxe s/d T12,000/24,000, luxe T15,000/30,000) Even though all the rooms here share the hot showers and only the half-luxe and luxe rooms have their own toilets, this is one of the cleanest hotels in town and good value.

Temujin Hotel HOTEL $

(☎9959 9599; Baga Toiruu; dm/d T9000/10,000, luxe tw T25,000; P) Somewhat of a Soviet dinosaur, the rooms here are a mishmash of '60s furniture and '80s decor. If the luxe rooms are full, the standard rooms lose access rights to the shower. It's in a white brick building, south of the main drag, a bit off Baga Toiruu.

Golden Gobi Hotel HOTEL $$$

(Altai Gobi; ☎22267; Zaluuchidiin Gudamj; r US$20-30, half-luxe US$25-40, luxe US$30-100) Popular with tour companies, the Golden Gobi features rooms that are no better than the others in town, but cost more. However, there are many options, all detailed on a bewildering price list in which no two rooms are priced the same. The US$100 per night luxe room has a sauna and king-sized bed.

Eating

All of the hotels listed under Sleeping have attached restaurants where a Mongolian main will set you back about T2500. While none are particularly terrible, none are going to thrill your taste buds. Self-caterers can pick up food items at the local **market**.

Oig Zoog MONGOLIAN $

(meals T2500-4000; ⌚9am-10pm) Look for this local cafe behind the Khan Bank in a yellow building. You may have to trawl through the menu before you find something that is actually available but we struck gold with the *sharsan bansh* (fried dumplings with salad).

Entertainment

Central Mongolian Concert Theatre TRADITIONAL MUSIC & DANCE
(Buyan Emekhiin Gudamj; ⏲Sep-Jun, Jul during Naadam) Performances are sporadic but worth checking out while you're in town.

Information

Ger to Ger Contact (☎9899 4237; zaanaa_999@chingiss.com; Apt 1, Old Khan Bank Bldg) Home of the local contact.

Internet cafe (per hr T500; ⏲8.30am-10pm) Located in the Telecom office.

Khan Bank (⏲9am-7pm Mon-Fri, 10am-3pm Sat) Can change US dollars and has an ATM.

Telecom office (⏲24hr) The post office is also located here.

Getting There & Away

BUS A bus leaves every day at 8am and 2pm for Ulaanbaatar (T12,000, six hours, 260km) and another every Monday and Thursday at 8am for Choir (T10,500, five hours, 187km). Tickets for Choir must be bought the morning before the day of departure. The bus from Ulaanbaatar on its way to Dalanzadgad (nine hours, 293km) passes sometime between 2pm and 3pm. If there is room, tickets cost T14,000.

JEEP & MINIVAN Daily share jeeps to Ulaanbaatar (T15,000, six hours) leave when full from the jeep stand outside the Telecom office and the bus station. You're unlikely to find a share jeep to Dalanzadgad (T15,000, seven hours), but Dalanzadgad-bound jeeps coming from Ulaanbaatar might be able to squeeze you in. Wait for these at the petrol station in the south of town. Share jeeps to Choir (T15,000, four hours) are even scarcer.

Baga Gazryn Chuluu
Бага Газрын Чулуу

This granite rock formation in the middle of the dusty plains sheltered Zanabazar during conflicts between the Khalkh and Oirat Mongols. Later it was home to two 19th-century monks who left **rock drawings** in the area. Locals who sometimes make pilgrimages here worship the rocks. Naturally, there is a legend that Chinggis Khaan grazed his horses here.

The **Delgeriin Choiriin Khiid**, one of the many monasteries destroyed in the purges of the 1930s, is in the process of being rebuilt and sequestered in a nearby ger is Luvsan Darjaa, a lama said to be the reincarnation of the famous Mongolia scholar Zava Damdin. Sometime in 2011 Luvsan is set to emerge from his ger after four years of solitary meditation.

Five kilometres away, the highest peak in the area, **Baga Gazryn Uul** (1768m), will take about an hour to climb. The mountain also contains a **cave** with an underground lake. The **mineral water springs** and trees in the region make it a great spot to camp, and there are plenty of rocky hills topped by *ovoos* (shamanistic offerings to the gods) to explore.

The **Bayan Bulag ger camp** (☎9825 0010; GPS: N 46°13.827', E 106°04.192'; with meals US$38) is one of the Gobi's more attractive ger camps and offers good food and hot showers. Guides (free) from the camp can show you sights in the area. It also has a greenhouse growing delicious tomatoes and cucumbers.

Baga Gazryn Chuluu is about 60km north by northwest of Mandalgov, and about 21km east of Süm Khökh Burd.

Süm Khökh Burd
Сум Хөх Бурд

The temple **Süm Khökh Burd** (GPS: N 46°09.621', E 105°45.590'), which sits on an island in the middle of a tiny lake, was built in the 10th century. Remarkably, the temple was built from rocks that can only be found more than 300km away. It was abandoned and left in ruins a few centuries after it was built.

Three hundred years ago a **palace** was built here, and 150 years later the writer Danzan Ravjaa (p165) built a stage on top of the ruins. Enough of the temple and palace remain to give you some idea of their previous magnificence.

The lake itself, **Sangiin Dalai Nuur**, only encircles the palace after heavy rains; at other times you slog through the mud to reach the palace. There is good **bird-watching** here: various species of eagle, goose and swan come to this spring-fed lake in summer and autumn.

The **Süm Khökh Burd Ger Camp** (☎9906 4388; per person with meals US$35) is an old socialist place that has a shower block with hot water and a generator.

The temple is located 72km northeast of Erdenedalai, 65km northwest of Mandalgov and 21km west of Baga Gazryn Chuluu.

CAMELS

They are known as the ships of the desert. The Mongolian Bactrian camel, a two-humped ornery beast with a shaggy wool coat, can still be seen hauling goods and people across the Gobi, as they have done for centuries.

Your first encounter with a camel may be a daunting experience: they bark, spit and smell like a sweaty armpit. Sitting atop one you may be reminded of the unruly ton tons from *Star Wars: The Empire Strikes Back*.

But, excusing its lack of graces, the camel is a versatile and low-maintenance creature: it can last a week without water and a month without food; it can carry a lot of gear (up to 250kg – equal to 10 full backpacks); it provides wool (on average 5kg per year) and milk (up to 600L a year); and is a good source of (somewhat gamey) meat. The camel also produces 250kg of dung a year, and you can never have too much camel crap.

Monitoring the hump is an important part of camel maintenance. A firm and tall hump is a sign of good health, while a droopy hump means the camel is in need of food and water. If a thirsty camel hasn't had a drink for some time, it can suck up 200L of water in a single day. Most camels are tame, but male camels go crazy during the mating season in January and February – definitely a time to avoid approaching one.

Of the 260,000 camels in Mongolia, two-thirds can be found in the five aimags that stretch across the Gobi – 80,000 in Ömnögov alone. They are related to the rare wild camel known as the *khavtgai*. The current number of *khavtgais* is considerably lower than it was 45 years ago, largely because they have been poached for their meat. In an attempt to stop the decline in numbers, several national parks in the Gobi have been established to protect the 300 or so remaining wild *khavtgais*.

Erdenedalai
Эрдэнэдалай

This sometime camel-herding community in the middle of nowhere (114km northwest of Mandalgov) is known for the **Gimpil Darjaalan Khiid** (admission T2000), an old monastery that survived Stalin's purges by becoming a warehouse and shop. The monastery was built in the late 18th century to commemorate the first ever visit to Mongolia by a Dalai Lama and was once used by about 500 monks. The monastery was reopened in 1990 and is now home to five monks.

The spacious temple has a central statue of Tsongkhapa (founder of the 'Yellow Hat' sect of Buddhism), some large parasols and huge drums. Seek permission if you want to take photographs inside the temple.

About 25km north of Erdenedalai, the **Middle Gobi Camp** (☎9912 8783, 011-367 316; GPS: N 46°08.816', E 105°11.013'; with/without meals US$35/12) is not a bad place to spend the night if you are headed in this direction.

Although the village is small, it is on a major jeep trail and a few vehicles come through every day.

Ongiin Khiid
Онгийн Хийд

This small mountainous area along the Ongiin Gol in the western *sum* (district) of Saikhan-Ovoo makes a pleasant place to break a trip between southern Gobi and either Ulaanbaatar or Arvaikheer for those with their own wheels; there is no public transport to Ongiin Khiid.

Sights

TOP CHOICE **Ongiin Khiid** HISTORIC SITE
(GPS: N 45°20.367', E 104°00.306'; admission US$2, photos US$1, video US$2) The bend in the river marks the remains of two ruined monasteries: the **Barlim Khiid** on the north bank and the **Khutagt Khiid** on the south. They're collectively known as Ongiin Khiid. Formerly one of the largest monasteries in Mongolia, and home to over a thousand monks, the complex was destroyed in the 1939 communist purges when over 200 lamas were murdered. Since 1990 a small but growing contingent of monks has set up shop amid the ruins, completing a small temple in 2004.

Locals claim that to reap the curative qualities of the **spring** (which apparently runs warm in winter and cool in summer), you must drink from it before sunrise. The ger in front of the temple houses a small **museum** showcasing some unimpressive artefacts found at the site.

The **views** of the ruins, river, ger camps and the surrounding area are impressive from any of the nearby hills. A good way to start is with the one with the **ibex monument** on top.

Sleeping & Eating

There are plenty of places to camp along the forested riverside and there are four ger camps, all next to each other near the monastery.

TOP CHOICE **Secret of Ongi Tourist Camp** TOURIST GER CAMP $$
(☎9909 6841; www.ongi.mongoliansecrethistory.mn; with/without meals US$48/17; P @) The big draw here is the log-and-stone **restaurant** (mains T3700-8500) reminiscent of a Chinese-style temple, the smart gers with curved wooden doors and some of the cleanest toilets in the Gobi. The whole complex is situated on the banks of the Ongiin Gol and the uniformed staff here can arrange guided camel treks, massages and laundry services. Nonguests are welcome to use the showers (T3000) or dine in the restaurant. If you do drop in, be sure to check out the fine ceremonial Buddhist dance costumes that are on display in reception.

Tsagaan Ovoo Ger Camp TOURIST GER CAMP $$
(☎9821 9592; with/without meals US$35/15) The camp features a small **restaurant** (mains US$5-8) and a games building with table tennis and a pool table. If you order your beast the day before, the staff can arrange horse and camel trekking in the surrounding countryside.

Ongiin Khiid Guest House TOURIST GER CAMP $
(☎9979 9721; per person T8000-10,000; P) This is the smallest of the ger camps in the vicinity and showers here cost an additional T2000. The best thing about this place is the outstanding view up the valley from the long drop toilet.

Saikhan-Ovoo Сайхан-Овоо

There is little to see in this nondescript settlement but Saikhan-Ovoo marks the jumping-off point for some excellent Ger to Ger trekking routes (p29).

Ger to Ger use the **Zambagiin Tal Guesthouse** (☎9301 3339; GPS: N 45°27.389', E 103°54.107'; with/without meals US$10/5) which has a very basic cafe and ger accommodation in the centre of town – look for the compound with the green roof and white walls near the hospital. The only other option is the **Saikhan-Ovoo Ger Camp** (GPS: N 45°22.996', E 103°58.143'), 10km south of town towards Ongiin Khiid.

Ikh Gazryn Chuluu
Их Газрын Чулуу

Caves, canyons and some excellent **rock-climbing** routes are a few of the reasons travellers head out to this remote Gobi area, 70km east of Mandalgov in Gurvan Saikhan *sum*. The Ulaanbaatar-based tour company Wind of Mongolia (p54), in association with Ger to Ger, have opened three routes in the granite massif ranging in technical levels from four to six. Climbers will have to negotiate cracks, chips and overhangs.

You can overnight at the comfortable **Töv Borjigan Ger Camp** (☎9976 9266; GPS: N 45°45.664', E 107°15.977'; with/without meals US$38/16). The people who run it can show you caves in the area.

Ulaan Suvraga
Улаан Суврага

In the southernmost *sum* of Ölziit is Ulaan Suvraga, an area that might be described as a 'badlands' or a 'painted desert'. The eerie, eroded landscape was at one time beneath the sea, and is rich in marine fossils and clam shells. There are also numerous **ancient rock paintings** in the region. About 20km east of Ulaan Suvraga is the equally stunning **Tsagaan Suvraga**, an area of 30m-high white limestone formations.

The best place to stay in the area is the **Tsagaan Suvraga Ger Camp** (☎9924 3138, 9861 0107; ts_suvarga@yahoo.com; GPS: N 44°34.405', E 105°48.542'; with/without meals US$44/18), 8km east of Tsagaan Suvraga.

DORNOGOV ДОРНОГОВЬ

POP (INCL GOV-SÜMBER) 71,600 / AREA 111,000 SQ KM

Dornogov (east Gobi) is the first place visited by many overlanders, as the train line from Beijing to Ulaanbaatar runs straight up its gut. The landscape seen from the train window is one of flat, arid emptiness and the occasional station where locals shuffle about on the platform. The railway supports local trade while the rest of the economy rides on the back of copper mining and small-scale oil extraction.

National Parks

Ergeliin Zuu (90,910 hectares) A small protected area with interesting rock formations and palaeontology sites that include 30-million-year-old mammalian fossils.

Ikh Nartiin Chuluu Nature Reserve (67,000 hectares) Easily accessible from Ulaanbaatar and home to argali sheep, ibex, black vulture and other wildlife

Sainshand Сайншанд

☎01522 / POP 19,540 / ELEV 938M

Thanks to Sainshand's railway and relative proximity to the Tavan Tolgoi mine, the world's largest, untapped coking coal deposit with 7.5 billion tonnes of the stuff, Sainshand (Good Pond) is slated for spectacular economic growth and heavy investment in its infrastructure.

If this comes to pass remains to be seen. As it stands today, the town is divided into two parts: a cluster around the train station, and the more developed city centre 2km to the south. Recently the city has drawn growing attention from Buddhist pilgrims, who use it as a jumping-off point for nearby Khamaryn Khiid.

Sights

Aimag Museum MUSEUM

(admission T1000; ⏰9am-1pm & 2-6pm) The well-appointed Aimag Museum houses plenty of stuffed Gobi animals, and a collection of seashells and marine fossils (Dornogov was once beneath the sea). There is also an impressive skeleton of a Protoceratops and a dinosaur egg. Upstairs, look out for the wooden breastplate used by a Mongol soldier of the imperial fighting days. Lighting here is poor so bring a torch (flashlight).

Museum of Danzan Ravjaa MUSEUM

(www.danzanravjaa.org; admission T1000; ⏰9am-1pm & 2-6pm) The life and achievements of Noyon Khutagt Danzan Ravjaa (1803–56), a well-known Mongolian writer, composer, painter and medic who was born about 100km southwest of Sainshand, are honoured in this small but well-put-together museum.

Look out for the large statue of Danzan Ravjaa looming in the darkness and the

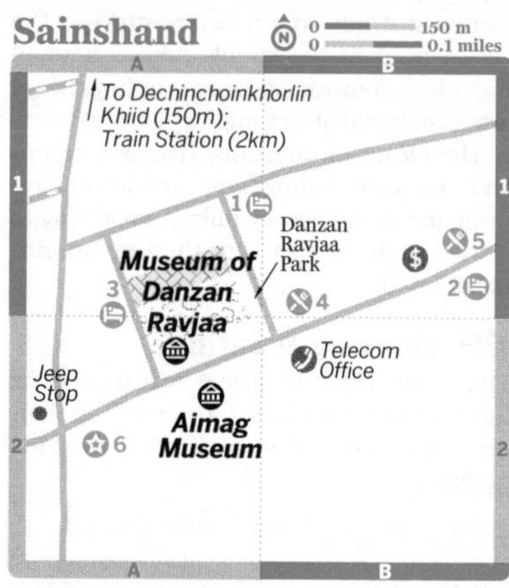

Sainshand

Top Sights

- Aimag Museum ... A2
- Museum of Danzan Ravjaa ... A2

Sleeping

1. Dornogobi Hotel ... A1
2. Lux Hotel ... B1
3. Shand Plaza ... A1

Eating

4. Altan Urag ... B1
5. Best Restaurant ... B1

Entertainment

6. Saran Khöökhöö Drama Theatre ... A2

small glass jar which contains Danzan Ravjaa's bones; the poet's mummified body was burned along with his monastery in the 1930s.

Dechinchoinkhorlin Khiid MONASTERY

(Дэчинчойнхорлин Хийд; ⏰10am-5pm Mon-Fri) This monastery, which opened in 1991, is in a large walled compound at the northern end of the central district. There is an active temple and, although visitors are welcome, photographs are not allowed inside. The 25 monks are very friendly. The best views are from the **tank monument** located behind the monastery.

Sleeping

Sainshand, like most aimag capitals in the Gobi, does not offer anywhere decent to pitch a tent. Try the cliffs north of the monastery.

Dornogobi Hotel HOTEL $$
(☎23657; dm/tw T10,000/40,000, d half-luxe/lux T50,000/55,000) The newest and largest hotel in Sainshand, its five floors and circular design mean it dominates the northeast corner of the park. The rooms are clean, smart and many have fine views over the surrounding town. There is a restaurant on the 2nd floor.

Lux Hotel HOTEL $$
(☎9301 1278; dm/tw T10,000/30,000, half-luxe d T40,000, luxe tw T50,000) On the outskirts of town, nearly all the rooms here have two beds apiece but ask to see a few as many smell rather smoky. The roomy dorm has six beds and an attached bathroom.

Shand Plaza HOTEL $$
(☎9914 8352, 23509; d/tr/half-lux/luxe T35,000/25,000/50,000/75,000) This reasonably comfortable hotel has a variety of rooms with TV and clean bathroom. The triple room has no shower but the basement has a shared shower and sauna that can be used even if you aren't staying here. The hotel also has a restaurant, disco and billiard room.

Eating & Drinking

Best Restaurant MONGOLIAN $$
(meals T2200-5000; ⏲10am-11pm) A local favourite, this place doles out excellent Mongolian dishes; we recommend the *bainshte shöl* (dumpling soup). There are no signs but it's on the 2nd floor of a light-brown brick building.

Altan Urag CHINESE $
(meals T1000-2500; ⏲9am-11pm) Another unsigned restaurant, this one can be found above a grocery store in a building that looks like an Arabian mini-castle (we thought it weird too). The draw here is authentic, if somewhat oily, Chinese meals. One dish is big enough for two people.

Entertainment

Saran Khöökhöö Drama Theatre THEATRE
(☎22796) This theatre is named after the famous play by local hero Danzan Ravjaa, who would be proud that this Sainshand theatre group is considered the best outside of Ulaanbaatar. It's in the centre of town on the west side of the park. Unfortunately, performances are sporadic.

Information

There are ATMs in the lobbies of both the Dornogobi and Shand Plaza hotels.

Internet cafe (per hr T500; ⏲24hr) In the Telecom office.

Telecom office (⏲24hr) The post office is also located here.

Trade & Development Bank (⏲9am-5pm Mon-Fri) Changes US-dollar travellers cheques and gives cash advances on MasterCard and Visa. The Mongol Post Bank is in the same building.

Getting There & Around

Because at least one train links Sainshand with Ulaanbaatar every day, there are no flights or scheduled bus services to or from Sainshand. A shared taxi from the train station to the city centre costs T500 per person or you can walk the 2km in around 25 minutes. Take the road that leads south from the train station and turn right at the T-intersection and then take the next left immediately after. This road runs south to the city centre.

JEEP Share jeeps park themselves at a stop south of the Sports Palace. These head out to the various villages in Dornogov, but it's nearly impossible to find a ride going to the neighbouring aimags.

TRAIN Local train 286 from Ulaanbaatar via Choir (daily) departs at 9.35am and arrives at 8.15pm. No 285 departs Sainshand for Ulaanbaatar at 9pm, arriving 8.05am. A second option is local train 276 to Zamyn-Üüd, which leaves Ulaanbaatar at 4.30pm, arriving at Sainshand at the inconvenient time of 1.38am. The return train (275) departs Sainshand at 11pm and arrives in Ulaanbaatar at 9.25am. Tickets from Ulaanbaatar cost T7400/13,200/21,500 for hard seat/hard sleeper/soft sleeper. If you book your ticket more than a day ahead there is a T800 to T1200 fee. Trains get crowded in both directions so book as far in advance as possible.

The Trans-Mongolian Railway and the trains between Ulaanbaatar and Ereen (Erlian; just over the Chinese border) and Hohhot (in Inner Mongolia) stop at Sainshand, but you cannot use these services just to get to Sainshand unless you buy a ticket all the way to China.

Around Sainshand

Although the desert in this part of the Gobi is typically flat and featureless, it is worth hiring a vehicle for a day to explore the attractions outside of town. Negotiate a trip with the drivers at the Sainshand's Sports Palace jeep stand.

Sights

Khamaryn Khiid MONASTERY
(Хамарын Хийд; www.khamarmonastery.mn, in Mongolian; GPS: N 44°36.038', E 110°16.650') This reconstructed monastery, an hour's drive south of Sainshand, has grown up around

RITUALS AT SHAMBHALA

There are several rituals to adhere to when you enter the Shambhala site. Do them in the following order.

» Write a bad thought on a piece of paper and burn it in the rocks to the left.

» Write down a wish, read it, throw some vodka in the air and drop some rice in the stone circles on the ground (representing the past, present and future).

» Take a white pebble from the ground, place it on the pile of other white pebbles and announce your family name.

» Take off your shoes and lie down on the ground, absorbing the energy of this sacred site.

» Circle the *ovoo* three times.

the cult of Danzan Ravjaa (p165), whom many locals believe to have been a living god. His image is sewn into a **carpet** that hangs in the main hall. The original monastery and three-storey theatre, built by Danzan Ravjaa in 1821, was destroyed in the 1930s.

From the monastery, a path leads for 3km to a **bell tower** which you must strike three times to announce your arrival at the 'energy centre,' known as **Shambhala** (admission T500). In 1853, Danzan Ravjaa told the local people that he would die in three years but they could forever come to this place and speak to his spirit. Indeed, he died three years later and the site was marked by an *ovoo*. Shambhala is now surrounded by 108 new stupas ('108' being a sacred number in Buddhism) and festivities are held here on 10 September.

A series of small **meditation caves** are located a short walk east of Shambhala. Here monks used to seal themselves inside the caves and meditate for 108 days.

Bayanzürkh Uul HISTORIC SITE
(GPS: N 44°41.644', E 110°02.707') Around 23km northwest of Khamaryn Khiid is the mountain home of the spirit of the third Noyon Khutagt (a predecessor of Danzan Ravjaa). The temple halfway up the mountain is as far as local women are allowed to go (although no one seems to mind if foreign women go to the top). At the summit (1070m) you are required to make three wishes and circle the peak along the well-worn path.

Sleeping & Eating

If you plan on making anything other than a day trip, it is worth noting that the monastery has only very basic facilities. You'll need to bring a tent or stay at either of the following ger camps, which are a 30-minute (20km) drive back towards Sainshand.

Gobi Sunrise Tavan Dohoi TOURIST GER CAMP $$
(☎9911 3820, 9909 0151; GPS: N 44°45.418', E 110°11.236'; with/without meals US$30/10; P) The 28 gers here can accommodate up to four people each and the shared facilities have flush toilets and clean showers with hot water. To arrange transport to the camp, which is about 20km south of Sainshand, ask Altangerel, the curator at the Museum of Danzan Ravjaa (p162).

Shand Ger Camp TOURIST GER CAMP $$
(☎9925 7883; with/without meals US$35/14; P) Located 15km south of Sainshand, this camp offers much the same facilities as the Gobi Sunrise although the mattresses here are no-

WORTH A TRIP

ROCK THIS WAY

The Gobi in Dornogov can at times seem a featureless wasteland, but hidden in its folds are some geological treats. Ancient volcanoes and eons of erosive winters have produced some intriguing rock formations.

Senjit Khad is a very impressive stone formation in the shape of an arch. It is about 95km northeast of Sainshand in Altanshiree *sum*.

Tsonjiin Chuluu looks rather like a set of hexagonal organ pipes. It's in the extreme northeast corner of Dornogov, in Delgerekh *sum*, about 160km along the northeast road from Sainshand.

The **Petrified Trees of Süikhent** (also known as Tsagaan Tsavyn) can be found lying buried in the sands of the remote southern *sum* of Mandakh, 200km southwest of Sainshand. Some of the fossilised trunks are 20m long.

As there is no public transport to any of these sites, they are best visited with your own vehicle and local guide.

THE LOST TREASURE OF DANZAN RAVJAA

Many tall tales exist about Danzan Ravjaa (1803–56), a hot-headed rebellious monk, a writer and popular leader of Mongolia's Red Hat Buddhists. It is said that he could fly to Tibet in an instant, disappear into thin air and turn water into whisky (a cherished feat in Mongolia). Displaying his powers to the local people, he once peed off the roof of his temple and 'magically' made the urine fly into the air. At age six he was proclaimed the Fifth Gobi Lord even though the Manchus had forbidden another after executing his predecessor.

Danzan Ravjaa's fame as a writer, artist and social critic spread far and wide. He was also an expert at martial arts, tantric studies, yoga and traditional medicine. He spent months in solitude writing, either in caves or in his ger. It is said that he so hated being disturbed that he built himself a ger with no door and his lousy temper was often exacerbated by protracted bouts of drinking.

Danzan Ravjaa's mysterious death came either at the hands of the rival Yellow Hat Buddhist sect or a jealous queen who failed to gain his love. During his life, Danzan Ravjaa had amassed a collection of statues, paintings, original manuscripts, opera costumes and ritual objects. It eventually fell to a man called Tuduv, the hereditary *takhilch* (caretaker) of Danzan Ravjaa's legacy, to protect these treasures during the 1937 communist purges. Every night, under the cover of darkness and in total secrecy, Tuduv buried a crate of treasure in the shifting sands of the Gobi. He only had time to bury 64 of the 1500 crates before they and the Khamaryn Khiid (monastery) were destroyed.

The only man alive today who knows their location is Zundoi Altangerel (Tuduv's grandson and the fifth *takhilch*), and in 1990 he retrieved all but 17 of them to found the Museum of Danzan Ravjaa in Sainshand. Then in 2009, much to the delight of a worldwide audience courtesy of a live **webcast** (www.gobi-treasure.com), Altangerel dug up two more crates.

For more information on Danzan Ravjaa, pick up a copy of his biography *Lama of the Gobi* (Maitri Books, 2006), by Michael Kohn, one of the authors of this guidebook.

ticeably thinner, which is a bonus if you like hard beds, not so great if you don't. Arrange transport through the Shand Plaza hotel in Sainshand (p163).

Getting There & Away

Both ger camps can arrange transport to Khamaryn Khiid, although the cheapest way to visit is to negotiate directly with the drivers at the Sports Palace jeep stand in Sainshand. Prices range from T40,000 to T60,000 and include waiting time.

Choir Чойр

Choir, about halfway between Sainshand and Ulaanbaatar, was once home to a large **Russian air-force base** that was abandoned in 1992. The base is still there, although most of the buildings have been stripped to their core, leaving empty shells and wreckage everywhere. The base and landing strip, around 15km north of Choir near the village of Lun, are part of a restricted zone that's off limits to travellers.

To get to Choir, take train 276 (departs Ulaanbaatar daily at 4.30pm and arrives at 9.22pm) or train 286 (departs at 9.35am and arrives at 3.07pm). The return trains 275 and 285 crawl out of town at the unspeakable times of 4.08am and 2am respectively. Tickets cost T4800/9700/14,900 for a hard seat/hard sleeper/soft sleeper.

Tickets for the 8am Tuesday and Friday bus to Mandalgov (T10,500, five hours) must be bought the day before.

Ikh Nartiin Chuluu
Их Нартын Чулуу

The **Ikh Nartiin Chuluu Nature Reserve** (Ikh Nart; www.ikhnart.com) is seeing an increasing trickle of visitors thanks to its accessibility from Ulaanbaatar, improving tourist facilities and a healthy population of the globally threatened argali sheep. As the Denver Zoo and a team of international biologists have been conducting a long-term study that has partly habituated the sheep to the presence of humans, you're almost guaranteed to see an argali here. In recent years the **Argali Project** has expanded to include the ibex and been joined by the **Carnivore Project** and the **Vulture Project**.

TO AND FROM CHINA

Jeeps, trains and buses all trundle to and from the Chinese border town of Ereen. See p264 for more information.

If you are on a Trans-Mongolian train, or the service between Ulaanbaatar and Hohhot or Ereen, you will stop at Zamyn-Üüd for an hour or so while Mongolian customs and immigration officials do their stuff – usually in the middle of the night. See p264 for details.

Several ancient **burial mounds** (GPS: N 45°75.546', E 108°65.454') and **petroglyphs** (GPS: N 45°60.787', E 108°57.201'; N 45°60.237', E 108°55.959'; N 45°59.175', E 108°61.397') can also be found throughout the park. The petroglyphs are found on rocky outcrops and take the form of Buddhist prayers written in the Tibetan script.

Some locals consider the **natural springs** near Khalzan Uul (Bald Mountain) a cure for everything from hangovers to HIV.

Sleeping

Red Rock Ger Camp TOURIST GER CAMP **$$$**
(in Ulaanbaatar 011-328 737; GPS: N 45°39.830', E 108°39.204'; 4/5 days with meals US$295/360; P) Nomadic Journeys (p54) operate this ger on the outskirts of the reserve. Advanced bookings are essential so that they can send a local driver (even with the GPS coordinates, local knowledge is invaluable when picking a route through the rocky formations) to collect you at either the Shiveegobi, Tsomog or Choir train stations. Transport to and from the train stations is included in the package.

Zamyn-Üüd Замын-Үүд

02524

The Trans-Mongolian Railway line serves as a life-sustaining artery for this small, otherwise insignificant village in the Gobi Desert. Indeed, cynics may say that Zamyn-Üüd is little more than a suburb of Chinese Ereen, uprooted and blown across the border in a Gobi sandstorm – locals would beg to differ.

Most of the town's activity can be found around the square in front of the train station. The chief attractions here are the disused water fountain, some outdoor pool tables and grabbing a bite at one of the many eateries that cater to transit travellers killing time.

Sleeping

Bank Hotel HOTEL **$**
(015245 100; d T35,000-50,000) The rooms here come in a range of sizes and prices but all are smartly decorated in restful greens and come with clean bathrooms and flat-screen TVs. You will find the hotel above a bank (Тѳрийн Банк) on the main road leading to the Chinese border.

Jintin HOTEL **$**
(025245 43289; dm T6500-9500, half-luxe d T26,000, luxe T28,000; P@) Painted a bold turquoise, this cheapie is next to the train station and boasts serviceable but threadbare rooms with showers that are more decorative than functional. Head to the hotel's basement for reliable hot water in the public shower (T500).

Information

The train station has several ATMs that accept international cards and moneychangers are on hand to change your tögrögs. Luggage storage is also available for T150 per item.

Getting There & Away

The daily train (276) to Zamyn-Üüd, via Choir and Sainshand, leaves Ulaanbaatar every day at 4.30pm, arriving around 7.10am. Tickets cost T9600/16,300/27,300 for hard seat/hard sleeper/soft sleeper.

The same train (now called 275) returns to Ulaanbaatar at 5.35pm, arriving the next morning at 9.25am. Tickets cost T4500/9300/14,300 to Sainshand and T7400/13,200/22,200 to Choir.

There is also an express train (33/34) that connects Zamyn-Üüd to Ulaanbaatar. It leaves Ulaanbaatar at around 8pm on Tuesdays and Saturdays, and arrives in Zamyn-Üüd at 7.55am. Departures from Zamyn-Üüd are on Mondays and Fridays at 9.25pm, reaching Ulaanbaatar at 9.20am. Tickets cost T22,100/39,200 for hard/soft sleeper to Ulaanbaatar, T13,500/18,800 to Sainshand and T17,500/31,100 to Choir.

ÖMNÖGOV ӨМНӨГОВЬ

POP 49,300 / AREA 165,000 SQ KM

Ömnögov (southern Gobi) is the largest aimag in Mongolia, and has a population density of only 0.3 people per square kilometre. With an average annual precipitation of only 130mm a year, and summer temperatures reaching an average of 38°C, this is the driest, hottest and harshest region in the entire country; it's not hard to see why humans prefer to live elsewhere.

Tourism is an important business in the region and there are plenty of ger camps throughout the aimag. Far more important, however, is the mining industry (legend has it that the aimag governor passes out business cards printed with gold dust), and in particular the massive Oyu Tolgoi copper and gold deposit in Khanbogd *sum*.

National Parks

Gurvan Saikhan National Park
(2,000,000 hectares) A wealth of sand dunes, canyons, dinosaur fossils and mountainous terrain. Desert wildlife includes argali sheep, ibex and snow leopard.

Small Gobi A Strictly Protected Area
(1,839,176 hectares) On the border with China, includes dunes and saxaul forest. It is the last great bastion of the *khulan* (wild ass).

Dalanzadgad
Даланзадгад

☎01532 / POP 13,900 / ELEV 1465M

The capital of Ömnögov, Dalanzadgad is a speck of civilisation in the desert, sitting in the shadow of Gurvan Saikhan Nuruu. As the capital of a mineral-rich aimag, there are some positive signs of development, including the construction of a massive new Government House.

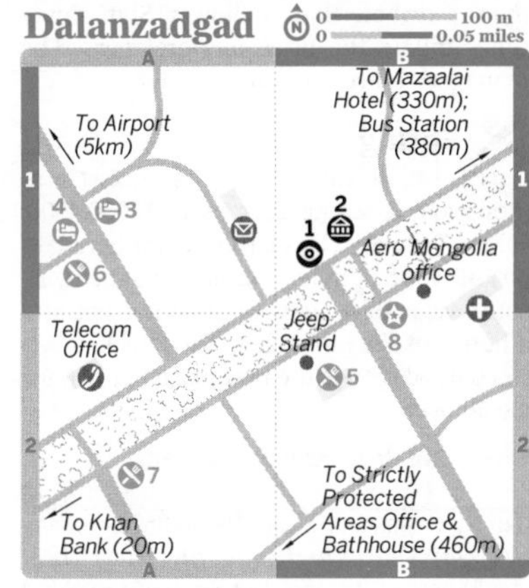

Dalanzadgad

Sights
1 Government House B1
2 South Gobi Museum B1

Sleeping
3 Dalanzadgad Hotel A1
4 Gobi Gurvan Saikhan Hotel A1

Eating
Dalanzadgad Hotel .... (see 3)
5 Department Store & Everyday Supermarket B2
6 Green Castle Center Restaurant A1
7 Market A2

Entertainment
8 Galaxy Cinema B2

Sights

South Gobi Museum MUSEUM
(☎23871; admission T2000, photos T5000, video T10,000; ⏲9am-6pm Mon-Fri) Surprisingly, this museum has little on dinosaurs – just a leg, an arm and a few eggs. (All of the best exhibits are in Ulaanbaatar or in other museums around the world.) There are a few nice paintings, a huge stuffed vulture and a display of scroll paintings and other Buddhist items.

Sleeping

Like other Gobi aimag capitals, there is no river or any decent place to camp in Dalanzadgad. You will have to walk 1km or 2km in any direction from town, and pitch your tent somewhere secluded.

Dalanzadgad Hotel HOTEL $$$
(☎24455; tw US$40, half-luxe/luxe with breakfast US$60/90) By far the nicest digs in town but often full of mining big-wigs. The half-luxe and luxe rooms here have flat-screen TVs, baths (as well as showers) and tea/coffee making facilities.

Mazaalai Hotel TOURIST GER CAMP $
(☎8898 4522; per person T10,000; P) This small and clean ger camp is on the eastern end of town and currently it's the best of the cheapies.

Kherleu 2 TOURIST GER CAMP $
(☎9953 1122; GPS N 43°34.214', E 104°23.869'; per person T5000; P) The four basic gers here with shared toilet and hot showers (T1000) are reasonably priced but difficult to find. Northwest of the centre.

Gobi Gurvan Saikhan Hotel HOTEL $
(☎23830; s/tr/tw T10,000/24,000/25,000) Most rooms come with a hot shower, although it's

more a dribble than a shower. Staff sometimes inflate the price for foreigners. The manager's office is on the 1st floor.

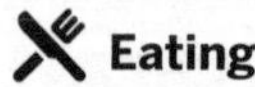

Eating

Dalanzadgad Hotel WESTERN/KOREAN $$
(Restaurant & Terrace Cafe; meals T2000-4500; ⏲7am-10pm; 📋) The picture menu here lays out all your options – salads, spaghetti, risotto, vegetable curry, Chinese hot pot and a bunch of Korean dishes. The attached **bar** (⏲6pm-midnight) is the best place in town for a cold beer.

Green Castle Center Restaurant MONGOLIAN $$
(Luxury Restaurant; meals T6000-8500; ⏲8am-midnight) The *ukhriin makhan steik* (beef steak) was a bit chewy but the *tsuivan* (fried noodles with mutton) got the nod of approval from our driver.

Also recommended:

Market MONGOLIAN $
Come here for fresh veggies (Gobi vegetables are renowned in Mongolia for their sweet taste). Nearby, you'll also see women selling jars of lovely *tarag* (yoghurt; T500) and packets of sugar.

Department Store & Everyday Supermarket WESTERN $
Self-caterers should check out the supermarket for dried goods.

☆ Entertainment

Galaxy Cinema CINEMA
(admission US$3) Hollywood blockbusters with Mongolian subtitles and a great foyer featuring murals of prehistoric life.

ⓘ Information

There is a good map of the city on the wall inside the bus station.

Bathhouse (shower T2000; ⏲9am-10pm) One street north of the Strictly Protected Areas office and near Secondary School 1.

Internet cafe (per hr T500; ⏲8am-11pm) In the Telecom office.

Khan Bank (⏲9am-9pm Mon-Fri, 9am-3pm Sat) Changes dollars and has an on-site ATM. It's 50m west of the market.

Strictly Protected Areas office (☎23973; gtzgobi@magicnet.mn) In the southwest of town, this office mostly deals in bureaucratic affairs. For information, you are better off at the information ger at the gate to Gurvan Saikhan National Park (p169).

Telecom office (☎24110; ⏲24hr)

ⓘ Getting There & Away

AIR At least one flight a day connects Dalanzadgad and Ulaanbaatar.

AeroMongolia (☎9606 0666; 2nd fl, Galaxy Cinema Bldg) One way T241,600.

EZ Nis (☎22969) One way T281,200.

BUS A twice-daily bus travels between Dalanzadgad and Ulaanbaatar (T22,500, 12 hours, 553km), departing at around 8am and 4pm via Mandalgov (T14,000, seven hours).

MINIVANS Minivans leave when full for Ulaanbaatar (T25,000) and Mandalgov (T20,000). They gather outside the Department Store & Everyday Supermarket. Jeeps and vans can be hired in Dalanzadgad for T600 to T700 per kilometre plus fuel if you ask around.

Around Dalanzadgad

Most travellers spend their time in the countryside around Dalanzadgad rather than in the town itself. While there is little of note besides fresh air and the empty grandeur, thanks to the relative proximity of both Yolyn Am and Bayanzag (the Flaming Cliffs), there are about 20 ger camps within 100km of Dalanzadgad.

As you travel about keep a look out for **black-tailed gazelle**, which you may see darting across the open plains, and herds of **domesticated camels**.

All of the ger camps listed below can organise a jeep (prices range from T650 to T850 per kilometre plus fuel) and guide (US$25 to US$30 per day) with advance notice.

Sleeping

TOP CHOICE **Three Camel Lodge** TOURIST GER CAMP $$$
(☎in Ulaanbaatar 011-330 998; www.threecamellodge.com; GPS: N 43°53.603', E 103°44.435'; std with/without meals US$137/103, luxe with/without meals US$193/160; 🅿) A veritable oasis in the desert 66km northeast of Dalanzadgad, Three Camels sets the bar for the Mongolian ger camp experience. Visitors stay in luxurious gers that share a central bathroom (only the luxe gers have private toilets) and a communal lounge with an open fire. Four-course meals (US$19) and a breakfast buffet are served in an elevated restaurant with a large terrace and spectacular views over a great, grassy plain. The basement Thirsty Camel Bar is refreshingly cool and a great place to escape the Gobi summer heat.

Gobi Mirage TOURIST GER CAMP $$
(☎9918 4809; www.gobimirage.mn; GPS: N 43°48.572', E 103°54.879'; with/without meals

US$38/20; P@) Run by a friendly family with local connections, the Gobi Mirage will collect clients from Dalanzadgad airport with advance notice. Buffet-style meals.

New Tovshin TOURIST GER CAMP $
(☎/fax 5053 5353; www.new-tovshin.mn; GPS: N 43°45.841', E 104°02.838'; with/without meals US$30/10; P) The 'new' in the name reflects the new owners, not the state of the gers or restaurant.

Juulchin-Gobi Camp 1 TOURIST GER CAMP $$
(☎5053 5355; GPS: N 43°45.236', E 104°07.578'; with/without meals US$45/20; P) Slightly rough around the edges but bird-watchers recommend the knowledgeable nature guide.

Gurvan Saikhan National Park Гурван Сайхан

With its iconic sand dunes, ice canyon, striped badlands and stunning mountain vistas, this is understandably one of Mongolia's most popular national parks. Most travellers only see a fraction of it, sticking to the main sites. With more time it's possible to drive to the remote western area – an eerie landscape so lacking in life that you may feel as if you've landed on the moon.

Gurvan Saikhan (Three Beauties) is named after its three ridges (though there are four). Besides its spectacular natural beauty it contains more than 200 bird species, including the Mongolian desert finch, cinereous vulture, desert warbler and houbara bustard. Spring brings further waves of migratory birds.

The park also has maybe 600 or more types of plants, many of which only bloom after (very infrequent) heavy rain. The sparse vegetation does manage to support numerous types of animals, such as the black-tailed gazelle, Kozlov's pygmy jerboa, wild ass and endangered species of wild camel, snow leopard, ibex and argali sheep.

Sights & Activities

TOP CHOICE **Yolyn Am** VALLEY
(Ёлын Ам) Yolyn Am (Vulture's Mouth) was originally established to conserve the birdlife in the region, but it's now more famous for its dramatic rocky cliffs and narrow, heavily shaded canyons that allow sheets of blue-veined ice to survive well into the summer. Yolyn Am is in the Zuun Saikhan Nuruu, 46km west of Dalanzadgad.

Nature Museum
(GPS: N 43°32.872', E 104°02.257'; admission T2000; ⌚8am-9pm) The small museum at the gate on the main road to Yolyn Am has a collection of dinosaur eggs and bones, stuffed birds and a snow leopard. Several souvenir shops and an 'information ger' can also be found here.

Gorge
(GPS: N 43°29.332', E 104°04.000') From the museum, the road continues for another 10km to a car park. From there, a pleasant 2km walk, following the Yol Stream, leads to an ice-filled gorge and one or two lonely souvenir salesmen. Locals also rent horses (T8000) and camels (T12,000) for the trip.

In winter, the ice is up to 10m high and continues down the gorge for another 10km, although it has largely disappeared by the end of July. It's possible to walk the length of the gorge – an experienced driver could pick you up on the other side (GPS: N 43°30.537', E 104°06.616'), about 8km east of the car park.

The surrounding hills offer plenty of opportunities for some fine, if somewhat strenuous, day **hikes**. If you are lucky you might spot ibex or argali sheep along the steep valley ridges.

Mukhar Shiveert
About 1km before the museum is a second ice valley called Mukhar Shiveert; visitors may be required to pay an additional T3000 to visit the site.

Dugany Am
(GPS: N 43°29.521', E 103°51.586') If you are headed from Yolyn Am to Khongoryn Els, an adventurous and rough alternative route takes you through the Dugany Am, a spectacular and narrow gorge barely wide enough to allow a jeep to pass that eventually leads to some spectacular views and a **small stupa** (GPS: N 43°29.115', E 103°51.043') that has been built on the remains of a former temple. The gorge is blocked with ice until July and can be impassable even after the ice has melted, so check road conditions with the rangers at the park entrance.

TOP CHOICE **Khongoryn Els** SAND DUNES
(Хонгорын Элс) Khongoryn Els are some of the largest and most spectacular sand dunes in Mongolia. Also known as the Duut Mankhan (Singing Dunes – from the sound they make when the sand is moved by the wind or as it collapses in small avalanches), they are up to 300m high, 12km wide and about 100km long. The largest dunes are at the northwestern corner of the

PIKA-BOO

The small, mouse-like creatures, often seen darting between rock crevices at Yolyn Am, are called pikas and are actually members of the rabbit family. Pikas are freakin' cute; so cute in fact that most people spend a considerable amount of time trying to photograph them. This is tricky because eagles find them conveniently bite-sized, and ever fearful of an aerial attack, pikas will scamper just out of shot the moment a camera is waved in their direction.

Surprisingly, pikas don't hibernate, preferring to spend their summers making hay while the sun shines and you may witness them dragging grass into their burrows for winter consumption.

range. Getting to the top is exhausting; every step forward is followed by a metre of backsliding but the views of the desert from the sandy summit are wonderful.

The sand dunes are also a popular place for organising **camel rides** (per hr/day T5000/15,000), and locals seem to appear from the woodwork when a jeep full of tourists arrives. A **mini Naadam** featuring horse racing and wrestling is held here on 15 August.

The dunes are about 180km from Dalanzadgad. There is no way to get there unless you charter a jeep or are part of a tour.

From Khongoryn Els it is possible to follow desert tracks 130km north to Bogd in Övörkhangai, or 215km northwest to Bayanlig in Bayankhongor. This is a remote and unforgiving area and you shouldn't undertake either trip without an experienced driver and full stocks of food, water and fuel.

Sleeping

YOLYN AM

Three local families near the Yolyn Am park entrance have **basic gers** (summer GPS N 43°33.725', E 104°00.985'; per person T5000; P) with outhouse toilets available for rent. In winter the families can be found close to the road near the museum, and in summer, just over the rise in a broad valley with rolling hills and a backdrop of tawny mountains. Meals typically cost from T2500 to T3000.

KHONGORYN ELS

Ganbold Delger TRADITIONAL GER $
(8853 8184; GPS: N 43°46.297', E 102°21.289'; per person with/without meals T10,000/7000; P) If you are prepared to rough it a little (there are no showers), staying with this family in their basic gers is great way to see a slice of daily Gobi life. If they are full, they'll soon direct you to another of the 10 or so family-run operations in the immediate vicinity.

Juulchin Gobi 2 TOURIST GER CAMP $$
(☎5053 5355; jgobi@magicnet.mn; with/without meals US$45/22; P) A tidy and welcoming camp with clean, if cramped, toilets.

Gobi Discovery TOURIST GER CAMP $$
(☎011-312 769; www.gobidiscovery.mn; GPS: N 43°46.495', E 102°20.307'; with meals US$45-50, without meal US$25; P) Offering much the same as the Juulchin Gobi 2, this camp is about 2km north of the dunes.

Information

There is a national park entry fee of T3000 per person. You can pay the fee at the park office in Dalanzadgad or, more conveniently, at the entrance to Yolyn Am or from the ranger at Khongoryn Els. Keep your entry ticket as you may need to show it more than once.

Conservation Ink (www.conservationink.org) publishes the excellent *Gobi Gurvan Saikhan National Park Map and Guide*, a satellite map with informative articles.

Bayanzag Баянзаг

Bayanzag (Flaming Cliffs; GPS: N 44°08.311', E 103°43.667'; admission T1000), which means 'rich in saxaul shrubs', is more commonly known as the 'Flaming Cliffs', penned by the palaeontologist Roy Chapman Andrews (see p172). First excavated in 1922, it is renowned worldwide for the number of **dinosaur bones and eggs** found in the area, which you can see in the Museum of Natural History in Ulaanbaatar or, mostly, in other museums around the world.

Even if you are not a 'dinophile', the eerie beauty of the surrounding landscape is a good reason to visit. It's a classic desert of rock, red sands, scrub, sun and awesome emptiness. There's not much to do once you're here except explore the area, hire a **camel** (per hr/day T5000/20,000) or grab a cold drink from the souvenir sellers who hang out on the edge of the cliff.

A further 22km northeast of Bayanzag is an area of sand dunes called **Moltzog Els**, which might be worth a visit if you're not planning to visit Khongoryn Els.

Sleeping & Eating

All of the accommodation listed below can rustle up a meal and a camel; occasionally this is one and the same. Alternatively you can do your own thing and camp near the *zag* (scrub) forest. The family-run gers charge about T3500 for a home-cooked meal. Thanks to a small stream, fresh veggies are available in the microscopic town of **Del** (GPS: N 44°05.105', E 103°42.945'), 12km from the cliffs.

Bayanzag Tourist Camp TOURIST GER CAMP $
(☎9314 9296; www.gobitour.mn; GPS: N 44°10.466', E 103°41.816'; with/without meals US$30/12; P) This 25-ger operation occupies a nice position on a low bluff looking towards the saxaul forest and within walking distance (4km) of the cliffs. Nonguests are welcome at its giant tortoise-shaped **restaurant** (meals T4000-5000) made from rocks. With a day's notice they can organise a guide and car for trips to Moltzog Els and local palaeolithic sites (US$100, including lunch).

Jamian Family Ger TRADITIONAL GER $
(☎9822 0998; GPS: N 44°10.268', E 103°41.693'; per person T7000; P) One of four families in the area that rent gers to overnighting tourists. When not in use by travellers, the family use the gers themselves so be sure not to touch their personal possessions tucked into the ger latticework. The long-drop toilet has a great view, mostly because the door is missing. There are no showers here.

Gobitour Camp TOURIST GER CAMP $$
(☎9909 3235; www.gobitourcamp.com; GPS: N 44°07.367', E 103°43.793'; with/without meals US$40/25) A pleasant camp on the up side of the cliffs, the Gobitour Camp opened in 2007 and has clean showers and 24-hour electricity. Some of the gers have double beds and if you're travelling in a group (or extremely hungry) the cook will BBQ a whole sheep *khorkhog* (hot-stone) style for around US$100.

Khanbogd Ханбогд

Despite its apparent remoteness, the Khanbogd *sum* is set to enrich the whole of Mongolia, thanks to an enormous copper and gold deposit at Oyu Tolgoi, about 40km southwest of the Khanbogd town centre. The field is currently being developed by a Canadian mining company (to the tune of US$5 billion) and when fully operational in 2018 the mine could boost Mongolia's GDP by more than 30% and become the world's largest copper mine.

Demchigiin Khiid MONASTERY
(Дэмчигийн Хийдийн Туйр; GPS: N 43°07.711', E 107°07.668') Unless you have a particular interest in copper mining, the main reason to come here is to visit one of the monasteries built by Danzan Ravjaa (see p165). The monastery, about 20km from the town, was destroyed in 1937 but is undergoing a renovation project funded by Ivanhoe Mines. Gobi people consider the rocky area around the monastery to be an important energy centre for Buddhism.

Lovon Chombin Agui RUINS
(Ловон Чомбын Агуй; GPS: N 42°35.305', E 107°49.529') Serious explorers may want to carry on to this 50m-long cave with numerous stalactites. The cave and adjacent monastery ruins are near the Chinese border, so you'll definitely need a border permit from Ulaanbaatar (see p72).

Bulgan Булган

By virtue of its central Gobi location, this ramshackle village 95km northwest of Dalanzadgad is home to large-scale **Tsagaan Sar** (Lunar New Year) festivities, which take place in January or February. The two-day festival includes camel racing, camel polo and a camel beauty contest (apparently they don't all look the same). During the event, temporary ger camps pop up to house tourists.

Nearby is **Ulaan Nuur** (Red Lake), the largest and just about the only lake in Ömnögov. It may not be there when you visit because it often dries out; it won't quench your thirst either – it is very salty.

The **Ankhsan Cooperative Guesthouse** (☎9898 2829; GPS: N 44°05.631', E 103°32.556'; per person T6000-8000) has a couple of cleanish gers and a long-drop outhouse to frighten small children.

BAYANKHONGOR БАЯНХОНГОР

POP 85,400 / AREA 116,000 SQ KM

One of the most diverse aimags in the Gobi, **Bayankhongor** (www.bayankhongor.com) has

ROY CHAPMAN ANDREWS

American adventurer Roy Chapman Andrews (1884–1960) had a restless spirit. 'I wanted to go everywhere', he wrote in *Under a Lucky Star*, 'I would have started on a day's notice for the North Pole or the South, to the jungle or the desert. It made not the slightest bit of difference to me.'

Adventures in his youth included filming whales in the Atlantic, trapping snakes in the East Indies and hunting game in Yunnan. But he is best known for his explorations of the Gobi in the 1920s, where he found the first dinosaur eggs, jaws and skulls in Central Asia. Andrews' most famous expeditions were based at Bayanzag, which he famously renamed the 'Flaming Cliffs'.

According to his books and biographies, he was an adventurer who took the expeditions' ambushes, raids, bandits, rebellions and vipers in his stride. He was never one for understatement: as one expedition member said, 'the water that was up to our ankles was always up to Roy's neck'. In reality, one of the few times an expedition member was seriously injured was when Andrews accidentally shot himself in the leg with his own revolver.

Andrews worked for US intelligence during WWI and also explored Alaska, Borneo, Burma, Korea and China. He wrote such boys' own classics as *Whale Hunting with Gun and Camera* (1916), *Across Mongolian Plains* (1921), *On the Trail of Ancient Man* (1926) and *The New Conquest of Central Asia* (1932). Always kitted out in a felt hat, khakis and a gun by his side, Andrews is widely regarded as the model on which the Hollywood screen character Indiana Jones was based.

For more information on RC Andrews, read *Dragon Hunter*, by Charles Galenkamp.

mountains in the north, deserts in the south, a handful of lakes and rivers, hot springs and a real oasis in the far south of the province.

Bayankhongor, which means 'rich chestnut' (named after the colour of horses – or your skin after a couple of hours in the Gobi sun), is home to wild camels and asses and the extremely rare Gobi bear.

Bayankhongor City
Баянхонгор

01442 / POP 23,800 / ELEV 1859M

The broad avenues, cantonment-style apartment blocks and parade ground in front of a monolithic Government House are straight out a Soviet planner's briefcase. There are also large patches of waste ground as if the builders gave up halfway through the project. Although the town itself is nothing special, the Khangai Nuruu, with several peaks of 3000m or more, is not too far away.

Sights

The skyline of the city is dominated by a **stupa** on a hill to the west of the square. If you are staying for a while, take a walk up there for views of the town and nearby countryside.

Lamyn Gegeenii Gon Gandan Dedlin Khiid MONASTERY

(Ламын Гэгээний Гон Гандан Дэдлин Хийд) The original monastery by this name was located 20km east of Bayankhongor city and was one of the biggest in the country. It was levelled by the communist government in 1937. The current monastery is home to only 15 monks. Foundations have been laid for a new prayer temple that is expected to be completed in 2011. Daily services start at 10am in the main 'brick ger' temple which features a statue of Sakyamuni (the historical Buddha) flanked by a green-and-white Tara.

Aimag Museum MUSEUM

(admission T2000, photos T5000; 9am-1pm & 2-6pm Mon-Fri) The Aimag Museum, inside the sports stadium in the park, is well laid out and worth a visit. There is a good display on Buddhist art, featuring two lovely statues of Tara, some fine old scroll paintings and *tsam* (lama dance) masks and costumes.

Natural History Museum MUSEUM

(admission T2000; 9am-1pm & 2-6pm Mon-Fri) The Natural History Museum across the street is filled with badly stuffed animals, a replica Tarbosaurus skeleton and some fossils, including a 130-million-year-old fossilised turtle.

Bayankhongor City

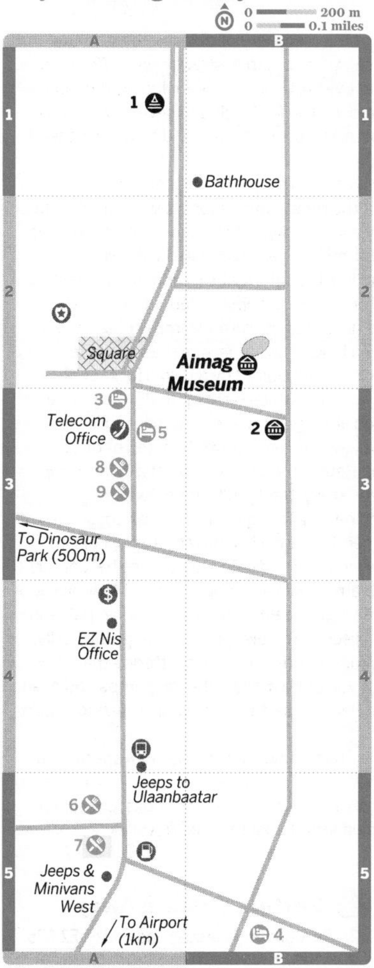

0 200 m
0 0.1 miles

A B
1 2 3 4 5
1 Bathhouse
Square
Aimag Museum
3 Telecom Office 5
2
8
9
To Dinosaur Park (500m)
EZ Nis Office
Jeeps to Ulaanbaatar
6
7
Jeeps & Minivans West
To Airport (1km)
4

Bayankhongor City

Top Sights

Aimag Museum B2

Sights

1 Lamyn Gegeenii Gon Gandan Dedlin Khiid A1
2 Natural History Museum B3

Sleeping

3 Khongor Hotel A3
4 Negdelchin Hotel B5
5 Seoul Hotel A3

Eating

6 Arvijikh Supermarket A5
7 Market A5
8 Soymbo A3
9 Uran Khairkhan A3

Dinosaur Park PARK

Still only half finished when we called, this park has several life-sized concrete dinosaurs including a family of Velociraptors, some kind of sauropod and a T-rex. We have no idea what the brown one with the stumpy tail is – nor did anyone else.

Sleeping

The best place to camp is probably by the Tüin Gol, a few hundred metres east of the city.

Khongor Hotel HOTEL $

(☎9972 3437; tw/q T25,000/25,000, half luxe/luxe incl breakfast T30,000/35,000; P) The rooms here are strictly no-frills but they are clean and functional and some even come with their own showers. The secure parking costs an additional T3000.

Negdelchin Hotel HOTEL $

(☎22278; s/d/tr/q/half-luxe/luxe T8000/16,000/24,000/32,000/30,000/40,000) Located at the southern end of the main street, the 'Workers Hotel' is Bayankhongor's old Soviet-era standby. Some rooms have seen renovation, all have a toilet but only the luxe rooms have a shower.

Seoul Hotel HOTEL $$

(☎22754, 9944 0884; s/tw US$20/36, luxe US$30/40) Considering the rooms rely on shared showers and toilets, this place is drastically overpriced.

Eating

All the hotels mentioned under Sleeping have restaurants. As always, you'll find a number of *guanz* (canteens) selling *buuz* (mutton dumplings) and *khuushuur* (mutton pancake) near the **market**. A number of supermarkets, including the **Arvijikh Supermarket**, can also be found here. Remember in these parts beef means yak.

Uran Khairkhan MONGOLIAN $

(meals T1500-6000; ⏰9am-10pm) With its cheery yellow tablecloths and cosy booth dining, jovial Uran Khairkhan is reminiscent of a Norman Rockwell painting c 1950. The iced cakes in the cabinet cost T1000 a slice.

Soymbo MONGOLIAN/WESTERN $

(meals T3500-6000; ⏰10am-11pm; 📋) Besides the usual mutton line, fried chicken is also

DINOSAURS

In the early 1920s, newspapers brought news of the discovery of dinosaur eggs in the southern Gobi Desert by American adventurer Roy Chapman Andrews (see p172). Over a period of two years Andrews' team unearthed over 100 dinosaurs, including Protoceratops Andrewsi, which was named after the explorer. The find included several Velociraptors (Swift Robbers), subsequently made famous by *Jurassic Park*, and a parrot-beaked Oviraptor (Egg Robber).

Subsequent expeditions have added to the picture of life in the Gobi during the late Cretaceous period 70 million years ago. One of the most famous fossils unearthed so far is the 'Fighting Dinosaurs' fossil, discovered by a joint Polish-Mongolian team in 1971 and listed as a national treasure. The remarkable 80-million-year-old fossil is of a Protoceratops and Velociraptor locked in mortal combat. It is thought that this and other fossilised snapshots were entombed by a violent sandstorm or by collapsing sand dunes. One poignant fossil is of an Oviraptor protecting its nest of eggs from the impending sands.

A picture of prehistoric Gobi has emerged – a land of swamps, marshes and lakes, with areas of sand studded with oases. The land was inhabited by a colourful cast of characters: huge duck-billed hadrosaurs; ankylosaurs, which were up to 25ft tall, were armour-plated and had club-like tails that acted like a giant mace; long-necked, lizard-hipped sauropods such as Nemegtosaurus, which may have grown to a weight of 90 tonnes; and the mighty Tarbosaurus (Alarming Reptile), a carbon copy of a Tyrannosaurus rex, with a 1.2m-long skull packed with razor-sharp teeth up to 15cm long.

Apart from the famous sites of Bayanzag and nearby Togrigiin Shiree, the richest sites of Bugiin Tsav, Ulaan Tsav, Nemegt Uul and Khermen Tsav are all in the remote west of Ömnögov aimag and impossible to reach without a jeep and dedicated driver (or a helicopter).

There are still plenty of fossils – in 2006 a team of palaeontologists from Mongolia and Montana unearthed 67 dinosaur skeletons in a single week! In 2007 a Canadian palaeontologist reported finding large numbers of fossilised carnivores near Nemegt Uul. Sadly, he also described how poachers remove the skulls, hands and feet, scattering the other bones in their dirty work. Locals may approach you at Bayanzag, the ger camps and even Dalanzadgad to buy dinosaur bones and eggs. Remember that it is *highly* illegal to export fossils from Mongolia.

Today the best places to come face to face with the dinosaurs of the Gobi are the Museum of Natural History in Ulaanbaatar and the **American Museum of Natural History** (www.amnh.org) in New York, which also has a fine website. As for books, check out *Dinosaurs of the Flaming Cliffs* by American palaeontologist Michael Novacek.

listed on the menu, although only occasionally is it successfully ordered. The glitzy gold leaf on the walls and neon 'open' sign in the window qualify this as the smartest restaurant in town.

Information

Bathhouse (shower T1500, sauna T8000; ⌚10am-10pm)

Internet cafe (per hr T500; ⌚9am-10pm) Next to the Telecom office.

Khan Bank (⌚9am-1pm & 2-6pm Mon-Fri) Changes US dollars and gives cash advances on Visa and MasterCard. There is an ATM in the shop next door.

Telecom office (⌚10am-10pm) The post office is also located here.

Getting There & Away

AIR On Monday, Thursday and Friday, **EZ Nis** (☎24444, 9904 9933) flies between Ulaanbaatar and Bayankhongor for T255,000 one way. The airport is about 1km south of the city.

BUS An 8am daily bus leaves for Ulaanbaatar (T21,000, 15 hours, 630km) via Arvaikheer (T10,000, five hours, 200km). It gets crowded so it is wise to purchase tickets the day before. It is not possible to travel further west by bus from Bayankhongor.

JEEP & MINIVAN Bayankhongor is connected by minivans to Ulaanbaatar (T30,000, 14 hours), which depart when full from the bus station. Minivans heading west to Altai (T20,000, 10 hours, 400km) and occasionally Khovd (T40,000, 24 hours) leave from in front of the market.

Shargaljuut Шаргалжуут

The major attraction in Bayankhongor aimag is the 300 or so hot- and cold-water springs at **Shargaljuut** (GPS: N 46°19.940', E 101°13.624'), about 60km northeast of Bayankhongor city and easily accessible from the aimag capital.

The springs and bathhouses cover the banks of the river between the peaks of Myangan Ugalzat Uul (3483m) and Shargaljuut Uul (3137m). The hot water, which can reach 50°C, is supposed to cure a wide range of complaints and many Mongolians come for treatment at the **sanatorium** (⌚9am-6pm Mon-Sat Apr-Dec).

Foreign guests can stay at the **Shargaljuut Resort** (☎9191 4077; ger/half-luxe/luxe US$35/35/60) at the sanatorium.

A number of small **guesthouses** also offer beds for T5000 to T10000. The best is a small ger camp on the west side of the river before the main complex; ask for Dr Burnee who is a mine of information on the area.

Alternatively, you can camp further upstream next to the river on the little-used road to Tsetserleg.

A minivan runs to Bayankhongor's market every morning from Shargaljuut (T4000, two hours, 70km). It returns in the afternoon when full. In summer a local named **Batbayar** (☎9975 1276) also makes runs directly to the springs for T20,000 one way from Ulaanbaatar.

Bayangovi Баянговь

The small town of Bayangovi is about 250km south of Bayankhongor (by road) in a beautiful valley dominated by Ikh Bogd Uul (3957m). While there is nothing of special interest in Bayangovi itself, the surrounding countryside offers some intriguing desert sites and ample opportunity for exploration.

Gobi Camels (☎9918 0916; GPS: N 44°45.750', E 100°20.585'; per person incl meals US$40) is an overpriced ger camp 6km northwest of town. It is possible to hire a jeep here for T55,000 plus fuel. The other alternative is the clean **Sumshig Hotel and Restaurant** (per person with shared bathroom T8000) within a compound on the western edge of the town 'square'.

Shared minivans or jeeps occasionally run to Bayangovi from outside the central market at Bayankhongor. To get back to Bayankhongor (T15,000) ask at the post office, shops or petrol station, and wait. The road around Bogd can become an impassable quagmire after heavy rain.

Amarbuyant Khiid Амарбуянт Хийд

Located 47km west of Shinejist, this ruined **monastery** (GPS: N 44°37.745', E 98°42.214') once housed around 1000 monks until its destruction in 1937 by Stalin's thugs. Its claim to fame is that the 13th Dalai Lama, while travelling from Lhasa to Urga in 1904, stayed here for 10 days. The extensive ruins today include temples, buildings and walls, and the main temple has been partially restored. Locals can also show you a small *ovoo* built by the Dalai Lama; out of respect no rocks were ever added to the *ovoo.*

Ekhiin Gol Эхийн Гол

This fertile **oasis** (GPS: N 43°14.898', E 90°00.295') located deep in the southern Gobi produces a tremendous amount of fruit and vegetables. This is probably the only place in Mongolia where, upon entering a ger, travellers are served tomato juice rather than tea. Until the 1920s, Chinese farmers tilled this soil and grew opium, an era that ended when a psychopathic lama-turned-bandit named Dambijantsan came by here and slaughtered them all. Ekhiin Gol is a good place to start or end a camel trek from Shinejist.

GOV-ALTAI ГОВЬ-АЛТАЙ

POP 59,400 / AREA 142,000 SQ KM

Mongolia's second-largest aimag is named after the Gobi Desert and Mongol Altai Nuruu, a mountain range that virtually bisects the aimag to create a stark, rocky landscape. There is a certain beauty in this combination, but there is considerable heartbreak too. Gov-Altai is one of the least suitable areas for raising livestock, and therefore one of the most hostile to human habitation.

Somehow a few Gobi bears, wild camels, ibex and even snow leopards survive, protected in several remote national parks. Most of the population live in the northeastern corner, where melting snow from Khangai Nuruu feeds small rivers, creating vital water supplies.

Mountaineers and adventurous hikers with a lot of time on their hands might want to bag an Altai peak. Opportunities include

WORTH A TRIP

EXPLORING THE GOBI

If you fancy yourself to be of the Indiana Jones ilk then you'll love the desert around Bayangovi. Few travellers make it this far and any DIY explorers need to carry plenty of water, fuel and spare parts for their 4WD vehicle. The area around Khermen Tsav is particularly barren and as water is extremely scarce, virtually no one lives here. A minimum of two vehicles and an experienced guide is recommended for this area.

From north to south, areas to explore in Bayankhongor include the following.

Galuut Canyon A 25m-deep canyon that narrows to around 1m wide in places. It is 20km southwest of Galuut *sum* centre, 85km northwest of Bayankhongor town.

Böön Tsagaan Nuur (GPS: N 45°37.114', E 99°15.350') A large saltwater lake at the end of Baidrag Gol with prolific birdlife, notably relic gull, whooper swan and goose.

Ikh Bogd Uul The highest mountain (3957m) in the Gobi Altai range. With a jeep and local guide it is possible to drive to the top for stupendous views. On Ikh Bogd's southern flank you'll also find the beautiful **Bituut rock**, formed after an earthquake in 1957.

Tsagaan Agui (GPS: N 44°42.604', E 101°10.187'; admission T1000) This is a cave with a crystal-lined inner chamber that once housed Stone Age people. It is about 90km east of Bayangovi in a narrow gorge.

Tsagaan Bulag (GPS: N 44°35.156', E 100°20.733') Also near Bayangovi, this white rock outcrop has the faint imprint of a strange helmeted figure, which locals believe was created by aliens.

Gunii Khöndii Gorge A beautiful, 4km-long gorge with vertical walls. It is about 70km southwest of Bayangovi.

Bayangiin Nuruu (GPS: N 44°17.218', E 100°31.329') A canyon with well-preserved rock engravings and petroglyphs depicting hunting and agricultural scenes dating from 3000 BC.

Bugiin Tsav (GPS: N 43°52.869', E 100°01.639') A large series of rift valleys running parallel to the Altan Uul mountain range and famous for its dinosaur fossils.

Yasnee Tsav An eroded hilly region with some impressive buttes. Local guides claim they can point out authentic fossils at this site.

Khermen Tsav (GPS: N 43°28.006', E 99°49.976') The most spectacular canyons in the area. The closest town is **Gurvantes** (GPS: N 43°13.599', E 101°02.798'), from which you can buy fuel and basic supplies.

Sevrei Petroglyphs (GPS: N 43°33.678', E 102°01.052') These depict herds of animals including deer, ibex and gazelle; 20km from the town of Sevrei.

Khuren Tovon Uul (3802m) in Altai *sum,* Burkhan Buuddai Uul (3765m) in Biger *sum,* or the permanently snow-capped peak of Sutai Uul (4090m), the highest peak in Gov-Altai located right on the border with Khovd aimag. Most climbers approach Sutai Uul (p178) from the Khovd side.

National Parks

The beauty of Gov-Altai's diverse and sparsely populated mountain and desert environment has led to the designation of large portions of the aimag as national parks.

Alag Khairkhan Nature Reserve (36,400 hectares) Protected Altai habitat with rare plants, snow leopard, argali and ibex.

Eej Khairkhan Nature Reserve (22,475 hectares) About 150km directly south of Altai, the reserve was created to protect the general environment.

Great Gobi Strictly Protected Area Divided into 'Gobi A' (Southern Altai Gobi, 4.4 million hectares) and 'Gobi B' (Dzungarian Gobi, 881,000 hectares), collectively this is the fourth-largest biosphere reserve in the world and protects a number of endangered animals.

Khasagt Khairkhan Strictly Protected Area (27,448 hectares) The area protects endangered argali sheep and the Mongol Altai mountain environment.

Sharga Nature Reserve Like the Mankhan Nature Reserve in Khovd aimag, it helps to preserve highly endangered species of antelope.

Takhiin Tal (150,000 hectares) On the border of the northern section of Gobi B (Dzungarian Gobi). *Takhi* (the Mongolian wild horse) have been reintroduced into the wild here since 1996 through the Research Station.

Altai Алтай

☎01482 / POP 19,100 / ELEV 2181M

Nestled between the mountains of Khasagt Khairkhan Uul (3579m) and Jargalant Uul (3070m), the aimag capital is a pleasant tree-lined place, with friendly locals. It's a poor city, but as it's a long way to anywhere else, you'll definitely need to stop for a short while to refuel and plot your next move.

Sights

Aimag Museum MUSEUM

(admission T2500; ⊙9am-1pm & 2-6pm Mon-Fri) The Aimag Museum includes some excellent bronze statues, scroll paintings, some genuine Mongol army chainmail, and an interesting shaman costume and drum. Look out for the 200kg statue of Buddha, which was hidden in a cave during the purges and recovered in 1965.

FREE **Mongol Rally Auto Service Graveyard** MUSEUM

Mongol Rally participants call in here to have their cars repaired before making the mad dash to UB but this is as far as many of them get. By September there is an interesting collection of abandoned ambulances, taxis and various other clapped-out bombs in their automobile graveyard.

Khun Chuluu HISTORIC SITE

(GPS: N 46°15.830', E 96°16.484') If headed south on the road to Biger, check out this *khun chuluu*, stone figures or *balbal,* said to date back to the 13th century (possibly earlier).

Khongor Hairhan Ovoo HISTORIC SITE

(GPS: N 46°22.590', E 96°52.057') This impressive *ovoo* on a small hill 50km east of the city has commanding views over the surrounding steppes.

Shuteen Park PARK

Situated on a hill from which you can see Altai in all its glory (such as it is), this newly finished park has a small temple at the top (not to be confused with the drab monastery at its base) and some fountains that actually contain water.

TIME TO COME CLEAN?

After driving around the dusty Gobi for a few days, don't be surprised if you take on a reddish tinge under the accumulated layers of dirt and sweat. Most ger camps have hot showers but if you're camping, the easiest place to come clean is at a public bathhouse once you reach town.

Public bathhouses are far from luxurious. Upon entering you pay for your visit at a little kiosk where you can also buy soap, shampoo and other beauty products. You'll be directed to a shower that usually comprises a small changing room and a flickering light bulb with exposed wiring. Mildew, rusty pipes and plug-holes choked full of hair round out the prison-like experience – but don't let all this put you off – just be brave and bring jandals (flip-flops).

Sleeping

The road from Altai towards Khovd city goes through a surprisingly lush plain for about 10km. If you have a tent and your own vehicle, head out here. Another great patch of ground is only a 20-minute walk northwest of town.

Altai is home to a large contingent of vocal dogs. No matter where you sleep you'll be able to appreciate their nightly cacophony of barks, snarls, howls and growls.

Zaiver Ger Camp TOURIST GER CAMP $

(☎9948 4300; GPS: N 46°14.391', E 96°21.682'; per ger T25,000; P) This pretty camp is nestled into the crook of a forested hillside, 16km from Altai. The staff will pick you up from town if you call ahead (T15,000 per person) and can prepare meals if notified in advance. There is no shower here.

Sutai HOTEL $

(Zaluur Altai; ☎9948 2424; tw/tr T10,000/15,000, luxe tw US$40) Thanks to the nearby karaoke, rooms here are acoustically challenged. The luxe rooms have hot showers.

Tulga Altai HOTEL $$

(☎23747; tw/d/tr/T20,000/24,000/42,000, half-luxe T36,000, luxe T48,000-72,000) Although not so pretty from the outside, it's pretty clean on the inside. Cold showers are available in some rooms.

Juulchin Altai TOURIST GER CAMP **$$**
(☎9119 4946, in Ulaanbaatar 9191 4946; juulchin-altai@yahoo.com; GPS: N 46°21.764', E 96°12.978'; with meals US$35; P) A small ger camp 3km west of town.

Altai Hotel HOTEL **$$**
(☎24134; q/half-luxe US$25/55, luxe d US$100) You have to wait a while (possibly days) for the hot water to make its way through the antique plumbing in this overpriced Soviet relic. There is some serious bling in the restaurant.

Eating

Sutai MONGOLIAN **$**
(Zaluur Altai; meals T2000-6000; ⌚8am-8pm) The goulash- and mutton-based fare comes in full or half portions. The restaurant includes an attached billiards hall and karaoke bar.

Most Altai MONGOLIAN **$**
(meals T2000-3000; ⌚10am-10pm Mon-Sat) Patrons can sit on the upstairs terrace and order mains with or without rice. Evening meals come with a side order of karaoke.

Market MONGOLIAN
(⌚8am-8pm Mon-Sat) Reasonably well stocked with foodstuffs (and warm clothing).

Information

Bathhouse (admission T1500; ⌚9am-9pm) The taps have to be 'just so' to get any hot water.

Internet cafe (per hr T500; ⌚9am-10pm) Inside the Telecom office.

Khan Bank (⌚9am-8pm Mon-Fri, to 4pm Sat) Currency exchange, an ATM and Western Union.

Mongol Rally Auto Service (☎9948 7153) Supports Mongol Rally drivers with mechanical repairs.

Telecom office (⌚8am-10pm) The post office is also here.

Getting There & Away

AIR **Eznis** (☎23232) flies every Monday, Thursday and Friday to Ulaanbaatar (T384,000 one way) via Bayankhongor (T270,000 one way). The airport is 2km northwest of the centre.

BUS A bus leaves every Monday, Wednesday, Friday and Saturday at 11am for Ulaanbaatar (T37,000, 26 hours, 1000km) via Bayankhongor (T20,000, 371km), Arvaikheer (T20,000, 571km), several *guanz* stops, a couple of breakdowns and a small river crossing.

MINIVAN & JEEP A minivan leaves every day for Ulaanbaatar (T42,000, 20 hours) and will reluctantly take passengers for Bayankhongor (T25,000) and Arvaikheer (T30,000). Despite being on the main road to Khovd, it is quite difficult to find transport west as passing buses are invariably full and it is hit and miss finding a share jeep travelling this way.

THE MONGOLIAN DEATH WORM

Worms aren't generally regarded as much of a menace but the *olgoi-khorkhoi*, aka the Mongolian death worm, is regarded by some as the deadliest creature in the Gobi. According to folklore, the only sensible thing to do if you see a large, red, sausage-shaped thing sticking out of the sand is to run like hell. Even this probably won't help because death worms are quick, far quicker than tourists, and if you don't die from the sulphuric acidlike venom they spray, the electrical discharge from its rear end most certainly will do you in.

This may sound like a job for Kevin Bacon (yes, tremors attract them) but renewed sightings in 2005 led to the launch of several hastily mounted expeditions, including one sponsored by National Geographic, to determine once and for all the veracity of their existence. So far the fearful worm has proved elusive.

Eej Khairkhan Nature Reserve
Ээж Хайрхан Уул

Near the base of the Eej Khairkhan Uul (2275m), part of the Eej Khairkhan Nature Reserve just north of 'Gobi A' National Park, you can camp at some delightful **rock pools** and explore the nearby **caves**. You will need a guide to show you around. Almost no suitable drinking water is available in the area, so take your own.

About 30 minutes' walk west of the rock pools are some spectacular ancient **rock paintings** of ibex, horsemen and archers. The mountain is about 150km south of Altai.

Sutai Uul Сутай Уул

A locally revered mountain, Sutai Uul (4090m) is a relatively easy climb that offers good views of the surrounding Gobi. You can drive to the base of the mountain from Tonkhil in Gov-Altai or Tsetseg village in Khovd. From the base it's a two-hour walk to the top, where you'll find permanent snow cover.

Great Gobi Strictly Protected Area

Говийн Их Дархан Газар

For both parts of the park you will need a very reliable vehicle and an experienced driver, and you must be completely self-sufficient with supplies of food, water and camping gear. A ranger will probably track you down and collect park entry fees (T3000 per person).

GOBI A (SOUTHERN ALTAI GOBI) ГОВЬ 'A'

The majority of this 4.4-million-hectare national park lies in southern Gov-Altai. Established more than 25 years ago, the area has been nominated as an International Biosphere Reserve by the UN.

The park is remote and very difficult to reach, which is bad news for visitors but excellent news for the fragile flora and fauna. To explore the park, start at Biger, turn southwest on the trail to Tsogt, and head south on any jeep trail you can find.

GOBI B (DZUNGARIAN GOBI) ГОВЬ 'B'

Although the majority of this 881,000-hectare park lies in neighbouring Khovd aimag, most travellers enter from the Gov-Altai side, where the **Takhiin Tal Research Station** (☎9983 6979; GPS: N 45°32.197', E 93°39.055'; per person T10,000) has been set up to protect the reintroduced *takhi* (Przewalski's horse). Most of the *takhi* (see the boxed text, p93) now run free, although a few still live in enclosures near the research station, which is about 15km southwest of Bij village. The ger accommodation is very basic but staff here can help arrange guides (T10,000 per day) and horses (T10,000 per day).

Western Mongolia

POP: 347,800 / AREA: 191,000 SQ KM

Includes »

Best Places to Stay

» Tsambagarau Hotel (p184)

» Uliastai Hotel (p202)

» Altai Tavan Bogd National Park (p188)

Best Places to Trek

» Altai Tavan Bogd National Park (p188)

» Kharkhiraa Uul & Türgen Uul (p199)

» Tsenkheriin Agui (p195)

» Tsambagarav Uul National Park (p187)

Why Go?

With its raw deserts, glacier-wrapped mountains, shimmering salt lakes and the hardy culture of nomads, falconry and cattle rustling, western Mongolia is a timeless slice of 'Central Asia'.

Squeezed between Russia, Kazakhstan, China and the Mongol heartland, this region has been a historical transition zone of cultures and traditions, the legacy of which is a patchwork of peoples including ethnic Kazakhs, Dörvöds, Khotons, Myangads and Khalkh Mongols. Lost arts such as *khöömii* throat singing and eagle hunting are still practised as they have been for thousands of years.

The region's wild landscape and the rugged mountain backbone of the Mongol Altai Nuruu create ample opportunity for trekkers to explore and mountaineers to challenge themselves on peaks that soar to over 4000m.

With time and flexibility, you too will discover why this region packs a powerful punch.

When to Go

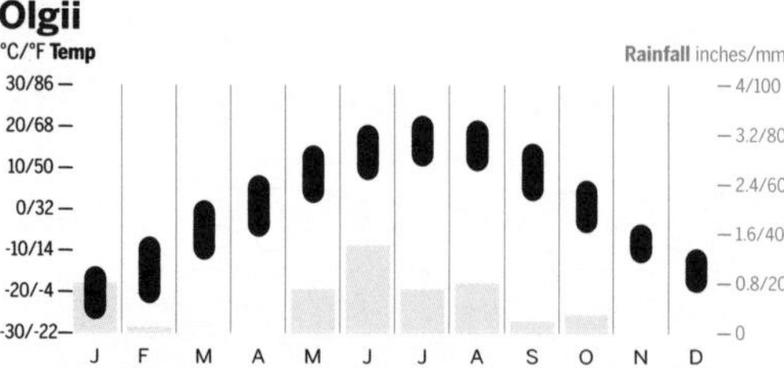

March Kazakh families celebrate Navrus with traditional games and feasting.

June–September Brief snowstorms occur in the Altai Mountains. Trekkers need sub-zero sleeping bags.

October–February The eagle-hunting season kicks off with Ölgii's Eagle Festival.

Western Mongolia Highlights

1. Soar above the borders of Mongolia, China and Russia when you climb to the top of **Tavan Bogd** (p189)
2. Rub shoulders with Kazakh eagle-hunters during Ölgii's **Eagle Festival** (p183)
3. Trek to the twin peaks of **Türgen Uul and Kharkhiraa Uul** (p199), a rugged landscape of glaciers, green meadows and boulder fields
4. Camp by the shores of **Üüreg Nuur** (p199), a lovely, accessible freshwater lake filled with fish
5. Strike a chord with a **khöömii throat singer** in the village of Chandmani (p194)
6. Walk around **Khoton Nuur** (p189), a beautiful alpine lake dotted with Kazakh settlements around its shore
7. Horse trek around the lakes and valleys beneath **Otgon Tenger Uul** (p203), abode of the gods and Mongolia's holiest peak

History

The Mongol Altai Nuruu (commonly referred to as the Altai Mountains) was once the easternmost territory inhabited by the Scythians, a vast empire of nomadic pastoralists who dominated Central Asia from 700 BC to AD 300.

Prior to Mongol domination in the 13th century, western Mongolia was a stronghold of the Oirads, a warrior tribe that initially resisted the expansionary tactics of Chinggis Khaan, but later submitted. Following the collapse of the Mongol empire, the Oirads reasserted their domination over the area and expanded to the Volga. These pioneers became known as Kalmyks and still inhabit the Caspian shores of Russia.

Manchu military outposts were created in Khovd City and Uliastai during the Qing dynasty. Both capitulated soon after the fall of the Manchu empire in 1911. The fighting was particularly bloody in Khovd, where a mystic Kalmyk named Dambijantsan (also known as Ja Lama) gathered an army of 5000 Oirads and Mongols, razed the fortress to the ground and skinned the Chinese soldiers inside.

Under Ulaanbaatar rule, western Mongolia was called Chandmandi until it was broken up into three aimags (provinces) in 1931. One of the three, Bayan-Ölgii, was designated as a homeland for ethnic Kazakhs living in the region.

Getting There & Away

Transport between western Mongolia and Ulaanbaatar is mainly by plane and flights are often very full. Transport by land from Ulaanbaatar is a rough and tedious six days. The northern route via Arkhangai has several points of interest, but most share vehicles travel along the mind-numbingly dull southern route via Khovd, Altai and Bayankhongor.

Though not yet a main traveller route, it is possible to enter or leave Mongolia at the Tsagaannuur border crossing to Russia or fly to Ölgii from Almaty (Kazakhstan) or to Khovd from Urumqi (China).

Note that western Mongolia is in a different time zone from the rest of the country: it's one hour behind.

Getting Around

Hiring a jeep is relatively easy in Ölgii but can be more difficult elsewhere. All of the three western aimag capitals are linked by decent jeep trails. You'll waste a lot of time if hitchhiking in the area; trucks will most likely be heading for the nearest border post and jeeps will be packed full of people. You are better off with the buses and the share jeeps that congregate at the markets. As it is easier to get off a bus heading back to Ulaanbaatar than trying to hop on an already full one on its way out, a good plan is to fly out and overland it back to the capital.

BAYAN-ÖLGII
БАЯН-ӨЛГИЙ

POP 101,900 / AREA 46,000 SQ KM

Travelling to Mongolia's westernmost province gives one the distinct feeling of reaching the end of the road, if not the end of the earth. High, dry, rugged and raw, the isolated, oddly shaped province follows the arc of the Mongol Altai Nuruu as it rolls out of Central Asia towards the barren wastes of the Dzungarian Basin.

Many peaks in the province are more than 4000m and permanently covered with glaciers and snow, while the valleys have a few green pastures that support about two million head of livestock, as well as bears, foxes and wolves.

Ethnic groups who call Bayan-Ölgii home include the Kazakh, Khalkh, Dörvöd, Uriankhai, Tuva and Khoshuud. Unlike the rest of Mongolia, which is dominated by the Khalkh Mongols, about 90% of Bayan-Ölgii's population are Kazakh.

National Parks

Most parks come under the jurisdiction of the Mongol Altai Nuruu Protected Areas Administration office (Manspaa).

Altai Tavan Bogd National Park (636,161 hectares) Fauna includes argali sheep, ibex, maral (Asiatic red deer), stone marten, deer, elk, Altai snowcock and eagle.

Develiin Aral Nature Reserve (10,300 hectares) A remarkable habitat around Develiin Island in the Usan Khooloi and Khovd Rivers. It is home to pheasant, boar and beaver.

Khökh Serkh Strictly Protected Area (65,920 hectares) A mountainous area on the border with Khovd, which protects argali sheep and ibex.

Siilkhem Nuruu National Park (140,080 hectares) This park has two sections, one around Ikh Türgen Uul, the other further west.

ICE WARRIOR OF THE ALTAI

In 2006 archaeologists in the Mongol Altai made headlines when they uncovered a 2500-year-old mummy believed to have been a Scythian warrior. The scientists noted that the mummy, well preserved in the permafrost, had blond hair and sported tattoos. He was believed to be a chieftain of some importance, between 30 and 40 years old. Clothed in a fur coat, he was entombed with two horses, saddles and weapons. Some of these treasures have been displayed in Ulaanbaatar's National History Museum, while the mummy was packed off to Berlin for research.

Tsambagarav Uul National Park (110,960 hectares) Protects glaciers and the snow-leopard habitat; borders on Khovd.

Ölgii Өлгий

☎01422 / POP 27,800 / ELEV 1710M

Ölgii city is a windblown frontier town that will appeal to anyone who dreams of the Wild West. It's a squat, concrete affair, meandering along the Khovd Gol and surrounded by ger (traditional circular felt yurt) districts and rocky escarpments. Thunderclouds brew in the mountains above town, making for some dramatic climatic changes throughout the day and brilliant light shows in the late afternoon.

The town is predominantly Kazakh, and you'll soon start feeling it has more in common with Muslim-influenced Central Asia than Buddhist Mongolia: there are signs in Arabic and Kazakh Cyrillic, and the market, which is called a bazaar rather than the Mongolian *zakh,* sells the odd *shashlik* (kebab) and is stocked with goods from Kazakhstan.

Sights

Aimag Museum MUSEUM

(admission T3000; ⏲9am-noon & 1-5pm Mon-Fri, 10am-5pm Sat) The Aimag Museum gives an excellent overview of Kazakh culture and the geography of Bayan-Ölgii. The 2nd floor is devoted to history, and the 3rd floor has some interesting ethnographic displays.

Tours

Ger to Ger work with local families and run community-based tours in this region. See p29 for further details.

Kazakh Tour TOUR AGENCY

(☎9942 2006; www.kazakhtour.com; 2nd fl NHU Bldg) This excellent tour company specialises in tailor-made trips throughout Bayan-Ölgii and consistently gets great reviews from travellers. The Kazakh owner, Dosjan Khabyl, has many contacts in the area and can organise trekking, horse treks and visits to local eagle-hunters, *khöömii* singers and the local *böö* (shaman). He can also purchase domestic airline tickets for within Mongolia and international tickets to Kazakhstan for clients in advance.

Blue Wolf Travel TOUR AGENCY

(☎22772, 9910 0303; www.bluewolftravel.com) Blue Wolf is the original tour operator in Ölgii and offers a variety of trips including winter eagle-hunting tours and guided treks in Tsambagarav Uul and Altai Tavan Bogd National Parks. It is also a good source of information for Sagsai's Altai Eagle Festival.

Other local guides:

Bek Travel LOCAL GUIDE

(☎9909 6385; www.backtobektravel.com) This one-man operation is run by Aynabek Khavduali, who speaks English, French, Russian, Turkish and Kazakh.

Altai Peaks TOUR AGENCY

(☎9942 7003; beku800@yahoo.com) A traveller-recommended tour company based at the ger camp of the same name.

Discover Western Mongolia LOCAL GUIDE

(☎9910 7676; maksum_agii@yahoo.com) Local guide 'Aggi' can also arrange personalised tours.

Festivals

TOP CHOICE **Eagle Festival** TRADITIONAL CULTURE

(admission US$35, video camera US$35; ⏲1st weekend in Oct) There are 360 eagle-hunters in Bayan-Ölgii and every year around 70 of them converge at Sayat Tube (Hunter's Hill), 8km east of Ölgii, for the annual Eagle Festival.

Although the tradition dates back about 2000 years (Marco Polo mentions it in his *Travels*), the inaugural festival was only held in 1999. The program differs from year to year but the opening ceremony usually kicks off around 10am, followed by the judging of how well the competitors are attired in traditional dress. This is followed by various competitions, including one called *shakhyru* during which the eagle must catch a piece of fox fur pulled behind a galloping horse. The festival culminates on Sunday, when a live fox (and sometimes a wolf pup) is released as bait for the top three eagles to hunt (animal lovers may find this somewhat cruel as the fox is killed).

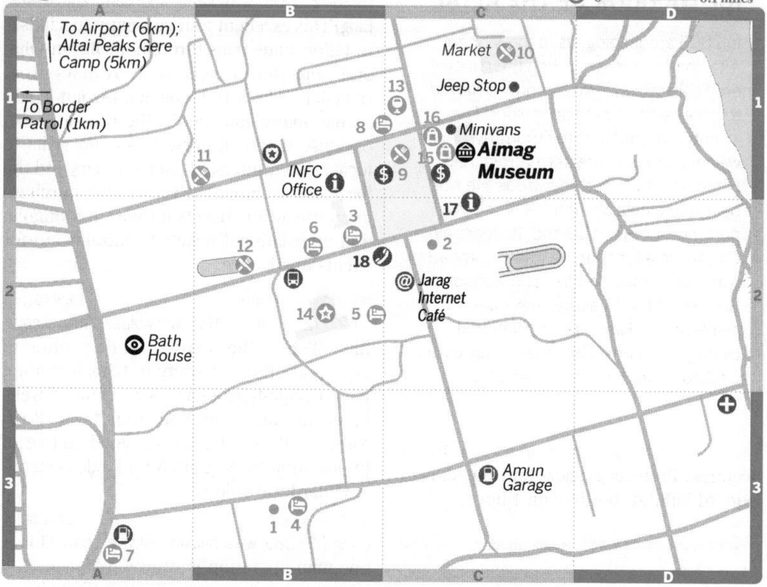

The traditional **horse games** and **camel races** that are staggered over the two-day event are probably more thrilling than the actual eagle-hunting competitions. The most exciting are *kokbar* (a tug-of-war with an animal skin between two riders) and *tenge ilu* (a competition in which riders must swoop down to pick up a scrap of material from the ground at full gallop).

Be sure to hang onto your admission ticket as it will get you into the Saturday-night **traditional music concert** held in the Kazakh National Theatre.

The easiest way to get to the festival grounds is on the bus operated by Kazakh Tour (T5000 per person return, tickets available from its office) or by taxi (T10,000 one way).

Smaller eagle festivals are also held in Sagsai (p187) and Tolbo (p187).

Navrus — SPRING FEAST

The spring festival of Navrus (22 March) is celebrated with family visits and feasting. You may see traditional games and contests at this time, including one in which men attempt to lift an ox off the ground.

Altai Horse Games — HORSE GAMES

(admission US$30; ⏲3rd weekend in Jul) Blue Wolf Travel sponsors a weekend of horse racing and horse games including *kokbar* (tug of war with a goat) and *kyz kul* (kiss the girl) between the two lakes in Tavan Bogd National Park.

Sleeping

To camp, walk east of the square to Khovd Gol and then head southeast, away from the market and ger suburbs.

TOP CHOICE Tsambagarav Hotel — HOTEL $$

(Green Hotel; ☎9555 9365; s/tw T35,000/40,000, d luxe T50,000) This is by far the nicest hotel in Ölgii (not that there is much competition), with clean, comfy beds, modern bathrooms in working order and friendly staff. The reception is on the 3rd floor past the restaurant and karaoke bar (closed Fridays).

TOP CHOICE Traveller's Guest House — TOURIST GER CAMP $

(☎9942 9699, 9942 4505; nazkana@fastmail.fm; per person T6000; Ⓟ) This small, no-frills, family-run operation is excellent value. The owner, Nazgul, speaks perfect English and has extensive knowledge about the whole aimag (she once worked for Manspaa). She'll rent you a mountain bike (T10,000 per day),

Ölgii

Top Sights
Aimag Museum C1

Activities, Courses & Tours
1 Blue Wolf Travel B3
2 Kazakh Tour C2

Sleeping
3 Bastau Hotel B2
4 Blue Wolf B3
5 Duman B2
6 Tavan Bogd Hotel B2
7 Traveller's Guest House A3
8 Tsambagarav Hotel B1

Eating
9 Arvin Restaurant & Pub C1
10 Market C1
11 Pamukkale B1
12 Sunkhar Supermarket B2
Tsambagarau Hotel .... (see 8)

Drinking
13 Aulum Sayajim Beer Garden C1

Entertainment
14 Kazakh National Theatre B2

Shopping
15 Aimag Museum Gift Shop C1
16 Kazakh Craft C1
Market .... (see 10)

Information
AeroMongolia Office .... (see 17)
Ez Niz .... (see 18)
17 Mongol Altai Nuruu Protected Areas Administration Office C2
18 Telecom Office B2

put on a load of your laundry (T10,000) and drop you off at the airport (T5000). Better yet, her gers and shared shower are spotless.

Blue Wolf TOURIST GER CAMP **$**
(22772, 9910 0303; www.bluewolftravel.com; per person US$10; P@) Blue Wolf offers three large Kazakh-style and two smaller Mongolian-style gers, all with stoves. The toilet and shower block have recently been upgraded with better flush toilets and hot showers. It's located behind the Blue Wolf cafe and tour office in a secure, walled compound.

Eagle Tour TOURIST GER CAMP **$$**
(9942 2100; eagle_tour@mongol.net; with/without meals US$35/15; P) Located 7km out of Ölgii in the direction of Sagsai, Eagle Tour has gers, flush toilets and hot showers.

Altai Peaks TOURIST GER CAMP **$$**
(9942 7003; beku800@yahoo.com; with/without meals US$34/14; P) Offering pretty much the same as its neighbour Eagle Tour, Altai Peaks also run a tour guide service here.

If all these places are full you might consider some of Ölgii's other hotels. Unfortunately most of these have had only a fleeting acquaintance with a mop.

Duman HOTEL **$$**
(9942 1515; s/d T18,000/32,000, luxe T23,000/46,000; P) A place that seems to be coming apart at the seams. Construction has started on a new Duman next door.

Bastau Hotel HOTEL **$**
(23629; s/d/tr T10,000/20,000/30,000, luxe d T25,000) The wooden hall and stairwell make for noisy comings and goings from patrons of the attached bar.

Tavan Bogd Hotel HOTEL **$**
(9942 8899; lenahidir@yahoo.com; s/d/tr/q T20,000/35,000/45,000/60,000;) This is the oldest hotel in town and so far the gradual renovations have done little to halt the ravages of time.

Eating

In respect to the large Muslim population, alcohol is seldom served on Fridays. Self-caterers should head to the **market** (10am-5pm Tue-Sun), which has a decent selection of food supplies imported from Russia and China, or to one of the supermarkets dotted about town. We found **Sunkhar** (9am-7pm) to be well stocked.

TOP CHOICE **Arvin Restaurant & Pub** KAZAKH, MONGOLIAN **$**
(meals T2000-3500; 10am-9.30pm Mon-Sat;) Smartly turned-out waiting staff, snappy service, an upmarket vibe and some tasty Kazakh favourites make this popular with locals and travellers alike. We recommend the *sirne* (a Kazakh dish of meat cooked in a pressure cooker) or if the thought of more mutton, no matter how tender, makes your skin crawl, a salad.

Pamukkale TURKISH $$
(☎9909 4593; meals T2500-7500; ⊙10.30am-10pm; ▣) A welcome addition to the local restaurant scene, Pamukkale is a Turkish-run outfit that serves authentic kebabs, Turkish soups and tasty chicken dishes. The Turkish desserts are also excellent but portions are minuscule. Alcohol is not served here.

Tsambagarav Hotel WESTERN, MONGOLIAN $
(meals T2000-5000; ⊙9.30am-9pm) The menu promises hamburgers, sushi, chicken soup and pizza although we are yet to hear of anyone successfully ordering such exotic fare. You will definitely have more luck with the Mongolian meals and if you have a hankering for sheep's head (T5000), here is your big chance.

Drinking

Aulum Sayajim Beer Garden BEER GARDEN
(admission T300; ⊙noon-11pm Jun-Aug) For a beer in a quiet atmosphere, try this beer garden, near the police station. The walled compound contains several cabanas and a tent. On Fridays, the beer is covered with towels so as not to offend the local Muslim population, but they will still sneak you a bottle. The gers nearby are actually for rent, but would you really want to sleep in a beer garden?

Shopping

Aimag Museum Gift Shop HANDICRAFTS
(⊙9am-noon & 1-5pm Mon-Fri, 10am-5pm Sat) If you are on the hunt for Kazakh wall hangings, felt rugs, carpets and crafts, this is the best place to start. It has a great, if dusty, collection of new and antique items along with various bits-and-bobs you don't see elsewhere. We were particularly enamoured with a leather saddle with antique silver trim (US$1500).

Kazakh Craft HANDICRAFTS
(www.kazakhcraft.com; ⊙10am-7pm) This small store inside the blue railway carriage next to the museum has a good selection of Kazakh crafts (felt wall hangings, bags and cushion covers with chain-stitch embroidery), eagle-hunting accessories (gauntlets, eagle hoods and eagle-hunter hats) and leather goods (belts and wallets).

Also recommended:

Market MARKET
(⊙10am-5pm Tue-Sun) Traditional Kazakh skullcaps and jackets can be found amid the chaos here.

Information

Amun Garage (☎21660, 9942 2200) Helps Mongol Rally drivers with mechanical repairs.

Bathhouse (shower T3000; ⊙9am-10pm)

Immigration, Naturalisation & Foreign Citizens office (INFC; ☎9942 2616; Government House; ⊙9am-noon & 1-5pm Mon-Fri) Can register your passport if you have just arrived from Russia and issue an exit visa (US$43) if you are leaving and don't already have one. It cannot issue visa extensions.

Jarag Internet Cafe (per hr T600; ⊙9am-10pm)

Khan Bank (⊙8am-5.30pm Mon-Fri, 9am-3pm Sat) Changes US dollars and euros and has an ATM. If this is down, Golomt Bank on the square can give cash advances against Visa.

Mongol Altai Nuruu Protected Areas Administration office (Manspaa; ☎22111, 9942 6633; manspaa@mongol.net; ⊙9am-noon & 1.30-5pm Mon-Fri) The office doubles as an information centre, although local tour agencies are more informed.

Telecom office (⊙24hr) The post office is also located here.

Getting There & Away

AIR EZ Nis and AeroMongolia share the Ulaanbaatar–Ölgii route. Schedules are increased in times of high demand such as during the Eagle Festival although you will still need to book well in advance to secure a seat. The airport is 6km north of the centre, on the opposite side of the river. There is no bus but you can find cars for hire at the market (T500 per km).

EZ Nis (☎21331; Telecom Bldg) charges T496,900 one way and flies on Tuesday and Saturday. Occasionally this plane is routed through Mörön (T357,000).

AeroMongolia (☎8808 0025; 2nd fl Manspaa Bldg) charges T424,200 one way and flies every Monday, Wednesday and Friday.

ONWARDS TO RUSSIA & KAZAKHSTAN

Jeeps and minivans leave daily for the Russian town of Kosh-Agach, and planes and a long distance bus also leave Ölgii for Kazakhstan. For more information on these international routes, see p267 or visit shop.lonelyplanet.com to purchase a downloadable PDF of the Kazakhstan chapter from Lonely Planet's *Central Asia* guide or the Western Siberia chapter from Lonely Planet's *Russia* guide.

BUS Those with a masochistic streak will relish the 50- to 60-hour bus trip to Ulaanbaatar (T70,000, daily, 1636km) via Khovd (211km), Altai (635km), Bayankhongor (1006km) and Arvaikheer (1206km). Tickets for the latter destinations are only available if there are empty seats. The ticket office is in the basement of the Kazakh National Theatre.

MINIVAN & JEEP Public share jeeps to Khovd City (T20,000, six to seven hours) are far more frequent than those to Ulaangom (T40,000, 10 hours, 300km).

Like the bus, the Ulaanbaatar (T68,000, 60 hours) minivan passes through Altai (T45,000), Bayankhongor (T68,000) and Arvaikheer (T68,000). They assemble at the road next to the museum.

Hiring a random driver at the Ölgii market is not a good idea – these drivers are not accountable to anyone and are known to change prices and itineraries mid-trip. The Manspaa office and local tour companies will have drivers more familiar with tourists' needs.

Tsambagarav Uul National Park Цамбагарав Уул

The permanently snow-capped **Tsambagarav Uul** (park admission T3000) straddles the border between Khovd and Bayan-Ölgii aimags and is accessible from either side. Despite its altitude of 4208m, the summit is relatively accessible and easy to climb compared with Tavan Bogd, but you'll need crampons and ropes. A neighbouring peak, **Tsast Uul**, is slightly lower at 4193m and also good for climbing.

The southern side of the mountain (near the main Khovd–Ölgii road) contains the **Namarjin valley**, where there are outstanding views of Tsambagarav. From here you can head west and then south to rejoin the main Khovd–Ölgii road, via several **Kazakh settlements** and a beautiful **turquoise lake**.

An alternative route from the Khovd side leads from the town of **Erdeneburen** (where you can see a deer stone dating back to the pre-Mongol era) and up the mountainside to the Bayangol Valley. The valley itself is nothing special but there are fine views southeast to Khar Us Nuur and you might be able to rent a horse for the hour-long ride to the Kazakh-populated **Marra valley**.

The Bayan-Ölgii (northern) side of the mountain is even more impressive. To reach the massif, a steep pass runs between Tavan Belchiriin Uul and Tsast Uul. Between the mountains is a 7m-high **waterfall** (GPS: N 48°44.741', E 090°42.378') that flows down a narrow gorge. A couple of kilometres to the east of the waterfall is a **glacier** and small glacial lake.

From the glacier, the road dips through some spectacular **rocky gorges** before finally tumbling down to **Bayan Nuur**, a small, slightly salty lake.

The best time to visit the massif is late June to late August, when it's populated by Kazakh nomad camps. You can rent horses from the nomads to explore the area. Outside of these months it's a cold, empty and forbidding place.

From Bayan Nuur, a desert road travels east through a Martian landscape of red boulders and rocky mountains. Near the town of Bayannuur and close to the Khovd Gol is an interesting white-stone **balbal** (Turkic stone statue; GPS: N 48°50.533', E 091°16.525').

Tolbo Nuur Толбо Нуур

Tolbo Nuur (GPS: N 48°35.320', E 090°04.536') is a freshwater lake about 50km south of Ölgii, on the main road between Ölgii and Khovd City. It is high (2080m), expansive and eerie but the shoreline is treeless with few mosquitoes and a few families camp here every summer. A major battle was fought here between the Bolsheviks and White Russians, with the local Mongolian general, Khasbaatar, siding with the Bolsheviks. The Bolsheviks won and there are a couple of **memorial plaques** by the lake.

A further 14km on from the eastern edge of the lake and 3km off the main jeep trail is the tiny settlement of **Tolbo**, which hosts a small **Eagle Festival** (last Sun in September) that includes horse games as well as eagle hunting. Tolbo *sum* (district), along with Deluun *sum* to the south are famed for their **eagle-hunters** and this is a great place to meet them. In fact a local hunter often waits by the road around 95km from Ölgii where the road narrows (GPS: N 48°29.439', E 090°33.648') to show his eagle to passing travellers (T5000 to T10,000 for photos).

Kazakh Tour (p183) in Ölgii has contacts in this area and can arrange eagle-hunting trips, homestays, horse treks and transport to the eagle festival.

Sagsai Сагсай

Most travellers pass through Sagsai on their way to the lakes in Altai Tavan Bogd National

Park, with little reason to stop. That is until the third weekend in September when this tiny community hosts the Altai Eagle Festival (per person US$30). The festival is smaller than the one in Ölgii although it follows much the same program. One notable difference is that live animals are not used as bait. Blue Wolf Travel (p183) is a sponsor and a good source of information. It also operates a ger camp (9910 0303; with/without meals US$30/15) and arranges homestays (with meals US$10) and transport (T5000 return).

It's also possible to rent a raft from either of Ölgii's main tour operators and take a **rafting** trip down the Khovd Gol from Sagsai to Ölgii (five to six hours, 33km, grade 1 to 2) or from Mogoit Bridge to Tsengel (two days, 45km, grade 1 to 2). You will need to have some prior river experience as guides are not generally supplied and there will be no one to help you should you get into difficulties.

Tsengel Цэнгэл

Of the 12 *sums* in Bayan-Ölgii, Tsengel is the largest. Although the town itself is bigger than most, it is still just a collection of gravel roads and wooden fences that surround compounds, each containing an earth and log home, possibly a ger or two and invariably a guard dog in a foul mood.

The principal reasons to stop here are to visit Tuvan khöömii (9941 4816; 30min demonstration T10,000-20,000) throat singer Bapizan and to grab a bite at the surprisingly excellent Artysh Cafe & Hotel (mains T1500-2000, sandwiches T500; 9am-10pm Mon-Sat). The menu will likely bamboozle your guide (if you have one) as it is written in Tuvan but the food is mostly Mongolian. If you are heading to the Altai Tavan Bogd National Park you can grab sandwiches and drinks from the chiller out back. The attached hotel (9542 8279; s/d T15,000/30,000) is also good value with clean and simple rooms.

Tsengel is 75km from Ölgii on the road to the twin lakes of Khoton Nuur and Khurgan Nuur. A share jeep leaves at 7am for Ölgii's market (T5000) and returns at around 5pm.

Altai Tavan Bogd National Park Алтай Таван Богд

This beautiful park stretches south from Tavan Bogd and includes the twin lakes of Khoton Nuur and Khurgan Nuur (and the less interesting Dayan Nuur), which are the source of the Khovd Gol that flows to Khar Us Nuur in Khovd aimag.

Despite its remote location, the park and its stunning scenery make it the premier attraction in western Mongolia. Divided from China by a high wall of snow-capped peaks, the area is a trekker's paradise.

Sights & Activities

Archaeological Sites HISTORIC SITES

There are many archaeological sites in the region. Mogoit Valley (Snake Valley) contains a moustachioed balbal (GPS: N 48°44.099', E 88°38.930') and a Kazakh cemetery with an interesting beehive-shaped mausoleum about 2km to the north. Yet another balbal (GPS: N 48°39.506', E 88°37.863') can be found south of Mogoit Valley, on the way to Khurgan Nuur. More interesting Kazakh cemeteries and ancient burial mounds are easily spotted from the road. Closer to Tavan Bogd, Sheveed Uul (3350m) contains some fascinating petroglyphs (GPS: N 49°06.238', E 88°14.918') depicting wild animals and hunting scenes.

The best petroglyphs in the area, if not all of Central Asia, can be found at Tsagaan Sala (aka Baga Oigor), on the route between Ulaankhus and Tavan Bogd. The drawings, more than 10,000 of them, are scattered over a 15km area; you'll need a guide to find the best ones.

TOP CHOICE **Eagle-Hunting** TOUR

(mid-Sep–Apr) Surprisingly, there are more Kazakh eagle-hunters in Bayan-Ölgii than there are in Kazakhstan. Arguably, the areas in and around the park (along with the mountain region of Tsast Uul between Khovd and Bayan-Ölgii, and the Deluun, Tsengel and Bayannuur regions of Bayan-Ölgii) are the best places in the world to experience eagle-hunting first hand. It is only practised during winter once the birds have recovered from their summer moult.

All the tour companies in Ölgii (p183) arrange trips with eagle-hunters on horseback, although to avoid disappointment be prepared for either an unsuccessful hunt or the possibility that the eagle catches its quarry (usually a fox, rabbit or marmot) behind a hill or out of sight.

TOP CHOICE **Lake Region** TREKKING

This is one of the most beautiful regions in the park, with the scenery growing more spectacular the further west you travel. The area is best explored on foot or horse-

LOCAL KNOWLEDGE

BAYTOLDA: EAGLE-HUNTER

Eagles are like people; some are calm, some are lazy and some, like my eagle Sari Köz (Yellow Eye), become cantankerous in their old age.

I trapped Sari Köz 22 years ago in the Sairyn Mountains. Some people steal chicks from an eagle's nest but these birds lack killer instincts and never become good hunters. I think it is better to lure and trap a wild adult who has already learnt to hunt, using a previously caught eagle and some meat. Sari Köz, like all eagles used in hunting, is a *bürkit* (female). *Bürkits* are best as they are bigger, heavier and far more aggressive than the males (*sarsha*).

To train a *bürkit* takes patience. At first she will flap wildly and try to bite whoever approaches. To 'break' her we rig a perch that spins and throws her off balance and causes her to fall. After two or three days she is hungry, exhausted and calm enough to take food from your hand. Eventually she will trust you and learn to come to you to be fed. This is the first step in training a *bürkit*.

When an eagle is first taken outside she is kept tethered to her *tugir* (pole) and taught to chase small animal skins or lures called *shirgas*, until the day comes when you must untie the tether and trust that she does not fly away.

After much practice, the *bürkit* is ready to go on a hunt. It is best to go with another, experienced eagle so that she can learn from it. When a fox or marmot is spotted, the *tomaga* (hood) is removed and, if trained correctly and of a strong spirit, she will chase and capture it. If she has been successful in her hunt, she is rewarded with fresh meat from the kill.

back. Kazakh families living around Khoton Nuur in summer can rent you horses.

The shoreline of **Khurgan Nuur** is dry and exposed. Few people travel along its southern shore but if you are going this way there is a stupa-like construction and several burial sites. Nearby is a **balbal** (GPS: N 48°32.006', E 88°28.549').

The southern shore along **Khoton Nuur** has excellent camping spots, especially around **Ulaan Tolgoi** (Red Head), the spit of land that juts majestically into the lake. The northern tip of the lake is marked by **Aral Tolgoi** (Island Head), a unique hill surrounded by verdant pastureland and rocky escarpments. A border station at the northern end of the lake will check to see if your border permit is in order.

Coming around the southern shore of Khoton Nuur, you can camp in secluded coves or explore the valleys that lead towards China. There are some difficult river crossings on your way back to Syrgal.

About 25km northwest of Khoton Nuur you can also visit Rashany Ikh Uul, an area of 35 **hot springs** (GPS N48°55.655', E88°14.288'; admission US$10). The springs are only just lukewarm.

Northwest of Khoton Nuur the mountains close in and there's some fine hiking possibilities. For experienced backcountry walkers, it is even possible to travel up river to Tavan Bogd (110km, seven days). You'll need local help from the Tuvan families to cross the powerful **Tsagaan Gol** (T2000).

TOP CHOICE **Tavan Bogd Region** TREKKING

Tavan Bogd (Five Saints) is a soaring cluster of mountains that straddles the border between Mongolia, Russia and China. The highest peak in the range, **Khuiten Uul** (Cold Peak; 4374m), is the tallest mountain in Mongolia and is of interest to professional climbers who are properly equipped with ice axes, crampons and ropes. The best time to climb is August and September, after the worst of the summer rains.

Besides Khuiten, the range includes Naran (Sun), Ölgii (Land), Bürged (Eagle) and Nairamdal (Friendship) *uuls* (mountains). In 2006 the president of Mongolia climbed Khuiten and renamed it Ikh Mongol; however, no one seems to use this name.

Even if you are not a climber, it's worth trekking up to the Khuiten Uul **base camp** (3092m; GPS N 49°09.036', E 87°56.528'), where you can get stunning views of all the peaks as well as the 12km-long **Potanii glacier**, which tumbles out of the range. It's possible to walk onto the glacier but be very careful of deep snow and crevasses. If you're not too exhausted already, head to the top of **Malchin Peak**. The three-hour walk is rewarded with views of Russia and the surrounding mountains.

Note that there are two trails to the base camp. One starts from the end of the road in Tsagaan Gol valley. From here it's a 14km trek to the base camp. The trailhead has a ranger station and a place to camp. Across the river are some gers occupied by an extended family of Tuvans. They rent horses (T10,000) and one of the younger family members can guide you up to the base camp (for around T15,000 with horse).

The other trail to the base camp begins in the Sogoog Gol valley (north of Tsagaan Gol); from here it's 13km to the base camp. This trailhead also has a ranger station.

Sleeping & Eating

There is no official accommodation in the park but during summer, **Tuvan and Kazakh families** (per person T10,000) will often host trekkers and may even supply a hot meal, although you will need to bring your own sleeping bag. Besides camping, the only other option is the small, unofficial and overpriced **Aksu Rashan Suvlal** (☎9942 2979; with/without meals US$25/20, tent site US$10), a ger camp set up by a local entrepreneur at the hot springs 25km northwest of Khoton Nuur.

The best **camping spots** are around the lakes. Dayan Nuur has some nasty mosquitoes but the other two lakes are largely bug-free. Be aware that unattended tents are sometimes robbed.

At **Syrgal** (GPS: N 48°36.004', E 88°26.672'), between the lakes, there are a couple of very basic shops selling sweets, vodka, water and little else.

Information

Maps

Kazakh Tour (p183) sells the excellent satellite map *Altai Tavan Bogd National Park Map & Guide* published by **Conservation Ink** (www.conservationink.org) for T15,000 and topographic 1:500,000 maps for T18,000.

Permits

PARK ENTRY FEES Fees are the standard T3000 per person. The main entry to the park is by the bridge over the Khovd Gol, south of Tsengel. You can pay for permits there or at the Manspaa office in Ölgii (p186).

BORDER PERMITS These are also required and can be obtained in Ulaanbaatar or at the **Border Patrol office** (Khiliin Tserenk Alb; ☎22341; ⌚8-11am & 2-5pm Mon-Fri) in Ölgii. The permit costs T3000 and is good for an entire group provided the group does not separate midtrek. The border patrol office will only deal with Mongolians so you'll need a local, your guide or a tour agency in Ölgii to apply on your behalf. Border guards at Dayan Nuur, Tavan Bogd base camp, Aral Tolgoi (western end of Khoton Nuur) and Syrgal (the point where Khoton Nuur meets Khurgan Nuur) will all ask to see your paperwork (photocopies are not accepted), and those without permits are fined US$150 and charged the cost it takes the army to return them to Ölgii (around US$170).

FISHING PERMITS These cost T500 per day and are not issued for 15 May to 15 July.

Getting There & Away

The main road from Tsengel leads 45km south to the bridge over the Khovd Gol (there's a T2000 toll) and then continues 33km to the junction of Khoton and Khurgan *nuurs* (lakes), where there is a bridge across the wide water channel between the two lakes.

A more scenic route takes you from Sagsai over a pass and up the beautiful Khargantin Gol valley, past Tsengel Khairkhan Uul and Khar Nuur, and then down to Dayan Nuur. A good option would be to enter the park this way and exit via the main road.

There are two main ways to access Tavan Bogd. One is via Tsengel and up the Tsagaan Gol (although fording the Khovd Gol after heavy rain can be tricky) to the south ranger station. The other is via Sogoog following the Sogoog Gol straight to Tavan Bogd via the north ranger station or alternatively by going over Hagiin Davaa (Hagiin Pass) that leads to Tsagaan Gol.

There is no public transport to the park, although Ölgii tour agencies (p183) can arrange a jeep to drop you off and collect you at the end of your trek. A jeep for one to five people typically costs around US$150 to either ranger station. At the time of research there was talk of the Ölgii tour operators introducing a fixed schedule service so that solo travellers can band together to help defray costs.

KHOVD ХОВД

POP 88,500 / AREA 76,000 SQ KM

Khovd aimag has long been a centre for trade, business and administration in western Mongolia, a status that began during the Qing dynasty when the Manchus built a military garrison here. The aimag still does robust trade with China through the border at Bulgan and its agricultural university is the largest of its kind outside Ulaanbaatar.

Besides its developing economy, Khovd is notable for being one of the most heterogeneous aimags in Mongolia, with a Khalkh

KAZAKHS

Ask anyone in Kazakhstan for the best place to find genuine Kazakh culture and they will most likely point to a small plot of land, not in their own country, but in western Mongolia. Bayan-Ölgii, thanks to its isolation for most of the 20th century, is considered by many to be the last bastion of traditional Kazakh language, sport and culture.

Kazakhs first migrated to this side of the Altai in the 1840s to graze their sheep on the high mountain pastures during summer and returned to Kazakhstan or Xinjiang for the winter. After the Mongolian Revolution in 1921, a permanent border was drawn by agreement between China, the USSR and Mongolia.

The word 'Kazakh' is said to mean 'free warrior' or 'steppe roamer'. Kazakhs trace their roots to the 15th century, when rebellious kinsmen of an Uzbek khan (king or chief) broke away, and settled in present-day Kazakhstan.

Kazakh gers (traditional circular felt yurts) are taller, wider and more richly decorated than the Mongolian version. *Tush* (wall hangings) and *koshma* (felt carpets), decorated with stylised animal motifs, are common. *Chiy* (traditional reed screens) are becoming less common.

Kazakhs adhere rather loosely to Sunni Islam, but religion is not a major force. This is because of their distance from the centre of Islam, their nomadic lifestyle and the suppression of Islam during the communist era. Islam is making a comeback in Bayan-Ölgii, thanks to the lifting of restrictions against religion, aid packages from other Muslim countries, the construction of mosques and the annual hajj (pilgrimage) to Mecca. The main Kazakh holiday is the pre-Islamic spring festival of Navrus, celebrated on 21 March.

Kazakhs speak a Turkic language with 42 Cyrillic letters, similar to Russian and a little different from Mongolian.

majority and minorities of Khoton, Kazakh, Uriankhai, Zakhchin, Myangad, Oold and Torguud peoples. Its terrain is equally varied, with large salt lakes, fast-flowing rivers and the Mongol Altai Nuruu almost bisecting the aimag.

National Parks

Bulgan Gol Nature Reserve (1840 hectares) On the southwestern border with China, this reserve was established to help preserve *minj* (beavers), sable and stone marten. A border permit is required.

Great Gobi Strictly Protected Area (Gobi B) Created to protect *khulan* (wild ass), gazelle, jerboas and *takhi* (wild horses).

Khar Us Nuur National Park (850,272 hectares) Protects the breeding grounds for antelope and rare species of migratory pelican, falcon and bustard.

Khökh Serkh Strictly Protected Area (65,920 hectares) On the northwestern border with Bayan-Ölgii, it helps protect argali sheep, ibex and snow leopard.

Mankhan Nature Reserve (30,000 hectares) Directly southeast of Khovd City, it preserves an endangered species of antelope.

Mönkh Khairkhan National Park Established in 2006, this protects an important habitat for ibex and argali sheep.

Khovd City Ховд

☎01432 / POP 31,000 / ELEV 1406M

Khovd City is a pleasant tree-lined place developed by the Manchus during their 200-year rule in Outer Mongolia. Somewhat more developed than other cities in western Mongolia, it boasts an agricultural university and some food processing and textiles manufacturing. It also has the region's busiest airport, one reason why so many tourists end up here.

The town offers a few sights to keep you busy for a day and some pleasant ger camps outside town. Shops are well stocked and there are plenty of jeeps, making this a good place to launch a trip to the Altai Mountains or the lakes region.

Sights

Aimag Museum MUSEUM

(☎9943 4502; admission T2000; 8am-noon & 1-5pm Mon-Fri) This regional museum has the usual collection of stuffed wildlife, plus some excellent ethnic costumes, Buddhist and Kazakh art and a snow-leopard pelt tacked up on the wall. One of the more interesting exhibits is the excellent recreation of the cave paintings at Tsenkheriin Agui (p195). There are also several examples of the many deer stones scattered around the aimag, plus a model of the original Manchurian fortress.

Gandan Puntsag Choilon Khiid MONASTERY
Officially opened in 2010, this is the largest monastery in western Mongolia. The whole compound is surrounded by a wall (with a path on top) and 108 stupas. Morning prayers are held from 9am until 3pm inside the main temple, which features a statue of Buddha flanked by 10 divine protectors.

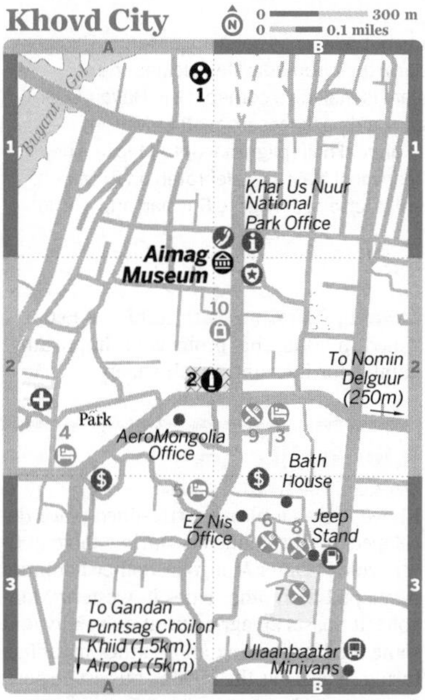

Sangiin Kherem HISTORIC SITE
At the northern end of the city are some crumbling walls built around 1762 by the Manchu (Qing dynasty) warlords who once brutally governed Mongolia. The 40,000 sq metre walled compound once contained several temples, a Chinese graveyard and the homes of the Manchu rulers, though there's little left to see. Three enormous gates provided access. At one time there was a moat (2m deep and 3m wide) around the 4m-high walls, but this has been completely filled in. The 1500-man Chinese garrison was destroyed after a 10-day siege and two-day battle in August 1912.

Town Square MONUMENT
Two statues in the town square honour local heroes. One of them, **Aldanjavyn Ayush** (1859–1939), was a local revolutionary hero who agitated against the Manchus to lower taxation, and the other statue is of **Galdan Boshigt** (1644–97), ruler of the Zuungar Mongols. Although only a blip on the pages of history, Galdan Boshigt's military victories in Central Asia gave him brief rule over the Silk Road cities Samarkand and Bukhara.

Tours

Khovd Handicraft & Tours TOURS
(☎9907 9485; markasl2002@yahoo.com; ⏲8am-10pm in summer) The friendly owner here is a great source of local information and can arrange tours to local attractions including Khar Us Nuur National Park, the caves of Tsenkheriin Agui and the *khöömii* singers in Chandmani. Guides (US$25 to US$30 per day), jeeps (T60,000 per day plus fuel) and homestays (US$5 to US$10) can also be arranged.

Sleeping

There are fine (if buggy) camping spots along the Buyant Gol; head out of the town

Khovd City

Top Sights
Aimag Museum B2

Sights
1 Sangiin Kherem A1
2 Town Square A2

Activities, Courses & Tours
Khovd Handicraft & Tours .... (see 10)

Sleeping
3 Buyant Hotel B2
4 Tsambagarav Hotel A2
5 Tusnig Hotel A3

Eating
6 Altai B3
7 Market B3
8 Tavan Erdene B3
9 Winners B2

Shopping
10 Khovd Handicraft and Tours B2

towards Ölgii, turn right (downstream) at the river, and pitch your tent anywhere.

Tsambagarav Hotel HOTEL $
(☎22260; tw/q T20,000/20,000, half-luxe tw T25,000, luxe d T40,000) Although it may not appear so from the outside, this is the newest hotel in town and locally regarded as the best. The luxe rooms here are smaller than elsewhere but smarter and cleaner. The worst of the standard rooms are trapped within the building and have no outside windows.

Möngön Uul TOURIST GER CAMP $$
(☎9943 2120; ganbold_h@yahoo.com; GPS: N 47°56.425', E 091°34.803'; with/without meals US$35/17) Set on a dry plain with a pretty backdrop of hills and mountains, Möngön Uul can be slightly exposed to the prevailing wind but is otherwise hard to fault. It's 3km southwest of the airport.

Buyant Hotel HOTEL $$
(☎23807; byanthotel@yahoo.com; dm/tr T12,000/T30,000, half-luxe tw T30,000, luxe T40,000; @) Though nothing extravagant, the rooms here are bright (especially 207) and all have hot showers except the dorm whose bathroom is two floors below. The luxe room is particularly spacious and resembles an apartment your nana might have decorated.

Shuutiin Tokhoi TOURIST GER CAMP $$
(☎9943 8200; bayarhuub@yahoo.com; GPS: N 48°02.960', E 091°40.253'; with/without meals US$27/10) About 6km to the northwest of town, this basic camp has a gorgeous location along the Buyant Gol, at the foot of a rocky escarpment.

Tusnig Hotel HOTEL $
(☎22245; tw/tr T16,000/24,000, luxe tw/d T25,000/25,000) This small, centrally located hotel offers good value, particularly the luxe rooms, which have their own large bathrooms.

Eating & Drinking

Self-caterers should head to the daily **market** or **Nomin Delguur** (⏱10am-7pm), the largest supermarket in town.

TOP CHOICE **Altai** MONGOLIAN, RUSSIAN $
(meals T2000-3500; ⏱9am-midnight) Justifiably popular, Altai's chef trained in Moscow and seems to care more about the quality of the food he serves than most. Some meals are served on a sizzling hotplate and salads are available (although these also come with meat).

Winners MONGOLIAN, RUSSIAN $
(meals T2000-3500; ⏱10am-midnight) Another good choice, the two dining rooms are separated by a small and cosy bar. Goulash is the house speciality and desserts in the form of cream cakes are also available.

Tavan Erdene MONGOLIAN $
(snacks T300; ⏱8am-10pm) The best *khuushuur* (mutton pancakes) are currently being served in this no-frills cafe behind the jeep stand. Four or five is enough grease for most people but a Mongolian with an appetite can easily finish 10.

Shopping

Khovd Handicraft & Tours HANDICRAFTS
(⏱8am-10pm summer) This charming little shop specialises in Kazakh embroidery, felt products and a few leather items. A 1.2m x 2m felt carpet costs around US$80 while a pair of felt slippers will only set you back US$10.

Information

Bathhouse (shower/sauna T1500/5000; ⏱9am-10pm)

Internet cafe (per hr T600; ⏱8am-10pm Mon-Fri, to 8pm Sat & Sun) Inside the Telecom office.

Khar Us Nuur National Park office (☎/fax 22539; kharus2006@chinggis.com; ⏱8am-5pm Mon-Fri) This office gives information on, and permits for, nearby Khar Us Nuur National Park.

Telecom office (☎22471; ⏱8am-10pm Mon-Fri, to 8pm Sat & Sun) The post office is also located here.

Khan Bank (⏱8am-7pm Mon-Fri, 9am-3pm Sat) Changes money and has a 24-hour ATM opposite the park in the multicoloured building.

Getting There & Away

AIR At least one plane a day travels the Khovd–Ulaanbaatar route. **AeroMongolia** (☎9982 1265; Turiin Bank Bldg) flies one way for T400,100 and **EZ Nis** (☎9943 9937; XAC Bldg) flies for T459,800, which occasionally is routed via Mörön (T323,000). The airport is 5km south of the city.

BUS Once a day a bus leaves for the gruelling 42- to 50-hour, nonstop trek to Ulaanbaatar (T60,000, 1425km, daily except Tuesdays) via Altai (T30,000, 15 hours, 424km) and Bayankhongor (T50,000, 28 hours, 795km). Typically there are two drivers who will rotate driving duties and it is standard practice for one to drive excruciatingly slowly and the other alarmingly fast. If you are game, buy your tickets in advance from the green railway carriage that serves as the bus station.

TO CHINA FROM KHOVD

For information on travelling directly to Urumqi in Xinjiang (China) from Khovd, see p262. For further information, head to shop.lonelyplanet.com to purchase a downloadable PDF of the Xinjiang chapter from Lonely Planet's *China* guide.

MINIVAN & JEEP Minivans leave from the jeep stand near the market for Ölgii (T15,000 to T20,000, six to seven hours, 238km) and Ulaangom (T18,000, seven to eight hours, 238km) if enough passengers show up (usually around four to eight hours after any suggested departure time).

Tickets for the daily Ulaanbaatar-bound minivan (T65,000, 45 hours) are sold in advance at the 'bus station'.

Jeeps cost around T500 per kilometre, including petrol, around town. Share jeeps for local *sums* leave from the local jeep stand behind the market.

Khar Us Nuur National Park Хар Ус Нуур

About 40km to the east of Khovd City is **Khar Us Nuur** (Dark Water Lake), the second-largest freshwater lake (15,800 sq km) in Mongolia – but with an average depth of only 4m. Khovd Gol flows into this lake, creating a giant marsh delta. Khar Us Nuur is the perfect habitat for wild ducks, geese, wood grouse, partridges and seagulls, including rare relict gulls and herring gulls – and by late summer a billion or two of everyone's friend, the common mosquito.

Bird-watchers, however, may be a little disappointed: the lake is huge, difficult to reach because of the marshes and locals know very little, if anything, about the birdlife. The best idea would be to go with one of the national park workers and head for the delta where the Khovd Gol enters the lake in May or late August.

The easiest place to see the lake is from the main Khovd–Altai road at the southern tip of the lake, where a metal **watchtower** (GPS: N 47°50.541', E 092°01.541') has been set up to view the nearby reed islands.

The outflow from Khar Us Nuur goes into a short river called Chono Khairkhan, which flows into another freshwater lake, **Khar Nuur** (Black Lake), home to some migratory pelicans. The southern end of Khar Nuur flows into **Dörgön Nuur**, which is a large alkaline lake good for swimming. The eastern side of Dörgön Nuur is an area of bone-dry desert and extensive sand dunes.

Just to the south, and between the Khar and Khar Us lakes, are the twin peaks of **Jargalant Khairkhan Uul** (3796m) and **Yargaitin Ekh Uul** (3464m). You can see the massif as you drive to Ölgii from Altai in Gov-Altai aimag. With the help of a guide you'll find numerous springs in these mountains. The canyons also hide a 22m high **waterfall**.

In 2004, 22 *takhi* (Przewalski's horse) were introduced to the **Khomyn Tal** buffer zone and became the third herd of this critically endangered horse to be re-established in Mongolia.

Sleeping

Area accommodation includes the following.

Jargalant Orgil TOURIST GER CAMP
(☎8843 8800; tseveenravdand@yahoo.com; per person T20,000) Between Khar Us Nuur and Jargalant Khairkhan Uul.

 **Torgon Els Tourist Camp** TOURIST GER CAMP
(☎8843 1811; baagii_nats@yahoo.com; with/without meals T25,000/15,000) On the southern shore of Khar Nuur.

Bortsgor Khoton Community Ger Camp TOURIST GER CAMP
(☎9890 8584; per person T20,000) Next to the metal watchtower.

Chandmani Чандмань

Chandmani, on the southeastern side of Khar Us Nuur National Park, is a renowned centre for **khöömii** (www.khoomei.com), or throat singing, along with Khovd and, more famously, the republic of Tuva in Russia.

Thanks to some resident old masters (Tserendavaa, Tsenee and Davaajav), it is quite easy to arrange some informal training or an impromptu demonstration (three songs, T30,000 per group). Apparently *khöömii* isn't as difficult to learn as you might imagine, although to attain any degree of proficiency you will need at least a week. If you're lucky, your visit may coincide with one of the small concerts that are held in the purpose-built *khöömii ordon* (palace), although your best chance of this is during the third week of July when a **khöömii competition** is planned as part of

THE GREEN TARA OF DÖRGÖN

In Dörgön *sum*, two hours' drive from Khovd City, an elderly woman is performing miracles. Megjin, 60, has spent the past several years clearing out a demon-infested charnel ground near the shores of Khar Us Nuur. The once-barren ground has been planted with more than 3500 trees and shrubs; several Buddhist temples have also been erected here.

In 2006 Megjin, clearly no ordinary granny, was officially recognised as a Green Tara (Buddha of enlightened activity) by the Mongolian Government and was given an enthronement ceremony in Ulaanbaatar.

a festival to celebrate traditional Mongolian arts (the inaugural festival held in 2011).

Also in town you'll find the women's cooperative, **Bisness Enkhbator Töv**, which produces a small selection of garments and hats made from camel and yak wool.

The only official place to stay, and rather a dire option at that, is in an empty wing of the town hospital. This **hotel** (☎8808 1811; per person T10,000) is very basic with steel-framed beds and the kind of atmosphere that would give Jack Nicholson in *The Shinning* the creeps. Most of the *khöömii* masters indicated that they could arrange **homestays** for around T5000 per night.

Once a day a shared jeep leaves for Khovd (T10,000, five hours, 150km).

Tsenkheriin Agui
Цэнхэрийн Агуй

Sights

TOP CHOICE Tsenkheriin Agui HISTORIC SITE

(Khoid Tsenkher; GPS: N 47°20.828', E 091°57.225'; admission T3000) This huge cave about 100km southeast of Khovd City looks deceptively small from the parking area but once you scramble up the loose rock path, you realise how big it is and how it must have afforded considerable shelter to the prehistoric humans who once lived here.

Tsenkheriin Agui is famous for its **cave paintings** and some of them depict long-extinct fauna including mammoths and ostrich-like birds. Today this area is known as a great place to spot **saiga antelopes**, especially on the road to Chandmani.

Unfortunately, this ancient art (c 13,000 BC) has inspired others and recent graffiti (c AD 2001) has seen much of it destroyed. In 2005 the area was incorporated into the Khar Us National Park and some of the paintings 'restored'.

To explore the cave you will need a strong torch (flashlight) and whatever kind of footwear you feel copes well with the dusty bird shit that blankets the cave floor.

Burial Mounds HISTORIC SITE

Only a few hundred metres further up the valley are some burial mounds that to the uninitiated would be just piles of rocks.

Petroglyphs HISTORIC SITE

More interesting than the burial mounds are these petroglyphs on the rise just behind the rock mounds.

Museum Ger MUSEUM

(admission T1000) This disappointing museum ger, run by the ranger, displays traditional Zakhchin clothing and little else.

Sleeping

The ranger has three wonderfully clean **gers** (☎9890 9130; per ger T15,000-25,000) set up for visiting travellers. He, or more likely

LOCAL KNOWLEDGE

D TSERENDAVAA: KHÖÖMII SINGER

Khöömii (throat singing) has been part of my family for generations. I was six when my father first started teaching me and I continued to study *khöömii* when I moved away to start school.

When foreigners first hear me sing they are amazed as they don't realise the human body is capable of producing such sounds. They are even more surprised to learn that I use seven different techniques to produce a whole harmonic range and that the 'song' is formed in the larynx, throat, stomach and palate. By singing this way I am able to produce two notes and melodies simultaneously: one a low growl, the other an ethereal whistle.

The best places to hear *khöömii* are in Western Mongolia, particularly in Chandmani and Khovd or at a concert in Ulaanbaatar.

his sons, can arrange hot showers (T2000), meals (T1500) and point out the best of the cave paintings (T1000).

Mönkh Khairkhan National Park
Мөнх Хайрхан Уул

At 4362m, **Mönkh Khairkhan Uul** (Tavan Khumit; park entrance T3000) is the second-highest mountain in Mongolia. You can walk up the peak if you approach from the northern side. There is plenty of snow and ice on top, so you'll need crampons, an ice axe and rope, but the climb is not technically difficult. A jeep trail runs to the base from Mankhan.

UVS УВС

POP 78,800 / AREA 69,000 SQ KM

After travelling around this aimag for a while you may start to wonder why they named it Uvs (Grass), as most of the region is classified as high desert. Really the main feature of this diverse aimag is its lakes, which come in all shapes, sizes and levels of salinity. The biggest, Uvs Nuur, is more like an inland sea, while smaller lakes such as Khökh Nuur make excellent hiking destinations. Together, the lakes and the surrounding deserts make up the Ikh Nuuruudin Khotgor: the 39,000 sq km Great Lakes Depression that includes bits of neighbouring Khovd and Zavkhan aimags.

However, the main attraction of Uvs has to be the twin peaks of Kharkhiraa Uul (4037m) and Türgen Uul (3965m). From these mountains spill permanent glaciers, fast-flowing rivers and verdant plateaus.

National Parks

The Great Lakes Depression is a globally important wetland area for migratory birds and is a Unesco World Biosphere Reserve. Many other parks have been established in the aimag and, together with parks in Russia, Tuva, China and Kazakhstan, form a Central Asian arc of protected areas.

Altan Els Strictly Protected Area (148,246 hectares) Contains the world's northernmost sand dunes and protects threatened desert plants.

Khan Khökhii National Park (220,550 hectares) An important ecological indicator and home to musk deer, elk, red deer and wolf.

Khyargas Nuur National Park (332,800 hectares) An area of springs and rocky outcrops that harbours abundant waterfowl.

Tes River Reserve (712,545 hectares) The newest conservation area in Uvs protects waterfowl, beaver and fish.

Uvs Nuur Strictly Protected Area (712,545 hectares) Consists of four separate areas: Uvs Nuur, Türgen Uul, Tsagaan Shuvuut Uul and Altan Els. Contains everything from desert sand dunes to snowfields, marsh to mountain forest. Snow leopard, wolf, fox, deer and ibex are among the animals protected.

Ulaangom Улаангом

☎01452 / POP 22,900 / ELEV 939M

Ulaangom (Red Sand) has had a recent makeover and is now looking rather smart. Many of the roads have been sealed, including a 13km stretch that leads into the city following the pretty Kharkhiraa Gol (T300 toll applies), and the main square is positively bristling with newly installed street lamps – most of which are working.

Sights

Aimag Museum MUSEUM

(admission T3000; 9am-noon & 1-6pm Mon-Fri, 10am-2pm Sat & Sun) The comprehensive Aimag Museum has the usual stuff plus a section on the 16th-century Oirad leader Amarsanaa (the chainmail jacket is supposedly his). There's a newly built wing dedicated solely to the reign of one-time dictator Yu Tsedenbal (who was born in Uvs), featuring photos of the man with other commie leaders like Fidel Castro and Ho Chi Minh.

Dechinravjaalin Khiid MONASTERY

Dechinravjaalin Khiid was originally founded in 1738 and contained seven temples and 2000 monks. The place was pulverised in 1937 thanks to Stalin, and its current incarnation consists of a concrete ger and about 20 welcoming monks.

Ulaan Uulyn Rashaan SPRING

(GPS: N 49°57.427', E 092°03.142') Just outside of town on the south side of Ulaan Uulyn (Red Mountain), a small spring draws a steady crowd of picnicking locals who come here to drink the medicinal water and knock back vodka shots.

Ulaangom

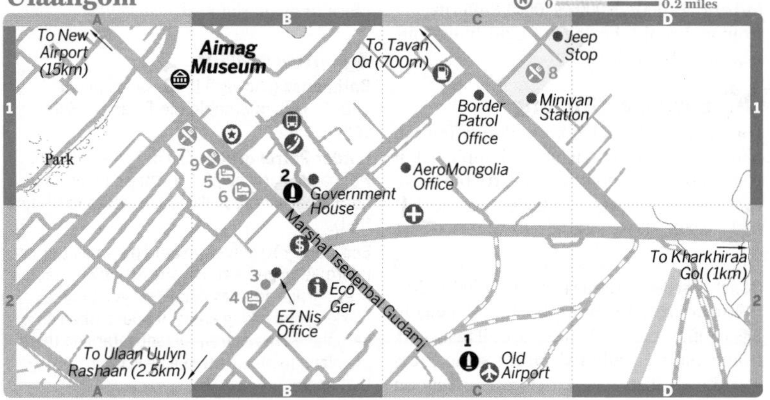

Ulaangom

Top Sights

Aimag Museum A1

Sights

1 Dechinravjaalin Khiid C2
2 Main Square B1

Activities, Courses & Tours

3 Strictly Protected Area Office B2

Sleeping

4 Bayalag Od Hotel B2
5 Khyargas Nuur Hotel B1
6 Tsogtsolbor Hotel B1

Eating

7 Ikh Mongol A1
8 Market C1
9 Qinggis Pub & Restaurant B1

Main Square MONUMENT

The **bronze statue** in front of Government House is of Yumjaagiin Tsedenbal, who ruled Mongolia for about 40 years until 1983, and was born near Ulaangom. Opposite the town square, another **statue** honours Givaan, a local hero who was killed in 1948 during clashes with Chinese troops.

Tours

Strictly Protected Areas office ECO TOUR

(22184; delhii novuvsnuur_mn@yahoo.com; 8am-5pm Mon-Fri) This government run office is better organised than most and runs the eco-ger which helps promote sustainable tourism throughout the Uvs aimag. Besides being an invaluable source of information, the staff can organise jeeps (T40,000 per day plus fuel), guides (US$30 per day), treks in the Türgen Uul and homestays with nomadic families.

Sleeping

Accommodation isn't Ulaangom's strong point and the rooms are often rented by the hour. We found camping along the Kharkhiraa Gol or anywhere south of the city on the road to Khovd to be the best option.

Tavan Od HOTEL $$

(23409, 9945 9418; tw/q incl breakfast T20,000/25,000, luxe tw incl breakfast T35,000; P) This 10-room hotel on the north edge of town offers a variety of rooms. Only the luxe rooms have their own bathrooms but all are fairly clean (by Ulaangom standards). It also has a restaurant-cum-bar that gets favourable reviews from locals but the meat they served us tasted like the cow had died of old age.

Bayalag Od Hotel HOTEL $$

(22445, 9984 3261; dm/d incl breakfast T10,000/18,000, luxe tw incl breakfast T36,000) The good news is that all the rooms have their own toilets and showers, the bad news is that not all the toilets have seats and the hot water only works when the central heating is turned on in winter.

If the above are full there are few more options around town. All are rundown and specialise in peeling paint and threadbare carpet.

Khyargas Nuur Hotel HOTEL

(9145 7492; s/tw T18,000/20,000) Small and smells funny.

Tsogtsolbor Hotel HOTEL
(d/tw/tr T15,000/25,000/30,000) Suffering from a chronic shortage of light bulbs and next to a noisy disco.

Eating & Drinking

For some really cheap *khuushuur* (mutton pancakes) or *buuz* (steamed dumplings), if you're not fussy about hygiene, try the train-car *guanz* (canteen) outside the **market** (⌚Tue-Sun).

Qinggis Pub & Restaurant FUSION $
(Marshal Tsedenbal Gudamj 27; meals T3000-5000; ⌚9am-midnight) Currently the best Ulaangom has to offer; the steak meals are all tasty and, from what we could tell, all the same – it is just the garnish that varies. One exception may be the 'boiled and tasted head' but we weren't game to try.

Ikh Mongol MONGOLIAN/CHINESE $
(Marshal Tsedenbal Gudamj 29; meals T3000-5000; ⌚9am-midnight) Once the best place in town, Ikh Mongol has seen better days and its reputation has taken a beating of late. The seating in the big red booths and its atmospheric ger-like interior make it a better place to drink than eat.

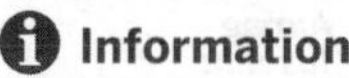

Information

Bathhouse (shower T1500, sauna per hr T5000; ⌚8am-8pm) In the Tavan Od Hotel compound.

Border Patrol office (Khiliin Tserenk Alban) Not particularly helpful, as they cannot issue border permits (you'll need to return to UB for that).

Eco Ger (⌚10 May–20 Sep) This small tourist-information ger is run by the Strictly Protected Areas office and has details on good horse-trekking and hiking areas. It opens when an aeroplane arrives from Ulaanbaatar and there are plans to move it to the new airport once that opens.

Internet cafe (☎23370; per hr T500; ⌚8am-5pm Mon-Sat) At the Telecom office.

Khan Bank (⌚8am-5pm Mon-Fri, 9am-2pm Sat) Will exchange US dollars. Its ATM is inside the M-Mart department store on the main road.

Strictly Protected Areas office (☎22184; delhiinovuvsnuur_mn@yahoo.com; ⌚8am-5pm Mon-Fri) Located at the western end of the main

WORTH A TRIP

ULAANGOM TO ÖLGII

This two-day jeep journey begins with a 40km tarmac road heading northwest out of Ulaangom before turning into a jeep trail just past Türgen village as it heads up **Ulaan Davaa** (Red Pass; elev 1972m), notable for its enormous *ovoo* (shamanistic offering).

From the pass there are two routes. One heads due south and then southeast to Khökh Nuur (p200). The other leads west to lovely Üüreg Nuur (p199).

From Üüreg Nuur, cargo trucks take a less-rugged (but longer) route (301km) via **Bohmörön village** (where you can check out the 8th-century Turkic *balbal*, or anthropomorphic statue). Light vehicles (jeeps and vans) bypass Bohmörön and take the short cut (254km) over the steep **Bairam Davaa**. Look out for several **ancient graves and balbals** (GPS: N 50°00.484', E 091°02.932') on this route a few kilometres south of Üüreg Nuur. The 8th-century *balbals* represent either local heroes or, possibly, enemies killed in battle. Another set of **graves and balbals** (GPS: N 50°00.220', E 091°02.713') is a further 550m south. The circular piles of stones in the area are *kurgans* (burial mounds).

On the south side of Bairam Davaa, the road passes more *kurgans* and standing stones (thin, stone pillars used as grave markers). The most impressive, 7km north of Khotgor, include two **mounds** (GPS: N 49°54.910', E 090°54.527') surrounded by concentric circles and radiating spokes.

Khotgor is a desolate coal-mining village but long-distance cyclists take note: this is the only place to pick up supplies between Ulaangom and Ölgii. Most maps show no road via Bairam Davaa but, rest assured, you can make it with a halfway decent vehicle or bike (and the lungs of a yeti).

From Khotgor you could opt for a detour into the **Yamaat Valley**, which leads to Türgen Uul (p199). Otherwise, continue south for 60km to the **Achit Nuur** bridge. From here it's another 75km to Ölgii. The road passes the surprisingly lush riverside forests of the **Develiin Aral Nature Reserve**, a 16km stretch along the fast-flowing Khovd Gol.

road, this office provides information on, and permits to, the protected areas in the aimag.

Telecom office (⌚8am-8pm) The post office is also here.

Getting There & Away

AIR Ulaangom's new airport (15km northwest of town) was due to open in 2009 but planes were still flying to the old airport 1km southeast of town at the time of writing.

EZ Nis (☎25252, 9904 9939) Charges T455,000 one way and flies on Wednesday and Sunday occasionally via Mörön (T328,000).

AeroMongolia (☎88080043) Charges T392,100 one way and flies every Tuesday, Thursday and Saturday.

BUS The **bus ticket office** (⌚8am-8pm Tue-Sun), which is nothing but a kiosk inside the Telecom office building, sells tickets to Ulaanbaatar (T55,000, 46 to 53 hours, 1336km) and Tosontsengel (T40,000, 26 hours, 540km) for the Wednesday, Friday and Sunday morning buses.

JEEP & MINIVAN If you are heading south to Ölgii it is generally easier to catch a share jeep or minivan to Khovd (T20,000, seven to eight hours, 238km) and make your way from there, as vehicles heading directly to Ölgii (T30,000, 10 hours, 300km) are few and far between. Even rarer are vans heading to Mörön (about 25 hours, 680km); if there is nothing available, consider riding a UB-bound minivan as far as Tariat (T25,000, 26 hours, 700km) and then attempt to bum a lift to Mörön from other backpackers at Terkhiin Tsagaan Nuur.

Share minivans to Ulaanbaatar (via Tosontsengel and Tsetserleg; T60,000, about 48 hours) leave daily. Note that the jeeps and minivans leave from different parts of the market and that the Khovd City–Ulaangom road sometimes suffers from flooded rivers and collapsed bridges.

Uvs Nuur Увс Нуур

Uvs Nuur is a gigantic inland sea in the middle of the desert. The lake's surface occupies 3423 sq km, making it Mongolia's largest lake, though it's very shallow at an average depth of 12m. (Still, legend has it that the lake is bottomless.)

Uvs Nuur is five times saltier than the ocean and devoid of edible fish. It has no outlet, so a lot of the shoreline is quasi-wetland. This environment, plus the clouds of mosquitoes, make Uvs Nuur tourist unfriendly.

Ornithologists have documented more than 200 bird species around Uvs Nuur, including crane, spoonbill, goose and eagle, as well as gulls that fly thousands of kilometres from the southern coast of China to spend a brief summer in Mongolia.

The small **Argai Az Ger Camp** (GPS: N 50°04.156', E 092°22.329'; with meals US$30) on the southwestern side of the lake is rather neglected and sees few guests.

Üüreg Nuur Үүрэг Нуур

Large and beautiful **Üüreg Nuur** (GPS: N 50°05.236', E 091°04.587'), at an elevation of 1425m, is surrounded by stunning 3000m-plus peaks, including **Tsagaan Shuvuut Uul** (3496m), which are part of the Uvs Nuur Strictly Protected Area. The freshwater Üüreg Nuur has some unidentified minerals and is designated as 'saltwater' on some maps, so it's best to boil or purify all water from the lake. There is a freshwater well on the southeastern edge of the lake near some deserted buildings.

The lake is great for swimming (albeit a little chilly) and locals say there are plenty of fish. One added attraction is that it's one of the few bug-free lakes in the region. Camping is the only sleeping option.

Tourist facilities in the area are limited to the **OT Tour Camp** (☎9913 6772; with/without meals US$42/20), located 25km southeast of the lake. The camp has a restaurant, modern toilet, hot water and horse-riding tours.

Kharkhiraa Uul & Türgen Uul Хархираа Уул & Түргэн Уул

The twin peaks of Kharkhiraa Uul (4037m) and Türgen Uul (3965m), which dominate the western part of the aimag, are vital sources of the Uvs Nuur and the mountains are also part of the Uvs Nuur Strictly Protected Area.

In summer, the area has some excellent hiking opportunities and the chance to meet Khoton nomads who graze their flocks in here. The village of **Tarialan** makes a good base for exploration. It is 11km off the main Ulaangom–Khovd road, about 20km out of Ulaangom (watch for the blue Тариалан sign).

The Strictly Protected Areas office in Ulaangom maintains a list of families in the area who accept travellers in informal **homestays** (per person T5000-10,000).

FAMILY PLANNING FOR GOATS

Depending on the time of year, you may notice many male goats wearing nifty, little leather aprons tied around their bellies in front of their hind legs. This age-old device, called a *khög*, is a trick employed by herdsmen to thwart the buck's attempts to successfully mount any does.

In Mongolia a kid born during the harsh winter months is not only likely to die itself, but also to imperil the life of its mother, who will struggle to find enough food to produce milk and maintain her own health. By selective employment of this device, farmers are able to restrict kidding to the warmer months when grass is more readily available.

Activities

Trekking

The mountains can be approached from different directions. Most hikers walk from east to west, from Tarialan to Khotgor. In Tarialan you can organise horses (T10,000), guides (T20,000) and pack camels (T20,000), but you will have to bring all other provisions with you.

From Tarialan follow the **Kharkhiraa Gol** into the mountains; you'll need to cross the river up to nine times as you go up the valley. Three days and 50km later you'll cross over the **Kharkhiraa Davaa** (2974m), which is accessible on foot but difficult going for pack camels.

From the pass you descend into the pretty **Olon Nuur Valley**, a marshy area of lakes and meadows. Turn north to walk over **Yamaat Davaa** (2947m) into Yamaat Valley, an area inhabited by snow leopards. In summer a ger camp is sometimes open in this valley. At the end of the valley you can easily reach the town of Khotgor.

It's 50km from Kharkhiraa Davaa to Khotgor, so you should plan six days for the entire route. Alternatively, you could save a day by starting from the Har Tarvagatay mining community, 36km to the south of Tarialan.

If you start in Khotgor, it's possible to drive into Olon Nuur valley, but it's pretty boggy here so stick to existing jeep tracks.

A third route leads from Khökh Nuur (see right).

Tseren Tours (p54), Mongolia Expeditions (p54) and Off the Map Tours (p264) all run walking trips through this area.

Getting There & Away

An 8am minivan leaves Tarialan for the jeep stand in Ulaangom (T5000) every day. It returns when full, usually sometime between 3pm and 4pm.

Khökh Nuur Хөх Нуур

This pretty alpine lake (elev 6322; GPS: N 49°50.413', E 91°41.141') is surrounded by mountains and makes a great destination on foot or horse from Tarialan; the trip is about 15km up Davaan Uliastai (one valley north of the Kharkhiraa Gol).

It's possible for a car to reach the lake in a very roundabout manner (120km) and only an experienced driver could do it. The road route involves driving up Ulaan Davaa (from Ulaangom), sweeping around the mountains close to Üüreg Nuur, and then heading southeast.

Trekkers can continue from the lake for 25km to the glacier-wrapped Türgen Uul (p199). The walk takes about two days through a harsh landscape of prairie, mountains, glaciers and rivers, but the topography is wide open so it's fairly easy to navigate. There are good camping spots (GPS: N 49°42.485', E 91°29.525') along the Türgen Gol, near the northern base of Türgen Uul.

Khar Us Nuur Хар Ус Нуур

To confuse things a little, another freshwater lake in the region is called Khar Us Nuur, but is sometimes referred to as Ölgii Nuur. You can swim and fish in Ölgii Nuur, and it makes a logical camping spot if travelling between Ulaangom and Khovd City. The lake is 102km south of Ulaangom.

Achit Nuur Ачит Нуур

The largest freshwater lake in Uvs, Achit Nuur is on the border of Uvs and Bayan-Ölgii aimags, and is an easy detour between Ulaangom and Ölgii. It offers stunning sunsets and sunrises and good fishing.

The lake is home to flocks of geese, eagles and other **birdlife**. One drawback is the absolute plethora of mosquitoes during the summer. Some camping spots are better than others for mozzies, so look around.

Locals claim they are almost bearable by October.

The small Kazakh encampment on the southeastern edge has a *guanz*.

A **bridge** (GPS: N 49°25.446', E 90°39.677') just south of the lake allows for relatively steady traffic between Ulaangom and Ölgii.

Khyargas Nuur National Park Хяргас Нуур

Khyargas Nuur, a salt lake amid desert and scrub grass, provides an attractive summer home for birds but sees little tourist traffic.

On the northwestern side of Khyargas Nuur, there is a **cold spring** (GPS: N 49°18.952', E 093°13.257') that dribbles out of the mountain – locals say drinking from it has health benefits. Five kilometres further on is **Khar Temis** (☎9945 6796; GPS: N 49°18.954', E 093°09.625'; with meals T25,000), an old Soviet holiday camp that is falling into serious disrepair. It has lake views and a sandy beach.

The main attraction of the lake is **Khetsuu Khad**, an enormous rock sticking out of the water that attracts migratory cormorant birds. The birds arrive in April and hatch their young in large nests built on the rock. When the chicks hatch, their squawking is constant and deafening. The aura created by the white cliffs, shrill birds and the prevailing smell of guano makes you feel as if you've arrived at the ocean. By mid-September the cormorants are off, migrating back to their wintering grounds in southern China.

Besides camping, the only option is the **Khetsuu Khad Ger Camp** (☎9911 7524, 9945 6796; GPS: N 49°01.968', E 093°28.783'; with meals US$25-30) set down here in the middle of absolutely nowhere. It has hot showers, flush toilets, a **restaurant** (meals T5000-6000) and lonely staff.

The last 15km of the road to Khetsuu Khad is very sandy and it's easy to get stuck, so don't attempt it without a reliable 4WD. The turn-off from the main road is signposted.

A national park fee of T3000 applies around the lake, though you'd be lucky (or unlucky) to find a ranger to pay it to.

ZAVKHAN ЗАВХАН

POP 79,000 / AREA 82,000 SQ KM

Zavkhan aimag occupies a transitional zone between the well-watered Khangai mountain range of central Mongolia and the harsh Great Lakes Depression of western Mongolia. In between the two regions, Zavkhan has its own microclimates and varied terrain that ranges from snowy peaks to steppe to lakes surrounded by sand dunes.

The aimag is in an awkward location and very few travellers are likely to pass through much or any of Zavkhan. This is a pity because the scenery is some of the most dramatic and varied in the country; one minute you are travelling through lush valleys and hills, and then a few kilometres further you are in a desert reminiscent of *Lawrence of Arabia*.

National Parks

Otgon Tenger Uul Strictly Protected Area (95,510 hectares) Protects the environment around one of Mongolia's most sacred mountains; Otgon Tenger Uul.

Uliastai Улиастай

☎01462 / POP 19,100 / ELEV 1760M

Along with Khovd, Uliastai is one of Mongolia's oldest cities, founded by the Manchus during their reign in Mongolia. The old garrison is long gone but the town has retained a pleasant, antiquated feel. Rivers flowing nearby and a lush valley surrounded by mountains complete the picture and make a great place to camp.

History

Manchurian generals established a military garrison here in 1733 to keep one eye on the Khalkh Mongols to the east and the other on the unruly Oirad Mongols who lived west of the Khangai mountains. The fortress once housed 3500 soldiers and was surrounded by an inevitable Chinese trading quarter called Maimaicheng.

The fort was emptied in 1911 with the disintegration of the Manchu dynasty, but Chinese troops made an attempt to retake the fort four years later, only to be booted out once and for all in March 1921, following the taking of Urga (Ulaanbaatar) by White Russian forces.

Sights

History Museum MUSEUM
(☎23097; admission T2000; ⌚9am-6pm Mon-Fri) The History Museum contains a mammoth bone, some fine religious art and a *tsam* mask, worn during lama dances, made from coral. There is also a fine collection of

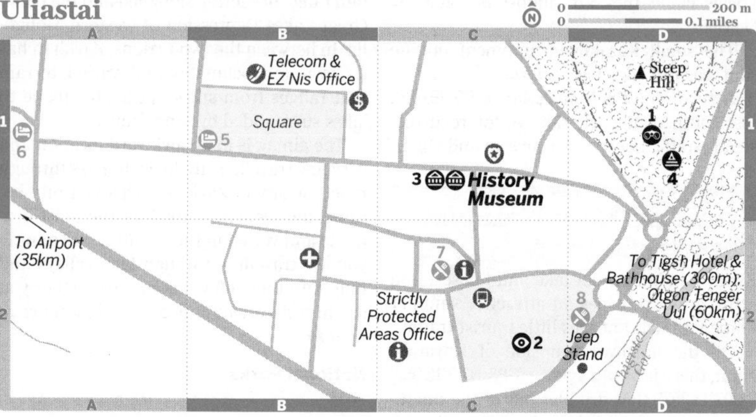

Uliastai

Top Sights
History Museum ... C1

Sights
1 Javkhlant Tolgoi ... D1
2 Market ... C2
3 Museum of Famous People ... C1
4 Tögs Buyant Javkhlant Khiid ... D1

Activities, Courses & Tours
Chigistei Restaurant ... (see 7)

Sleeping
5 Bolorjin Hotel ... B1
6 Uliastai Hotel ... A1

Eating
7 Chigistei Restaurant ... C2
8 Tesiin Gol Supermarket ... D2

photographs of Uliastai taken in the early 20th century and a few grisly reminders of the Manchu era in the form of shackles and torture devices. Next door, the **Museum of Famous People** (9am-6pm Mon-Fri) features well-known Zavkhanites (including Mongolia's first two democratically elected presidents, P Ochirbat and N Bagabandi), and is included in the price.

Javkhlant Tolgoi LANDMARK
(Жавхлант Толгой) This hilltop near the river and just to the north of the main street features a pavilion, nine stupas and the concrete likenesses of an elk, ibex and argali sheep. The views from the top are good. To the northeast, about 3km away, you can barely make out the remains of the old **Manchu military garrison** (GPS: N 47°44.922', E 96°52.198'). It is possible to walk to the garrison in about 30 minutes, though there's not much to see and is generally regarded by locals as a waste dump.

Tögs Buyant Javkhlant Khiid MONASTERY
(Төгс Буянт Жавхлант Хийд) This small monastery has around 20 monks with daily ceremonies at 10am.

Courses

Mr Enkhjargal is a professional music teacher at the local music college and gives **khöömii (throat singing) lessons**. He can be reached through the Chigistei restaurant.

Tours

Chigistei Restaurant HORSE TREKS
(9946 0506, 9811 2507; chigesteituya@yahoo.com) Tuya who owns the Chigistei Restaurant and speaks excellent English also organises tours, particularly horse treks in the Otgon Tenger Uul Strictly Protected area. She can arrange transport, tents, guides (T15,000 per day) and horses (T20,000 per day).

Sleeping

Along the lush valley that hugs the Chigistei Gol for 15km from town, and parallel to the northern road to Tosontsengel, there are some gorgeous camping spots.

TOP CHOICE **Uliastai Hotel** HOTEL $$
(2414; s/tw/half-luxe/luxe incl breakfast T20,000/20,000/30,000/40,000, half-luxe tw incl breakfast T60,000, luxe incl breakfast T100,000) A

polished marble foyer, glass chandeliers and a swanky, some might say over-the-top, restaurant create a fine first impression at the Uliastai Hotel. A trifle disappointingly this standard isn't maintained but, when all is said and done, these digs are the cleanest in town. Not all rooms have their own showers and hot water is only available from 7am to 10am and 7pm to 10pm.

Tigsh Hotel HOTEL $
(☎8846 6969; dm/d T10,000/20,000; P) The Tigsh is looking a little forlorn these days but the basic rooms are good value if all you want is a bed and roof over your head. It's a 15-minute walk from the centre of town in a white building labelled Зочид Вудал (Hotel).

Bolorjin Hotel HOTEL $
(☎9946 7142; d with/without toilet T16,000/13,000, tw T16,000-25,000) Bolorjin is a small establishment – only five rooms; all of which are simple, clean and share the hot shower.

Ikh Mongol Ger Camp TOURIST GER CAMP $
(☎9946 2222; GPS: N 47°48.621', E 96°50.218'; per person incl meals T18,000) Thirteen kilometres towards the northeast of town in the pretty rock-strewn Khoid Soloni Am (valley), this camp has four gers and a few wooden shacks.

Eating & Drinking

All the hotels listed also serve passable food in their attached restaurants, and by 'passable' we mean if it isn't mutton, it'll smell like mutton. Self-caterers can explore the busy **market** (⏲11am-6pm Mon-Sat) or try the **Tesiin Gol Supermarket** (⏲10am-6pm) near the roundabout.

TOP CHOICE **Chigistei Restaurant** ASIAN FUSION $
(meals T2000-5000; ⏲9am-midnight; ✎) A large restaurant with retro-Soviet decor and Mongolian and Chinese/Korean meals. Sit near the bar to be shown the Mongolian menu and at the far end of the restaurant to be given the Asian menu. A third menu is available in the VIP rooms from which you can order *aduu* (horse). Pizza is also planned and will undoubtedly necessitate a fourth menu.

Information

Khan Bank (⏲10am-7pm Mon-Fri, to 4pm Sat) On the 2nd floor of a yellow-and-white building. Changes US dollars and has an ATM.

Strictly Protected Areas office (☎22361, 9809 9466; ⏲9am-1pm & 2-5pm Mon-Fri) This office contains a small information room with brochures and pictures, though no English is spoken. The staff can also sell you entry tickets to Otgon Tenger Uul Strictly Protected Area.

Telecom internet cafe (☎21120; per hr T500; ⏲9am-10pm Mon-Fri, 11am-5pm Sat & Sun)

Telecom office (☎24117; ⏲24hr) The post office is also located here (but has a separate entrance).

Tigsh Bathhouse (shower T1200, sauna per hr T2000; ⏲9.30am-10pm) Located behind the Tigsh Hotel.

Getting There & Away

AIR **EZ Nis** (☎2112, 9904 9982) flies between Ulaanbaatar and Uliastai on Tuesdays, Thursdays and Saturdays (T384,000 one way). The airport is about 35km west of Uliastai; a taxi will cost about T9000.

BUS A Monday, Thursday and Saturday bus leaves for Ulaanbaatar (T33,000, 30 hours) from near the Chigistei Restaurant at 9am.

MINIVAN & JEEP Several minivans and jeeps leave each day for Ulaanbaatar (T40,000, 26 hours, 984km) via Tosontsengel (T15,000, five to six hours, 181km). If you want to get off at Tariat (for Terkhiin Tsagaan Nuur; 10 to 11 hours, 399km) or Tsetserleg (15 hours, 531km), you may have to pay the full Ulaanbaatar fare.

It is virtually impossible to find a vehicle heading north to Mörön, south to Altai or even west to Ulaangom, although that doesn't stop people trying. You may be forced to hire a jeep privately at the jeep station to head in these directions (T45,000 per day plus fuel).

In the last week of August it is easy to get a ride to Khovd City (T35,000, 18 hours, 480km) when vans fill up with students headed back to university.

The road between Uliastai and Tosontsengel is unpaved, but pretty reasonable and easy to follow. The turn-off to Tosontsengel is 148km north of Uliastai and 33km west of Tosontsengel.

Zagastain Davaa Загастайн Даваа

Forty-eight kilometres northeast of Uliastai on the Uliastai–Tosontsengel road is a spectacular mountain pass with the unusual name of **Zagastain Davaa** (Fish Pass; GPS: N 48°04.157', E 097°09.900'). At the top, there are fine views, a large *ovoo* and infamously changeable weather. Look out for the two **balbals and burial mounds** (GPS: N 47°56.396', E 097°00.824') 20km south of the pass.

WORTH A TRIP

WESTERN ZAVKHAN

If you are travelling overland from Uliastai to western Mongolia (or vice versa) there are a few places of interest to stop on the way.

Khar Nuur (Хар Нуур) Located in the *sum* of Erdenekhairkhan, this is a pretty freshwater lake bordering on alpine and desert zones. Most of the lake is ringed by sand dunes, making vehicle access difficult.

Ikh Khairkhan Nuruu (Их Хайрхан) An area of cliffs that provides shelter for ibex and wolf. There are caves in the area, including **Ikh Agui** (Big Cave; GPS: N 47°57.080', E 94°59.854').

Ereen Nuur (Эрээн Нуур) A beautiful lake surrounded by rolling sand dunes, some of them high enough to resemble small mountains. It's technically in Gov-Altai aimag but most travellers reach the lake via Uliastai.

Otgon Tenger Uul Strictly Protected Area Отгон Тэнгэр Уул

One of Mongolia's most sacred mountains, **Otgon Tenger Uul** (3905m), 60km east of Uliastai, is the spiritual abode of the gods and an important place of pilgrimage for many Mongolians. The mountain is the highest peak in the Khangai Nuruu and part of the **Otgon Tenger Strictly Protected Area** (admission T3000). The mountain's sanctity means that climbing is prohibited, and attempting to do so will incur the wrath of park rangers and the authorities in Uliastai.

You'll need to be content with viewing Otgon Tenger from **Dayan Uul**, a 30-minute drive past the children's camp (passing pretty Tsagaannuur en route), where you'll also get views of lovely **Khökh Nuur** (GPS: N 47°37.447', E 97°20.546'). A second route into the area is via the town of **Otgon**, 138km southeast of Uliastai, where a decent road heads up the Buyant Gol towards the southeastern flank of the mountain. This route is littered with impressive pre-Mongol-era **burial mounds**.

Otgon Tenger is a great area for **horse trekking** (guide/horse per day T15,000/20,000). Tuya at the Chigistei Restaurant (in Uliastai, see p202) and the rangers at the ranger station in Dayan Uul can put you in touch with horse wranglers.

Tosontsengel Тосонцэнгэл

☎014546 / ELEV 1716M

Occupying a pretty valley along the Ider Gol, with forested mountains on all sides, Tosontsengel is Zavkhan's second-biggest city and a transit hub for west-bound traffic. Tosontsengel once supported a booming timber trade and its many wood-fronted buildings, coupled with unpaved lanes and wandering horsemen, give it a Wild West atmosphere.

The **Gandiras Hotel** (☎9601 0571; s/d T15,000/25,000; P), on the main road is one of the many small hotels that cater to people on their way to the capital. While most specialise in crumbling walls and dank smells, the Gandiras is clean and comfortable but alas, it doesn't have any showering facilities and the toilet is still an outhouse. It's opposite the Sports Center, behind a shop in an apricot-coloured building.

As a transit hub between eastern and western Mongolia there is plenty of traffic, including a daily minivan to Ulaanbaatar (T35,000) and Tariat (T15,000, five hours, 190km). Occasionally you may find one heading to Uliastai (T15,000, five hours, 181km) and Mörön (seven hours, 273km) but this is by no means guaranteed. The Uliastai–Ulaanbaatar bus calls into the **Buunz Cafe** (mains T2500; ⌚24hr; 📵) at around 2pm and if there is room, will take you to Ulaanbaatar for T30,000.

If you are heading to Mörön from Uliastai or Ulaangom, you don't need to come to Tosontsengel at all; the turn-off to Mörön is 33km to the west of the city.

Telmen Area Тэлмэн

Around 65km west of Tosontsengel is the town of Telmen, which has a well-preserved **deer stone** in the centre of town. A collection of **burial mounds and deer stones** (GPS: N48°30.674', E97°27.169') can be seen a further 21km south of Telmen, on the main road to Uliastai.

Understand Mongolia

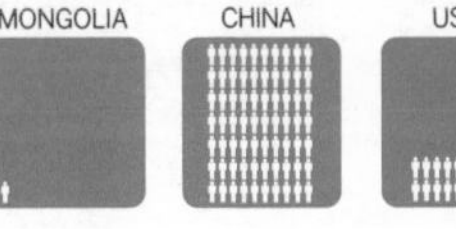

Mongolia Today

Mongolia may be just a little fish in the big pond of globalisation but its importance on the world stage has only just started to grow. Pundits have dubbed the country 'Mingolia', a nod to its enormous mineral wealth. Indeed, the country is rich in copper, gold, coal and other minerals and the government is being wooed by international firms hoping to grab a piece of the pie. Mongolians are stepping cautiously ahead, wary of the fact that other natural resource rich countries have been over-exploited and ruined by corruption and mismanagement. All the talk now is what path the government will take – rapid development and a reduction of poverty, or corruption and a greater split between the rich and poor.

The Great Leap Forward

The hot topic of conversation in Mongolia these days centres on Oyu Tolgoi, a massive copper and gold deposit in the Gobi. The US$5 billion mine under construction is expected to be operational by 2013. Within 10 years, this solitary mine could account for a third of Mongolia's GDP.

China is a ready market for Mongolia's raw materials and the government is rapidly trying to build up its infrastructure to deliver the goods. New rail and road links to China are being planned, and in a bid to diversify its markets, Mongolia is also planning a 1000km railway from Ömnögov all the way to Russia (via Choibalsan).

Mongolia's political leaders seem keenly aware of the need to invest their newfound wealth back into the country. Plans have been laid to build a copper smelter, oil refinery and coal washing plant.

Investment is also being made in education. A sparkling new university and IT complex is planned for the city of Nalaikh. For now, however,

Fast Facts

» Population: 3,086,000 (2010)

» GDP: US$3100 per capita, ranking Mongolia 135 out of 182 listed countries

» Literacy rate: 98%

» Voter turnout: often over 80%

» Number of livestock: 44 million

» Horse-to-human ratio: 13 to 1

Top Books

When Things Get Dark to End, by Matthew Davis

Dateline Mongolia, by Michael Kohn

Wild East, by Jill Lawless

Hearing Birds Fly, by Louisa Waugh

The Secret History of the Mongol Queens, by Jack Weatherford

Dos

» Do accept a snuff bottle with your right hand (as if you were shaking hands). If you don't take the snuff, at least sniff the top part of the bottle. But don't grab the bottle from the top.

» Do keep ger visits to less than two hours to avoid interrupting the family's work.

» If you have stepped on anyone, or kicked their feet, immediately shake their hand.

belief systems

(% of population)

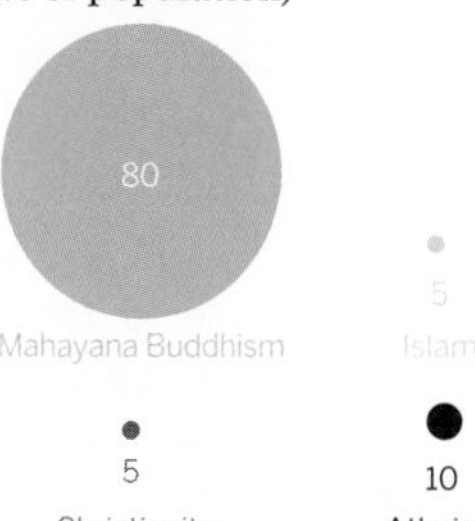

if Mongolia were 100 people

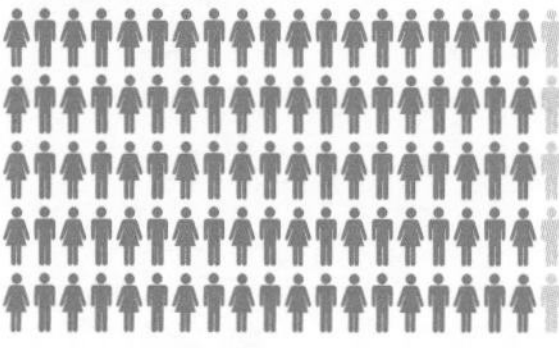

95 would be Mongol (mostly Khalkh)
5 would be Turkic (mostly Kazakh)

the government seems intent on pleasing voters by keeping taxes low and distributing money through various economic support schemes.

Power Sharing

On 1 July 2008 supporters of the Democratic Party took to the streets to protest recent election results, claiming the rival MPRP had rigged the vote. The MPRP headquarters were attacked and by nightfall the building was on fire and hundreds had been arrested. Four protestors were shot dead in the melee – the worst political violence in Mongolia's post-communist period.

Although the MPRP was declared winner of the election, it offered an olive branch to the Democrats, giving several of their senior members positions in the government. Power sharing is not a new thing in Mongolia: between 2004 and 2008 the two main parties even shared the position of prime minister. The ability of Mongolia's political parties to cooperate is unique in Central Asia and may provide lessons for neighbours. Even China has sent election observers to Mongolia to witness a legitimate democracy in action.

The Future

For Mongolia, the challenge lies largely in the task of nation building. From a cultural point of view, Mongolia has moved on from the Soviet period and has established a new path of strong nationalism fused with Western influences. One only needs to look at urban youth culture in Ulaanbaatar – tattooed with *soyombos* and rapping about the blue skies – to realize that the country is forging a unique new identity.

But on the ground, life is still hard. Poverty, especially in rural areas, has forced thousands to the city in search of work. Many end up jobless

Sample Prices

» Can of Chinggis beer T1200

» *Guanz* (canteen) lunch T2500

» Internet per hour T700

» Taxi from the airport to Sükhbaatar Sq T10,000

» Best seat at the Naadam opening US$25

Don'ts

» Don't point your feet at the hearth, the altar or another person in a ger. Sleep with your feet pointing towards the door.

» Don't walk in front of an older person or turn your back to the altar (except when leaving a ger).

» Don't stand on or lean over the threshold.

» Don't lean against a support column.

» Don't touch another person's hat.

Top Films

The Weeping Camel (2004)
Cave of the Yellow Dog (2006)
Mongol (2007)
Tracking the White Reindeer (2008)

When offered some vodka, dip your ring finger of right hand into the glass and flick three times into the air (to the sky, earth and wind). Then put the same finger to your forehead and drink the vodka.

in the sprawling ger districts. The struggle for work, housing, food and education remains ever-present for some, while others, business leaders involved in mining, construction, import/export and supply-side business, are rocketing to riches.

Despite the challenges ahead, surveys show widespread support for the path the government has taken, with only 10% of people still hoping for a return to communism. The reality is that there is no turning back and those that wish for bygone days tend to be from the older generation. There is strong optimism among most of the population, but the country still most certainly has a long way to go before it can claim success.

Top Phrases

» Hold the dog! *Nokhoi khor!*

» Are your sheep fattening up nicely? *Mal sureg targan tavtai uu?*

» Not too much, please (food, tea, vodka). *Dunduur*. Or, *jaakhan, jaakhan*.

» I would like to ride a calm (nonaggressive) horse. *Bi nomkhon mori unmaar baina.*

» Please write down your address and I will send your photo later. *Ta nadad hayagaa bichij ogno uu. Bi tand zurag ilgeene.*

Top Culture Sites

» www.artscouncil.mn

» www.uma.mn

» www.mongoliatoday.com

» www.mongolianculture.com

» www.mongolculture.blogspot.com

History

By Jack Weatherford & Dulmaa Enkhchuluun

Over the past 2000 years, there is possibly no other place on the planet that has exported as much history as Mongolia. Hordes of warriors rode their small but powerful horses down from the Mongolian Plateau in three dramatic waves – Hun, Turk and, finally, Mongol – to challenge and transform the world. The steppe warriors not only conquered nations, they swept up whole civilisations and reassembled them into intercontinental empires of a scale never before reached by any other people.

Although each of the three waves produced its distinctive influence, the name of Chinggis Khaan has achieved a unique spot in the world's imagination. He created the nation in 1206 and named it after his Mongol lineage. Mongols still maintain an intimate tie to him, but beyond the use of his iconic image and name, there seems to be surprisingly little to show of him in the nation. Chinggis Khaan did not leave a monument to himself, a temple, pyramid, palace, castle or canal, and even his grave was left unmarked in the remote area where he grew up and hunted as a boy. As he himself wished, his body could wither away so long as his great Mongol nation lived – it is that nation today that is his monument.

The lack of tangible ties to Chinggis Khaan presents both a challenge and an opportunity to visitors; Mongolia does not yield its history promiscuously to every passer-by. Its story is not told in great books, large stone monuments or bronze statues. A hiker crossing a hilltop can easily find etchings of deer with baroque configurations of antlers, soaring falcons or shamans without faces, but how would they know if the image was etched last year by a bored herder, a century ago by a pious lama or 25,000 years ago by a passing hunter? A small stone implement could have been abandoned on that same site centuries ago by a Hun mother preparing a family meal or by a Turk warrior on a raid; the modern visitor might easily be the first human to clutch it in 3000 years. These artefacts don't come labelled, classified and

Khan means Chief or King; *Khaan* means Emperor or Great Khan.

A Mongol is a member of the Mongol ethnic group; a Mongolian is a citizen of Mongolia. Kazakhs of Bayan-Ölgii are Mongolians but not Mongols; the Kalmyks of New Jersey are Mongols but not Mongolians.

TIMELINE

209–174 BC

Reign of Modun, as *shanyu* of the Huns; the first great steppe empire of Mongolia stretches from Korea to Lake Baikal in Siberia and south into northern China.

AD 552–744

Succession of two Turkic empires; greatest ruler is Bilge Khan. Following his death in 734, a monument is erected near Lake Ögii.

744–840

The Uighur empire occupies central Mongolia until expelled by the Kyrgyz tribe; the Uighur move south into western China and control the Silk Route for nearly 1000 years.

explained – the stories of the steppe are incomplete – but you'll find that Mongolia's history emerges slowly, from the objects, the soil and the landscape around you.

Turkic-Era Sites

- » Uushigiin Uver
- » Stele of Tonyukok
- » Kul-Tegenii Monument
- » Tavan Bogd balbals

People of the Sun

The first of the steppe nomads to make an impact beyond Mongolia were the Hunnu, whom the Mongols now call the 'People of the Sun', better known as the Huns. They created the first steppe empire in 209 BC under Modun, a charismatic leader who took the title *shanyu* (king) and ruled until his death in 174 BC. Modun created a disciplined and strong cavalry corps personally devoted to him, and used the corps to overthrow and kill his father, the tribal chief.

Between the creation of the Qing dynasty in China in 221 BC and the collapse of the Han dynasty in AD 220, the Chinese became the dominant economic power in East Asia. Even still, under the Huns, the steppe tribes grew into a great military power. During this period, the Chinese and the Huns vied for dominance through protracted wars with intermittent truces, during which the Chinese lavished the steppe warriors with tributes of goods and women, including imperial princesses (in exchange the Huns agreed not to slaughter them all). Using the merchandise extracted from the Chinese, the Huns extended their trade routes, connecting the civilisations around them.

CHINGGIS KHAAN

Known to the world as a conqueror, Mongolians remember Chinggis Khaan as the great lawgiver and proudly refer to him as the Man of the Millennium (a title bestowed on him by the *Washington Post* in 1995). His laws derived from practical considerations more than from ideology or religion.

After the abduction of his wife Borte, Chinggis recognised the role of kidnapping in perpetuating feuds among clans and outlawed it. Similarly, he perceived religious intolerance as being a source of violence in society, and so decreed religious freedom for everyone and exempted religious scholars and priests from taxes.

To promote trade and communications, Chinggis built an international network of postal stations that also served as hostels for merchants. He decreased and standardised the taxes on goods so that they would not be repeatedly taxed. Under these laws, the Mongol empire formed the first intercontinental free-trade zone.

In an era when ambassadors served as hostages to be publicly tortured or killed during times of hostilities, Chinggis Khaan ordered that every ambassador be considered an envoy of peace. This law marked the beginning of diplomatic immunity and international law. Today nearly every country accepts and promotes, at least in theory, the ideas and policies behind the 'Great Law of Chinggis Khaan'.

1162

Birth of Temujin, the child destined to become Chinggis Khaan, near the Onon River. According to legend, Temujin emerges with a blood clot clutched in his fist.

1204

Chinggis Khaan establishes the Mongolian state script based on the Uighur alphabet; it had Semitic origins but was written vertically from top to bottom.

TONY WHEELER

» Chinggis Khaan statue (p41), Ulaanbaatar

Following the collapse of the Hun empire in the 4th century AD, various newly independent tribes left the Mongolian homeland, wandering from India to Europe in search of new pastures and new conquests. By the 5th century, one of these branches reached Europe and created a new Hun empire that stretched from the Ural Mountains to Germany. Under their most famous leader, Attila the Hun, they threatened Rome and ravaged much of Western Europe. For the first time in history, mounted archers from the Mongolian steppe created an intercontinental reputation for their fierceness and tenacity in battle.

At Noyon Uul in Selenge aimag archaeologists have made curious finds inside Hunnu-era tombs. Unearthed objects include Hellenistic mirrors and jewellery from Afghanistan. Historians believe these were brought from Persia or Central Asia and traded by steppe nomads until they reached the Siberian border.

Descendents of the Wolf

In the 6th century, a new sense of order returned to the Mongolian Plateau with the rise of a series of tribes speaking Turkic languages. These tribes claimed descent from a boy who was left for dead but was saved and adopted by a mother wolf who raised him and then mated with him, creating from their offspring the ancestors of the various steppe clans. Compared with both the Huns before them and the Mongols after them, the literate Turks sought to blend traditional nomadic herding with a life of agriculture, urbanisation and commerce; consequently, they left more physical remains than the others in the ruins of Turkic cities and ceremonial centres. Along the Orkhon Gol in central Mongolia, they built their small cities of mud, the most famous of which were erected during the time of the Uighurs, the last of the great Turkic empires of Mongolia. The Turkic era reached its zenith in the early 8th century under Bilge Khan and his brother Kultegen, the military general. Their monuments near the Orkhon Gol are probably the oldest known examples of writing in a Turkic language.

Like the Huns before them, the Turks moved down off the Mongolian Plateau, spreading from what is today China to the shores of the Mediterranean. Another invading Turkic tribe, the Kyrgyz, overthrew the Uighur empire in AD 840, destroying its cities and driving the Uighur people south into the oases of western China. But the Kyrgyz showed no inclination to maintain the cities or the empire they had conquered. With the expulsion of the Uighurs came another period of decentralised feuding and strife, before the greatest of all Mongolian empires arose at the beginning of the 13th century: the rise to power of Chinggis Khaan.

Chinggis Khaan never erected any statues or grand monuments to himself, but recent years have seen modern Mongolians trying to rectify this. Statues of Chinggis can be seen at Sükhbaatar Sq in UB, on the Ulaanbaatar–Khentii road, in Öndörkhaan and in Dadal.

Children of the Golden Light

The decline of the Turkic tribes gave the opening for a new tribe to emerge. Scholars offer varying explanations for when and where these new people arrived, but the Mongols ascribe their origins to the mating of a blue wolf and a tawny doe beside a great sea, often identified as Lake Baikal (in Russia). They further credit the origin of Chinggis Khaan's

1206

Chinggis Khaan calls a massive conclave at Kherlen Gol and creates his empire – he calls it the Great Mongol Nation.

1235

Ögedei Khaan completes the imperial capital at Karakorum. In addition to a great palace, the city has Muslim mosques, Christian churches and Buddhist temples.

1258

Mongolian soldiers destroy Baghdad and kill some 100,000 people. The siege marked the end of the 500-year-old Abbasid Caliphate.

1260

The end of Mongol expansion with their defeat by the Mamluk army of Egypt at the Battle of Ayn Al-Jalut near the Sea of Galilee.

own clan to a mysterious and sacred woman called Alan Goa, who gave birth to two sons during her marriage, and had an additional three sons after her husband died. The elder sons suspected that their younger brothers had been fathered by an adopted boy (now a man) whom their mother had also raised and who lived with her.

Anthropologist Chris Kaplonski maintains an excellent site devoted to Mongolian culture and history at www.chriskaplonski.com.

Upon hearing of their suspicions and complaints, Alan Goa sat her five sons around the hearth in her ger and told them that the three younger sons were fathered by a 'Golden Light'. She then handed each an arrow with the command to break it. When they had done this, she handed each a bundle of five arrows with the command to break them all together. When the boys could not do so, she told them that it mattered not where the brothers came from so long as they remained united.

No matter what the Mongol origin, the story of Alan Goa has had a persistent and profound influence on the development of Mongolian culture, on everything from the role of women and attitudes towards sexuality to the political quest for unity and the herder's value of practical action over ideology or religion.

The *Encyclopedia of Mongolia and the Mongol Empire*, by Christopher P Atwood, is an authoritative historical reference book with special emphasis on Buddhism.

The Mongol Empire

The Mongols were little more than a loose confederation of rival clans until the birth of Temujin in 1162. Overcoming conditions that would have crushed lesser men, Temujin rose to become the strongest ruler on the steppe, and in AD 1206 founded the Mongol empire and took the title 'Chinggis Khaan'. He was already 44 years old at this stage, but since the age of 16, when his bride was kidnapped, he had been fighting one clan feud and tribal war after another. Frustrated with the incessant chaos, he began killing off the leaders of each clan as he defeated them and incorporating the survivors into his own following. Through this harsh but effective way, Chinggis Khaan forced peace onto the clans around him.

He named his new state Yeke Mongol Ulus (Great Mongol Nation). His followers totalled probably under a million people, and from this he created an army of nine units of 10,000 and a personal guard of another 10,000. With a nation smaller than the workforce of a large, modern multinational corporation, and an army that could fit inside a modern sports stadium, the Mongols conquered the greatest armies of the era and subdued hundreds of millions of people.

Anthropologist Jack Weatherford wrote *Genghis Khan and the Making of the Modern World*, for which he received the Order of the Polar Star, Mongolia's highest state honour.

In battle, Chinggis Khaan was merciless, but to those who surrendered without fighting, he promised protection, religious freedom, lower taxes and a heightened level of commerce and prosperity. His law did more to attract people into his empire than his military power. Based on military success and good laws, his empire continued to expand after his death until it stretched from Korea to Hungary and from India to Russia.

1271
Kublai Khaan claims the office of Great Khan and also makes himself Emperor of China by founding the Yuan dynasty.

1368
Yuan dynasty collapses in China but the Mongol government return to Mongolia refusing to submit to the newly created Ming dynasty. They continue ruling as the 'Northern Yuan'.

1448
Birth of Mongolia's greatest queen, Manduhai the Wise, who reunites Mongolia by the end of the century.

1449
Esen Taishi defeats the Chinese and captures the Ming emperor. His reign marks the rise of western Mongolia and the Oirat people as major powers of inner Asia.

The Decline

After Chinggis Khaan's death, his second son Ögedei ruled from 1229 to 1241, followed by Ögedei's widow Töregene Khatun and the brief 18-month reign of Ögedei's son Guyuk from 1246 through 1248. Tensions began to develop among the branches of his descendants, and broke into open civil war in 1259 when Arik Boke and Kublai each claimed the office of Great Khan after the death of their brother Möngke. Arik Boke controlled all of Mongolia, including the capital Karakorum, and enjoyed widespread support from the ruling Borijin clan. Yet Kublai controlled the vast riches of northern China, and these proved far more powerful. Kublai defeated his brother, who then perished under suspicious circumstances in captivity.

Geoffrey Chaucer's *The Canterbury Tales* (1395), recognised as the first book of poetry written in English, includes an early account of Chinggis Khaan in the 'Squire's Tale'.

Kublai had won the civil war and solidified his hold over China, but it had cost him his empire. Although they still claimed to be a single empire, the nation of Chinggis Khaan had been reduced to a set of oft-warring sub-empires. The Mongols of Russia became in effect independent, known later as the Golden Horde, under the lineage of Chinggis Khaan's eldest son Jochi. Persia and Mesopotamia drifted off to become the Ilkhanate, under descendants of Kublai's only surviving brother Hulegu, the conqueror of Baghdad.

Rivers in Mongolia are female and may be called *ej* (mother). A river, spring or lake that never runs dry is called a *khatun* (queen).

Kublai went on to create a Chinese dynasty named Yuan, took Chinese titles and, while still claiming to be the Great Khan of the Mongols, looked southward to the remaining lands of the Sung dynasty, which he soon conquered.

Much of Central Asia, including Mongolia, pursued an independent course and acknowledged the Yuan dynasty only when forced to by military invasion or when enticed with extravagant bribes of silk, silver and other luxuries. By 1368, the subjects had mostly overthrown their Mongol overlords, and the empire withdrew back to the Mongolian steppe where it began. Although most Mongols melted into the societies that they conquered, in some distant corners of the empire, from Afghanistan to Poland, small vestiges of the Mongolian empire still survive to the present.

In 1368, the Ming army captured Beijing, but the Mongol royal family refused to surrender and fled back to Mongolia with the imperial seals and their bodyguards. Much to the frustration of the Ming emperors in China, the Mongols continued to claim to be the legitimate rulers of China and still styled themselves as the Yuan dynasty, also known as the Northern Yuan. However, even within Mongolia, the Imperial Court exerted little power. Unaccustomed to the hardships of the herding life, and demanding vast amounts of food, fuel and other precious resources for their large court and retainers, the Mongol rulers devastated their own country, alienated the increasingly impoverished herders and eventually became the captive pawns of the imperial guards.

The best source for information on the life of Chinggis Khaan can be found in *The Secret History of the Mongols*, which was written in the 13th or 14th century and not made public until the 20th century.

1585

Founding of Erdene Zuu Khiid, the first Buddhist monastery in Mongolia, at the site of the Mongol capital, Karakorum (modern Kharkhorin).

TIM MAKINS

» *White stupas at Erdene Zuu Khiid (p95), Kharkhorin*

1603

A descendant of Chinggis Khaan and great-great grandson of Queen Manduhai is enthroned in Lhasa Tibet as the fourth Dalai Lama, the only Mongolian Dalai Lama.

WARRIOR QUEENS OF MONGOLIA

Chinggis Khaan's greatest disappointment in life was the quality of his sons, but his greatest pride was in his daughters. He left large sections of his empire under the control of his daughters, although they did gradually lose power to his sons.

Mongol women presented a strange sight to the civilisations they helped conquer – they rode horses, shot arrows from their bows and commanded the men and women around them. In China, the Mongol women rejected foot-binding; in the Muslim world, they refused to wear the veil.

At the death of Ögedei (Chinggis Khaan's second son), in 1241, probably in an alcoholic stupor, his widow Töregene assumed complete power. She replaced his ministers with her own, the most important of whom was another woman, Fatima, a Tajik or Persian captive from the Middle Eastern campaign. In addition to the rule of Töregene and Fatima from Karakorum in Mongolia, two of the other three divisions of the empire also had female governors – only the Golden Horde of Russia remained under male rule. Never before had such a large empire been ruled by women.

Töregene passed power on to her inept son Guyuk in 1246, but he died mysteriously within 18 months and was replaced by his widow Oghul Ghamish, who had to face Sorkhokhtani, the most capable woman in the empire. With the full support of her four sons, whom she trained for this moment, Sorkhokhtani organised the election of her eldest son Möngke on 1 July 1251. So great was her achievement that a Persian chronicler wrote that if history produced only one more woman equal to Sorkhokhtani, then surely women would have to be judged the superior sex.

While Kublai Khaan ruled China, his cousin Khaidu continued to fight against him from Central Asia and, true to the Mongol tradition, Khaidu's daughter Khutlun fought with him. According to Marco Polo, who called her Aiyaruk, she was both beautiful and powerful. She defeated so many men in wrestling that today, Mongolian wrestlers wear an open vest in order to visibly distinguish the male from the female wrestlers.

After the fall of the Mongol empire, in 1368, the men returned to squabbling over sheep and stealing horses, but the women kept the imperial spirit alive. In the late 15th century, a new conqueror arose, determined to restore the empire. Known to the grateful Mongols as Manduhai the Wise Queen, she took to the battlefield and united the scattered tribes into a single nation. She fought even while pregnant and was once injured while carrying twins; she and the twins survived, and her army won the battle.

Faced with Manduhai's tenacity and skill, the Chinese frantically expanded the Great Wall. Although she left seven sons and three daughters, the era of the great warrior queens of Mongolia had passed with her death. Even so, Mongolians still watch and wait for a new Manduhai.

1634
Death of Ligden Khaan, the last of Chinggis Khaan's descendants to rule as Great Khaan. Eastern Mongolia becomes part of the Manchu empire, but western Mongolia holds out.

1639
Zanabazar, a direct descendent of Chinggis Khaan and the greatest artist in Mongolian history, is recognised as the first Jebtzun Damba, the supreme religious leader of Mongolia.

1644
The Manchus expel the Ming dynasty and with the support of their Mongolian allies create the Qing dynasty in China.

1696
The Manchus defeat Galdan Khaan of Zungaria and claim western Mongolia for the Qing Dynasty, but some western Mongolians continue to resist foreign rule for several generations.

In the 15th century, the Mongols united with the Manchus, a Tungusic people related to Siberian tribes, for a new conquest of China and the creation of the Qing dynasty (1644–1911). Initially, the ruling Manchus treated the Mongols with favour, gave them an exalted place in their empire and intermarried with them. Gradually, however, the Manchus became ever more Sinicised by their Chinese subjects and less like their Mongol cousins. The Mongols were reduced to little more than a colonised people under the increasingly oppressive and exploitative rule of the Manchus.

The English word 'horde' derives from the Mongol *ordu*, meaning 'royal court'.

Revolutions

In 1911 the Qing dynasty crumbled. The Mongols broke away and created their own independent country under their highest Buddhist leader, the

THE MAD BARON

Baron Roman Nikolaus Fyodirovich von Ungern-Sternberg, an unusual character in Mongolia's history, was a renegade officer of a group of White Russians (anti-communists), who believed he was the reincarnation of Chinggis Khaan, destined to restore the Mongol warlord's previous empire. Contemporaries paint a fine picture of Baron von Ungern-Sternberg, later known as the Mad Baron, describing him as haunted-looking, with a psychotic stare that fixed on people 'like those of an animal in a cave'. He spoke with a high-pitched voice and his bulging forehead bore a huge sword scar, which pulsed with red veins whenever he grew agitated. As a finishing touch, one of his eyes was slightly higher than the other.

The Bolshevik victory in Russia forced the Baron east, and he slowly accumulated a desperate army of renegade mercenaries. He enforced discipline with a reign of terror, roasting deserters alive, baking defiant prisoners in ovens and throwing his rivals in locomotive boilers. He was also a fervent Buddhist, convinced that he was doing his victims a favour by packing them off to the next life sooner rather than later.

With an army of 6000 troops (and tacit backing of the Japanese), the Baron crossed the Mongolian border in the summer of 1920 with the aim of establishing a Pan-Mongol empire. By October, his forces attacked Urga, but were driven back four times before finally taking the city. He freed the Bogd Khan (who had been imprisoned by the Chinese), but Mongol joy turned to horror as the next three days saw an orgy of looting, burning and killing. In May 1921 the Baron declared himself the Emperor of Russia.

After only a few months, the Bolshevik advance forced the Baron to abandon Urga. Out on the steppes, his own followers tried to kill him, shooting him in his tent, but he managed to escape. A group of Mongolian herders later found him wounded in the grass, tortured by biting ants. He was eventually taken by the Bolsheviks, deported to Novosibirsk and shot on 15 September 1921, presumed mad. Dr Ferdinand Ossendowski, a Polish refugee living in Mongolia in the early 1920s, offers an excellent account of the 'Mad Baron' in his book *Beasts, Men and Gods*.

1911
Mongolia declares independence from the dying Manchu empire and sets up religious leader the Bogd Khan as the head of state.

1915
Treaty of Khyakhta is signed by Mongolia, China and Russia, granting Mongolia limited autonomy.

1921
The mad Russian baron, von Ungern-Sternberg, briefly conquers Mongolia but the Red Army and Mongolian forces under D Sükhbaatar defeat him.

1924
The Bogd Khan, the eighth reincarnation of the Jebtzun Damba, dies; the People's Republic of Mongolia is created on 26 November.

Voltaire's *The Orphan of China*, the first European play on the life of Chinggis Khaan, debuted in Paris in 1755.

Jebtzun Damba (Living Buddha), who became both spiritual and temporal head of the nation as the Bogd Khan (Holy King). When the Chinese also broke free of the Manchus and created the Republic of China, the new nation did not recognise Mongolia's independence, claiming portions of the Manchu empire, including Tibet and Mongolia. In May 1915 the Treaty of Khyakhta, which granted Mongolia limited autonomy, was signed by Mongolia, China and Russia.

The Russian Revolution of October 1917 came as a great shock to Mongolia's aristocracy. Taking advantage of Russia's weakness, a Chinese warlord sent his troops into Mongolia in 1919 and occupied the capital. In February 1921, retreating White Russian (anti-communist) troops entered Mongolia and expelled the Chinese. At first the Bogd Khan seemed to welcome the White Russians as saviours of his regime, but it soon became apparent that they were just another ruthless army of occupiers.

Mongolian nationalists believed their best hope for military assistance was to ask the Bolsheviks for help. The White Russians disappeared from the scene when their leader, Baron von Ungern-Sternberg, was captured, tried and shot. In July 1921, Damdin Sükhbaatar, the leader of the Mongolian army, marched uncontested into Urga (modern-day Ulaanbaatar) alongside Bolshevik supporters. The People's Government of Mongolia was declared and the Bogd Khan was retained as a ceremonial figurehead with no real power. Led by a diverse coalition of seven revolutionaries, including Sükhbaatar, the newly formed Mongolian People's Party (MPP), the first political party in the country's history (and the only one for the next 69 years), took the reins of power. Soon after its birth the MPP adopted the name, the Mongolian People's Revolutionary Party (MPRP). The party re-instated the original name in 2010.

In the mid-1950s, Howard Hughes cast John Wayne as Chinggis Khaan in *The Conqueror*, one of the worst films ever made by Hollywood.

Soviet Control

After Lenin's death in Russia in 1924, Mongolian communism remained independent of Moscow until Stalin gained absolute power in the late 1920s. Then the purges began in Mongolia – MPRP leaders were disposed of until Stalin finally found his henchman in one Khorloogiin Choibalsan.

Following Stalin's lead, Choibalsan seized land and herds from the aristocrats, which was then redistributed to nomads. Herders were forced to join cooperatives and private business was banned. The destruction of private enterprise without time to build up a working state sector had the same result in Mongolia as in the Soviet Union: famine. Choibalsan's policy against religion was just as ruthless – in 1937 some 27,000 people were executed or never seen again (3% of Mongolia's population at that time), 17,000 of whom were monks.

Russian Cossacks adopted the Mongol battle cry of 'hurray!' and spread it to the rest of the world.

Choibalsan died in January 1952 and was replaced by Yumjaagiin Tsedenbal – no liberal, but not a mass murderer – and Mongolia enjoyed a

1937

Choibalsan's Buddhist purge leaves 700 monasteries destroyed and 27,000 monks and civilians dead.

1937

Former Mongolian Prime Minister Genden is tried in Moscow on trumped up espionage charges, found guilty and executed by firing squad on 26 November.

1939

Japan invades Mongolia from Manchuria in May. With help from the Soviet Union, and after heavy fighting along the Khalkh Gol, the Mongols defeat Japan by September.

1945

In a UN-sponsored plebiscite, Mongolians vote overwhelmingly to confirm their independence but the USA and China refuse to admit Mongolia to the UN.

THE MONGOL WHO SLAPPED STALIN

In 1932 P Genden became the ninth prime minister of Mongolia, using the slogan 'Let's Get Rich!' to inspire Mongolians to overcome the troubled fighting since the breakup of the Manchu Empire and the establishment of an independent country. Mongolia was the second communist state, after the Soviet Union, but at this time Genden was trying to establish Mongolia as an ally of the Soviets rather than a colony or satellite.

Genden, standing up to Stalin, resisted demands that Mongolia purge the Buddhist monks and charged the Russians with 'Red Imperialism' for seeking to send Soviet troops into Mongolia. Amid much drinking at a reception in the Mongolian embassy in Moscow in 1935, the two men clashed, literally. Stalin kicked Genden's walking stick and Genden slapped Stalin and broke Stalin's trademark pipe, which always accompanied him.

Stalin held Genden under house arrest until he was convicted as a Japanese spy and executed by firing squad on 26 November 1937 – a day of great symbolic importance to the Mongols because it was the date of their declaration of independence and the creation of the Mongolian People's Republic.

In 1996, Genden's daughter, G Tserendulam, opened the Victims of Political Persecution Memorial Museum (p47) in Ulaanbaatar in memory of her father and all those who died in defence of Mongolian independence.

period of relative peace. With the Sino-Soviet split in the early 1960s, the Mongolians sided with the Soviet Union. The Mongolian government expelled thousands of ethnic Chinese and all trade with China came to a halt.

Throughout the 1970s, Soviet influence gathered strength. Young Mongolians were sent to the USSR for technical training, and Tsedenbal's wife, a Russian woman of modest background named Filatova, attempted to impose Russian culture – including food, music, dance, fashion and even language – on the Mongolians.

Modern composer N Jantsannarov created a series of symphonies and other musical works covering Mongolian history including Chinggis Khaan and Queen Manduhai.

The Great Transition

The unravelling of the Soviet Union resulted in decolonisation by default. In March 1990, in sub-zero temperatures, large pro-democracy protests erupted in the square in front of the parliament building in Ulaanbaatar. Hunger strikes were held and in May 1990, the constitution was amended to permit multiparty elections in July of the same year.

The political liberation of Mongolia from the Soviets came as an economic disaster for Mongolia because of the heavy subsidies that the Soviets had paid to keep Mongolia as a buffer state between itself and China. The Mongols lost much of their food supply and, unable to pay their electrical bills to the Russian suppliers, the western districts were plunged

1956

The Trans-Siberian railroad through Mongolia is completed, connecting Beijing with Moscow; the Chinese and Russian trains still operate on different gauges, requiring the bogies to be swapped at the border.

TIM MAKINS

» All aboard (p242)!

1961

Mongolia is admitted to the UN as an independent country, but the Soviet Union continues to occupy Mongolia with troops and run the country as a satellite state.

1990

Democracy demonstrations break out in Ulaanbaatar. In June the first free, multiparty elections are held, with the Mongolian People's Revolutionary Party (MPRP) winning 85% of the vote.

into a blackout that lasted for several years. The economy of Mongolia withered and collapsed.

The harsh conditions called for stringent measures and Mongolians created a unique approach to the new challenges. They began a radical privatisation of animals and large state-owned corporations. Unlike the other Soviet satellites in Eastern Europe and Central Asia that expelled the communist party, the Mongolians created a new democratic synthesis that included both the old communists of the MPRP and a coalition that became known as the Democrats. Freedom of speech, religion and assembly were all granted – the era of totalitarianism had ended.

The Mongolians gradually found their way towards the modern global economy and embraced their own brand of capitalism and democracy that drew heavily on their ancient history while adjusting to the modern realities of the world around them. Despite difficult episodes, such as the unsolved murder of the Democratic leader S Zorig in 1998 and some heated clashes between government and citizens, Mongolia managed to move forward with tremendous cultural vigour. While maintaining staunch friendships with old allies such as North Korea, Cuba and India, Mongolia reached out to Europe, South Korea, Japan and, most particularly, to the USA, which they dubbed their 'Third Neighbour' in an effort to create a counterpoint to China and Russia.

WWII

During WWII, Mongolia donated 300kg of gold and more than six million animals to Soviet and Allied forces. More than 2000 Mongolians died fighting Japan.

1996

The Democratic Coalition becomes the first non-communist government to win an election (although a series of scandals causes the fall of four successive governments).

2000

The MPRP trounces the Democratic Coalition in June elections, winning 72 of the 72 seats in Parliament. N. Enkhbayar becomes prime minister.

2004

In closely contested elections the MPRP wins 37 seats in Parliament while the Democratic Coalition wins 35 seats. The two parties enter into a 'national unity coalition'.

2008

In hotly contested Parliamentary elections the MPRP narrowly defeats the Democratic Coalition. Protestors allege vote rigging and subsequent riots end with four people shot dead and hundreds arrested.

The Mongolian Way of Life

Every Mongolian, no matter how long he or she has lived in a city, is a nomad at heart. The nomadic way of life was born out of necessity in this region as herders were forced to move their animals over the steppes in search of grasslands. But even as new technologies were introduced, the country remained a nomadic one, in large part because the nomadic way of life became more than a necessity – it became an unbreakable lifestyle. While today, more than ever, Mongolians are lured to the city in search of work, many choose to stay on the land with their animals, unable to give up the freedom and independence afforded to them by their traditional lifestyle.

Ingredients for Life

Mongolian nomads have two crucial tools at their disposal. The first and most essential is the *ger*, the ubiquitous Mongolian felt and canvas tent that provides shelter for the nomad family.

The second tool (or tools) are the animals pastured by nomads. Cows, sheep, goats, camels and horses provide all of life's necessities, including food (mutton and beef), milk, fuel (in the form of dung) and transportation.

Mongolians are attached to their animals in the same way that Westerners feel a certain affinity for their cars. The horse in particular is a much beloved animal, forming an intimate part of the Mongolian lifestyle. It was the horse that allowed ancient tribesman to spread across the steppes and cover its great distances. Later, it was the horse that carried the Mongolian warriors across Asia as they built their empire. An old Mongolian proverb says: 'A man without a horse is like a bird without wings.'

Today you'll see symbolic images of horses everywhere, from the tops of fiddles to the tail of MIAT aeroplanes. It is frequently stated that Mongolian children start riding a horse at the age of two; in fact the horse

MONGOL GAMES

Day-to-day life may be a struggle on the steppes but families will still find time for games and leisure activities. In the evenings, children (and sometimes adults) play with their *shagai* (ankle bones), which have four distinct sides representing horse, sheep, goat and camel. There are numerous *shagai* games but the most common is *moir uraldulakh* (horse race), which entails rolling four *shagai* (like dice) and then moving your 'horse *shagai*' a certain number of moves depending on the roll (roll four camels, move four spaces). The first person to reach the end of their *ger* wins the 'race'. Other indoor games include ankle-bone shooting (like darts but with *shagai*), *shatar* (chess), *hözör* (cards) and *duu dulakh* (singing songs).

riding begins earlier, essentially from birth, as parents will carry babies in their *dels* (traditional coat or dress) when they need to travel by horse.

The Forces of Nature

Nomadic peoples are, for all intents and purposes, on a lifelong camping trip. As such, they are greatly affected by the climate and other natural forces around them. Reverence towards the land, a product of their shamanic beliefs, has attuned them to nature; the thought of degrading the land or altering nature strikes many locals as profane. For Mongolians, nature is not something that must be tamed or dominated, but something that thrives on balance and harmony.

Modern Mongolia, Reclaiming Genghis Khan, edited by Paula Sabloff, is a pictorial account of recent developments in Mongolia. Written with a sometimes controversial edge, it discusses the economy, ger etiquette, social issues and Chinggis Khaan's principles, suggesting these are the foundations of modern Mongolia.

Mongolia's reverence towards nature can still be seen in modern daily ritual. For example, the act of flicking milk into the sky is seen as an offering to the sky spirits. Tossing a rock on an *ovoo* (a shamanistic collection of stones) and walking around it three times is a way to give thanks to earthly spirits. In the modern world some compromises do need to be made – for example, pits need to be dug for buildings and mines. In such cases lamas are often summoned to not only bless the project but also to pray for the damaged earth

Reverence to nature is seen in all aspects of Mongolian culture, especially song, dance and art. Ride in a van full of Mongolians and you'll soon hear them break out into song, crooning about the clear rivers and high mountains. These influences seem to have also affected the very nature of the Mongolian character. A Mongolian is typically humble, stoic and reserved; it is unusual to see a Mongolian express emotions vocally or in public. These personality traits must certainly be rooted in the quiet, motionless steppes that remain unchanged through the eons of time.

Seasons also shape Mongolian life. Spring in particular is a crucial time for Mongolians. Because the country's rainy season comes towards the end of summer, spring is dry, dusty, windy and unforgiving. This is the time when the weaker animals die and, it is said, when people die. Despite the severe temperatures, it is during winter that Mongolians feel most comfortable. After a difficult summer filled with chores and tending to livestock, winter is generally a time of relaxation.

One Mongolian tradition you might see is the annual horse-branding ceremony, which involves rounding up the foals for branding. Following the special ceremony, the family and their invited guests will sit down to a night of singing, feasting and drinking.

Steppe Rules

Mongolia's vast, open steppes and great distances have made hospitality a matter of sheer necessity rather than a social obligation. It would be difficult for anyone to travel across the country without this hospitality, as each ger is able to serve as a hotel, restaurant, pub and repair shop. As a result, Mongolians are able to travel rapidly over long distances without the weight of provisions. This hospitality is readily extended to strangers and usually given without fanfare or expectation of payment.

FUNERARY RITES

Up until the early 20th century Mongolians typically disposed of their dead by leaving them out in the elements, where dogs, birds and wild animals would devour the body. The practice followed the tradition of Sky Burial, common in Tibet. This act was seen to be the best way to return a body to the natural world, while the soul could safely be reincarnated into another body (either human or animal). When the Russians forbade the practice, Mongolians began following the Russian tradition of burying their dead. In the post-communist era, some families are reverting to the old method of 'Sky Burial', although this is still quite rare. The more popular option now is cremation and several crematoriums have been built around Ulaanbaatar in recent years.

A WOMAN'S WORLD

Mongolian women enjoy a great amount of freedom in Mongolian society. They always have, dating back to a time when Mongol queens helped rule the great Mongolian empire (see p214).

In the countryside Mongolian women are often in charge of managing household activities, such as selling sheep, bartering for flour and rice or managing the family cash reserves. These responsibilities usually fall upon the woman of the house because the men are often busy herding livestock, making repairs around the home or travelling to market.

Women also tend to achieve higher levels of education because, on average, they go to school longer than men (80% of higher-education students are women). Men often need to stay behind in the countryside to take care of aging parents and their livestock. As a result of this lopsided male-female ratio, it's estimated that women hold some 70% to 80% of skilled jobs in Ulaanbaatar.

Nomads tend to move two to four times a year, although in areas where grass is thin they move more often. One nuclear family may live alone or with an extended-family camp of three or four gers (known as an *ail*); any more than that would be a burden on the grassland. A livestock herd should contain around 300 animals per family to be self-sustaining, although some wealthy herders may have 1000 head of livestock.

Mongolia's nomads are surprisingly well-informed. Nearly all families have a short-wave radio to get national and world news. Some can receive satellite TV and certainly everyone reads newspapers when they are available (98% of Mongolians are literate). In winter, children of the ger go to school in the nearest town (where they live in dorms), visiting their parents during holidays and summer.

Life on the steppes is by no means easy or idyllic. Constant work is required to care for the animals, cook food and collect dung and water. It is also a precarious life – one bad winter can kill an entire herd, instantly wiping out a family's fortune. Life is even harder in the Gobi Desert, where grass is sparse and just one dry summer can threaten livestock.

The 'haircut' ceremony is a traditional rite of passage for Mongolian children. Their heads are shaved (girls at the age of two and boys at the age of three) and a special party is held in their honour. The person who cuts the hair must have been born in a year that corresponds to the child's year, and lamas sometimes come to the ceremony and read prayers. Afterwards, the hair is usually burnt.

City Slickers

Mongolians have carried their nomadic roots with them into the 21st century. One only needs to look at the city of Ulaanbaatar to see nomadic practices at work. For example, the layout of buildings across the city resembles a scattering of assorted gers across a fertile valley. Wags also note that driving habits in UB tend to mirror the way Mongols ride their horses. Mongolia's strong democratic values are also another reflection of nomadic traditions and their basic tenets – freedom, independence and pluralism.

Life in the city is changing as more Mongolians become accustomed to an urban lifestyle. Ger districts in Ulaanbaatar, for example, once considered a regular part of the fabric, are on their way out as developers transform the areas into modern apartment complexes. Western media, especially MTV, now carries significant weight in influencing youth culture.

The Mongolian way of life in Ulaanbaatar is still far from dead; in fact, its restoration is a unique blend of foreign trends and Mongolian culture. In Ulaanbaatar you'll see young Mongols who look like they've just stepped off the streets of New York or London, so convincing is their Western fashion sense. But talk to some of them and you'll soon realise that their hopes and dreams lie not only in the West but also in the future of Mongolia, its success, prosperity and continuation of its unique culture.

Naadam

A Mongolian legend recounts that one Amazonian female entered a wrestling competition and thrashed her male competitors. In order to prevent such an embarrassing episode from happening again, the wrestling jacket was redesigned with an open chest, forcing women to sit on the sidelines.

Mongolia's penchant for war games comes to a head each summer on the vast grasslands, where competitors show off their skills in wrestling, archery and horse racing. The annual Naadam Festival is the much-anticipated culmination of these events, and it's a colourful spectacle enjoyed by locals and tourists alike.

Every village and city has a naadam; most (including the one in Ulaanbaatar) are held on 11 and 12 July, coinciding with Independence Day. Some rural naadams are held a few days before or after this date, so some planning is required if you want to see one.

The most traditional and authentic naadams occur in small countryside villages. Almost every family in the village contributes in some way; children march in the opening parade, men sign up for the wrestling tournament and any kid with a horse participates in the horse races. Everyone in town will don their finest *del* (traditional cloak) and join together for the celebration. On the downside, you might not see archery at a small naadam.

By comparison, the naadam in Ulaanbaatar feels less like a community festival and more like a big sporting event, with huge crowds, souvenir salesmen, traffic, loudspeakers and a definite separation between the athletes and the spectators. Celebrities and professional actors will perform in the opening ceremony and the majority of locals will simply watch the events at home on TV. Although it's less intimate than small naadams, it is nice to see Ulaanbaatar in a more relaxed mood with plenty of associated concerts and theatre events.

Naadam Basics

If you are in UB in the days before 11 July take a walk down to the Naadam Stadium to see the archers going through some practice rounds.

OFF TO THE RACES

Mongolians hold a special place in their hearts for horse racing and naadam is the best time of year to watch this sport.

Jockeys – traditionally children between the ages of five and 12 years – race their horses over open countryside rather than around a track. Courses can be either 15km or 30km and are both exhausting and dangerous – every year jockeys tumble from their mounts and horses collapse and die from exhaustion at the finish line.

Winning horses are called *tümnii ekh*, or 'leader of 10,000'. Riders and spectators rush to comb the sweat off the best horses with a scraper traditionally made from a pelican's beak. Pelicans being quite rare these days, most people use a wooden curry-comb called a *khusuur*.

The five winning riders must drink some special *airag* (fermented mare's milk), which is then often sprinkled on the riders' heads and the horses' backsides. During the Naadam Festival, a song of empathy is also sung to the two-year-old horse that comes in last.

TITANS OF THE STEPPES

Mongolian-style wrestling is similar to wrestling found elsewhere, except there are no weight divisions, so the biggest wrestlers (and they are big!) are often the best. Out on the steppes matches can go on for hours, but matches for the national naadam have a time limit – after 30 minutes a referee moves the match into something akin to 'penalty kicks' (the leading wrestler gets a better position from the get go). The match ends only when the first wrestler falls, or when anything other than the soles of the feet or open palms touches the ground. Tournaments can vary in size; the Ulaanbaatar naadam tournament is the biggest with 512 competitors.

Then on 11 July get out to Sükhbaatar Sq (around 9.30am) to watch an honour guard march into the Parliament (Government) House to collect the nine yak-tail banners that will be brought to the stadium.

The opening ceremony, which starts at about 11am at the Naadam Stadium, includes an impressive march of monks and athletes, plus song and dance routines. The wrestling starts immediately after the ceremony and continues all day.

By comparison, almost nothing happens at the closing ceremony. The winning wrestler is awarded, the ceremonial yak banners are marched away, and everyone goes home. It is held at about 7pm on the second day, but the exact time depends on when the wrestling finishes.

Archery is held in an open archery stadium next to the main stadium but the horse racing is held about 40km west of the city on an open plain called Hui Doloon Khutag. Buses and minivans go there from the Naadam Stadium for around T1000 (vehicles also depart from the Dragon bus stand).

The horse racing can be disappointing from a spectator's point of view because although the race lasts about two hours you can only see the finish. Traffic to and from the racecourse can also be a nightmare. What is nice about the event is not so much the race itself but the generally festive atmosphere around the horse-race grounds.

To get a good feel for it all, consider camping out at the horse-race area, which will give you some insight into the rigorous lives of the trainers. A good day to visit is 13 July when a mini-naadam is held for the benefit of trainers who missed the archery and wrestling events. You could even ride your own horse to the racing grounds. Steppe Riders does four-day trips from its base near Bogd Khan Uul.

A recent addition to the naadam programme is ankle-bone shooting. This entails flicking a ball-like projectile made of cowhide at a small target (about 3m away) made from ankle bones. The competition is held in the Ankle-Bone Shooting Tent near the archery stadium.

> The website www.nadaam.viahistoria.com has pictures and historical information on naadam and the associated sporting events.

> The greatest naadam champion of all time was B Bat-Erdene, who won 11 straight naadams from 1988 to 1999. In 2000 he did not lose the naadam but rather stepped aside in order to give younger wrestlers a chance at the championship. His title translates loosely as 'Renowned by all, oceanic, joy-giving, forever titan Bat-Erdene'.

Naadam Tickets

Admission to the stadium (except for the two ceremonies), and to the archery and horse racing are free, but you'll definitely need a ticket for the opening ceremony and possibly the last round or two of the wrestling and closing ceremony. Ticket costs vary per section; the north side of the stadium (which is protected from the sun and rain by an overhang) is more expensive with tickets going for US$25 or more. This section is also less crowded and everyone will get a seat. These tickets are distributed via the tour operators and hotels.

There is no ticket window for general seating but you can buy a ticket from scalpers who hang around the stadium. The cheapest tickets will cost around T6000. Guesthouse owners normally help their guests buy tickets.

TAKING AIM

The third sport of Eriin Gurvan Naadam (Three Manly Sports; the other two being horse racing and wrestling) is archery, which is actually performed by men and women alike. Archers use a bent composite bow made of layered horn, bark and wood. Usually arrows are made from willow and the feathers are from vultures and other birds of prey. After each shot judges, who stand near the target, emit a short cry called *uukhai,* and raise their hands in the air to indicate the quality of the shot.

The website www.atarn.org has a number of informative articles on Mongolian archery.

The general seating sections are always oversold, so unless you get in early you'll end up sitting in the aisle or standing by the gate. The bandstand on the west end of the stadium offers some shade.

To find out what is going on during the festival, look for the events program in the two English-language newspapers.

Traditional Gers

Of all the different types of homes in our great world, the Mongolian ger has to be one of the most useful, versatile and perfectly adapted for the user. Here is a home that one can take apart in less than hour, move to a different location (with the help of a camel or two) and set up again, all on the same day. Gers are not unique to Mongolia; versions can be found across Central Asia, from Xinjiang to Turkmenistan. But while other traditions are fading, use of the ger is still common. For travellers, a visit inside a ger is part of the great Mongolian experience.

Timothy Allen of BBC Earth filmed the set-up of a ger using time-lapse photography. Check out the 80 second clip on YouTube – search 'Timothy Allen BBC Earth'.

Structural Integrity

The outermost and innermost material of the ger is usually canvas, with an insulating layer of felt sandwiched in between (more layers in winter and fewer in summer), supported by a collapsible wooden frame. Ropes made from horsehair are cinched around the perimeter to hold the ger together. The roof tends to be low, which helps in deflecting wind. During hot weather the sides can be rolled up and mosquito netting added.

The felt (*esgi*) is made in the autumn by stretching out several layers of sheep's wool on the ground, sprinkling it with water, adding grass and rolling it up tight, wetting it again and then rolling the whole thing back and forth over the steppe. As the wool dries the threads tighten up and harden into a stiff (yet still flexible) mat. The poles traditionally come

DOS & DON'TS IN THE GER

Do

- sleep with your feet pointing towards the door
- say hello (*sain bain uu*) when you first arrive, but don't repeat it when you see the same person again
- try to converse in Mongolian as much as possible (have a phrasebook handy) and avoid long conversations in your own language
- bring a gift (even if it's just small) for the family or children. Your host will likely accept it humbly, so don't feel bad if they don't look too thrilled.

Don't

- touch another person's hat (even to move it out of the way)
- whistle
- lean against the support column
- touch a child's (or anyone else's) head
- open drawers (or look at personal items)
- serve yourself (wait for the host to serve you).

from Mongolia's forests but recent limits on wood use have forced ger makers to acquire timber from Russia.

Inside a Ger

The 2010 documentary *Babies* featured four newborns from different corners of the globe: Namibia, San Francisco, Tokyo and Mongolia. Not only are the kids cute but watching the film also gives great insight on the life of a typical Mongolian family. This was made by French filmmaker Thomas Balmes. For more information, see www.filminfocus.com/film/babies.

The internal layout of the ger is universal throughout Mongolia. Anywhere from Khovd to Dornod you will see the same set up and go through the same motions. The door always faces south, primarily because the wind come from the north and a south-facing door will catch the most sunlight. Visitors should not step on the threshold as they enter, as this is symbolic of stepping on the neck of the ger patriarch.

Once inside, men move to the left (to the west, under the protection of the great sky god, Tengger), women to the right (east, under the protection of the sun). Towards the back, and a little to the west, is the place of honour set aside for guests. After two or three ger visits, this routine becomes like clockwork and you'll be amazed how everyone in your group easily falls into the same place during each ger visit.

The back of the ger is the *khoimor*, the place for the elders, where the most honoured people are seated and treasured possessions are kept. On the back wall is the family altar, decorated with Buddhist images and family photos (mostly taken during trips to Ulaanbaatar). Near the door, on the male side are saddles, ropes and a big leather milk bag and churn, used to stir *airag* (fermented mare's milk). On the female side of the door are the cooking implements and water buckets. Around the walls there are two or three low beds and cabinets. In the centre sits a small table with several tiny chairs. Hanging in any vacant spot, or wedged between the latticed walls, are toothbrushes, clothes, children's toys and plenty of slabs of uncooked mutton.

Building Your Ger

The small cartwheel-shaped opening at the top, called a *toon*, allows smoke to exit and sunlight to enter. It is covered with an *örkh*, which can be adjusted from the ground using ropes. The wooden roof poles (*uni*) are orange (the colour of the sun); the concertina-like latticed walls are called *khan*.

Kazakh gers differ a little from the Mongolian variety. They are darker, larger and decorated inside with bright carpets and rugs.

Most gers have five *khan*, although they can be bigger or smaller depending on the preference (and sometimes wealth) of the family. Each wall has about 10 to 15 roof poles. Depending on the mobility and wealth of the family, the ger is placed on a wooden platform or bare earth floor.

The first part of the ger to be assembled is the floor (if there is one). Next, the stove is placed in the centre. It is symbolic of the ritual fire worship practised by Central Asian nomads for centuries, and is therefore considered holy. The walls and the brightly painted door (*khaalga*) are erected along with the two central columns that support the roof. Once the frame is put together the felt coverings are wrapped around the ger.

GER CARTS

It is said that the great Mongol *khaans* (emperors) had enormous gers that they placed on ox carts to be pulled around their empire, like some sort of ancient Winnebago. This is depicted on some Mongolian banknotes. Some modern scholars, however, dispute this story. Whatever the case, the Mongols certainly did use their gers everywhere they went, only rarely adopting the life of the settled peoples they conquered. It is even said that the Mongols never lived in their own capital, Karakorum. Instead they parked their gers on the plains outside the city walls, used to the freedom they provided. The city itself was inhabited by foreign artisans, traders, labourers and priests, accustomed to the stone houses and to life within the city walls.

21ST CENTURY GERS

Some gers today sport many of the mod cons found in apartments. Most have a TV, radios are common and some have DVD players. Many families also own a generator (sometimes small solar panels or mini windmills), which allows them to watch the tube, charge their mobile phones and turn on the lights.

Everyone in the family is expected to contribute to this process in some way. However, once the ger is set up it's the sole responsibility of the woman of the home to hang the curtain (*khushig*) that covers the lattice frame. Voila! You have a ger.

An average ger weighs about 250kg and can be carried by one camel. These days most families tend to hire a truck to transport their ger to a new location.

The ger plays a vital role in shaping both the Mongolian character and family life. The small confines compel family members to interact with one another, to share everything and work together, tightening relationships between relatives. It prevents privacy but promotes patience and makes inhibitions fade away. It also creates self-sufficiency; ger dwellers must fetch their own water and fuel, and subsist on the food they themselves produce.

Nomads tend to move two to four times a year, although in areas where grass is thin they move more often. One nuclear family may live alone or with an extended-family camp of three or four gers (known as an *ail*); any more than that would be a burden on the grassland.

Spiritualism in Mongolia

Mongolians are a deeply spiritual people. This, however, is not always apparent, as organised religion is but one small part of the spiritual matrix. Spirituality comes in many other forms, much of it day-to-day rituals rooted in Mongolia's shamanic past. The ancient animist beliefs of the Siberian and steppe tribes who worshipped the sun, earth and sky are still very much alive, woven intimately into the fabric of modern Mongolia.

Ovoos, the large piles of rocks found on mountain passes, are repositories of offerings for local spirits. Upon arriving at an *ovoo*, walk around it clockwise three times, toss an offering onto the pile (another rock should suffice) and make a wish.

Shamanism

Throughout Mongolia's history most steppe and taiga tribes believed in the spirit world as their shamans described it to them. Their cosmic view of the universe did not differentiate between the worlds of the living and dead nor did they consider themselves any greater than other creatures in this or other worlds. Any imbalance between the human and natural world could cause calamity.

Shamanism is based around the shaman – called a *bo* if a man or *udgan* if a woman – who has special medical and religious powers (known as *udmyn* if inherited; *zlain* if the powers become apparent after a sudden period of sickness and apparitions).

Two of a shaman's main functions are to cure sickness caused by the soul straying, and to accompany souls of the dead to the other world. As intermediaries between the human and spirit worlds, they communicate with spirits during trances, which can last up to six hours.

Shamanist beliefs have done much to shape Mongolian culture and social practices. The lack of infrastructure throughout Mongolia's history can be traced to shamanic rules on maintaining a balance with nature, ie not digging holes or tearing up the land. Even today when nomads move their camps they fill in the holes created by horse posts. The fact that Mongolia's landscape is being torn up in search of minerals is inexcusable according to shamans, and may lead to retribution from the *tengers* (sky gods).

Sky worship is another integral part of shamanism; you'll see Mongolians leaving blue scarves (representing the sky) on *ovoos*. Sky gods are honoured by flicking droplets of vodka in the air before drinking.

Around 80% of Mongolians are Buddhist of the Mahayana variety, as practised in Tibet. Some 5% follow Islam (mainly Kazakhs living in Bayan-Ölgii aimag). Approximately 5% of Mongolians are Christians, Mongolia's fastest-growing religion. Around 10% are atheist (the creed of the former communist state).

Buddhism

The Mongols had limited contact with organised religion before their great empire of the 13th century. It was Kublai Khaan who first found himself with a court in which all philosophies of his empire were represented, but it was a Tibetan Buddhist, Phagpa, who wielded the greatest influence on the *khaan* (emperor).

In 1578 Altan Khaan, a descendant of Chinggis Khaan, met the Tibetan leader Sonam Gyatso, was converted, and subsequently bestowed on

Sonam Gyatso the title Dalai Lama (*dalai* means 'ocean' in Mongolian). Sonam Gyatso was named as the third Dalai Lama and his two predecessors were named posthumously.

Mass conversions occurred under Altan Khaan. As Mongolian males were conscripted to monasteries, rather than the army, the centuries of constant fighting seemed to wane (much to the relief of China, which subsequently funded more monasteries in Mongolia). This shift from a warring country to a peaceful one persists in contemporary society – Mongolia is the world's only UN-sanctioned 'nuclear weapons-free nation'.

Buddhist opposition to needless killing reinforced strict hunting laws already set in place by shamanism. Today Buddhist monks are still influential in convincing local populations to protect their environment and wildlife.

Buddhism in Mongolia was nearly destroyed in 1937 when the young communist government, fearing competition, launched a purge that wiped out nearly all of the country's 700 monasteries. Up to 30,000 monks were massacred and thousands more sent to Siberian labour camps. Freedom of religion was only restored in 1990 with the dawn of democracy.

Restoring Buddhism has been no easy task as two generations had been essentially raised as atheists. Most people no longer understand the Buddhist rituals or their meanings but a few still make the effort to visit the monasteries during prayer sessions. Numbers swell when well-known Buddhist monks from Tibet or India (or even Western countries) visit Mongolia.

In 1903, when the British invaded Tibet, the 13th Dalai Lama fled to Mongolia and spent three years living in Gandan Khiid in Urga (modern-day Ulaanbaatar).

THE NINTH JEBTZUN DAMBA

In 1924 the eighth Jebtzun Damba ('Bogd Khan' in Mongolian) passed away, marking the end of two centuries of Buddhist rule in Mongolia. Soon after his death Mongolia was declared a republic and the then-communist government forbade the recognition of a ninth Jebtzun Damba.

But the great lamas of Tibet had other plans. Tradition held that new incarnations of the Jebtzun Damba would be found in Tibet, so when the time was right, the Regent of Lhasa recognised a ninth incarnation. His identity was kept secret to protect him from the Russian secret police, which was busy ridding Mongolia of its Buddhist clergy. The young Jebtzun Damba, named Jampal Namdrol Chokye Gyaltsen, undertook Buddhist studies at Drepung Monastery for 14 years.

At the age of 21 he left the monastery to live as a hermit, practising meditation at sacred caves throughout central Tibet. When he was 29 he fled Tibet for India, following the Dalai Lama and thousands of other Tibetans attempting to escape Chinese persecution. The Jebtzun Damba lived in obscurity for decades until being re-recognised by the Dalai Lama in 1991.

In 1999, at the age of 67, he turned up unannounced in Ulaanbaatar, having received a tourist visa in Moscow. (One can only imagine the customs form: 'Occupation: Reincarnation of Tibetan deity Vajrapani'!).

He stayed in Mongolia for 60 days, visiting monasteries in both Ulaanbaatar and the countryside. Although mobbed by adoring fans wherever he went, he was deemed persona non grata by the Mongolian government, which at the time was unsure of his motives. He was finally pressured to leave after overstaying his visa.

In 2010 he was allowed to return to Mongolia, where a more confident government welcomed him and even granted him Mongolian citizenship. He currently resides at Gandan Monastery. Sadly, the Jebtzun Damba recently suffered a stroke and is now in poor health. He has indicated, however, that there is a real possibility his 10th incarnation will be found in Mongolia, when that time comes.

For more information on Mongolia's spiritual leader, see www.jetsundhampa.com.

Religions of Mongolia, by Walther Heissig, provides an in-depth look at the Buddhist and shamanist faiths as they developed in Mongolia.

Islam

In Mongolia today, there is a significant minority of Sunni Muslims, most of them ethnic Kazakhs, who live primarily in Bayan-Ölgii. Because of its great isolation and distance from the major Islamic centres of the Middle East, Islam has never been a major force in Bayan-Ölgii. However, most villages have a mosque and contacts have been established with Islamic groups in Turkey. Several prominent figures in the community have been on a haj to Mecca. Besides the Kazakhs, the only ethnic Mongols to practice Islam are the Khoton tribe, who live primarily in Uvs aimag.

Christianity

Nestorian Christianity was part of the Mongol empire long before the Western missionaries arrived. The Nestorians followed the doctrine of Nestorious (358–451), patriarch of Constantinople (428–31), who proclaimed that Jesus exists as two separate persons: the man Jesus and the divine son of God. Historically the religion never caught hold in the Mongol heartland, but that has changed in recent years with an influx of Christian missionaries, often from obscure fundamentalist sects. In Mongolia, there are an estimated 65,000 Christians and more than 150 churches.

Mongolian Cuisine

The culinary masters of Mongolia's barren steppes have always put more stock in survival than taste. Mongolian food is therefore a hearty, if somewhat bland, array of meat and dairy products. In the countryside, green vegetables are often equated with animal fodder and spices may be an alien concept. In the summer months, when animals provide milk, dairy products become the staple food. Meat (and copious amounts of fat) takes over in winter, supplemented with flour (in some form) and potatoes or rice if available.

In contrast, in Ulaanbaatar there's a wide variety of food available and a surprisingly cosmopolitan restaurant scene.

The well-researched www.mongolfood.info includes notes on Mongolian cuisine, plus cooking techniques and recipes to dispel the myth that Mongolian menus stop at 'boiled mutton'.

Staples & Specialties

Almost any Mongolian dish can be created with meat, rice, flour and potatoes. Most meals consist of *talkh* (bread) in the towns and cities and *bortzig* (fried unleavened bread) in the gers, and the uncomplicated *shölte khool* (literally, soup with food) – a meal involving hot broth, pasta slivers, boiled mutton and a few potato chunks.

Two of the most popular menu options you'll find in restaurants are *buuz* (steamed dumplings filled with mutton and sometimes slivers of onion or garlic) and *khuushuur* (fried mutton pancakes). Miniature *buuz*, known as *bansh*, are usually dunked in milk tea.

The classic Mongolian dinner staple, and the one most dreaded by foreigners, is referred to simply as '*makh*' (meat) and consists of boiled

It is customary to flick spoonfuls of milk in the direction of departing travellers, whether they are going by horse, car, train or plane.

WHAT'S YOUR DRINK?

Mongolians are big tea drinkers and will almost never start a meal until they've had a cup of tea first, as it aids digestion.

Süütei tsai, a classic Mongolian drink, is milk tea with salt. The taste varies by region; in Bayan-Ölgii it may even include a dollop of butter. If you can't get used to the salty brew, try asking for *khar tsai* (black tea), which is like European tea, with sugar and no milk.

Alcoholic drinks are readily available and Mongolians can drink you under the table if challenged. There is much social pressure to drink, especially on males – those who refuse to drink *arkhi* (vodka) are considered wimps.

Locally produced beer labels such as Mongol, Chinggis and Khan Brau are growing in popularity, as most young people prefer beer to vodka. The very smooth Chinggis black label vodka costs just US$8 a bottle.

While it may not be immediately apparent, every countryside ger doubles as a tiny brewery or distillery. One corner of the ger usually contains a tall, thin jug with a plunger that is used for fermenting mare's milk. The drink, known as *airag* or *koumiss*, has an alcohol content of about 3%. Go easy on it at the start or your guts will pay for it later.

DOS & DON'TS AT THE TABLE

Do

» cut food towards your body, not away

» accept food and drink with your right hand; use the left *only* to support your right elbow if the food is heavy

» drink tea immediately after receiving it; don't put it on the table until you have tried some

» take at least a sip, or a nibble, of the delicacies offered, even if they don't please you

» hold a cup by the bottom, not by the top rim

» cover your mouth when using a toothpick.

Don't

» point a knife at anyone; when passing the knife, offer the handle

» get up in the middle of a meal and walk outside; wait until everyone has finished

» cross your legs or stick your feet out in front of you when eating – keep your legs together if seated, or folded under you if on the floor.

sheep bits (bones, fat, various organs and the head) with some sliced potato, served in a plastic bucket.

The other main highlight of Mongolian cuisine is *khorkhog,* made by placing hot stones from an open fire into a pot or urn with chopped mutton, some water and sometimes vodka. The container is then sealed and left on the fire. While eating this, it's customary to pass the hot, greasy rocks from hand to hand, as this is thought to be good for your health.

In summer, you can subsist as the Mongols do on *tsagaan idee* (dairy products; literally 'white foods'): yogurt, milk, delicious fresh cream, cheese and fermented milk drinks. When you visit a ger, you will be offered dairy snacks such as *aaruul* (dried milk curds), which are as hard as a rock and often about as tasty.

Finally, if you get a chance, don't miss the opportunity to try blowtorched marmot (prairie dog), a delicacy of the steppes.

Imperial Mongolian Cooking: Recipes from the Kingdoms of Genghis Khan (2001), by Marc Cramer, describes a variety of recipes from Mongolia, China, Central Asia and other lands that were once part of the Mongol empire. Many recipes are from the author's grandfather, who worked as a chef in Siberia.

Celebrations

Tsagaan Sar, the Mongolian New Year, is a festival for a new beginning. Everything about the holiday is symbolic of happiness, joy and prosperity in the coming year, and it is food that represents many of these rites.

Mongolians are an optimistic lot – a full belly during Tsagaan Sar is said to represent prosperity in the year ahead; *buuz* in their thousands are prepared and consumed during the holiday. The central meal of the holiday must be the biggest sheep a family can afford; pride is at stake over how much fat appears on the table.

During Tsagaan Sar, food is even part of the decoration: the centrepiece is made from layers of large biscuits called *ul boov*. Young people stack three layers of biscuits, middle-aged folk five layers and grandparents seven layers.

Habits & Customs

While traditions and customs do surround the dinner table, Mongolian meals are generally casual affairs and there is no need to be overly concerned about offending your hosts.

In a ger in the countryside, traditional meals such as boiled mutton do not require silverware or even plates; just trawl around the bucket of bones until a slab catches your fancy. Eat with your fingers and try to nibble off as much meat and fat as possible; Mongolians can pick a bone clean and consider leftovers to be wasteful. There'll be a buck knife to slice off larger chunks.

Most other meals in the rest of Mongolia are eaten with bowls, knives, forks and spoons. Chopsticks are only used at Chinese restaurants in Ulaanbaatar.

It is always polite to bring something to contribute to the meal; drinks are easiest, or in the countryside you could offer a bag of rice or sweets for dessert.

'Bon appétit' in Mongolian is *saikhan khool loorai.*

Meals are occasionally interrupted by a round of vodka. Before taking a swig, there's a short ritual to honour the sky gods and the four cardinal directions. There is no one way of doing this, but it usually involves dipping your left ring finger into the vodka and flicking into the air four times before wiping your finger across your forehead. This tradition began centuries ago. Its original motive was to determine whether the vodka was poisoned – namely, if the silver ring on your finger changed colour after being submerged, it was probably best not to drink it!

Price categories used in this guide per main course are as follows: **$** budget, less than T5000; **$$** midrange, T5000 to T10,000; **$$$** top end, more than T10,000.

Because of his failing health, the advisors of Ögedei Khaan (a son of Chinggis) suggested that he halve the number of cups of alcohol he drank per day. Ögedei readily agreed, then promptly ordered that his cups be doubled in size.

Tribal Mongolia

You may hear people from western Mongolia refer to themselves as Oirats, an umbrella term under which sit a number of tribes. Oirats have long been rivals of Khalkh Mongols, at times vying for power and other times coexisting as part of the same empire.

Mongolia is an ancient tribal society that can be broken down into more than a dozen ethnic sub-groups. A thousand years ago these tribes regularly squared off against each other in seasonal warfare and bouts of bride theft. They went by the names of Kerait, Tatar, Merkit and Naiman, to name a few; linked by culture, they were divided by old feuds and rivalries.

The tribes were united during the great Mongol empire (1206 to 1368) but after its demise they went back to their periodic squabbles. To this day, Mongolia still counts around 20 different *undesten* (nations), with numerous sub-clans. Most of these tribes are located along the borders of modern Mongolia and in some cases they spill over the borders into Russia and China. Inner Mongolia (in China) also has a tribal order that persists today.

Tribes in Modern Mongolia

The tribes of modern Mongolia lack the political, economic or social independence that one might encounter in tribal areas of Pakistan, southern Africa, India or the Americas. However, many Mongols still associate closely with their tribal roots and actively promote their unique identities. The Buriats, for example, sponsor the bi-annual Altargana Festival, which draws Buriats from all over the country as well as Buriats from Russia and China.

While it can be difficult to differentiate between some of these tribes, a few are starkly unique. The Tsaatan, who live in tepees, speak a distinct Turkic language and herd reindeer, are one of the most identifiable ethnic groups. The Khoton people in western Mongolia are also easily distinguished as the only Mongols to practice Islam.

When meeting minority groups, ask about their traditional clothing, which can be quite distinctive, as is the case with the Dariganga peoples of Sükhbaatar aimag. The Kazakhs, who live primarily in Bayan-Ölgii aimag, are a Turkic tribe with cultural roots in Islamic Central Asia.

If you want to impress your Mongol friends, try to identify their subnationality and ask them about the particular features of their clan. It's a great conversation starter as well as a good way to gain an in-depth understanding of the country. Mongols will be impressed if you are able to cite specific characteristics of their ethnic group or geographic features of their homeland.

Numbers sometimes figure into the names of Mongol tribes. The tribe Dörvöd means 'four'. The tribe Naiman means 'eight'.

The following is a list of some of the main ethnic groups you may encounter:

» **Barga** Originally from the Lake Baikal region of Siberia, they number about 2000 and live in remote border areas of Dornod aimag. Many Barga also live in Inner Mongolia (China) around Dalai Nuur and Hailar. Barga consider themselves descended from Alan Goa, a mythical figure described in *The Secret History of the Mongols*.

» **Bayad** Descendants of Oirat Mongols; about 50,000 live in the Malchin, Khyargas and Züüngov *sums* of Uvs aimag. The most famous Bayad was the 13th century princess Kököchin (Blue Dame), whom Kublai Khaan betrothed to the Il-Khanate khan Argun. It was Marco Polo who was selected to escort Kököchin on her journey to Persia.

» **Buriat** There are around a half million Buriats in north Asia (around 50,000 live in Mongolia with others in Russia and China), making them the largest ethnic minority in Siberia. Buriats are known for their strong associations with shamanism. Among Mongols, they are also unique in their lifestyle; most live in log cabins instead of gers. You'll meet many Buriats in northern Khentii and Dornod aimags.

» **Dariganga** During the Qing dynasty era, this ethnic group received special recognition from the emperor. They were responsible for supplying horses to the emperor in Beijing and today they are still regarded as excellent horse breeders. During the Qing era, the Dariganga also gained skills as blacksmiths and silversmiths. Their traditional headdress, chock-full of silver, is considered the most elegant and valuable of its kind.

» **Darkhad** This 20,000 member tribe can be found in the Darkhad valley in northern Khovsgol aimag. During the Qing era, they served as ecclesiastical serfs to the Bogd Gegeens and were required to perform service such as pasturing his animals. Darkhads are known as powerful shamans but are also beloved for their great sense of humour. A pastime is to sing humorous songs about each other; ask politely and they may make one up about you!

» **Dörvöd** There are around 66,000 Dörvöds in western Mongolia. In the 17th century, a group of Dörvöds split from the main clan and trekked west to settle in the Volga region of Russia. Historically, the Dörvöd have sometimes clashed with Khalkh Mongols (during the communist era some proposed ceding their territory to the Soviet Union). Yu Tsedenbal (ruled 1954 to 1984) and J Batmönkh (ruled 1984 to 1990) were both Dörvöd.

» **Khalkh** The majority (about 86%) of Mongolians are Khalkh Mongolians. The origin of the word Khalkh is a topic of great debate: some believe it means shield, while others suggest it's derived from the Turkic word Halk, which means people.

NAMES

In the 1990s, when the government of Mongolia asked its citizens to choose a clan name, 20% of the population adopted the name 'Borjigan', the clan of Chinggis Khaan.

THE MONGOLIAN NAME GAME

Early in the 20th century the communist government of Mongolia forbade the use of clan names, a dedicated effort to stamp out loyalties that might supersede the state. Mongolians managed to tread along with one name, which proved do-able thanks to the small and scattered population. When it was needed, a father's name was added to differentiate people with the same names.

Decades later, when communism finally crumbled, few families were able to recall their own clan name. As a result, when the first phone books were made in the 1990s, you'd see pages listing just one name. Elections also proved confusing when six or seven candidates with the same name would appear on one ballot.

A more serious problem was inbreeding, the result of cousins inadvertently marrying each other. Historians pointed out that this problem could be avoided by employing an old tradition, which stated that seven generations must pass before a family member could again marry within their clan.

In order to reverse this trend, the government took a more modern approach, ordering all citizens to start using their clan names again. The identity crisis that ensued sparked a boom in amateur genealogy, with families contacting relatives to uncover possible clan names. Authorities have encouraged creativity and people who could not retrace their name simply made one up – usually after a hobby, a profession, favourite mountain or nickname. Mongolia's lone spaceman, Gurragchaa, named his family 'Cosmos.' Another clan name currently up for grabs is 'Family of Seven Drunks', which hasn't had many takers.

In November 2010 the Oirats organized the first ever Ikh Khogsuu Oirat Festival, a three-day celebration in Ulaanbaatar. The organizers plan to make the festival an annual event.

» **Torguud** About 7000 live in Khovd aimag. Originally from northern Xinjiang, a large group of them moved to the Volga to become the core Kalmyks. Today most Torguuds in Mongolia live in Bulgan *sum*.

» **Tsaatan** About 500 of these reindeer herders live in northern Khövsgöl; for more information, see p135.

» **Uriankhai (Tuvans)** About 21,000 live in western Mongolia – you'll meet some if you visit Tsengel Sum, near Tavan Bogd National Park. The Uriankhai are renowned for their throat-singing abilities. Today, most Uriankhai live in the Tuva Region of Russia.

» **Uzemchin** Most Uzemchin live in Inner Mongolia. In 1945, about 2000 of them migrated to Outer Mongolia and they can still be found in some remote corners of Dornod aimag. Uzemchin are well known for their elegant embroidered *dels*. During Naadam, Uzemchin wrestlers wear badass leather jackets with brass studs.

Wild Lands & Wildlife

Mongolia is the sort of country that naturalists dream about. With the world's lowest population density, huge tracts of virgin landscape, minimal infrastructure, varied ecosystems and abundant wildlife, Mongolia is rightfully considered to be the last bastion of unspoiled land in Asia. Mongolia's nomadic past, which did not require cities or infrastructure, along with shamanic prohibitions against defiling the earth, have for centuries protected the country from overdevelopment.

Traditional beliefs, however, are always at odds with modern economics. The Soviets were the first to bring heavy industry to Mongolia but the human impact has been even greater during the age of capitalism. With no more subsidies coming from the USSR, Mongolia has spent nearly two decades looking for ways to earn revenue, and the easiest solution has been the sale of its resources. Consequently, the wildlife and landscape are now being degraded at an alarming rate, but there is hope among conservationists that ecotourism will provide a new direction for government fiscal policy.

The Wildlife Conservation Society's Mongolia programme strives to address wildlife conservation issues through various approaches that reach local communities, wildlife biologists, provincial governments and national ministries. Read more at www.wcs.org/Mongolia.

The Land

Mongolia is a huge landlocked country. At 1,566,500 sq km in area, it's about three times the size of France. The southern third of Mongolia is dominated by the Gobi Desert, which stretches into China. Only the southern sliver of the Gobi is 'Lawrence of Arabia'–type desert with cliffs and sand dunes. The rest is desert steppe and has sufficient grass to support scattered herds of sheep, goats and camels. There are also areas of desert steppe in low-lying parts of western Mongolia.

Much of the rest of Mongolia is covered by grasslands (or mountain forest steppe). Stretching over about 35% of the country, these steppes are home to vast numbers of gazelle, birdlife and livestock.

The far northern areas of Khövsgöl and Khentii aimags are essentially the southern reaches of Siberia and are covered by larch and pine forests known by the Russian word 'taiga'.

Near the centre of Mongolia is the Khangai Nuruu range, with its highest peak, Otgon Tenger Uul, reaching 3905m. On the northern slope of these mountains is the source of the Selenge Gol, Mongolia's largest river, which flows northward into Lake Baikal in Siberia.

Just to the northeast of Ulaanbaatar is the Khentii Nuruu, the highest mountain range in eastern Mongolia and by far the most accessible to hikers. It's a heavily forested region with meandering rivers and impressive peaks, the highest being Asralt Khairkhan Uul (2800m). The range provides a major watershed between the Arctic and Pacific oceans.

The *takhi* horse also goes by the name Przewalski's horse. It was named after Colonel Nikolai Przewalski, an officer in the Russian Imperial Army who made the horse's existence known to Europe after an exploratory expedition to Central Asia in 1878.

Mongolia has numerous saltwater and freshwater lakes, which are great for camping, bird-watching, hiking, swimming and fishing. The

Silent Steppe: The Illegal Wildlife Trade Crisis (July 2006), published by the Netherlands-Mongolia Trust Fund for Environmental Reform (NEMO), is an important publication that highlights the decimation of wildlife in Mongolia. You can download the document by going to the World Bank website (www.worldbank.org/nemo).

largest is the low-lying, saltwater Uvs Nuur, but the most popular is the magnificent Khövsgöl Nuur, the second-oldest lake in the world, which contains 65% of Mongolia's (and 2% of the world's) fresh water.

Other geological and geographical features include caves (some with ancient rock paintings), dormant volcanoes, hot and cold mineral springs, the Orkhon Khürkhree (Orkhon Waterfall), the Great Lakes Depression in western Mongolia and the Darkhad Depression west of Khövsgöl Nuur.

Wildlife

In Mongolia, the distinction between domestic and wild (or untamed) animals is often blurry. Wild and domesticated horses and camels mingle on the steppes with wild asses and herds of wild gazelle. In the mountains there are enormous (and horned) wild argali sheep and domesticated yaks along with wild moose, musk deer and roe deer. Reindeer herds are basically untamed, but strangely enough they can be ridden and are known to return to the same tent each night for a salt-lick.

Animals

Despite the lack of water in the Gobi, numerous species (many of which are endangered) somehow survive. These include the Gobi argali sheep *(argal),* wild camel *(khavtgai),* Asiatic wild ass *(khulan),* Gobi bear *(mazaalai),* ibex *(yangir)* and black-tailed gazelle *(khar suult zeer).*

In the wide-open steppe you may see the rare saiga antelope, Mongolian gazelle *(tsagaan zeer),* several species of jerboa *(alag daaga),* which is a rodent endemic to Central Asia, and thousands of furry marmots *(tarvaga),* waking up after their last hibernation or preparing for the next.

Further north in the forests live the wild boar *(zerleg gakhai),* brown bear *(khuren baavgai),* roe deer *(bor görös),* wolf *(chono),* reindeer *(tsaa buga),* elk *(khaliun buga),* musk deer *(khuder)* and moose *(khandgai),* as well as plenty of sable *(bulga)* and lynx *(shiluus),* whose fur, unfortunately, is in high demand. Most of the mountains are extremely remote, thus providing an ideal habitat for argali sheep, ibex, the very rare snow leopard *(irbis),* and smaller mammals such as the fox, ermine and hare.

The International Crane Foundation (www.savingcranes.org) works to preserve important crane habitats and wetland areas in Mongolia.

CRANES

Birds

Mongolia is home to 469 recorded species of bird. In the desert you may see the desert warbler, saxaul sparrow *(boljmor)* and McQueen's bustard *(toodog),* as well as sandgrouse, finch *(byalzuuhai)* and the cinereous vulture *(tas).*

On the steppes, you will certainly see the most charismatic bird in Mongolia – the demoiselle crane *(övögt togoruu)* – as well as the hoopoe *(övöölj)* and the odd falcon *(shonkhor),* vulture *(yol),* and golden and steppe eagle *(bürged).* Other steppe species include the upland buzzard *(sar),* the black kite *(sokhor elee)* and some varieties of owl *(shar shuvuu)* and hawk *(khartsaga).* Some black kites will even swoop down and catch pieces of bread in mid-air if you throw the pieces high enough. These magnificent raptors, perched majestically on a rock by the side of the road, will rarely be disturbed by your jeep or the screams of your guide ('Look. Eagle!! Bird!! We stop?') but following the almost inaudible click of your lens cap, these birds will move and almost be in China before you have even thought about apertures.

In the mountains, you may be lucky to spot species of ptarmigan *(tsagaan yatuu),* bunting *(khömrög byalzuuhai),* woodpecker *(tonshuul),* owl and endemic Altai snowcock *(khoilog).* The lakes of the west and north are visited by Dalmatian pelican *(khoton),* hooded crane *(khar togoruu),* relict gull *(tsakhlai)* and bar-headed goose.

Eastern Mongolia has several species of crane, including the hooded and Siberian varieties and the critically endangered white-naped crane *(tsen togoruu)*, of which only 4500 remain in the wild.

Fish

Rivers such as the Selenge, Orkhon, Zavkhan, Balj, Onon and Egiin, as well as dozens of lakes, including Khövsgöl Nuur, hold 76 species of fish. They include trout, grayling *(khadran)*, roach, lenok *(zebge)*, Siberian sturgeon *(khilem)*, pike *(tsurkhai)*, perch *(algana)*, the endemic Altai osman and the enormous taimen, a Siberian relative of the salmon, which can grow up to 1.5m in length and weigh up to 50kg.

Endangered Species

According to conservationists, 28 species of mammals are endangered in Mongolia. The more commonly known species are the wild ass, wild camel, argali sheep, Gobi bear and ibex; others include otter, wolf, saiga antelope and some species of jerboa. The red deer is also in dire straits; over the past two decades its numbers have dropped from 130,000 to just 8000. Poachers also prize brown bears for their gall bladders, which are used in traditional medicine.

There are 22 species of endangered birds, including many species of hawk, falcon, buzzard, crane and owl. Cranes are endangered due to habitat loss; there are just 5000 breeding pairs left in the wild. The best place to see them is the Dornod's Mongol Daguur Strictly Protected Area.

Every year the government allows up to 300 falcons to be captured and sold abroad; the major buyers are the royal families of Kuwait and the United Arab Emirates. A licence for each bird costs US$12,000. In the late 1990s the press frequently reported stories on smugglers caught at the airport with falcons stuffed in their overcoats (presumably many made it out without detection). The illegal export of these birds still occurs albeit on a much smaller scale. There are an estimated 2200 breeding pairs left in Mongolia.

One positive news story is the resurrection of the *takhi* wild horse. The *takhi* was actually extinct in the wild in the 1960s. It has been successfully

Mongolians consider wolf parts and organs to have curative properties. The meat and lungs are good for respiratory ailments, the intestines aid in digestion, powdered wolf rectum can soothe the pain of haemorrhoids and hanging a wolf tongue around ones neck will cure gland and thyroid ailments.

PROTECTED AREAS

The Ministry of Nature, Environment & Tourism (MNE) and its Department of Special Protected Areas Management control the national park system with an annual budget of around US$2.1 million.

The 65 protected areas in Mongolia now constitute an impressive 14.5% of the country (22.3 million hectares). The strictly protected areas of Bogdkhan Uul, Great Gobi, Uvs Nuur Basin, Dornod Mongol and Khustain Nuruu are biosphere reserves included in Unesco's Man and Biosphere Network.

At the time of independence in 1990, some proposed that the *entire country* be turned into a national park, but the government settled on 30% (potentially creating the world's largest park system). This goal, however, has stalled in recent years as the government has given favour to expanding mining operations and the sale of mining rights.

The MNE classifies protected areas into four categories (from most protected to least):

Strictly Protected Areas Very fragile areas of great importance; hunting, logging and development is strictly prohibited and there is no established human influence.

National Parks Places of historical and educational interest; fishing and grazing by nomadic people is allowed and parts of the park are developed for ecotourism.

Natural & Historical Monuments Important places of historical and cultural interest; development is allowed within guidelines.

Nature Reserves Less important regions protecting rare species of flora and fauna, and archaeological sites; some development is allowed within certain guidelines.

NATIONAL PARKS

NATIONAL PARKS	FEATURES	ACTIVITIES	TIME TO VISIT
Altai Tavan Bogd National Park (p188)	mountains, glaciers, lakes; argali sheep, ibex, snow leopard, eagle, falcon	mountaineering, horse trekking, backpacking, fishing, eagle hunting (winter)	Jun-Sep
Gorkhi-Terelj National Park (p87)	rugged hills, boulders, streams	river rafting, hiking, mountain biking, rock climbing, camping, cross-country skiing, horse riding	yr-round
Gurvan Saikhan National Park (p169)	desert mountains, canyons, sand dunes; Gobi argali sheep, ibex, black-tailed gazelle	hiking, sand-dune sliding, camel trekking, bird-watching	May-Oct
Khorgo-Terkhiin Tsagaan Nuur National Park (p107)	lake and mountains; wolf, deer, fox	fishing, hiking, horse trekking, bird-watching	May-Sep
Khövsgöl Nuur National Park (p127)	lake, mountains, rivers; fish, moose, wolverine, bear, sable, elk, roe deer	mountain biking, kayaking, fishing, hiking, horse trekking, bird-watching	Jun-Sep
Khustain National Park (p91)	rugged hills, Tuul River; *takhi* horse, gazelle, deer, wolf, lynx, manul wild cat	trekking, wildlife spotting	Apr-Oct
Otgon Tenger Uul Strictly Protected Area (p203)	mountains, rivers, lakes; argali sheep, roe deer, wolf	horse trekking, hiking, swimming	May-Sep

reintroduced into three special protected areas after an extensive breeding program overseas. For more on the *takhi,* see p93.

In preserved areas of the mountains, about 1000 snow leopards remain. They are hunted for their pelts (which are also part of some shamanist and Buddhist traditional practices), as are the leopards' major source of food, marmots.

Each year the government sells licences to hunt 200 ibex and 40 argali sheep, both endangered species, netting the government nearly US$1 million.

Plants

Mongolians collect various wild herbs and flowers for their medicinal properties: yellow poppies to heal wounds, edelweiss to add vitamins to the blood, and feather grass to cure an upset stomach.

Mongolia can be roughly divided into three zones: grassland and shrub land (55% of the country); forests, which only cover parts of the mountain steppe (8%); and desert (36%). Less than 1% of the country is used for human settlement and crop cultivation. Grasslands are used extensively for grazing, and despite the vast expanses, overgrazing is not uncommon.

Forests of Siberian larch (sometimes up to 45m in height), Siberian and Scotch pine, and white and ground birch cover parts of northern Mongolia.

In the Gobi saxaul shrub covers millions of hectares and is essential in anchoring the desert sands and preventing degradation and erosion. Saxaul takes a century to grow to around 4m in height, creating wood so dense that it sinks in water.

Khentii aimag and some other parts of central Mongolia are famous for the effusion of red, yellow and purple wildflowers, mainly rhododendrons and edelweiss. Extensive grazing is the major threat to Mongolia's flowers, trees and shrubs; more than 200 species are endangered.

Environmental Issues

Mongolia's natural environment remains in good shape compared with that of many Western countries. The country's small population and nomadic subsistence economy have been its environmental salvation.

However, Mongolia does have its share of problems. Communist production quotas in the past put pressure on grasslands to yield more crops and support more livestock than was sustainable. The rise in the number of herders and livestock has wreaked havoc on the grasslands; some 70% of pastureland is degraded and near village centres around 80% of plant species have disappeared.

Forest fires, nearly all of which are caused by careless human activity, are common during the windy spring season. The fires destroy huge tracts of forest and grassland, mainly in Khentii and Dornod aimags.

Other threats to the land include mining, which has polluted 28 river basins in eight aimags (there are more than 300 mines in Mongolia). The huge Oyu Tolgoi mine in Ömnögov will require the use of 360L of water *per second,* which environmentalists say might not be sustainable. China's insatiable appetite for minerals and gas is opening up new mines, but the bigger threat is China's hunt for the furs, meat and body parts of endangered animals. Chinese demand has resulted in an 80% decline in the number of marmots and an 85% drop in the number of saiga antelope.

Urban sprawl, coupled with a demand for wood to build homes and for heating and cooking, is slowly reducing the forests. This destruction of the forests has also lowered river levels, especially the Tuul Gol near Ulaanbaatar. In recent years the Tuul has actually gone dry in the spring months due to land mismanagement and improper water use.

Large-scale infrastructure projects are further cause for concern. The 18m-tall Dörgön hydropower station, built on the Chon Khairkh Gol in Khovd, has submerged canyons and pastures. The dam threatens fish and will only run in summer when electricity is in lower demand compared with winter.

Conservationists are also concerned about the 'Millennium Road', which will likely cut through important gazelle migration routes in eastern Mongolia. Its completion is sure to increase mining and commerce inside fragile ecosystems. A proposed railway from the Gobi Desert east to Sainshand and Choibalsan would cause similar problems, especially if fences are built along the railway.

PRIZE

In 2007 Tsetsegee Munkhbayar, a herder from central Mongolia, was awarded the prestigious Goldman Environmental Prize for his efforts to block aggressive mining on the Ongii River. You can watch a short video on his heroic story at www.goldmanprize.org/node/606.

Trans-Mongolian Railway

Mongolia uses the Russian standard 5ft gauge track for its railways, rather than the 4ft 8.5in track used everywhere else in the world. It's believed the Russians adopted a different width track to prevent invaders from easily crossing into Russia by train.

The Trans-Mongolian Railway is a segment of the vast network of track that links Beijing and Moscow, a crucial piece of the world's longest continuous rail route. For rail enthusiasts, a journey along Trans-Siberian Railway is the railroad equivalent of climbing Mt Everest.

The idea of building a rail route between Moscow and Vladivostok was hatched in the mid-19th century. This was the Age of Imperialism, when the powers of Europe were expanding across continents in a race to gobble up as much land and resources as possible. In 1916, after some 25 years of planning and building, the final link along the Moscow-Vladivostok route was complete. The section across Mongolia on the other hand was only completed in 1956.

The names of the rail lines can be a bit confusing. The Trans-Mongolian Railway goes from Beijing through Ulaanbaatar and onto a junction called Zaudinsky, near Ulan Ude in Russia, where it meets the Trans-Siberian line and continues on to Moscow. The Trans-Siberian Railway runs between Moscow and the eastern Siberian port of Vladivostok – this route does not go through either China or Mongolia. The Trans-Manchurian Railway crosses the Russia-China border at Zabaikalsk-Manzhouli, also completely bypassing Mongolia.

Transsiberian (2008) is a Hollywood thriller starring Woody Harrelson as a wayward American traveller and Ben Kingsley as a hardnosed Russian detective. While watching the film look out for the Lonely Planet guidebook the Americans use while kicking back in their cabin.

General Train Information

At the stations in Mongolia and Russia, there may be someone on the platform selling basic food (dumplings, soft drinks). Vendors in China offer better variety of foods, including fruit and a range of snacks and drinks.

The restaurant cars on the Russian and Chinese trains have decent food and drinks on offer for around US$2 to US$4.

Remember that toilets are normally locked whenever the train is pulled into a station and for five minutes before and after. Showers are only available in the deluxe carriages. In 2nd and 1st class, there is a washroom and toilet at the end of each carriage – which gets filthier as the trip progresses.

The trains are reasonably safe but it's still a good idea to watch your bags closely. For added safety, lock your cabins from the inside and also make use of the security clip on the upper left-hand part of the door. The clip can be flipped open from the outside with a knife, but not if you stuff the hole with paper.

If you want to get off or on the Trans-Mongolian at Sükhbaatar, Darkhan or Sainshand, you'll still have to pay the full Ulaanbaatar fare. If you're not actually getting *on* the train in Ulaanbaatar, you should arrange for someone (your guesthouse manager, guide or a friend) to let the attendant know that you'll be boarding the train at a later stop. This is to ensure that your seat is not taken.

Tickets list the train's departure times. Get to the station at least 20 minutes before *arrival* to allow enough time to find the platform and struggle on board, as the train only stops in Ulaanbaatar for about 30 minutes.

What to Bring

It is handy to have some US dollars in small denominations, as they are useful to buy meals and drinks on the train, and to exchange for the local currency so you can buy things at the train stations. It's also a good idea to buy some Russian roubles or Chinese yuan at a bank or licensed moneychanger in Ulaanbaatar before you leave Mongolia.

Stock up on munchies such as biscuits, chocolate and fruit before you depart, and bring some bottled water or juice. A small samovar at the end of each carriage provides constant boiling water, a godsend for making tea and coffee, as well as instant meals of packet noodles or soup.

Other essential items include thongs (flip flops) or slippers, an enamel mug, toilet paper, a jumper, plenty of reading material and comfortable long pants. Tracksuits are a must for blending in with the locals.

Total railway in Mongolia: 1810km

World rank: 76

Total railway in Russia: 87,157km

World rank: 2

Total distance of the Moscow–Vladivostok Railway: 9259km (spanning seven time zones)

Classes

With a few exceptions, all international trains have two or three classes. The names and standards of the classes depend on whether it is a Mongolian, Russian or Chinese train.

On the Russian (and Mongolian) trains, most travellers travel in 2nd class – printed on tickets and timetables as '1/4' and known as 'hard sleeper', 'coupé' or *kupeynyy* in Russian. These are small, but perfectly comfortable, four-person compartments with four bunk-style beds and a fold-down table.

First class (printed as '2/4') is sometimes called a 'soft sleeper' or *myagkiy* in Russian. It has softer beds but hardly any more space than a Russian 2nd-class compartment and is not worth the considerably higher fare charged. Smoking is not allowed in any of the cabins but many travellers will smoke at the ends of the train cars.

The real luxury (and expense) comes with Chinese deluxe class (printed as '1/2'): it involves roomy, two-berth compartments with a sofa, and a shower cubicle shared with the adjacent compartment. The deluxe class on Russian trains (slightly cheaper than the Chinese deluxe) has two bunks but is not much different in size from 2nd class and has no showers.

Google has put the entire Moscow to Vladivostok rail journey online. Sit behind your computer for a week and watch the entire traverse, or pick and choose the place you want to visit. It even comes with a soundtrack of Russian music or audiobooks. Go to: www.google.ru/intl/ru/landing/transsib/en.html.

Customs & Immigration

There are major delays of three to six hours at both the China-Mongolia and Russia-Mongolia borders, usually at night. The whole process is not difficult or a hassle, just annoying because they keep interrupting your sleep.

Your passport will be taken for inspection and stamping. When it is returned, inspect it closely – sometimes they make errors such as cancelling your return visa for China. Foreigners generally sail through customs without having their bags opened, which is one reason people on the train may approach you and ask if you'll carry some of their luggage across the border – *this is not a good idea.*

During these stops, you can alight and wander around the station, which is just as well because the toilets on the train are locked during the inspection procedure.

Tickets

The international trains, especially the Trans-Mongolian Railway, are popular, so it's often hard to book this trip except during winter. Try to plan ahead and book as early as possible.

If you are in Ulaanbaatar and want to go to Irkutsk, Beijing or Moscow, avoid going on the Beijing-Moscow or Moscow-Beijing trains; use the other trains mentioned on p265 and p268, which *originate* in Ulaanbaatar. In Ulaanbaatar, you cannot buy tickets in advance for the Beijing-Moscow or Moscow-Beijing trains, because staff in UB won't know how many people are already on the train. For these trains, you can only buy a ticket the day before departure, ie on Wednesday for trains from Ulaanbaatar to Moscow, and on Saturday for trains from Ulaanbaatar to Beijing. You'll need to get to the ticket office early and get into the Mongolian scramble for tickets.

For details on buying tickets in Ulaanbaatar, see p76.

Overseas branches of China International Travel Service (CITS) or China Travel Service (CTS) can often book train tickets from Beijing to Ulaanbaatar. Or try the following places:

Gateway Travel (☎02-9745 3333; www.russian-gateway.com.au) In Australia.
Intourist (☎020-7538 8600; www.intourist.com) In the UK.
Lernidee Reisen (☎030-786 0000; www.lernidee-reisen.de) German company.
Mir Corporation (☎206-624-7289; www.mircorp.com) In the USA.
Regent Holidays (☎0845-277 3317; www.regent-holidays.co.uk) In the UK.
The Russia Experience Ltd (☎020-8566 8846; www.trans-siberian.co.uk) In the UK.
Trek Escapes (☎866-338 8735; www.trekescapes.com) In Canada.

Survival Guide

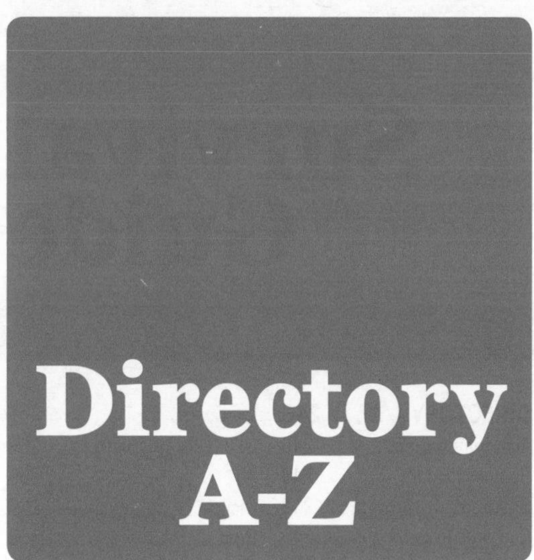

Directory A-Z

Accommodation

The prices listed in this book are for a standard double room in the high season (summer). Tax (10%) is almost always built into the price.

Outside Ulaanbaatar accommodation price ranges are defined as follows:

$	Less than T25,000
$$	T25,000 to T50,000
$$$	More than T50,000

In Ulaanbaatar, accommodation price ranges are defined as follows:

$	Less than US$40 (under T57,000)
$$	US$40 to US$90 (T57,000 to T115,000)
$$$	More than US$90 (more than T115,000)

Seasons

Rates listed in this guide are generally high season. High season is May to September. Some places may keep the same rates year round while others will offer a discount in the off-season.

Bookings

It's a good idea to book ahead for any accommodation. In rural areas, accommodation is limited, so if you turn up at the same time as a big tour group or if a government conference is underway, you may find every bed already booked out. You also need to book ahead for accommodation in Ulaanbaatar, especially the guesthouses, which get packed in summer. Booking ahead at a ger camp also allows your hosts to have enough food available for your party. Your tour operator can help make bookings.

Camping

Mongolia is probably the greatest country in the world for camping. With 1.5 million sq km of unfenced and unowned land, spectacular scenery and freshwater lakes and rivers, it is just about perfect. The main problem is a lack of public transport to great camping sites, though there are some accessible sites near Ulaanbaatar, such as in Gachuurt and Terelj. Camping is also well worth considering given the poor choice of hotels and the expense of ger camps.

Local people may come to investigate your camping spot, but you are very unlikely to encounter any hostility. However, be mindful of your security. If drunks spot your tent, you could have a problem. If you are hitching, it is not hard to find somewhere to pitch your tent within walking distance of most aimag (provincial) capitals and towns.

To wash yourself, you'll probably need to use the local town's bathhouse. Many are listed under the Information entries in this book. Be aware, though, that the bathhouses aren't like what you'd find in Turkey, for example; in Mongolia they are simply for getting a hose down.

If the owners (and their dog) give you permission, camping near a ger is a good idea for extra security; otherwise camp at least 300m from other gers. Mongolians have little or no idea of the Western concept of privacy, so be prepared for the locals to open your tent and look inside at any time – no invitation is needed.

You can often get boiled water, cooked food, uncooked meat and dairy products from nearby gers in exchange for other goods or money, but always leave something and don't rely on nomads, who may have limited supplies of food, water and fuel. It is also best to bring a portable petrol stove rather than use open fires, which are potentially dangerous, use precious wood and may not be possible where wood is scarce.

A few extra tips:

» Burn dried dung if you are being eaten alive by mosquitoes (you may then have to decide which is worse: mozzies or burning cow shit) and bring strong repellent with as much DEET as possible. Other anti-mosquito measures include wearing light-coloured clothing, avoiding perfumes or aftershave, impregnating clothes and mosquito nets with permethrin (nontoxic insect repellent), making sure your tent has an insect screen and camping away from still water or marshes (camping in hills or mountains is always better than low-lying areas).

» Make sure your tent is waterproof before you leave home and always pitch it in anticipation of strong winds and rain.

» Ensure your gear is warm enough for sub-zero temperatures, or you'll freeze. Cheap and flimsy Chinese-made tents and sleeping bags bought in UB won't cut it, especially for camping in the mountains. Bring the best stuff you can get your hands on for an enjoyable trip.

» Store your food carefully to protect it from creatures of the night.

» Don't pitch your tent under trees (because of lightning) or on or near riverbeds (flash floods are not uncommon).

Ger Buudals

Ger buudals (ger hotels) are found in popular tourist destinations, including Khövsgöl National Park, Terkhiin Tsagaan Nuur and Terelj. These are family-run operations and usually consist of an extra ger next to the family's ger. Basically, these are homestays with local families. They are very basic: no toilets, no showers and thin bedding. Expect to pay around T5000 per night. Be aware that some families running *ger buudals* might not be able to cope with the trash you produce and may dispose of it improperly. For this reason, the ranger at Khövsgöl National Park will hand you a plastic bag when you enter the park (you're expected to carry your own rubbish out of the park). Bags are not handed out at other national parks, so bring a few of your own if you plan to camp or stay at a ger buudal.

Ger Camps

One unique option, particularly popular with organised tours, is to stay in tourist gers, which are like those used by nomads – except for the hot water, toilets, sheets and karaoke bars.

The camps are found all over Mongolia. They may seem touristy and are often surprisingly expensive, but if you are going into the countryside, a night at one is a great way to experience a Western-oriented, 'traditional Mongolian nomadic lifestyle' without the discomforts or awkwardness of staying in a private ger.

A tourist ger camp is a patch of ground consisting of several (or sometimes dozens of) traditional gers, with separate buildings for toilets, hot showers and a ger-shaped restaurant/bar. Inside each ger, there are usually two to four beds, a table, tiny chairs and a wood stove that can be used for heating during the night – ask the staff to make it up for you.

Toilets are usually the sit-down types, though they may be (clean) pit toilets.

Prices for tourist camps often depend on the location. Where there is lots of competition, ie Lake Khövsgöl, Kharkhorin and Terkhiin Tsagaan Nuur, you can find basic camps for under T10,000 per night. Better camps or camps in remote areas may charge US$20 to US$30 (or more) per person per night, including meals. Activities such as horse or camel riding will cost extra. A surprising amount of the charge goes to the food bill, so you may be able to negotiate a discount of 50% by bringing your own food. This is pretty reasonable for a clean bed and a hot shower.

Meals are taken in a separate restaurant ger. With only a few exceptions, expect the usual Mongolian fare of meat, rice and potatoes. Most camps have a bar (and sometimes satellite TV). There's often little to differentiate between ger camps; it's normally the location that adds the charm and makes your stay special.

If you plan to stay in a ger camp, you may want to bring a torch for nocturnal visits to the toilets, candles to create more ambience than stark electric lights (though not all have electricity), towels (the ones provided are invariably smaller than a handkerchief), and toilet paper (it may run out).

Except for a handful of ger camps in Terelj, most ger camps are only open from June to August, although in the Gobi they open a month earlier and close a little later.

Traditional Gers

If you are particularly fortunate you may be invited to spend a night or two out on the steppes in a genuine ger, rather than a tourist ger camp. This is a wonderful chance to experience the 'real' Mongolia.

If you are invited to stay in a family ger, only in very rare cases will you be expected to pay for this accommodation. Leaving a gift is strongly recommended. While cash payment is usually OK as a gift, it's far better to provide worthwhile gifts for the whole family, including the women (who look after the guests). Cigarettes, vodka and candy are customary gifts, but with some creativity you can offer more

BOOK YOUR STAY ONLINE

For more accommodation reviews by Lonely Planet authors, check out hotels.lonelyplanet.com/mongolia. You'll find independent reviews, as well as recommendations on the best places to stay. Best of all, you can book online.

PRACTICALITIES

» **Currency** tögrög; 1210 tögrög = US$1.

» **Electricity** Power is 220V, 50Hz. The sockets are designed to accommodate two round prongs in the Russian/European style. Some sockets will accommodate multiple prong styles.

» **Expat Information** Mongol Expat (www.mongolexpat.com) is an online resource for housing, jobs, classifieds, events etc.

» **English-language newspapers** *Mongol Messenger* (www.mongolmessenger.mn) and the *UB Post* (http://ubpost.mongolnews.mn) both have good articles, events listings and classified sections.

» **Floors** As in the USA, the ground floor is called the 1st floor, as opposed to the UK system, where the next floor above ground level is the 1st floor.

» **Mongolian-Language newspapers** *Ardiin Erkh* (People's Right), *Zunny Medee* (Century News), *Odriin Sonin* (Daily News) and *Önöödör* (Today).

» **Radio** BBC World Service has a nonstop service at 103.1FM. Local stations worth trying include Jag (107FM), Blue Sky (100.9FM) and Radio Ulaanbaatar (102.5FM). Voice of America news programs are occasionally broadcast on 106.6FM.

» **Smoking** Some hotels and restaurants have designated smoking and nonsmoking areas. Smoking is not permitted on public buses. In December 2010, the government launched a campaign to ban smoking in all public areas.

» **TV & Video** TV and video are both PAL.

» **Weights & Measures** Mongolia follows the metric system.

useful items. Constructive presents include sewing kits, multi-tools, fleece sweaters, toothbrushes/toothpaste, Mongolian-language books and newspapers, and hand-powered flashlights and radios. Children will enjoy colouring books, pens, paper, puzzles and postcards from your home country.

Your host may offer to cook for you; it is polite for you to offer to supply some food, such as biscuits, bread, fruit, salt, rice and pasta. Pack out any garbage or packaging leftover from these items. Mongolians love being photographed. If you take pictures of your host family, remember to take down their name and a mail them a copy. For address purposes, you'll need their name, *sum* (district) and aimag.

If you stay longer than a night or two (unless you have been specifically asked to extend your visit), you will outstay your welcome and abuse Mongolian hospitality, making it less likely that others will be welcome in the future. Never rely on families to take you in; only stay if you have been invited.

Guesthouses

Ulaanbaatar now has around 20 guesthouses firmly aimed at foreign backpackers. Most are in apartment blocks and have dorm beds for around US$5, cheap meals, a laundry service, internet connection and travel services. They are a great place to meet other travellers to share transportation costs, but can get pretty crowded before and during Naadam (11 and 12 July).

Outside Ulaanbaatar only a handful of places, including Kharkorin and Khatgal, have accommodation aimed at backpackers.

Hotels

Most *zochid budal* (hotels) in the countryside (and budget hotels in Ulaanbaatar) have three types of rooms: a luxe (deluxe) room, which includes a separate sitting room, usually with TV and private bathroom; a *khagas lux* (half-deluxe), which is only a little smaller but often much cheaper; and an *engiin* (simple) room, usually with a shared bathroom. Sometimes, *niitiin bair* (dorm-style) beds are also available. Invariably, hotel staff will initially show you their deluxe room, so ask to see the standard rooms if you're on a budget. Simple rooms cost around T10,000 per person per night.

Budget hotels in Ulaanbaatar, lying on the fringe areas of the city, mainly cater to Mongolian truck drivers – guesthouses are a much better idea. If you plan to stay in budget hotels in the countryside, you should bring a sleeping bag. An inner sheet (the sort used inside sleeping bags) is also handy if the sheets are dirty. Blankets are always available, but are generally dirty or musty.

Midrange places are generally good but rather overpriced, charging US$40 to US$50 for a double. These rooms will be comfortable and clean and probably have satellite TV. Hot water and heating is standard for most buildings and hotels in Ulaanbaatar, and air-conditioning is rarely needed. The staff in midrange and top-end places will speak English. A private room or apartment, available through the guesthouses, may be a better idea.

In Ulaanbaatar, prices are usually quoted in dollars while in the countryside you'll get the price in tögrög. Either way, you should pay in tögrög because it is now the law. Payment for accommodation is usually made upon checkout, but some receptionists will ask for money upfront.

In the countryside, most hotels are generally empty and falling apart, though facilities continue to improve and almost every aimag capital will have one decent new place. Even at the best places you can expect dodgy plumbing, broken locks, rock hard beds and electrical outages. The quality of hotels in the countryside is reason enough to take a tent and go camping.

As for service, it is generally poor, except for top-end places in Ulaanbaatar. You'll gain little by getting angry; just be businesslike and eventually you'll get what you want. If the staff haven't seen guests for a long time (very possible in the countryside), they might have to search for some sheets, blankets, even a bed, washstand and water, and then rouse a cook to light a fire to get some food ready a few hours later.

If the hotel has no hot water (most likely outside UB) or no water at all, it's worth knowing that most aimag capitals have a public bathhouse.

Security should be a consideration. Always keep your windows and door locked (where possible). Be aware that staff may enter your room while you're not around. Err on the side of caution by keeping your valuables with you, at the very least lock up valuables inside your luggage. Most hotels have a safe where valuables can be kept.

Rental Accommodation

Apartment rental is really only an option in Ulaanbaatar; see p55 for details.

Business Hours

In the countryside, banks, museums and other facilities may close for an hour at lunch, sometime between noon and 2pm.

Outdoor markets are usually open from 9am to 7pm daily (or sunset in winter), while indoor markets open from 10am to 8pm.

Museums have reduced hours in winter and are normally closed an extra couple of days a week.

BUSINESS HOURS IN ULAANBAATAR

Banks	9am-6pm Mon-Fri 10am-3pm Sat
Government offices	9am-5pm Mon-Fri
Restaurants	10am-10pm
Shops	10am-10pm

Children

Children can be a great icebreaker and are a good avenue for cultural exchange with the local people; however, travelling in Mongolia is difficult even for a healthy adult. Long jeep rides over nonexistent roads are a sure route to motion sickness and the endless steppe landscape may leave your children comatose with boredom. Also, Mongolian food is difficult to stomach no matter what your age. That said, children often like the thrill of camping, for a night or two at least. There are also lots of opportunities to sit on yaks, horses and camels, and plenty of opportunities to meet playmates when visiting gers. Check out LP's *Travel with Children* for more general tips.

Practicalities

- Items such as formula, baby food, nappies (diapers) and wipes are sold in nearly every supermarket in Ulaanbaatar and many of these items are now available in other cities too. In the countryside, the best place to get milk is directly from a herder, but make sure it has been boiled.
- It's unlikely that your tour company will have a child seat for the vehicle. This is something to clarify when booking your tour. Chinese-made safety seats are sold in some Ulaanbaatar shops. Another option is to bring your own car seat. Note that Air China and MIAT will weigh the car seat and count it as part of your luggage (some other airlines won't count it against your luggage allotment).
- When travelling in the countryside, deluxe hotel rooms normally come with an extra connecting room, which can be ideal for children.
- Many restaurants in Ulaanbaatar have a high chair available. This will be rare in the countryside.
- Diaper-changing facilities are rare.
- Breastfeeding in public is common in the countryside but is slightly rarer in the city.

Customs Regulations

When you enter Mongolia, you should fill out an English-language customs declaration form to declare any prohibited items, all precious stones and all 'dutiable goods'. You are also asked to list all monies in your possession. Retain this form until your departure. Travellers entering at the airport with extra baggage can expect to have their luggage opened and inspected.

You can bring 1L of spirits, 2L of wine, 3L of beer, three bottles of perfume and 200 cigarettes into Mongolia duty-free.

If you are legally exporting any antiques, you must have a receipt and a customs certificate from the place you bought them. Most reliable shops in Ulaanbaatar can provide this. If the shop cannot produce a receipt or if you buy the item from a roadside stall, you can still get a customs certificate from the **Centre of Cultural Heritage** (☎7011 0877) in the Cultural Palace in Ulaanbaatar. You'll need to fill in a form with your passport number and where the antique was purchased and include two photos of the antique itself.

If you have anything that even *looks* old, it is a good idea to get a document to indicate that it is not an antique. That goes for Buddha images and statues as well.

At some sites (especially Kharkhorin and Bayanzag) you'll be offered furs of rare animals and even fossilised dinosaur bones and eggs. Please do not take up these offers. The fine for illegally exporting fossils is from US$100 to US$150, or five years in jail.

For more information on customs regulations, call ☎1281.

Discount Cards

An ISIC student card will get a 25% discount on train tickets plus discounts with some tour operators. Check the **ISIC website** (www.isiccard.com) for updates.

A student price might not always be listed but may be available; it's a good idea to inquire if you've got a student card on you.

Electricity

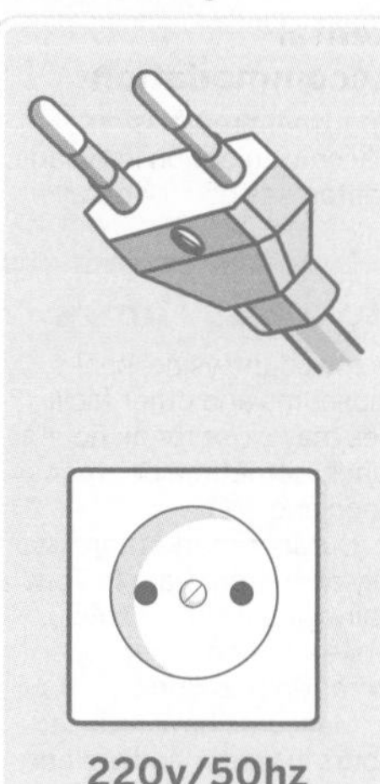

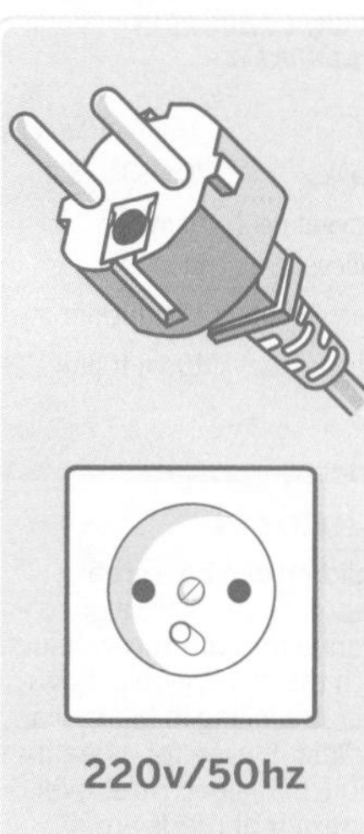

Embassies & Consulates

Mongolian Embassies & Consulates

You'll find a full listing of Mongolia's embassies and consulates at www.mongolianconsulate.com.au/mongolia/embassies.shtml.

Embassies & Consulates in Mongolia

A few countries operate embassies in Ulaanbaatar, though for most nationalities the nearest embassies are in Beijing or Moscow. If your country has an embassy in Ulaanbaatar, it's a good idea to register with it if you're travelling into the remote countryside, or in case you lose your passport.

Note that the German embassy also looks after the interests of Dutch, Belgian, Greek and Portuguese citizens. The British embassy handles normal consular duties for most Commonwealth countries.

For details on getting visas for China, Kazakhstan and Russia, see p259. For updates on the location/contact details, check: www.mfat.gov.mn.

Canada (Map p42; ☎328 285; fax 328 289; www.mongolia.gc.ca; Central Tower 6th floor, Peace Ave)

China (Map p42; ☎323 940; fax 311 943; http://mn.china-embassy.org; Zaluuchuudyn Örgön Chölöö 5) The consular section is actually on Baga Toiruu.

France (Map p42; ☎324 519; www.ambafrance-mn.org, in French; Peace Ave 3)

Germany (Map p42; ☎323 325; fax 323 905; www.ulan-bator.diplo.de; Negdsen Undestnii Gudamj 7)

Japan (Map p42; ☎320 777; www.mn.emb-japan.go.jp; Olympiin Gudamj 6)

Kazakhstan (Map p42; ☎345 408; kzemby@mbox.mn; Zaisan Gudamj, Khan Uul District)

Russia (Map p42; ☎327 191, 312 851; fax 327 018; www.mongolia.mid.ru; Peace Ave A6)

South Korea (Map p42; ☎321 548; fax 311 157; www.mofat.go.kr; Olympiin Gudamj 10)

Switzerland (Map p42; ☎331 422; fax 331 420; www.

swissconsulate.mn; Olympiin Gudamj 12)

UK (Map p42; ☎458 133; fax 458 036; britemb@mongol.net; Peace Ave 30)

US (Map p42; ☎329 095; http://ulaanbaatar.usembassy.gov; Ikh Toiruu 59/1)

Gay & Lesbian Travellers

Mongolia is not a gay-friendly place and not a place to test local attitudes towards homosexuality. While homosexuality is not specifically prohibited, some laws could be interpreted to make it appear illegal. Harassment by police has been reported, thus it should come as no surprise to hear that Ulaanbaatar's small gay and lesbian community is not well-organised.

Meeting places come and go quickly, so you'll need to quietly tap into the scene and ask. As you never know what sort of reaction you'll get from a Mongolian in person, try making contacts through the web. Insight can be found at www.globalgayz.com/g-mongolia.html and www.gay.mn.

Insurance

A policy covering loss, theft and medical expenses, plus compensation for delays in your travel arrangements, is essential for Mongolia. If items are lost or stolen you'll need to show your insurance company a police report. You may also need to prove damage or injury, so make sure to take photos. All policies vary, so check the fine print. For more on insurance, see p278.

Internet Access

Internet cafes in Ulaanbaatar are widespread and you'll spot them as you walk around town. Signs are often in English or Mongolian (Интэрнэт Кафэ).

Every aimag capital has an internet cafe at the central Telecom office and most cities have a couple of private internet cafes as well. A handful of *sum* (district) centres also have internet access. Expect to pay between T400 and T800 per hour at internet cafes, double or triple that for hotel business centres.

Wi-fi (wireless) access is widespread in Ulaanbaatar; see the boxed text, p71. However, wi-fi in rural areas is still uncommon.

Places in this book with free wi-fi, or internet connected computers, are indicated with a 📶 icon. Some hotels will just have an internet cable sticking out of the wall but require you to have your own laptop; if this is the case, it is described in the hotel listing.

Many apartment rentals will offer internet access of some kind, either wi-fi or with a cable hook-up. If you don't mind a slow connection you can even use dial-up – a card that will last for 10 hours is available from the Central Post Office for T3000.

Internet service providers include Magicnet, Citinet, Skytel and Mobicom. **Citinet** (Map p42; ☎011-7011 1010; www.citinet.mn; Ikh Toiruu) is one of the most popular. Rates are reasonable, costing around T20,000 per month for a 1mbs (megabyte per second) connection. However, not all buildings are internet-cable ready. In this case you can sign up for internet service with **Ulusnet** (Map p42; ☎321 434; www.ulusnet.mn; Sambugiin Gudamj 18), which gives you an internet connection via WiMax technology (no cable required). WiMax service plans start from T38,000 per month for 170kbps (kilobytes per second) and you'll need to buy or rent the router.

For expats living in Mongolia, especially in rural areas where internet is limited, mobile broadband is available. Mobile phone companies in Ulaanbaatar sell the USB stick (T100,000 to T200,000) and monthly plans (unlimited data usage costs around T50,000).

Legal Matters

Foreigners' rights are generally respected in Mongolia, although you may bump into the occasional bad cop or customs inspector who won't be satisfied unless they've gotten a piece of what's inside your wallet. If caught, drug use will give you a peek into Mongolia's grim penitentiary system.

The most common offence committed by foreigners is straying too close to a border without a permit. Violators end up paying a fine and a few unlucky souls have been imprisoned for a few days. If you run into serious trouble, ask to contact your embassy.

The police get mixed reports from travellers who have had to deal with them. Some have reported fast response and results while others have been let down with lacklustre work. Overall, police are harmless, but can be unreliable when you really need them.

Maps

Among the maps produced outside Mongolia, the best is the 1:200,000 Mongolia map published by **Gizi Maps** (www.gizimap.hu). The map is in both Latin and Cyrillic letters, handy for both you and your driver. It's available at Seven Summits (p68) in Ulaanbaatar for T19,200.

While shopping for maps in Ulaanbatar, look out for the 1:1,500,000 *Road Network Atlas* (T14,990) produced by MPM Agency. Another handy map is the 1:2,000,000 *Road Map of Mongolia* (T9990). It has the most accurate road layout and town names and usefully marks the kilometres between all towns. Also useful is the *Tourist Map of Mongolia* (T7500), which marks a host of obscure historical, archaeological and natural sights, as well as ger camps. Most maps are updated every couple of years.

Explorers will want to check out the 1:500,000 series of topographic maps, which covers Mongolia in 37 maps. Each sheet costs around T7000 to T8000, but don't count on all being available. The topographic maps are particularly useful if travelling by horse or foot or using a GPS unit, but they can get expensive. A cheaper alternative is a series of all 21 aimag maps (T25,000).

You will also spot handy regional maps (T4000 each) to the most popular tourist areas, including Khövsgöl Nuur (1:200,000), Gobi Gurvan Saikhan (1:200,000), Terelj (1:100,000) and the stretch of road between Ulaanbaatar and Kharkhorin (1:500,000).

Conservation Ink (www.conservationink.org) produces maps (US$8) using satellite images combined with useful information on culture, wildlife and tourist facilities. The national park series includes Altai Tavan Bogd, Khövsgöl Nuur, Gobi Gurvan Saikhan, Gorkhi-Terelj and Khustain Nuruu.

Chinggis Khaan junkies will want to check out the *Chinggis Khaan Atlas*, available around Ulaanbaatar for about T8000, which maps his every presumed movement in obsessive detail.

In many Western countries, you can buy the ONC and TPC series of topographical maps published by the Defense Mapping Agency Aerospace Center in the USA. The maps are topographically detailed but dated and are not reliable for place names or road layout. Mongolia is covered by ONC (1:1,000,000) and TPC (1:500,000) maps E-7, E-8, F-7 and F-8. Order from www.omnimap.com.

Money

The Mongolian unit of currency is the tögrög (T), which comes in notes of T5, T10, T20, T50, T100, T500, T1000, T5000, T10,000 and T20,000. (T1 notes are basically souvenirs.) The highest-value note is worth around US$17.

Banks and exchange offices in Ulaanbaatar will change money with relative efficiency. Banks in provincial centres are also fine; they change dollars and give cash advances against debit and credit cards.

When paying out large sums of money (to hotels, tour operators and sometimes airlines), its fine to use either US dollars or tögrögs. Other forms of currency aren't usually accepted, although the Euro is probably the next best. Cash offers the best exchange rates and you won't be paying any commission charge, but for security purposes you can also use debit cards. It's also possible to cash travellers cheques in Mongolia, usually for a 2% fee. American Express travellers cheques can be cashed at the Trade & Development Banks and Golomt Banks in Ulaanbaatar but getting cheques cashed outside Ulaanbaatar is more difficult.

Remember to change all your tögrög when leaving the country, as it's worthless elsewhere.

See the inside front cover for exchange rates at the time of publication and p14 for the costs of everyday items.

ATMs

Golomt, Trade & Development Bank, Khan Bank and Khas Bank all have ATMs in their Ulaanbaatar and countryside branches. These ATMs accept Visa and MasterCard and work most of the time, allowing you to withdraw up to T600,000 per day. Ordinary ATM cards issued from your bank at home probably won't work; try to get a 'debit' card linked to your bank account. It should be associated with a credit-card company. Before leaving home check with your bank about fees for making ATM transactions overseas. A 3% charge is standard nowadays but some banks will only charge 1%. If you plan to use your debit card a lot, it may be worth opening an account at a bank that has the lowest ATM fees.

Credit Cards

You can't rely on plastic for everything, but credit cards are becoming more widely accepted in upmarket hotels, travel agencies and antique shops. Most of these, however, charge an additional 3% if you use a credit card. Banks can give cash advances off credit cards, often for no charge if you have Visa, but for as much as 4% with MasterCard.

Tipping

Traditionally, Mongolians don't tip. However, Mongolians working in tourism-related fields (guides, drivers, bellhops and waitresses at restaurants frequented by foreigners) are now accustomed to tips. If you do feel service was good, a 10% tip is appreciated.

Photography & Video

Mongolia's remote and beautiful landscapes make for some incredible photography, but it's this same remoteness that requires extra planning when taking pictures. As you may go several days in a row without seeing a shop, internet cafe or electrical outlet, you'll need extra batteries and memory cards for your digital camera. These are best bought at home or in Ulaanbaatar as electronic goods in aimag centres can be hard to find. Once you reach an aimag capital you can go to an internet cafe and burn your pictures to a CD or save them to a USB storage drive.

In summer, days are long, so the best time to take photos is before 10am and between 6pm and 8pm, when Mongolia basks in gorgeous light. As bright, glaring sunshine is the norm, a polarising filter is essential. If you do a jeep trip on an unsurfaced road, you can expect plenty of dust, so keep the camera well sealed in a plastic bag.

For professional tips on how to take better photos, check out LP's *Travel Photography*, by Richard I'Anson.

Photographing People

Always ask before taking a photograph. Keep in mind that monks and nomads are not photographic models, so if they do not want to be photographed, their wishes should be respected. Point a camera at an urban Mongol on the street and chances are they will cover their face. Don't try sneaking around for a different angle as this may lead to an argument. Markets are also often a place where snap-happy foreigners are not welcome.

On the other hand, people in the countryside are often happy to pose for photographs if you ask first. If you have promised to send them a copy, please do it. One way to do this is to print out the photos at an aimag centre or in Ulaanbaatar. To simplify matters, bring blank envelopes and ask them to write their address on the outside. On the inside, make a note to yourself about who they were in case you forget.

When Mongolians pose for a portrait they instantly put on a face that looks like they are in mourning at Brezhnev's funeral. You may need to take this Soviet-style portrait in order to get a more natural shot later. 'Can I take your photograph?' in Mongolian is '*Bi tany zurgiig avch bolokh uu?*'

Restrictions

Photography is prohibited inside monasteries and temples, although you may photograph building exteriors and monastery grounds. You can sometimes obtain special permission to take photographs for an extra fee.

In most museums throughout the country you need to pay an extra fee (often outrageously high) to use your still or video camera. It is best to have a look around first before you decide whether to fork out the extra tögrög.

Don't photograph potentially sensitive areas, especially border crossings and military establishments.

Post

The postal service is generally reliable. Allow at least a couple of couple of weeks for letters and postcards to arrive home from Mongolia. Foreign residents of Ulaanbaatar find it much faster to give letters (and cash to buy stamps) to other foreigners who are departing.

You won't find letter boxes on the streets. In most cases, you will have to post your letters from the post office. You can buy stamps in post offices (and top-end hotels) in Ulaanbaatar and aimag capitals.

The poste restante at the Central Post Office in Ulaanbaatar seems to work quite well; bring along your passport as proof of identification. Don't even think about using poste restante anywhere else in the country.

Contact details for the more reliable courier services, including DHL and FedEx, are found on p72.

Postal Rates

Normal-sized letters cost T1100 and postcards cost T880 to all countries. A 1kg airmail parcel to the UK will cost T29,480, or T36,130 to the USA.

Public Holidays

Mongolians do not get many holidays. Naadam Festival and Tsagaan Sar each warrant three days off, plus there's a day off for New Year's. Most tourist facilities remain open during holidays, but shops and offices will close down. The following holidays are observed:

Shin Jil (New Year's Day) 1 January

Constitution Day 13 January; to celebrate the adoption of the 1992 constitution (generally a normal working day)

Tsagaan Sar (Lunar New Year) January/February; a three-day holiday celebrating the Mongolian New Year (for more information, see p232)

Women's Day 8 March (generally a normal working day)

Mothers' & Children's Day 1 June; a great time to visit parks

Naadam Festival 11 & 12 July; also known as National Day celebrations

Mongolian Republic Day 26 November (most government offices and banks are closed)

Safe Travel

Mongolia is a reasonably safe country in which to travel, but given the infrastructure of the country, state of the economy and other development problems, you are bound to run into hiccups along the way. With a bit of patience, care and planning, you should be able to handle just about anything.

Alcoholism

Alcoholism is a problem in Mongolia and you are bound to encounter drunks in both the city and countryside. Drunks (*sogtuu khun*) are more annoying than dangerous, except when they are driving your vehicle. Drivers who work for tour companies have been disciplined to hold their alcohol on trips, but hitchhikers may encounter drunk drivers.

Drinking is pretty common on the trains, which is another reason to travel in coupe class or 'soft seat' (you can close your cabin door). If the offending drunk happens to be in *your* cabin, ask the attendant to move you to another cabin.

If camping, always make sure that you pitch your tent somewhere secluded, and that no drunks see you set up camp; otherwise, they will invariably visit you during the night.

Dogs

Stray dogs in the cities and domestic dogs around gers in the countryside can be vicious and possibly rabid. In the countryside, some dogs are so damn lazy that you wouldn't get a whimper if 100 lame cats hobbled past; others will almost head-butt your vehicle and chase it for a kilometre or two. Before approaching any ger, especially in the countryside, make sure the dogs are friendly or under control and shout the phrase *'Nokhoi khor'*, which roughly translates as 'Can I come in?' but literally means 'Hold the dog!'. Getting rabies shots is no fun; it's easier to just stay away from dogs, even if they appear friendly.

If you need to walk in the dark in the countryside, perhaps for a midnight trip to the toilet, locals have suggested that if you swing a torch in front of you it will stop any possible dog attacks.

Scams

Professional scamming is not common; the main thing to be aware of is dodgy tour companies that don't deliver on their promises. We've had letters from readers who booked tours where the promised accommodation, food and service standards fell short of expectations. It might be good to get in writing exactly what is offered, and ask about compensation if things don't work out as planned. The riskiest tour companies are the ones operated by guesthouses and the ones that specialise in onward trips to Russia.

Theft

Petty theft is a fact of life in Ulaanbaatar and you need to stay vigilant of bag slashers and pickpockets, especially around naadam time when muggers do a brisk trade on all the starry-eyed tourists wandering about. In the countryside, keep an eye on your gear and don't leave valuables lying around your campsite if you wander off. Lock your kit inside your jeep or hotel whenever possible (drivers do a good job of watching your stuff). When horse trekking, be wary of Mongolians who seem to be following you; they may be after your valuables or even your horses, which are easily stolen while you sleep. For information on the dangers of theft in Ulaanbaatar, see p73.

Other Annoyances

Heating and hot-water shortages and electricity blackouts are common in aimag capitals. Some villages go for days (or weeks) without any utility services at all. In terms of official policies, although they have relaxed considerably since the arrival of democracy, some of the old KGB-inspired thinking still occurs among the police, especially in rural backwaters and border areas.

Quarantine sometimes affects travel in Mongolia. Foot-and-mouth disease, malignant anthrax and the plague pop up all the time and may prevent you from travelling to certain areas. Some regions that have been hit by foot-and-mouth require drivers to decontaminate their cars when they enter and leave cities. This requires the spraying of tyres (or the whole car) and can cost a few thousand tögrög.

Telephone

It's easy to make international or domestic calls in Ulaanbaatar and the aimag capitals. Technology is still lagging in many *sum* centres; however, it's now possible to use cell phones in most of the country.

Ulaanbaatar landline phone numbers have six digits, while most countryside numbers have five. Every aimag has its own area code; we have listed them in this book under the aimag capital headings. Note that Ulaanbaatar now has several area codes: 11 is the most widely used. If a phone number begins with a 23, 24 or 25, then the area code is 21. If the phone number begins with a 26, the code is 51.

If you are calling out of Mongolia and using an IDD phone, just dial ☎00 and then your international country code. On non-IDD phones you can make direct long-distance calls by dialling the international operator (☎106), who may know enough English to make the right connection; ask an English-speaking Mongolian to help you speak with the operator.

Pre-paid, international phone cards are available at the Central Post Office, starting from T3000. You can use these when calling from a landline.

These days, most travellers make international calls with **Skype** (www.skype.com) or a similar service. Calls to landlines are cheap, only around US$0.02 a minute to most Western countries (or free for computer to computer calls). You can do this on your own device at a wi-fi hotspot or use an internet cafe.

GOVERNMENT TRAVEL ADVICE

The following government websites offer travel advisories and information on current hot spots.

Australian Department of Foreign Affairs (☎1300 139 281; www.smarttraveller.gov.au)

British Foreign Office (☎020 7008 1500; www.fco.gov.uk/travel-and-living-abroad)

Canadian Department of Foreign Affairs (☎800-267 8376; www.dfait-maeci.gc.ca)

US State Department (☎888-407 4747; www.travel.state.gov)

Calls from the central Telecom offices in any city will be more expensive, but not outrageous: T560 per minute to the USA and UK, T820 per minute to Australia. To make the call, you need to pay a deposit in advance (a minimum equivalent of three minutes).

A couple of the top-end hotels have Home Country Direct dialling, where the push of a button gets you through to international operators in the USA, Japan and Singapore. You can then make a credit card, charge card or reverse charge (collect) call.

To make a call *to* Mongolia, dial the international access code in your country (normally ☎00) and then the Mongolian country code (☎976). Then, for a landline number, dial the local code (minus the '0' for Ulaanbaatar, but include the '0' for all other areas) and then the number. Be aware, though, that there are different requirements for area codes if using or phoning a mobile phone; see p255.

In Ulaanbaatar, the domestic operator's number is ☎1109.

Mobile Phones

The main companies are Mobicom, Skytel, Unitel and G-Mobile. Mobicom and Unitel operate on GSM (Global System for Mobile communication) 900/1800. G-Mobile and Skytel are both on the CDMA network. (Make sure you buy a SIM card appropriate for your phone.)

Buying a SIM card in Mongolia will probably work out cheaper than paying roaming charges on your home country network.

The process is simple – just go to a mobile-phone office (a good one is the Tedy Centre on Baruun Selbe Gudamj in UB), buy a SIM card (around T7000), and top up with units as needed. It is free to receive calls and text messaging charges are almost negligible. If you are abroad, and calling a mobile-phone number in Mongolia, just dial the country code (☎976) without the area code. Note that you drop the '0' off the area code if dialling an Ulaanbaatar number *from* a mobile phone but you retain the '0' if using other area codes.

Every aimag capital (and many *sum* centres) has mobile-phone service, and calls are fairly cheap, making this a good way to keep in touch with home. If a *sum* centre is not covered by Mobicom, it probably will be covered by an alternative network, such as G-Mobile.

It's a good idea to have a phone while travelling in the countryside, as it allows you to communicate with your tour operator should problems arise on your trip. You can also use it to call ger camps or hotels to make a reservation.

If you have a smart phone (Edge, 3G or 4G), you should be able to access the internet with a local SIM card.

Buying/Renting a Mobile Phone

New and used mobile phone shops are everywhere in UB and also in some rural cities. The cheapest phones will cost around US$35. In UB, try the Tedy Centre on Baruun Selbe Gudamj.

If you want to rent a phone ask **Robert** (☎9521 8521) at American Burgers & Fries (p60). At the time of research he was setting up a phone-rental business.

Satellite Phones

If you're planning a serious mountaineering or horse-trekking expedition, considering bringing or renting a satellite phone, which isn't too bulky and can be used anywhere. If you haven't already purchased one in your home country these are available for sale at the Mobicom office in the **Royal Castle building** (cnr Sambuugiin Örgön Chölöö & Tokyogiin Gudamj).

Time

Mongolia is divided into two time zones: the three western aimags of Bayan-Ölgii, Uvs and Khovd are one hour behind Ulaanbaatar and the rest of the country. Mongolia does not observe daylight-saving time, which means that the sun can rise at very early hours in summer.

The standard time in Ulaanbaatar is UTC/GMT plus eight hours. When it is noon in Ulaanbaatar, it is also noon in Beijing, Hong Kong, Singapore and Perth; 2pm in Sydney; 8pm the previous day in Los Angeles; 11pm the previous day in New York; and 4am in London. The 24-hour clock is used for plane and train schedules.

Toilets

In most hotels in Ulaanbaatar, aimag capitals and most ger camps, toilets are

MARGASH & YOU

There is another form of 'Mongolian time': add two hours' waiting time to any appointments you make. Mongolians are notorious for being late, and this includes nearly everyone likely to be important to you, such as jeep drivers, your guide or the staff at a museum you want to visit. You could almost adjust your watch to compensate for the difference. The Mongolian version of *'mañana'* (tomorrow) is *margash*.

the sit-down European variety. In other hotels and some more remote ger camps, you will have to use pit toilets and hold your breath.

In the countryside, where there may not be a bush or tree for hundreds of kilometres, modesty is not something to worry about – just do it where you want to, but away from gers. Also, try to avoid such places as *ovoos* (sacred cairns of stones), rivers and lakes (water sources for nomads) and marmot holes.

The plumbing is decrepit in many of the older hotels, and toilet paper can easily jam up the works. If there is a rubbish basket next to the toilet, this is where the waste paper should go. Most of the toilet paper in hotels resembles industrial-strength cardboard, or may be pages torn from Soviet-era history books or recently distributed bibles. To avoid paper cuts, stock up on softer brand toilet paper, available in the larger cities.

Tourist Information

There are three tourist information desks in Ulaanbaatar: at city hall, the post office and inside the Erel Bank on Peace Ave. Each is run by a separate entity. They all stock books, maps and brochures and have English-speaking staff. Outside UB, the only similar tourist desk is in Mörön.

Travellers with Disabilities

Mongolia is a difficult place for wheelchair travellers. Sidewalks are rough and buildings and buses are generally not wheelchair accessible. Still, travel to Ulaanbaatar and jeep trips to places such as Khustain Nuruu shouldn't cause too many insurmountable problems.

If any specialised travel agency might be interested in arranging trips to Mongolia, the best bet is the US company **Accessible Journeys** (☎800-846-4537; fax 610-521 6959; www.disabilitytravel.com) in Pennsylvania. At the very least, hire your own transport and guide through one of the Ulaanbaatar agencies (see p52). If you explain your disability, these agencies may be able to assist you.

Visas

Currently, a 30-day tourist visa is easily obtained at any Mongolian embassy consulate, consulate-general or honorary consul.

To get a visa for longer than 30 days, you must be invited or sponsored by a Mongolian citizen, foreign resident (expat) or Mongolian company, or be part of an organised tour. It is therefore possible to get a 90-day visa for most nationalities; you just need to pay the inviting agency a fee of around US$30 (most guesthouses can do this).

If you cannot get to a Mongolian consulate, you can pick up a 30-day tourist visa on arrival at the airport in Ulaanbaatar. You'll need US$53 and two passport photos – you should also have an invitation from an organisation or company in Mongolia.

Israeli and Malaysian citizens can stay visa-free for up to 30 days and Hong Kong and Singaporean citizens can stay visa-free for up to 14 days.

US citizens can stay in Mongolia for up to 90 days without a visa. If you stay less than 30 days, nothing needs to be done, other than having your passport stamped when you enter and leave the country. If you stay more than 30 days, you need to register.

In fact, all visitors who plan to stay more than 30 days must be registered within seven days of their arrival (see p257).

Mongolian honorary consuls can issue transit visas and nonextendable tourist visas, but only for 14 days from the date of entry. However, these visas are for entry only; they cannot issue normal entry/exit visas, so you will have to spend some of your precious time in Ulaanbaatar arranging an exit visa (see p257) from the **Office of Immigration, Naturalisation & Foreign Citizens** (INFC; ☎011-1882; ⏲9am-1pm & 2-6pm Mon-Fri). This office is located about 1.8km east of the airport (next to the large sports arena), an inconvenient 15km trek from the city centre. The office is usually quite busy, so you should expect to spend an hour or two here getting your stuff done. There is a small cafe here that serves lunch if you get stuck during the lunch hour. An information desk with English-speaking staff can help answer your questions and point you to the correct line.

To check current regulations, try the website of the Mongolian embassy in Washington DC at www.mongolianembassy.us. Another website to check is www.immigration.gov.mn.

For information on getting visas to China, Kazakhstan or Russia from Mongolia, see p259.

Tourist Visas

Standard tourist visas generally last 30 days from the date of entry and you must enter Mongolia within three months of issue. Tourist visas usually cost US$25 for a single entry/exit, though there may be a 'service fee'. Each embassy or consulate sets its own price. For single entry/exit visas you can expect to pay: A$100 in Sydney, UK£40 in London, C$90 in Ottawa and Y250 in Beijing.

Visas normally take several days, or even up to two weeks, to issue. If you want your visa quicker, possibly within 24 hours, you will have to pay an 'express fee', which is double the normal cost. If you want to stay longer than 30 days, tourist visas can be extended in Ulaanbaatar (see p257).

Multiple-entry/exit tourist visas are usually only issued to foreign residents who do a lot of travel.

Transit Visas

These visas last 72 hours from the date of entry. This period will only allow you to get off the Trans-Mongolian train for a very short time before catching another train to Russia or China. A single-entry/exit transit visa costs between US$25 and US$60, depending on where you apply for it, but cannot be extended. You will need to show the train or plane ticket and a visa for the next country (Russia or China).

Visa Extensions

If you have a 30-day tourist visa, you can extend it by another 30 days. For extensions, go to the INFC office (the one near the airport). The only catch is that if you stay longer than 30 days you have to be registered at this office (which you should have done within seven days after arrival).

The INFC office is a branch of the main visa office of the **Ministry of External Relations** (Map p42; cnr Peace Ave & Olympiin Gudamj; ⌚9.30am-noon Mon-Fri). You may be sent to the ministry if your visa situation is complicated (ie you require a work permit). The entrance is around the back. In Mongolian it's known as: Gadaadiin Irgen Haryatiin Asuudal Erhleh Gazar (Гадаадын Иргэн Харьяатын Асуудал Эрхлэх Газар).

If you have already registered, you should apply for an extension about a week before your visa expires. It costs US$2 per day but the minimum extension is seven days. You will need a passport-sized photo and must pay a T5000 processing fee. The extension will be issued on the same day. Credit cards may be accepted, but it's best to bring cash in case the machine isn't working.

Several guesthouses in Ulaanbaatar will take care of visa extensions (and registration) for a small fee. If you don't have a letter of support, you can write your own (handwritten is OK); the letter should state the date of your arrival, the date of extension and the reason for travel.

Getting a visa extension outside Ulaanbaatar is difficult, as officials would need to send your passport back to Ulaanbaatar. In an extreme situation this might be possible at the INFC office in Ölgii (p186).

Exit Visas

Transit and tourist visas are good for one entry and one exit (unless you have a double or multiple-entry/exit visa). If you are working in Mongolia, or if you obtained your visa at an honorary consul, you are usually issued a single-entry visa (valid for entry only). In this case, another visa is required to *leave* the country. These visas are available from the INFC office (see p256). For most nationalities the exit visa costs around US$15, plus an additional US$2 per day that you stay beyond the expiry of your entry visa. It is valid for 10 days, which means that you can stay 10 days after your normal visa has expired. The exit visa situation in particular applies to Israeli and US passport holders (who usually enter without visas). Israelis need an exit visa if they stay more than 30 days and Americans need one if they stay more than 90 days.

Registration

If you intend to stay in Mongolia for more than 30 days you must register before the end of your first 30 days of being in the country. (US passport holders must register within the first seven days.)

Registration takes place at the INFC office. The process is free, but you have to pay T1200 for the one-page application. You'll need one passport-sized photo. Most guesthouses can rustle up an invitation to Mongolia for you if you require one.

As a formality, the registration also needs to be 'signed out'; however, the official you are dealing with will usually do this when you register so you won't have to come back. A specific date is not needed, just set the exit date as far out as possible and you can leave anytime before that date.

If you've arrived in western Mongolia from Russia, the INFC office in Ölgii (p186) can get you registered.

VISAS FOR ONWARD TRAVEL

China

The best place to get a visa for China is in your home country. Applying at home will require less paperwork and you'll have a better shot at getting a multiple-entry visa. If you cannot get one in your home country, the Chinese embassy in Ulaanbaatar is another option. Drop off passports between 9.30am and noon Monday, Wednesday and Friday (pick up is 4pm to 5pm). Transit visas (single or double entry) last up to seven days from each date of entry, and single- and double-entry tourist visas are valid for 30 days from the date of each entry – you must enter China within 90 days of being issued the visa. Single-/double-entry tourist visas cost US$30/60 and take a week to issue. For three-day or same-day service, you'll have to fork out an extra US$20 or US$30. You must pay in US dollars. Visas for US citizens are US$140, regardless of type.

When you apply for the visa you must provide one passport photo, proof of departure from China (eg, an air or train ticket), proof of a booked hotel stay of three nights and a bank statement. This is not as difficult as it sounds. For the proof of departure, you can go to any travel agent in Ulaanbaatar, make a booking for a flight and get a print out (you don't need to actually buy the ticket). As for the hotel bookings, the best way to do this is to book three nights at a hostel in Beijing using your credit card. These bookings are usually 90% refundable so even if you never stay at the hostel this exercise should only cost a few dollars.

Note that in August and early September the lines at the embassy will be very long (Mongolian students come to pick up visas before the start of the academic year). People will start lining up at 6am (or earlier). Before the embassy opens, the guard will give out a limited number of tickets. If you don't get a ticket, it's highly unlikely you'll get inside that day.

For updated information, see http://mn.china-embassy.org.

Kazakhstan

The Kazakhstan embassy is open from 10am to noon and 3pm to 5pm Monday to Friday. Single-entry, one-month visas cost US$60 and take five days to process (or pay double to get it the next day). A double-entry, three-month visa costs US$100. A multiple-entry visa

If you don't register, you are liable for a fine (theoretically from US$100 to US$300) when you leave the country.

Note that you can only register one time per calendar year at the INFC office.

Long-Term Stays

The only way to remain in Mongolia on a long-term basis (ie more than three months) is to get a work or study permit. The company or organisation you are working for should handle this for you, but if you are working independently you need to go it alone. You will almost certainly need a letter from an employer providing a legitimate reason for your stay. You may need to pay a visit to the **Labour Registration Department** (Map p42; ☎011-260 376, 260 363) in the Supreme Court building on Sambuugiin Örgön Chölöö (in Mongolian 'Hodolmor, Halamjiin Uilchilgeenii Gazar, Хөдөлмөр халамжийн Үйлчилгээний Газар)

Independent researchers and students are usually registered through the Ministry of Education, Culture and Science (in Mongolian 'Bolovsrol Soyol Shinjleh Uhaanii Yam, Боловсрол Соёл Шинжлэх Ухааны Яам), in a building behind the Ulaanbaatar Hotel.

Volunteering

Some organisations are anxious to receive help from qualified people, particularly in education, health and IT development. Agencies are more interested in committed people who are willing to stay two years or more, although short-term projects are available. In most instances, you will be paid in local wages (or possibly a little more). Besides the following, a good starting reference is **Golden Gate Friends of Mongolia** (www.ggfom.org).

Adventure Meg (☎9964 3242; www.adventuremeg.com) Small tour operator that organises volunteer projects for short-term travellers. The work usually involves assisting at an orphanage.

Asral (☎011-304 838; fax 011-304 898; www.asralmongolia.org; PO Box 467, Ulaanbaatar-23) Travellers can volunteer as English teachers at this Buddhist social centre or work on the project farm in Gachuurt.

Australian Youth Ambassadors for Development (AYAD; ☎1800 225 592; www.

valid for one year costs US$205. Before trekking down here, call the embassy to make sure the consul is in town (and to check that they are even issuing visas as this service periodically stops). It's open Monday, Tuesday, Thursday and Friday, 10am to noon and 4pm to 6pm. The embassy is located on the way to Zaisan; take the last right turn before the bridge, into an alley with hideous-looking villas. Look for the Kazakh flag on the right.

Russia

Getting a visa is by no means a straightforward process, but it is not impossible. The consular section is open for visas from 2pm to 3pm daily. Almost everyone ends up paying a different price for their visa; costs vary between US$25 and US$200, depending on your itinerary and nationality. You will need one photo, an invitation or sponsor, and possibly vouchers for hotels. You can get a visa for 21 days. You will also need 'health insurance', which local agents can organise for about US$2 per day.

Americans, Australians, French, Dutch and Italians are a few of the nationalities that can get a tourist visa here. Processing time is two to three weeks and the visa is 21 days. Prices change all the time, but as a point of reference, an American will pay US$131 while an Australian will pay US$55.

Citizens of Germany, UK and New Zealand are a few of the nationalities that cannot get a tourist visa here (unless the applicant has been living in Mongolia over 90 days). However, they can get a transit visa. You must have all your tickets into and out of Russia to get the visa (you need to show the physical tickets to the consul). The length of the transit visa depends on your travel route but you are usually given a maximum of seven days (which is enough to take the Trans-Siberian to Europe). Regular processing time for a transit visa is four days, although rush visas can be done the following day. A transit visa costs US$55 while a rush transit visa costs US$115.

However things pan out at the embassy, you will almost certainly be directed to Legend Tour (see p72) for vouchers and visa support. For additional information, contact http://waytorussia.net.

ayad.com.au) AYAD has a handful of Australian volunteers in Mongolia.

Itgel Foundation (☎9972 2667; www.itgel.org) An organisation that assists the Tsaatan people in Khövsgöl. Various opportunities, from IT support to veterinary assistance.

Khustain National Park (www.ecovolunteer.org) The park runs a three-week eco-volunteer program where you can help with research.

Peace Corps (Enkh Tavnii Korpus; ☎011-311 518) The organisation is well represented throughout the country. Alternatively, contact your local Peace Corps office in the **USA** (☎1-800-424 8580; www.peacecorps.gov).

UN Development Program (UNDP; ☎011-327 585; www.undp.mn; PO Box 46/1009, Ulaanbaatar, Negdsen Undestnii Gudamj 12) The UNDP is always on the lookout for committed and hard-working volunteers but normally recruits abroad.

Voluntary Service Overseas (VSO; ☎/fax 011-313 514; www.vso.org.uk; PO Box 678, Ulaanbaatar) This British-run organisation is set up mainly for Brits. It prefers you to contact the organisation through its **UK head office** (☎020-8780 7500).

Women Travellers

Mongolia doesn't present too many problems for foreign women travelling independently. The majority of Mongolian men behave in a friendly and respectful manner, without ulterior motives. However, you may come across an annoying drunk or the occasional macho idiot. The phrase for 'Go away!' is '*Sasha be!*'

There are occasional incidents of solo female travellers reporting being harassed by their male guide. If your guide is male, it is best to keep in touch with your tour agency in Ulaanbaatar (having a mobile phone with a local SIM card makes it easier to contact them). Better yet, take a female guide whenever possible.

Tampons and pads are available in Ulaanbaatar and most other main aimag capitals, though these will be very hard to find the deeper you go into the countryside. Many women also find it useful to wear long skirts while in the countryside, so that they can relieve themselves in some semblance of privacy on the open steppes.

Although attitudes towards women are more conservative in the mostly Muslim Bayan-Ölgii aimag, you don't need to cover up as you would in other areas of Central Asia.

Work

Work opportunities for foreigners in Mongolia are few but are steadily growing as the economy picks up. However, if you do get work, the pay will be poor (possibly the same as the locals), unless you can score a job with a development agency or a mining company.

If you are keen to work in Mongolia and are qualified in teaching or health, contact the organisations listed in the Volunteering section of this chapter, network through the internet or check the English-language newspapers in Ulaanbaatar.

Permission to work is fairly easy to obtain if you have been hired locally. In most cases, your employer will take care of this for you. See also Long-Term Stays on p258.

For any project you get involved with, ask the organisation to put you in touch with former volunteers or workers to get a better idea of what you may be in for.

Language Teaching

Many Mongolians are hungry to learn a second language, particularly English, so there is a demand for teachers. Colleges and volunteer agencies are ever on the lookout for qualified teachers who are willing to stay for a few terms (if not a few years), but not just for a week or two.

In Ulaanbaatar try the following options:

American School of Ulaanbaatar (☎011-345 359; www.asu.edu.mn)

Ikh Zasag University (☎7015 7761; www.ikhzasag.edu.mn)

International School (☎7016 0012; www.isumongolia.edu.mn)

National University of Mongolia (☎011-320 159; www.num.edu.mn)

Orchlon School (☎011-353 519; www.orchlon.mn).

Turkish School (☎011-462 606; www.monturkub.edu.mn)

Transport

For most international travellers, getting to Mongolia will involve at least two legs: the first to the gateways of Moscow, Beijing or Seoul, and the second from these cities onward to Mongolia. The first section of this chapter details long-haul options to/from Mongolia, while the second section details the practicalities of actually getting into and around country.

Once you are within the region, the most popular options into Mongolia are flights from a hub like Moscow or Beijing or overland on the train from China or Russia.

There are few bureaucratic obstacles to reaching the country; it's simply a matter of getting a visa and a plane or train ticket.

Flights, tours and rail tickets can be booked online at www.lonelyplanet.com/bookings.

GETTING THERE & AWAY

Entering the Country

When entering Mongolia, by land or air, fill out straightforward immigration and customs forms. You shouldn't have to pay anything if your visa is in order (see p256 for visa information). You'll have to register if you plan to be in Mongolia for more than 30 days; see p257 for details. Registering in Ulaanbaatar is fairly straightforward, and it's also possible in Ölgii if you arrive in western Mongolia.

Passport

Make sure that your passport is valid for at least six more months from the date of arrival. If you lose your passport, your embassy in Ulaanbaatar can replace it, usually in one day. Before leaving Mongolia, check whether you'll need an exit visa from the Office of Immigration, Naturalisation & Foreign Citizens (INFC; p256).

Air

Airports & Airlines

Ulaanbaatar's **Chinggis Khaan airport** (☎198, 011-983 005; 📶) is Mongolia's major international airport; the code is ULN. There are constant rumours of a new international airport in Töv aimag, though nothing has been established formally.

Other airports with international flights include Ölgii (connected to Almaty, Kazakhstan), Choibalsan (connected to Hailar, China) and Khovd (connected to Xinjiang, China).

The tables in this section indicate sample high-season prices for midweek travel (Monday and Tuesday flights are generally cheaper than Friday and Saturday flights). In July and August, most flights are full, so book well in advance.

Airlines flying to and from Mongolia:

AeroMongolia (airline code MNG; ☎in UB 011-330 373; www.aeromongolia.mn) Mongolia-based airline that uses Fokker 50 propeller aircraft and Fokker 100 jets.

Aeroflot (airline code SU; ☎in UB 011-320 720; www.aeroflot.ru)

Air China (airline code CA; ☎in UB 011-452 458; www.airchina.cn)

EZ Nis (airline code ZY; ☎in UB 011-333 311; www.eznisairways.com) Mongolia-based airline with a handful of Saab 340B aeroplanes.

Korean Air (airline code KE; ☎in UB 011-317 100; www.koreanair.com)

MIAT (airline code OM; ☎in UB 011-333 999; www.miat.com) Mongolia's national airline, MIAT, has brought its safety practices for international flights to near-Western standards. Online booking is available through its website. On international flights, MIAT allows 30kg of baggage for business travellers and 20kg for economy travellers, though see p262 for a way around this.

TO/FROM ULAANBAATAR

Flights to/from Ulaanbaatar can be pricey, as there are a limited number of carriers. The main carriers are MIAT, Air China, Korean Air and Aeroflot.

TO/FROM CHOIBALSAN

EZ Nis has a twice-weekly flight to/from Hailar (which will possibly increase to three times per week). The flight originates in Ulaanbaatar, makes a pit stop in Choibalsan and continues to Hailar. The fare for Choibalsan–Hailar is US$74 each way.

Buying a ticket in Hailar can be a little tricky. If you want to fly *from* Hailar all the way to Ulaanbaatar (and you have a Mongolian visa) you can buy the ticket online. However, if Choibalsan is your final stop you will need to contact EZ Nis so that they can get approval from the immigration officials in Choibalsan (allow one to two working days).

Going *to* Hailar from Mongolia requires similar logistics hurdles; eg you will need to get approval from immigration. The staff at an EZ Nis office in Ulaanbaatar (or Choibalsan) will do this for you.

Immigration procedures are likely to ease within the lifetime of this book.

TO/FROM KHOVD

AeroMongolia connected Mongolia to Urumqi in late 2010. The once-weekly flight originates in Ulaanbaatar, stops in Khovd and continues to Urumqi, returning to Ulaanbaatar (via Khovd) on the same day.

The immigration procedures in Khovd are new and untested so travellers should confirm with AeroMongolia that they can get stamped in/out of Khovd. The fare for Khovd–Urumqi is about US$170 each way.

To buy a ticket in Urumqi, contact the **AeroMongolia representative** (☎150 2292 3901, 150 2292 3902) at the Urumqi airport.

EZ Nis also had plans to fly this same route, possibly starting in 2011.

TRANSITING AT BEIJING'S T3

The Beijing International Airport (PEK) is one of the world's largest. Most travellers use the new Terminal 3, often shortened to T3. You will almost certainly pass through here if you're travelling to/from Mongolia by air. Here is what you need to know:

» Your luggage weight is determined by the airline with which you begin your journey, not any middle segment or final segment. So if you are flying from overseas it doesn't matter that MIAT's baggage allowance is only 20kg; you can bring as much as your original flight allows. (This applies only if you check your baggage *all the way through* to Ulaanbaatar. If you pick up your luggage midway through the journey you will be subject to luggage restrictions when you check in with MIAT or Air China.)

» If you have an onward ticket for Mongolia, you can stay in Beijing for 24 hours without a visa. Luggage storage is available at the airport for about Y30 per bag. T3 also has a tiny hotel on the arrivals level where you can stay in between flights (rooms start from Y100 per hour). Alternatively, if you want to pop into the city for a few hours, take the new Airport Line light rail (Y25), which runs every 15 minutes to Dongzhimen subway station.

» In the event that one of your flights is landing at or taking off from Terminal 2 (T2), you can use a free shuttle bus to connect with T3.

» The airport is open all night; if you get in late and have an early flight to UB you can wait in the lounge on the 3rd level. There's usually a few other transit travellers here to keep you company.

» The airport has free wi-fi. To use it, you must first get a chit that will have a numbered code giving you five hours of internet use. The chits are available from machines that require you to scan your passport. One such machine is next to the payphones on the departure level (near the dragon sculpture close to Starbucks). It's also possible to have the code sent to your mobile phone.

» Most midrange to high-end hotels near the airport will send a free shuttle to pick you up. Call ahead and they will meet you at the gate, holding a sign with your name. Always have their number handy in case you don't see them at the gate. One decent option is the **Best Western Grandsky Hotel** (☎134-3996-3176; www.bestwestern.com; wi-fi), just a few kilometres from the airport, where you can usually get a room for around US$60.

» When leaving Mongolia, if you are catching a connecting flight, you must be able to show proof of your onward ticket at the counter in Ulaanbaatar and in Beijing (so have a printout handy). If you cannot show an onward ticket and you have no visa for China, you won't be allowed on the flight.

FLIGHTS TO/FROM ULAANBAATAR

FROM	AIRLINE	FREQUENCY	ONE WAY/ RETURN FARE
Beijing	Air China	6 weekly	US$330/512
Beijing	MIAT	6 weekly	US$218/481
Berlin	MIAT	2 weekly (via Moscow)	US$899/1237
Hailar (via Choibalsan)	EZ Nis	2 weekly	US$198/396
Hohhot	AeroMongolia	3 weekly	US$215/430
Irkutsk	AeroMongolia	2 weekly	US$205/370
Moscow	Aeroflot	2 weekly	US$639/892
Moscow	MIAT	2 weekly	US$593/815
Seoul	Korean	4 weekly	US$415/510
Seoul	MIAT	6 weekly	US$446/666
Tokyo	MIAT	1 weekly	US$792/1087
Ulan Ude	EZ Nis	3 weekly	US$154/308
Urumqi	AeroMongolia	1 weekly	US$385/770

TO/FROM BAYAN-ÖLGII

A twice-weekly flight connects Almaty (Kazakhstan) and Ölgii via Üst-Kamenogorsk. The flight, operated by **Trans-Olgii** (☎9942 8162, 318 000; Ölgii Government House) costs T310,000 to Üst-Kamenogorsk or T420,000 to Almaty. Tickets can only be bought in Ölgii so if you want to reserve a ticket you'll need to get in touch with an Ölgii-based tour operator (see p183).

If at all possible, don't change the date of your ticket, as this always leads to ticketing problems and your new ticket may be invalid. Flights are always crowded and you may be asked to pay a dubious health tax (just ignore it).

Tickets

Full-time students and people aged under 26 years (under 30 in some countries) have access to better deals than other travellers. You have to show a document proving your date of birth or a valid International Student Identity Card (ISIC) when buying your ticket. Airfares to Mongolia peak between June and August.

Overlanders should consider purchasing an open-jaw ticket. This option could involve, for example, flying into Beijing and then flying out of Moscow. This would allow you to travel slowly along the Trans-Siberia Railway.

The following online ticket agencies book flights originating in the USA, but they have links to specific country websites across the world:

Cheapflights.com (www.cheapflights.com)

Expedia (www.expedia.com)

Last Minute.com (www.lastminute.com)

Lonely Planet (www.lonelyplanet.com) Click on 'Flights' to book flight tickets.

Orbitz (www.orbitz.com)

Priceline (www.priceline.com)

STA Travel (www.statravel.com)

Travelocity (www.travelocity.com)

Travel Agencies & Organised Tours

In this section we list reliable agencies outside Mongolia that can help with the logistics of travel in Mongolia, including visas, excursions or the whole shebang. These include travel agencies, adventure-tour operators and homestay agencies. The following can hook you up with tickets, individual itineraries or group packages. For Ulaanbaatar-based travel companies, see p52.

Asia

Monkey Business Shrine (☎8610-6591 6519; www.monkeyshrine.com; room 201, Poachers Inn, 43 Beisanlitun Nan, Chao Yang District, 100027, Beijing, China)

Moonsky Star Ltd (☎852-2723 1376; www.monkeyshrine.com; flat D, 11th fl, Liberty Mansion, 26E Jordan Rd, Yau Ma Tei, Kowloon, Hong Kong)

Australia

Intrepid Travel (☎03-9473 2626; www.intrepidtravel.com.au; 11 Spring St, Fitzroy, Victoria 3065)

Peregrine Adventures (☎03-8601 4444; www.peregrine.net.au; 258 Lonsdale St, Melbourne, Victoria 3000)

UK & Continental Europe

Equitour (☎061-303 3105; www.equitour.com; Herrenweg, 60 CH-4123 Allschwil, Switzerland) Specialises in horse-riding tours.

In the Saddle (☎01299-272 997; www.inthesaddle.co.uk; Reaside, Neen Savage, Cleobury Mortimer, Shropshire, DY14 8ES, UK) Runs horse-riding tours.

KE Adventure (☎017687-73966; www.keadventure.com; 32 Lake Rd, Keswick, Cumbria, CA12 5DQ, UK) Organises mountain-biking tours and guided ascents of Tavan Bogd Uul.

CLIMATE CHANGE & TRAVEL

Every form of transport that relies on carbon-based fuel generates CO_2, the main cause of human-induced climate change. Modern travel is dependent on aeroplanes, which might use less fuel per kilometre per person than most cars but travel much greater distances. The altitude at which aircraft emit gases (including CO_2) and particles also contributes to their climate change impact. Many websites offer 'carbon calculators' that allow people to estimate the carbon emissions generated by their journey and, for those who wish to do so, to offset the impact of the greenhouse gases emitted with contributions to portfolios of climate-friendly initiatives throughout the world. Lonely Planet offsets the carbon footprint of all staff and author travel.

Mongolei Reisen GmbH (☎3303-214 552; www.mongoliajourneys.com; Am Spargelfeld 3, 16540 Hohen Neuendorf, Berlin, Germany)

Off the Map Tours (☎0116-2402625; www.mongolia.co.uk; 2 The Meer, Fleckney, Leicester, LE8 8UN, UK) A Mongolia specialist with motorcycling, mountain-biking, horse riding and hiking trips.

Panoramic Journeys (☎1608 811183; www.panoramicjourneys.com; Noah's Ark, Market St, Charlbury, Oxon, OX7 3PL, UK) A specialist in Mongolia trips, with highly regarded tailor-made tours to off-the-beaten-path destinations as well as standard tours. Excellent sustainable development philosophy. Especially recommended for trips to visit the Tsaatan.

Steppes Travel (☎01285-880 980; www.steppeseast.co.uk; 51 Castle St, Cirencester, GL7 1QD, UK)

USA & Canada

Boojum Expeditions (☎1-800-287-0125, 406-587-0125; www.boojum.com; 14543 Kelly Canyon Rd, Bozeman, MT 59715, USA) Offers horse-riding, mountain-biking, fishing and trekking trips. In Ulaanbaatar, Boojum's local office is called Khövsgöl Lodge Company.

Geographic Expeditions (☎1-800-777-8183; www.geoex.com; 2nd fl, 1008 General Kennedy Ave, San Francisco, CA 94129, USA) Horse-riding trips to Khentii and jeep trips combining western Mongolia and Tuva in western Siberia.

Hidden Trails (☎604-323-1141; www.hiddentrails.com; 659A Moberly Rd, Vancouver, BC V5Z 4B3, Canada) Horse-riding tours to Terelj and Darkhad Depression, in conjunction with Equitour.

Mir Corporation (☎1-800-424-7289; www.mircorp.com; Suite 210, 85 South Washington St, Seattle, WA 98104, USA)

Nomadic Expeditions (☎1-800-998-6634, 609-860-9008; www.nomadicexpeditions.com; Suite 20A, 1095 Cranbury-South River Rd, Jamesburg, NJ 08831, USA) One of the best Mongolia specialists, offering everything from palaeontology trips to eagle hunting and camel trekking. It also has an office in Ulaanbaatar.

Land

There are two main land border crossings open to foreigners: Ereen (Erenhot or Erlian in Chinese) and Zamyn-Üüd, on the Chinese-Mongolian border; and Naushki-Sükhbaatar, on the Russian-Mongolian border. It's possible to cross borders by minivan or train, though the latter is the more common and convenient option. There are also other border crossings between Russia and Mongolia; see p267.

China

BORDER CROSSINGS

The only border open to foreigners is the one between Zamyn-Üüd and Ereen. It's open daily but note that on holidays only the train (not the road) crossing will operate. For vehicles the border is open 8am to 6pm. It's not possible to walk across the border.

If you are heading for Mongolia and need a visa, there is a **Mongolian consulate** (Měnggǔ Lǐngshìguǎn; ☎151-6497-1992; Weijian Binguan, 206 Youyi Beilu; ⏲8.30am-4.30pm Mon-Fri) in Ereen. To find the consulate from the bus station, walk east half a block to the T-junction and make a left. Walk north along this road (Youyi Beilu) for 10 minutes until you see the red, blue and yellow Mongolian flags on your left. A 30-day rush tourist visa (Y495) can be issued on the same day you apply; you'll need one passport-sized photo. A taxi can take you there for Y4. See p256 for more visa information.

Most travellers end up here in the middle of the night on the international through train. If you are taking local transport you'll need to navigate Ereen, a mid-sized Chinese city with efficient rail and bus links, and a slew of hotels, restaurants, shops and markets. If you have just come from Mongolia, change any remaining tögrög here or you'll be keeping it as a souvenir. If you need to spend the night there are some cheap and reliable hotels opposite the train station.

Zamyn-Üüd, on the Mongolian side, is not an interesting place, so you aren't missing anything if you are on the overnight train. Mongolian customs and immigration officials take about two hours to do their stuff.

Remember that if you are carrying on to rural China there is absolutely no need to go to Beijing first. From Ereen you can travel to the rail junction at Datong and then catch trains or buses to Pingyao, Xi'an and points south. For western China, get off at Jining where you can change to Hohhot, Lanzhou and beyond. Read Lonely Planet's *China* guide for details on connections from these cities.

CAR & MOTORCYCLE

As long as your papers are in order there is no trouble crossing the Chinese–Mongolian border in your own car. Driving around Mongolia is a lot easier than China, where drivers require a guide and Chinese driving permit.

MINIVAN

Minivans shuttle between the train stations of Zamyn-Üüd, on Mongolia's southern border, and Ereen, the Chinese border town. On the Mongolian side it costs T15,000 (or about Y50) for a seat in a van.

When the train arrives in Zamyn-Üüd there is a frantic rush for minivans and then a jockeying for position at the border. Keeping up with the crowd will get you to Ereen more quickly, so don't dally!

By minivan the price is the same if coming from Ereen. Jeeps assemble at the Ereen bus station and the market; ask the Mongolian drivers. There is a Y5 tax that you need to pay going either way (you can pay the driver in tögrög or US dollars and they will pay the tax for you).

TRAIN

Mongolia has trains to both Russia and China. Getting a ticket in Ulaanbaatar can be very difficult during the summer tourist season, so you need to plan ahead.

The yellow International Railway Ticketing Office (Map p39) is about 200m northwest of the train station. Inside the office, specific rooms sell tickets to Beijing, Irkutsk (Russia), Moscow, and Ereen and Hohhot (both in China), but as a foreigner you'll be directed to a **foreigners' booking office** (☎24133, enquiries 243 848; room 212; ⏰8am-7pm). It's upstairs and staff here speak some English. On weekends you can use the downstairs booking desk. You'll need your passport to buy a ticket. You can book the ticket by phone for a T4500 booking fee. If you cancel a ticket there is a minuscule T1000 charge. There is no departure tax if travelling on the train.

You can book a ticket for international trains out of Ulaanbaatar up to one month in advance, but for the Moscow–Beijing or Beijing–Moscow trains you will have to scramble for a ticket on the day before departure (although you could try asking two days in advance). If you have trouble booking a berth, ask your guesthouse manager or hotel reception desk for assistance.

A taxi between Sükhbaatar Sq and the train station costs about T2000.

Refer to the boxed text, p266, for international train services.

Direct Trains

Most travellers catch the direct train between Beijing and Ulaanbaatar.

There are two direct trains a week each way between Beijing and Ulaanbaatar. One of these (3 and 4) is the Trans-Mongolian Railway, which runs between Beijing and Moscow. It's easier to get a ticket for the other train (23 and 24).

It is also possible to travel directly between Ulaanbaatar and Hohhot twice a week, allowing you to either bypass Beijing completely or catch a train or flight (Y480) on to Beijing from there.

Trains leave from **Beijing Train Station** (☎5101 9999). If your luggage weighs over 35kg, on the day before departure you'll have to take it to the Luggage Shipment Office, which is on the right-hand side of the station. The excess is charged at about US$11 per 10kg, with a maximum excess of 40kg allowed.

The best place to buy tickets in China is at the **China International Travel Service** (CITS; ☎010-6512 0507; www.cits.net; ⏰8.30am-noon & 1.30-5pm) in the International Hotel, Jianguomenwai Dajie, Beijing. Tickets are also available at **BTG Travel & Tours** (☎010-6515 8010; Beijing

ULAANBAATAR–CHINA TRAINS

The costs (in tögrög) for destinations in China from Ulaanbaatar are found in the following table.

DESTINATION	2ND CLASS (HARD SLEEPER)	1ST CLASS (SOFT SLEEPER)	DELUXE* (COUPÉ)
Beijing	130,050	217,750	184,550
Datong	113,250	188,450	160,250
Ereen	80,050	131,350	111,650
Hohhot	118,150	166,650	

*Prices are for Chinese trains. Deluxe cars are not available on Mongolian trains. Mongolian trains are about 5% to 10% cheaper for 1st class.

Tourism Bldg, 28 Jianguomenwai Dajie), between the New Otani and Gloria Plaza hotels.

With CITS it is possible to book up to six months in advance for trains originating in Beijing if you send a deposit of Y100, and you can collect your ticket from one week to one day before departure. There is a Y150 cancellation fee.

CITS only sells tickets from Beijing to Moscow or Ulaanbaatar – no stopovers are allowed. Tickets to Ulaanbaatar cost Y1128/1619 in hard/soft sleeper on the K23 Saturday train and Y1225/1710 in hard/soft sleeper on the K3 Wednesday train.

You can also buy train tickets privately; they will be more expensive than at CITS, but you may also be able to arrange a stopover and visas. In Beijing, **Monkey Business Shrine** (☎8610-6591 6519; fax 6591 6517; www.monkeyshrine.com) can put together all kinds of stopovers and homestay programs. The company has a lot of experience in booking international trains for independent travellers. In Hong Kong, it goes under the name **Moonsky Star Ltd** (☎852-2723 1376; fax 2723 6653).

Note that the Russian embassy in Beijing is only accepting visa applications from official residents of China. You are more likely to get a visa from the Russian consulate in Hong Kong. See the boxed text (p265) for train fares from Ulaanbaatar to China.

Local Trains

If you're on a tight budget it's possible to take local trains between UB and Beijing. This will save some money but involves more hassle and uncertainty and requires more time. During the summer season, from mid-June to mid-August, international train bookings are almost impossible to get, unless you have booked your seats weeks or months in advance. The local train may be your only option.

The first option is train 21 or 22, which runs between Ulaanbaatar and Ereen just inside China. This Mongolian train leaves Ulaanbaatar at 10pm on Thursday and Sunday and arrives in Ereen at about 10.35am the next morning, after completing immigration and customs formalities. In reverse, train 21 leaves Ereen on Tuesday and Saturday evenings and arrives the next day. The schedules for this train change regularly.

TRAINS TO/FROM MONGOLIA

Schedules change from one summer to another, and services reduce in winter, and can increase in summer. The durations below refer to the journey time to/from Ulaanbaatar.

TRAIN	TRAIN NO	DAY OF DEPARTURE	DEPARTURE TIME	DURATION
China-Mongolia				
Beijing-Ulaanbaatar	23	Sat	7.40am*	30hr
Beijing-Ulaanbaatar-(Moscow)	3	Thu	1.50pm	30hr
Hohhot-Ulaanbaatar	215	Sun, Wed	10.40pm	30hr
Mongolia-China				
Ulaanbaatar-Beijing	24	Thu	7.15am	30hr
(Moscow)-Ulaanbaatar-Beijing	4	Thu	7.15am	30hr
Ulaanbaatar-Hohhot	34	Mon, Fri	8pm	24hr
Mongolia-Russia				
Ulaanbaatar-Irkutsk	263	daily	9.10pm	36hr
Ulaanbaatar-Moscow	5	Tue, Fri	1.50pm	70hr
(Beijing)-Ulaanbaatar-Moscow	3	Thu	1.50pm	100hr
Russia-Mongolia				
Irkutsk-Ulaanbaatar	264	daily	7.10pm	36hr
Moscow-Ulaanbaatar	6	Wed, Thu	9pm	70hr
Moscow-Ulaanbaatar-(Beijing)	4	Sun	7.55pm	100hr

*Train 23 passes through Datong at approximately 2.15pm, Jining at 4.15pm, Ereen at 8.45pm and Zamyn-Üüd at 11.45pm.

BOGIES

Don't be concerned if you get off at Ereen (on the Chinese side of the border) and the train disappears from the platform. About an hour is spent changing the bogies (wheel assemblies) because the Russians (and, therefore, the Mongolians) and the Chinese use different railway gauges. Train buffs may want to see the bogie-changing operation. Stay on the train after it disgorges passengers in Ereen. The train then pulls into a large shed about 1km from the station. You can watch the whole operation from the window of your train car.

The second option is to take local trains to Zamyn-Üüd in Mongolia (see p166) and then cross the border by minivan or jeep. From Ereen you can go deeper into China by either train or bus.

From Beijing, the local train for Jining departs at 11.42am and takes about nine hours. A second train departs at 9.20pm and continues to Hohhot. The train from Jining to Ereen (Erlian) departs around noon and takes six hours. (Alternatively, a 7am bus takes just four hours.) If you have to stay the night in Jining, there's a budget hotel on the right (south) side of the plaza as you walk out of the train station. Most transport between Ereen and the border takes place in the morning. If you need help with the logistics of train travel, a good contact is freelance guide **Daka Nyamdorj** (☎9984 4844; www.happymongolia.net), who specialises in tours by train.

Russia

BORDER CROSSINGS

Most travellers go in and out of Russia at the Naushki–Sükhbaatar train border crossing. In addition, there are three road crossings: Tsagaannuur–Tashanta in Bayan-Ölgii aimag, Altanbulag–Kyakhta in Selenge and Ereentsav–Solovyevsk in Dornod. The crossings are open from 9am to noon and 2pm to 6pm daily except holidays.

The Khankh–Mondy border in northern Khövsgöl is not open to third country nationals.

Both the road and rail crossings can be agonisingly slow, but at least on the road journey you can get out and stretch your legs. Train travellers have been stranded for up to 10 hours on the Russian side, spending much of this time locked inside the train cabins. Procedures on the Ulaanbaatar–Moscow train are faster than on the local trains.

We have received a number of complaints about scams and problems with customs on the Russian side of the border, so be ready for anything.

One thing to be careful about is the Russian exit declaration form. The currency you list on the form must match the currency you listed on the customs form you received when you entered the country. If the form shows that you are leaving with more dollars or euros than you had when you arrived, you will have to get off the train and change all the excess money into roubles. Further, if the entry form was not stamped when you arrived in Russia (or if you never received one) it will be considered invalid, so have the form stamped even if you have nothing to declare.

To avoid these problems, either don't cross the border with foreign currency (roubles are OK) or be vigilant with that exit declaration form. Lying about not having foreign cash is one option, but you run the risk of being searched. Telling the border guard you plan to use a credit card may work.

Russian & Mongolian Border Towns

Customs and immigration between Naushki and Sükhbaatar can take at least four hours. You can have a look around Naushki, but there is little to see and the border crossing usually takes place in the middle of the night. Surprisingly, you may have difficulty finding anyone at the Naushki station to change money, so wait until Sükhbaatar or Ulaanbaatar, or somewhere else in Russia. (Get rid of your tögrög before you leave Mongolia, as almost no one will want to touch them once you are inside Russia.)

The train may stop for one or two hours at, or near, the pleasant Mongolian border town of Sükhbaatar, but there is no need to look around. You may be able to buy some Russian roubles or Mongolian tögrög from a moneychanger at the train station, but the rate will be poor. If there aren't any moneychangers, you can use US dollars cash to get by until you change money elsewhere.

BUS

Bus is probably the fastest form of public transport between Mongolia and Russia. A daily bus operated by **Vostok Trans** (☎7011 0696) departs Ulaanbaatar bound for Ulan Ude. It departs at 8pm, and the journey takes 12 hours and costs T45,600. Buses leave from the parking lot at the Avto Terveriin Gazar, the vehicle registration office; it is also known as Discovery Mongolia Centre. Buy tickets from a small office inside this building.

An Ulan Ude bus (R950) departs at the same time

for Ulaanbaatar, leaving from the Hotel Baikal in Ulan Ude. In Ulan Ude contact **Trio-Impex** (☎3012-217 277; trio-tour@mail.ru) or **Buryat-Intour** (☎3012-210 056; bintur@yandex.ru).

CAR & MOTORCYCLE

It's possible to drive between Russia and Mongolia at Tsagaannuur (Bayan-Ölgii), Altanbulag (Selenge) and Ereentsav (Dornod). However, these road crossings can be difficult and time consuming – up to six hours if traffic is backed up or if you have visa problems.

In order to speed things up, it may help to have a letter written by the Mongolian consular (or Russian consular if you are headed that way) when you get your visa. The letter should state that you are authorised to take a car or motorcycle across the border. A carnet (passport for your car) may be useful but is not necessary.

Foreigners are currently not allowed to 'walk' across the Kyakhta–Altanbulag border, but they are allowed to pass through in a car or even on a motorcycle, so you may have to pay someone to drive you across.

Among the borders, the trickiest is the one at Ereentsav (the Russian side is Solovyevsk). Some travellers have reported getting through and others being turned back. Travellers going from Russia into Mongolia seem to have more success. In either direction you will most likely need to be in a private vehicle as you cannot walk across the border. This isn't a problem if you have your own car but if you need a car to take you across you could be in for a long wait.

TRAIN

Besides the Trans-Mongolian Railway (p242) connecting Moscow and Beijing, there is a direct train twice a week connecting Ulaanbaatar and Moscow, which is easier to book from Ulaanbaatar. The epic trip takes four days.

If you are headed to Lake Baikal, there is a daily train between Ulaanbaatar and Irkutsk, which stops en route in Darkhan. These trains stop at every village, however, and train 263 travels past Lake Baikal at night, so if you are in a hurry or want to see the lake, take the Ulaanbaatar–Moscow train (5) as far as Irkutsk. Note that departure and arrival times at Irkutsk are given in Moscow time, although Irkutsk is actually five hours ahead of Moscow.

This trip can be done more cheaply by travelling in stages on local trains (eg from Ulan Ude to Naushki, Naushki to Sükhbaatar, and Sükhbaatar to Ulaanbaatar), but this would involve more hassles, especially as Russian visas are more difficult to arrange than Chinese ones due to Russian officials wanting full details of your itinerary.

In Moscow you can buy tickets at the building on Ulitsa Krasnoprudnaya 1, next door to the Yaroslavl train station, from where the trains to Ulaanbaatar and Beijing leave.

Unifest Travel (☎495-234 6555; www.unifest.ru; Komsomolsky pr 16/2, Bldg 3-4) in Moscow is a reliable travel agent that can sell train tickets on the Trans-Siberian Railway.

A reliable agency in Ulan Ude is **Buryat-Intour** (☎3012-216 954; www.buryatintour.ru; Kirova 28a). In Irkutsk, you can try **Irkutsk Baikal Travel Inc** (☎3952-200 134; www.irkutsk-baikal.com; 1a Cheremhovsky Ln, 664025). See the boxed text (p265) for train fares from Ulaanbaatar to Russia.

ULAANBAATAR–RUSSIA TRAINS

Approximate costs (in tögrög) for major destinations in Russia from Ulaanbaatar are listed below. Exact costs depend on whether the train is Russian, Chinese or Mongolian; we have listed the most expensive.

DESTINATION	2ND CLASS	1ST CLASS
Irkutsk	97,850	146,950
Krasnoyarsk	142,750	220,350
Moscow	266,250	445,050
Naushki	42,250	66,750
Novosibirsk	164,450	268,950
Omsk	183,450	301,650
Perm	226,350	373,950
Ulan Ude	64,150	99,050
Yekaterinburg	216,350	359,950

GETTING AROUND

Travelling around the countryside independently is the best way to see Mongolia and meet the people, but there are several matters you need to be aware of. Annual outbreaks of forest fires, the plague, foot-and-mouth and even cholera may affect your travel plans if there are quarantine restrictions.

Generally, shortages of petrol and spare parts are uncommon, except in remote regions. Accidents are not uncommon. Try to avoid travelling at night, when unseen potholes, drunk drivers and wildlife can wreak havoc. Driving in the dark is also a great way to get completely lost.

Air

Mongolia, a vast, sparsely populated country with very little infrastructure, relies heavily on air transport. It has 46 functioning airports, although only 14 of those have paved airstrips.

Almost all of the destinations are served directly from Ulaanbaatar, so flying from, say, Dalanzadgad to Bayan-Ölgii is impossible without first returning to UB.

Airlines in Mongolia

AeroMongolia (☎011-330 373; www.aeromongolia.mn) Operates two Fokker aircraft. Routes change but in 2010 it flew domestic services to Ölgii, Khovd, Dalanzadgad, Mörön, Ulaangom, Gov-Altai, Choibalsan and Khovd. It is really stingy on baggage allowance, allowing only 15kg (including hand luggage); any kilogram over the limit costs around T3000. Credit card and cash payments are accepted. AeroMongolia also serves Hohhot in China, and Irkutsk in Russia.

Blue Sky Aviation (☎011-312 085; www.blueskyaviation.mn) Has a nine-seat Cessna that can be chartered for any part of the country.

EZ Nis (☎011-333 311; www.eznisairways.com) Operates Swedish-built Saab 340B propeller aeroplanes. Has domestic flights to/from UB and Choibalsan, Mörön, Donoi (Uliastai), Ulaangom, Khovd, Bayan-Ölgii, Bayankhongor, Gov-Altai, Dalanzadgad and Oyu Tolgoi. Schedules change frequently so check the website for the latest information. It's a slick and reliable operation, but more expensive than AeroMongolia.

MIAT (☎011-322 118; http://miat.com) The state-owned airline that once flew to every corner of the country. It no longer operates any domestic routes.

Checking In

Get to the airport at least one hour before your flight. Even if you have a ticket, flight number and an allocated seat number, don't assume the plane won't be overbooked. Try to make certain your luggage has gone on the plane. Gas canisters are not allowed on any flight.

Costs

The foreigner price is often higher than what locals pay for tickets. Anyone can buy a ticket on your behalf, but you will always have to pay in US dollars (or by credit card in Ulaanbaatar). Tickets can be pricey; a one-way fare to Dalanzadgad costs US$200 while a flight to Bayan-Ölgii goes for about US$350. However, considering the overland alternative to Ölgii is a 50-hour trip in an overstuffed van, it's not surprising many choose to fly. Children aged between five and 16 years pay half; under fives fly free. If you've come on a student visa you can get 25% to 50% off the cost of the ticket.

Ask about baggage allowances when you buy your aeroplane ticket. EZ Nis allows you to carry 20kg without extra charges.

Reservations & Tickets

A domestic ticket reservation isn't worth diddly-squat until you have a ticket in your hand. In the countryside, buy your ticket as soon as you arrive.

It's now possible to buy a domestic airline e-ticket with Mongolia's domestic carriers (EZ Nis and AeroMongolia). Try to book your domestic flights as soon as you can as flights fill up in summer.

You can buy a return ticket in Ulaanbaatar but it's still a good idea to reconfirm your reservation at the airport as soon as you arrive at your destination.

If you wish to fly in one direction and return by road in the other (for example to Mörön), it's best to fly from Ulaanbaatar, where you are more likely to get a ticket and a seat, and then return overland – otherwise you may wait days or more for a flight and ticket in Mörön.

Seats can be difficult to get in summer, especially in the July tourist peak and in late August as students return to college.

> **DEPARTURE TAX**
>
> A T2000 domestic departure tax is payable at the airport.

Bicycle

For keen bikers with a sense of adventure, Mongolia offers an unparalleled cycling experience. The vast, open steppes make for rough travel but if properly equipped there is nothing stopping you from travelling pretty much anywhere (although a trip to the Gobi could only be done with vehicle support). For details on cycle touring, see p27.

Boat

Although there are 397km of navigable waterways in Mongolia, rivers aren't used for transporting people or cargo. The biggest boat in the country is the *Sükhbaatar*, which occasionally travels around Khövsgöl Nuur. There's also a customs boat that patrols the Selenge Gol on the border of Russia and Mongolia. Some ger camps at Khövsgöl Nuur also own small boats that can be chartered.

ROAD DISTANCES (KM)

	Altai (Gov-Altai aimag)	Arvaikheer	Baruun-Urt	Bayankhongor	Bulgan	Choibalsan	Dalanzadgad	Darkhan	Khovd	Mandalgov	Mörön (Khövsgöl aimag)	Ölgii	Öndörkhaan	Sainshand	Sükhbaatar	Tsetserleg	Ulaanbaatar	Ulaangom
Arvaikheer	571																	
Baruun-Urt	1561	990																
Bayankhongor	371	200	1190															
Bulgan	874	373	878	503														
Choibalsan	1656	1085	191	1285	973													
Dalanzadgad	948	377	856	577	725	1074												
Darkhan	1122	596	779	751	248	874	772											
Khovd	424	995	1985	795	1180	2080	1372	1519										
Mandalgov	879	308	613	508	578	741	293	479	1303									
Mörön (Khövsgöl aimag)	583	679	1231	627	353	1326	1056	601	853	913								
Ölgii	635	1206	2196	1006	1344	2291	1583	1582	211	1314	991							
Öndörkhaan	1332	761	229	961	649	324	710	550	1756	417	1002	1967						
Sainshand	1234	663	340	863	781	531	516	682	1658	355	1134	1869	302					
Sükhbaatar	1214	688	871	830	340	966	864	92	1612	571	693	1823	642	774				
Tsetserleg	502	266	1013	218	289	1108	643	537	438	500	413	1220	784	855	629			
Ulaanbaatar	1001	430	560	630	326	655	553	219	1425	260	671	1636	331	463	311	430		
Ulaangom	662	1188	1896	988	1033	991	1585	1281	238	1383	680	311	1667	1738	1373	883	1336	
Uliastai	218	659	1544	497	807	1639	1074	989	465	967	388	676	1315	1355	1147	531	984	529

Bus

Private bus companies connect Ulaanbaatar to the other aimag capitals. Large buses that can accommodate 40-plus passengers make a daily run to most cities. However, cities in the far west such as Khovd, Bayan-Ölgii and Uvs are served by minivans that run every other day.

The benefit of the regularly scheduled buses and vans is that they leave on time and drive straight to their destination, as opposed to private vans, which run on Mongolian time. With the government buses you also get an assigned seat.

However, the government buses have their share of discomforts. One problem is that there seems to be no restriction on luggage so boxes and bags tend to pile up in the aisles, which makes getting on and off the bus at breaks a real chore. Try getting a seat closer to the front of the bus to avoid the pile. Note that in winter, the heater will be turned to maximum, which is fine if you're up front or in the back (the heater is in the middle). However, if you are unfortunate enough to get the seat over the heater it will feel like you are hovering over a blast furnace. No matter what time of year it is, the driver will probably crank up the music. This is fine for an hour or two but if you want to get some sleep consider bringing noise-cancelling headphones.

Camel & Yak

Intractable yaks and confrontational camels are recognised forms of transport in Mongolia. Camels can carry the weight of an average-sized sumo wrestler. Yaks are also a useful and environmentally friendly way of hauling heavy cargo.

At Ongiin Khiid and Khongoryn Els you can arrange a multiple-day camel trek. A few travel agencies include a ride on a camel or yak in their program. Otherwise, you can always ask at a ger.

Car & Motorcycle

Travelling around Mongolia with your own car or motorcycle – without a driver – is dangerous business. What look like main roads on the map are often little more than tyre tracks in the dirt, sand or mud, and there is hardly a signpost in the whole country. In Mongolia, roads connect nomads, most of whom by their nature keep moving, so even the roads are seminomadic, shifting like restless rivers. Remote tracks quickly turn into eight-lane dirt highways devoid of any traffic, making navigation tricky – some drivers follow the telephone lines when there are any, or else ask for directions at gers along the way. Towns with food and water are few and far between, and very few people in the countryside will speak anything but Mongolian or, if you are lucky, Russian.

Having said that, people with an adventurous spirit do attempt to drive around Mongolia. To help you find your way around, use the GPS Coordinates Table (p274), which contains many towns and villages, and some sights. The coordinates for a number of other sights are included in the regional chapters.

Car Hire & Purchase

If you want to hire a car, contact **Drive Mongolia** (☎011-312 277, 9911 8257; www.drivemongolia.com), a tour operator that rents out Land Cruisers and other suitably rugged vehicles. Another company that offers self-drive trips is **Happy Camel** (☎9911 2075; www.happycamel.com), with rates somewhat higher than Drive Mongolia.

If you want to buy a vehicle, you will have to ask around, or check out the *tsaiz zakh* (car market) in the northeastern part of Ulaanbaatar. An old Russian 4x4 could go for around $3500. A good condition, used Ij Planeta – the Russian-made motorcycle you see all over the countryside – sells for around US$900. These tend to break down often but people in the countryside can help with repairs. A Japanese motorcycle will be more reliable. In markets the sign *'zarna'* (Зарна) on a jeep means 'for sale'.

Driving Licences

Travellers can use an international driving licence to drive any vehicle in Mongolia; expat residents need to apply for a local licence. If you buy a vehicle, enquire about registration at the local police station.

Fuel

Two types of Russian fuel are available: '95' is the best and the type used by Japanese jeeps, but it's only generally available in Ulaanbaatar; all Russian-made vehicles use '76', which is all that is available in the countryside. Petrol stations are marked by the initials 'ШТС', which is Mongolian for station.

Hitching

Hitching is never entirely safe in any country in the world and we don't normally recommend it. People who choose to hitch will be safer if they travel in pairs and let someone know where they are planning to go.

Mongolia is different, however. Because the country is so vast, public transport so limited and the people so poor, hitching (usually on trucks) is a recognised – and, often, the only – form of transport in the countryside. Hitching is seldom free and often no different from just waiting for public transport to turn up. It is *always* slow; after stopping at gers to drink, fixing flat tyres, breaking down, running out of petrol and getting stuck in mud and rivers, a truck can take 48 hours to cover 200km.

Hitching is not generally dangerous personally, but it is still hazardous and often extremely uncomfortable. Don't expect much traffic in remote rural areas; you might see one or two vehicles a day on many roads, and sometimes nobody at all for several days. In the towns, ask at the market, where trucks invariably hang around, or at the bus/truck/jeep station. The best place to wait is the petrol station on the outskirts of town, where most vehicles stop before any journey.

If you rely on hitching entirely, though, you will just travel from one dreary aimag town to another. You still need to hire a jeep to see, for example, the Gobi Desert, the mountains in Khentii or some of the lakes in the far west.

Truck drivers will normally expect some negotiable payment, which won't be much cheaper than a long-distance bus or shared jeep; figure on around T3000 per hour travelled.

Bring a water- and dust-proof bag to put your backpack in. The most important things to bring, though, are an extremely large amount of patience and time, and a high threshold for discomfort. Carry camping gear for the inevitable breakdowns, or suffer along with your travel mates.

Local Transport

Bus, Minibus & Trolleybus

In Ulaanbaatar, crowded trolleybuses and buses ply the main roads for around T300 a ride. Cities such as Darkhan and Erdenet have minibuses that shuttle from one end of town to the other, but you are unlikely to need them because most facilities are located centrally.

Taxi

Only in UB and a couple of the bigger cities is there taxi service, though in UB any vehicle on the street is a potential taxi – just flag down the driver and agree on a price. The rate at the time of writing was T400 per kilometre, but this will certainly increase.

Minivan & Jeep

Both minivans and jeeps are used for long- and short-distance travel in the

THE MONGOL RALLY

In an age when getting from point A to point B has been simplified to the point of blandness, the Mongol Rally attempts to put a bit of spark back into the journey to Mongolia. According to rally rules, the London-to-Mongolia trip must be made in a vehicle that has an engine capacity of 1L or less. In other words, you have to travel 16,000km (10,000 miles) across some of the world's most hostile terrain in an old clunker barely capable of making it over the A83 to Campbeltown.

The wacky idea of driving from London to Mongolia in a clapped-out banger was dreamt up in 2001 by Englishman Thomas Morgan, whose own attempt to accomplish the feat failed miserably somewhere east of Tabriz. Morgan had another go in 2004 and completed the trip, along with a few friends who were inspired by the utter lunacy of it all. Since then the Mongol Rally has become an annual rite of passage for English adventurers.

The journey begins by selecting a vehicle. Gutless wonders such as old Fiat Pandas and Citroëns are suitable (so long as it's a 1.0ish-litre engine). Next, assemble your team – you can have as many people as you can squeeze into the damn thing. Then pay your dues: it's £714 to enter and then you must raise another £1000, which will go to a charity in Mongolia or another country en route (the Mongol Rally has raised over £1.6 million in charity money so far). Finally, zoom out of London with 500 other likeminded drivers in July.

The organisers give absolutely no advice on how to actually get to Mongolia; that you've got to figure out on your own. Teams have travelled as far north as the Arctic Circle and as far south as Afghanistan on their way across the Asian landmass. This is by no means a race – whether you arrive first or last, your only reward is a round of free beers at the finish line. Some teams make the trip in around five weeks, while others have taken as long as three months, stopping off at places en route.

The rally is organised by the grandly titled **League of Adventurists International** (www.theadventurists.com). If you want to sign up, contact the organisers early as there are only a limited number of spots available and these sell out a year in advance.

countryside. They can be shared among strangers, which is good for a group of people headed from one aimag centre to another (or usually to/from Ulaanbaatar). Alternatively, they can be hired privately. In most cases, the grey 11-seat Furgon minivans are used for longer cross-country trips that see a lot of traffic. Jeeps, khaki-coloured or green, are found in more remote areas such as *sum* (district) centres. They are nicknamed *jaran yös* (shortened to *jaris*), which means '69' – the number of the original model. The large and comfortable Toyota Land Cruiser–style jeeps are owned by wealthy Mongolians and never used for share purposes (though some travel agencies might have them for hire, but expect to pay at least 30% more than for a good Russian jeep).

On the terrible Mongolian roads, these jeeps and minivans are an important form of transport, and are mandatory when visiting more remote attractions. They can typically only travel between 30km/h and 50km/h. The Gobi region generally has the best roads and here you can average 60km/h.

SHARE MINIVAN & JEEP

Share jeeps and minivans are the most common form of public transport in Mongolia. Private vehicles go from Ulaanbaatar to all aimag capitals, major cities and tourist destinations. Less frequent and reliable services operate between most aimag capitals, but very few jeeps go to the *sums*.

If you rely solely on share vehicles to get around, you'll see surprisingly little of Mongolia. Most vehicles drive between uninteresting cities with little to see on the way. You'll still need to hire a car from the aimag or *sum* centres to see anything, and it's usually easier to organise this from Ulaanbaatar.

For a long-distance trip bring snacks and water; stops at a roadside *guanz* (canteen or cheap restaurant) can be few and far between. You can expect at least one breakdown and it would be a good idea to bring a sleeping bag and warm clothes just in case you have to spend the night somewhere. Long-distance travel of over 10 hours is fiendishly uncomfortable. Most people who take a long-distance minivan to Mörön or Dalanzadgad end up flying back.

Costs & Departure Times

Minivan or jeep fares are usually about 10% more than a bus fare, largely because they can drive faster than a bus. In the countryside, the post office operates postal vans, which accept passengers. They have fixed departure times, normally running once a week between an aimag capital and a *sum* capital. The local post office should have a list of departure times and fares.

HIRING A MINIVAN OR JEEP

The best way to see the countryside of Mongolia independently is to hire your own minivan or jeep, which will come with a driver and, for a little extra, a guide. If you share the costs with others it doesn't work out to be too expensive. With enough time, camping equipment, water and food, and a reliable jeep and driver, you'll have the time of your life.

You can save money by using public transport to major regional gateways – that is Mörön for Khövsgöl Nuur, Khovd for the west, Dalanzadgad for the south Gobi and Choibalsan for the far east. Then, from these places, you will be able to rent a jeep fairly easily, though drivers outside Ulaanbaatar will have little experience of dealing with tourists. You may not find a local English-speaking guide, so bring one from Ulaanbaatar.

Don't expect to rent a jeep outside of an aimag capital. Villages do have jeeps, but they may not be available or running.

Note that when hiring a vehicle in the countryside to take you to another rural city you will have to pay for the return fare because the driver will have to go back with an empty van. This does not apply when travelling to Ulaanbaatar as the driver can find passengers there. The upshot of this is that it will cost almost the same to hire a driver to take you from, for example, Ulaangom to Mörön as it would from Ulaangom to Ulaanbaatar.

Where to Hire

In Ulaanbaatar, the best place to start looking for a driver and a guide is at the various guesthouses. These guesthouses will take a commission, but you'll get a driver and/or guide who understands the needs of a tourist. More importantly they know the tourist routes and can locate hard-to-find attractions such as caves, deer stones and ruined monasteries. Finding a driver from the market, and negotiating on your own, will be cheaper, but the driver will probably be in a hurry to get back home, which won't work well if you want to take it slow and see the sights.

Costs

On a long-distance trip, tour operators will have a per-day charge (usually US$100) that will probably include petrol. This may be more if they throw in camping and cooking gear.

Vehicles that you hire on your own (from a market) usually charge T60,000 per day without petrol. Russian jeeps have terrible fuel economy: you'll need 20L to travel around 100km. Petrol was around T1350 per litre at the time of research. Some drivers may want to charge a per-kilometre rate; in the countryside this is around T600 to T800. Vehicle hire is more expensive the further you get from Ulaanbaatar.

Agreeing on Terms

It is vital that you and the driver agree to the terms and conditions – and the odometer reading – before you start. Ask about all possible 'extras' such as waiting time, food and accommodation. There are several private bridges and tolls around the countryside (each costing about T500), which are normally paid for by you. If you arrange for a jeep to pick you up, or drop you off, agree on a reduced price for the empty vehicle travelling one way.

Numbers

Three can sit in the back seat of a Russian jeep, but it may be uncomfortable on longer trips. Five or six people can ride in a minivan. If you also take a guide, rather than just a driver, you can therefore take a maximum of three passengers in a jeep, though two would be more comfortable.

THE MINIVAN WAITING GAME

A real problem with share vehicles is that they are privately operated and won't leave until they are packed tighter than a sardine tin. The waiting game sometimes has the effect of turning your hair grey.

In the countryside, most vans just park at the local market and wait for passengers to turn up, which means that if the van isn't already mostly full you'll be waiting around all day for the seats to fill up, if they ever do.

The process can be agonising. Even after the 11-seat van has 20 or so passengers, the driver will vanish for an hour or two for lunch, or to find more cargo, spare parts and petrol.

One solution is to ask the driver to pick you up at your hotel or the local internet cafe when they are ready to go, which they usually agree to. This arrangement works out well and allows you to do something productive (such as sleep or catch up on your email) while the other passengers sweat it out at the market. If you have a mobile phone, give the driver your number and they will call you when they are ready to go.

The waiting time from Ulaanbaatar isn't as bad, but you can still count on two hours or more.

The table shows latitude and longitude coordinates for various locations in Mongolia, in degrees, minutes and decimal minutes (DMM). To convert to degrees, minutes and seconds (DMS) format, multiply the number after the decimal point (including the decimal point) by 60. The result is your seconds, which can be rounded to the nearest whole number. The minutes is the number between the degree symbol and the decimal point. For example: 43°52.598′ DMM is equal to 43°52′36" DMS.

CENTRAL MONGOLIA	Latitude (N)	Longitude (E)
Arvaikheer	46°15.941	102°46.724
Bat-Ölzii	46°49.028	102°13.989
Battsengel	47°48.157	101°59.040
Bayan-Öndör	46°30.018	104°05.996
Bayan Önjuul	46°52.859	105°56.571
Bayangol	45°48.505	103°26.811
Bayantsagaan	46°45.806	107°08.709
Bogd	44°39.971	102°08.777
Burenbayan Ulaan	45°10.276	101°25.989
Chuluut	47°32.830	100°13.166
Delgerkhan	46°37.097	104°33.051
Eej Khad (Mother Rock)	47°18.699	106°58.583
Erdenemandal	48°31.445	101°22.265
Erdenesant	47°19.071	104°28.937
Guchin Us	45°27.866	102°23.726
Gunjiin Süm	48°11.010	107°33.377
Ikh Tamir	47°35.221	101°12.413
Jargalant	48°43.716	100°45.120
Khandgait	48°07.066	106°54.296
Khangai	47°51.553	99°26.126
Kharkhorin	47°11.981	102°50.527
Khashant	47°27.034	103°09.708
Khotont	47°22.196	102°28.746
Khujirt	46°54.225	102°46.545
Khustain National Park	47°45.459	105°52.418
Mandshir Khiid	47°45.520	106°59.675
Möngönmorit	48°12.192	108°28.291
Naiman Nuur	46°31.232	101°50.705
Ögii Nuur (Lake)	47°47.344	102°45.828
Ögii Nuur	47°40.319	102°33.051
Ölziit	48°05.573	102°32.640
Ondor Ulaan	48°02.700	100°30.446
Orkhon Khürkhree	46°47.234	101°57.694
Övgön Khiid	47°25.561	103°41.686
Stele of Tonyukuk	47°41.661	107°28.586
Tariat	48°09.574	99°52.982
Terelj	47°59.193	107°27.834
Tögrög	45°32.482	102°59.657
Tövkhön Khiid	47°00.772	102°15.362
Tsakhir	49°06.426	99°08.574
Tsenkher	47°26.909	101°45.648
Tsetseguun Uul	47°48.506	107°00.165
Tsetserleg City	47°28.561	101°27.282
Tsetserleg Soum	48°53.095	101°14.305
Ulaanbaatar	47°55.056	106°55.007
Uyanga	46°27.431	102°16.731
Zaamar	48°11.843	104°46.629
Züünbayan-Ulaan	46°31.176	102°34.971
Zuunmod	47°42.357	106°56.861

EASTERN MONGOLIA	Latitude (N)	Longitude (E)
Asgat	46°21.724	113°34.536
Baldan Bereeven Khiid	48°11.910	109°25.840
Baruun-Urt	46°40.884	113°16.825
Batnorov	47°56.952	111°30.103
Batshireet	48°41.405	110°11.062
Bayan Tumen	48°03.076	114°22.252
Bayan Uul	49°07.550	112°42.809
Bayandun	49°15.276	113°21.565
Binder	48°36.967	110°36.400
Chinggis Statue	47°06.157	109°09.356
Choibalsan	48°04.147	114°31.404
Chuluunkhoroot	49°52.163	115°43.406
Dadal	49°01.291	111°37.598
Dashbalbar	49°32.794	114°24.720
Delgerkhaan	47°10.735	109°11.423
Erdenetsagaan	45°54.165	115°22.149
Galshar	46°13.324	110°50.606
Khalkhgol	47°59.565	118°05.760
Khalzan	46°10.019	112°57.119
Kherlen Bar Khot	48°03.287	113°21.865
Khökh Nuur (Blue Lake)	48°01.150	108°56.450
Matad	46°57.007	115°16.008
Mönkh Khaan	46°58.163	112°03.418
Norovlin	48°41.449	111°59.596
Öglöchiin Kherem	48°24.443	110°11.812
Ömnödelger	47°53.469	109°49.166
Öndörkhaan	47°19.416	110°39.775
Ongon	45°21.509	113°08.297
Shiliin Bogd	45°28.350	114°35.349
Sükhbaatar	46°46.285	113°52.646
Sümber	47°38.174	118°36.421
Tsagaan Ovoo	48°33.864	113°14.380
Tsenkhermandal	47°44.673	109°03.909
Uul Bayan	46°30.036	112°20.769

NORTHERN MONGOLIA	Latitude (N)	Longitude (E)
Altanbulag	50°19.225	106°29.392
Amarbayasgalant Khiid	49°28.648	105°05.122
Arbulag	49°54.949	99°26.537
Baruunburen	49°09.753	104°48.686
Bayangol	48°55.472	106°05.486
Borsog	50°59.677	100°42.983
Bugat	49°02.874	103°40.389
Bulgan City	48°48.722	103°32.213
Chandman-Öndör	50°28.436	100°56.378
Chuluut and Ider	49°10.415	100°40.335
Darkhan	49°29.232	105°56.480
Dashchoinkhorlon Khiid	48°47.821	103°30.687
Dashinchinlen	47°51.179	104°02.281
Dulaankhaan	49°55.103	106°11.302
Erdenebulgan	50°06.880	101°35.589
Erdenet	49°01.855	104°03.316
Five Rivers	49°15.475	100°40.385
Gurvanbulag	47°44.499	103°30.103

Jiglegiin Am	51°00.406	100°16.003
Khangal	49°18.810	104°22.629
Khankh	51°30.070	100°41.382
Khar Bukh Balgas	47°53.198	103°53.513
Khatgal	50°26.517	100°09.599
Khishig-Öndör	48°17.678	103°27.086
Khötöl	49°05.486	105°34.903
Khutag-Öndör	49°22.990	102°41.417
Mogod	48°16.372	102°59.520
Mörön	49°38.143	100°09.321
Orkhon	49°08.621	105°24.891
Orkhontuul	48°49.202	104°49.920
Renchinlkhumbe	51°06.504	99°40.234
Saikhan	48°39.448	102°37.851
Selenge	49°26.647	103°58.903
Shine-Ider	48°57.213	99°32.297
Sükhbaatar	50°14.196	106°11.911
Teshig	49°57.649	102°35.657
Toilogt	50°39.266	100°14.961
Tosontsengel	49°28.650	100°53.074
Tsagaan Uur	50°32.391	101°31.806
Tsagaannuur (Khövsgöl)	51°21.778	99°21.082
Tsagaannuur (Selenge)	50°05.835	105°25.989
Tsetserleg	49°31.959	97°46.011
Ulaan Uul	50°40.668	99°13.920
Uran Uul	48°59.855	102°44.003
Züünkharaa	48°51.466	106°27.154

THE GOBI	Latitude (N)	Longitude (E)
Altai City	46°22.388	96°15.164
Altai Soum	44°37.010	94°55.131
Altanshiree	45°32.046	110°27.017
Baatsagaan	45°33.266	99°26.188
Baga Gazryn Chuluu	46°13.827	106°04.192
Bayan Dalai	43°27.898	103°30.763
Bayan-Ovoo	42°58.607	106°06.994
Bayan-Uul	46°59.129	95°11.863
Bayanbulag	46°48.223	98°06.189
Bayangovi	44°44.017	100°23.476
Bayankhongor	46°11.637	100°43.115
Bayanlig	44°32.555	100°49.809
Bayanzag	44°08.311	103°43.667
Biger	45°42.583	97°10.354
Bömbogor	46°12.279	99°37.234
Böön Tsagaan Nuur	45°37.114	99°15.350
Bugat	45°33.440	94°20.571
Bulgan	44°05.312	103°32.297
Buutsagaan	46°10.411	98°41.637
Choir	45°47.994	109°18.462
Dalanzadgad	43°34.355	104°25.673
Delger	46°21.074	97°22.011
Delgerekh	45°48.157	111°12.823
Erdenedalai	46°00.418	104°56.996
Erdentsogt	46°25.080	100°49.234
Galuut	46°42.061	100°07.131
Govi-Ugtal	46°01.916	107°30.377
Gurj Lamiin Khiid	43°29.030	103°50.930
Gurvantes	43°13.759	101°03.360
Jargalant	47°01.480	99°30.103
Khamaryn Khiid	44°36.038	110°16.650
Khanbogd	43°12.000	107°11.862
Khatanbulag	43°08.882	109°08.709
Khökhmorit	47°21.248	94°30.446
Khövsgöl	43°36.314	109°39.017
Khüreemaral	46°24.523	98°17.037
Mandakh	44°24.122	108°13.851
Mandal-Ovoo	44°39.100	104°02.880
Mandalgov	45°46.042	106°16.380
Manlai	44°04.441	106°51.703
Nomgon	42°50.160	105°08.983
Ondorshil	45°13.585	108°15.223
Ongiin Khiid	45°20.367	104°00.306
Orog Nuur	45°02.692	100°36.314
Saikhan-Ovoo	45°27.459	103°54.110
Sainshand	44°53.576	110°08.351
Sevrei	43°35.617	102°09.737
Shinejist	44°32.917	99°17.349
Süm Khökh Burd	46°09.621	105°45.590
Taihshir	46°42.671	96°29.623
Takhi Research Station	45°32.197	93°39.055
Tsagaan Agui	44°42.604	101°10.187
Tseel	45°33.266	95°51.223
Tsogt	45°20.813	96°37.166
Tsogt-Ovoo	44°24.906	105°19.406
Tsogttsetsii	43°43.541	105°35.040
Ulaanbadrakh	43°52.598	110°24.686
Yolyn Am	43°29.332	104°04.000
Zag	46°56.168	99°09.806
Zamyn-Üüd	43°42.967	111°54.651

WESTERN MONGOLIA	Latitude (N)	Longitude (E)
Altai	45°49.115	92°15.497
Altantsögts	49°02.700	100°26.057
Batuunturuun	49°38.578	94°23.177
Bulgan (Bayan-Ölgii)	46°55.559	91°04.594
Bulgan (Khovd)	46°05.486	91°32.571
Chandmani	43°39.100	92°48.411
Darvi	46°56.181	93°37.158
Deluun	47°51.553	90°44.160
Dörgon	48°19.768	92°37.303
Erdeneburen	48°30.131	91°26.811
Erdenkhairkhan	48°07.228	95°44.229
Khökh Nuur	47°37.207	97°20.546
Khovd (Uvs)	49°16.720	90°54.720
Khovd City	48°00.430	91°38.474
Mankhan	47°24.557	92°12.617
Möst	46°41.626	92°48.000
Naranbulag	49°23.164	92°34.286
Nogoonuur	49°36.923	90°13.577
Ölgii (Uvs)	49°01.306	92°00.411
Ölgii City	48°58.070	89°58.028
Öndörkhangai	49°15.849	94°51.154
Otgon	47°12.488	97°36.391
Sagsai	48°54.688	89°39.429
Telmen	48°38.197	97°09.900
Tes	49°39.013	95°49.029
Tolbo	48°24.557	90°16.457
Tolbo Nuur	48°35.320	90°04.536
Tosontsengel	48°45.286	98°05.992
Tsagaanchuluut	47°06.531	96°39.497
Tsagaankhairkhan	49°24.209	94°13.440
Tsagaannuur	49°31.437	89°46.697
Tsengel	48°57.213	89°09.257
Tsenkheriin Agui	47°20.828	91°57.225
Tüdevtei	48°59.390	96°32.229
Ulaangom	49°58.764	92°04.028
Ulaankhus	49°02.525	89°26.929
Uliastai	47°44.591	96°50.582
Urgamal	48°30.653	94°16.046
Üüreg Nuur	50°05.236	91°04.587
Zavkhan (Uvs)	48°49.463	93°06.103
Zavkhanmandal	48°19.071	95°06.789

There is usually ample room at the back of the jeep and minivan for backpacks, tents, water and so on.

Trip Preparation

There are several other factors you should consider when embarking on a jeep or minivan tour of Mongolia. Before the trip, explain your itinerary in detail to the driver and make sure they have a map and agree to the route. For long expeditions, also ensure your driver has jerry cans, for extra petrol, and a water drum. A wide-mouthed plastic drum is also very useful for storing food, as boxes will rapidly disintegrate. Resealable bags are useful for opened bags of sugar, pasta and so on. Your backpacks will get filthy so it's a good idea to put them in a water- and dust-proof bag.

Supplies

Drivers from tourist agencies will assume that you will feed them along the way. On a longer trip it's easiest for everyone to cook, eat and wash up together. If you don't want to do this, you will have to agree on a fee for the driver's food or buy them the food yourself. This shouldn't cost more than T7000 per day.

Experienced drivers will have their own Soviet-built petrol stove, though it's a good idea to bring your own stove as a backup, and to boil water for tea while the other stove is cooking dinner. If you are cooking for a group you'll need a big cooking pot and a ladle. Everyone should bring their own penknife, cutlery, bowl and torch. Avoid drinking from the same water bottles as this spreads viruses around the group.

On the Road

Shop as a group when you reach a city or town. If you are travelling with strangers, it's a good idea to keep everyone happy by rotating seats so that everyone (including the guide) has a go in the front seat. Don't push the driver or guide too hard; allow them (and the vehicle) to stop and rest. However, regular and lengthy stops for a chat and a smoke can add time to the journey.

Lastly, if you are on a long trip, you'll find morale boosted by a trip to a bathhouse (hot water!) in an aimag capital. Another morale booster is the occasional meal in a decent *guanz*. If you are camping a lot then add in at least one night in a decent hotel to clean up and sort out your stuff.

Guides

Few people in the countryside speak anything other than Mongolian and Russian, so a guide-cum-translator is very handy, and almost mandatory. A guide will explain local traditions, help with any hassles with the police, find accommodation, explain captions in museums and act as linguistic and cultural interpreter.

In Ulaanbaatar you can find guides through travel agencies and guesthouses. In the countryside, there is nothing to do but ask – try the hotels and schools. Guides are easier to find between 15 June and 1 August, when schools and universities are on summer break.

For getting around Ulaanbaatar, a nonprofessional guide or a student will cost a negotiable US$8 to US$15 per day. To take one around the countryside from the capital you will have to include expenses for travel, food and accommodation. In an aimag capital, a guide (if you can find one) costs about US$5 per day, plus any expenses. For a professional guide who is knowledgeable in a specific interest, such as bird-watching, and fluent in your language, the bidding starts at US$20 per day.

Shortcuts

The quickest distance between two points is a straight

TAKING A GPS

When you are travelling around the featureless plains of eastern Mongolia, the deserts of the Gobi or a tangle of confusing valleys in the west, a Global Positioning System (GPS) can be very useful in determining where exactly you are, as long as you have a reliable map on which to pinpoint your coordinates. We have given GPS coordinates for many hard-to-find places in this book, plus coordinates for *sum* (district) and aimag centres. Many places are listed in the table on p274.

A GPS won't help you every time, as you'll still need to know which road to take, even if you know the rough direction. Gobi and steppe areas are particularly tricky – except for the main routes there probably won't be any one road between places. Every few kilometres the track you're on will veer off in the wrong direction, requiring constant corrections and zigzagging.

It is always a good idea to ask about road conditions at gers along the way. Often a good-looking road will become impassable, running into a river, swamp or wall of mountains; herders can offer good info on the best route to take. If all else fails, you can always rely on Mongolian GPS (Ger Positioning System), which requires following the vague sweep of the ger owner's hand over the horizon, until you reach the next ger.

line, and the only thing that could (but not always) put off a Mongolian jeep driver from taking a shortcut is a huge mountain range or raging river. If renting a jeep by the kilometre, you will welcome a shortcut, especially to shorten an uncomfortable trip.
If you have an experienced driver, allow him to take shortcuts when he feels it is worthwhile, but don't insist on any – he is the expert. The downside of shortcuts is the possibility of breaking down on more isolated roads.

Breakdowns

Serious mechanical breakdowns are a definite possibility. Should your vehicle break down irreparably in a rural area, you'll be faced with the task of trying to get back to civilisation either on foot (not recommended), by hitching, or by whatever means is available. The safest solution is to travel with a small group using two jeeps. Make sure your driver has tools and at least one spare tyre.

A warning: Russian jeeps easily overheat. There is no easy solution, but it helps to travel during the early-morning or late-afternoon hours when temperatures are relatively low.

Getting Bogged

Most of Mongolia is grassland, desert and mountains. You might think that mountain driving would pose the worst problems, but forests cause the most trouble of all. This is because the ground, even on a slope, is often a springy alpine bog, holding huge amounts of water in the decaying grasses, which are instantly compacted under tyres, reducing a wildflower meadow to slush.

Mongolian drivers have one of two reactions when they get bogged. Some will sit on their haunches, have a smoke and then send word to the nearest farm or town for a tractor to come and tow the vehicle out. Other drivers will get out a shovel and start digging; you can help by gathering flat stones to place under the wheels (drivers usually try to jack the tyres out of the mud).

Taxi

Mongolia claims to have about 49,250km of highway – of which only around 2800km is actually paved. Taxis are only useful along these paved roads, eg from Ulaanbaatar to Zuunmod, Terelj, Darkhan, Erdenet, Bulgan, Kharkhorin and Öndörkhaan. But just as a Humvee is impractical on Hong Kong's backstreets, so is a Hyundai-style taxi on the unpaved steppes. The general appalling quality of roads around the countryside means that most travel is by jeep or Furgon minivan.

Train

The 1810km of railway line is primarily made up of the Trans-Mongolian Railway (p242), connecting China with Russia. (Both the domestic and international trains use this same line.) In addition, there are two spur lines: to the copper-mining centre of Erdenet (from Darkhan) and the coal-mining city of Baganuur (from Ulaanbaatar). Another train runs weekly from Choibalsan, the capital of Dornod aimag, to the Russian border.

From Ulaanbaatar, daily express trains travel north to Darkhan, and on to Sükhbaatar or Erdenet. To the south, there are daily direct trains from Ulaanbaatar to Zamyn-Üüd, via Choir and Sainshand. There are also trains terminating at Choir twice a week. You can't use the Trans-Mongolian Railway for domestic transport.

When travelling in hard-seat class (see below), you will almost certainly have to fight to get a seat. If you're not travelling alone, one of you can scramble on board and find seats and the other can bring the luggage on board. The food available on the local trains is usually of poor quality so it's best to bring snacks, fruit and instant noodles.

Classes

There are usually three classes on domestic passenger trains: hard seat, hard sleeper and soft seat. In hard-seat class, the seats are actually padded bunks but there are no assigned bunks or any limit to the amount of tickets sold, so the carriages are always crowded and dirty. A hard sleeper *(platzkartnuu)* looks just like the hard seat but everyone gets their own bunk and there is the option of getting a set of sheets and a blanket (T1000). Upgrades are available to soft seat if you decide you can't stand the hard seats.

Soft seats are only a little bit softer, but the conditions are much better: the price difference (usually at least double the price of the hard seat) is prohibitive for most Mongolians. The soft-seat carriages are divided into compartments with four beds in each. You are given an assigned bed, and will be able to sleep, assuming, of course, that your compartment mates aren't rip-roaring drunk and noisy. If you travel at night, clean sheets are provided for about T1100, which is a wise investment since some of the quilts smell like mutton. Compared with hard-seat class, it's the lap of luxury, and worth paying extra.

If you're travelling from Ulaanbaatar, it is important to book a soft seat well in advance – this can be done up to 10 days before departure. There may be a small booking fee. In general, booking ahead is a good idea for any class, though there will always be hard-seat tickets available.

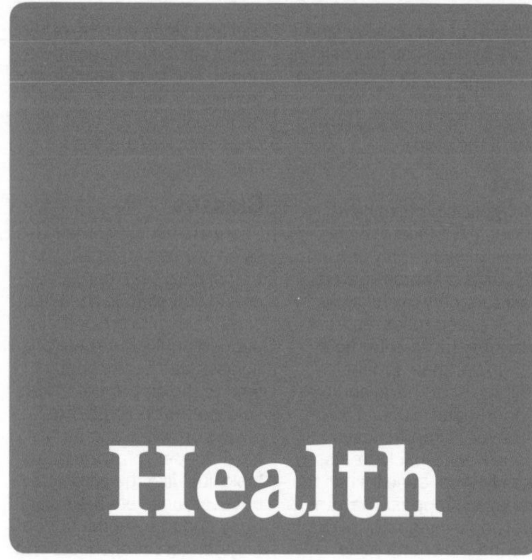

Health

Mongolia's dry, cold climate and sparse human habitation means there are few of the infectious diseases that plague tropical countries in Asia. The rough-and-tumble landscape and lifestyle, however, presents challenges of its own. Injuries sustained from falling off a horse are common in the summer season. In winter, the biggest threats are the flu and pneumonia, which spread like wildfire in November.

If you do become seriously ill in Mongolia, your local embassy can provide details of Western doctors. Serious emergencies may require evacuation to Seoul or Beijing. If in the countryside, make a beeline for Ulaanbaatar to have your ailment diagnosed.

The following advice is a general guide only; be sure to seek the advice of a doctor trained in travel medicine.

BEFORE YOU GO

Prevention is the key to staying healthy while abroad. A little planning before departure, particularly for pre-existing illnesses, will save trouble later. See your dentist before going on a long trip, carry a spare pair of contact lenses and glasses, and take your optical prescription with you. Bring medications in their original, clearly labelled containers. A signed and dated letter from your physician describing your medical conditions and medications, including generic names, is also a good idea.

Western medicine can be in short supply in Mongolia. Most medicine comes from China and Russia, and the labels won't be in English, so bring whatever you think you might need from home. Take extra supplies of prescribed medicine and divide it into separate pieces of luggage; that way if one piece goes astray, you'll still have a backup supply.

Insurance

If your health insurance does not cover you for medical expenses abroad, consider supplemental insurance. (Check the Lonely Planet website at www.lonelyplanet.com/travel_services for more information.)

While you may prefer a policy that pays hospital bills on the spot, rather than paying first and sending in documents later, the only place in Mongolia that might accept this is the SOS Medica clinic (see p71).

Declare any existing medical conditions to the insurance company; if your problem is pre-existing, the company will not cover you if it is not declared. You may require extra cover for adventurous activities – make sure you are covered for a fall if you plan on riding a horse or a motorbike. If you are uninsured, emergency evacuation is expensive, with bills over US$100,000 not uncommon.

Medical Checklist

Following is a list of items you should consider including in your medical kit – consult your pharmacist for brands available in your country.

- Antibacterial cream (eg Muciprocin)
- Antibiotics (prescription only) – for travel well 'off the beaten track', carry the prescription with you in case you need it refilled
- Antifungal cream or powder (eg Clotrimazole) – for fungal skin infections and thrush
- Antinausea medication (eg Prochlorperazine)
- Antiseptic (such as povidone-iodine) – for cuts and grazes
- Aspirin or paracetamol (acetaminophen in the USA) – for pain or fever
- Bandages, Band-Aids (plasters) and other wound dressings
- Calamine lotion, sting-relief spray or aloe vera – to ease irritation from sunburn and insect bites or stings
- Cold and flu tablets, throat lozenges and nasal decongestant
- Insect repellent (DEET-based)
- Loperamide or diphenoxylate – 'blockers' for diarrhoea
- Multivitamins – consider them for long trips, when dietary vitamin intake may be inadequate

» Rehydration mixture (eg Gastrolyte) – to prevent dehydration, which may occur during bouts of diarrhoea (particularly important when travelling with children)

» Scissors, tweezers and a thermometer – note that mercury thermometers are prohibited by airlines

» Sunscreen, lip balm and eye drops

» Water purification tablets or iodine (iodine is not to be used by pregnant women or people with thyroid problems)

Internet Resources

There is a wealth of travel health advice on the internet. For further information, the Lonely Planet website at www.lonelyplanet.com is a good place to start. The WHO publishes a superb book called *International Travel & Health*, which is revised annually and is available online at no cost at www.who.int/ith. Another website of general interest is MD Travel Health at www.mdtravelhealth.com, which provides complete travel health recommendations for every country and is updated daily.

Further Reading

Lonely Planet's *Healthy Travel Asia & India* is a handy pocket-sized health guide. Other recommended references include *Traveller's Health* by Dr Richard Dawood and *Travelling Well* by Dr Deborah Mills (www.travellingwell.com.au). Lonely Planet's *Travel with Children* is useful for families.

IN MONGOLIA

Availability & Cost of Health Care

Health care is readily available in Ulaanbaatar, but choose your hospital and doctor carefully. Ordinary Mongolians won't know the best place to go, but a reputable travel agency or top-end hotel might. The best advice will come from your embassy. Consultations cost around US$5, although SOS Medica (see p71), a reliable clinic in Ulaanbaatar with Western doctors, charges around US$180. Most basic drugs are available without a prescription. Health services in the countryside are generally poor but improving in some aimag capitals. Taking very small children to the countryside is therefore risky. Female travellers will need to take pads and tampons with them, as these won't be available outside the main cities.

Infectious Diseases

Brucellosis

The most likely way for humans to contract this disease is by drinking unboiled milk or eating home-made cheese. People with open cuts on their hands who handle freshly killed meat can also be infected.

In humans, brucellosis causes severe headaches, joint and muscle pains, fever and fatigue. There may be diarrhoea and, later, constipation. The onset of the symptoms can occur from five days to several months after exposure, with the average time being two weeks.

Most patients recover in two or three weeks, but people can get chronic brucellosis, which recurs sporadically for months or years and can cause long-term health problems. Fatalities are rare but possible.

Brucellosis is a serious disease and requires blood tests to make the diagnosis. If you think you may have contracted the disease, seek medical attention, preferably outside Mongolia.

Bubonic Plague

This disease (which wiped out one-third of Europe during the Middle Ages) makes an appearance in remote parts of Mongolia in late summer. Almost 90% of reported cases occur in August and September.

The disease (also known as the Black Plague) is normally carried by rodents and can be transmitted to humans by bites from fleas that make their home on the infected animals. It can also be passed from human to human by coughing. The symptoms are fever and enlarged lymph nodes. The untreated disease has a 60% death rate, but if you get to a doctor it can be quickly treated. The best (but not only) drug is the antibiotic Gentamicin, which is available in Mongolia.

During an outbreak, travel to infected areas is prohibited, which can greatly affect overland travel. All trains, buses and cars travelling into Ulaanbaatar from infected areas are also thoroughly checked when an outbreak of the plague has been reported, and vehicles are sprayed with disinfectant.

Hepatitis

This is a general term for inflammation of the liver. The symptoms are similar in all forms of the illness, and include fever, chills, headache, fatigue and aches, followed by loss of appetite, nausea, vomiting, abdominal pain, dark urine, light-coloured faeces, jaundiced (yellow) skin and yellowing of the whites of the eyes. People who have hepatitis should avoid alcohol for some time after the illness, as the liver needs time to recover.

Hepatitis A is transmitted by contaminated food and drinking water. You should seek medical advice, but there is not much you can do apart from resting, drinking lots of fluids, eating lightly and avoiding fatty foods. Hepatitis E is transmitted in the same way as hepatitis A; it can be particularly serious in pregnant women.

Hepatitis B is endemic in Mongolia. It is spread through contact with infected blood, blood products or body fluids. The symptoms of hepatitis B may be more severe than type A and the disease can lead to long-term problems such as chronic liver damage, liver cancer or long-term carrier state. Hepatitis C and D are spread in the same way as hepatitis B and can also lead to long-term complications.

There are vaccines against hepatitis A and B, but there are currently no vaccines against the other types of hepatitis.

Rabies

In the Mongolian countryside, family dogs are often vicious and can be rabid; it is their saliva that is infectious. Any bite, scratch or even a lick from an animal should be cleaned immediately and thoroughly. Scrub with soap and running water, and then apply alcohol or iodine solution. Medical help should be sought promptly to receive a course of injections to prevent the onset of the symptoms and death. The incubation period for rabies depends on where you're bitten. On the head, face or neck it's as little as 10 days, whereas on the legs it's 60 days.

Tuberculosis (TB)

TB is a bacterial infection usually transmitted from person to person by coughing but which may be transmitted through consumption of unpasteurised milk. Milk that has been boiled is safe to drink, and the souring of milk to make yogurt or cheese also kills the bacilli. Travellers are usually not at great risk

REQUIRED & RECOMMENDED VACCINATIONS

Ask your doctor for an International Certificate of Vaccination (otherwise known as the yellow booklet), which will list all of the vaccinations you have received, and take it with you. The WHO recommends the following vaccinations for travel to Mongolia:

» **Adult Diphtheria & Tetanus** Single booster recommended if none in the previous 10 years. Side effects include sore arm and fever.

» **Hepatitis A** Provides almost 100% protection for up to a year; a booster after 12 months provides at least another 20 years' protection. Mild side effects such as headache and sore arm occur with some people.

» **Hepatitis B** Now considered routine for most travellers, it provides lifetime protection for 95% of people. Immunisation is given as three doses over six months, though a rapid schedule is also available, as is a combined vaccination for Hepatitis A. Side effects are mild and uncommon, usually headache and sore arm.

» **Measles, Mumps & Rubella (MMR)** Two doses of MMR are recommended unless you have had the diseases. Occasionally a rash and flu-like illness can develop a week after receiving the vaccine. Many young adults need a booster.

» **Typhoid** Recommended unless your trip is less than a week. The vaccine offers around 70% protection, lasts for two to three years and comes as a single dose. Tablets are also available, although the injection is usually recommended, as it has fewer side effects. A sore arm and fever may occur.

» **Varicella** If you haven't had chickenpox discuss this vaccination with your doctor.

The following are recommended for long-term travellers (more than one month) or those at special risk:

» **Influenza** A single jab lasts one year and is recommended for those over 65 years of age or with underlying medical conditions such as heart or lung disease.

» **Pneumonia** A single injection with a booster after five years is recommended for all travellers over 65 years of age or with underlying medical conditions that compromise immunity, such as heart or lung disease, cancer or HIV.

» **Rabies** Three injections are required. A booster after one year will then provide 10 years' protection. Side effects are rare – occasionally headache and sore arm.

» **Tuberculosis (TB)** A complex issue. High-risk adult long-term travellers are usually recommended to have a TB skin test before and after travel, rather than a vaccination. Only one vaccine is given in a lifetime. Children under five spending more than three months in China and/or Mongolia should be vaccinated.

as close household contact with an infected person is usually required before the disease is passed on. You may need to have a TB test before you travel, as this can help diagnose the disease later if you become ill.

DRINKING WATER

» Bottled water is generally safe – check that the seal is intact at purchase.

» Tap water in Ulaanbaatar and other cities probably won't make you sick but because of antiquated plumbing the water may contain traces of metals that won't be good for your long-term health.

» Be cautious about drinking from streams and lakes, as they are easily polluted by livestock. Water is usually OK if you can get it high up in the mountains, near the source. If in doubt, boil your water.

» The best chemical purifier is iodine, although it should not be used by pregnant women or those with thyroid problems.

» Water filters should filter out viruses. Ensure your filter has a chemical barrier such as iodine and a small pore size (eg less than four microns).

Environmental Hazards

Heatstroke

This serious, occasionally fatal condition can occur if the body's heat-regulating mechanism breaks down and the body temperature rises to dangerous levels. Long, continuous exposure to high temperatures and insufficient fluids can leave you vulnerable to heatstroke.

The symptoms are feeling unwell, not sweating very much (or at all) and a high body temperature. Where sweating has ceased, the skin becomes flushed and red. Victims can become confused, aggressive or delirious. Get victims out of the sun, remove their clothing and cover them with a wet sheet or towel and fan continually. Give fluids if they are conscious.

Hypothermia

In a country where temperatures can plummet to -40°C, cold is something you should take seriously. If you are trekking at high altitudes or simply taking a long bus trip across the country, particularly at night, be especially prepared. Even in the lowlands, sudden winds from the north can send the temperature plummeting.

Hypothermia occurs when the body loses heat faster than it can produce it and the core temperature of the body falls. It is best to dress in layers; silk, wool and some of the new artificial fibres are all good insulting materials. A hat is important, as a lot of heat is lost through the head. A strong, waterproof outer layer is essential (and a 'space' blanket for emergencies if trekking). Carry basic supplies, including fluid to drink and food containing simple sugars to generate heat quickly.

Bites & Stings

Bee and wasp stings are usually painful rather than dangerous. Calamine lotion or sting-relief spray will give relief and ice packs will reduce the pain and swelling. However, people who are allergic to bees and wasps may require urgent medical care.

Mongolia has four species of venomous snakes: the Halys viper *(agkistrodon halys)*, the common European viper or adder *(vipera berus)*, Orsini's viper *(vipera ursine)* and the small *taphrometaphon lineolatum*. To minimise your chances of being bitten, always wear boots, socks and long trousers where snakes may be present. Don't put your hands into holes and crevices, and be careful when collecting firewood.

Bedbugs live in various places, but particularly in dirty mattresses and bedding, evidenced by spots of blood on bedclothes or on the wall. Bedbugs leave itchy bites in neat rows. Calamine lotion or a sting-relief spray may help. All lice cause itching and discomfort. They make themselves at home in your hair, your clothing, or in your pubic hair. You catch lice through direct contact with infected people or by sharing combs, clothing and the like. Powder or shampoo treatment will kill the lice and infected clothing should then be washed in very hot, soapy water and left in the sun to dry.

Language

WANT MORE?

For in-depth language information and handy phrases, check out Lonely Planet's *Mongolian Phrasebook*. You'll find it at **shop.lonelyplanet.com**, or you can buy Lonely Planet's iPhone phrasebooks at the Apple App Store.

Mongolian is a member of the Ural-Altaic family of languages, and as such it is distantly related to Turkish, Kazakh, Uzbek and Korean. It has around 10 million speakers worldwide. The traditional Mongolian script (cursive, vertical and read from left to right) is still used by the Mongolians living in the Inner Mongolia Autonomous Region of China. In 1944 the Cyrillic alphabet was adopted and it remains in use today in Mongolia and two autonomous regions of Russia (Buryatia and Kalmykia).

Mongolian also has a Romanised form, though the 35 Cyrillic characters give a better representation of Mongolian sounds than the 26 of the Roman alphabet. Different Romanisation systems have been used, and a loose standard was adopted in 1987 – so the capital city, previously written as Ulan Bator, is now Ulaanbaatar.

It's well worth the effort to familiarise yourself with the Cyrillic alphabet so that you can read maps and street signs. Otherwise, just read the coloured pronunciation guides given next to each word in this chapter as if they were English, and you'll be understood.

Mongolian pronunciation is explained in the alphabet table on the next page. It's important to pronounce double vowel letters as long sounds, because vowel length can affect meaning. In our pronunciation guides the stressed syllables are in italics.

BASICS

Hello.	Сайн байна уу?	sain *bai*·na uu
Yes./No.	Тийм./ Үгүй.	tiim/ü·*güi*
Thank you.	Баярлалаа.	ba·yar·la·*laa*
You're welcome.	Зүгээр.	zü·*geer*
Excuse me.	Уучлаарай.	uuch·*laa*·rai
Sorry.	Уучлаарай.	uuch·*laa*·rai
Goodbye.	Баяртай.	ba·yar·*tai*

What's your name?
Таны нэрийг хэн гэдэг вэ? — ta·*ny* ne·*riig* khen *ge*·deg ve

My name is ...
Миний нэрийг ... гэдэг. — mi·*nii* ne·*riig* ... *ge*·deg

Do you speak English?
Та англиар ярьдаг уу? — ta an·*gliar yair*·dag uu

I don't understand.
Би ойлгохгүй байна. — bi *oil*·gokh·güi *bai*·na

ACCOMMODATION

Do you have any rooms available?
Танайд сул өрөө байна уу? — ta·*naid* sul ö·*röö bai*·na uu

How much is it per night/week?
Энэ өрөө хоногт/долоо хоногт ямар үнэтэй вэ? — e·ne ö·*röö kho*·nogt/do·*loo kho*·nogt *ya*·mar ün·*tei* ve

I'd like a single/double room.
Би нэг/хоёр хүний өрөө авмаар байна. — bi neg/*kho*·yor khü·*nii* ö·*röö* av·*maar bai*·na

air-con	агааржуулалт	a·gaar·*juul*·alt
bathroom	угаалгын өрөө	u·*gaal*·gyn ö·*röö*
cot	хүүхдийн ор	khüükh·*diin* or
dormitory	нийтийн байр	*nii*·tiin bair
hotel	зочид буудал	*zo*·chid *buu*·dal
window	цонх	tsonkh
youth hostel	залуучуудын байр	za·*luu*·chuu·dyn bair

DIRECTIONS

Where's ...?
... хаана байна вэ? ... khaan *bai*·na ve

How can I get to ...?
... руу би яаж очих вэ? ... ruu bi yaj *o*·chikh ve

Can you show me on the map?
Та газрын зураг дээр зааж өгнө үү? ta gaz·*ryn zu*·rag deer zaaj *ög*·nö *üü*

address	хаяг	*kha*·yag
after	ард	ard
before	урд	urd
behind	хойно	*khoi*·no
in front of	өмнө	*öm*·nö
straight ahead	чигээрээ урагшаа	chi·*gee*·ree u·rag·*shaa*
to the left	зүүн тийш	züün tiish
to the right	баруун тийш	ba·*ruun* tiish

EATING & DRINKING

Can I have a menu, please?
Би хоолны цэс авч болох уу? bi *khool*·nii tses avch *bo*·lokh uu

What food do you have today?
Өнөөдөр ямар хоол байна вэ? ö·nöö·dör *ya*·mar khool *bai*·na ve

I'd like to have this.
Би энэ хоолыг авъя. bi en *khoo*·lyg a·*vi*

I don't eat (meat).
Би (мах) иддэггүй. bi (makh) *id*·deg·gui

Cheers!
Эрүүл мэндийн төлөө! e·*rüül* men·*diin* tö·*löö*

The bill, please.
Тооцоогоо бодуулъя. too·*tsoo*·goo bo·*duu*·li

Key Words

appetisers	хүйтэн зууш	*khüi*·ten zuush
bottle	шил	shil
breakfast	өглөөний хоол	ög·*löö*·nii khool
canteen	гуанз	guanz
cold	хүйтэн	*khüi*·ten
cup	аяга	*a*·yag
dessert	амтат зууш	*am*·tat zuush
dinner	оройн хоол	o·*roin* khool
dining room	зоогийн газар	*zoo*·giin *ga*·zar
dumplings	банштай	*ban*·shtai
food	хоол	khool
fork	сэрээ	se·*ree*
fried	шарсан	*shar*·san
fried food	хуураг	*khuu*·rag
glass	шилэн аяга	*shi*·len *a*·yag
hot	халуун	kha·*luun*
knife	хутга	*khu*·tag
lunch	үдийн хоол	ü·*diin* khool
market	зах	zakh
menu	хоолны цэс	khool·*ny* tses
plate	таваг	*ta*·vag
restaurant	ресторан	res·to·*ran*
set dish	бэлэн хоол	*be*·len khool
spoon	халбага	*khal*·bag
tea shop	цайны газар	*tsai*·ny *ga*·zar
vegetarian	ногоон хоолтон	no·*goon* *khool*·ton

CYRILLIC ALPHABET

Cyrillic	Sound	
А а	a	as the 'u' in 'but'
Г г	g	as in 'get'
Ё ё	yo	as in 'yonder'
И и	i	as in 'tin'
Л л	l	as in 'lamp'
О о	o	as in 'hot'
Р р	r	as in 'rub'
У у	u	as in 'rude'
Х х	kh	as the 'ch' in Scottish *loch*
Ш ш	sh	as in 'shoe'
Ы ы	y	as the 'i' in 'ill'
Ю ю	yu	as the 'yo' in 'yoyo'
	yü	long, as the word 'you'
Б б	b	as in 'but'
Д д	d	as in 'dog'
Ж ж	j	as in 'jewel'
Й й	i	as in 'tin'
М м	m	as in 'mat'
Ө ө	ö	long, as the 'u' in 'fur'
С с	s	as in 'sun'
Ү ү	ü	long, as the 'o' in 'who'
Ц ц	ts	as in 'cats'
Щ щ	shch	as in 'fresh chips'
Ь ь		'soft sign' (see below)
Я я	ya	as in 'yard'
В в	v	as in 'van'
Е е	ye	as in 'yes'
	yö	as the 'yea' in 'yearn'
З з	z	as the 'ds' in 'suds'
К к	k	as in 'kit'
Н н	n	as in 'neat'
П п	p	as in 'pat'
Т т	t	as in 'tin'
Ф ф	f	as in 'five'
Ч ч	ch	as in 'chat'
Ъ ъ		'hard sign' (see below)
Э э	e	as in 'den'

The letters ь and ъ never occur alone, but simply affect the pronunciation of the previous letter – ь makes the preceding consonant soft (pronounced with a faint 'y' after it), while ъ makes the previous consonant hard (ie not pronounced with a faint 'y' after it).

Signs

ГАРЦ	Exit
ЛАВЛАГАА	Information
ОРЦ	Entrance
ХААСАН	Closed
ХАДГАЛСАН	Reserved/Engaged
ЭРЭГТЭЙН	Men
ЭМЭГТЭЙН	Women

Meat & Fish

antelope	цагаан зээр	tsa·*gaan* zeer
beef	үхрийн мах	ü·*khriin* makh
carp	булуу цагаан	bu·*luu* tsa·*gaan*
chicken	тахианы мах	ta·khia·*ny* makh
duck	нугас	*nu*·gas
fillet	гол мах	gol makh
fish	загас	*za*·gas
goat	ямаа	ya·*maa*
kebab	шорлог	*shor*·log
marmot	тарвага	*tar*·vag
meat	мах	makh
(fried) meat pancake	хуушуур	*khuu*·shuur
meat with rice	будаатай хуураг	bu·*daa*·tai *khuu*·rag
mutton	хонины мах	kho·ni·*ny* makh
mutton dumplings (steamed)	бууз	buuz
patty	бифштекс	*bif*·shteks
perch	алгана	*al*·gan
pike	цурхай	tsurh·*kai*
pork	гахайн мах	ga·*khain* makh
salmon	омуль	o·*mul*
sausage	хиам/зайдас/ сосик	khiam/*zai*·das/ *so*·sisk
sturgeon	хилэм	*khi*·lem
antevenison	бугын мах	bu·*gyn* makh
wild boar	бодон гахай	*bo*·don ga·*khai*

Fruit & Vegetables

apple	алим	*a*·lim
banana	гадил	*ga*·dil
cabbage	байцаа	*bai*·tsaa
carrot	шар лууван	shar *luu*·van
cucumber	өргөст хэмэх	*ör*·göst *khe*·mekh
fruit	жимс	jims
onion	сонгино	*son*·gin
potato	төмс	töms
radish	улаан лууван	u·*laan luu*·van
salad	салат	*sa*·lad
tomato	улаан лооль	u·*laan loo*·il
turnip	манжин	*man*·jin
vegetable	ногоо	no·*goo*

Other

bread	талх	talkh
butter	цөцгийн тос	tsöts·*giin* tos
cake	бялуу	bya·*luu*
camel yogurt	хоормог	*khoor*·mog
cheese	бяслаг	*byas*·lag
cream	өрөм	ö·röm
dairy	цагаан-идээ	tsa·*gaan* i·*dee*
(dried) curds	ааруул	*aa*·ruul
egg	өндөг	*ön*·dög
honey	зөгийн бал	zö·*giin* bal
ice cream	зайрмаг	*zair*·mag
jam	жимсний чанамал	jims·*nii* *cha*·na·mal
noodle soup	гоймонтой шөл	*goi*·mon·toi shöl
pasta	хөндий гоймон	khön·*diin* *goi*·mon
pepper	поваарь	po·*vaair*
rice	цагаан будаа	tsa·*gaan* bu·*daa*
salad	ногоон зууш	no·*goon* zuush
salt	давс	davs
soup	шөл	shöl
sour cream	тараг/цөцгий	*ta*·rag/tsöts·*gii*
stewed fruit	компот	kom·*pot*
sugar	чихэр	*chi*·kher
sweets	цаастай чихэр	*tsaas*·tai *chi*·kher
with rice	будаатай	bu·*daa*·tai

Drinks

beer	пиво	piv
coffee	кофе	*ko*·fi
(buckthorn) juice	(чацарганы) шүүс	(cha·tsar·ga·*ny*) shüüs
koumiss (fermented mair milk)	айраг	*ai*·rag
lemonade	нимбэгний ундаа	nim·beg·*nii* un·*daa*
milk	сүү	süü
milk tea	сүүтэй цай	*süü*·tei tsai
milk with rice	сүүтэй будаа	*süü*·tei bu·*daa*
mineral water	рашаан ус	ra·*shaan* us
tea	цай	tsai
vodka	архи	*a*·rikh
wine	дарс	dars

EMERGENCIES

Help!	Туслаарай!	tus·*laa*·rai
Go away!	Зайл!	zail
I'm lost.	Би төөрчихлөө.	bi töör·chikh·*löö*

There's been an accident.
Осол гарчээ. *o*·sol gar·*chee*

Call a doctor/the police!
Эмч/Цагдаа дуудаарай! emch/tsag·*daa* duu·*daa*·rai

I'm ill.
Би өвчтэй байна. bi övch·*tei bai*·na

It hurts here.
Энд өвдөж байна. end öv·döj *bai*·na

I'm allergic to (antibiotics).
Миний биед (антибиотик) харшдаг. mi·*nii bi*·ed (an·ti·bi·o·tik) *harsh*·dag

SHOPPING & SERVICES

I'd like to buy ...
Би ... авмаар байна. bi ... av·*maar bai*·na

I'm just looking.
Би юм үзэж байна. bi yum *ü*·zej *bai*·na

Can you show me that?
Та үүнийг надад үзүүлнэ үү? ta *üü*·niig *na*·dad ü·*züü*·len üü

I don't like it.
Би үүнд дургүй байна. bi üünd *dur*·güi *bai*·na

How much is it?
Энэ ямар үнэтэй вэ? en *ya*·mar ün·*tei* ve

That's very expensive.
Яасан үнэтэй юм бэ. *yaa*·san ün·*tei* yum be

Can you reduce the price?
Та үнэ буулгах уу? ta ün *buul*·gakh uu

exchange rate	мөнгөний ханш	möng·*nii* khansh
post office	шуудан	*shuu*·dan
public phone	нийтийн утас	*nii*·tiin *u*·tas
signature	гарын үсэг	ga·*ryn ü*·seg
travellers check	жуулчны чек	*juulch*·ny chek

TIME & DATES

What time is it?
Хэдэн цаг болж байна? *khe*·den tsag bolj *bai*·na

Question Words

What?	Юу?	yuu
When?	Хэзээ?	khe·*zee*
Where?	Хаана?	khaan
Which?	Ямар?	*ya*·mar
Who?	Хэн?	khen

It's (nine) o'clock.
(Есөн) цаг болж байна. (*yö*·sön) tsag bolj *bai*·na

It's half past (four).
(Дөрөв) хагас болж байна. (*dö*·röv) *kha*·gas bolj *bai*·na

morning	өглөө	ög·*löö*
afternoon	өдөр	*ö*·dör
evening	орой	o·*roi*

yesterday	өчигдөр	ö·*chig*·dör
today	өнөөдөр	ö·*nöö*·dör
tomorrow	маргааш	mar·*gaash*

Monday	даваа	da·*vaa*
Tuesday	мягмар	*myag*·mar
Wednesday	лхагва	*lkha*·vag
Thursday	пүрэв	*pü*·rev
Friday	баасан	*baa*·sang
Saturday	бямба	byamb
Sunday	ням	nyam

Remember to add the word **сар** sar (literally 'month', 'moon') after each of the following words:

January	нэгдүгээр	neg·dü·*geer*
February	хоёрдугаар	kho·yor·du·*gaar*
March	гуравдугаар	gu·rav·du·*gaar*
April	дөрөвдүгээр	dö·röv·dü·*geer*
May	тавдугаар	tav·du·*gaar*
June	зургадугаар	zur·ga·du·*gaar*
July	долдугаар	dol·du·*gaar*
August	наймдугаар	naim·du·*gaar*
September	есдүгээр	yes·dü·*geer*
October	аравдугаар	a·rav·du·*gaar*
November	арваннэгдүгээр	ar·van·neg·dü·*geer*
December	арванхоёрдугаар	ar·van·kho·yor·du·*gaar*

TRANSPORT

Public Transport

What times does the ... leave/arrive?	... хэдэн цагт явдаг/ирдэг вэ?	... *khe*·den tsagt *yav*·dag/*ir*·deg ve
bus	Автобус	av·*to*·bus
plane	Нисэх онгоц	*ni*·seh *on*·gots
train	Галт тэрэг	galt *te*·reg
trolleybus	Троллейбус	trol·*lei*·bus

Numbers

1	нэг	neg
2	хоёр	*kho*·yor
3	гурав	*gu*·rav
4	дөрөв	*dö*·röv
5	тав	tav
6	зургаа	zur·*gaa*
7	долоо	do·*loo*
8	найм	naim
9	ес	yös
10	арав	*ar*·av
20	хорь	*kho*·ri
30	гуч	guch
40	дөч	döch
50	тавч	taiv
60	жар	jar
70	дал	dal
80	ная	*na*·ya
90	ер	yör
100	зуу	zuu
1000	мянга	*myang*·ga

I want to go to ...
Би ... руу явмаар байна. bi ... ruu yav·*maar bai*·na

Can you tell me when we get to ...?
Бид хэзээ ... хүрэхийг хэлж өгнө үү? bid khe·*zee* ... khu·re·*hiig* helj *ög*·nö uu

I want to get off!
Би буумаар байна! bi *buu*·maar *bai*·na

1st class	нэгдүгээр зэрэг	neg·dü·*geer* *ze*·reg
2nd class	хоёрдугаар зэрэг	kho·yor·du·*gaar* *ze*·reg
one-way ticket	нэг талын билет	neg ta·*lyn* bi·*let*
return ticket	хоёр талын билет	*kho*·yor ta·*lyn* bi·*let*

first	анхны	ankh·*ny*
next	дараа	da·*raa*
last	сүүлийн	*süü*·liin

airport	нисэх онгоцны буудал	*ni*·sekh on·gots·*ny* *buu*·dal
bus stop	автобусны зогсоол	av·*to*·bus·ny zog·*sool*
platform	давцан	*dav*·tsan
ticket office	билетийн касс	bi·le·*tiin* kass
timetable	цагийн хуваарь	tsa·*giin* khu·*vaair*
train station	галт тэрэгний буудал	galt te·re·ge·*nii* *buu*·dal

Driving & Cycling

Excuse me, am I going in the right direction for ...?
Уучлаарай, би ... руу зөв явж байна уу? uuch·*laa*·rai bi ... ruu zöv yavj *bai*·na uu

How many kilometres is it?
Замын урт хэдэн километр вэ? za·*myn* urt *khe*·den ki·lo·*metr* ve

bicycle	унадаг дугуй	*u*·na·dag du·*gui*
map	газрын зураг	gaz·*ryn zu*·rag
mechanic	механик	me·*kha*·nik
motorcycle	мотоцикл	mo·to·*tsikl*
petrol	бензин	ben·*zin*

Visiting the Locals

We'd like to see inside a herder's yurt.
Бид малчны гэрт орж үзэх гэсэн юм. bid malch·*ny* gert orj *ü*·zekh *ge*·sen yum

We'd like to drink some koumiss.
Бид айраг уух гэсэн юм. bid *ai*·rag uukh *ge*·sen yum

I hope your animals are fattening up nicely.
Мал сүрэг тарган тавтай юү? mal *sü*·reg *tar*·gan tav·*tai* yü

Please hold the dogs!
Нохой хогио! nok·*hoi kho*·ri·o

I'd like to ride a ...	Би ... явах гэсэн юм.	bi ... *ya*·vakh *ge*·sen yum
camel	тэмээгээр	te·*mee*·geer
horse	мориор	mo·*rior*
yak	сарлагаар	sar·la·*gaar*

camel	тэмээ	te·*mee*
chicken	тахиа	*ta*·khia
cooking pot	тогоо	to·*goo*
cow	үнээ	ü·*nee*
cowdung box	араг	*a*·rag
donkey	илжиг	*il*·jig
felt material	эсгий	es·*gii*
goat	ямаа	ya·*maa*
herding	мал аж ахуй	mal aj ak·*hui*
horse	морь	*mo*·ri
koumiss bag	хөхүүр	khö·*khüür*
pig	гахай	ga·*khai*
saddle	эмээл	e·*meel*
sheep	хонь	*kho*·ni
summer camp	зуслан	*zus*·lan
yak	сарлаг	*sar*·lag
yurt	гэр	ger

GLOSSARY

agui – cave or grotto
aimag – a province/state within Mongolia
am – mouth, but often used as a term for canyon
aral – island
arkhi – the common word to describe home-made vodka
ashkhana – restaurant (Kazakh)

baatar – hero
bag – village; a subdivision of a *sum*
baga – little
balbal – stone figures believed to be Turkic grave markers; known as *khun chuluu* (man stones) in Mongolian
baruun – west
bayan – rich
bodhisattva – Tibetan-Buddhist term; applies to a being that has voluntarily chosen not to take the step to nirvana in order to save the souls of those on earth
Bogd Gegeen – the hereditary line of reincarnated Buddhist leaders of Mongolia, which started with Zanabazar; the third-holiest leader in the Tibetan Buddhist hierarchy; also known as *Jebtzun Damba*
Bogd Khaan (Holy King) – title given to the Eighth Bogd Gegeen (1869–1924)
bökh – wrestling
bugan chuluu (deer stones) – upright grave markers from the Bronze and Iron ages, on which are carved stylised images of deer
bulag – natural spring
Buriat – ethnic minority living along the northern frontier of Mongolia, mostly in Khentii and Dornod

chuluu – rock; rock formation

davaa – mountain pass
deer stones – see *bugan chuluu*
del/deel – the all-purpose, traditional coat or dress worn by men and women
delger – richness, plenty
delgüür – a shop
dombra – two-stringed lute (Kazakh)
dorje – thunderbolt symbol, used in Tibetan Buddhist ritual
dorno – east
dov – hill
dund – middle

els – sand; sand dunes
erdene – precious

Furgon – Russian-made 11-seater minivan

gegeen – saint; saintlike person
ger – traditional circular felt *yurt*
gol – river
gov – desert
guanz – canteen or cheap restaurant
gudamj – street

hard seat – the common term to describe the standard of the 2nd-class train carriage

ikh – big
ikh delgüür– department store
Inner Mongolia – a separate province within China
irbis – snow leopard

Jebtzun Damba – see *Bogd Gegeen*

Kazakh – ethnic minority, mostly living in western Mongolia
khaan – emperor; great *khan*
khad – rock
khagan – *khaan*; generally used for leaders during the Turkic (pre-Mongol) period
khaganate – Turkic (pre-Mongol) empire
khagas – half-size
Khalkh – the major ethnic group living in Mongolia
khan – king or chief
khar – black
khashaa – fenced-in *ger*, often found in suburbs
kherem – wall
khetsuu – difficult/hard
khiid – a Buddhist monastery
khödöö – countryside
khoid – north
khöndii – valley
khoroo – district or subdistrict
khot – city
khulan – wild ass
khun chuluu (man stones) – see *balbal*
khuree – originally used to describe a 'camp', it is now also in usage as 'monastery'
khuriltai – nomadic congress during the Mongol era
khürkhree – waterfall
khutukhtu – reincarnated lama, or living god
kino – cinema

lama – Tibetan Buddhist monk or priest
Lamaism – an outdated term, and now properly known as Vajramana, or Tibetan Buddhism
Living Buddha – common term for reincarnations of Buddha; Buddhist spiritual leader in Mongolia (see *Bogd Gegeen*)
loovuuz – fox-fur hat

malchin – herder
man stones – see *balbal*
maral – Asiatic red deer
mod – tree
morin khuur – horse-head fiddle
mörön – another word for river, usually a wide river
MPRP – Mongolian People's Revolutionary Party

naadam – games; traditional festival with archery, horse racing and wrestling

nairamdal – friendship
nuruu – mountain range
nuur – lake

ömnö – south
ordon – palace
örgön chölöö – avenue
Outer Mongolia – northern Mongolia during Manchurian rule (the term is not currently used to describe Mongolia)
ovoo – a shamanistic collection of stones, wood or other offerings to the gods, usually found in high places

rashaan – mineral springs

shaykhana – tea house (Kazakh)
soft seat – the common term to describe the standard of the 1st-class train carriage
soyombo – the national symbol
stupa – a Buddhist religious monument composed of a solid hemisphere topped by a spire, containing relics of the Buddha; also known as a pagoda, or *suvrag* in Mongolian
sum – a district; the administrative unit below an *aimag*
süm – a Buddhist temple
suvrag – see *stupa*

taiga – subarctic coniferous evergreen forests (Russian)
takhi – the Mongolian wild horse; also known as Przewalski's horse
tal – steppe
talbai – square
thangka – scroll painting; a rectangular Tibetan Buddhist painting on cloth, often seen in monasteries
tögrög – the unit of currency in Mongolia
töv – central
Tsagaan Sar – 'white moon' or 'white month'; a festival to celebrate the Mongolian New Year (start of the lunar year)
tsainii gazar – tea house/café
tsam – lama dances; performed by monks wearing masks during religious ceremonies
tsas – snow
tsuivan gazar – noodle stall
tuuts – kiosk selling imported foodstuffs

ulaan – red
urtyn duu – traditional singing style, literally 'Long Song'
us – water
uul – mountain
uurga – traditional wooden lasso used by nomads

yavakh – depart
yurt – the Russian word for *ger*

zakh – a market
zochid budal – hotel
zud – a particularly bad winter, involving a huge loss of livestock
zun – summer
zuu – one hundred
züü – needle
zuun – century
züün – east

behind the scenes

SEND US YOUR FEEDBACK

We love to hear from travellers – your comments keep us on our toes and help make our books better. Our well-travelled team reads every word on what you loved or loathed about this book. Although we cannot reply individually to postal submissions, we always guarantee that your feedback goes straight to the appropriate authors, in time for the next edition. Each person who sends us information is thanked in the next edition – and the most useful submissions are rewarded with a free book.

Visit **lonelyplanet.com/contact** to submit your updates and suggestions or to ask for help. Our award-winning website also features inspirational travel stories, news and discussions.

Note: we may edit, reproduce and incorporate your comments in Lonely Planet products such as guidebooks, websites and digital products, so let us know if you don't want your comments reproduced or your name acknowledged. For a copy of our privacy policy, visit lonelyplanet.com/privacy.

OUR READERS

Many thanks to the travellers who used the last edition and wrote to us with helpful hints, useful advice and interesting anecdotes:

Tom Allen, Lavergne Annick, Cameron Asam, Zoljargal Batjargal, Rene Boerkamp, Lee Boyd, Francesca Broom, Ulrike Brunner, Sarnai Byambajav, Coral Camps, Rachel Cotterill, Maurizio D'antonio, Henk Edelman, Stephen Edwards, Hagai Elron, Tomer Farkash, Glen Fi, Kenneth Gavin, Horst Gudemann, Dan Hennenfent, Marc Hens, Peter Jansen, Olaf Jensen, Tyler Keys, Robert Klein, Angelika Lange, Vanesa Lee, David Lowe, Beatriz Lucas, Seumas Macdonald, Ramona Materi, Asta Olafsdottir, Linda Parton, François Pavé, Igor Polakovic, Jiri Preclik, Matthew Raiche, Antonio Ranada, Pyry Rechardt, Sue Rowe, Hugh Scrine, Alexandra Sfintesco, Dan Straw, Daniel Suman, Bihonegn Timur, Ilona Väätänen, Andrea Votavova, Max Walsh, Tom Winser, Peter Young, Andrew Ziaja, Guenther Zippel

AUTHOR THANKS

Michael Kohn

First and foremost, thanks to the editors and cartographers that saw this project from start to finish, including David Carroll, David Connolly and Brigitte Ellemor. And thanks to Dean for his mighty contributions in the Gobi and West.

In Mongolia, special thanks to Toroo for answering my endless questions about Mongolia. I also received support and advice from Peter Weinig, Ron Zeidel, Kirk Olson, Andy Parkinson, Aldra and Batbayar, Jan Wigsten, Baigalmaa Begzsuren, Murray Benn and Spiro Deligiannis

Cheers also to travellers Susan Fox and Yuval Kesary, as well as the Mongol Ralliers who kept me company in the line outside the Chinese Embassy. As always, a heartfelt thanks to Baigalmaa and Molly for being such great troopers on our journey around Mongolia.

Dean Starnes

It would be wrong not to acknowledge the legacy of work from previous editions and help from author-extraordinaire Michael Kohn. I'm also indebted to the team at LP, including David Carroll, David Connolly and Brigitte Ellemor.

Those long drives were greatly enhanced by the wit and expertise of Frederik Halewyck, Oyunbayar Ganbat, Lhagvasuren Dorjsuren and Dosjan Khabyl. Thanks also to Jan Wigsten, Canat Cheryiasdaa, Marima Haumen, Enkhtuya Tsieregzen and Rik and Tseren for sharing their hard-won knowledge.

This Book

This 6th edition of Lonely Planet's Mongolia guidebook was researched and written by Michael Kohn and Dean Starnes. The history chapter was written by Jack Weatherford and Dulmaa Enkhchuluun. The 5th and 4th editions were written by Michael Kohn, Bradley Mayhew wrote the 3rd edition and Paul Greenway wrote the 2nd edition. The 1st edition was written by Robert Storey. This guidebook was commissioned in Lonely Planet's Melbourne office, and produced by the following:

Commissioning Editor David Carroll
Coordinating Editors Elizabeth Harvey, Simon Williamson
Coordinating Cartographer Xavier Di Toro
Coordinating Layout Designer Jacqui Saunders
Senior Editor Anna Metcalfe
Managing Editors Brigitte Ellemor, Liz Heynes
Managing Cartographers Shahara Ahmed, David Connolly
Managing Layout Designers Jane Hart, Celia Wood
Assisting Editors Janet Austin, Janice Bird, Monique Perrin
Assisting Cartographers Katalin Dadi-Racz, Julie Dodkins, Jennifer Johnston
Cover Research Naomi Parker
Internal Image Research Rebecca Skinner
Language Content Annelies Mertens, Branislava Vladisavljevic
Thanks to Lisa Knights, Baigalmaa Kohn, Chris Lee Ack, Raphael Richards, Juan Winata

At home my love and thanks go to my wife, Debbie, and my Mum and Dad for all their unfailing support.

ACKNOWLEDGMENTS

Climate map data adapted from Peel MC, Finlayson BL & McMahon TA (2007) 'Updated World Map of the Köppen-Geiger Climate Classification', Hydrology and Earth System Sciences, 11, 163344.

Cover photograph: Camel riders, Gobi Desert, Obert Obert/Photolibrary. Many of the images in this guide are available for licensing from Lonely Planet Images: www.lonelyplanetimages.com.

000 Map pages
000 Photo pages

N

000 Map pages
000 Photo pages

000 Map pages
000 Photo pages

U

V

W

Y

Z

OUR STORY

A beat-up old car, a few dollars in the pocket and a sense of adventure. In 1972 that's all Tony and Maureen Wheeler needed for the trip of a lifetime – across Europe and Asia overland to Australia. It took several months, and at the end – broke but inspired – they sat at their kitchen table writing and stapling together their first travel guide, *Across Asia on the Cheap*. Within a week they'd sold 1500 copies. Lonely Planet was born.

Today, Lonely Planet has offices in Melbourne, London and Oakland, with more than 600 staff and writers. We share Tony's belief that 'a great guidebook should do three things: inform, educate and amuse'.

OUR WRITERS

Michael Kohn

Coordinating Author, Ulaanbaatar, Central Mongolia, Northern Mongolia, Eastern Mongolia Michael first visited Mongolia in 1997. The first years were spent working as a reporter and editor for the *Mongol Messenger* newspaper. During that period, he interviewed the president, played a lead role in a Mongolian film, hosted a radio talk show and had a brief stint as a news presenter for a local TV station. His travels have led him to all 21 aimags, occasionally by bicycle or in the back of trucks, and when he is lucky by Hummer with politicians and diplomats. Michael's articles on Mongolian culture, politics and history have appeared in the *New York Times*, *Wall Street Journal* and *San Francisco Chronicle*. He is also the author of two books, *Dateline Mongolia* and *Lama of the Gobi*. He splits his time between Ulaanbaatar and California. Find him on the web at www.michaelkohn.us.

Dean Starnes

The Gobi, Western Mongolia Dean has travelled extensively throughout central and northeast Asia, but it wasn't until 2005 while researching his book *Roam: the Art of Travel* that he finally made it to Mongolia. That trip, which involved several near-death experiences and a growing dependency on vodka, confirmed his belief that Mongolia remains one of the best places on earth to experience genuine adventure. This trip, however, may have been his last. A shaman he met in Ölgii foretold that he would return to New Zealand and father four children. Until then, Dean is happy to spend his days writing for Lonely Planet, freelancing as a graphic designer and shirking responsibilities. Check out his website, www.deanstarnes.com, for photography and more.

Published by Lonely Planet Publications Pty Ltd
ABN 36 005 607 983
6th edition – July 2011
ISBN 978 1 74179 317 8

10 9 8 7 6 5 4 3 2 1
Printed in China

how to use this book

These symbols will help you find the listings you want:

- Sights
- Activities
- Courses
- Tours
- Festivals & Events
- Sleeping
- Eating
- Drinking
- Entertainment
- Shopping
- Information/ Transport

These symbols give you the vital information for each listing:

- Telephone Numbers
- Opening Hours
- Parking
- Nonsmoking
- Air-Conditioning
- Internet Access
- Wi-Fi Access
- Swimming Pool
- Vegetarian Selection
- English-Language Menu
- Family-Friendly
- Pet-Friendly
- Bus
- Ferry
- Metro
- Subway
- London Tube
- Tram
- Train

Reviews are organised by author preference.

Look out for these icons:

TOP CHOICE Our author's recommendation

FREE No payment required

A green or sustainable option

Our authors have nominated these places as demonstrating a strong commitment to sustainability – for example by supporting local communities and producers, operating in an environmentally friendly way, or supporting conservation projects.

Map Legend

Sights
- Beach
- Buddhist
- Castle
- Christian
- Hindu
- Islamic
- Jewish
- Monument
- Museum/Gallery
- Ruin
- Winery/Vineyard
- Zoo
- Other Sight

Activities, Courses & Tours
- Diving/Snorkelling
- Canoeing/Kayaking
- Skiing
- Surfing
- Swimming/Pool
- Walking
- Windsurfing
- Other Activity/ Course/Tour

Sleeping
- Sleeping
- Camping

Eating
- Eating

Drinking
- Drinking
- Cafe

Entertainment
- Entertainment

Shopping
- Shopping

Information
- Bank
- Embassy/ Consulate
- Hospital/Medical
- Internet
- Police
- Post Office
- Telephone
- Toilet
- Tourist Information
- Other Information

Transport
- Airport
- Border Crossing
- Bus
- Cable Car/ Funicular
- Cycling
- Ferry
- Metro
- Monorail
- Parking
- Petrol Station
- Taxi
- Train/Railway
- Tram
- Other Transport

Routes
- Tollway
- Freeway
- Primary
- Secondary
- Tertiary
- Lane
- Unsealed Road
- Plaza/Mall
- Steps
- Tunnel
- Pedestrian Overpass
- Walking Tour
- Walking Tour Detour
- Path

Geographic
- Hut/Shelter
- Lighthouse
- Lookout
- Mountain/Volcano
- Oasis
- Park
- Pass
- Picnic Area
- Waterfall

Population
- Capital (National)
- Capital (State/Province)
- City/Large Town
- Town/Village

Boundaries
- International
- State/Province
- Disputed
- Regional/Suburb
- Marine Park
- Cliff
- Wall

Hydrography
- River, Creek
- Intermittent River
- Swamp/Mangrove
- Reef
- Canal
- Water
- Dry/Salt/ Intermittent Lake
- Glacier

Areas
- Beach/Desert
- Cemetery (Christian)
- Cemetery (Other)
- Park/Forest
- Sportsground
- Sight (Building)
- Top Sight (Building)